Chinese Environmental Law

China has industrialized and urbanized at unprecedented scale and speed since its economic take-off began in the 1980s. It has become the world's second largest economy, but pollution has pushed the environment to the limits of its carrying capacity. *Chinese Environmental Law* provides a comprehensive and structured analysis of the increasingly sophisticated Chinese environmental legal regime. It examines the regulation of pollution in detail, covering key environmental statutes, policies and plans, and investigates judicial innovation in the interpretation and application of environmental legal instruments. The book presents Chinese environmental law in action and in context. By discussing key institutions and processes, readers will understand the operation of the environmental law and policy, the dynamic interactions between state and non-state actors, and the special challenges to the implementation and enforcement of environmental law in the socio-economic and political context of China.

YUHONG ZHAO is Associate Professor at the Faculty of Law of The Chinese University of Hong Kong. Her research interests and teaching expertise include environmental law and civil law. She has published widely on aspects of Chinese environmental law in leading academic law journals and books, and has been invited to speak on China's environmental law reform and its climate policies at international conferences hosted by prestigious universities and professional bodies in Asia, Europe, Australia and the United States.

Chinese Environmental Law

Yuhong Zhao
The Chinese University of Hong Kong

CAMBRIDGE
UNIVERSITY PRESS

CAMBRIDGE
UNIVERSITY PRESS

University Printing House, Cambridge CB2 8BS, United Kingdom

One Liberty Plaza, 20th Floor, New York, NY 10006, USA

477 Williamstown Road, Port Melbourne, VIC 3207, Australia

314–321, 3rd Floor, Plot 3, Splendor Forum, Jasola District Centre, New Delhi – 110025, India

79 Anson Road, #06–04/06, Singapore 079906

Cambridge University Press is part of the University of Cambridge.

It furthers the University's mission by disseminating knowledge in the pursuit of education, learning, and research at the highest international levels of excellence.

www.cambridge.org
Information on this title: www.cambridge.org/9781107039445
DOI: 10.1017/9781139600316

First published 2021

A catalogue record for this publication is available from the British Library.

ISBN 978-1-107-03944-5 Hardback
ISBN 978-1-107-69628-0 Paperback

Contents

Detailed Contents

Tables

Preface

Chinese environmental law has experienced fascinating and dynamic development since the late 1970s. The first wave of environmental legislation started with the Environmental Protection Law (EPL) (for trial implementation) (1979) and continued throughout the 1980s and 1990s, a period that also witnessed the growth of environmental lawmaking and institution building. The Water Pollution Prevention and Control Law (WPPCL) (1984), the Air Pollution Prevention and Control Law (APPCL) (1987), the Environmental Protection Law (EPL) (1989) and the Law on the Prevention and Control of Pollution by Solid Waste (SWL) (1995) were among laws enacted to address pollution from varied sources. China's command-and-control approach relies heavily on government agencies to set standards, monitor performance and impose sanctions to punish or deter violations. Political and systemic constraints in the context of China's large-scale and rapid economic growth have, however, impeded effective environmental enforcement by local agencies. Despite the enactment of the Environmental Impact Assessment Law (EIAL) (2001) and amendments of the APPCL, WPPCL and SWL in the 1990s and at the turn of the twenty-first century, pollution continues to threaten public health and cause substantial damage to public and private property.

China's most recent environmental law reform has taken place in the second decade of the twenty-first century, with unprecedented active engagement by its supreme executive body, the State Council, as well as the national legislature, the courts and the procuratorates. The most significant Action Plans – the Action Plan on Prevention and Control of Air Pollution (Air Action Plan) (2013), the Action Plan on Prevention and Control of Water Pollution (Water Action Plan) (2015) and the Action Plan on Prevention and Control of Soil Pollution (Soil Action Plan) (2016) – were issued by the State Council to tackle serious pollution as a matter of urgency. The National People's Congress Standing Committee (NPCSC) revised the EPL (1989) in 2014 to strengthen government responsibility and accountability, expand the enforcement powers of local agencies, enhance public participation and information disclosure, and substantially increase the cost of non-compliance. Specialized environmental statutes have been revised or amended, and include the APPCL (2018), WPPCL (2017), EIAL (2018) and SWL (2020). In addition, the Soil Pollution Prevention and Control Law (SPPCL) (2018) was enacted to tackle China's lack of regulatory control of soil pollution. To promote full implementation and effective enforcement of law, the party-state has initiated institutional reform and judicial innovation. The State Council's institutional reform of 2018 further expanded the powers of the Ministry of Ecology and Environment (MEE), facilitating an integrated approach to regulation and to managing and protecting the environment from pollution. The recent establishment of specialized environmental courts and tribunals, active trialling of public interest litigation (PIL) and the amendment of the Civil Procedure Law (CPL) (2017) and Administrative Litigation Law (ALL) (2017) provide the infrastructure for public access to judicial redress and more effective scrutiny and supervision of both polluters and agencies by social organizations and procuratorates.

This book presents China's increasingly sophisticated environmental legal regime in the context of its social, economic and political transformation. Chapter 1 highlights the country's major environmental crisis of air and water pollution, soil contamination and pollution by solid waste and provides an overview of the legal responses. This overview includes a discussion of the sources of environmental law and the legal hierarchy in China. Chapter 2 examines key institutions and operators of the environmental legal regime, including government organs, judicial institutions and civil society. Chapters 3–8 analyse the command-and-control approach to pollution taken by key environmental statutes, including the EPL (2014), EIAL (2018), APPCL (2018), WPPCL (2017), SWL (2016) and SPPCL (2018). The chapters examine issues ranging from basic environmental legal principles and regulatory control mechanisms to specialized instruments targeting different types of pollution from a variety of sources. Chapters 9 to 12 focus on law in action and investigate how statutory provisions are applied and interpreted by courts in civil, criminal, administrative and PIL cases. These chapters demonstrate how individuals and organizations have been able to use litigation to protect private and public rights and interests from pollution, and how they have made an impact on China's environmental law reform.

This book could not have been completed without the enormous support and assistance of many individuals and institutions. I appreciate very much the excellent professional service and patient support I received from Caitlin Lisle, Marianne Nield, Laura Blake and the editorial team at Cambridge University Press, as well as Indra Siddharthan, Orvil Matthews and Katherine Demopoulos. I completed part of the research and writing while on sabbatical from the Chinese University of Hong Kong. I am grateful to Professor Vivienne Bath, Director of the Centre for Asian and Pacific Law of Sydney Law School for hosting my sabbatical visit to work on this book. I have benefited tremendously from the knowledge and wisdom of my environmental law colleagues and friends as I conducted research for this book. It is impossible to name them all, but I particularly appreciate the insightful guidance of Professor Wang Canfa and Professor Yang Sujuan of the China University of Political Science and Law, Professor Li Yanfang of Renmin University of China, Professor Luo Li of the Beijing Institute of Technology, Professor Wang Mingyuan of Tsinghua University and Professor Li Zhiping of Sun Yat-sen University. My special thanks are reserved for Bing, Cindy and Vicky for their encouragement and genuine interest in what I do.

Author's Note

This is a brief note to clarify matters of contents, translation, citation, format and related issues.

CONTENTS

The manuscript was completed in February 2020 and covers Chinese environmental law to the end of that month. Later legislative developments, such as the revision of the SWL in April 2020 and the promulgation of the Civil Code in May 2020, are not included. Where possible, however, minor updates on cases that occurred after February 2020 were adopted during the editorial process.

TRANSLATION

This book does not follow any specific version of commercial or academic translation of China's statutes or other legal instruments. The author's translation may or may not be the same as other translations. Where there are well-established translations of titles of statutes or other legal instruments, they are used in this book. Otherwise, the author has provided her own translations. Where the contents of a statute, a judgment or other legal instrument are quoted, they are mostly the author's own translation.

ONLINE RESOURCES

Online resources provide abundant information to readers studying the development of Chinese environmental law and practice. They include, but are not limited to, the official websites of key legal institutions, such as the National People's Congress (NPC), the Supreme People's Court (SPC), the Ministry of Ecology and Environment (MEE) and their corresponding bodies at provincial, municipal and county levels. In addition, the websites of major domestic and international media are also valuable resources. A few examples are *China Environment News*, *Legal Daily*, *People's Daily*, *China Daily*, South China Morning Post, The Guardian and The New York Times. However, many of the weblinks are short-lived and therefore this book keeps their use to a minimum. In comparison, the legal database managed by Peking University, known as Beida Fabao and accessed at www .pkulaw.cn, provides a relatively stable source of primary and secondary legal resources for the research of Chinese law. Unless otherwise specified in the footnotes, the sources of the statutes, regulations, measures, state plans, party policies, judicial interpretations and cases discussed in this book are Beida Fabao at www.pkulaw.cn. For the sake of simplicity, the weblink is not repeated for every single item.

FOOTNOTE CITATIONS

This book uses the short-title system of referencing, whereby the full information of a source appears in the first footnote citation and in the Bibliography at the end of the book. Second and subsequent footnote citations use a simplified format and include only key information. For example, for the second and subsequent footnote citations of a single-author book, only the author's surname, the first few words of the book title and a page reference, if relevant, appear. However, given the generic nature of Chinese surnames, such as Wang, Li and Zhang, the full names of Chinese authors are used in all footnotes in order to assist readers in quickly locating a source in the Bibliography. Footnote citations are in English only, while the Chinese version of key sources are given either in the relevant table or the Bibliography. The Pinyin system of romanization is used in the translation of Chinese names, including authors, cities, counties and provinces. Where a Chinese author publishes in English, the author's English name as it appears in the publication is used.

TABLES OF STATUTES AND OTHER LEGAL INSTRUMENTS

The tables cover major environmental statutes, state plans, regulations and judicial interpretations in bilingual versions to assistant readers to locate the original Chinese sources. The tables do not include every legal instrument mentioned in this book, but focus on the most crucial under which China's environmental legal regime operates.

ABBREVIATIONS

All statutes contain 'of the People's Republic of China' in the full title of the original Chinese version: for example, the Environmental Protection Law of the People's Republic of China. For simplicity's sake, both the Chinese title and English translation in this book omit the phrase 'of the People's Republic of China'. For ease of reference, the Environmental Protection Law is further abbreviated to the EPL. In addition, abbreviated forms of some legal instruments are used instead of the full title. For example, the State Council's Decision on Implementing Scientific Development and Strengthening Environmental Protection (2005) is abbreviated to State Council Decision (2005) for the second and subsequent appearances in a chapter.

Weights and Measures

°C	degree Celsius
μg	microgram
dB	decibel
km	kilometre
km^2	square kilometre
kV	kilovolt
kW	kilowatt
l	litre
m	metre
m^2	square metre
m^3	cubic metre
mg	milligram
mu	Chinese unit of land measurement equal to 666.7 m^2
$PM_{2.5}$	particulates with a diameter of less than 2.5 microns
PM_{10}	particulates with a diameter of less than 10 microns
ppm	parts per million
t	tonne

Statutes

- Administrative Compulsion Law (2011)
  行政强制法
- Administrative Licence Law (2003, amended 2019)
  行政许可法
- Administrative Litigation Law (1989, amended 2014 and 2017)
  行政诉讼法
- Administrative Penalty Law (1996, amended 2009 and 2017)
  行政处罚法
- Air Pollution Prevention and Control Law (1987, amended 1995, revised 2000 and 2015, amended 2018)
  大气污染防治法
- The Basic Law of the Hong Kong Special Administrative Region (1990)
  香港特别行政区基本法
- The Basic Law of the Macau Special Administrative Region (1993)
  澳门特别行政区基本法
- Civil Procedure Law (1991, amended 2007, 2012 and 2017)
  民事诉讼法
- Constitution (1982, amended 1988, 1993, 1999, 2004 and 2018)
  宪法
- Criminal Law (1979, revised 1997, with 10 amendments, the latest in 2017)
  刑法
- Criminal Procedure Law (1979, amended 1996, 2012 and 2018)
  刑事诉讼法
- Decision of the First Session of the 13th NPC on State Council Institutional Reform (2018)
  第十三届全国人民代表大会第一次会议关于国务院机构改革方案的决定
- Decision of the Standing Committee of the National People's Congress on Authorizing the Supreme People's Procuratorate to Launch the Pilot Programme of Initiating Public Interest Actions in Certain Areas (2015)
  全国人民代表大会常务委员会关于授权最高人民检察院在部分地区开展公益诉讼试点工作的决定
- Emergency Response Law (2007)
  突发事件应对法

- Environmental Impact Assessment Law (2002, amended 2016 and 2018)
  环境影响评价法
- Environmental Protection Law (for trial use) (1979)
  环境保护法（试行）
- Environmental Protection Law (1989, revised 2014)
  环境保护法
- Environmental Protection Tax Law (2016, amended 2018)
  环境保护税法
- Fishery Law (1986, amended 2000, 2004, 2009 and 2013)
  渔业法
- Forestry Law (1984, amended 1998 and 2009, revised 2019)
  森林法
- General Principles of Civil Law (1986, amended 2009)
  民法通则
- General Rules of Civil Law (2017)
  民法总则
- Government Procurement Law (2002, amended 2014)
  政府采购法
- Law on Energy Conservation (2007, amended 2016 and 2018)
  节约能源法
- Law on Legislation (2000, amended 2015)
  立法法
- Law on the Prevention and Control of Pollution by Solid Waste (1995, revised 2004, amended 2013, 2015 and 2016)
  固体废物污染环境防治法
- Law on Promotion of the Circular Economy (2008, amended 2018)
  循环经济促进法
- Law on the Promotion of Clean Production (2002, amended 2012)
  清洁生产促进法
- Law on the Quality and Safety of Agricultural Products (2018)
  农产品质量安全法
- Marine Environmental Protection Law (1982, revised 1999, amended 2013, 2016 and 2017)
  海洋环境保护法
- Mineral Resources Law (1986, amended 1996 and 2009)
  矿产资源法
- Noise Pollution Prevention and Control Law (1996, amended 2018)
  环境噪声污染防治法
- Organic Law of Local People's Congresses and Local People's Governments (1979, amended 1982, 1986, 1995, 2004 and 2015)
  地方各级人民代表大会和地方各级人民政府组织法
- Organic Law of the National People's Congress (1982)
  全国人民代表大会组织法
- Organic Law of the People's Courts (1979, amended 1983, 1986 and 2006, revised 2018)
  人民法院组织法

- Organic Law of the People's Procuratorates (1979, amended 1983 and 1986, revised 2018)
  人民检察院组织法
- Organic Law of the State Council (1982)
  国务院组织法
- Soil Pollution Prevention and Control Law (2018)
  土壤污染防治法
- Tort Law (2009)
  侵权责任法
- Water Law (1988, revised 2002, amended 2009 and 2016)
  水法
- Water Pollution Prevention and Control Law (1984, amended 1996, revised 2008, amended 2017)
  水污染防治法
- Wildlife Protection Law (1988, amended 2004, 2009 and 2018, revised 2016)
  野生动物保护法

Regulations and Measures

STATE COUNCIL REGULATIONS AND OPINIONS

- Decision on Implementing Scientific Development and Strengthening Environmental Protection (2005)
  国务院关于落实科学发展观加强环境保护的决定
- Notice to Adjust the Criteria for the Size of Cities (2014)
  国务院关于调整城市规模划分标准的通知
- Recent Work Arrangement on Soil Environmental Protection and Comprehensive Treatment (2013)
  近期土壤环境保护和综合治理工作安排
- Regulation on the Control of Clinical Waste (2003, revised 2011)
  医疗废物管理条例
- Regulation on Environmental Impact Assessment of Plans (2009)
  规划环境影响评价条例
- Regulation on Government Information Disclosure (2007, revised 2019)
  政府信息公开条例
- Regulation on the Implementation of the Environmental Protection Tax Law (2017)
  环境保护税法实施条例
- Regulation on the Levy and Use of Pollution Discharge Fees (2003, repealed 2018)
  排污费征收使用管理条例
- Regulation on the Management of Environmental Protection of Construction Projects (1998, revised 2017)
  建设项目环境保护管理条例
- Regulation on Pesticide Administration (1997, revised 2001 and 2017)
  农药管理条例
- Regulation on the Recovery and Disposal of Waste Electrical and Electronic Products (2009)
  废弃电器电子产品回收处理管理条例
- State Council General Office, Guiding Opinion on Further Promoting Pilot Exercises of Paid Use and Trading of Pollution Discharge Allowances (2014)
  国务院办公厅关于进一步推进排污权有偿使用和交易试点工作的指导意见

- State Council General Office, Opinion on Building an Ecological Protection Compensation Mechanism (2016)
国务院办公厅关于健全生态保护补偿机制的意见

ADMINISTRATIVE MEASURES

- Catalogue of Stationary Sources Subject to Pollution Discharge Permit Control (2017)
固定污染源排污许可分类管理目录
- GAC and MEE, 'Announcement on designated ports for waste import', (announcement) 27 June 2018.
海关总署和生态环境部，关于发布限定固体废物进口口岸的公告（2018年6月27日）
- Guideline on Government Information Disclosure of Construction Project EIA (for trial use) (2013)
建设项目环境影响评价政府信息公开指南（试行）
- Healthy China Promotion Committee, *Healthy China Action (2019–2030)* (2019). www.pkulaw.cn
健康中国行动推进委员会，健康中国行动（2019–2030年）
- Inventory of EIA Categories of Construction Projects (latest revised 2018)
建设项目环境影响评价分类管理名录
- Measures for the Administration of the Soil Environment of Agricultural Land (for trial use) (2017)
农用地土壤环境管理办法（试行）
- Measures for the Administration of the Soil Environment of Industrial and Mining Land (for trial use) (2018)
工矿用地土壤环境管理办法（试行）
- Measures on Administration of the Special Fund for Soil Pollution Prevention and Control (2016)
土壤污染防治专项资金管理办法
- Measures on the Collection and Use of Wastewater Treatment Fees (2014)
污水处理费征收使用管理办法
- Measures on Environmental Administrative Sanction (2010)
环境行政处罚办法
- Measures on Environmental Emergency Response (2015)
突发环境事件应急管理办法
- Measures on Environmental Information Disclosure by Enterprises and Institutions (2014)
企业事业单位环境信息公开办法
- Measures on Environmental Management of Contaminated Sites (for trial use) (2016)
污染地块土壤环境管理办法（试行）
- Measures on Environmental Supervision (2012)
环境监察办法
- Measures on Fines Calculated on Daily Basis (2014)
环境保护主管部门实施按日连续处罚办法
- Measures on the Importing of Solid Waste (2011)
固体废物进口管理办法

- Measures on the Levy, Use and Management of the Waste Electrical and Electronic Equipment Treatment Fund (2012)
  废弃电器电子产品处理基金征收使用管理办法
- Measures on Management of Automatic Monitoring Devices by Polluting Sources (2008)
  污染源自动监控设施运行管理办法
- Measures on Management of the Soil Pollution Prevention and Control Fund (2020)
  土壤污染防治基金管理办法
- Measures on On-Site Inspection of Automatic Monitoring Devices of Polluting Sources (2012)
  污染源自动监控设施现场监督检查办法
- Measures on Permit Control of Pollution Discharge (for trial implementation) (2018)
  排污许可管理办法（试行）
- Measures on Permit Control over Hazardous Waste Operations (2004, revised 2013 and 2016)
  危险废物经营许可证管理办法
- Measures on Pollution Prevention and Control at Drinking-Water-Source Reserves (1989)
  饮用水水源保护区污染防治管理规定
- Measures on Post-Approval EIA of Construction Projects (for trial use) (2015)
  建设项目环境影响后评价管理办法（试行）
- Measures on Prevention and Control of Pollution by Electronic Waste (2007)
  电子废物污染环境防治管理办法
- Measures on Public Participation in Environmental Impact Assessment (2018)
  环境影响评价公众参与办法
- Measures on Qualification Management of Construction Project Environmental Impact Assessment (2015)
  建设项目环境影响评价资质管理办法
- Measures on Regional Environmental Impact Assessment Suspension of Construction Projects (for trial use) (2015)
  建设项目环境影响评价区域限批管理办法（试行）
- Measures on Restriction and Suspension of Production for Treatment (2014)
  环境保护主管部门实施限制生产、停产整治办法
- Measures on Seal-up and Seizure (2014)
  环境保护主管部门实施查封、扣押办法
- Measures on Self-Monitoring and Information Disclosure by Key Enterprises under State Supervision (trial use) (2013)
  国家重点监控企业自行监测及信息公开办法（试行）
- Measures on the Standards for Levying Pollution Discharge Fees (2003, repealed 2018)
  排污费征收标准管理办法
- MEE et al., 'Announcement on adjustment of Catalogues on Waste Import', (announcement) 13 April 2018.
  生态环境部、商务部、国家发展和改革委员会、海关总署，关于调整《进口废物管理目录》的公告（2018年4月13日）
- MEE et al., 'Announcement on adjustment of Catalogues on Waste Import', (announcement) 21 December 2018.

生态环境部、商务部、国家发展和改革委员会、海关总署，关于调整《进口废物管理目录》的公告（2018年12月21日）

- MEP Implementation Plan on EIA Reform during the 13th FYP Period (2016)
环保部'十三五'环境影响评价改革实施方案
- MEP Notice on Coordination between EIA and Permit Control (2017)
环保部关于做好环境影响评价与排污许可制衔接工作的通知
- MEP Notice on Pollution Prevention and Control in Industrial Enterprise Close-down, Relocation and Redevelopment of the Industrial Sites (2014)
环保部关于加强工业企业关停、搬迁及原址场地再开发利用过程中污染防治工作的通知
- MEP Opinion on Strengthening Regulation of Project EIA Focusing on EIA and Post-EIA Stages (2018)
环保部关于强化建设项目环境影响评价事中事后监管的实施意见
- MEP Opinion on Strengthening the Work on Soil Pollution Prevention and Control (2008)
环保部关于加强土壤污染防治工作的意见
- MEP Plan on Information Disclosure for EIA of Construction Projects (2015)
环保部建设项目环境影响评价信息公开机制方案
- MEP and CIRC, Guideline on Pilot Schemes of Compulsory Environmental Pollution Liability Insurance (2013)
环境保护部、中国保险监督管理委员会关于开展环境污染强制责任保险试点工作的指导意见
- MEP and MPS Opinion on Strengthening Cooperation in Law Enforcement between Environmental Protection and Public Security Departments (2013)
环境保护部、公安部关于加强环境保护与公安部门执法衔接配合工作的意见
- MEP et al., 'Announcement on the ban of production, circulation, use, import and export of DDT, chlordane, mirex and HCB (2009)', (announcement) 16 April 2009. www.mee.gov.cn/gkml/hbb/bgg/200910/t20091022_174552.htm
关于禁止生产、流通、使用和进出口滴滴涕、氯丹、灭蚁灵及六氯苯的公告
- MEP et al., 'Announcement on the promulgation of Catalogues on Waste Import (2017)', (announcement) 10 August 2017.
环境保护部、商务部、发展改革委、海关总署、质检总局，关于发布《进口废物管理目录》（2017年）的公告（2017年8月10日）
- MPS et al., Provisional Measures on the Transfer of Environmental Violation Cases by Administrative Agencies in Charge of Administrative Detention (2014)
行政主管部门移送适用行政拘留环境违法案件暂行办法
- National Catalogue of Hazardous Waste (2016)
国家危险废物名录
- NDRC et al., 'Announcement', (announcement no. 29 of 2016) 26 December 2016. www.ndrc.gov.cn/xxgk/zcfb/gg/201612/t20161226_961172.html
- NDRC et al., 'Announcement', (announcement no. 16 of 2018) 29 December 2018. www.ndrc.gov.cn/xxgk/zcfb/gg/201812/t20181229_961214.html
- Provisions on the Approval Authorities over EIA Documents of Construction Projects (2009)
建设项目环境影响评价文件分级审批规定

- Provisional Measures on the Management of Revenues from Emissions Trading (2015)
  排污权出让收入管理暂行办法
- Provisional Measures on Pollution Discharge Permits (2016)
  排污许可证管理暂行规定
- SEPA Circular on Earnestly Accomplishing Pollution Prevention Work in the Enterprise Relocation Process (2004)
  关于切实做好企业搬迁过程中环境污染防治工作的通知
- SEPA and CIRC, Guideline on Environmental Pollution Liability Insurance (2007)
  国家环境保护总局、中国保险监督管理委员会关于环境污染责任保险工作的指导意见
- SPC, MOA, MEP Notice on Implementing the Environmental Civil Public Interest Litigation System (2014)
  最高人民法院、民政部、环境保护部关于贯彻实施环境民事公益诉讼制度的通知
- State Council et al., 'Joint announcement on the complete ban of DDT and other POPs pesticides', 12 May 2009.

Judicial Interpretations

- SPC Interpretation on the Application of the Administrative Litigation Law (2000, 2015, 2018)
  最高人民法院关于适用《中华人民共和国行政诉讼法》的解释
- SPC Interpretation on the Application of Laws in Adjudicating Environmental Tort Cases (2015)
  最高人民法院关于审理环境侵权责任纠纷适用法律若干问题的解释
- SPC Interpretation on Several Issues Concerning the Application of Law in Environmental Civil Public Interest Litigation (2015)
  最高人民法院关于审理环境民事公益诉讼案件适用法律若干问题的解释
- SPC Interpretation on Several Issues in Determining Emotional Damages in Tort (2001)
  最高人民法院关于确定民事侵权精神损害赔偿责任若干问题的解释
- SPC Notice on Pilot Exercise of Centralized Jurisdiction over Administrative Cases (2012)
  关于开展行政案件相对集中管辖试点工作的通知
- SPC Opinion on the Legal Protection of Parties' Rights to Sue in Administrative Litigations (2009)
  最高人民法院关于依法保护行政诉讼当事人诉权的意见
- SPC Opinion on Several Issues in the Application of the Civil Procedure Law (1992)
  最高人民法院关于适用《中华人民共和国民事诉讼法》若干问题的意见
- SPC Opinion on Strengthening Adjudication Work on Environment and Resources to Provide Judicial Guarantee to the Construction of Ecological Civilization (2014)
  最高人民法院关于全面加强环境资源审判工作为推进生态文明建设提供有力司法保障的意见
- SPC Provisions on Jurisdiction over Administrative Cases (2008)
  关于行政案件管辖若干问题的规定
- SPC Several Provisions on Evidence for Civil Litigation (2001)
  最高人民法院关于民事诉讼证据的若干规定
- SPC and SPP Interpretation on the Application of Laws in Procuratorial Public Interest Litigation (2018)
  最高人民法院、最高人民检察院关于检察公益诉讼案件适用法律若干问题的解释
- SPC and SPP Interpretation on the Application of Law in Smuggling Cases (2014)
  最高人民法院、最高人民检察院关于办理走私刑事案件适用法律若干问题的解释

- SPC and SPP Interpretation on Several Issues Concerning the Application of Law in Environmental Criminal Cases (2013, 2016)
  最高人民法院、最高人民检察院关于办理环境污染刑事案件适用法律若干问题的解释
- SPP Implementation Measures on Pilot Projects of Public Interest Litigation Initiated by People's Procuratorates (2015).
  人民检察院提起公益诉讼试点工作实施办法
- SPP Reform Plan on a Pilot Project for Instituting Public Interest Litigation by Procuratorial Organs (2015)
  检查机关提起公益诉讼改革试点方案

State Plans and Party Policies

- 10th Five-Year Plan on Environmental Protection (2001–5)
  国家环境保护'十五'计划
- 11th Five-Year Plan on the Construction of Municipal Solid Waste Disposal Facilities (2006–10) (2007)
  全国城市生活垃圾无害化处理设施建设"十一五"规划
- 11th Five-Year Plan on Environmental Protection (2007)
  国家环境保护'十一五'规划
- 11th Five-Year Plan on National Economic and Social Development (2006–10)
  国民经济和社会发展第十一个五年规划纲要
- 12th Five-Year Plan on Air Pollution Prevention and Control in Key Regions (2012)
  重点区域大气污染防治'十二五'规划
- 12th Five-Year Plan on the Construction of Safe Disposal Facilities for Municipal Solid Waste (2012)
  '十二五'全国城镇生活垃圾无害化处理设施建设规划
- 12th Five-Year Plan on Environment and Development (2011)
  国家环境保护'十二五'环境与健康工作规划
- 12th Five-Year Plan on Environmental Protection (2011)
  国家环境保护'十二五'规划
- 12th Five-Year Plan on National Economic and Social Development (2011–15)
  国民经济和社会发展第十二个五年规划纲要
- 12th Five-Year Plan on Prevention and Control of Pollution by Toxic and Hazardous Waste (2012)
  '十二五'危险废物污染防治规划
- 12th Five-Year Plan on Safe Drinking Water Projects in Rural China (2011–15)
  全国农村饮水安全工程'十二五'规划
- 13th Five-Year Plan on the Construction of Safe Disposal Facilities for Municipal Solid Waste (2016)
  '十三五'全国城镇生活垃圾无害化处理设施建设规划
- 13th Five-Year Plan on the Construction of Wastewater Treatment, Recycling and Reuse Facilities (2016–20)
  '十三五'全国城镇污水处理及再生利用设施建设规划

- 13th Five-Year Plan on Ecological and Environmental Protection (2016)
  '十三五'生态环境保护规划
- 13th Five-Year Plan on Energy Development (2016)
  国家发展改革委、国家能源局关于印发能源发展"十三五"规划的通知(2016）
- 13th Five-Year Plan on Environment and Development (2017)
  国家环境保护'十三五'环境与健康工作规划
- 13th Five-Year Plan on National Economic and Social Development (2016–20)
  国民经济和社会发展第十三个五年规划纲要
- Action Plan on Air Pollution Prevention and Control (2013)
  大气污染防治行动计划
- Action Plan on Prevention and Control of Soil Pollution (2016)
  土壤污染防治行动计划
- Action Plan on Prevention and Control of Water Pollution (2015)
  水污染防治行动计划
- Beijing Municipal Heavy-Pollution-Weather Emergency Response Plan (2016)
  北京市空气重污染应急预案
- CCP Central Committee Plan on Deepening Reform of the Party and State Institutions (2018)
  中共中央深化党和国家机构改革方案
- CCP Central Committee and State Council Guiding Opinion on Pilot Work of Institutional Reform and Vertical Management of Local Environmental Monitoring and Supervision Bodies below the Provincial Level (2016)
  中共中央办公厅、国务院办公厅关于省以下环保机构监测监察执法垂直管理制度改革试点的指导意见
- CCP Central Committee and State Council Integrated Reform Plan for Promoting Ecological Civilization (2015)
  生态文明体制改革总体方案
- CCP Central Committee and State Council Measures on the Accountability of Party and Government Leaders for Eco-environmental Damage (for trial implementation) (2015)
  中共中央办公厅、国务院办公厅党政领导干部生态损害责任追究办法（试行）
- CCP Central Committee and State Council Opinion on Accelerating the Construction of Ecological Civilization (2015)
  关于加快推进生态文明建设的意见
- CCP Central Committee and State Council Opinion to Improve Eco-environmental Protection and Continue Fighting Against Pollution (2018)
  关于全面加强生态环境保护坚决打好污染防治攻坚战的意见
- CCP Central Committee and State Council Opinion on the Promotion of River Chief System (2016)
  中共中央办公厅、国务院办公厅关于全面推行河长制的意见
- CCP Central Committee and State Council Provisions on the Work of Supervision over Ecological and Environmental Protection by Central Authorities (2019)
  中央生态环境保护督察工作规定
- CCP Central Committee and State Council Reform Plan on the Compensation Regime for Eco-environmental Damage (2017)
  生态环境损害赔偿制度改革方案

- Comprehensive Treatment Plan on Chromium Waste Contamination (2005)
  铬渣污染综合整治方案
- Detailed Implementation Plan of the Action Plan on Air Pollution Prevention and Control for Beijing–Tianjin–Hebei and Surrounding Areas (2013)
  京津冀及周边地区落实大气污染防治行动计划实施细则
- Implementation Plan on the Ban of Foreign Garbage to Promote Reform of the Waste Import Control System (2017)
  禁止洋垃圾入境推进固体废物进口管理制度改革实施方案
- Implementation Plan on Permit Control of Pollution Discharge (2016)
  控制污染物排放许可制实施方案
- National Plan on the Construction of Disposal Facilities for Hazardous Waste and Clinical Waste (2004)
  全国危险废物和医疗废物处置设施建设规划
- National Plan to Ensure Drinking Water Hygiene and Safety in Cities (2011–20)
  全国城市饮用水卫生安全保障规划
- National Plan on Environmental Emergency Response (2006, revised 2014)
  国家突发环境事件应急预案
- National Plan on Groundwater Pollution Prevention and Control (2011–20)
  全国地下水污染防治规划
- National Plan on Protection of Drinking-Water-Source Reserves in Cities (2008–20)
  全国城市饮用水水源地环境保护规划
- NEPA and State Planning Commission, China's Environmental Protection Action Plan for 1991–2000 (1994)
  国家环境保护局和国家计划委员会中国环境保护行动计划: 1991–2000
- Opinion on Improving the Eco-compensation Mechanism (2016)
  关于健全生态保护补偿机制的意见
- Opinion on the Recovery and Utilization of Waste from Livestock and Poultry Farming (2017)
  国务院办公厅关于加快推进禽畜养殖废弃物资源化利用的意见
- Plan on the Construction of an Eco-environmental Monitoring Network (2015)
  生态环境检测网络建设方案
- Plan on National Agricultural Modernization (2016–2020) (2016)
  全国农业现代化规划（2016–2020年）
- Plan on Water Pollution Prevention and Control at Key River Basins (2011–15)
  重点流域水污染防治规划
- Three-Year Action Plan on Winning the Battle of Blue-Sky Protection (2018)
  打赢蓝天保卫战三年行动计划

Table of Cases

SPC GUIDING CASES

- SPC 15th Batch of Guiding Cases (case nos. 70–7) (2016)
  最高人民法院第15批指导性案例
- SPC 24th Batch of Guiding Cases (case nos. 127–39) (2019)
  最高人民法院第24批指导性案例
- SPC Guiding Case No. 75: China Biodiversity Conservation and Green Development Foundation *v.* Ningxia Ruitai Science and Technology Co. and Seven Others (2016)
  指导案例75号：中国生物多样性保护与绿色发展基金会诉宁夏瑞泰科技股份有限公司环境污染公益诉讼案

SPP GUIDING CASES

- SPP 2nd Batch of Guiding Cases (case nos. 4–8) (2012)
  最高人民检察院第二批指导性案例
- SPP 8th Batch of Guiding Cases (case nos. 28–32) (2016)
  最高人民检察院第八批指导性案例
- SPP 13th Batch of Guiding Cases (case nos. 49–51) (2018)
  最高人民检察院第十三批指导性案例

SPC MODEL CASES

- SPC Four Model Cases on Environmental Crimes (2013)
  最高人民法院公布四起环境污染犯罪典型案例
- SPC Seven Model Cases on Protection of Livelihoods (2014)
  最高人民法院公布七起保障民生典型案例
- SPC Eight Model Cases on Environmental Crimes (2016)
  最高人民法院公布八起环境污染犯罪典型案例
- SPC Nine Model Cases on Environment and Resources (2014)
  最高人民法院公布的九起环境资源审判典型案例

- SPC 10 Important Administrative Cases on Environmental Protection (2014)
  最高人民法院公布环境保护行政案件十大案例
- SPC 10 Important Administrative Cases on Environmental Protection (second batch) (2016)
  最高法院发布环境保护行政案件十大案例（第二批）
- SPC 10 Model Cases of Environment and Resource Adjudication at the Yangtze River Basin (2017)
  最高人民法院发布长江流域环境资源审判十大典型案例
- SPC 10 Model Cases of Environment and Resources Adjudication to Guarantee High-Quality Development along the Yangtze River Economic Belt (2018)
  最高人民法院发布10起人民法院环境资源审判保障长江经济带高质量发展典型案例
- SPC 10 Model Cases of Environmental Public Interest Litigation (2017)
  最高人民法院发布十起环境公益诉讼典型案例
- SPC 10 Model Cases on Environmental Torts (2015)
  最高人民法院发布10起环境侵权典型案例
- SPC 10 Model Cases on Maritime Trials (2014)
  最高人民法院公布海事审判十大典型案例
- SPC 10 Model Cases on Services Provided by Courts and Guarantees for the Development of Eco-civilization in the New Era (2018)
  最高人民法院发布10起人民法院服务保障新时代生态文明建设典型案例
- SPC 10 Model Criminal, Civil and Administrative Cases on Environment and Resources (2017)
  最高人民法院发布10起环境资源刑事、民事、行政典型案例
- SPC Model Cases on Guaranteeing the Reform of the System of Compensation for Eco-environmental Damage (2019)
  最高人民法院发布人民法院保障生态环境损害赔偿制度改革典型案例

SPP MODEL CASES

- SPP 10 Model Cases of Procuratorial Public Interest Litigation (2018)
  最高人民检察院发布检察公益诉讼十大典型案例
- SPP 10 Model Cases on Strengthening Judicial Protection of the Eco-environment (2015)
  最高人民检察院发布10起检察机关加强生态环境司法保护典型案例
- SPP 15 Model Cases on Crimes against the Ecological Environment (2014)
  最高人民检察院发布15个涉生态环境领域犯罪典型案例
- SPP 26 Model Cases of Public Interest Litigation (2017)
  最高人民检察院公布26起检察机关提起公益诉讼试点工作典型案例

JOINT SPC AND SPP MODEL CASES

- SPC and SPP 10 Model Cases of Procuratorial Public Interest Litigation (2018)
  最高人民法院、最高人民检察院发布10起检察公益诉讼典型案例

OTHER CASES

- All-China Environment Federation *v.* Xiuwen County Environmental Protection Bureau, Guizhou Province (Guizhou Guiyang Intermediate Court, 12 March 2012), *Supreme People's Court Gazette*, 1 (2013)
  中华环保联合会诉贵州省贵阳市修文县环境保护局信息公开案（贵州省贵阳市中级人民法院2012年3月12日二审审结）《最高人民法院公报》2013年第1期
- Cao Baozhang (Shanghai Intermediate Court, 17 August 1992)
  曹保章投毒案（上海市中级人民法院1992年8月17日审结）
- Chunyang Villagers' Committee *v.* Hua'nan Gold Mine Bureau (Jiamusi Intermediate Court, 30 January 1988), *Supreme People's Court Gazette*, 4 (1988), 28–29.
  春阳村村民委员会诉桦南金矿局采金船排污污染水田损害赔偿纠纷案（佳木斯市中级人民法院1988年1月30日二审审结）《最高人民法院公报》1988年第4期
- Friends of Nature and Chongqing Green Volunteer League *v.* Yunnan Luliang Chemical Industry and Yunnan Luliang Peace Technology Ltd (Yunnan Qujing Intermediate Court, 3 August 2020)
  自然之友和重庆绿联与云南省陆良化工实业有限公司和陆良和平科技有限公司（云南省曲靖市中级人民法院2020年8月3日调解结案）
- Geng Yuping and Another (Jiangsu High Court, 20 March 2013)
  耿玉萍等走私废物案（江苏省高级人民法院2013年3月20日二审审结）
- Kunming Sannong Ltd and Another *v.* Kunming Environmental Protection Bureau (Yunnan High Court, 26 May 2011)
  昆明三农农牧有限公司等与昆明市环境保护局环境污染侵权纠纷上诉案（云南省高级人民法院2011年5月26日二审审结）
- Li Jian and Others (2005) (Sichuan Chengdu Jinjiang District Court, 9 September 2005)
  李俭重大环境污染事故案（四川省成都市锦江区人民法院2005年9月9日一审审结）
- Lu Yaodong v. Yongda Co. (Shanghai Pudong New District Court, 1 November 2004), Supreme People's Court Gazette, 5 (2005), 40–42.
  陆耀东诉永达公司环境污染损害赔偿纠纷案（上海市浦东新区人民法院2004年11月1日一审审结）《最高人民法院公报》2005年第5期
- Pinghu Aquatic Farm v. Jiaxing Buyun Dye and Chemical Co. and Others (SPC, 2 April 2009)
  浙江省平湖师范农场特种养殖场与嘉兴市步云染化厂等水污染损害赔偿纠纷案（最高人民法院2009年4月2日再审审结）
- Shen Xixian and 181 Others v. Beijing Urban Planning Commission (Beijing No. 2 Intermediate Court, 24 October 2003), *Supreme People's Court Gazette*, 3 (2004), 40–43.
  沈希贤等182人诉北京市规划委员会颁发建设工程规划许可证纠纷案（北京市第一中级人民法院2003年10月24日二审审结）《最高人民法院公报》2004年第3期
- Shenzhen Shekou Environmental Monitoring Station *v.* Hong Kong Kaida Enterprise Ltd (Shenzhen Intermediate Court, 14 July 1984) *Supreme People's Court Gazette*, 3 (1985), 44–46
  深圳市蛇口区环境监测站与香港凯达企业有限公司环境污染案（深圳市中级人民法院1984年7月14日一审结案）《最高人民法院公报》1985年第3期

- Song Shiying and Others (Sichuan Chengdu Jinjiang District Court, 9 September 2005)
  宋世英环境监管失职案（四川省成都市锦江区人民法院2005年9月9日一审审结）
- William Ping Chen (Shanghai High Court, 28 February 1997), *Supreme People's Court Gazette*, 1 (1997), 20–21.
  威廉 平 陈走私案（上海市高级人民法院1997年2月28日二审审结）《最高人民法院公报》1997年第1期
- Wu Shengli (Guangdong Huizhou Intermediate Court, 18 May 2000)
  吴胜利走私固体废物案（广东省惠州市中级人民法院2000年5月18日一审审结）
- Yang Junwu (1998) (Shanxi Yuncheng Intermediate Court, 7 December 1998), *Supreme People's Court Gazette*, 2 (1999), 63–64.
  杨军武重大环境污染事故案（山西省运城市中级人民法院1998年12月7日二审审结）《最高人民法院公报》1999年第2期
- Zhang Changlin (criminal judgment no. 26, Jiangsu Suzhou Intermediate Court, 27 October 1979)
  张长林案（江苏省苏州市中级人民法院1979年10月27日审结）

Table of Treaties

- Declaration of the UN Conference on the Human Environment, Stockholm, 16 June 1972. *International Legal Materials*, 11 (1972), 1416–69.
- Convention on International Trade in Endangered Species of Wild Fauna and Flora, Washington, 3 March 1973, treaty no. 14537. *International Legal Materials*, 12 (1973), 1085–104.
- Montreal Protocol on Substances that Deplete the Ozone Layer, Montreal, 16 September 1987, *International Legal Materials*, 26 (1987), 1541–61.
- Vienna Convention for the Protection of the Ozone Layer, Vienna, 22 March 1985, *International Legal Materials*, 26 (1987), 1516–40.
- Basel Convention on the Control of Transboundary Movements of Hazardous Wastes and their Disposal, Basel, 22 March 1989, treaty no. 28911. *United Nations Treaty Series*, 1673, 57–336.
- United Nations Framework Convention on Climate Change, New York, 9 May 1992, treaty no. 30822. *United Nations Treaty Series*, 1771, 107–322.
- Convention on Biological Diversity, Rio de Janeiro, 5 June 1992, treaty no. 30619. *United Nations Treaty Series*, 1760, 79–308.
- Rio Declaration on Environment and Development, Rio de Janeiro, 14 June 1992, *International Legal Materials*, 31 (1992), 874–80.
- Kyoto Protocol to the United Nations Framework Convention on Climate Change, Kyoto, 11 December 1997, treaty no. 30822. *United Nations Treaty Series*, 2303, 162–331.
- Stockholm Convention on Persistent Organic Pollutants, Stockholm, 22 May 2001, treaty no. 40214. *United Nations Treaty Series*, 2256, 119–404.
- International Convention for the Control and Management of Ship's Ballast Water and Sediments, London, 13 February 2004. https://treaties.un.org/doc/Publication/UNTS/No%20Volume/55544/Part/I-55544-080000028053b465.pdf
- Paris Agreement (2015), Paris, 12 December 2015, treaty no. 54113. *International Legal Materials*, 55 (2016), 743–55.

Abbreviations

AAQ	Ambient Air Quality
AAQS	Ambient Air Quality Standards
ACEF	All-China Environment Federation
ALL	Administrative Litigation Law
APL	Administrative Penalty Law
APPCL	Air Pollution Prevention and Control Law
AQI	Air Quality Index
CBCGDF	China Biodiversity Conservation and Green Development Foundation
CCP	Chinese Communist Party
CEPL	Law on Promotion of the Circular Economy
CFC	Chlorofluorocarbon
CIRC	China Insurance Regulatory Commission
CL	Criminal Law
CLAPV	Center of Legal Aid for Victims of Pollution
CO	Carbon Monoxide
CO_2	Carbon Dioxide
COD	Chemical Oxygen Demand
CPL	Civil Procedure Law
CPPCC	Chinese People's Political Consultative Conference
Cr^{6+}	Hexavalent Chromium
CRC	China Resources Cement Holdings Ltd
DDT	Dichlorodiphenyltrichloroethane
DWSR	Drinking-Water-Source Reserve
EA	Environmental Assessment
EEB	Ecology and Environmental Bureau
EEP	Electrical and Electronic Product
EIA	Environmental Impact Assessment
EIAL	Environmental Impact Assessment Law
EPA	Environmental Protection Agency
EPB	Environmental Protection Bureau
EPC	Environmental Protection Commission

EPIL	Environmental Public Interest Litigation
EPL	Environmental Protection Law
EPR	Extended Producer Responsibility
EPTL	Environmental Protection Tax Law
ERD	Environment and Resources Division
ERPC	Environment and Resources Protection Committee
FGB	Forestry and Grassland Bureau
FON	Friends of Nature
FYP	Five-Year Plan
GAC	General Administration of Customs
GDP	Gross Domestic Product
GEV	Green Earth Volunteers
GHG	Greenhouse Gas
GONGO	Government-Organized Non-governmental Organization
GPCL	General Principles of Civil Law
GRCL	General Rules of Civil Law
GVB	Global Village Beijing
HCH	Hexachlorocyclohexane
HW	Hazardous Waste
IPE	Institute of Public and Environmental Affairs
ISW	Industrial Solid Waste
KPS	Key Polluting Source
KPU	Key Polluting Unit
KWP	Key Water Pollutant
LAC	Legislative Affairs Commission
LAO	Legislative Affairs Office
MARA	Ministry of Agriculture and Rural Affairs
MEE	Ministry of Ecology and Environment
MEP	Ministry of Environmental Protection
MEPL	Marine Environmental Protection Law
MIIT	Ministry of Industry and Information Technology
MLR	Ministry of Land and Resources
MNR	Ministry of Natural Resources
MOA	Ministry of Agriculture
MOC	Ministry of Commerce
MOF	Ministry of Finance
MOFTEC	Ministry of Foreign Trade and Economic Cooperation
MOHURD	Ministry of Housing and Urban–Rural Development
MOYP	Management Office of the YuanMingYuan Park
MPS	Ministry of Public Security
MSA	Maritime Safety Administration
MSW	Municipal Solid Waste
MURCEP	Ministry of Urban–Rural Construction and Environmental Protection

MWR	Ministry of Water Resources
NDRC	National Development and Reform Commission
NEERP	National Environmental Emergency Response Plan
NEMC	National Environmental Monitoring Center
NEPA	National Environmental Protection Agency
NFGA	National Forestry and Grassland Administration
NGO	Non-governmental Organization
NH	Ammonia Nitrogen
NH_3	Ammonia
NIMBY	Not In My Backyard
NOx	Nitrogen Oxides
NPC	National People's Congress
NPCSC	National People's Congress Standing Committee
NPPCL	Noise Pollution Prevention and Control Law
NRDC	Natural Resources Defense Council
ODS	Ozone-Depleting Substances
OECD	Organization for Economic Cooperation and Development
OGV	Ocean-Going Vessel
PCSC	People's Congress Standing Committee
PIL	Public Interest Litigation
PITI	Pollution Information Transparency Index
$PM_{2.5}$	Particulate Matter Less Than 2.5 Microns in Diameter
PM_{10}	Particulate Matter Less Than 10 Microns in Diameter
POP	Persistent Organic Pollutant
PSB	Public Security Bureau
RGID	Regulation on Government Information Disclosure
SAQSIQ	State Administration for Quality Supervision, Inspection and Quarantine
SARS	Severe Acute Respiratory Syndrome
SEA	Strategic Environmental Assessment
SEPA	State Environmental Protection Administration
SO_2	Sulphur Dioxide
SOA	State Oceanic Administration
SPC	Supreme People's Court
SPP	Supreme People's Procuratorate
SPPCL	Soil Pollution Prevention and Control Law
SPPCP	Soil Pollution Prevention and Control Plan
SWL	Law on the Prevention and Control of Pollution by Solid Waste
TL	Tort Law
UNEP	United Nations Environment Programme
UNFCCC	United Nations Framework Convention on Climate Change
UVB	Ultraviolet B Radiation
VAT	Value-Added Tax
VOC	Volatile Organic Compound

WHO	World Health Organization
WPPCL	Water Pollution Prevention and Control Law
WPPCP	Water Pollution Prevention and Control Plan
WQS	Water Quality Standard

Abbreviations of Legal Instruments

10th FYP	10th Five-Year Plan on National Economic and Social Development
11th FYP	11th Five-Year Plan on National Economic and Social Development
12th FYP	12th Five-Year Plan on National Economic and Social Development
13th FYP	13th Five-Year Plan on National Economic and Social Development
Air Action Plan (2013)	Action Plan on Air Pollution Prevention and Control (2013)
Catalogue (2017)	Catalogue of Stationary Sources Subject to Pollution Discharge Permit Control (2017)
Catalogue (2019)	Catalogue of Stationary Sources Subject to Pollution Discharge Permit Control (2019)
Construction Plan (2004)	National Plan on the Construction of Disposal Facilities for Hazardous Waste and Clinical Waste (2004)
Detailed Implementation Plan (2013)	Detailed Implementation Plan of the Action Plan on Air Pollution Prevention and Control for Beijing–Tianjin–Hebei and Surrounding Areas (2013)
Draft Measures (2017)	Measures on Compulsory Liability Insurance for Environmental Pollution (draft for consultation) (2017)
EIA Regulation (1998)	Regulation on the Management of Environmental Protection of Construction Projects (1998)
EIA Regulation (2017)	Regulation on the Management of Environmental Protection of Construction Projects (2017)
Guideline (2007)	Guideline on Environmental Pollution Liability Insurance (2007)
HW Catalogue (2016)	National Catalogue of Hazardous Waste (2016)

Implementation Plan (2016)	Implementation Plan on Permit Control of Pollution Discharge (2016)
Inventory (2018)	Inventory on Environmental Impact Assessment Categories of Construction Projects (2018)
Measures on HW Permit Control (2016)	Measures on Permit Control over Hazardous Waste Operations (2016)
Measures on Permit Control (2018)	Measures on Permit Control of Pollution Discharge (for trial implementation) (2018)
Measures on Public Participation (2018)	Measures on Public Participation in Environmental Impact Assessment (2018)
Measures on Waste Import (2011)	Measures on the Importing of Solid Waste (2011)
MEP Measures (2015)	Measures on Qualification Management of Construction Project Environmental Impact Assessment (2015)
MEP Provisions (2017)	Provisions on the List of Key Polluting Units (for trial use) (2017)
New Guideline (2013)	Guideline on Pilot Schemes of Compulsory Environmental Pollution Liability Insurance (2013)
Notice on MSW Disposal Fees (2002)	Notice on Implementing Municipal Solid Waste Disposal Fees to Foster the Waste Disposal Industry (2002)
Plan on EPR (2016)	Plan on Implementation of the Extended Producer Responsibility Scheme (2016)
Plan on DWSRs (2008–2020)	National Plan on the Protection of Drinking-Water-Source Reserves in Cities (2008–2020)
Provisional Measures (2006)	Provisional Measures on Public Participation in Environmental Impact Assessment (2006)
Provisional Measures on Reporting (1987)	Provisional Measures on Reporting of Environmental Pollution and Destruction Incidents (1987)
Provisions on Environmental Case Transfer (2007)	Provisions on the Transfer of Suspected Environmental Criminal Cases by the Environmental Protection Agencies (2007)
Recent Work Arrangement (2013)	Recent Work Arrangement on Soil Environmental Protection and Comprehensive Treatment (2013)
Reform Plan on PIL Pilots (2015)	Reform Plan on a Pilot Project for Instituting Public Interest Litigation by Procuratorial Organs (2015)
Regulation on Discharge Fees (2003)	Regulation on the Levy and Use of Pollution Discharge Fees (2003)
Regulation on Environmental Tax (2017)	Regulation on the Implementation of the Environmental Protection Tax Law (2017)

Regulation on ODS (2010) and (2018)	Regulation on the Administration of Ozone-Depleting Substances (2010) and (2018)
Regulation on Plan EA (2009)	Regulation on Environmental Assessment of Plans (2009)
SEPA Circular (2004)	Circular on Earnestly Accomplishing Pollution Prevention Work in the Enterprise Relocation Process (2004)
SEPA Guidance (2006)	Guidance on Solid Waste Information Disclosure by Large and Medium-Sized Cities (2006)
Soil Action Plan (2016)	Action Plan on Prevention and Control of Soil Pollution (2016)
SPC Interpretation (2015)	Interpretation on the Application of Laws in Adjudicating Environmental Tort Cases (2015)
SPC Interpretation on Civil EPIL (2015)	Interpretation on Several Issues Concerning the Application of Law in Environmental Civil Public Interest Litigation (2015)
SPC Interpretation on Environmental Crime (2006)	Interpretation on the Application of Law in Adjudicating Environmental Criminal Cases (2006)
SPC Interpretation on the ALL (2000)	Interpretation on the Application of the Administrative Litigation Law (2000)
SPC and SPP Interpretation on Environmental Crime (2013) and (2016)	Interpretation on Several Issues Concerning the Application of Law in Environmental Criminal Cases (2013) and (2016)
SPC and SPP Interpretation on Smuggling (2014)	Interpretation on the Application of Law in Smuggling Cases (2014)
SPC Opinions on Judicial Guarantee and Services (2010)	Several Opinions on Providing Judicial Guarantee and Services for Accelerating the Transformation of the Economic Development Mode (2010)
SPC and SPP Interpretation (2013) and (2016)	Interpretation on the Application of Laws in Adjudicating Environmental Criminal Cases (2013) and (2016)
SPP Implementation Measures (2015)	Implementation Measures on Pilot Projects of Public Interest Litigation Initiated by People's Procuratorates (2015)
SPP Provisions (2006)	Provisions on Standards for Accepting Cases Involving the Crimes of Dereliction of Duties and Infringement of Rights (2006)
State Council Decision (2005)	Decision on Implementing Scientific Development and Strengthening Environmental Protection (2005)
Water Action Plan (2015)	Action Plan on Prevention and Control of Water Pollution (2015)
Work Plan on EEP Pilots (2015)	Work Plan on a Pilot Exercise of Extended Producer Responsibility on Electrical and Electronic Products (2015)

1

Environmental Problems and Legal Responses

China's unprecedented economic growth since the late 1970s is rapidly depleting its natural resources and the environmental carrying capacities of air, water and land. 'Environmental pollution has become one of the main factors threatening human health, public security and social stability.'[1] 'There is a huge gap between the quality of the environment and people's demands and expectations.'[2] China addresses environmental problems with a range of legal instruments issued by national and local lawmaking bodies and administrative and judicial organs. In addition to the formal sources of law, state and party policies and plans often lead and shape the development of environmental law in China.

This chapter is divided into three sections. Section 1.1 exposes China's environmental crisis, the scale and impact of its air and water pollution and land contamination. Section 1.2 discusses the sources of environmental law in China: (i) the Constitution; (ii) specialized environmental statutes that regulate human conduct and the operation of legal persons and other organizations to prevent and control pollution; (iii) civil, criminal, administrative and procedural laws that are crucial in legal resolution of environmental problems; (iv) state regulations and administrative rules that implement national laws; (v) judicial interpretations that bind the courts and procuratorates in adjudication and procuratorial work, ensuring correct and consistent application of environmental law; (vi) local regulations that implement national laws, regulations and plans at a local level and (vii) international environmental treaties that China has ratified. Section 1.3 examines state and party policies and plans that have significant impact on the development of Chinese environmental law.

1.1 CHINA'S ENVIRONMENTAL CRISIS

The large-scale and high-speed economic growth seen in China since 1978 when the pragmatic leader Deng Xiaoping came to power has changed the lives of 1.3 billion Chinese and lifted 850 million out of poverty.[3] He initiated an 'open-door' policy to facilitate

[1] State Council, 12th Five-Year Plan (FYP) on Environmental Protection (2011), part I.

[2] State Council, 13th FYP on Ecological and Environmental Protection (2016), chapter 1.

[3] The poverty rate of the rural population in China fell from 97.5 per cent in 1978 to 3.1 per cent in 2017. See State Council, *Human Rights Development in China during Forty Years of Reform* (2018). www.pkulaw.cn, part II.

China's economic reform and take-off after decades of chaotic political campaigns and class struggles during the Mao era. Within just forty years, China was transformed from a low-income developing country with a gross domestic product (GDP) of 367.9 billion yuan in 1978 to a powerhouse with a GDP of 82,712.2 billion yuan in 2017.[4] In 2011, China overtook Japan to become the world's second largest economy.[5] Such rapid economic ascendance has brought severe adverse impacts to the environment and to ecosystems, given the size and scale of China's population and economy. Environmental degradation caused by large-scale industrialization and urbanization has turned blue sky, clear water and green mountains into heavy smog, dark rivers, contaminated land and poisoned produce. Access to clean air and safe drinking water has become a luxury for China's citizens, rather than a basic staple.

By the early 1990s, seven areas had been identified as top priorities for action by state departments: (i) water pollution, especially contamination by organic waste; (ii) urban air pollution, as measured by particulates and sulphur dioxide (SO_2); (iii) pollution caused by industrial toxic and hazardous waste and municipal solid waste; (iv) water shortages, particularly in northern China; (v) soil erosion; (vi) low forest coverage and grassland deterioration and (vii) loss of species and habitats, especially wetlands.[6] Key elements of the environment, including air, water and land, continued to deteriorate, causing serious harm to human health and heavy losses to public and private property, and threatening and constraining China's long-term sustainable development.

1.1.1 Air Pollution

Coal is the primary source of air pollution in China. As the world's largest producer and consumer of coal, China burns as much coal as the rest of the world combined.[7] Its coal-fired power plants and industrial furnaces operate inefficiently and fail to control pollution effectively. Coal consumption contributes to 70 per cent of smoke and dust emissions and 90 per cent of SO_2 emissions in China.[8] Vehicles are another major source of air pollution. An expansion in car ownership, heavy traffic and low-grade petrol have made vehicles the leading source of air pollution in major cities. Particulate matters, major pollutants contributing to China's bad air and emitted by coal burning, industry and vehicles, are fine dust and soot, as well as aerosol particles less than 10 microns in diameter (PM_{10}) and less than 2.5 microns in diameter ($PM_{2.5}$).

4 State Council, *Human Rights Development* (2018), part III.

5 Justin McCurry and Julia Kollewe, 'China overtakes Japan as world's second-largest economy', *The Guardian*, 14 February 2011; 'China's economy is now the world's second largest', BBC News, 14 February 2011.

6 NEPA and State Planning Commission, China's Environmental Protection Action Plan for 1991 to 2000 (1994), at 118–21. The NEPA was elevated in 1998 and renamed the State Environmental Protection Administration (SEPA), which was further upgraded to the Ministry of Environmental Protection (MEP) in 2008. It was then restructured and renamed the Ministry of Ecology and Environment (MEE) in 2018. The State Planning Commission (1952–98) became the State Development Planning Commission (1998–2003), and then the National Development and Reform Commission (NDRC) in March 2003. The NDRC is the most powerful of China's ministries and is in charge of socio-economic development.

7 Adam Vaughan, 'China burns half of coal consumption worldwide, figures show', *The Guardian*, 30 January 2013. China's coal consumption peaked in 2013 at 4.24 billion t. Government efforts to improve the country's energy structure and tackle pollution resulted in a fall in coal use from 2014 to 2016. Coal consumption rose slightly in 2017 and again in 2018, but has not returned to 2013 levels. See Feng Hao and Tom Baxter, 'China's coal consumption on the rise', *China Dialogue*, 1 March 2019.

8 State Council, *Environmental Protection in China* (1996). www.pkulaw.cn, part III.

TABLE 1.1 WHO AIR QUALITY GUIDELINES (AQG) ON ANNUAL MEAN CONCENTRATION LEVELS OF PM_{10} AND $PM_{2.5}$

	WHO interim targets (stage I) (μg/m³)	WHO interim targets (stage II) (μg/m³)	WHO interim targets (stage III) (μg/m³)	WHO goal (μg/m³)
PM_{10}	70	50	30	20
$PM_{2.5}$	35	25	15	10

Sources: WHO, *Air Quality Guidelines for Particulate Matter, Ozone, Nitrogen Dioxide and Sulfur Dioxide: Global update 2005: Summary of Risk Assessment* (World Health Organization, 2006), at 11.

In order to protect public health, the World Health Organization (WHO) has made recommendations on air quality targets, as seen in Table 1.1.

For years after the promulgation of the WHO AQG (2006), however, China continued to implement its Ambient Air Quality Standards (GB3095-1996, amended 2000), which applies limits on major air pollutants, including SO_2, NO_2 and PM_{10}, for three different types of zone:

(i) Grade I: nature reserves, scenic areas and other special protection areas;
(ii) Grade II: residential areas, mixed commercial and residential areas, cultural areas, ordinary industrial zones and rural regions and
(iii) Grade III: special industrial zones.

The national ambient air quality standard for PM_{10} was 40 μg/m³ for Grade I areas, 100 μg/m³ for Grade II and 150 μg/m³ for Grade III.[9] They were much higher than the maximum recommended by the WHO. In 2006, of 559 cities monitored, 33.5 per cent had an annual mean PM_{10} concentration level of more than 100 μg/m³ and 7 per cent had excessively high PM_{10} levels of more than 150 μg/m³.[10] Worse still, $PM_{2.5}$ was not monitored. Air quality continued to deteriorate, especially in the economically most-advanced regions, including the Pearl River Delta, Yangtze River Delta and the Beijing–Tianjin–Hebei region. By 2010, megacities, including Guangzhou, Shenzhen, Shanghai, Nanjing, Suzhou and Tianjin, had smoggy days on 30 per cent to 50 per cent of all days of the year. In 2010, 17.2 per cent of the cities monitored failed to achieve Grade II air quality.[11]

Faced by both domestic and international pressure and demand for clean air, China finally adopted the new Ambient Air Quality Standards (AAQS) (GB3095-2012) to include $PM_{2.5}$ and revised concentration levels for other pollutants, including PM_{10}.[12] It replaced the three categories of zones with two:

(i) Grade I: nature reserves, scenic zones and special protection areas;
(ii) Grade II: residential, mixed commercial and residential, industrial and rural areas.

[9] Ambient Air Quality Standards (GB3095-1996, amended 2000).

[10] SEPA, *2006 China Environment Gazette* (2007). www.mee.gov.cn/hjzl/sthjzk/, at 43.

[11] Zhou Shengxian, *Report on Environmental Protection Work* (2011). www.pkulaw.cn. On 25 October 2011, Zhou Shengxian, the then minister of environmental protection, presented the report to the 23rd session of the 11th NPCSC.

[12] The Ambient Air Quality Standards (GB3095-2012) were issued by the MEP and the State Administration for Quality Supervision, Inspection and Quarantine (SAQSIQ) on 29 February 2012. It came into force on 1 January 2016.

TABLE 1.2 ANNUAL MEAN CONCENTRATION LEVELS OF PM_{10} AND $PM_{2.5}$ ($\mu G/M^3$) IN BEIJING

	AAQS (2012) target		2016	2017	2018	2019
	Grade I	Grade II				
PM_{10} ($\mu g/m^3$)	40	70	92	84	78	68
$PM_{2.5}$ ($\mu g/m^3$)	15	35	73	58	51	42

Sources: AAQS (GB3095-2012); MEP, *2016 China Environment Gazette.* www.mee.gov.cn/hjzl/sthjzk/; MEE, *2017 to 2019 China Ecology and Environment Gazette.* www.mee.gov.cn/hjzl/sthjzk/.

The 2012 AAQS was implemented across China in stages, finally covering the whole country on 1 January 2016. As a result of tightened quality standards for major and newly monitored and controlled pollutants, an overwhelming majority of cities failed to meet the requirements of the AAQS. Of 338 cities monitored, 75.1 per cent failed to achieve the required standard in 2016,[13] 70.7 per cent failed in 2017[14] and 64.2 per cent failed in 2018.[15] The new AAQS was first implemented in 2012 in the Yangtze River Delta, Pearl River Delta and the Beijing–Tianjin–Hebei region, areas in which significant efforts had already been made to abate air pollution from all sources. Despite this, many cities, including the capital Beijing, were still in violation in 2019, notwithstanding steady improvement over the years.

PM_{10} and $PM_{2.5}$ are suspended particulates – these include sulphates, nitrates, metals and organic chemicals – that are largely emitted by vehicles, manufacturing, power plants and farming. Most Chinese cities have dangerously high levels of PM_{10} and $PM_{2.5}$ that exceed the WHO guidelines several times, and lead to health conditions, including asthma, lung cancer, heart disease, stroke and chronic obstructive pulmonary disorder. Another major air pollutant in China is SO_2, which is emitted by burning coal and diesel. It can cause respiratory and cardiovascular diseases, as well as acid rain. China became the world's largest emitter of SO_2 in 2005.[16] As per Table 1.3, acid rain affected around 50 per cent of cities monitored in 2005, at the end of the 10th Five-Year Plan on National Economic and Social Development (for the period 2000–5) (10th FYP), and in 2010, at the end of the 11th Five-Year Plan on National Economic and Social Development (for the period 2006–10) (11th FYP). Cities affected by acid rain dropped to 40 per cent in 2015, at the end of the 12th FYP on National Economic and Social Development (for the period 2011–15) (12th FYP). During the 13th FYP on National Economic and Social Development

[13] MEP, *2016 China Environment Gazette*, at 7.

[14] MEE, *2017 China Ecology and Environment Gazette*, at 7.

[15] MEE, *2018 China Ecology and Environment Gazette*, at 7.

[16] At a press conference in 2006, the SEPA said China emitted 25.49 million t of SO_2 in 2005, making it the world's largest emitter. See Xia Mingqun, 'State Environmental Protection Administration: China's sulfur dioxide emissions ranked first in the world in 2005', *Sina Finance*, 4 August 2006. http://finance.sina.com.cn/g/20060804/09052792219.shtml

TABLE 1.3 CHINESE CITIES AFFECTED BY ACID RAIN

	2005	2010	2015	2016	2017	2018
Total cities monitored	696	494	480	474	463	471
Per cent of cities affected (%)	51.3	50.4	40.4	38.8	36.1	37.6

Sources: SEPA, *2005 China Environment Gazette*; MEP, *2010 China Environment Gazette*; MEP, *2015 China Environment Gazette*; MEP, *2016 China Environment Gazette*; MEE, *2018 China Ecology and Environment Gazette*.

(for the period 2016–20) (13th FYP), the proportion of cities affected has remained below 40 per cent.

Acid rain directly affects ecosystems. Acid deposition of rain, snow, fog and dew damages forests and agricultural crops, while deposition on lakes and rivers harms aquatic flora and fauna. Acid rain also corrodes metals and building materials and impacts on human health. A conservative estimate of the economic costs of crop and forestry losses was more than 4 billion US dollars a year, perhaps as much as 5 billion US dollars a year.[17]

1.1.2 The Water Crisis: Water Pollution and Water Shortage

China's water crisis is an even more acute challenge.[18] Serious water pollution and shortage not only threaten public health, but also restrict China's ability to sustain its industrial and agricultural output. China is home to 20 per cent of the world's population, but only 7 per cent of its fresh water.[19] Pollution by untreated industrial effluent and household sewage has intensified the water shortage. In contrast to the large-scale and swift industrialization and urbanization seen in China since 1978, pollution treatment infrastructure remains a weakness. By the mid-1990s, only 20 per cent of municipal wastewater received treatment before discharge and less than 50 per cent of solid waste was disposed of safely.[20] By the end of 2004, the municipal wastewater treatment rate had reached 46 per cent and the rate for safe disposal of municipal solid waste (MSW) was 52 per cent.[21] The 11th FYP on Environmental Protection (2007) accepted that the discharge of major pollutants far exceeded China's environmental carrying capacity and had caused serious pollution. In 2005, more than a quarter of surface water had quality below Grade V, the lowest grade, and was not safe for use. More than 60 per cent of surface water did not meet quality standards for Grade III and was thus unsafe for use as drinking water, even with treatment.[22] In China, the quality of surface water is divided into five grades, each of

[17] World Bank, *Clear Water, Blue Skies: China's Environment in the New Century* (Washington, DC, World Bank Group, 1997), at 21–2, 26–8; see also Thorjorn Larssen et al., 'Acid rain in China', *Environmental Science and Technology*, 40:2 (2006), 418–25.

[18] Ma Jun, *China's Water Crisis* (Beijing: China Environmental Sciences Publishing House, 1999).

[19] World Affairs Council of Pittsburgh, 18 April 2014, 'China's struggle to access water'. Blog. https://worldpittsburgh.wordpress.com/2014/04/18/chinas-struggle-to-access-water/

[20] State Council, *Environmental Protection in China* (1996), part III.

[21] State Council, *Environmental Protection in China 1996–2005* (2006). www.pkulaw.cn, part IV.

[22] State Council, 11th FYP on Environmental Protection (2007), part I.

which is suitable for different uses, under the Surface Water Quality Standards (GB3838-2002):

> Grade I: water flowing through state nature reserves;
> Grade II: drinking-water-source reserve (DWSR) (I); conservation areas for rare aquatic species; areas for fish spawning;
> Grade III: DWSR (II); conservation areas for common aquatic species; areas for swimming;
> Grade IV: industrial water use; recreational use other than skin-contact activities;
> Grade V: agricultural water use; for use in view-only water features in parks or gardens.

By 2010, the municipal wastewater treatment rate had increased to 77 per cent, and the rate for safe disposal of MSW had reached 72.4 per cent.[23] Water quality had improved slightly by the end of 2010 when more than half of surface water reached Grade III and above, compared to 38 per cent in 2005.[24] The toxic water that had lost all function, sub-Grade V, dropped to 20.8 per cent, a slight improvement compared to 26 per cent in 2005.[25] By the end of the 12th FYP period in 2015, roughly two-thirds of surface water had achieved water quality of Grade III and above and the proportion of water that fell into the worst sub-Grade V category had dropped to 9.7 per cent.[26] This slow improvement continued during the 13th FYP period (2016–20).[27]

Groundwater quality is even more alarming. In 2010, 57 per cent of the groundwater monitored was rated as 'poor' or 'very poor'.[28] Under China's Standard for Groundwater Quality, there are five categories of groundwater, each with different uses:[29]

> Grade I (very good): low levels of chemicals detected, suitable for any use;
> Grade II (good): relatively low levels of chemicals detected, suitable for any use;
> Grade III (average): medium levels of chemicals detected, suitable for use as source of centralized drinking water supply and other industrial and agricultural use;
> Grade IV (poor): relatively high levels of chemicals detected, suitable for agricultural and certain industrial use, may be used as drinking water subject to proper treatment;
> Grade V (very poor): high levels of chemicals detected, not suitable for drinking water supply, may be used for other purposes.

[23] Zhou Shengxian, *Report on Environmental Protection Work.*
[24] State Council, 12th FYP on Environmental Protection (2011), part I.
[25] Zhou Shengxian, *Report on Environmental Protection Work*, part I.
[26] State Council, 13th FYP on Environmental Protection (2016), part I. Note that the annual report by the MEP recorded a slightly different set of data: 64.5 per cent for Grades I to III, 26.7 per cent for Grades IV and V, and 8.8 per cent for sub-Grade V. See MEP, *2015 China Environment Gazette*, at 5.
[27] MEP, *2016 China Environment Gazette*; MEE, *2017 China Ecology and Environment Gazette*; MEE, *2018 China Ecology and Environment Gazette.*
[28] Zhou Shengxian, *Report on Environmental Protection Work*; see also MEP, *2010 China Environment Gazette.*
[29] Standard for Groundwater Quality (GB/T 14848-2017), s. 4.1. The Standard for Groundwater Quality (GB/T 14848-2017, replacing GB/T 14848-1993) was issued by the SAQSIQ and State Standardization Commission on 14 October 2017. It came into force on 1 May 2018.

TABLE 1.4 SURFACE WATER QUALITY AS A PERCENTAGE OF MONITORED RIVERS AND LAKES

	Grades I–III (%)	Grades IV–V (%)	Sub-grade V (%)
2005	38	36	26
2010	51.9	27.3	20.8
2015	66	24.3	9.7
2016	67.8	23.7	8.6[a]
2017	67.9	23.8	8.3
2018	71	22.3	6.7
2019	74.9	21.7	3.4

Sources: MEP, *2005 China Environment Gazette* to *2016 China Environment Gazette*; MEE, *2017 China Ecology and Environment Gazette* to *2019 China Ecology and Environment Gazette.*
[a] Due to rounding, percentages in this table may not total 100 per cent.

In 2010, the MEP started to publish – in its annual gazette – more detailed data on groundwater quality. Table 1.5 shows China has experienced further deterioration of groundwater quality since 2010, with the 'poor' and 'very poor' categories going up from 57 per cent in 2010 to 86.2 per cent in 2018.

China's water resources face serious risks of being contaminated by secret or hidden discharge of untreated wastewater and illegally dumped hazardous waste (HW), as well as by environmental emergencies caused by chemical explosions or spills. China has approximately 44,600 chemical factories, of which 72 per cent are located along the Yangtze, Yellow and Pearl rivers and Lake Tai, while 12.2 per cent are within 1 km of a DWSR or other eco-sensitive region.[30] Damage caused by water pollution includes a reduction in the land available for farming following irrigation with wastewater, human health problems caused by unsafe drinking water that has been contaminated with pesticides, fertilizers and toxic discharges, and declines in fish catches.[31]

The other aspect of China's water crisis is a water shortage, which is directly linked to pollution. Serious pollution means that water cannot be used as drinking water, or as an industrial or agricultural input. Pollution of surface waters drives an over-reliance on groundwater. Aquifers in northern China have been depleted faster than they can be replenished. Levels have dropped by 50 m to 90 m in the Hai River Basin, and in cities such as Tianjin and Beijing serious subsidence has occurred.[32] Inefficient use of water intensifies the problem. Some estimates suggest that up to 60 per cent of water used for irrigation is lost to evaporation from canals and fields and to poor maintenance of an outdated supply

[30] Zhou Shengxian, *Report on Environmental Protection Work.*

[31] Xiaoying Ma and Leonard Ortolano, *Environmental Regulation in China: Institutions, Enforcement, and Compliance* (Lanham, MD: Rowman & Littlefield, 2000), 3.

[32] World Bank, *China: Agenda for Water Sector Strategy for North China (Summary Report)*, (Washington, DC: World Bank Group, 2002), at 32–4.

TABLE 1.5 GROUNDWATER QUALITY

	Number of monitoring wells	Grade I (very good) (%)	Grade II (good) (%)	Grade III (average) (%)	Grade IV (poor) (%)	Grade V (very poor) (%)
2010	4,110	10.2	27.6	5	40.4	16.8
					57.2	
2015	5,118	9.1	25	4.6	42.5	18.8
					61.3	
2016	6,124	10.1	25.4	4.4	45.4	14.7
					60.1	
2017	5,100	8.8	23.1	1.5	51.8	14.8
					66.6	
2018	10,168	1.9	9.0	2.9	70.7	15.5
					86.2	
2019*	10,168	14.4 (Grades I to III)			66.9	18.8
					85.7	

Sources: MEP, *2010 China Environment Gazette* to *2016 China Environment Gazette* ; MEE, *2017 China Ecology and Environment Gazette* to *2019 China Ecology and Environment Gazette.*
* Due to rounding, percentage is not 100.

infrastructure. China's extremely unbalanced distribution of water resources further intensifies the water shortage: 80 per cent of water supply is found in the south, primarily in the Yangtze River basin. The north, home to approximately half China's population and 66 per cent of its agriculture, is an immense and parched region that threatens to become the world's biggest desert. From 1982 to 2000, the Yellow River ran dry for as much as two-thirds of each year.[33] To address the challenge of water scarcity in the north, China has undertaken the South-to-North Water Diversion Project, one of the most ambitious engineering projects in history. It consists of a network of canals, rivers and lakes to transport water from the flood-prone Yangtze River to feed dry areas in the north. This long-distance water transfer project may well be the inconvenient solution to the problems of inadequate surface water supply and over-exploitation of groundwater resources.

1.1.3 Soil Contamination

Until the beginning of this century, soil contamination was believed to be restricted to rural China and caused by excessive use of fertilizers and pesticides (dichlorodiphenyltrichloroethane (DDT) and hexachlorocyclohexane (HCH)) in agricultural

[33] Eric Zusman, 'The river runs dry: examining water shortages in the Yellow River Basin' in *Economic, Social and Legal Issues in China's Transition to a Market Economy* (University of California, Los Angeles: Asia Institute, 2000).

fields in the 1950s, 1960s and 1970s, and a lack of household waste disposal facilities.[34] Farmland contamination was further aggravated in the 1980s and 1990s by increased industrial and mining operations that released heavy metals, including lead, mercury and cadmium. China's initial response to soil contamination was narrowly focused. The first Soil Environmental Quality Standard (1995)[35] applied solely to agricultural land and covered only eight heavy metals (cadmium, mercury, arsenic, copper, lead, chromium, zinc and nickel) and two organic compounds (DDT and HCH). Toxic contaminants in the soil have been absorbed by crops and have entered the food chain. Media exposure of lead poisoning and cadmium-tainted rice has drawn public attention to food safety in China and beyond.[36] Lead is especially harmful to children's behavioural and cognitive development, while cadmium affects liver function and bone health, and nitrogen from fertilizers can cause blood disorders in infants that result in brain damage or death.[37] Clearly, soil pollution poisons more than China's farmland.[38]

Urbanization since the 1990s has been characterized by industrial relocation from city centres to the outskirts, construction of roads and subways, and property development. This has exposed the hidden risks of contamination at sites previously used by industry.[39] The toxic site at SongJiaZhuang in Beijing, at which three subway construction workers were poisoned in April 2004, revealed the serious historical contamination left by industrial operators, including a pesticide factory and subsequently Beijing Hongshi Paint Co.[40] In July 2006, six road construction workers fainted as they dug into soil at a site at Guoxiang, near the southern ring road in Suzhou, which had been contaminated by a chemical factory that had since relocated. In February 2007, a construction worker at the Heshan property development site in Hanyang district in Wuhan was poisoned and rushed to hospital for

[34] State Council, *Environmental Protection in China 1996–2005* (2006). www.pkulaw.cn; see also the 9th FYP on Environmental Protection (1996–2000), 10th FYP on Environmental Protection (2001–5) and 11th FYP on Environmental Protection (2006–10); Yang Meng, 'The damaging truth about Chinese fertiliser and pesticide use', *China Dialogue*, 7 September 2012; Dominique Patton, 'China farm pollution worsens, despite moves to curb excessive fertilisers, pesticides', *Reuters*, 14 April 2015.

[35] Soil Environmental Quality Standard (GB15618-1995). It was recently replaced by the Soil Environmental Quality Risk Control Standard for Soil Contamination of Agricultural Land (GB15618-2018).

[36] Xinhua, 'Pollutants, pesticides threaten farm land', *China Daily*, 12 June 2012; Sharon LaFraniere, 'Lead poisoning in China: the hidden scourge', *New York Times*, 15 June 2011; Liu Hongqiao, 'The polluted legacy of China's largest rice-growing province', *China Dialogue*, 30 May 2014; Chen Huamian et al., 'Heavy metal pollution in soils in China: status and countermeasures', *Royal Swedish Academy of Science*, 28 (1999), 130–4, at 132; Gong Jing, 'Toxic rice tainted by cadmium', *New Century Weekly*, 14 February 2011.

[37] Dustin D. Drenguis, 'Reap what you sow: soil pollution remediation reform in China', *Pacific Rim Law and Policy Journal*, 23 (2014), 171–201.

[38] Li Jing, 'Soil pollution poisons more than farmland', *China Daily*, 10 March 2011.

[39] Zhao Yuhong, 'Land contamination in urban China: developing a national cleanup legal regime', *Hong Kong Law Journal*, 39 (2009), 627–48; Jian Xie and Fasheng Li, *Overview of the Current Situation on Brownfield Remediation and Redevelopment in China* (Washington, DC: World Bank Group, 2010). China has been trying to transform its economy from one dependent on its secondary industrial sector to one focused on tertiary service provision. In the course of this transformation, industry has relocated from city centres and residential areas, often leaving behind contaminated land. The relocation of hundreds of Beijing's old industrial facilities to the city outskirts left behind 8 million m^2 of brownfield sites in need of redevelopment.

[40] Zhao Yuhong, 'Land contamination in urban China'; 'Hidden toxic sites', *Caijing*, 4 June 2012; 'Toxic site clean-up at SongJiaZhuang section of subway line no. 10', *Jianghua Times*, 7 December 2009; Liu Wei, 'Beijing: after the subway workers fell ill', *Outlook Weekly*, 9 (2009), 49–50; Liu Yang, 'Soil at the site of Beijing Hongshi Coatings factory removed for incineration', *Beijing Daily*, 16 August 2007; Pan Hongtao, 'Relocation of chemical enterprises and the building of residential housing', *China Environment News*, 25 December 2008.

emergency treatment. More workers then fell ill at the site, which had been contaminated by the relocated Wuhan Pesticide Factory.[41] These seemingly isolated cases are only the tip of the iceberg of land contamination in urban China. In contrast to these cases of acute poisoning of construction workers by sudden exposure to exceptionally high levels of toxins accumulated in soil, there are more cases that cause harm quietly in a chronic manner to humans, property and the environment. People with long-term exposure by direct skin contact, through drinking contaminated water or eating contaminated food, are at high risk of being harmed by land contamination. In December 2015, nearly 500 students of the Changzhou Foreign Language School fell ill after moving to a new campus in September of the same year. They suffered headaches, skin rashes and, from December 2015 and into early 2016, some were diagnosed with lymphoma and leukaemia. Less than 100 m to the north of the school campus, the Changlong toxic site was being treated by an environmental remediation firm – organized by the local government – for contamination. The site had been occupied since the late 1970s by three chemical factories, Changlong, Changyu and Huada.[42]

The National Soil Pollution Survey, conducted from 2005 to 2013, confirmed the extremely bleak picture for land contamination in rural and urban China, and the serious threat posed to the health and safety of humans and the environment. The survey, jointly led and coordinated by the MEP (now MEE) and the Ministry of Land Resources (MLR, now part of the Ministry of Natural Resources, MNR), covered roughly 6.3 million km^2, and included all China's farmland, and part of its forestland, grassland, unutilized land and land for development. In 2014, the MEP and MLR issued a brief report, the *National Soil Pollution Survey Report*, that started with an unusually pessimistic tone for a government report:

> The overall national soil environmental quality does not allow us to be optimistic. Soil pollution in some regions is quite severe. Soil environmental quality of farmland is of great concern. Soil pollution at sites historically used by industrial and mining operators is particularly problematic.[43]

From the limited data released,[44] we gain a very general understanding of the nature, type, distribution, causes, extent and degree of soil pollution in China. Overall, 16.1 per cent of

[41] Luo Jingyun and Zhou Hui, 'Lack of information disclosure on toxic sites, investigation of chaotic treatment sector', *21st Century Economic Report*, 29 September 2012; Zhang Yanchun et al., 'Wuhan Heshan "toxic site" cleaned up at high cost', *People's Daily*, 4 January 2013, 1; Zhou Hui, 'Wuhan toxic site in city centre sold for 1.44 billion yuan', *21st Century Economic Report*, 23 December 2014; Michael I Jeffery and Xiaobo Zhao, 'Developing a national contaminated land liability scheme in China: the Comprehensive Environmental Response, Compensation, and Liability Act Revisited', *Journal of Energy and Natural Resources Law*, 30 (2012), 423–65.

[42] Li Jing, 'Hundreds of pupils at school near toxic site in East China fall ill, some with cancer, state TV reports', *South China Morning Post*, 17 April 2016; 'School campus 100 meters from the toxic site: Changzhou school chemical pollution incident', *Xinhua News*, 19 April 2016.

[43] MEP and MLR, *National Soil Pollution Survey Report*, 17 April 2014, part I. www.mee.gov.cn/gkml/sthjbgw/qt/201404/t20140417_270670.htm

[44] The government refused to release the full report or raw survey data to the public, presumably in order to avoid public concern over the seriousness of rural and urban soil contamination in China. Public requests for disclosure of the survey data were rejected on the basis that it was a state secret. Li Jing, 'Report on mainland China's soil pollution a "state secret"', *South China Morning Post*, 26 February 2013; see also discussion on

the total number of monitored points were in violation of the soil environmental quality standards.[45] A closer look reveals that 19.4 per cent of farmland, 10 per cent of forestland and grassland and 11.4 per cent of unutilized land was in violation of the relevant standards.[46] Of the fifty-five farmlands that were irrigated with sewage, thirty-nine were contaminated. Of the 1,378 monitoring points tested on sewage-irrigated farmland, 26.4 per cent violated relevant standards.[47] The more serious pollution is found at and near heavily polluting industrial operators, abandoned industrial sites, industrial parks, waste disposal sites, oilfields and mining zones.[48] As far as distribution is concerned, more severe soil contamination is found in the south than the north. Large areas within southern and south-west China are contaminated with heavy metals, including cadmium, mercury, arsenic and lead. In particular, the Pearl River Delta, Yangtze River Delta and the old industrial base in north-east China have particularly serious soil pollution compared to other regions.[49]

1.1.4 The Waste Problem

Improper waste management in China has further aggravated the country's air, water and soil pollution. Regulatory control of solid waste, including industrial solid waste (ISW), MSW and HW, only started in the mid-1990s. Despite improvement in the last ten years, there remains a serious shortage of waste disposal infrastructure for all types of solid waste. Safe disposal of MSW in urban China increased from 34.8 per cent in 2005 to 63.5 per cent in 2010 and 90.2 per cent in 2015, but the figures do not include the vast rural areas where rubbish dumps pose environmental and public health hazards.[50] Disposal of industrial waste and HW is the responsibility of waste generators or industrial operators. A significant portion of waste is often stockpiled on and off factory premises for a prolonged period without any treatment, and this can kill and injure animals and people. Toxic contamination in Qujing, Yunnan province killed seventy-seven goats and cattle in June 2011 and was traced to chromium waste generated by Luliang Chemical, which had stockpiled 288,400 t on its site since 1989. Of this, 148,000 t had not been treated.[51] The village of Xinglong, known as a 'cancer village', was located 2 km away, and had a population of more than 3,000. From 2002 to 2011, eleven out of fourteen villagers diagnosed with cancer died, according to government data, and villagers claimed that at least thirty villagers had suffered from cancer caused by chromium-contaminated water and soil.[52] The Severe Acute Respiratory Syndrome (SARS) epidemic of 2003 exposed

government data control by Takashi Itakura, 'Current issues with the regulatory framework for managing soil contamination in China', *Asia Pacific Journal of Environmental Law* 18 (2015), 119–46.

45 MEP and MLR, *National Soil Pollution Survey Report*, part I. The standards are: the Soil Environmental Quality Standard (GB15618-1995); Environmental Quality Evaluation Standards for Farmland of Edible Agricultural Products (HJ/T 332-2006); and Environmental Quality Evaluation Standards for Farmland of Greenhouse Vegetable Production (HJ/T 333-2006).

46 MEP and MLR, *National Soil Pollution Survey Report*, part III.

47 MEP and MLR, *National Soil Pollution Survey Report*, part IV (7).

48 MEP and MLR, *National Soil Pollution Survey Report*, part IV.

49 MEP and MLR, *National Soil Pollution Survey Report*, part I.

50 State Council, 12th FYP on the Construction of MSW Disposal Facilities (2012); 13th FYP on the Construction of MSW Disposal Facilities (2016).

51 Fiona Tam, 'Yunnan plant dumped toxic dregs for two decades', *South China Morning Post*, 17 August 2011.

52 Yang Jian, ' "Cancer village" blames chrome plant', *Shanghai Daily*, 18 August 2011, A03.

China's decades-long mishandling of clinical waste – most clinical waste was disposed of with MSW, while a small amount was incinerated by hospitals without any pollution control.[53] In general, disposal facilities, including landfills and incinerators, have failed to prevent leachate or control emissions.

In contrast to the low capacity of waste disposal is the daunting speed and scale of waste growth in China. By 2016, the annual generation of industrial waste had reached 3.3 billion t, while MSW generated in large- and medium-sized cities hit 200 million t, and HW generation came to 40 million t. In addition, China produced 1.8 billion t of construction waste, 1.35 million t of clinical waste, 4 billion t of animal waste and 1 billion t of crop straws. Further, the historically accumulated industrial waste stockpiled by generators on or off factory premises had reached 60–70 billion t.[54] While the state has made serious efforts to plan and expand waste disposal infrastructure, illegal dumping of waste of all types remains widespread. By the end of 2016, HW disposal capacity had reached 64.71 million t/year, but actual disposal that year was around 16.29 million t.[55] More than half of the 40 million t of HW generated in 2016 did not reach centralized facilities for safe disposal. While safe disposal of MSW had reached 96.6 per cent in cities by the end of 2016,[56] this figure excludes the vast suburban areas on the outskirts of cities and rural villages. In rural China, only 43 per cent of villages provide collection and transport of household waste, and nearly 40 per cent of animal waste is not treated for safe disposal.[57] Random dumping and disposal of waste has created open rubbish dumps surrounding cities, towns and villages, posing serious threat to the health and safety of the environment and human lives.

Growth in prosperity and the urban population naturally increases the generation of MSW. That increase has been boosted exponentially by the emergence of the internet economy. Online shopping platforms, including Alibaba, have unfortunately fostered a culture of excessive shopping and consumption and a wasteful lifestyle. Online transactions have become so pervasive that orders for food delivery alone have triggered astronomical growth in the number of takeout containers, utensils and bags flooding China. The vast amount of plastic waste ends up discarded, buried or burnt with other rubbish. Scientists estimate that the online takeout business in China was responsible for 1.6 million t of packaging waste in 2017, a ninefold jump from two years previously. The 2017 figure includes 1.2 million t of plastic containers, 175,000 t of disposable chopsticks, 164,000 t of plastic bags and 44,000 t of plastic spoons.[58] The sudden rise of numerous bicycle-sharing companies, including OfO, MoBike, BlueGogo, since 2016 flooded city streets with millions of bright yellow, orange and blue bicycles for easy use with a simple scan of a QR-code. However, rapid and unregulated overgrowth of the market – more than forty platforms – vastly outpaced demand within just

[53] SEPA and NDRC, National Plan on the Construction of Disposal Facilities for Hazardous Waste and Clinical Waste (2004), chapter 1.

[54] Zhang Dejiang, *Inspection Report on the Implementation of the Solid Waste Law* (2017). www.pkulaw.cn. The report was presented on 1 November 2017 by Zhang Dejiang, NPCSC chairman, to the 30th session of the 12th NPCSC.

[55] Zhang Dejiang, *Inspection Report on the Implementation of the Solid Waste Law.*

[56] Zhang Dejiang, *Inspection Report on the Implementation of the Solid Waste Law.*

[57] Zhang Dejiang, *Inspection Report on the Implementation of the Solid Waste Law.*

[58] Raymond Zhong and Carolyn Zhang, 'Food delivery apps are drowning China in plastic', *New York Times*, 28 May 2019.

eighteen months. As a result, a huge surplus of bicycles old and new was discarded in vast vacant lots and even rubbish dumps.[59]

Despite China's inability to safely dispose of its own waste, by the time restrictions were imposed on waste imports in 2017, it had become the world's number one dumping ground. For a quarter of a century, China had received about 70 per cent of the world's waste, including plastics, paper, glass and all sorts of metals and e-waste for processing and recycling.[60] Countries that imported products from China shipped waste and garbage back to China at relatively low cost, using containers that would otherwise have been transported empty before being refilled with more consumer goods.[61] It was a loop of exported products and imported junk that left China with all the toxic pollution, both at the stage of manufacturing and of waste disposal. In parallel with the legal waste trade, but more harmful to people and the environment, has been the smuggling of mixed MSW, clinical waste and e-waste that cannot be recycled or recovered for resources, all of which was banned from being imported.

1.1.5 The Cost of Pollution

In the mid-1990s, the annual economic cost to China of air and water pollution was estimated by the World Bank to be between 24 billion US dollars and 54 billion US dollars, approximately 3.5 per cent to 7.7 per cent of China's GDP, depending on which of two valuation approaches was taken: human capital or willingness to pay.[62] By 2003, the total cost of pollution under the human-capital approach was 362 billion yuan or 2.68 per cent of GDP, rising to 781 billion yuan or 5.78 per cent of GDP under the willingness-to-pay approach.[63] The official conservative estimate of the cost of environmental degradation to China was at 511.8 billion yuan in 2004, accounting for 3.05 per cent of GDP; the cost of treatment would reach 6.8 per cent of GDP if all air and water pollution and pollution caused by solid waste was effectively treated and disposed of safely in the same year.[64] The cost of pollution

[59] Sarah Dai, 'Winter descends on China's once-hot bike sharing market as another player goes bust', *South China Morning Post*, 27 November 2017; Alan Taylor, 'The bike-share oversupply in China: huge piles of abandoned and broken bicycles', *The Atlantic*, 22 March 2018; Thomas Bird, 'China's bike sharing bubble has burst: drone photography captures its casualties rusting in "bicycle graveyards"', *South China Morning Post*, 27 July 2018.

[60] Richard James Havis, 'Plastic China documentary focuses on human impact of imported waste', *South China Morning Post*, 19 May 2018; David Dodwell, 'More than a year after China's ban on waste imports, the world is still learning to clean up after itself', *South China Morning Post*, 8 June 2019.

[61] Adam Minter, *Junkyard Planet: Travels in the Billion-Dollar Trash Trade* (New York, Bloomsbury Press, 2013).

[62] World Bank, *Clear Water, Blue Skies*, at 23–5. The human-capital approach values mortality and morbidity impacts as lost productivity and out-of-pocket expenditure. The willingness-to-pay approach measures the value of human life and health in the market – that is, the amount people are willing to pay to reduce the risk of injury or death. Under the former approach, the cost is 24 billion US dollars and 3.5 per cent of GDP, and, under the latter, 54 billion US dollars and 7.7 per cent of GDP.

[63] World Bank, *Cost of Pollution in China: Economic Estimates of Physical Damages* (Washington, DC: World Bank Group, 2007), xvii.

[64] SEPA and the State Bureau of Statistics, 'Report on China's green GDP for 2004', *Environmental Protection*, 98 (2006), 22–9, at 27. This estimate may be on the low side, as the study excluded many items, such as the cost of groundwater pollution and soil contamination, due in part to a lack of data.

continued to increase and, by 2010, had reached more than 1.5 trillion yuan or approximately 3.5 per cent of GDP, according to the MEP.[65]

The impacts of pollution on public health in China are devastating. According to Chen Zhu, former minister of health (2007–13), between 350,000 and 500,000 people die prematurely each year as a result of outdoor air pollution in China.[66] By 2017, air pollution by particulate matter (PM_{10} and $PM_{2.5}$) was the fourth leading risk factor for deaths in China.[67] The death toll caused by pollution has been increasing and, in 2018, the WHO released data showing that air pollution was responsible for about two million deaths in China per year, with more than one million caused by outdoor ambient air pollution and one million by indoor air pollution.[68] Cancer is the leading cause of death in urban China, and the second highest cause of death in rural regions.[69] Notably, high incidences of cancer have been reported in villages in different parts of China,[70] drawing academics to study the causes and consequences of 'cancer villages'.[71] However, it was not until 2013 that the government first officially acknowledged the emergence of these 'cancer villages'.[72]

While there is still a lack of regularly released and comprehensive data on the cost of pollution, existing reports and studies from the government, international organizations and researchers clearly indicate that China is paying heavily for pollution and that this cost goes beyond economic loss calculated as a percentage of GDP. Serious pollution has become a significant risk factor for social unrest, threatening the political regime of the Chinese Communist Party (CCP). During the 11th FYP period (2006–10), thirty-seven environmental incidents developed into large-scale protests. Nineteen of these also involved health issues. There were thirty-one serious heavy metal pollution incidents in cities and counties – including Shanxi Fengxiang, Henan Jiyuan and Hunan Wugang – that severely threatened public health and social stability.[73] The main state environmental protection authority, in its various incarnations (the MEE, MEP, SEPA and NEPA), has

[65] Wang Erde, 'China's cost of pollution reached 1.5 trillion yuan in 2010', *21st Century Economic Report*, 15 January 2013. Since 2004, the Chinese Academy of Environmental Planning has been working on green-GDP accounting, a concept that deducts the cost of pollution and damage to resources from the calculation of GDP.

[66] Zhu Chen et al., 'China tackles the health effects of air pollution', *The Lancet*, 382:14 December (2013), 1959–60.

[67] Maigeng Zhou et al., 'Mortality, morbidity, and risk factors in China and its provinces, 1990–2017: a systematic analysis for the global burden of disease study 2017', *The Lancet* , 394:10204 (2019), 1145–58.

[68] WHO, 'Greater cooperation needed to win the war on pollution', (press release) 8 May 2018; see also WHO, n.d., 'Air pollution in China'. Online article. www.who.int/china/health-topics/air-pollution.

[69] Healthy China Promotion Committee, *Healthy China Action (2019–2030)* (2019). www.pkulaw.cn, part III, section 12. The Healthy China Promotion Committee is a high-level cross-department committee established by the State Council on 9 July 2019. The Committee is chaired by Vice Premier Sun Chunlan and composed of members who are ministers or vice ministers of state council departments, as well as experts and representatives of the NPC and Chinese People's Political Consultative Conference (CPPCC).

[70] '"Cancer village" in spotlight', *China Daily*, 10 May 2004; Tan Ee Lyn, 'China's "cancer villages" bear witness to economic boom', *Reuters*, 17 September 2009; Jonathan Watts, 'China's "cancer villages" reveal dark side of economic boom', *The Guardian*, 7 June 2010.

[71] Lee Liu, 'Made in China: cancer villages', *Environment*, 52 (2010), 8–21; Lora-Wainwright, Anna, 'An anthropology of "cancer villages": villagers' perspectives and the politics of responsibility', *Journal of Contemporary China*, 19 (2010), 79–99.

[72] MEP, 12th FYP on the Prevention and Control of Environmental Risk of Chemicals (2013), part I; see also 'China's environmental ministry acknowledges "cancer villages" ', *Science*, 339:6123 (2013), 1018–19.

[73] MEP, 12th FYP on Environment and Health (2011), part I.

realised that the issue of environment and health is not purely a subject for scientific investigation or economic analysis, but is also a highly sensitive political issue directly affecting social harmony and stability and the long-term administration by the party-state.[74] Pollution-related health problems have increasingly become the cause of social conflict, as reported by the media and studied by researchers from the perspectives of civil society movements, public participation, access to justice and dispute resolution, among others.[75] Chapters 2 to 12 will engage in in-depth discussion – with reference to high-impact cases – on how these crucially important issues have been addressed by China's evolving environmental regime, in order to understand both progress made and lessons learnt.

1.2 SOURCES OF ENVIRONMENTAL LAW

Sources of Chinese environmental law include: (i) the Chinese Constitution, which is the supreme law of China and lays the foundation for environmental law making; (ii) specialized environmental statutes enacted to protect the environment and prevent pollution, including the Environmental Protection Law (EPL) and the Environmental Impact Assessment Law (EIAL) and others directly targeting air, water, waste and soil pollution; (iii) civil, criminal, administrative and procedural statutes that are of crucial importance in addressing environmental problems; (iv) state regulations and administrative rules that are issued to implement national laws; (v) judicial interpretations that bring environmental law into operation; (vi) local regulations set by local lawmaking bodies to address local issues and (vii) international environmental legal instruments that China has signed and ratified.

1.2.1 Chinese Constitution

As the supreme law of the land, the Chinese Constitution establishes the structure of the state and defines the powers and duties of key state organs. The first Constitution (1954)[76] was short-lived, derailed by the anti-rightist movement in 1957 and the ten-year Cultural Revolution (1966–76). In 1975, towards the end of the Cultural Revolution, the Constitution was amended to reflect the ideology of Mao Zedong and his followers. Mao's death in 1976 ended China's chaotic period of political campaigns. Important constitutional developments then occurred in 1978 and 1982 when Deng Xiaoping was in power; he was determined to shift the national priorities from political and ideological struggles to

74 MEP, 13th FYP on Environment and Health (2017), part I.

75 See Jennifer Holdaway, 'Environment and health research in China: the state of the field', *The China Quarterly* 214 (2013), 255–82; Yanhua Deng and Guobin Yang, 'Pollution and protest in China: environmental mobilization in context', *The China Quarterly* 214 (2013), 321–36; Thomas Johnson, 'The health factor in anti-waste incinerator campaigns in Beijing and Guangzhou', *The China Quarterly* 214 (2013), 356–75; Elizabeth Economy, 'The great leap backward?', *Foreign Affairs*, 86 (2007), 38–59; Benjamin van Rooij, 'The people vs. pollution: understanding citizen action against pollution in China', *The Journal of Contemporary China*, 19:63 (2010), 55–77.

76 The Constitution was adopted on 20 September 1954 by the first session of the first National People's Congress (NPC).

economic development. The new 1982 Constitution was amended five times to accommodate China's unprecedented socio-economic reform and development.[77]

Two articles in the Constitution directly address the environment, one on natural resources and the other on pollution. On natural resources, article 9 provides that '[t]he State ensures the rational use of natural resources and protects rare and precious animals and plants. It is prohibited for any organization or individual to appropriate or damage natural resources by any means.'[78] The Constitution has thus laid down the fundamental approach to natural resources, which is 'rational use' for socio-economic development, rather than conservation for the health and well-being of ecosystems. The state only protects 'rare and precious' animals and plants, instead of protecting flora and fauna in general to ensure biological diversity. To implement article 9, the national legislature has enacted laws to promote rational use of natural resources, including the Forestry Law,[79] the Grassland Law,[80] the Fishery Law,[81] the Land Administration Law,[82] the Mineral Resources Law,[83] the Water Law[84] and the Wildlife Protection Law.[85]

As for environmental protection and pollution control, article 26 of the Constitution provides that '[t]he State protects and improves both the living and the ecological environments. It prevents and controls pollution and other public hazards.'[86] It stipulates the state's duty to protect and improve the environment and serves as the legal basis for environmental legislation to prevent and control pollution. To implement article 26, the national legislature has enacted laws to protect the environment and control pollution, including the EPL,[87] the EIAL,[88] the Marine Environmental Protection Law (MEPL),[89] the Air Pollution Prevention and Control Law (APPCL),[90] the Water Pollution Prevention and Control Law

[77] The Constitution was amended in 1988, 1993, 1999, 2004 and 2018. For further discussion, see Albert H. Y. Chen, *An Introduction to the Legal System of the People's Republic of China*, 4th ed. (Hong Kong: LexisNexis, 2011).

[78] Constitution (1982), art. 9(2).

[79] The Forestry Law was first enacted on 20 September 1984 by the 6th NPCSC at its 7th session. It was amended in 1998 and 2009, and revised in 2019.

[80] The Grassland Law was first enacted on 18 June 1985 by the 6th NPCSC at its 11th session. It was revised in 2002, and amended in 2009 and 2013.

[81] The Fishery Law was first enacted on 20 January 1986 by the 6th NPCSC at its 14th session. It was amended in 2000, 2004, 2009 and 2013.

[82] The Land Administration Law was first enacted on 25 June 1986 by the sixth NPCSC at its 16th session. It was amended in 1988, 2004 and 2019, and revised in 1998.

[83] The Mineral Resources Law was first enacted on 19 March 1986 by the 6th NPCSC at its 15th session. It was amended in 1996 and 2009.

[84] The Water Law was first enacted on 21 January 1988 by the 6th NPCSC at its 24th session. It was revised in 2002, and amended in 2009 and 2016.

[85] The Wildlife Protection Law was first enacted on 8 November 1988 by the 7th NPCSC at its 4th session. It was amended in 2004, 2009 and 2018, and revised in 2016.

[86] Constitution (1982), art. 26(1).

[87] The EPL was enacted on 26 December 1989 by the 7th NPCSC at its 11th session to replace the EPL (for trial use) (1979). It was substantially revised in 2014.

[88] The EIAL was first enacted on 28 October 2002 by the 9th NPCSC at its 30th session. It was amended in 2016 and 2018.

[89] The MEPL was first enacted on 23 August 1982 by the 5th NPCSC at its 24th session. It was revised in 1999 and amended in 2013, 2016 and 2017.

[90] The APPCL was first enacted on 5 September 1987 by the 6th NPCSC at its 22nd session. It was amended in 1995 and 2018, and revised in 2000 and 2015.

(WPPCL),[91] the Soil Pollution Prevention and Control Law (SPPCL),[92] the Law on the Prevention and Control of Pollution by Solid Waste (SWL),[93] and the Noise Pollution Prevention and Control Law (NPPCL).[94]

The 2018 Amendment to the Constitution[95] has far-reaching and significant impact on the environment. It introduces 'ecological civilization' in the seventh paragraph of the preamble and places it as an aspect of development equally important to four elements already stipulated in the Constitution: 'material civilization', 'political civilization', 'spiritual civilization' and 'social civilization'. Implementation of the 'new development concept' and coordinated development of the five civilizations will make China not only prosperous and strong, democratic and civilized, but also 'harmonious and beautiful'.[96] The rhetoric of 'ecological civilization', 'new development concept' and 'beautiful China', all adopted from the policy statements of the CCP, are interrelated and highlight the importance of the environment.

'Ecological civilization' was first given top priority in 2012 as one of the five important aspects of China's national development strategy – 'economic, political, cultural, social and ecological civilization construction' – in former president Hu Jintao's report to the 18th National Congress of the CCP.[97] The essence of 'ecological civilization' is human respect for and protection of nature, which require the implementation of the fundamental national policies of resource conservation and environmental protection. Only by integrating ecological civilization into all aspects and all stages of economic, political, cultural and social construction can a beautiful China with long-term sustainable development be built.[98] The term 'beautiful China' encompasses blue skies, clear water and green mountains. The new development concept, which embodies 'innovative, coordinated, green, open and shared development', was introduced by President Xi Jinping in 2015 at the CCP Central Committee meeting in the context of making recommendations on the upcoming 13th FYP on Socio-Economic Development.[99] Green development requires a departure from the conventional economic growth that for three decades relied on energy- and resource-intensive heavily polluting industries. The focus of green development is resource conservation, environmental protection and sustainable development. The goal of a beautiful China is based on a society that is resource-saving and environmentally friendly, where humans and nature co-exist in harmony.[100] The three concepts were given high priority by

[91] The WPPCL was first enacted on 11 May 1984 by the 6th NPCSC at its 5th session. It was amended in 1996 and 2017, and revised in 2008.

[92] The SPPCL was adopted on 31 August 2018 by the 13th NPCSC at its 5th session. It came into force on 1 January 2019.

[93] The SWL was first enacted on 30 October 1995 by the eighth NPCSC at its 16th session. It was revised in 2004, and amended in 2013, 2015 and 2016.

[94] The NPPCL was first enacted on 29 October 1996 by the eighth NPCSC at its 22nd session. It was amended in 2018.

[95] The Amendment to the Constitution (2018) was adopted on 11 March 2018 by the 13th NPC at its first session.

[96] Amendment to the Constitution (2018), art. 32; Constitution (2018), preamble.

[97] Hu Jintao, *Report to the 18th National Congress of the Chinese Communist Party* (2012), part I.

[98] Hu Jintao, *Report to the 18th National Congress*, part VIII.

[99] The Communique of the Fifth Plenary Session of the 18th CCP Central Committee was adopted on 29 October 2015.

[100] Communique of the Fifth Plenary Session of the 18th CCP Central Committee.

Xi Jinping in his report to the 19th National Congress of the CCP.[101] Among the fourteen fundamental strategies of China's development in the new era are: strategy (iv) on the new development concept; and strategy (ix) on harmonious co-existence of humans and nature through the construction of an ecological civilization.[102] The report further elaborates on the construction of the ecological civilization and a beautiful China with more detailed measures that prioritize conservation, protection and remediation.[103]

In practice, the Constitution is seldom litigated in courts. It does, however, provide the foundation and guiding principles for lawmaking as '[n]o law or administrative or local regulation may contravene the Constitution'.[104]

1.2.2 Environmental Statutes

China's first wave of environmental legislation started with the EPL (for trial implementation) (1979).[105] It set out basic principles and mechanisms for environmental management and established key administrative agencies for environmental protection. Ten years of trialling the law resulted in the revised EPL (1989),[106] which incorporated more sophisticated environmental legal principles and developed a range of mechanisms and institutions to protect the environment and control pollution. The law was substantially revised in the EPL (2014),[107] which improved environmental governance through public participation and strengthened enforcement and sanction of violations. The EPL (for trial implementation) (1979) was followed by specialized environmental statutes to tackle the most visible pollution problems that directly affected human lives and well-being. These statutes include the MEPL (1982), WPPCL (1984) and APPCL (1987).

The EPL (1989) led a second wave of environmental legislation, including the making of new laws and the revision or amendment of existing statutes. These included the SWL (1995), NPPCL (1996) and EIAL (2002), which were designed to fill the gaps in regulatory control on pollution by solid waste and noise nuisance, and to implement the preventative principle of environmental law by strengthening the environmental impact assessment (EIA) regime. During this period, the MEPL (1982) was revised in 1999 and amended in 2013, the WPPCL (1984) was amended in 1996 and revised in 2008, and the APPCL (1987) was amended in 1995 and revised in 2000 to incorporate more sophisticated regulatory mechanisms.

The latest and third wave of environmental lawmaking was led by the EPL (2014) and has focused on improving environmental governance through public participation, effective enforcement and sanction of violations, and better use of economic instruments, such as taxation, insurance and emissions trading. New laws have been made and key statutes

[101] Xi Jinping, *Secure a Decisive Victory in Building a Moderately Prosperous Society in All Respects and Strive for the Great Success of Socialism with Chinese Characteristics in the New Era* (2017). www.pkulaw.cn. Xi Jinping presented the Report to the 19th National Congress of the CCP on 18 October 2017.

[102] Xi Jinping, *Secure a Decisive Victory*, part III.

[103] Xi Jinping, *Secure a Decisive Victory*, part IX.

[104] Constitution (2018), art. 5.

[105] The EPL (for trial implementation) was passed on 13 September 1979 by the 5th NPCSC at its 11th session. It was repealed on 26 December 1989 with the enactment of the EPL (1989).

[106] The EPL was enacted on 26 December 1989 by the 7th NPCSC at its 11th session. It came into force immediately and was revised in 2014.

[107] The EPL (1989) was substantially revised on 24 April 2014 by the 12th NPCSC at its 8th session. It came into force on 1 January 2015.

revised or amended. The Environmental Protection Tax Law (EPTL) (2016) was enacted to implement the fees-to-tax reform,[108] which replaced the pollution fees charged by local environment bureaus with taxes collected by the tax authority. The SPPCL (2018) was enacted to provide the missing piece of China's pollution-control puzzle – soil pollution. To improve environmental governance and ensure consistency with the EPL (2014), the National People's Congress Standing Committee (NPCSC) revised or amended the APPCL (2000) in 2015 and 2018, the WPPCL (2008) in 2017 and the EIAL (2002) in 2016 and 2018.

1.2.3 Other Relevant Statutes

To prevent and control pollution, specialized environmental statutes regulate human behaviour and the way in which legal persons or other organizations operate. They do this by setting standards, monitoring performance and punishing violations. Where harm is caused by pollution to the environment, damaging the interest of any citizen, legal person or the state, the injured party or any party with standing to initiate public interest litigation (PIL) may seek remedies under civil law. Administrative inaction or failure to enforce environmental law often causes or aggravates environmental harm. Agencies liable may be sued by the affected party, a relevant party or the people's procuratorate. Where serious intentional violations are involved or grave harm is caused to the environment, parties liable will be investigated and prosecuted for criminal liability. The operation of environmental law in courts requires the support of civil law, criminal law and administrative law. The latest reforms to the laws on civil procedure and administrative litigation are of crucial importance to the development of environmental public interest litigation (EPIL).

Civil Law

The General Principles of Civil Law (GPCL) (1986)[109] was the first comprehensive statute to regulate civil legal relationships. It served as the basis for further lawmaking: the Contract Law (1999), Property Law (2007) and Tort Law (TL) (2009). Codification work has consolidated major civil law statutes into a civil code that was completed early in 2020. Part I of the Civil Code on general provisions of civil law was issued in 2017 as the General Rules of Civil Law (GRCL) (2017).[110] It is based on the GPCL (1986) and more than thirty years of civil law practice, both of which facilitated China's transition from planned to market economy. A significant part of the GPCL (1986) on civil law principles and rules has been adopted, while important improvements have also been made to respond to new challenges. One of the most important highlights of the GRCL (2017) is the introduction of a green principle in the first chapter, which stipulates that 'civil subjects shall engage in civil legal acts in a manner that facilitates resource conservation and environmental protection'.[111] It is a fundamental principle and guides both civil lawmaking and judicial interpretation in

[108] The EPTL was first enacted on 25 December 2016 by the 12th NPCSC at its 25th session. It was amended in 2018.

[109] The GPCL was issued on 12 April 1986 by the 6th NPC at its 4th session. It came into force on 1 January 1987, and was amended in 2009.

[110] The GRCL was adopted on 15 March 2017 by the 12th NPC at its 5th session. It came into force on 1 October 2017.

[111] GRCL (2017), art. 9.

the development and application of civil legal rules and mechanisms in contract, tort and property law.

Prior to the GRCL (2017), the GPCL (1986) addressed environmental liabilities by reference to the risk level of an operation. 'Any person causing damage to others by engaging in ultra-hazardous operations such as operations ... involving high pressure, high voltage, combustibles, explosives, highly toxic or radioactive substances ... shall bear civil liability; he shall not be liable if it can be proved that the damage was deliberately caused by the victim.'[112] In the case of pollution caused by operations not falling within that category, fault-based liability was applied. That is, 'any person who pollutes the environment and causes damage to others in violation of state provisions for environmental protection and pollution prevention shall bear civil liability in accordance with the law'.[113] However, operations that comply with pollution measures may still harm the environment and cause loss to the victims. The polluter-pays principle requires polluters to bear the cost of pollution, including the cost of prevention and remediation. This principle was adopted by the EPL (1989). The EPL (1989) stipulated that 'any person causing environmental harm by polluting shall be liable for elimination of the harm and compensation for the losses suffered by units and individuals'.[114] In practice, however, many courts took the view that as long as the pollution discharge was in compliance with state standards, polluters should not be held liable to compensate victims for the loss and injury caused by pollution.

The TL (2009)[115] made important changes to the rules of environmental tort,[116] and expressly makes polluters liable for the harm caused by pollution, regardless of fault. It states that '[p]olluters bear tort liability for the harm caused by pollution'.[117] In addition, the TL (2009) provides for special rules of burden of proof, for the liabilities of multiple polluters in one incident and third-party liability to make it easier for victims to access judicial redress. Conventional rules of civil law require the plaintiff to prove a causal link between the defendant's act and the plaintiff's loss or suffering. This burden of proof can be a mission impossible for most victims of pollution, due to their lack of expertise, skills, financial resources and access to pollution information. The TL (2009), however, reversed the burden and placed it on the defendant so that 'polluters bear the burden to prove that they shall not be liable or the liability shall be mitigated according to law, or that there is no causation between the act and the harm'.[118] Where harm is caused by pollution as a result of the fault of a third party, the victim may claim compensation from either the polluter or the third party. After making compensation, the polluter may claim against the third party.[119]

[112] GPCL (1986), art. 123. [113] GPCL (1986), art. 124.

[114] EPL (1989), art. 41(1). 'Unit' is a term used widely in China to refer to any legal person or non-legal-person organization. A unit may be a company, a factory, a school, a hospital or an institution, among others.

[115] The TL was enacted on 26 December 2009 by the 11th NPCSC at its 12th session. It came into force on 1 July 2010.

[116] TL (2009), chapter 8.

[117] TL (2009), art. 65. While both polluters in violation of law and those in compliance are liable to victims of pollution for compensation and other remedies, liabilities are apportioned differently when pollution is caused by multiple polluters, some of whom are in compliance and some in violation. Under art. 67, where environmental harm is caused by multiple polluters, the liability of each is calculated on the basis of the types of pollutants, the total emission or discharge and other factors.

[118] TL (2009), art. 66. [119] TL (2009), art. 68.

Civil Procedure Law

Civil procedure law stipulates rules of civil litigation. Of particular relevance to environmental law reform are the rules of standing in PIL provided by amendments to the Civil Procedure Law (CPL)[120] in 2012 and 2017. The CPL expands the landscape of civil litigation to offer channels through which civil PIL can be initiated and involve more parties in environmental protection in order to make polluters pay. The 2012 amendment formally established the standing of 'legally prescribed state organs and relevant organizations to file civil litigation against parties who harm the public interest in the environment, such as environmental pollution or infringement of a large number of consumers' rights and interests'.[121] The 2017 amendment expressly grants standing to people's procuratorates to initiate PILs in designated areas, including environment and natural resources, and issues of food and drug safety involving consumer rights and interests. However, the procuratorial right to sue is subject to the absence of a PIL initiated by another state organ or social organization.[122]

Administrative Law

To improve legal supervision of administrative agencies by judicial review and to protect the legal rights and interests of citizens, legal persons and other organizations, the Administrative Litigation Law (ALL) (1989)[123] was amended twice to lower the threshold requirements for standing to sue. The 2014 amendment extends standing from parties 'whose lawful rights and interests are infringed by the concrete administrative acts of administrative agencies or their staff'[124] to include 'citizens, legal persons or other organizations with an interest in the administrative acts'.[125] This amendment has made an important change to environmental administrative litigation in the context of EIAs. Prior to the 2014 amendment, only project proponents who submitted EIA documents for agency approval had standing to sue agencies, as they were the parties directly affected by the agency decisions. The 2014 amendment granted standing to others with an interest in agency decisions, meaning that those potentially adversely affected by the construction and operation of a project were given standing to challenge agencies on their approval decisions.

The 2017 amendment took administrative litigation one step further to enhance legal supervision of agencies. That is, '[w]here people's procuratorates become aware of agency acts or omissions in violation of law, causing damage to the state interest or social public interest in the areas of environment and resource protection, food and drug safety, protection of state assets and transfer of the state's land-use rights, they shall issue procuratorial advice to agencies urging performance of statutory duties according to law. People's procuratorates may sue agencies that fail to rectify as requested by the procuratorial advice.'[126]

[120] The CPL was first enacted on 9 April 1991 by the 7th NPC at its 4th session. It was amended in 2007, 2012 and 2017.

[121] CPL (2012), art. 55; CPL (2017), art. 55(1).

[122] CPL (2017), art. 55(2).

[123] The ALL was first enacted on 4 April 1989 by the 7th NPC at its 2nd session. It was amended in 2014 and 2017.

[124] ALL (1989), art. 2.

[125] ALL (2014), art. 25(1); ALL (2017), art. 25(1).

[126] ALL (2017), art. 25(4).

Criminal Law

Environmental statutes provide for administrative penalties to sanction and deter violations, but for the most serious environmental violations or violations causing grave environmental harm, they typically provide general reference to criminal sanctions, as occurs in the EPL (1989).

> If a violation of this Law causes a serious environmental pollution incident, leading to the grave consequences of heavy losses of public or private property or human injuries or deaths of persons, the persons directly responsible for such an incident shall be investigated for criminal responsibility according to law.[127]
>
> Any person in charge of supervision and management of environmental protection who abuses his power, neglects his duty or engages in malpractice for personal gains shall be imposed administrative sanction by the unit to which he belongs or the competent higher authorities; if his act constitutes a crime, he shall be investigated for criminal responsibility according to law.[128]

The revised EPL (2014) simply provides that 'any party in violation of this law who has committed a crime shall be investigated for criminal liability according to *law*'[emphasis added].[129] The reference 'according to law' means according to the Criminal Law (CL) (1997),[130] its relevant amendments,[131] and the judicial interpretations of the Supreme People's Court (SPC). Crimes relating to pollution control include the crime of environmental pollution,[132] the crime of illegal disposal of imported waste,[133] the crime of importing waste without permission[134] and the crime of waste smuggling.[135] The crimes against natural resources include illegal fishing, hunting, mining and logging.[136] Where it is a legal person that commits an offence under articles 338 to 345 of the CL (2017), the legal person will be fined, and the individuals directly in charge and others directly liable will be sanctioned under the relevant articles.[137]

1.2.4 State Regulations and Administrative Rules

Chinese environmental law cannot be implemented or enforced without the support of more detailed and specific rules found in state regulations[138] and administrative rules.[139] The State Council issues regulations to implement laws or to perform its administrative duties under article 89 of the Constitution.[140] The MEE, as well as the SEPA and MEP, its predecessors, have issued rules on detailed procedures for environmental enforcement, on emission and discharge standards, and technical methods of environmental monitoring,

[127] EPL (1989), art. 43. [128] EPL (1989), art. 45. [129] EPL (2014), art. 69.

[130] The CL was first enacted on 1 July 1979 by the 5th NPC at its 2nd session. It was substantially revised on 14 March 1997 by the 8th NPC at its 5th session.

[131] The CL (1997) has been amended ten times. [132] CL (2017), art. 338. [133] CL (2017), art. 339(1).

[134] CL (2017), art. 339(2). [135] CL (2017), art. 339(3) and art. 152(2) and (3). [136] CL (2017), arts. 340–45.

[137] CL (2017), art. 346.

[138] State regulations are issued by the State Council in accordance with the Constitution and laws. See Constitution (2018), art. 89(1); Law on Legislation (2015), art. 65(1).

[139] Administrative rules are issued by the ministries or commissions of the State Council in accordance with relevant laws and regulations. See Law on Legislation (2015), art. 80.

[140] Law on Legislation (2015), art. 65(2).

appraisal and assessment, among others, to guide both the regulators and the regulated in the implementation and enforcement of environmental law. State regulations are of higher status than administrative rules in China's hierarchy of legal instruments, which means administrative rules cannot contravene laws or state regulations.[141]

The State Council has issued many regulations to implement environmental laws. Examples are: the Regulation on the Implementation of the Environmental Protection Tax Law (Regulation on Environmental Tax) (2017),[142] the Regulation on the Management of Environmental Protection of Construction Projects (EIA Regulation) (2017),[143] and the Regulation on Environmental Impact Assessment of Plans (2009).[144] In exercising its power in pollution prevention and control, the State Council has issued action plans to tackle air, water and soil pollution including: the Action Plan on Prevention and Control of Air Pollution (Air Action Plan) (2013),[145] the Action Plan on Prevention and Control of Water Pollution (Water Action Plan) (2015),[146] the Action Plan on Prevention and Control of Soil Pollution (Soil Action Plan) (2016),[147] and the Three-Year Action Plan on Winning the Battle of Blue-Sky Protection (2018).[148]

The state ministry in charge of environmental protection, the MEE, has issued a large number of administrative rules to protect the environment and control pollution. The MEE, and the MEP (2008–18) and SEPA (1998–2008), its predecessors, issued administrative rules to implement environmental mechanisms, including permit control, public participation and emergency response, adopted by environmental laws and regulations. Examples of the rules include the Measures on Permit Control of Pollution Discharge (Measures on Permit Control) (for trial implementation) (2018),[149] the Catalogue of Stationary Sources Subject to Pollution Discharge Permit Control (Catalogue) (2017),[150] the Measures on Public Participation in Environmental Protection (2015),[151] the Measures on Public Participation in Environmental Impact Assessment (Measures on Public Participation) (2018),[152] the Measures on Environmental Emergency Response (2015),[153] the Measures on

[141] Law on Legislation (2015), art. 88.

[142] The Regulation on Environmental Tax was issued by the State Council on 25 December 2017. It came into force on 1 January 2018.

[143] The EIA Regulation was first enacted in 1998 to implement the EIA mechanism for construction projects, which had been provided for in the EPL (1989). It was substantially revised in 2017.

[144] The Regulation on Environmental Impact Assessment of Plans was issued by the State Council on 17 August 2009. It came into force on 1 October 2009.

[145] The State Council issued the Air Action Plan on 10 September 2013 with immediate effect.

[146] The State Council issued the Water Action Plan on 2 April 2015 with immediate effect.

[147] The State Council issued the Soil Action Plan on 28 May 2016 with immediate effect.

[148] The State Council issued the Three-Year Action Plan on Blue-Sky Protection on 27 June 2018 with immediate effect.

[149] The MEP issued the Measures on Permit Control (for trial implementation) on 10 January 2018 with immediate effect.

[150] The MEP issued the Catalogue on 28 July 2017 with immediate effect.

[151] The MEP issued the Measures on Public Participation in Environmental Protection on 13 July 2015. The Measures came into force on 1 September 2015.

[152] The Measures on Public Participation were issued by the MEE on 16 July 2018 and came into force on 1 January 2019.

[153] The Measures on Environmental Emergency Response were issued by the MEP on 16 April 2015 and came into force on 5 June 2015.

Investigation and Handling of Environmental Emergencies (2014)[154] and Measures on Information Reporting of Environmental Emergencies (2011).[155]

1.2.5 Judicial Interpretations

Judicial interpretations are issued separately or jointly by the SPC and the Supreme People's Procuratorate (SPP), and sometimes with other State Council ministries. The practice of the promulgation of judicial interpretations was first regulated by the SPC's Several Provisions on Judicial Interpretation Work (1997)[156] and the SPP's Provisional Provisions on Judicial Interpretation Work (1996).[157] The former was revised and repealed by the SPC Provisions on Judicial Interpretation Work (2007)[158] and the latter by the SPP Provisions on Judicial Interpretation Work (2006, 2015 and 2019).[159]

According to the SPC Provisions on Judicial Interpretation Work (2007), judicial interpretations issued by the SPC have the force of law[160] and, where relevant, may be cited in court judgments.[161] There are four types of judicial interpretation: interpretations, provisions, replies and decisions.[162] Interpretations deal with the application of the law in adjudication, while provisions stipulate norms and opinions on adjudication work in accordance with the spirit of the law, replies are written responses to lower-court requests for guidance on specific legal issues arising from adjudication, and decisions are made to amend or repeal existing judicial interpretations.[163] Similarly, the SPP Provisions on Judicial Interpretation Work (2019) provide that judicial interpretations issued by the SPP have legal force and may be cited as needed in matters including indictments, protest applications and procuratorial advice, among others.[164] They are issued in the form of interpretations, rules, provisions, replies and decisions.[165] Judicial interpretations are an important source of law in China, including in the field of environmental law. Such interpretations cover important areas of civil, criminal and administrative cases and PIL.

For the adjudication of civil cases, the SPC has issued judicial interpretations on civil procedure and evidence that provide special rules for environmental cases. Examples include the SPC Opinion on Several Issues Concerning the Application of Civil Procedure

[154] The MEP issued the Measures on Investigation and Handling of Environmental Emergencies on 19 December 2014. The Measures came into force on 1 March 2015.

[155] The MEP issued the Measures on Information Reporting of Environmental Emergencies on 18 April 2011. The Measures came into force on 1 May 2011.

[156] The SPC Several Provisions on Judicial Interpretation Work were issued on 23 June 1997. It came into force on 1 July 1997 and was repealed by the SPC Provisions (2007) on 1 April 2007.

[157] The SPP issued the Provisional Provisions on Judicial Interpretation Work on 9 December 1996 with immediate effect. They were repealed by the SPP Provisions on Judicial Interpretation Work (2006) on 10 May 2006, which was revised in 2015.

[158] The SPC Provisions on Judicial Interpretation Work were issued on 9 March 2007 and came into force on 1 April 2007.

[159] The revised SPP Provisions on Judicial Interpretation Work were issued by the SPP on 31 December 2015 and came into force on 12 January 2016.

[160] SPC Provisions on Judicial Interpretation Work (2007), art. 5.

[161] SPC Provisions on Judicial Interpretation Work (2007), art. 27.

[162] SPC Provisions on Judicial Interpretation Work (2007), art. 6.

[163] SPC Provisions on Judicial Interpretation Work (2007), art. 6.

[164] SPP Provisions on Judicial Interpretation Work (2019), art. 5.

[165] SPP Provisions on Judicial Interpretation Work (2019), art. 6.

Law (1992), which stipulates special rules for the burden of proof in environmental tort litigation,[166] and the SPC Several Provisions on Evidence in Civil Litigation (2001), which further provides that in environmental tort litigation the defendant bears the burden to prove either that circumstances exist that exempt liability or that there is no causal link between the defendant's acts and the harm caused to the plaintiff.[167] The SPC has also issued specialized judicial interpretations, such as the Interpretation on the Application of Laws in Adjudicating Environmental Tort Cases (SPC Interpretation) (2015).[168]

To guide the prosecution and adjudication of environmental criminal cases, the SPC and SPP have jointly issued the Interpretation on the Application of Laws in Adjudicating Environmental Criminal Cases (SPC and SPP Interpretation) (2016).[169] To tackle especially difficult issues and enhance the enforcement and sanction of environmental crimes, five state organs – the SPC, SPP, Ministry of Public Security (MPS), Ministry of Justice and MEE – issued the Minutes of the Meeting on Handling Environmental Criminal Cases (2019)[170] for implementation by the relevant bodies.

In recent developments in the area of PIL, the SPC issued the Interpretation on Several Issues Concerning the Application of Law in Environmental Civil Public Interest Litigation (SPC Interpretation on Civil EPIL) (2015),[171] the Measures on Adjudication of Pilot Procuratorial Public Interest Litigation (2016),[172] and the Working Rules on the Adjudication of Environmental Public Interest Litigation (for trial implementation) (2017).[173] To test procuratorial PIL in both civil and administrative cases, the SPP carried out pilot exercises from 2015 to 2017 under special powers delegated by the NPCSC.[174] For implementation of the pilot schemes, the SPP issued the Reform Plan on a Pilot Project for Instituting Public Interest Litigation by Procuratorial Organs (Reform Plan on PIL Pilots) (2015),[175] and the Implementation Measures on Pilot Projects of Public Interest Litigation Initiated by People's Procuratorates (SPP Implementation Measures) (2015).[176] Upon completion of the pilot programme, the SPC and SPP issued the Interpretation on the

[166] Section 74 of the SPC Opinion on Several Issues Concerning the Application of Civil Procedure Law (1992) reverses the burden of proof from plaintiff to defendant in environmental tort litigation.

[167] SPC Several Provisions on Evidence in Civil Litigation (2001), s. 4.

[168] The SPC Interpretation (2015) was issued on 1 June 2015 and came into force on 3 June 2015.

[169] The SPC and SPP Interpretation was issued on 23 December 2016 and came into force on 1 January 2017. On the same day, the SPC and SPP Interpretation (2013) was repealed.

[170] The SPC, SPP, MPS, Ministry of Justice and MEE jointly issued the Minutes of the Meeting on Handling Environmental Criminal Cases on 20 February 2019 with immediate effect.

[171] The SPC Interpretation on Civil EPIL was issued on 6 January 2015 and came into force on 7 January 2015.

[172] The SPC issued the Measures on Adjudication of Pilot Procuratorial Public Interest Litigation on 25 February 2016. The Measures came into force on 1 March 2016.

[173] The SPC issued the Working Rules on the Adjudication of Environmental Public Interest Litigation (for trial implementation) on 1 April 2017 with immediate effect.

[174] NPCSC Decision on Authorizing the Supreme People's Procuratorate to Launch the Pilot Programmes of Public Interest Litigation in Designated Areas (2015). This was a two-year programme that began on 1 July 2015. It was conducted in the four subject areas of environment and resources protection, protection of state assets, transfer of land use rights, and food and drug safety. The thirteen designated provinces were Beijing, Inner Mongolia, Jilin, Jiangsu, Anhui, Fujian, Shandong, Hubei, Guangdong, Guizhou, Yunnan, Shaanxi and Gansu.

[175] The SPP Reform Plan on PIL Pilots was issued on 2 July 2015 with immediate effect.

[176] The SPP Implementation Measures were issued on 24 December 2015 and took effect immediately in the thirteen provinces.

Application of Law in Procuratorial Public Interest Litigation (2018)[177] for nationwide implementation.

On eco-environmental damage litigation, the SPC issued the Several Provisions on the Adjudication of Eco-environmental Damage Litigation (for trial implementation) (2019).[178] It sets the rules and procedures for a new type of environmental litigation that can be initiated by provincial and municipal governments or their designated departments against liable parties to seek remedies to restore an eco-environment damaged by serious pollution or eco-destruction.

1.2.6 Local Regulations

Local authorities have the power to issue stricter regulations than those existing nationally or to fill gaps in national regulations. A provincial-level people's congress and its standing committee are granted the lawmaking power to issue local regulations that do not contravene the Constitution, laws or administrative regulations. Provincial regulations are reported to the NPCSC for the record.[179] In relatively large cities (known as 'cities in which districts are established'), the municipal people's congress and its standing committee may promulgate local regulations that do not contravene the Constitution, laws, administrative or local regulations. They are implemented upon approval by the standing committee of the provincial people's congress.[180] These local regulations are of higher authority than local rules made by the local people's governments at the same level or lower.[181]

Using Guangdong province as an example, its People's Congress Standing Committee (PCSC) has issued many local regulations to protect the environment from pollution. These include the Guangdong Provincial Environmental Protection Regulation (2018),[182] the Guangdong Provincial Regulation on Prevention and Control of Environmental Pollution by Solid Waste (2018),[183] the Guangdong Provincial Regulation on the Protection of Water Quality of the East River (2018),[184] and the Guangdong Provincial Regulation on the Prevention and Control of Pollution by Vehicle Emissions (2018).[185]

[177] The SPC and SPP Interpretation on the Application of Law in Procuratorial Public Interest Litigation was issued on 1 March 2018 and came into force on 2 March 2018.

[178] The SPC Several Provisions on the Adjudication of Eco-environmental Damage Litigation (for trial implementation) was issued on 4 June 2019 and came into force on 5 June 2019.

[179] Constitution (2018), art. 100(1); Law on Legislation (2015), art. 72(1).

[180] Constitution (2018), art. 100(2); Law on Legislation (2015), art. 72(2).

[181] Law on Legislation (2015), art. 89(1).

[182] The Guangdong Provincial Environmental Protection Regulation was first enacted by the 10th Guangdong Provincial PCSC on 24 September 2004 at its 13th session. It was revised by the 12th Guangdong PCSC on 13 January 2015 at its 13th session, and amended by the 13th Guangdong PCSC on 29 November 2018 at its 7th session.

[183] The Guangdong Provincial Regulation on Prevention and Control of Environmental Pollution by Solid Waste was first enacted in 2004, was amended twice in 2012 and revised by the 13th Guangdong PCSC on 29 November 2018 at its 7th session.

[184] The Guangdong Provincial Regulation on the Protection of Water Quality of the East River was first enacted in 2002, and was amended in 2010, 2014 and 2018.

[185] The Guangdong Provincial Regulation on the Prevention and Control of Pollution by Vehicle Emissions was first enacted in 2000, was amended in 2004, revised in 2010 and further amended in 2018.

1.2.7 International Environmental Treaties

China has been an active participant in the international environmental regime since the 1980s, has been a vocal representative of developing countries since the Rio Summit (1992)[186] and an important player in building the global climate governance since the Paris Agreement (2015).[187] It has signed and ratified a great number of the treaties that tackle the global environmental problems of ozone depletion,[188] loss of biodiversity,[189] transboundary movement of waste[190] and climate change,[191] among others.

In practice, China has implemented its international environmental legal obligations through domestic laws, regulations and government plans. For example, to phase out the production and consumption of ozone-depleting substances (ODS), China incorporated its international obligations into the APPCL since 2000 by providing that the state must implement total control and quota management on the production, consumption, import and export of ODS.[192] This was further implemented by the Regulation on the Administration of Ozone-Depleting Substances (Regulation on ODS) (2018)[193] issued by the State Council.

1.3 STATE AND PARTY POLICIES AND PLANS

Discussion of the 2018 amendment to the Constitution in Section 1.2.1 highlighted the CCP's leading role in the adoption of the ideas of ecological civilization, the new

[186] The United Nations (UN) Conference on Environment and Development was held in Rio de Janeiro in June 1992. The important legal instruments adopted include the Rio Declaration on Environment and Development, the Convention on Biological Diversity and the UN Framework Convention on Climate Change (UNFCCC). See Rio Declaration on Environment and Development, Rio de Janeiro, 14 June 1992, *International Legal Materials*, 31 (1992), 874–80; Convention on Biological Diversity, Rio de Janeiro, 5 June 1992, treaty no. 30619. *United Nations Treaty Series*, 1760, 79–308; UN Framework Convention on Climate Change, New York, 9 May 1992, treaty no. 30822. *United Nations Treaty Series*, 1771, 107–322.

[187] The Paris Agreement was adopted by the parties to the UNFCCC on 12 December 2015 at the 21st Conference of the Parties in Paris. It opened for signature on 22 April 2016 and China was among the first to sign it. Paris Agreement (2015), Paris, 12 December 2015, treaty no. 54113. *International Legal Materials*, 55 (2016), 743–55.

[188] China signed and ratified the Vienna Convention for the Protection of the Ozone Layer (Vienna Convention) (1985) and the Montreal Protocol on Substances that Deplete the Ozone Layer (Montreal Protocol) (1987) to phase out the production and consumption of ozone-depleting substances. See Vienna Convention for the Protection of the Ozone Layer, Vienna, 22 March 1985, *International Legal Materials*, 26 (1987), 1516–40; Montreal Protocol on Substances that Deplete the Ozone Layer, Montreal, 16 September 1987, *International Legal Materials*, 26 (1987), 1550.

[189] Convention on Biological Diversity; Convention on International Trade in Endangered Species of Wild Fauna and Flora, Washington, 3 March 1973, treaty no. 14537. *International Legal Materials*, 12 (1973), 1085–104. China signed and ratified both conventions to conserve biological diversity and protect endangered species.

[190] China signed and ratified the Basel Convention on the Control of Transboundary Movements of Hazardous Wastes and their Disposal (1989) to prevent and control environmental harm caused by cross-border movement of hazardous waste. See Basel Convention on the Control of Transboundary Movements of Hazardous Wastes and their Disposal, Basel, 22 March 1989, treaty no. 28911. *United Nations Treaty Series*, 1673, 57–336.

[191] China signed and ratified the UNFCCC (1992), the Kyoto Protocol (1997) and the Paris Agreement (2015) to enhance its commitments on the mitigation of greenhouse gas emissions. See Kyoto Protocol to the UN Framework Convention on Climate Change, Kyoto, 11 December 1997, treaty no. 30822. *United Nations Treaty Series*, 2303, 162–331.

[192] APPCL (2015), art. 85. Also see APPCL (2000), art.45 on the control of production and import of ODS.

[193] The Regulation on ODS was issued on 8 April 2010 and amended on 19 March 2018.

development concept and beautiful China. Party influence certainly goes beyond constitutional development. It is well known that Chinese law is highly policy oriented and environmental law is no exception; party and state policies play an indispensable role in environmental protection, leading and shaping the development of environmental laws and regulations at both national and local levels.

1.3.1 The Five-Year Plans on National Economic and Social Development

China's FYPs on National Economic and Social Development are the core of central government policymaking. In the FYPs, the government lays out its socio-economic development strategies, sets targets to be achieved by the end of the five-year period and clarifies key tasks. In accordance with the Constitution, the State Council draws up the FYP and implements it.[194] In practice, FYPs are drafted by the NDRC based on recommendations made by the Party Central Committee, which determines the broad themes and goals of the FYP. The State Council receives and endorses the NDRC's draft and submits it to the NPC for review and approval.[195]

The FYP is implemented by the State Council through specialized plans made by its departments, which guide the work of central and local governments and send signals to market players, including those who do business with China. The goals and measures laid out in FYPs focused solely on socio-economic development until the 11th FYP (2006–10), which, for the first time, set binding targets for a 10 per cent reduction of key pollutants SO_2 and chemical oxygen demand (COD).[196] The 12th FYP (2011–15) devotes one part – six chapters – to environmental protection and green development.[197] It advocates an active response to climate change, strengthening of resource conservation and management, promoting a circular economy, enhancing environmental protection, improving ecological conservation and restoration, and building hydraulic infrastructure and disaster prevention capacity. The 13th FYP (2016–20) continues the tradition with Part X entitled 'Accelerate the improvement of the ecological environment'.[198] It urges accelerating the creation of zones designated for specific ecological functions, promoting resource conservation and efficient utilization, enhancing comprehensive environmental governance, strengthening ecological conservation and restoration, actively responding to climate change, building mechanisms to ensure ecological security, and developing a green environmental protection industry.

Carbon intensity refers to carbon emissions per unit of GDP, while energy intensity refers to energy consumption per unit of GDP. China failed to achieve its target for reducing energy intensity by 20 per cent by the end of the 11th FYP period in 2010, which resulted in a more conservative approach in setting targets for the next two FYPs.

1.3.2 Party Policies Jointly Promulgated with the State Council

Party policies play an important role in China's environmental lawmaking and enforcement. The CCP is a body of supreme power,[199] making decisions on important national socio-

194 Constitution (2018), art. 89(5). 195 Constitution (2018), art. 62(10). 196 11th FYP, part I, chapter 3.
197 12th FYP, part VI, chapters 21–26. 198 13th FYP, part X, chapters 42–48.
199 Constitution (2018), preamble. It expressly states the important leadership position of the CCP in China.

TABLE 1.6 ENVIRONMENTAL ABATEMENT TARGETS SET IN THE FYPs

	11th FYP targets (%)	11th FYP achievement (%)	12th FYP targets (%)	12th FYP achievement (%)	13th FYP targets (%)
SO_2	−10	−14.29	−8	−18	−15
NOx	Nil	Nil	−10	−18.6	−15
COD	−10	−12.45	−8	−12.9	−10
Ammonia nitrogen	Nil	Nil	−10	−13	−10
Carbon intensity	Nil	Nil	−17	−20	−18
Energy intensity	−20	−19.1	−16	−18.2	−15

Sources: China's 11th FYP (2006–10), 12th FYP (2011–15) and 13th FYP (2016–20).

economic and political policies that directly guide the lawmaking work of the state legislature.[200] The CCP controls the work of the central, provincial, municipal and county governments through a system of party committees. It approves the appointment of government officials, assesses their performance and monitors and controls the routine operation of government.[201]

The CCP plays a crucial role in making environmental law and policies and, since Xi Jinping came to power, increasingly also in implementation and enforcement. It is worth noting that important environmental reform policies and decisions of recent years have been issued jointly by the CCP Central Committee and the State Council, in sharp contrast to the previous practice of the State Council acting alone. A few examples are the Opinion on Accelerating the Construction of the Ecological Civilization (2015),[202] the Integrated Reform Plan for Promoting Ecological Civilization (2015),[203] Reform Plan on the Compensation Regime for Eco-environmental Damage (2017),[204] the Opinion to Improve Eco-environmental Protection and Continue Fighting Against Pollution (2018)[205] and the Provisions on the Work of Supervision over Ecological and Environmental Protection by Central Authorities (2019).[206]

200 In practice, the Party Congress is held towards the end of each year, a few months before the annual meeting of the NPC, which is normally held in March.

201 Albert Chen, *An Introduction to the Legal System*, at 105–21.

202 The CCP Central Committee and State Council issued the Opinion on Accelerating the Construction of the Ecological Civilization on 25 April 2015.

203 The CCP Central Committee and State Council issued the Integrated Reform Plan for Promoting Ecological Civilization on 21 September 2015.

204 The General Offices of both the CCP Central Committee and the State Council issued the Reform Plan on the Compensation Regime for Eco-environmental Damage in December 2017.

205 The CCP Central Committee and the State Council issued the Opinion to Improve Eco-environmental Protection and Continue Fighting Against Pollution on 16 June 2018.

206 The General Offices of both the CCP Central Committee and the State Council issued the Provisions on the Work of Supervision over Ecological and Environmental Protection by Central Authorities on 17 June 2019.

China faces daunting environmental challenges, but change is happening. Coal consumption in the primary energy mix has dropped from 70.7 per cent in 1978 to 59 per cent in 2018, while clean energy, including natural gas, hydropower, nuclear and wind, increased from 6.6 per cent in 1978 to 22.1 per cent in 2018. The annual mean concentration level of PM_{10} in 338 cities had dropped 22.7 per cent by 2017 compared to the 2013 level, and that of $PM_{2.5}$ in 74 key cities had fallen 34.7 per cent during the same period as a result of tight control over sources of air pollution.[207] China's evolving environmental law and governance are making these changes, slowing environmental degradation and improving environmental quality as the country pursues continuing economic growth by green and sustainable development.

[207] State Council, *Human Rights Development*, part II; MEE, *2018 China Ecology and Environment Gazette*, at 54.

2

Key Institutions of Environmental Protection

This chapter examines key institutions involved in making, implementing and enforcing China's environmental laws, policies, regulations and plans. These key institutions are important players in the reform and improvement of China's environmental governance, which is evolving dynamically through interaction between the state and civil society, and among different government bodies, the procuratorates and the courts. This chapter is divided into seven sections focusing on the evolving roles and functions of: the people's congress at national and local levels (Section 2.1); the State Council and local governments (Section 2.2); agencies in charge of environmental protection (Section 2.3); other agencies and departments involved in environmental protection (Section 2.4); the courts (Section 2.5); the procuratorates (Section 2.6); and environment NGOs (Section 2.7).

2.1 PEOPLE'S CONGRESS AT NATIONAL AND LOCAL LEVELS

The National People's Congress (NPC) is the supreme power organ of the state. Its working body is the NPC Standing Committee (NPCSC).[1] The NPCSC is accountable to – and reports to – the NPC.[2] Local people's congresses exist at provincial, municipal, county/district, village and township levels.[3] These local congresses are the state's power organs at local levels.[4] The standing committee exists at county level and above.[5]

2.1.1 The NPC and NPCSC

The NPC and NPCSC exercise the lawmaking power of the state.[6] The NPC has more than 3,000 deputies and meets once a year.[7] The NPC at its annual meeting only passes laws that are considered to be the most important and fundamental, such as the Criminal Law (CL), Contract Law, General Rules of Civil Law (GRCL), Criminal Procedure Law, Civil Procedure Law (CPL). It relies routinely on its standing committee to discharge most of its lawmaking

[1] Constitution (2018), art. 57. [2] Constitution (2018), art. 69. [3] Constitution (2018), art. 95(1).
[4] Constitution (2018), art. 96(1); Organic Law of Local People's Congresses and Local People's Governments (2015), art. 4.
[5] Constitution (2018), art. 96(2); Organic Law of Local People's Congresses and Local People's Governments (2015), art. 2.
[6] Constitution (2018), art. 58. [7] Constitution (2018), art. 61.

functions. According to Professor Albert Chen, the NPCSC plays a more significant legislative role than the NPC, having enacted more than 80 per cent of national laws.[8] The NPCSC meets every two months to deliberate and pass bills.[9] All environmental statutes have been enacted, amended and revised by the NPCSC.

The Legislative Affairs Commission (LAC) of the NPCSC provides administrative and professional support to the NPC and NPCSC. It is in charge of preparing most bills that will be deliberated by the NPC and NPCSC. The LAC drafts five-year lawmaking plans for approval by the NPCSC at the start of a new NPC term and annual lawmaking plans. While not all laws are enacted and issued as scheduled, these plans indicate national lawmaking priorities.

2.1.2 Special Committee: The ENRPC

In addition to the standing committee, special committees exist within the NPC to provide expertise in the drafting and deliberation of bills and to supervise the implementation of the laws.[10] In 1993, the NPC set up a special committee on environmental protection, in response to the pressing need to address China's environmental pollution and ecological degradation with more sophisticated and effective lawmaking. In 1994, this committee was renamed the Environment and Natural Resources Protection Committee (ENRPC), and the conservation and use of natural resources were added to its remit, which previously was limited to environmental protection.[11] The ENRPC is in charge of drafting and amending environmental laws arising from the annual and five-year lawmaking plans. It is also responsible for supervising and monitoring the implementation of environmental laws. Further, it reviews the environmental regulations and rules issued by the State Council and its ministries or commissions, as well as local regulations, to ensure they do not contravene national laws or the Constitution.[12]

2.1.3 Lawmaking Process

A typical NPC lawmaking process begins when the LAC assigns the task of drafting the legislation to a government agency with expertise in the subject matter. Once the LAC receives the initial draft, it consults with state ministries and provincial governments to collect feedback. Disputes often arise given the different interest groups and stakeholders involved, leading to changes in the draft in order to reach consensus. At the end of this consultation process, a revised compromise draft is produced and submitted to the NPC's Constitution and Law Committee and to a specialized committee for review. In the case of environmental legislation, it is the ENRPC that fulfils the specialist role. The two committees report to the NPCSC with or without making further revisions. The NPCSC then either

[8] Albert Chen, *An Introduction to the Legal System*, 132.

[9] Organic Law of the National People's Congress (1982), art. 29.

[10] Constitution (2018), art. 70. They are: the Nationalities Committee, Constitution and Law Committee, Financial and Economic Affairs Committee, Education, Science, Culture and Public Health Committee, Foreign Affairs Committee, Overseas Chinese Affairs Committee and other special committees established as needed.

[11] The NPC Decision to Rename the Environmental Protection Committee as the Environment and Natural Resources Protection Committee was adopted on 22 March 1994 by the 8th NPC at its 2nd session.

[12] Organic Law of the NPC (1982), art. 37.

forwards the approved draft to the NPC (this occurs in the case of the most important statutes) or places it on its own agenda for deliberation.

Once on the agenda of the NPC annual meeting and presented to the general assembly by the bill proponents, bills are deliberated within different delegations,[13] voted on at a scheduled time during the annual session, and adopted if supported by a simple majority of all delegates.[14] Only amending the Constitution requires a two-thirds majority.[15]

In contrast, NPCSC lawmaking takes longer as each bill normally goes through three readings. This applies to both the enactment of new laws and the revision of existing laws. The first reading presents the draft bill to the whole session of the NPCSC, after which it is usually published for public consultation. Deliberation of the draft bill begins at breakout sessions of the NPCSC. At the second reading, the Constitution and Law Committee reports to the whole session of the NPCSC on major issues and revisions resulting from deliberations and public comment.[16] Further deliberation of the revised bill continues at breakout sessions. At the third reading, the Constitution and Law Committee reports to the whole session of the NPCSC on the deliberations that have taken place, and the revised bill is subject to further deliberation at breakout sessions.[17] A bill may, however, be voted on after two readings if there is already a general consensus. In the case of an amendment or revision to a law, where there is general consensus the bill may be voted on after one reading.[18] A simple majority is required to pass the bill into law.[19] Where bills or revision involve a high degree of controversy among different stakeholders and interest groups, it may take years and more than three readings to pass the bill into law. The enactment of the Environmental Impact Assessment Law (EIAL) (2002)[20] and the revision of the Environmental Protection Law (EPL) (2014)[21] both took years of consultation to reach compromise over a range of contentious issues.

2.1.4 Supervision of Implementation of Laws

In addition to lawmaking, people's congresses and their standing committees play crucially important roles in supervising same-level people's governments.[22] The EPL (2014) strengthened this supervisory role by requiring governments at county level and above to report annually to the same-level people's congress or its standing committee on the state of environmental quality and the achievement of environmental protection targets in their region. In the case of serious pollution incidents, the relevant government must make

[13] Law on Legislation (2015), art. 18. [14] Constitution (2018), art. 64(2); Law on Legislation (2015), art. 24.
[15] Constitution (2018), art. 64(1).
[16] The Constitution and Law Committee, consisting of NPCSC members with legal qualifications and experience, is in charge of revising draft bills in between the first and second reading, and the second and third reading. The revisions are based on the results of breakout group discussions and public consultation.
[17] Law on Legislation (2015), art. 29. [18] Law on Legislation (2015), art. 30.
[19] Law on Legislation (2015), art. 41.
[20] The EIAL bill was first presented on 22 December 2000 to the 9th NPCSC at its 19th session. After deliberation and consultation, the revised bill was adopted on 28 October 2002 at the 30th session of the 9th NPCSC. It came into force on 1 September 2003.
[21] The draft amendment of the EPL (1989) was presented on 31 August 2012 to the 28th session of the 11th NPCSC for a first reading. The revised EPL was adopted on 24 April 2014 by the 8th session of the 12th NPCSC.
[22] Constitution (2018), arts. 67(6), 92, 104, 110(1).

timely report to the same-level people's congress standing committee (PCSC) and accept its supervision.[23] In 2016, the State Council made a first annual report to the NPCSC on China's 2015 environmental quality and the achievement of environmental protection targets.[24]

Apart from reporting annually to the people's congress of the same level, the NPCSC conducts inspections, as needed, to analyse the implementation of the law and uncover problems. The NPCSC decides whether, when and how often to conduct such inspections. It forms a special inspection task force divided into several inspection teams that visit selected provinces over two to three months. In the case of provinces that will not be visited by NPCSC inspection teams, the task force delegates to provincial people's congresses the power to conduct concurrent inspections. The NPCSC has clearly been paying increasing and closer attention to environmental law implementation in recent years. In June and July 2016, less than two years after the revised EPL (2014) was implemented,[25] the NPCSC sent inspection teams to eight provinces or autonomous regions: Hebei, Henan, Shanxi, Heilongjiang, Guangxi, Guizhou, Yunnan and Ningxia. The provincial PCSCs of the twenty-three provinces, autonomous regions and centrally controlled municipalities not covered by the inspection teams were authorized to conduct inspections during the same period. The inspection teams heard reports from local governments and agencies at 21 meetings and visited 106 units and projects.[26] They also made unscheduled visits without prior notice to check and understand the real picture of local implementation and enforcement. The purpose of NPCSC inspection is to identify problems and recommend improvements to be made by government from central to local levels. Similarly, less than two and a half years after the revised APPCL (2015) was implemented,[27] an NPCSC inspection task force was formed and teams were sent to eight provinces – Hebei, Henan, Inner Mongolia, Shanxi, Shaanxi, Shandong, Anhui and Jiangsu – in May and June 2018. Twenty-three provinces not visited by the teams were instead inspected by the provincial PCSCs. The NPCSC inspection teams had 29 meetings to hear reports from local governments and agencies and visited 107 units and projects. In addition, they met deputies from five levels of people's congresses, as well as experts and community representatives to collect views from different sources and identify problems and difficulties in implementing the APPCL (2015).[28]

2.1.5 Local People's Congress

Each provincial-level local people's congress and its standing committee is granted lawmaking power to issue local regulations that do not contravene the Constitution or

[23] EPL (2014), art. 27.

[24] Chen Jining, *Report on Environmental Status and Achievement of Environmental Protection Targets* (2015). On 25 April 2016, Chen Jining, minister of environmental protection, presented the Report to the 20th session of the 12th NPCSC.

[25] The EPL (2014) was adopted on 24 April 2014 at the 8th session of the 12th NPCSC. It came into force on 1 January 2015.

[26] Shen Yueyue, *Inspection Report on the Implementation of the Environmental Protection Law.*

[27] The APPCL (2015) was adopted on 29 August 2015 at the 16th session of the 12th NPCSC. It came into force on 1 January 2016.

[28] Li Zhanshu, *Inspection Report on the Implementation of Air Pollution Prevention and Control Law* (2018). www.pkulaw.cn. On 9 July 2018, Li Zhanshu, NPCSC chairperson, presented the report to the 4th session of the 13th NPCSC.

national laws and regulations, and are applicable within that administrative jurisdiction.[29] These local regulations are reported to the NPCSC for the record.[30] In cities in which administrative districts are established, a municipal people's congress and its standing committee may promulgate local regulations on rural and urban construction and management, environmental protection and historical and cultural conservation that do not contravene the Constitution, national laws and regulations or provincial regulations. Municipal regulations are implemented following approval by the provincial PCSC.[31]

In the battle against pollution, many provincial people's congresses have been actively involved in local environmental lawmaking in recent years. For example, the Beijing Municipal People's Congress enacted the Beijing Water Pollution Prevention and Control Regulation (2010)[32] and the Beijing Air Pollution Prevention and Control Regulation (2014).[33] Both were amended by the Beijing PCSC in 2018 to incorporate legal developments effected by the EPL (2014), APPCL (2015) and WPPCL (2017).[34]

Under the EPL (2014), a local people's congress at county level and above and its standing committee play a supervisory role over the same-level people's government.[35] They receive annual reports on local environmental quality and progress towards achievement of environmental targets. In 2016, fourteen provincial governments, including Henan, Chongqing and Jiangxi, made their first annual report on environmental performance (2015 performance) to provincial people's congresses.[36]

2.2 STATE COUNCIL AND LOCAL PEOPLE'S GOVERNMENTS

The State Council, also known as the Central People's Government, is the supreme executive body of the state.[37] It is accountable to the NPC, and to the NPCSC when the NPC is not in session.[38]

2.2.1 The State Council's Lawmaking Power

The State Council has extensive lawmaking powers. In addition to introducing bills to the NPC or NPCSC, it is also empowered to enact administrative regulations.[39] In particular, it promulgates regulations in accordance with the Constitution and law in the following circumstances: (i) where they are necessary to implement a national law; (ii) when it is exercising its executive powers under article 89 of the Constitution, which provides for State Council leadership and management of a wide range of affairs and (iii) when it has

[29] Constitution (2018), art. 100(1); Law on Legislation (2015), art. 72(1);
[30] Constitution (2018), art. 100(1).
[31] Constitution (2018), art. 100(2); Law on Legislation (2015), art. 72(2).
[32] The Beijing Water Pollution Prevention and Control Regulation was adopted on 19 November 2010 at the 21st session of the 13th Beijing Municipal PCSC.
[33] The Beijing Air Pollution Prevention and Control Regulation was adopted on 22 January 2014 at the 2nd session of the 14th Beijing Municipal People's Congress.
[34] On 30 March 2018, the 3rd session of the 15th Beijing Municipal PCSC amended seven local regulations, including regulations on the control of air and water pollution.
[35] EPL (2014), art. 27.
[36] Shen Yueyue, *Inspection Report on the Implementation of the Environmental Protection Law* (2016). www.pkulaw.cn. Shen Yueyue, vice chairperson of the NPCSC, presented the report on 2 November 2016 to the 24th session of the 12th NPCSC.
[37] Constitution (2018), art. 85.
[38] Constitution (2018), art. 92.
[39] Constitution (2018), art. 89.

been empowered by an enabling decision of the NPC or NPCSC to set administrative regulations on an issue that should be regulated by national law, and is beyond the scope of (i) and (ii).[40] Each year, the State Council sets an annual regulation-making plan that is consistent with and complementary to the lawmaking plans of the NPCSC.[41] The Legislative Affairs Office (LAO) of the State Council played a crucial role in making environmental laws and regulations through its special division devoted to environmental issues, known as the Agricultural, Natural Resources and Environmental Protection Department. Institutional reforms in 2018 transferred the LAO to the Ministry of Justice without much change to its role.[42] There are now four Ministry of Justice bureaus in charge of making regulations, one of which is tasked with regulating ecological civilization, meaning environmental protection, resources conservation and green development.[43]

To implement the EPL (2014), the State Council has issued the National Environmental Emergency Response Plan (NEERP) (2014),[44] the Plan on the Construction of Eco-environmental Monitoring Network (2015),[45] the Implementation Plan on Permit Control of Pollution Discharge (2016),[46] the Opinion on Improving the Eco-compensation Mechanism (2016),[47] and the Opinion on Recovery and Utilization of Waste from Livestock and Poultry Farming (2017).[48] To address China's serious pollution problems as a matter of urgency – prior to the amendment of the APPCL (2000) and WPPCL (2008) – the State Council issued the Action Plan on Air Pollution Prevention and Control (Air Action Plan) (2013),[49] the Action Plan on Prevention and Control of Water Pollution (Water Action Plan) (2015),[50] the Action Plan on Prevention and Control of Soil Pollution (Soil Action Plan) (2016),[51] and the Three-Year Action Plan on Winning the Battle of Blue-Sky Protection (2018).[52] Many of the regulatory and market mechanisms in the action plans were later adopted by the NPCSC in the APPCL (2015), WPPCL (2017) and SPPCL (2018).

2.2.2 Government Environmental Responsibilities

The EPL (2014) emphasizes the importance of government responsibility and accountability by stipulating that local governments at all levels are responsible for the environmental

[40] Law on Legislation (2015), art. 65. [41] Law on Legislation (2015), art. 66.

[42] On 17 March 2018, the 1st session of the 13th NPC approved the State Council Institutional Reform Proposal with immediate effect. See State Council Institutional Reform Proposal, part I, s. 9.

[43] For details, see Ministry of Justice, 27 June 2019, 'The fourth bureau of legislation'. Online article. http://en.moj.gov.cn/2019-06/27/c_384623.htm

[44] The State Council issued the revised NEERP on 29 December 2014 with immediate effect.

[45] The State Council issued the Plan on the Construction of an Eco-environmental Monitoring Network on 26 July 2015 with immediate effect.

[46] The State Council issued the Implementation Plan on Permit Control of Pollution Discharge on 10 November 2016 with immediate effect.

[47] The State Council issued the Opinion on Improving the Eco-compensation Mechanism on 28 April 2016 with immediate effect.

[48] The State Council issued the Opinion on Recovery and Utilization of Waste from Livestock and Poultry Farming on 31 May 2017 with immediate effect.

[49] The State Council issued the Air Action Plan on 10 September 2013 with immediate effect.

[50] The State Council issued the Water Action Plan on 2 April 2015 with immediate effect.

[51] The State Council issued the Soil Action Plan on 28 May 2016 with immediate effect.

[52] The State Council issued the Three-Year Action Plan on Blue-Sky Protection on 27 June 2018 with immediate effect.

quality within their jurisdictions[53] and must take effective measures to improve it.[54] Similar provision in the previous EPL (1989)[55] failed in practice, as local governments tend to pursue short-term GDP growth at the cost of the environment. However, the EPL (2014) expressly mandates a 'target responsibility system' and a mechanism for government appraisal that takes into account environmental performance.[56] National environmental goals or pollution abatement targets are assigned to provincial governments as specific tasks to be achieved within a time limit.[57] Provincial governments further assign the tasks to lower-level people's governments for implementation. The target responsibility system operates in the form of an agreement between a higher-level authority and its subordinate regarding targets to be achieved and measures to be taken. It aims to transform national targets into local implementation effectively and will only work if the outcome matters to individuals in charge. Therefore, achieving the assigned targets and implementing the measures forms an important basis for assessing performance in the appraisal mechanism.

2.2.3 Equal Accountability of Party and Government Leaders

The enactment of the EPL (2014) and the new emphasis, since 2018, by party and state leadership on ecological civilization brought to the fore a new concept of 'equal accountability of party and government leaders'. This concept seeks to make party leaders accountable for the decisions they make, given their substantial power at all levels of government. As part of this new focus, the CCP Central Committee and the State Council issued the Measures on the Accountability of Party and Government Leaders for Eco-environmental Damage (2015).[58] Now both the government and those holding leadership positions in the CCP committees are responsible for protecting the environment.

2.2.4 Supervision and Inspection by the Central Authorities

The State Council exercises uniform leadership over local governments at all levels, stipulating the division of power between central and provincial governments.[59] There are three levels of local government: provincial (including four municipalities directly under the Central People's Government and five ethnic-minority autonomous regions), municipal (including prefecture and county) and township (including district in urban areas and township in rural regions).[60] It is the local governments and local agencies that implement and enforce the environmental laws, regulations, targets and standards set by the national legislature, the State Council and its departments.

The State Council issued the Notice to Enhance Environmental Supervision and Enforcement (2014)[61] to strengthen enforcement and sanction of environmental violations and to improve supervision of environmental enforcement. In 2018, it also set up a special

[53] EPL (2014), art. 6(2). [54] EPL (2014), art. 28(1). [55] EPL (1989), art. 16.

[56] EPL (2014), art. 26. For further discussion, see Alex L. Wang, 'The search for sustainable legitimacy: environmental law and bureaucracy in China', *Harvard Environmental Law Review*, 37 (2013), 365–440.

[57] See Section 3.2.2 in Chapter 3 of this book.

[58] The Measures on the Accountability of Party and Government Leaders for Eco-environmental Damage were issued by the CCP Central Committee and the State Council on 17 August 2015.

[59] Constitution (2018), art. 89. [60] Constitution (2018), art. 30.

[61] The State Council issued the Notice to Enhance Environmental Supervision and Enforcement on 12 November 2014.

environmental supervision body, the Office on Supervision of Eco-environmental Protection, under the Ministry of Ecology and Environment (MEE) to take charge of the supervision and inspection of local governments and relevant agencies in relation to their implementation of environmental laws, regulations, standards, policies and plans.[62] In July 2015, the CCP Central Committee's Leadership Group on Deepening Reform issued the Environmental Protection Supervision Plan (for trial implementation) to strengthen environmental supervision by extending it to local party committees.[63] It took two years – 2016 and 2017 – for the first round of environmental supervision by the central authorities to cover all thirty-one provinces, autonomous regions and municipalities that fall directly under the Central People's Government. The supervision team normally visits each province for a month, meeting provincial party and government leaders and heads of relevant agencies to hear reports, reading files and checking records, conducting site visits to enterprises and receiving public complaints by phone and post. It is a process through which the central authority can inspect both the environmental work of local governments and the operation of polluting enterprises, with a focus on supervising the provincial party committees and governments in their implementation of environmental laws, regulations, plans and policies issued by central authorities. The supervision teams identify local environmental problems and pass them to the provincial governments for action.[64]

During the two-year period, the supervision and inspection teams received 135,000 complaints from the public and passed 104,000 cases to provincial governments for action. More than 17,000 people were held accountable and sanctioned.[65] To maintain pressure on the local governments and to ensure they fully implement and enforce environmental laws and regulations, the central authorities have clearly wanted to make the supervision and inspection a routine practice, not just a one-off political event. In 2018, follow-up visits were conducted, targeting twenty provinces, autonomous regions and centrally controlled municipalities with serious environmental problems. The focus of these visits was to ensure that the specific environmental problems identified in 2016 and 2017 had been rectified. The first ten provinces – Hebei, Inner Mongolia, Heilongjiang, Jiangsu, Jiangxi, Henan, Guangdong, Guangxi, Yunnan and Ningxia – were inspected in June and July 2018.[66] The second ten – Shanxi, Liaoning, Jilin, Anhui, Shandong, Hubei, Hunan, Sichuan, Guizhou and Shaanxi – were inspected in November and December.[67] In total, 8,644 people were held accountable and sanctioned by the end of 2018.[68]

[62] The State Council's Notice to Enhance Environmental Supervision and Enforcement (2014), part III, s. 9.

[63] Zhang Ke, 'The central environmental supervision and inspection teams: members and rules', *Environmental Education*, 194:12 (2016), 20–1.

[64] Zhang Lujing et al., 'Powerful environmental supervision and inspection by the central authorities', *China Economic Weekly*, 43:6 November (2017), 17–29. More details on individual provinces can be found at Central Supervision and Inspection Office of the MEE (n.d.). Website. http://dcb.mee.gov.cn/

[65] Zhang Lujing et al., 'Powerful environmental supervision'.

[66] MEE, 'Central environmental supervision and inspection follow-up visits receiving 38,000 complaints, holding 4,305 accountable', (press release) 9 July 2018. www.mee.gov.cn/gkml/sthjbgw/qt/201807/t20180709_446306.htm.

[67] MEE, 'Second batch of revisits by central eco-environmental supervision and inspection teams completed', (press release) 8 December 2018. www.mee.gov.cn/xxgk2018/xxgk/xxgk15/201812/t20181208_680881.html.

[68] Deng Qi, 'Second round of central eco-environmental supervision and inspection starts this year', *New Beijing News*, 27 February 2019.

TABLE 2.1 FIRST ROUND OF SUPERVISION BY THE CENTRAL AUTHORITIES (2016–2017)

	Inspection visits	Province visited	Publishing date of supervision report
Pilot exercise	January to February 2016	Hebei	May 2016
First batch	July to August 2016	Inner Mongolia, Heilongjiang, Jiangsu, Jiangxi, Henan, Guangxi, Yunnan, Ningxia	November 2016
Second batch	November to December 2016	Beijing, Shanghai, Hubei, Guangdong, Chongqing, Shaanxi, Gansu	April 2017
Third batch	April to May 2017	Tianjin, Shanxi, Liaoning, Anhui, Fujian, Hunan, Guizhou	August 2017
Fourth batch	August to September 2017	Jilin, Zhejiang, Shandong, Hainan, Sichuan, Tibet, Qinghai, Xinjiang	December 2017

Sources: Central Supervision and Inspection Office of the MEE (n.d.). Website. http://dcb.mee.gov.cn/

2.3 ENVIRONMENTAL PROTECTION AGENCIES

The MEE and local environmental protection bureaus (EPBs), assisted by environmental monitoring stations and regional environmental supervision centres, are the bodies in charge of environmental law implementation and enforcement. The EPL (2014) provides that the environmental protection authority of the State Council is in charge of overall supervision of environmental protection work nationwide. Local environmental protection authorities at the county level and above are in charge of overall supervision of environmental protection work within the relevant jurisdiction.[69] There is vertical administrative hierarchy within the environmental protection authorities. That is, EPBs receive guidance from their supervisory authorities, the superior EPB. Superior EPBs set the broad agenda for lower-level EPBs in the form of annual and five-year plans (FYPs). Local EPBs periodically report to the supervisory EPBs on the progress they are making to achieving their objectives. Horizontally, EPBs vary in size and in quality of staff, with those in wealthier regions on the east coast usually equipped with better-trained personnel than their less-developed counterparts in western China.

Environmental protection authorities play a crucially important role in implementing and enforcing environmental law. Their main statutory duties are: (i) making environmental protection plans,[70] (ii) setting environmental quality and emission/discharge standards,[71] (iii) establishing environmental monitoring systems,[72] (iv) approving EIA documents,[73] (v) routine enforcement including on-site inspections[74] and imposing administrative sanctions to punish violations[75] and (vi) disclosing environmental information to

[69] EPL (2014), art. 10(1). [70] EPL (2014), art. 13. [71] EPL (2014), arts. 15 and 16.
[72] EPL (2014), art. 17. [73] EPL (2014), arts. 19 and 44. [74] EPL (2014), art. 24.
[75] EPL (2014), arts. 59, 61 and 62.

the public.[76] The functional division between central and local authorities is that the MEE focuses more on national-level plan making, standards and target setting, while local EPBs are responsible for implementing the national plans in order to achieve the MEE's targets and standards.

2.3.1 MEE: A Historical Review

Environmental institution building started in the early 1970s and it has been a long and winding road for the MEE to achieve its current political status and administrative powers within the State Council. The first government entity with an explicit focus on environmental protection was the Office of the State Council Environmental Protection Leadership Group, which was established in 1974 after the first National Conference on Environmental Protection Work in 1973.[77] It was the start of the Chinese government's initiative on environmental protection, which began after a toxic-fish incident in Beijing in 1971 and China's participation in the United Nations (UN) Conference on the Human Environment in 1972.

Toxic Fish and the Contaminated Guanting Reservoir (1971)

Serious pollution occurred at Guanting Reservoir in Hebei province in the winter of 1971. In March 1972, some Beijing residents who consumed fish from the reservoir fell ill, showing symptoms of fatigue, headache, stomach ache, nausea and vomiting. Premier Zhou Enlai took it seriously and ordered a thorough investigation to identify the sources of pollution. The State Planning Commission and the State Construction Commission formed an investigation group headed by Wan Li, a senior leader and chairman of the seventh NPCSC (1988–93). The *Report on Guanting Reservoir Pollution and Recommended Solutions* was submitted by the two commissions on 8 June 1972. They found that untreated industrial wastewater had been discharged from factories, including a pesticide factory, in the river basin in which Xuanhua county and the cities of Zhangjiakou and Datong were located. This untreated wastewater was the primary source of the water contamination that killed the fish and poisoned the consumers. The State Council circulated the report on 20 June 1972 and the Guanting Reservoir Protection Task Force headed by Wan Li was formed with representatives from the governments of Beijing and Tianjin, Hebei and Shanxi. The task force investigated and reported directly to the State Council with proposals for action. Measures were then taken to control the industrial polluting sources and improve the water quality of Guanting Reservoir.[78]

The toxic-fish incident happened at a time when China was guided by the political ideology that pollution belonged exclusively to capitalist economies and indicated the decay and collapse of capitalist societies. However, the investigation had revealed serious

[76] EPL (2014), art. 54.

[77] Qu Geping, *Qu's Pursuit: China's Environmental Protection Strategy* (Beijing: China Environmental Science Press, 2010), at 381–2.

[78] Xu Yijie, 'Environmental protection regional cooperation in the new China: the case of Guanting Reservoir', *Contemporary China History Studies*, 22:6 (2015), 69–81; also see Qu Geping, *Qu's Pursuit*, at 379–81; and Wang Yongchen, *Green Action in China* (Beijing: Foreign Languages Press, 2006), at 6–7.

industrial pollution threatening human health in China's capital Beijing. The Guanting Reservoir case was, in fact, the very first environmental project undertaken by the Chinese government to tackle pollution. Unfortunately, more and worse pollution was soon found in Shandong, Wuhan, Shanghai and Guangzhou, among others.[79]

In 1972, when China was overwhelmed by the political campaigns and class struggles initiated by Chairman Mao during the Cultural Revolution (1966–76), Premier Zhou Enlai managed to send a small delegation to attend the UN Conference on the Human Environment in Stockholm. Although the members of China's delegation, which included scientists and policymakers, were fairly passive participants, it was an eye-opening experience for many and raised their environmental awareness. Upon hearing reports from the delegates, Premier Zhou Enlai realized that many pollution problems that had previously been seen as western were already happening in China. Consequently, he ordered a national conference on environmental protection to be held immediately to address the issues of air and water pollution, pollution by waste, and ecological destruction.[80]

The first National Conference on Environmental Protection was held in August 1973 and it produced a set of guiding principles: 'comprehensive planning, rational arrangements, integrated use, turning harm into benefit, relying on the masses, full participation, protecting the environment, and bringing benefit to the people'.[81] In order to strengthen work on environmental protection, the State Council established the Environmental Protection Leadership Group in October 1974, which comprised the heads of approximately twenty State Council departments. It was a high-level body focusing on general environment planning but, unfortunately, it only met twice in nine years.[82] The daily environmental planning work was handled by the Environmental Protection Office attached to the Group.[83]

As part of the institutional reform of the early 1980s, the State Council, in 1982, dissolved the Environmental Protection Leadership Group and transferred the Environmental Protection Office to the newly established Ministry of Urban–Rural Construction and Environmental Protection (MURCEP), renaming it the Environmental Protection Agency (EPA).[84] Though staff numbers doubled from thirty to sixty, it lost its independent status and became embedded in the bureaucracy in charge of construction. It was soon found that the EPA under the MURCEP had great difficulty in promoting environmental protection among different ministries and different levels of local government. Qu Geping, head of the EPA, proposed to the State Council that a higher-level body be set up to lead and coordinate national environmental protection. In May 1984, the State

79 Qu Geping, *Qu's Pursuit*, at 381. 80 Qu Geping, *Qu's Pursuit*, at 381.

81 The guiding principles, containing thirty-two Chinese characters, were found in the Provisions on Environmental Protection and Improvement issued after the State Council held the first National Conference on Environmental Protection Works in August 1973. They were incorporated into article 4 of the EPL (for trial implementation 1979). The term 'rational arrangements' in the guiding principles refers to rational geographic layout of industry, while 'integrated use' refers to integrated use of resources and waste recycling.

82 Abigail Jahiel, 'The organization of environmental protection in China', *China Quarterly*, 156 (1998), 757–87, at 767.

83 Jahiel, 'The organization of', at 767.

84 Zhao Ziyang, *Report on State Council Institutional Reform* (1982). www.pkulaw.cn. Premier Zhao Ziyang presented the report on 2 March 1982 to the 5th NPCSC at its 22nd session.

Council issued the Decision on Environmental Protection Work to establish the Environmental Protection Commission (EPC), which was to decide on environmental protection strategy and policy, and plan, lead and coordinate environmental protection work. It comprised the heads of twenty-four ministries and commissions initially and was headed by a vice premier, Li Peng, who served as the first director of the commission.[85] It met once every three months from 1984 to 1997 to discuss and decide on environmental protection plans, policies and provisions and request relevant ministries and local governments to report their environmental protection work. The EPC was a powerful body that put pressure on governments at all levels to take environmental issues seriously.[86] In December 1984, the EPA was renamed the National Environmental Protection Agency (NEPA) and staff numbers were increased from 60 to 120. From December 1984, it functioned as the executive office of the EPC, and gained some independence. The NEPA, however, remained part of the MURCEP until 1988, when the MURCEP was formally divided into two – the Ministry of Construction and the NEPA.[87]

In 1988, the NEPA formally gained independent status at sub-ministerial level and staff numbers increased from 120 to 321.[88] Under the EPL (1989), the NEPA exercised overall supervision and management of environmental protection work nationwide.[89] In 1998, the NEPA was further elevated to become the State Environmental Protection Administration (SEPA) at a time when many ministries were being closed down or consolidated. However, the SEPA was not yet at cabinet level, meaning it was not yet on an equal footing with other ministries or commissions and that its head did not have a vote in the State Council.[90]

It took another ten years for the SEPA to be further upgraded; in 2008 it became the Ministry of Environmental Protection (MEP). At this point, the minister of environment became a member of the State Council with voting power. The MEP was primarily engaged in the development of China's environmental policies, plans and legislation. It drafted or assisted the NPC's ENRPC in drafting environmental laws, regulations and standards, guided and directed the work of environmental management, promoted environmental education and publicity programmes, supported technology innovation, promoted best-available technologies and coordinated international environmental programmes and inter-ministry environmental initiatives.[91]

The institutional reform of the State Council in 2018 substantially expanded the powers of the MEP and renamed it the MEE. The MEE took over statutory responsibilities relating to the environment from a range of state departments. These responsibilities were: (i) climate change mitigation and adaptation taken from the National Development and Reform Commission (NDRC); (ii) groundwater pollution control from the Ministry of Land and

[85] Li Peng (1928–2019) served as vice premier (1983–88), premier (1988–98) and chairman of the 9th NPCSC (1998–2003).

[86] The EPC was abolished in 1998. See Qu Geping, *Qu's Pursuit*, at 416.

[87] Qu Geping, *Qu's Pursuit*, at 415–6; also see Jahiel, 'The organization of', at 769.

[88] Xiaoying Ma and Ortolano, *Environmental Regulation in China*, at 79.

[89] EPL (1989), art. 7(1).

[90] Xin Qiu and Honglin Li, 'China's environmental super ministry reform: background, challenges and the future', *Environmental Law Reporter*, 39 (2009), 10152–63 at 10153.

[91] Charles McElwee, *Environmental Law in China: Mitigating Risk and Ensuring Compliance* (Oxford University Press, 2011), at 84–8.

Resources (MLR); (iii) water-function regional planning, wastewater discharge outlet set-up and river basin water protection from the Ministry of Water Resources (MWR); (iv) rural non-point-source pollution control from the Ministry of Agriculture (MOA), (v) marine environmental protection from the State Oceanic Administration (SOA) and (vi) environmental protection of the South-to-North Water Diversion Project from the Office of the Project Construction Commission.[92]

2.3.2 Local Environment Agencies

Local environment agencies at the provincial, municipal and county levels are in charge of implementing and enforcing environmental laws and regulations. Most of these agencies were known as EPBs prior to the institutional reform of 2018, which changed the local agencies to ecological environment bureaus (EEBs). These bureaus make and implement local plans for environmental protection, formulate local environmental rules, regulations and standards, investigate pollution incidents and mediate environmental disputes. Their routine enforcement work includes: (i) reviewing and approving EIA documents; (ii) conducting on-site inspections of facilities discharging pollutants; (iii) ensuring compliance with the three-simultaneities requirement, conducting environmental examination and approval of new facilities before they are put into operation; (iv) issuing pollutant discharge permits; (v) monitoring and collecting data on local discharge of pollutants; (vi) calculating and levying pollutant discharge fees prior to the implementation of the Environmental Protection Tax Law (EPTL) (2016) on 1 January 2018; (vii) monitoring ambient environmental quality and publishing monitoring data and (viii) imposing penalties on entities in violation of environmental laws and regulations.

Most environmental law enforcement is carried out at the county or district level by environmental inspection teams, which are authorized by the local environment bureau to conduct on-site inspections to monitor performance. However, they are not law enforcement bodies and do not have the power to impose compulsory administrative measures, such as the seizure or seal-up of polluting devices and equipment, measures provided for by the EPL (2014).[93] Nor are they entitled to the same logistic support as law enforcement bodies, including the use of vehicles to conduct on-site inspections. In addition, environmental inspection teams suffer from a serious shortage of well-qualified staff, technological support and financial resources, hampering their ability to perform their duties.[94] Pilot exercises started to address the problem by introducing local-level institutional reform. Local environmental monitoring and supervision bodies are now directly supervised and instructed by municipal EEBs and are independent from county governments. Their staffing and work budgets come from municipal governments and they are formally categorized as administrative enforcement bodies to be equipped with the items necessary for collection of

[92] The 13th NPC at its 1st session on 17 March 2018 approved the State Council's Institutional Reform Proposal by issuing the Decision on State Council's Institutional Reform Proposal with immediate effect. For details, see part I, section (2) of the Reform Proposal.

[93] EPL (2014), art. 25.

[94] Shen Yueyue, *Inspection Report on the Implementation of the Environmental Protection Law.*

evidence and enforcement with mobile devices, as well as enforcement uniforms and enforcement vehicles.[95]

One fundamental reason for weak enforcement and the lenient sanctions placed on polluters by local environmental agencies is control and interference by local governments, which are generally focused on protecting local industry and attracting investment to boost the local economy. Local environmental agencies are subordinate to the governments of the same level in terms of personnel decisions and budget allocation. Although local governments have legal responsibility under the EPL (1989) to ensure environmental quality within their jurisdictions and take measures to improve the environment,[96] this responsibility was vague compared to the clear targets for local GDP growth that directly determine a government's and an individual's performance during their term of office. The EPL (2014) has strengthened local government responsibilities in environmental protection through the target responsibility scheme and performance appraisal,[97] but it will take time to implement it fully at local levels. To address the problem more directly and as a matter of urgency, in 2016 the central government started pilot exercises to implement institutional reform of local environment agencies, so that county-level agencies become branch offices of municipal environmental agencies.[98] This means that the basic-level environmental agencies performing the primary function of environmental enforcement are no longer subject to the control of county governments. Consequently, they should be able to perform their statutory duties with substantially improved independence, authority and effectiveness.

2.3.3 Environmental Monitoring Stations

Environmental monitoring stations are professional entities established at all levels of government. They collect technical data on air and water quality, solid waste and noise pollution, and provide relevant information to environmental protection authorities for formulating and implementing environmental regulations. Local monitoring stations fall under the leadership of local EEBs and are responsible for both ambient and emission monitoring. The latest pilot exercise on institutional reform and vertical management of local environmental agencies has redefined the roles of county environmental monitoring stations to focus on monitoring for the purposes of enforcement of law. Their staffing and budgets are decided by the municipal governments and tasks are assigned by the county environmental agencies to ensure they provide effective support and a fast response to local environmental enforcement teams. Current municipal environmental monitoring stations have become extensions of provincial environmental bureaus and fall directly under their administrative supervision, with staffing and budgets from provincial governments. They are independent of municipal governments, which helps to tackle the problem of local

95 Party Central Committee and State Council, Guiding Opinion on Pilot Work of Institutional Reform and Vertical Management of Local Environmental Monitoring and Supervision Bodies under the Provincial Level (2016), part III, s. 9.

96 EPL (1989), art. 16.

97 EPL (2014), art. 26. For more discussion, see Alex L. Wang, 'The search for sustainable legitimacy'.

98 Party Central Committee and State Council, Guiding Opinion on Pilot Work of Institutional Reform and Vertical Management of Local Environmental Monitoring and Supervision Bodies under the Provincial Level (2016), part III, s. 6.

protectionism. Both the provincial and municipal environmental monitoring stations focus on monitoring the ambient environmental quality.[99]

The National Environmental Monitoring Center (NEMC), established in 1993, manages and guides the work of the nationwide environmental monitoring system. It provides technical support to the MEE's (previously the MEP's) environmental supervision and management functions, including routine monitoring of state-controlled pollution sources, on-site supervision and inspection of three-simultaneities compliance where projects have been directly approved by the State Council, and inspection of major pollutant dischargers. The NEMC's National Environmental Quality Monitoring Network has more than 200 stations to collect data on air and water quality, acid rain, radioactive waste and ecologically sensitive areas. It reports directly to the MEE.

2.3.4 Regional Environmental Inspection Bureaus

To strengthen central supervision of local implementation and enforcement, six regional environmental inspection bureaus have been set up.[100] They are extensions of the MEE and are directly accountable to it. Each bureau supervises provincial governments and environmental agencies in three to seven provinces, autonomous regions or municipalities directly under the central government.

The bureaus' major responsibilities include: (i) supervising the implementation of national environmental policies, laws, regulations and standards, (ii) undertaking the environmental inspection of local governments on behalf of the central authorities, (iii) participating in the inspection of emergency responses and investigating serious environmental emergencies, (iv) resolving major environmental disputes that cut across provincial boundaries or river basins, (v) investigating serious cases of environmental pollution or ecological destruction and (vi) undertaking any other tasks assigned by the MEE.[101]

An important task in recent years has been the verification of environmental data reported by local governments to show their achievement of pollution abatement targets.[102] Regional environmental supervision centres engage in an annual verification exercise and carry out routine inspections of polluters to tackle the problem of data falsification by local governments. The verification exercise consists of both documentary reviews and on-site inspections. The verification normally starts with a report by provincial government leaders on their pollution reduction work and progress, followed by a review of government records and documents on emission reductions. The regional environmental supervision centres are thereby able to identify problematic cases, which are then subject to on-site inspection to uncover potential violations.[103] In addition to the annual verification exercises, the

[99] Party Central Committee and State Council, Guiding Opinion on Pilot Work of Institutional Reform and Vertical Management of Local Environmental Monitoring and Supervision Bodies under the Provincial Level (2016), part III, s. 8.

[100] General Office of CPC Central Committee and General Office of State Council, Provisions on the Functions, Structure and Staffing of the Ministry of Ecology and Environment (2018), art. 6(1).

[101] For details, see the websites of the regional inspection bureaus.

[102] For further discussion of the verification scheme and central supervision over local implementation of environmental laws and policies, see Xuehua Zhang, 'Implementation of pollution control targets in China: has a centralized enforcement approach worked?', *The China Quarterly*, 231 (2017), 749–74.

[103] Xuehua Zhang, 'Implementation of pollution control targets', at 762–3.

TABLE 2.2 REGIONAL INSPECTION BUREAUS UNDER THE MEE

Regional bureau	Office location	Regions under inspection
North China Inspection Bureau	Beijing	Beijing, Tianjin, Tianjin, Hebei, Henan, Shanxi, Inner Mongolia
Northeast China Inspection Bureau	Shenyang	Heilongjiang, Jilin, Liaoning
Northwest China Inspection Bureau	Xi'an	Shaanxi, Gansu, Ningxia, Qinghai, Xinjiang
East China Inspection Bureau	Nanjing	Shandong, Jiangsu, Shanghai, Zhejiang, Fujian, Anhui, Jiangxi
South China Inspection Bureau	Guangzhou	Hubei, Hunan, Guangxi, Guangdong, Hainan
Southwest China Inspection Bureau	Chengdu	Sichuan, Chongqing, Guizhou, Yunnan, Tibet

Sources: North China Inspection Bureau, MEE (n.d.). Website. https://hbdc.mee.gov.cn/; East China Inspection Bureau, MEE (n.d.). Website. https://hddc.mee.gov.cn/; South China Inspection Bureau, MEE (n.d.). Website. https://hndc.mee.gov.cn/; Northwest Inspection Bureau, MEE (n.d.). Website. https://xbdc.mee.gov.cn/; Southwest Inspection Bureau, MEE (n.d.). Website. https://xndc.mee.gov.cn/; Northeast China Inspection Bureau, MEE (n.d.). https://dbdc.mee.gov.cn/

regional centres also conduct routine inspections to deter illegal discharge of pollutants and non-operation of pollution treatment facilities. It should be noted, however, that while regional bureaus have powers to monitor and inspect local governments, agencies and polluters, they are not agencies with regulatory powers to enforce the law. In other words, they cannot impose sanctions when they detect violations, but instead must pass cases to local EPBs for follow-up sanction or, where a local agency fails to impose a sanction, to the MEE.[104]

2.3.5 River Basin Environmental Regulatory Bureaus

Seven river basin environmental regulatory bureaus have been set up to manage the water resources and water quality of the Yangtze, Yellow, Huai, Hai, Pearl and Songliao rivers and Lake Tai. They fall under the dual leadership of the MEE and MWR.[105]

2.4 OTHER RELEVANT DEPARTMENTS

While the MEE and local EEBs play primary roles in environmental law implementation and enforcement, they cannot single-handedly prevent and control pollution from all sources or ecological destruction. The EPL (2014) provides that other administrative departments at the county level and above have the power to supervise and manage the work of resource

[104] Xuehua Zhang, 'Implementation of pollution control targets', at 764–5.

[105] General Office of CPC Central Committee and General Office of State Council, Provisions on the Functions, Structure and Staffing of the Ministry of Ecology and Environment (2018), art. 6(2).

protection and pollution prevention as provided for by relevant laws.[106] Previously, the EPL (1989) provided a list of administrative bodies involved in pollution prevention[107] and in protection of natural resources.[108] The 2014 amendment substitutes that long list with a general reference to 'relevant departments'.

Even after the institutional reform of 2018, which substantially expanded the regulatory powers of the newly established MEE by shifting to it many environmental protection functions from other departments, many State Council commissions and ministries and their counterparts at local levels continue to play important roles in improving environmental governance in collaboration with the MEE and EEBs.

2.4.1 The NDRC

Prior to the 2018 institutional reform, the NDRC had been a key player in China's participation in the global climate change regime. As China perceives climate change fundamentally as an issue of development rather than environment,[109] the NDRC was entrusted with the responsibility of taking the lead in climate change negotiations, developing domestic climate change policies, strategies and plans and drafting climate change law. In 2018, these responsibilities relating to climate change and emissions reduction shifted to the MEE.[110] Despite the 2018 institutional reform, however, the NDRC will continue to impact significantly on China's environmental law and policy through its five-year socio-economic development plans.

The NDRC was established in March 2003 to replace its predecessors, the State Development Planning Commission (1998–2003) and the State Planning Commission (1952–98), which operated during the period in which China had a highly centralized planned economy. The NDRC's role in managing the macroeconomy has profound environmental implications. It is in charge of the implementation of *China's Agenda 21*,[111] the sustainable development programme China developed as part of commitments made at the Rio de Janeiro UN Conference on Environment and Development in 1992. The NDRC drafts China's FYPs on socio-economic development, which contain national targets for the abatement of key pollutants and cuts in energy and carbon intensity.[112]

As the body in charge of economic development, the NDRC plays a critical role in promoting clean production and pollution control at the source. The EPL (2014) provides that the state must promote clean production and resource recovery, recycling and reuse,[113]

[106] EPL (2014), art. 10(2).

[107] EPL (1989), art. 7(3). They included the state administrative department of marine affairs, the harbour supervision administration, the fisheries administration and fishing harbour supervision agencies, the environmental protection department of the armed forces and the administrative departments of public security, transportation, railways and civil aviation at various levels.

[108] EPL (1989), art. 7(4). They included the administrative departments for land, minerals, forestry, agriculture and water conservancy of governments at or above the county level.

[109] 'Climate change is both an environmental issue and a development issue. But, fundamentally, it is a development issue.' See China's National Plan on Climate Change (2007), preamble.

[110] NPC, Decision on State Council's Institutional Reform Proposal (17 March 2018), part I, s. 2.

[111] State Council, *China's Agenda 21: White Paper on China's Population, Environment, and Development in the 21st Century* (Beijing: China Environmental Science Press, 1994). It was passed by the State Council on 25 March 1994, published on 4 July 1994 and serves as a guide for the long-term planning of China's socio-economic development.

[112] 11th FYP (2006–10); 12th FYP (2011–15); 13th FYP (2016–20).

[113] EPL (2014), art. 40(1).

TABLE 2.3 ENVIRONMENTAL TARGETS IN CHINA'S FYPs

	Energy intensity (%)	Carbon intensity (%)	Sulphur dioxide (SO_2) (%)	Chemical oxygen demand (COD) (%)	Nitrogen oxides (NOx) (%)	Ammonia nitrogen (NH) (%)
11th FYP (2006–10)	−20	Nil	−10	−10	Nil	Nil
12th FYP (2011–15)	−16	−17	−8	−8	−10	−10
13th FYP (2016–20)	−15	−18	−15	−10	−15	−10

Sources: 11th FYP (2006–10); 12th FYP (2011–15); 13th FYP (2016–20).

all of which are crucial for preventing pollution at the source. At regular intervals, the NDRC issues national catalogues designed to restructure industry by phasing out energy- and resource-intensive production processes, equipment and products.[114] The NDRC is the key institution responsible for: (i) organizing and coordinating the work of clean production under the Law on the Promotion of Clean Production (2012);[115] (ii) promoting reduction, reuse, recycling and recovery of resources from both production and consumption under the Law on Promotion of the Circular Economy (CEPL) (2008)[116] and (iii) improving energy conservation and energy efficiency in both production and consumption under the Law on Energy Conservation (2007).[117]

2.4.2 The MWR

Prior to the institutional reform of 2018, the MWR formulated protection plans for water resources to achieve national goals on resources and environmental protection. It also designated the functional use (for example, conservation or drinking water supply) of waterbodies and controlled the setting-up of wastewater discharge outlets. It monitored the quantity and quality of water resources to determine their pollutant carrying capacities and made proposals to the State Council on total control of wastewater discharge. There were overlaps in the responsibilities for water pollution control and water resources management between the MEP and the MWR and conflicts on the designation of waterbodies. While the MEP divided waterbodies into functional zones based on water quality for the purpose of setting pollutant discharge limits, the MWR divided the same waterbodies

[114] EPL (2014), art. 46. The state phases out processes, equipment and products that cause serious environmental pollution. No unit or individual may engage in the production, sale, transfer or use of such processes, equipment and products.

[115] The Law on the Promotion of Clean Production (2012) was first enacted on 29 June 2002. It came into force on 1 January 2003. It was amended on 29 February 2012.

[116] The CEPL (2008) was enacted by the 11th NPCSC at its 4th session on 29 August 2008. It came into force on 1 January 2009.

[117] The Law on Energy Conservation was first enacted on 1 November 1997. It was amended by the 10th NPCSC at its 30th session on 28 October 2007, with the amended Law coming into force on 1 April 2008.

into functional zones for purposes of water usage and allocation. As they designate water zones based on different criteria and for different purposes, serious confusion was caused at local levels for both the regulators and regulated as to which pollution discharge standards and caps were applicable.[118]

The institutional reform of 2018 shifted the responsibilities of regional water-function planning, setting-up of wastewater discharge outlets, and river basin water protection from the MWR to the MEE.[119] The MWR now focuses on the management and utilization of water resources. New responsibilities of the MWR include the management of the Three Gorges Hydropower Project and the South-to-North Water Diversion Project, which were formerly administered by two separate State Council committees.[120]

2.4.3 MLR to MNR

Prior to the 2018 institutional reform, the MLR was responsible for the administration, protection and rational utilization of land, mineral and marine resources.[121] The MLR and its local departments supervised mining operations and operated the registration and licensing schemes that granted the rights to explore for and exploit mineral resources. The MLR also designated areas where foreign investment in mineral resources was permitted. The geological hazard assessment reports and water and soil conservation plans carried out by project proponents were, prior to the 2018 reforms, subject to the approval of local land and resources bureaus before project proponents conducted EIAs.

The 2018 reform abolished the MLR and replaced it with the new Ministry of Natural Resources (MNR). The new MNR inherited the responsibilities of the MLR, except for groundwater pollution control, as well as the responsibilities of the SOA, except for marine environmental protection, and of the State Bureau of Surveying, Mapping and Geo-information. The MNR also acquired additional functions from other departments: (i) planning major functional zones, acquired from the NDRC; (ii) urban and rural planning and management, from the Ministry of Housing and Urban–Rural Development (MOHURD); (iii) water resources surveying and registration of water-use rights, from the MWR; (iv) grassland resources surveying and registration, from the MOA; (v) forests and wetlands surveying and registration of rights, from the State Forestry Bureau.[122]

A new Forestry and Grassland Bureau (FGB) was also established in 2018 based on the former State Forestry Bureau. It is supervised and managed by the MNR. The FGB has taken over responsibility for grassland management from the former MOA and also functions as the National Park Administration, managing nature reserves, scenic zones, natural heritage and geoparks, among others, that were formerly managed by departments including the MLR, MOHURD, MWR, MOA and SOA.[123]

118 Xin Qiu and Honglin Li, 'China's environmental super ministry reform', at 10158–9.
119 NPC, Decision on State Council's Institutional Reform Proposal (17 March 2018), part I, s. 2.
120 NPC, Decision on State Council's Institutional Reform Proposal (17 March 2018), part I, s. 10.
121 Marine fishery resources are managed by the MOA.
122 NPC Decision on State Council's Institutional Reform Proposal (17 March 2018), part I, s. 1.
123 NPC Decision on State Council's Institutional Reform Proposal (17 March 2018), part II, s. 8.

2.4.4 The SOA

The SOA was established directly under the State Council in 1964. It became a subordinate body of the National Commission of Science and Technology in 1993, though maintained its previous status in the bureaucratic hierarchy. The institutional reform of 1998 turned the SOA into a national bureau under the then newly established MLR.[124] The SOA was put in charge of planning and management of China's marine environmental resources, including coastal zones, marine islands, internal seas and the continental shelf, in accordance with the Marine Environmental Protection Law (MEPL) (2013).[125] In particular, the SOA protected the marine environment by organizing surveys, monitoring, surveillance, assessment and scientific research. It regulated and controlled marine pollution caused by marine construction projects and by the dumping of waste at sea.[126] The SOA and its local bureaus ran the review and approval of EIAs of offshore operations and monitoring and enforcement work at sea. The 2018 institutional reform, however, relocated the SOA to the newly established MNR,[127] and reassigned its responsibilities for marine environmental protection to the MEE.[128]

2.4.5 The MOHURD

The MOHURD was established in March 2008, replacing its predecessors, the Ministry of Construction (1988–2008) and the MURCEP (1982–8). Prior to the 2018 reforms, it set housing policies and plans, regulated construction activity and prepared urban and rural development plans. Following the reforms, its responsibilities for urban and rural planning were reassigned to the MNR.[129]

So far as environment is concerned, the MOHURD provides guidance and supervision to municipal governments on issues of water supply, water conservation, gas supply, heat supply, urban infrastructure building, greening, landscaping and the construction of municipal wastewater treatment facilities and networks.[130] The MOHURD plays the key role in the planning, supervision and regulation of the construction and operation of wastewater treatment facilities and solid waste disposal facilities. It issued the 13th FYP on the Construction of Municipal Wastewater Treatment and Recycling Facilities (2016)[131] and the 13th FYP on the Construction of Municipal Waste Disposal Facilities (2016)[132] to substantially improve China's wastewater infrastructure and solid waste treatment during

[124] On 6 March 1998, State Councillor Luo Gan presented the State Council Institutional Reform Plan to the 9th NPC at its 1st session. The NPC approved the plan in a decision on 10 March 1998 with immediate effect.

[125] The MEPL (2013) was first enacted on 23 August 1982 by the 5th NPCSC at its 24th session. It came into force on 1 March 1983. A substantial revision made on 25 December 1999 by the 9th NPCSC at its 13th session came into force on 1 April 2000. Minor amendments were made on 28 December 2013, while further amendments were made in 2016 and 2017.

[126] MEPL (2013), art. 5(2).

[127] NPC Decision on State Council's Institutional Reform Proposal (17 March 2018), part I, s. 1.

[128] NPC Decision on State Council's Institutional Reform Proposal (17 March 2018), part I, s. 2.

[129] NPC Decision on State Council's Institutional Reform Proposal (17 March 2018), part I, s. 1.

[130] State Council Provisions on Major Functions, Internal Structures and Staffing of MOHURD (2008), part II, s. 7; part III, s. 9.

[131] The 13th FYP on the Construction of Municipal Wastewater Treatment and Recycling Facilities was issued by the NDRC and MOHURD on 31 December 2016.

[132] The 13th FYP on the Construction of Municipal Waste Disposal Facilities was issued by the NDRC and MOHURD on 31 December 2016.

the five-year period from 2016 to 2020 and to abate and eliminate direct discharge of untreated wastewater and dumping of untreated waste that would cause serious contamination of water and soil. It is in charge of planning and supervising the construction of urban drainage and sewage systems,[133] and of licensing sewage discharge into the drainage network.[134]

2.4.6 MOA to MARA

The MOA played a major role in protecting the rural environment. It protected grassland and fishery resources, and regulated the use of pesticides, fertilizers and feed additives through registration systems in order to promote rational application of these chemicals in agriculture and farming. The Fisheries Bureau of the MOA protected the eco-environment of fishery waters and investigated serious fishery pollution incidents. It also controlled the use of veterinary drugs in order to prevent aquaculture pollution. The 2018 institutional reform reassigned responsibility for the regulation of non-point-source pollution in rural China to the MEE[135] and established the new Ministry of Agriculture and Rural Affairs (MARA) to replace the MOA.[136]

2.4.7 The GAC

The General Administration of Customs (GAC) plays an important role in implementing and enforcing environmental laws and regulations that involve cross-border control, including the import and export of solid waste, ozone-depleting substances (ODS) and heavily polluting and outdated equipment and products that have been phased out by the NDRC and are banned from being imported. Since the State Council's decision to ban the entry of foreign waste in stages from 2017,[137] the GAC has taken a range of measures to tighten control over waste imports. First, in 2017 it promulgated updated catalogues of waste prohibited from being imported, waste under import restriction and waste not under import restriction. These were revised several times in 2018 to phase in the waste import ban.[138]

In addition to increasing the types of solid waste prohibited from being imported, enforcement at the border and control at the source have been strengthened. To improve the efficiency and effectiveness of border inspection and control, the GAC and MEE announced a list of eighteen ports designated for the importing of solid waste that may be used as a raw material. These are ports with both the human resources and technological

[133] The Regulation on Urban Drainage and Sewage Treatment was issued by the State Council on 2 October 2013. It came into force on 1 January 2014.

[134] The MOHURD issued the Measures on Licensing of Urban Sewage Discharge into the Drainage Network on 22 January 2015. It came into force on 1 March 2015.

[135] NPC Decision on State Council's Institutional Reform Proposal (2018), part I, s. 2.

[136] NPC Decision on State Council's Institutional Reform Proposal (2018), part I, s. 3.

[137] The General Office of the State Council issued the Implementation Plan on the Reform of the Solid Waste Import System to Ban Entry of Foreign Waste on 18 July 2017.

[138] The GAC issued the Catalogues of Waste Import (2017) jointly with the MEP, Ministry of Commerce (MOC), NDRC and the State Administration for Quality Supervision, Inspection and Quarantine (SAQSIQ) on 10 August 2017. Two more revisions were announced jointly with the MEE, MOC and NDRC on 13 April 2018 and 21 December 2018. They re-categorized some restricted and non-restricted wastes into the prohibited category. Further types of waste were re-categorized from non-restricted to restricted.

TABLE 2.4 PHASED-IN WASTE IMPORT BAN

Waste type	Previous category	New category	Effective dates
Twenty-four types of waste, including waste plastic from domestic sources, unsorted waste paper, waste textiles, vanadium slag	Waste under import restriction	Waste prohibited from being imported	31 December 2017 (announcement on 10 August 2017)
Sixteen types of waste, including waste tools, machinery and equipment, waste ships, waste vehicle parts, smelter slag, waste plastics from industrial sources	Waste under import restriction	Waste prohibited from being import	31 December 2018 (announcement on 13 April 2018)
Sixteen types of waste, including scrap stainless steel, titanium scrap and scrap wood	Waste under import restriction and waste not under import restriction	Waste prohibited from being imported	31 December 2019 (announcement on 13 April 2018)
Eight types of waste, including waste iron and steel, scrap copper and aluminium	Waste not under import restriction	Waste under import restriction	1 July 2019 (announcement on 21 December 2018)

Sources: GAC, Catalogues on Waste Import (2017); MEP et al., 'Announcement on the promulgation of Catalogues on Waste Import (2017)', (announcement) 10 August 2017; MEE et al., 'Announcement on adjustment of Catalogues on Waste Import', (announcement) 13 April 2018; MEE et al., Announcement on adjustment of Catalogues on Waste Import, (announcement) 21 December 2018.

capacity to inspect the imported waste.[139] To control waste imports at the overseas source, the GAC implements a registration system that requires foreign suppliers of solid waste that may be used as a raw material to register.[140] It also requires pre-shipment inspection of the solid waste at the place of origin by a professional inspection and certification body on the GAC register.[141]

2.4.8 The MPS

The Ministry of Public Security (MPS) and its local public security bureaus (PSBs) are in charge of law enforcement and investigation of crimes in order to ensure public safety and social order. They have important roles to play in punishing serious environmental violations, investigating suspected cases of environmental crimes, and regulatory control of vehicle emissions in collaboration with environmental agencies. To implement the revised APPCL (2015), the MPS, with the MEP and the Certification and Accreditation Administration, issued

[139] GAC and MEE, 'Announcement on designated ports for waste import', (announcement) 27 June 2018. The rules came into force on 1 January 2019.

[140] The GAC issued the Implementation Rules on the Registration of Foreign Suppliers of Solid Wastes that May Be Used as Raw Materials on 6 July 2018. The Rules came into force on 1 August 2018.

[141] The GAC issued a first list of professional inspection bodies on 7 November 2018 and a second on 2 January 2019. These bodies conduct and certify pre-shipment inspections.

the Notice to Improve Regulation of Emission Testing to Control Vehicle Pollution (2016).[142] This was designed to strengthen regulatory control over vehicle emission testing and to accelerate the phasing out of yellow-label vehicles and old vehicles.[143]

PSBs are the only administrative agencies with the power, granted by the Administrative Penalty Law (APL), to impose administrative penalties that restrict personal freedom and liberty.[144] While environmental agencies may impose a range of administrative sanctions to punish violation, they transfer cases where liable parties may be liable to receive 'administrative detention' to PSBs for review and decision. Such cases involve most serious intentional violations, including: (i) construction projects in violation of EIA requirements that have been ordered by environmental agencies to suspend construction, but refuse to do so; (ii) anyone discharging pollutants without a permit and in violation of the law who has been ordered by environmental agencies to stop discharge, but refuses to do so; (iii) anyone discharging pollutants by evading regulatory monitoring through the use of, for example, hidden pipes, anyone falsifying monitoring data or tampering with monitoring devices; (iv) anyone producing or using pesticides expressly banned by the state, who has been ordered to rectify, but refuses to do so.[145]

Where environmental violation cases may involve criminal liability, they will be investigated under China's CL (2017). This provides for the crimes of environmental pollution,[146] illegal disposal of imported waste[147] and crime of waste smuggling.[148] PSBs must investigate environmental crimes in a timely manner, making good use of the technical expertise of environmental agencies. Where necessary, joint enforcement action by the local counterparts of the MPS and MEP is encouraged.[149] The transfer of suspected environmental criminal cases to PSBs is subject to legal supervision by people's procuratorates.[150]

2.5 THE COURTS

Courts are the state's adjudication bodies.[151] At the top of the hierarchy is the Supreme People's Court (SPC), which supervises the adjudication work of local courts at all levels and special courts. Higher-level courts supervise the adjudication work of courts at lower levels.[152] Through the adjudication of criminal, civil and administrative cases, courts impose sanctions to punish crimes, settle civil disputes and ensure agencies perform their statutory duties.[153] Courts play an indispensable role in setting the law in motion. In the past, however,

[142] The MEP, MPS and Certification and Accreditation Administration issued the Notice to Improve Regulation of Emission Testing to Control Vehicle Pollution on 21 July 2016.

[143] Yellow-label vehicles are old and heavily polluting vehicles manufactured before 1996. If such a vehicle passes its annual test, a yellow sticker is placed on the windshield and it may be used on the roads, subject to restrictions on time and location.

[144] APL (2017), art. 16.

[145] EPL (2014), art. 63. To implement case transfer under article 63, the MPS, with the Ministry of Industry and Information (MIIT), MEP, MOA and SAQSIQ, issued the Provisional Measures on Transfer of Environmental Violation Cases Subject to Administrative Detention by Administrative Agencies in Charge on 24 December 2014.

[146] CL (2017), art. 338. [147] CL (2017), art. 339. [148] CL (2017), art. 152(2).

[149] On 4 November 2013, the MEP and MPS issued the Opinion on Strengthening Enforcement Cooperation between Environmental Agencies and Public Security Bureaus.

[150] On 25 January 2017, the MEP, MPS and SPP issued the Measures on Coordination Work between Administrative Enforcement and Criminal Justice in Environmental Protection.

[151] Constitution (2018), art. 128; Organic Law of the People's Courts (2018), art. 2(1).

[152] Constitution (2018), art. 132. [153] Organic Law of the People's Courts (2018), art. 2(2).

they were criticized for their relatively passive role in addressing environmental issues.[154] Lawyers, NGOs and victims of pollution often felt frustrated and defeated when they attempted to seek judicial redress for harm caused by pollution. It was common for most environmental claims to fail at the first hurdle of having the case accepted by the court. Even for the cases accepted by the court, plaintiffs often lost legal battles they should have won.[155] If, against all odds, a plaintiff won a case, they rarely received the full compensation they had claimed.[156] Even if a plaintiff obtained a court ruling in their favour, they may still have been no better off, as defendants often failed to comply with the judgment, and enforcement of judgments was weak. Professor Wang Canfa uses the Chifeng case (2001)[157] to explain the extreme difficulties of gaining access to judicial redress.

Han Xiang v. *Chifeng Jinfeng Copper Smelter* (2001)

The construction of the Chifeng Jinfeng Copper Smelter (Jinfeng) was a major achievement for the Chifeng city government in its endeavour to attract investment and boost local GDP. The plant started trial production on 28 December 1997, but the required EIA had not been conducted, nor had equipment to remove sulphur or dust been installed. According to monitoring data supplied by Chifeng EPB, the plant's emissions of SO_2 varied from 9.6 to 46 times over the national emission standard. After the rainy season of April and May 1998, farmers in Chifeng suffered serious damage to their agricultural produce, trees and plants. They approached the local government for assistance. The government investigation confirmed that the damage was caused by acid rain resulting from the high concentration of SO_2 emitted by Jinfeng. The government tried to settle the dispute by ordering Jinfeng to pay 131,974.71 yuan in total to victims within 2.3 km of the factory.

Han Xiang was not covered by the government's compensation proposal, but his fruit trees had suffered serious damage from the acid rain, according to an expert report. With legal help from the CLAPV headed by Professor Wang Canfa, Han Xiang sued Jinfeng, seeking compensation of 1.4 million yuan for the loss of his fruit trees.

Chifeng Intermediate Court (2000) ruled that there was no causation between the plaintiff's loss and the defendant's pollution, following an appraisal report produced by a court-appointed certification body. The appraisal report concluded that the fruit trees were killed by pests rather than sulphur pollution. Han Xiang appealed.

The **High Court of Inner Mongolia Autonomous Region** (2001) dismissed the appeal and upheld the first-instance decision.

[154] Wang Doudou, 'The Supreme People's Court exploring public interest litigation to protect water resources', *Legal Daily*, 12 April 2010, 5.

[155] Wang Canfa, 'The rapid development of environmental protection law' in Cai Dingjian and Wang Chenguang (eds.), *China's Journey toward the Rule of Law: Legal Reform, 1978–2008* (Leiden and Boston, MA: Brill, 2010), 495–548, at 539–40. The Center for Legal Assistance to Pollution Victims (CLAPV) provided legal assistance to victims of pollution in 110 cases and won one-third of these.

[156] In the calculation of damages, courts often consider a polluter's ability to pay and the impact the payment will have on the ongoing financial viability of the polluter's operations. One example is the Rongping case discussed in Chapter 9.

[157] Wang Canfa, 'The rapid development', at 539–40; details of the case are found in Wang Canfa, 'The case of air pollution compensation caused by copper smelter in Chifeng of Inner Mongolia' in Wang Canfa and Feng Jia (eds.), *China's Environmental Litigation* (Beijing: Chinese University of Politics and Law Press, 2015), 21–39.

The way in which this case unfolded is a common experience for pollution victims fighting legal battles against polluters protected by local government. In this case, even the presiding judges admitted their inability to be impartial. Jinfeng was set up with close ties to the local government – its deputy general manager was also the deputy director of the Economic and Trade Commission, part of the local government.[158]

The SPC has made efforts to enhance the role of courts in environmental protection. In its Several Opinions on Providing Judicial Guarantee and Services for Accelerating the Transformation of the Economic Development Mode (2010) (SPC Opinions on Judicial Guarantee and Services), the SPC emphasized that courts must properly conduct trials of environmental cases to provide timely and adequate compensation to victims of pollution, must support and supervise the environmental enforcement work of administrative agencies and punish violations of environmental rules and crimes against the environment so as to promote social and economic sustainable development. In particular, courts will hear cases where environmental agencies sue on behalf of the state for compensation of environmental harm caused by pollution. Environmental tribunals may be established in courts with many environmental cases in order to develop expertise in environmental law adjudication and improve the quality of judicial practice in environmental protection.[159]

However, the head of each local court is appointed by the local people's congress on the recommendation of the local party committee, and courts depend on the local governments for funding.[160] Given the strong power and influence wielded by local governments, courts often fail to render impartial adjudication or provide timely redress in environmental disputes where polluting firms are protected by the local government. Fundamental change is expected from the implementation of the revised EPL (2014), as it makes local governments accountable for environmental quality and the achievement of environmental targets set by the central government. They must balance the environment with development, instead of pursuing GDP growth at all cost. Also in 2014, the SPC announced the establishment of a new specialized Environment and Resources Division (ERD),[161] and has taken measures to engage actively in judicial reform for better protection of the environment. Through institutional specialization, judicial guidance and innovation in jurisdiction, adjudication and remedies, the SPC and courts at all levels try to play their role in China's battle against pollution. In addition to dealing with the conventional environmental civil, administrative and criminal cases, courts are exploring new rules and procedures for handling new types of litigation, including environmental public interest litigation (EPIL) and environmental damage compensation litigation, so that private and public interests are protected by civil remedies, administrative agencies are supervised to ensure they perform their statutory duties, serious environmental violations are sanctioned and potential offenders deterred.

158 Wang Canfa, 'The rapid development', at 539–40; details of the case are found in Wang Canfa, 'The case of air pollution compensation' in Wang Canfa and Feng Jia (eds.), *China's Environmental Litigation.*

159 SPC, Opinions on Judicial Guarantee and Services (2010), art. 13.

160 Albert Chen, *An Introduction to the Legal System*, 203–4.

161 SPC, 'Fully strengthening the environment and resources adjudication work', (press release) 3 July 2014. www.pkulaw.cn; see also 'SPC establishes environment and resources division', *People's Court News*, 4 July 2014.

2.5.1 Specialized Environmental Tribunals

The establishment of the specialized ERD within the SPC in 2014 is a landmark in the judicial reforms China is undertaking to strengthen and improve adjudication work on environment and resources cases. It was not, however, the first specialized environmental division set up in a Chinese court. The development of environmental tribunals in China has taken a bottom-up approach. Since 2007, pilot environmental tribunals have been taking place at basic-level and intermediate courts. The early pioneers promoting judicial environmental activism include the cities of Guiyang,[162] Wuxi[163] and Kunming.[164] An environment tribunal at Qingzhen, a city in Guizhou province, was the first to test specialized environmental adjudication, including EPILs, in China. It took on China's first civil EPIL – *Guiyang Two Lakes and One Reservoir Administration* v. *Guizhou Tianfeng Chemical Company Ltd* (2008) – in December 2007 and its first administrative EPIL – *All China Environment Federation* v. *Qingzhen Land Resources Bureau* (2009)– in September 2009.[165]

By mid-2014, 134 specialized environmental divisions, collegiate panels[166] and circuit tribunals had been established across China.[167] Institution building continued as reported by SPC White Papers in 2016, 2017 and 2019. By mid-2016, a total of 558 specialized environmental divisions, collegiate panels and circuit tribunals had been established across China, of which 191 were specialized environmental divisions and 15 were located at provincial high courts.[168] By April 2017, a total of 956 bodies had been set up – 296 specialized environmental divisions, 617 collegiate panels and 43 circuit tribunals – and 18 provincial high courts had established environment and resources divisions.[169] By the

[162] On 26 November 2007, Guizhou Provincial High Court approved the establishment of the Environmental Protection People's Tribunal at Qingzhen City Court in Guiyang. Guiyang Municipal Court issued the Decision on Designated Jurisdiction on 12 December 2007, providing that all first-instance environmental cases in the city of Guiyang, including EPIL, would fall under the jurisdiction of the newly established Environmental Protection People's Court. It also stipulated that procuratorates, the management authority of two lakes and one reservoir, environmental protection authorities and forest bureaus, among others, may initiate EPIL as plaintiff.

[163] Environmental tribunals were set up in Wuxi at both basic- and intermediate-level courts to accept environmental cases initiated by procuratorates, environmental protection authorities, environmental social organizations and management companies of residential premises. Wuxi Intermediate Court and Wuxi Procuratorate issued the Provisions on Handling Environmental Public Interest Litigations (for trial use) on 8 September 2008.

[164] On 5 November 2008, Kunming Intermediate Court, Kunming Procuratorate, Kunming Municipal PSB and Kunming EPB issued the Decision on Establishing Environmental Protection Coordinating Mechanisms. Under the Decision, Kunming Intermediate Court was to set up an environmental protection tribunal, which would have jurisdiction over environmental civil, criminal, administrative and enforcement cases. Procuratorates, environmental bureaus and social organizations were permitted to initiate PIL as plaintiff.

[165] SPC, *Environment and Resources Adjudication* (2016), chapter I.

[166] In China, trials are conducted by a collegiate panel of three judges. If a court does not have an environmental division, it will form a panel of judges specializing in the subject matter.

[167] SPC, 'Fully strengthening'; see also An Keming and Chen Yifang, 'To provide judicial guarantee for the construction of ecological civilization', *People's Court News*, 7 July 2014.

[168] SPC, *Environment and Resources Adjudication in China* (2016). The White Paper covers the period from 1 January 2014 to June 2016. The fifteen high courts that set up environment and resources divisions were Guizhou, Fujian, Hainan, Jiangsu, Hebei, Shandong, Guangxi, Jiangxi, Henan, Guangdong, Chongqing, Yunnan, Hunan, Sichuan and Jilin.

[169] SPC, *Environment and Resources Adjudication in China 2016–2017* (Beijing: People's Court Press, 2017). The White Paper covers the period of July 2016 to June 2017. The eighteen high courts that set up environmental and resources divisions include the high courts of Qinghai, Gansu and Xinjiang.

end of 2018, there were 1,271 bodies – 391 specialized environmental divisions, 808 collegiate panels and 72 circuit tribunals – and 23 provincial high courts had set up environment and resources divisions.[170]

2.5.2 SPC Judicial Guidance

The SPC's ERD performs judicial supervision of the adjudication work of courts at all levels by a range of different means. It reviews lower-court judgments and may bring a case up for retrial or issue an order for the lower court to retry it. It provides general guidance to lower-level courts by drafting judicial interpretations.[171]

Judicial Interpretation

The SPC guides the work of lower courts by issuing legally binding judicial interpretations to provide detailed rules on the application of law. On environmental tort, the SPC issued the Interpretation on Several Issues Concerning the Application of Law in the Adjudication of Environmental Tort Cases (2015).[172] On environmental crimes, the SPC and the Supreme People's Procuratorate (SPP) issued the Interpretation on Several Issues Concerning the Application of Law in Environmental Criminal Cases (SPC and SPP Interpretation on Environmental Crime) (2016).[173] To tackle especially difficult issues and enhance sanctions on environmental crimes, the SPC worked with the SPP, MPS, Ministry of Justice and the MEE to issue the Minutes of the Meeting on Handling Environmental Criminal Cases (2019)[174] for implementation by the relevant bodies.

On PIL, the SPC issued the Interpretation on Several Issues Concerning the Application of Law in Environmental Civil Public Interest Litigation (SPC Interpretation on Civil EPIL) (2015),[175] the Measures on Adjudication of Pilot Procuratorial Public Interest Litigations (2016)[176] and the Working Rules on the Adjudication of Environmental Public Interest Litigation (for trial implementation) (2017).[177] Upon completion of the pilot procuratorial PIL programme, the SPC and SPP issued the Interpretation on Several Issues Concerning the Application of Law in Procuratorial Public Interest Litigation (2018)[178] for nationwide implementation.

[170] SPC, *Environment and Resources Adjudication in China 2017–2018* (Beijing: People's Court Press, 2019). The White Paper covers the period from July 2017 to December 2018; see also Lü Zhongmei and Liu Changxing, 'Innovative development of specialization and professionalization of environmental adjudication: observation in 2017–18', *China Applied Legal Science*, 2 (2019), 1–35, at 2.

[171] SPC, 'Fully strengthening'.

[172] The SPC issued the Interpretation on Several Issues Concerning the Application of Law in the Adjudication of Environmental Tort Cases on 1 June 2015. It came into force on 3 June 2015.

[173] The SPC and SPP issued the Interpretation on Environmental Crime on 23 December 2016 and it came into force on 1 January 2017. The previous SPC and SPP Interpretation on Environmental Crime (2013) was repealed on 1 January 2017.

[174] The SPC, SPP, MPS, Ministry of Justice and MEE issued the Minutes of the Meeting on Handling Environmental Criminal Cases on 20 February 2019 with immediate effect.

[175] On 6 January 2015, the SPC issued the SPC Interpretation on Civil EPIL It came into force on 7 January 2015.

[176] The SPC issued the Measures on Adjudication of Pilot Procuratorial Public Interest Litigations on 25 February 2016. The Measures came into force on 1 March 2016.

[177] The SPC issued the Working Rules on the Adjudication of Environmental Public Interest Litigation (for trial implementation) on 1 April 2017 with immediate effect.

[178] The SPC and SPP issued the Interpretation on Several Issues Concerning the Application of Law in Procuratorial Public Interest Litigations on 1 March 2018. It came into force on 2 March 2018.

On eco-environmental damage litigation, the SPC issued the Several Provisions on the Adjudication of Eco-environmental Damage Litigation (for trial implementation) (2019).[179] This sets the rules and procedures for a new type of environmental litigation that may be initiated by provincial and municipal governments or their designated departments against liable parties to seek remedies to restore an eco-environment damaged by serious pollution or rectify ecological destruction such as that caused by harmful logging or mining.

Guiding Cases and Model Cases

In addition to judicial interpretation, the SPC is giving greater importance to the use of cases to supervise and guide the work of courts, in order to improve quality, consistence and justice in adjudication.[180] It issued the Provisions on Case Guidance Work (2010)[181] and started to promulgate carefully selected guiding cases in batches in 2011.[182] By the end of 2019, the SPC had issued 139 guiding cases in 24 batches.[183] Of these, fourteen are related to the environment. The case of *China Biodiversity Conservation and Green Development Foundation* v. *Ningxia Ruitai Science and Technology Co. and Seven Others*[184] addresses the new and difficult issue of standing in EPIL and the interpretation and application of article 58 of the EPL (2014).

Guiding cases are selected on the basis that the issues raised attract widespread social concern, the relevant legal rules are too general for correct and consistent application, and they are either typical or representative of a significant number of cases or involve difficult, complicated or new issues.[185] While guiding cases have significant force in directing, although not binding, adjudication work, they are still too few in number and too narrow in scope to fully guide environmental adjudication. Therefore, in addition to these highly authoritative guiding cases, the SPC has issued model cases in much larger numbers to improve the quality of environmental adjudication and ensure consistency among courts in different regions and at different levels. The following are batches of major environmental model cases issued by the SPC in recent years:

- Four Model Cases on Environmental Crimes (2013)
- Nine Model Cases on Environmental Adjudication (2014)
- 10 Important Administrative Cases on Environmental Protection (2014)
- 10 Model Cases on Environmental Torts (2015)
- 10 Important Administrative Cases on Environmental Protection (second batch) (2016)
- Eight Model Cases on Environmental Crimes (2016)
- 10 Model Cases of Environmental Public Interest Litigation (2017)
- 10 Model Criminal, Civil and Administrative Cases on Environment and Resources (2017)

[179] SPC issued the Several Provisions on the Adjudication of Eco-Environmental Damage Litigation (for trial implementation) on 4 June 2019. The Provisions came into force on 5 June 2019.
[180] In China, court cases are, in theory, not binding. However, under the guiding case system, a small number of cases are selected and published by the SPC to guide the adjudication work of all courts.
[181] The SPC issued the Provisions on Case Guidance Work on 26 November 2010 with immediate effect.
[182] The SPC issued the 1st batch of guiding cases on 20 December 2011.
[183] The SPC issued the 21st batch of guiding cases on 25 February 2019.
[184] SPC 15th Batch of Guiding Cases (2016), guiding case no. 75.
[185] SPC Provisions on Case Guidance Work (2010), art. 2.

- 10 Model Cases of Environment and Resources Adjudication at the Yangtze River Basin (2017)
- 10 Model Cases on Procuratorial Public Interest Litigation (2018)[186]
- 10 Model Cases on Services Provided by Courts and Guarantees for the Development of Eco-civilization in the New Era (2018)
- 10 Model Cases of Environment and Resources Adjudication to Guarantee High-Quality Development along the Yangtze River Economic Belt (2018)
- Model Cases of Guaranteeing the Reform of the System of Compensation for Eco-environmental Damage (2019)

These model cases have played an important role in guiding and supervising adjudication work by clarifying the application of law.

White Papers

The SPC has established a new tradition of publishing annual White Papers on environment and resources adjudication. By mid-2019, the SPC had published a White Paper in each of the years 2016, 2017 and 2019. The first, *Environment and Resources Adjudication in China* (2016), covered the two and a half years of judicial reform of environmental adjudication from January 2014 to June 2016. The second, *Environment and Resources Adjudication in China 2016–2017* (2017), covered the period July 2016 to June 2017. The third, *Environment and Resources Adjudication in China 2017–2018* (2019), covered the one and a half years from July 2017 to December 2018, and serves as the White Paper's transition to an annual report.

The SPC White Papers review the adjudication of five types of case: (i) environmental criminal, (ii) environmental civil, (iii) environmental administrative, (iv) EPIL initiated by social organizations and people's procuratorates and (v) cases filed by provincial and municipal governments for environmental damage compensation. They summarize the efforts made by the SPC to promote high-quality specialized environment and resources adjudication through the issuance of judicial policies, judicial interpretations and model and guiding cases. The White Papers also assess the successes or otherwise of reforms of specialized environmental tribunals and innovation in rules and procedures designed to boost judicial protection of the environment and resources.

Many provincial high courts have followed suit and issued environment and resources adjudication White Papers:[187]

- Yunnan Provincial High Court, *Environment and Resources Adjudication White Paper for 2017* (2018)
- Hubei Provincial High Court, *Hubei Environment and Resources Adjudication White Paper 2015–18* (2018)
- Anhui Provincial High Court, *Environment and Resources Adjudication White Paper for 2017* (2018)

[186] The 10 Model Cases on Procuratorial Public Interest Litigation (2018) were issued jointly with the SPP.
[187] Lü Zhongmei and Liu Changxing, 'Innovative development', at 11.

- Zhejiang Provincial High Court, *Zhejiang Environment and Resources Adjudication* (White Paper) (2018)
- Gansu Provincial High Court, *Gansu Environment and Resources Adjudication 2017–19* (White Paper) (2018)
- Guangdong Provincial High Court, *Guangdong Environment and Resources Adjudication 2016–18* (White Paper) (2018)

Issuing White Papers is a way of reviewing a court's environmental adjudication over the years in order to gain a deeper understanding of the strengths and weaknesses of new institutions and new rules of jurisdiction and adjudication. A White Paper can also act as a venue for experience sharing and lesson learning, in order for improvements to be made.

2.5.3 Jurisdiction

Traditionally, environmental and resources cases are adjudicated by a civil, criminal or administrative tribunal, depending on the nature of the case. The creation of new specialized environmental tribunals aims to address environmental problems more effectively and efficiently by employing courts and judges with expertise in handling cases involving environment and resources. It is necessary to define the jurisdictions of these tribunals in order to facilitate a streamlined transfer of relevant cases from civil, criminal and administrative to environmental divisions. In practice, expanding the jurisdiction of the environmental division takes time and is an ongoing process. For example, the SPC's ERD was first established in mid-2014 with civil jurisdiction over first- and second-instance civil disputes involving: (i) tort caused by air pollution, water pollution or soil contamination; (ii) mining rights and (iii) rights over development and use of natural resources, including forests, grassland, rivers, lakes, shoals and wetland.[188] In April 2016, the SPC expanded the ERD's jurisdiction to cover second-instance administrative cases and review for retrial of administrative cases in which environment agencies are the defendants.[189] Since then, the ERD has had jurisdiction over both civil and administrative cases involving environment or resources. In 2017, the SPC trialled a 'three-in-one' model at its Third Circuit Court, in which one adjudication team is in charge of all civil, criminal and administrative cases involving environment and resources.[190] The jurisdiction of the ERD was expanded again in June 2018 to cover administrative cases where agencies in charge of the eco-environment, natural resources, forestry and grassland are defendants.[191]

Under the guidance of the SPC, local courts also adopted combined jurisdictions in the form of two-in-one civil and administrative cases, three-in- one civil, administrative and criminal cases, and three-plus-one civil, administrative and criminal, plus enforcement cases.[192]

[188] SPC, 'Fully strengthening'; also see 'SPC establishes', *People's Court News*.
[189] SPC, *Environment and Resources Adjudication in China*, part III.
[190] SPC, *Environment and Resources Adjudication in China 2016–2017*, part III.
[191] SPC, *Environment and Resources Adjudication in China 2017–2018*, part III.
[192] SPC, *Environment and Resources Adjudication in China*, part III.

Depending on the need for environmental protection and local circumstances, different forms of cross-region and centralized jurisdiction are being trialled by provincial high courts. For example, Guizhou Provincial High Court has designated four intermediate courts and five basic-level courts to exercise jurisdiction over environment and resources cases. Jiangsu Provincial High Court has designated thirty-one basic-level courts to exercise centralized jurisdiction over environment and resources cases within Jiangsu province.[193] In 2019, the SPC approved a request from Jiangsu Provincial High Court to set up a specialized environment and resources division at Nanjing Intermediate Court. The division would exercise jurisdiction of second-instance adjudication of all environmental cases in Jiangsu province.[194]

Given that environment and resources cases can have an impact across administrative regions, the possibility of centralized jurisdiction that crosses provincial borders has been explored. For instance, to adjudicate cases involving pollution or eco-destruction of the Yangtze River basin, it is more effective and efficient for such cases to be handled by a court that has jurisdiction over more than one province.[195] The latest development on cross-provincial region jurisdiction is the SPC's designation of Beijing No. 4 Intermediate Court as the second-instance court for all environmental administrative cases adjudicated in Tianjin since 26 October 2017.[196]

2.5.4 Innovation in Adjudication, Judgment and Enforcement of Judgment

Given the special nature of environmental cases and the pressing need for timely remediation, courts are innovative in trying different approaches in adjudication, judgment and enforcement of judgment.

Combined Adjudication

Very often one pollution incident involves multiple parties with potential civil, criminal and administrative legal liabilities. Such cases are typically tried in courts as environmental tort cases, criminal prosecutions, administrative cases, cases of civil and administrative EPIL and cases for compensation of environmental damage. Courts are exploring combined adjudication, in which an administrative EPIL has civil EPIL attached, and a criminal prosecution has a civil EPIL attached. This is designed to promote efficiency in the use of judicial resources and consistency in the adjudication of a pollution incident involving multiple parties with different legal liabilities.

[193] SPC, *Environment and Resources Adjudication in China*, part III. In Jiangsu province, there is one provincial high court, 13 intermediate courts and 109 basic-level courts. Before this change, cases were heard based on geographical jurisdiction.

[194] SPC Reply to Jiangsu Provincial High Court on the Approval of Setting Up a Specialized Environment and Resources Division at Nanjing Intermediate Court (2 January 2019).

[195] See SPC Opinion on Providing Judicial Service and Guarantee for the Development of the Yangtze River Economic Belt (2016).

[196] SPC, *Environment and Resources Adjudication in China 2017–2018*, part III. The term 'provincial-level government' includes five autonomous regions and four municipalites directly under central government control, including Beijing and Tianjin, as well as governments of provinces.

Jilin Baishan City People's Procuratorate v. *Baishan Jiangyuan District Health and Family Planning Bureau and Baishan Jiangyuan District Chinese Medicine Hospital* (2016)[197]

The Baishan Jiangyuan District Chinese Medicine Hospital had operated without wastewater treatment facilities since 2012. It had discharged untreated medical wastewater directly to a permeation well within the hospital grounds and a pit outside the grounds, causing serious pollution of the soil and groundwater nearby. The hospital was sanctioned by the local EPB in 2014, but continued the illegal discharge. Despite the violations, the Baishan Jiangyuan District Health and Family Planning Bureau approved an extension to the hospital's operating permit in May 2015. In February 2016, the procuratorate sued both the Bureau and the hospital for violations of the law causing environmental harm.

Baishan Intermediate Court (2016) held that the Bureau's approval of the hospital's operation permit was unlawful. It ordered the Bureau to exercise its supervision responsibility to ensure the hospital rectified the wastewater problem within three months. The hospital was found to bear tort liability for actual and potential harm to the groundwater and soil. It was ordered to stop the illegal discharge of untreated medical wastewater immediately and carry out rectification.

This was China's first administrative EPIL with attached civil EPIL. The court accepted the cases separately as one administrative EPIL and one civil EPIL, combined the two for joint adjudication by one collegiate panel, and issued judgments separately.[198]

Where a people's procuratorate prosecutes an environmental crime against polluters, it may simultaneously file a civil PIL attached to the criminal case. The court with jurisdiction over the criminal case also adjudicates the civil PIL.[199] In the case of *Anhui Wuhu Jinghu District Procuratorate* v. *Li and Others* (2018),[200] Jinghu District Court combined criminal prosecution and civil EPIL to sanction criminal violations and make liable parties bear the cost of emergency response, remediation and assessment and appraisal.

Use of Special Experts in Adjudication

In Guangdong, Guizhou and Chongqing, environmental tribunals invite environmental experts to serve as 'people's assessors' and participate in court trials.[201] Their specialist knowledge, training and expertise on complicated and highly technical environmental issues are valuable inputs to the collegiate panel. Seeking expert opinions is another way to tackle the technical difficulties of addressing environmental disputes. To facilitate this, many courts have built databases of environmental experts. For instance, Tianjin High Court established such a database jointly with the Tianjin EPB and Tianjin Justice Bureau. It includes nearly seventy experts specializing in environmental science and technology, assessment and appraisal, legal science, adjudication and enforcement. By 2018, Fujian High Court had a list of twenty-five experts for consultation in subject areas including

[197] SPC 10 Model Cases of Environmental Public Interest Litigation (2017), case no. 10.
[198] SPC, *Environment and Resources Adjudication in China 2016–2017*, part II.
[199] SPC and SPP Interpretation on Application of Law in Public Interest Litigation by People's Procuratorates (2018), art. 20.
[200] SPP 10 Model Cases of Procuratorial Public Interest Litigation (2018), case no. 10.
[201] Lü Zhongmei and Liu Changxing, 'Innovative development', at 3.

environmental protection, forestry, the atmosphere, marine and fishery, agriculture and animal husbandry, land and mineral resources, and hydraulic engineering.[202]

Judicial Redress and Enforcement of Judgment

Compensation and ecological restoration are typical remedies to ensure liable parties pay for the environmental harm caused by pollution. Courts are exploring various means to ensure that these remedies are actually carried out. Courts not only prioritize ecological remediation in civil EPILs over payment of damages, but also strive to ensure quality control of the remediation. Where timely and effective remediation by defendants is unlikely, the court can order remediation by a third party in line with remediation plans produced by experts, as well as monitoring by a local environmental authority. Where remediation at the original site is impossible, a court orders off-site substitute remediation. Full compensation takes into account the loss of ecosystem services and functions during the period from contamination or destruction to completion of restoration.[203]

2.5.5 Environmental Caseload

The surge in the environmental caseload occurred in 2014, the year the EPL was revised and the SPC set up the specialized ERD. The increase in environmental cases in 2014 was larger than for all other categories of criminal and civil first-instance cases. In criminal cases, the crime of environmental pollution increased 850 per cent over the previous year. In comparison, other types of criminal case increased at lower rates: the crime of production and sale of toxic and hazardous food increased 190 per cent, the crime of deliberate failure to pay wages rose 120 per cent, the crime of illegal collection of personal data rose 58 per cent, the crime of production and sale of fake medications rose 47.4 per cent, the crime of incitement and secession rose 40.7 per cent and bribery 32.9 per cent. Turning to civil cases, pollution compensation cases increased 51.15 per cent in 2014, compared to increases of 44.5 per cent in cases of product liability, 27.9 per cent in cases of the infringement of rights of reputation, 19.9 per cent in unregulated loans cases, 17.68 per cent in cases related to construction projects and 13.5 per cent for inheritance disputes.[204]

The SPC has pushed for courts to be actively engaged in environmental adjudication in civil, criminal and administrative cases and has supported the development of PIL, which can be initiated by social organizations and people's procuratorates. It has also explored the adjudication of eco-compensation litigation, which can be initiated by provincial and municipal governments, by issuing judicial interpretations and promulgating model civil, criminal and administrative environmental cases, as well as PIL initiated by environmental NGOs and people's procuratorates. The environmental courts have not only accepted and concluded a substantial number of environmental cases of conventional litigation (civil,

202 Lü Zhongmei and Liu Changxing, 'Innovative development', at 3.

203 See All-China Environment Federation v. Wuxi Lihu Huishan Scenic Zone Management Committee (2012), SPC Nine Model Cases on Environment and Resources (2014), case no.8; SPC Interpretation on EPIL (2015), art.21; Lü Zhongmei and Liu Changxing, 'Innovative development', at 28.

204 Zhou Qiang, *SPC's Work Report Presented to the 12th NPC at its Third Meeting* (2015), appendix II. Zhou Qiang, president of the SPC, presented the annual work report to the NPC on 12 March 2015 at its annual meeting.

TABLE 2.5 NATIONAL ENVIRONMENTAL CASELOAD

	Period	Cases accepted	Cases concluded
Environmental criminal cases	January 16–June 18	48,700	45,900
Environmental civil cases	January 16–June 18	481,000	442,000
Environmental administrative cases	January 16–June 18	77,600	67,300
Civil EPILs initiated by social organizations	January 15–April 18	183	92
Civil and administrative EPILs initiated by procuratorates	July 15–April 18	1,431	991
Eco-environmental damages litigation initiated by provincial and municipal governments	December 15–May 18	8	3

Sources: Jiang Bixin, 'Providing judicial service and guarantee for ecological civilization in the new era', *Zi Guang Ge*, 9 (2018), 29–30.

TABLE 2.6 ENVIRONMENT AND RESOURCES CASES (FIRST INSTANCE) IN 2018

	Number of cases accepted	Compared to 2017 (%)	Number of cases concluded	Compared to 2017 (%)
First-instance criminal cases	26,481	+16.51	25,623	+13.19
First-instance civil cases	192,008	+8.17	182,691	+0.79
First-instance administrative case	42,235	+7.35	41,725	+3
Environmental civil PILs initiated by social organizations	65	+12.07	16	−57.89
Environmental civil and administrative PILs initiated by people's procuratorates	1,737	+33.21	1,252	+28.41
Eco-environmental damages litigation initiated by provincial and municipal governments	20	No data available	8	No data available

Sources: SPC, *Environment and Resources Adjudication in China (2017–2018)*.

criminal and administrative), but have also made important progress on EPIL, although cases involving the latter remain much smaller in number.

The SPC White Paper *Environment and Resources Adjudication in China (2017–2018)* updates the 2018 environmental adjudication data to highlight the steady increase in the number of cases accepted by courts as compared to the year before.

Chinese courts have become a major force in the battle against environmental pollution and ecological destruction. Their active engagement in turning law on paper into law in operation has facilitated the implementation and enforcement of environmental legislation and regulations issued by lawmakers and regulators.

2.6 THE PROCURATORATES

The procuratorial system has a hierarchical structure similar to that of the courts. The SPP sits at the top of the hierarchy and directs the work of procuratorates at local levels.[205] Under the SPP are the provincial, municipal and district or county procuratorates.[206] There are also specialized procuratorates, such as military procuratorates.[207] The procuratorates prosecute crimes in order to maintain national security and social order and to protect the lawful rights and interests of individuals, organizations and the state, as well as the public interest.[208] They also have further important roles. They exercise legal supervision of the work of courts, public security bodies and administrative agencies.[209] They protest against incorrect civil or administrative judgments, serve procuratorial advice to agencies failing to perform their statutory duties, support civil PIL initiated by social organizations and initiate both civil and administrative PIL. According to the SPP, the procuratorates dealt with 59,312 cases involving natural resources and the environment in 2018. They prosecuted a total of 26,287 cases of crimes against the environment and resources involving 42,195 defendants.[210]

2.6.1 Prosecuting Environmental Crimes

Procuratorates play a crucially important role in prosecuting environmental crimes. The first environmental criminal case prosecuted under the CL (1997) was the Yang Junwu case (1998) in Shanxi province.[211]

The Yang Junwu Case (1998)

Yang Junwu owned and operated Tianma Paper Factory near the Yellow River Water Diversion Ditch in Yuncheng city, Shanxi province. The Diversion Ditch is a man-made project that diverts water from the Yellow River to a local reservoir to provide water for Yuncheng. The factory began operating in 1993 without any wastewater treatment facilities. Yang kept the toxic wastewater in a pit nearby, leaving it to evaporate and permeate into the soil. In early October 1997, the wastewater in the pit overflowed into a trench that was separated from the Diversion Ditch by a gate. On 14 October 1997, Yang instructed his employees to open the gate and discharge the wastewater into the Diversion Ditch. A total of 410,000 m^3 of contaminated water in the Diversion Ditch then flowed into the reservoir, resulting in the suspension of Yuncheng's water supply for three days and direct economic losses of 429,095 yuan.

205 Constitution (2018), art. 137; Organic Law of the People's Procuratorates (2018), art. 10.
206 Organic Law of the People's Procuratorates (2018), art. 13.
207 Organic Law of the People's Procuratorates (2018), art. 12.
208 Constitution (2018), art. 136; Organic Law of the People's Procuratorates (2018), art. 2(2).
209 Constitution (2018), art. 134; Organic Law of the People's Procuratorates (2018), art. 2(1) and art. 20.
210 Dong Fanchao, 'SPP releases the procuratorial work on eco-environmental protection', *Legal Daily*, 14 February 2019.
211 Yang Junwu (1998) (Shanxi Yuncheng Intermediate Court, 7 December 1998), *Supreme People's Court Gazette*, 2 (1999), at 63–64.

The Yuncheng People's Procuratorate prosecuted Yang for the crime of causing a serious water pollution incident. Three other bodies, the Water Diversion Bureau, the Reservoir Management Committee and the Water Supply Company, filed collateral civil claims against Yang for compensation: (i) the Water Diversion Bureau claimed 246,000 yuan, the amount that the Reservoir Management Committee had refused to pay, because the water was contaminated; (ii) the Reservoir Management Committee incurred costs of 73,495 yuan to clean up the contamination and sold the contaminated water for 36,000 yuan, meaning that it claimed 37,495 from Yang and (iii) the Water Supply Company claimed from Yang the 107,600 yuan in losses it had suffered.

Yuncheng City Basic-Level Court (1998) found that Yang, who had experience in the paper industry, should have known that volatile phenol was toxic and was in the wastewater. Nonetheless, he intentionally discharged the wastewater containing volatile phenol into the Diversion Ditch, causing serious pollution of the water supply and heavy losses to the state, which owns all natural resources, including water. Article 21 of the WPPCL (1984) prohibits the discharge of toxic effluent into the water, and article 338 of the CL (1997) imposes criminal liability for causing a serious environmental pollution incident. Yang was convicted of the crime of causing a serious pollution incident, sentenced to two years' imprisonment and fined 50,000 yuan. In terms of his civil liabilities, Yang was ordered to pay compensation of 246,000 yuan to the Water Diversion Bureau, 37,495 yuan to the Reservoir Management Committee, and 75,320 yuan to the Water Supply Company. Yang appealed.

Yuncheng Prefecture Intermediate Court (1998) found that the lower court had ascertained the facts clearly and convicted Yang correctly with an appropriate sentence. It further found that the civil compensation was reasonable and the trial procedure lawful. The court rejected the appeal and upheld the lower court's judgment.

Environmental legal reforms since the EPL (2014) have strengthened enforcement and sanction of violations. The number of defendants prosecuted for crimes against the environment and resources, including the crimes of environmental pollution, illegal mining, illegal logging and unlawful grassland reclamation, has been increasing: 20,969 in 2013, 25,863 in 2014, 27,101 in 2015, 29,173 in 2016, 34,872 in 2017 and 42,195 in 2018.[212]

2.6.2 Legal Supervision of Adjudication by Courts

Procuratorates are able to fulfil their function of supervision of a court's adjudication work by means of protest. Procuratorates may protest against legally effective judgments in cases in which courts have erred in the finding of facts, have incorrectly applied the law or violated legal procedure.[213] The Pinghu tadpole case[214] illustrates the role of local procuratorates in exercising legal supervision of the adjudication work of same-level people's courts. Although protests by Jiaxing City Procuratorate and Zhejiang Provincial

[212] SPP, *Annual Work Report* (2014 to 2019). www.pkulaw.cn

[213] Organic Law of the People's Procuratorates (2018), arts. 20 and 21. CPL (2017), arts. 200 and 208; APL (2017), arts. 91 and 93.

[214] *Pinghu Aquatic Farm v Jiaxing Buyun Dye and Chemical Co. and Others* (SPC, 2 April 2009). www.pkulaw.cn. See also Chapter 9 of this book.

Procuratorate failed to rectify the court's adjudication errors, they did help Yu Mingda, the pollution victim, to reach higher-level courts and ultimately the SPC. Yu's long legal journey exhausted the resources of four levels of courts before he finally achieved the justice he deserved – payment of more than 930,000 yuan (including interest) in June 2009.

2.6.3 Legal Supervision of Agencies

In exercising its role of legal supervision, a procuratorate may serve advice to administrative agencies and other entities to ensure the law is implemented and enforced.[215] In practice, little can be done if procuratorial advice is ignored.[216] But that is likely to change as procuratorates become increasingly engaged in the environmental PIL process.[217] Under the revised Administrative Litigation Law (ALL) (2017), a procuratorate must issue procuratorial advice to any regulatory agency that has violated the law or failed to perform its statutory duties in the areas of: (i) protection of eco-environment and resources; (ii) food and drug safety; (iii) protection of state assets and (iv) transfer of state-owned land-use rights, resulting in harm to the interests of the state or public interest. Its advice will urge the agency to take action. If the agency fails to rectify the situation, the procuratorate initiates a PIL.[218]

While the ALL (2017) expressly grants standing to the procuratorates to initiate an administrative PIL, litigation is seen as a last resort to urge agency performance. It is preferable for agencies to rectify upon receiving the procuratorial advice within the time limit as it saves public finances and the time and resources of the procuratorates. In the 13th Batch of Guiding Cases issued by the SPP,[219] two of the three cases involved the use of procuratorial advice to urge agencies to enforce environmental law. Of the two, the first was a case in Shaanxi province that ended up in court with a procuratorial PIL against a local EPB for its failure to fully perform its duties.[220] The second occurred in Hunan province and was resolved before litigation. Local agencies and the local government actively responded to the procuratorial advice and enforced the law against a company in violation.[221]

***Fengxiang Branch of Baoji EPB, Shaanxi Province* (2016)**

Particulate matter emissions from Shaanxi Changqing Energy and Chemical Company (Changqing Co.) violated local standards that had come into force on 1 January 2015. Fengxiang Branch of the Baoji EPB issued a notice on 7 July 2015 to Changqing Co. requesting rectification of the violations

[215] Organic Law of the People's Procuratorates (2018), art. 21. For further discussion, see Jingjing Liu, 'China's procuratorate in environmental civil enforcement: practice, challenges & implications for China's environmental governance', *Vermont Journal of Environmental Law*, 13 (2011), 41–68.

[216] Albert Chen, *An Introduction to the Legal System*, at 215.

[217] Organic Law of the People's Procuratorates (2018), art. 20(4); ALL (2017), art. 25(4).

[218] ALL (2017), art. 25(4). [219] SPP issued the 13th Batch of Guiding Cases on 21 December 2018.

[220] *Fengxiang Branch of Baoji EPB, Shaanxi Province* (2016), SPP 13th Batch of Guiding Cases (2018), case no. 49.

[221] *Changsha County Urban and Rural Planning and Construction Bureau, Hunan Province*, SPP 13th Batch of Guiding Cases (2018), case no. 50.

within a specified time limit. Failure to rectify would result in a fine at the higher end of the permitted range. Changqing Co. did not rectify the situation, but no sanction was imposed by Fengxiang Branch. It finally issued its overdue administrative sanction decision on 18 November 2015, imposing a fine of 50,000 yuan and ordering rectification to take place within one month. However, there was no improvement in Changqing Co.'s emissions of particulate matter, which continued to breach standards.

On 3 December 2015, Fengxiang county procuratorate issued procuratorial advice to Fengxiang Branch, urging it to perform its duty and ensure Changqing Co. complied with emission standards by installing and using emissions abatement equipment. Fengxiang Branch replied on 4 January 2016 that it had ordered Changqing Co. to cut its production and pay fees to cover the extra emissions of particulate matter. The Fengxiang procuratorate's investigation found that although Changqing Co. had cut its production, it was not using emissions abatement equipment and its emissions continued to breach the required standards.

Fengxiang county procuratorate initiated administrative PIL against the local EPB on 11 May 2016, seeking: (i) court confirmation that the failure of Fengxiang Branch to fully perform its duties was unlawful and (ii) a court order that the agency must fully perform its statutory duties and ensure Changqing Co. complied with particulate matter emissions standards. On 16 May 2016, Fengxiang Branch fined Changqing Co. 6.45 million yuan. By 22 August 2016, Changqing Co. had begun using emissions abatement equipment and had reached the required standards for emissions of particulate matter. The procuratorate withdrew the second claim on 20 December 2016.

Chencang District Court (2016) held that the failure of Fengxiang Branch to fully perform its duties of regulatory control over Changqing Co. was unlawful.

Initiating administrative PIL against agencies is a last resort and the overwhelming majority of disputes are resolved without litigation. In 2018 alone, procuratorial advices were successful in urging administrative agencies to rectify their errors in 97 per cent of cases.[222] Procuratorates have effectively promoted the protection of the ecological environment, including within nature reserves[223] and scenic zones,[224] by using procuratorial advices to urge agencies and local governments to take enforcement action against illegal construction, structures and operations within the protected zones.

2.6.4 Supporting or Initiating Environmental Civil PIL

The CPL (2017) provides that civil PIL may be initiated by relevant bodies and organizations in cases of environmental pollution or consumer protection.[225] Where a procuratorate becomes aware of a case with public interest implications in the subject areas of environmental pollution or food and drug safety, and no other body or organization has initiated a civil PIL, the procuratorate may do so. Where another body or organization has

[222] Dong Fanchao, 'SPP releases'.
[223] *Shuimoxi Wetland Nature Reserve in Shizhu County, Chongqing City*, SPP 10 Model Cases of Procuratorial Public Interest Litigation (2018), case no. 1.
[224] *Cihu Scenic Zone in Huangshi City, Hubei Province*, SPP 10 Model Cases of Procuratorial Public Interest Litigation (2018), case no. 2.
[225] CPL (2017), art. 55(1).

initiated a PIL, the procuratorate may support such litigation.[226] As such, the procuratorates' role in civil PIL is secondary to other bodies and organizations, but is a crucial final guarantee that PIL will be initiated against parties causing harm to the environment and resources. In practice, procuratorates enquire of municipal civil affairs bureaus whether any eligible non-governmental organization (NGO) is willing and able to initiate PIL against parties liable for environmental harm. In the absence of a willing NGO or other body, the procuratorate proceeds through PIL to make liable parties pay to clean up contamination and restore the ecological environment. The payment includes the fees for appraisal and assessment of the eco-damage. In the Lu Rongtai case, Liaocheng City Procuratorate sued to make Lu Rongtai pay 38,400 yuan to treat pollution and cover the restoration fee for land contamination caused by his illegal washing of waste-oil buckets and discharge of untreated wastewater.[227] In a bigger and more complicated pollution case in Yunnan, Pu'er city procuratorate initiated PIL against Yunnan Jinggu Mining and Metallurgy Co. to make it pay 829,700 yuan for the cost of eco-restoration and 400,000 yuan for the appraisal and assessment fee.[228]

One important development is the effort made by the procuratorates to restore the environment, in addition to prosecuting the environmental offence. Procuratorates may attach civil PIL to criminal prosecutions to make the best use of judicial resources to prosecute and punish crime and seek civil remedies to clean up contamination and restore the eco-environment in a timely manner.

Anhui Wuhu Jinghu District Procuratorate v. *Li and Others* (2018)[229]

Li founded an environmental services company in January 2017. Without having a licence for solid waste disposal, he collected more than 2,500 t of industrial sludge from nine enterprises in Jiangsu and Zhejiang provinces, brought it illegally to Anhui province and dumped it by the Yangtze River in Tongling. This caused serious contamination of the surface water, soil and groundwater. The losses and damage to public and private property amounted to more than 7.9 million yuan, including expenses incurred for emergency monitoring and removal and disposal of the sludge. In addition, restoration of the contaminated water and soil was estimated to cost more than 3.1 million yuan. On 16 July 2018, the Jinghu District Procuratorate prosecuted twelve people, including Li, for the crime of environmental pollution following the illegal transfer and dumping of the waste. At the same time, the procuratorate initiated civil PIL against the twelve individuals and the nine enterprises that had generated the industrial sludge for compensation amounting to 13.02 million yuan. This was to cover the cost of the emergency response, environmental restoration and pollution appraisal and assessment.

Jinghu District Court (2018) held the twelve defendants in the criminal case liable for the crime of environmental pollution and sentenced them to imprisonment ranging from eighteen months to

226 CPL (2017), art. 55(2).

227 *Liaocheng City Procuratorate of Shandong Province* v. *Lu Rongtai* (2017), SPC and SPP 10 Model Cases of Procuratorial Public Interest Litigation (2018), case no. 8.

228 *Pu'er City Procuratorate of Yunnan Province* v. *Yunnan Jinggu Mining and Metallurgy Co.* (2017), SPC and SPP, 10 Model Cases of Procuratorial Public Interest Litigation (2018), case no. 9.

229 SPP 10 Model Cases of Procuratorial Public Interest Litigation (2018), case no. 10.

six years. It also imposed fines ranging from 10,000 yuan to 200,000 yuan. In the civil litigation, the nine enterprises were each ordered to pay a share of the 13.02 million yuan proportionate to the amount of industrial sludge they had disposed of. They were also ordered to make a public apology through the provincial media.

According to the SPP, procuratorates, in 2018, made liable parties pay more than 360 million yuan in eco-restoration fees, and restore farmland, grassland and mountains damaged by mining operations.[230] By 2019, procuratorates, through PIL, had achieved the restoration of 3.21 million *mu* of farmland, wetland, forestry land and grassland.[231] Between July 2015, when a procuratorial PIL pilot exercise was conducted, and the end of December 2018, the procuratorates had issued procuratorial advices or public announcements as a form of pre-litigation procedure for about 120,000 cases and had initiated 4,611 PILs.[232]

2.7 ENVIRONMENTAL NGOS

In contrast to the legal institutions discussed above, environmental NGOs are not part of the government, but they play an increasingly important role in building sound environmental governance in China.[233] Before the 1990s, NGOs were barely known in China. However, international and domestic political and socio-economic change since the Rio Summit (1992) has provided an opportunity for the growth of green NGOs.[234] *China's Agenda 21* formally recognized the importance of environmental NGOs, emphasizing that they are key players in achieving sustainable development.[235] It also extended the role of 'participation by the public and social organizations' from the decision-making process only to also include monitoring the implementation of decisions.[236] National policies further encourage social organizations to play a role in environmental protection.[237] Meanwhile, domestic institutional reform of the 1990s and the limited capacity of local agencies to contain the

230 Dong Fanchao, 'SPP releases'.

231 Zhang Jun, *Report on Procuratorial Public Interest Litigation* (2019). www.pkulaw.cn. Zhang Jun, procurator general of the SPP, presented the Report on 23 October 2019 to the 13th NPCSC at its 14th session.

232 Dong Fanchao, 'SPP releases'.

233 For further discussion of environmental NGOs in China, see Yuhong Zhao, 'Environmental NGOs and sustainable development in China' in Robert Percival et al. (eds.), *Global Environmental Law at a Crossroads* (Cheltenham and Northampton, MA: Edward Elgar, 2014) 63–80.

234 See Qiusha Ma, *Non-Governmental Organizations in Contemporary China: Paving the Way to Civil Society?* (London and New York: Routledge, 2006); Yiyi Lu, *Non-Governmental Organizations in China: The Rise of Dependent Autonomy* (London and New York: Routledge, 2009); Wang Ming (ed.) *Emerging Civil Society in China, 1978–2008 (Leiden and Boston: Brill, 2008).*

235 State Council, *China's Agenda 21*, chapter 20, s. 20.1. It states that 'to achieve the goal of sustainable development depends on the support and participation of the public and social organizations. The form and level of their participation determines the journey to achieve sustainable development.'

236 State Council, *China's Agenda 21*, chapter 20, s. 20.2.

237 State Council, Decision on Several Issues of Environmental Protection (1996), s. 10; State Council, Decision on Implementing Scientific Development and Strengthening Environmental Protection (State Council Decision) (2005), s. 27.

ongoing degradation of the environment provided the socio-political context for dedicated individuals to found and lead environmental NGOs.

By the early 1990s, oversized central and local administrations were not only inefficient but also corrupt. Downsizing the government was deemed the only solution.[238] State Councillor Luo Gan presented the Government Reform Proposal (1998) to the NPC, explaining that China relied too heavily on the government to manage socio-economic affairs by administrative means. Further, a bloated and inefficient government was prone to corruption and placed too heavy a financial burden on the state.[239] The Government Reform Proposal (1998) was executed under the determined leadership of Premier Zhu Rongji to redefine the role of the government, slim down state bureaucracy and improve administrative efficiency.[240] The biggest challenge was how to relocate laid-off state employees. Later studies found a direct correlation between the downsizing of government apparatus and the growth of social organizations.[241] The Government Reform Proposal (1998) supported the development of social organizations to take on socio-economic responsibilities that the state was either unable or unwilling to undertake, and to absorb the former government employees laid off by the reform.

China's economic expansion since the 1980s has aggravated its pollution hugely and the consequences have snowballed. Pollution has become a major cause of concern for public health and social stability, and pollution-related illnesses have soared. Mass protests over contaminated water, damaged crops and air pollution have contributed to social unrest.[242] In contrast to the scale and severity of widespread pollution was the limited capacity and resources of local EPBs. The state had no choice but to encourage the growth of environmental NGOs to fill the gap between public demand for a cleaner and safer environment and the government's inability to provide it. China's top leaders have openly expressed their support for environmental NGOs and public participation in environmental activities on various public and formal occasions. In 1996, Song Jian, then vice premier and state councillor, praised the roles of environmental NGOs at the National Environmental Conference, commending organizations including Friends of Nature (FON) and calling for support for the healthy development of green NGOs.[243] At an NGO conference, Pan Yue,

[238] From 1991 to 1993, the ministries and bureaus of the State Council were cut from more than 100 to 59 and staffing was reduced by 20 per cent. The largest downsizing took place in 1998 under the leadership of Premier Zhu Rongji, when two million government employees left their positions nationwide. See Ma Qiusha, *Non-governmental Organizations in Contemporary China*, 56–8.

[239] Luo Gan, *An Explanation of the State Council's Reform Proposal* (1998). The document was presented to the ninth NPC at its 1st session on 6 March 1998.

[240] Zhu Rongji, *The Government Work Report* (5 March 1999).
www.npc.gov.cn/npc/index.shtml and www.pkulaw.cn. The report was presented by Zhu Rongji, the then premier of China, on 5 March 1999 to the 9th NPC at its 2nd session. By 1999, the number of ministries and departments of the State Council had been further cut from 40 to 29. Divisions within those ministries and departments were cut by one-quarter. More than 200 functions were transferred from the State Council to enterprises, social organizations and local authorities. The total number of employees working for the central government was cut by half.

[241] Wang Ming et al., *China's NGO Reform: From the Governmental Choice to Societal Choice* (Beijing: Social Sciences Academic Press, 2001), at 83.

[242] For more details, see Elizabeth Economy, 'China's environmental challenge' in David B. H. Denoon (ed.), *China: Contemporary Political, Economic, and International Affairs* (NYU Press, 2007), 204–15.

[243] Song Jian, 'Protect environment according to law and accomplish sustainable development', *China Environment News*, 25 July 1996, 2.

then vice minister of the MEP, spoke of the need to establish a mechanism for public participation in environmental affairs and allow green NGOs to play a more active role.[244] Political realities have forced the government to form alliances with environmental NGOs in the battle against pollution.

2.7.1 Grass-Roots NGOs and GONGOs

The state's recognition of its own limits and of the role of a stronger civil society in tackling serious environmental problems provides opportunities for green groups to grow in China.[245] Enthusiastic environmentalists, many of whom are accomplished and charismatic intellectuals with full-time jobs as professors, lawyers or journalists, began also to lead environmental NGOs. '[O]rganizations with resourceful leaders have an advantage, because these entrepreneurs can mobilize their cultural prestige, social networks, economic capital, political positions and personal skills to boost organizational development.'[246] One of the best known and most influential environmental NGOs in China, the FON, was China's first grass-roots environmental NGO, and was founded in 1994 by Professor Liang Congjie.[247] He was able to use his social status, political influence and personal connections to bring prestige and resources to his organization.[248] The Global Village Beijing (GVB) was established in 1996 by Liao Xiaoyi, an independent producer of TV programmes who had been a visiting scholar in the United States. In addition to producing a weekly programme, 'Time for the Environment', she has launched environmental campaigns to promote green communities and a green lifestyle.[249] Green Earth Volunteers (GEV) was co-founded in 1997 by Wang Yongchen, a veteran journalist and popular radio host. Her media experience and her personal and professional networks have proved to be her biggest assets – she knows how to draw media attention and how to use the media effectively to convey messages to the public and the state.[250] The CLAPV was established in 1998 by Professor Wang Canfa, a leading environmental law scholar of the China University of Political Science and Law (CUPL) and active environmental lawyer.[251] The CLAPV is best known for its expertise in

[244] 'Pan Yue speaks at conference on environmental culture and public participation', *Sina News*, 8 December 2003.

[245] Peter Ho, 'Sprouts of environmentalism in China?' in Christof Mauch et al., (eds.), *Shades of Green: Environmental Activism Around the Globe* (Lanham, MD: Rowman & Littlefield Publishers, 2006), 135–60, at 140.

[246] Guobin Yang, 'Environmental NGOs and institutional dynamics in China', *The China Quarterly*, 181 (2005), 46–66, at 60.

[247] Liang Congjie (1932–2010) was professor of history at Peking University, vice-president of the Academy of Chinese Culture, member of the Chinese People's Political Consultative Conference (CPPCC) and grandson of Liang Qichao, a prominent political and cultural figure in modern Chinese history. For more, see Guobin Yang, 'Environmental NGOs'.

[248] For more details on Liang Congjie, see Friends of Nature, n.d., 'Leadership'. Online article. www.fon.org.cn/index.php?option=com_k2&view=item&id=12931:leadership&Itemid=261

[249] Elizabeth Knup, 'Environmental NGOs in China: an overview', *China Environment Series*, 1 (1997), 9–15.

[250] Knup, 'Environmental NGOs in China'; for more details of Wang Yongchen and the GEV, Green Earth Volunteers (n.d.). Website. http://chinagev.org/

[251] Professor Wang Canfa and the CLAPV have been extensively covered by China's domestic media for their involvement in litigation against the government and polluters in Beijing and elsewhere. The high-impact cases have also been reported by international media. Professor Wang was named one of *Time* magazine's "Heroes of the Environment' in 2007. See Austin Ramzy, 'Wang Canfa', *Time*, 17 October 2007. http://content.time.com/time/specials/2007/article/0,28804,1663317_1663320_1669921,00.html

environmental litigation, representing victims of pollution in their legal battles against polluters and agencies.[252] The Institute of Public and Environmental Affairs (IPE) was founded in 2006 by Ma Jun, another journalist-turned-environmentalist who is known for his book, *China's Water Crisis*.[253] The IPE's most significant contribution is its promotion of access to environmental information. It has released interactive and user-friendly databases – China's Water Pollution Map, Air Pollution Map and Solid Waste Pollution Map[254] – to facilitate easy public access to pollution information.

In addition, many government bodies have established NGOs that fall directly under their supervision; these are known as government-organized NGOs (GONGOs). The well-known All-China Environment Federation (ACEF) was established by the SEPA (predecessor of the MEP and MEE) and registered with the Ministry of Civil Affairs upon approval by the State Council.[255] Song Jian, former vice premier and state councillor, was appointed chairman of the ACEF. Vice chairpersons have included former environmental protection ministers Xie Zhenhua and Zhou Shengxian.[256] In addition to promoting government policies and organizing public education and training programmes for lawyers and green NGOs, the ACEF has initiated EPIL against polluters and local governments. The ACEF has won several high-profile cases against local governments,[257] a clear message that GONGOs can be an important force in advocating for social, legal and political change.

2.7.2 Participation in Government Decision-Making

While public participation was not traditionally part of government decision-making in China, the environmental legal regime – especially the EIAL (2002)[258] – has opened up opportunities for public input into the EIA approval process. Now NGOs are able to intervene successfully and influence decisions on development plans and projects, ensuring environmental considerations become an integral part of the process. The FON and GEV both objected to the Nu River Hydropower Development Plan in Yunnan province, forcing the proponent to conduct an EIA and scale back the development, while the FON and GVB challenged proponents of Beijing's YuanMingYuan Park anti-seepage project at a public

[252] For more details, see Center for Legal Assistance to Pollution Victims (n.d.). Website. www.clapv.org/

[253] Ma Jun, *China's Water Crisis*. The English translation of the book was published in 2004 by EastBridge (Norwalk, CT). Ma started his investigation of China's water pollution in the 1990s when he worked for the *South China Morning Post*. He assessed seven major rivers in China and concluded that the country urgently needed a water management strategy or it would face a water crisis. In 2006, *Time* magazine named Ma Jun one of the 100 people shaping the world. See 'The 2006 Time 100', *Time*, 30 April 2006. http://content.time.com/time/specials/packages/article/0,28804,1975813_1975844_1976451,00.html. *China's Water Crisis* has been referred to as China's wake-up call to a potential environmental catastrophe, much like Rachel Carson's 1962 book, *Silent Spring* (London: Hamish Hamilton, 1962).

[254] For more details, see Institute of Public and Environmental Affairs (n.d.). Website. www.ipe.org.cn/

[255] The SEPA (now the MEE) serves as the supervisory body of the ACEF. For more, see MEE, n.d., 'All-China Environment Federation'. Online article. www.mee.gov.cn/gkml/zzjg/qt/200910/t20091030_180902.htm

[256] For more details, see ACEF, n.d., 'All-China Environment Federation'. Online article. www.acef.com.cn/a/about/#C1

[257] For more details on PIL, see ACEF, n.d., 'Environmental public interest litigation'. Online article. www.acef.com.cn/envlaw/index.shtml.

[258] The EIAL was adopted on 28 October 2002 by the 9th NPCSC at its 30th session and came into force on 1 September 2003. It was amended in 2016 and 2018; see also Yuhong Zhao, 'Assessing the environmental impact of projects: a critique of the EIA regime in China', *Natural Resources Journal*, 49 (2009), 485–524.

hearing hosted by the SEPA.[259] Both cases involved EIA, with one relating to a development plan and the other to a construction project. In addition, the promulgation of the Measures on Public Participation in Environmental Protection (2015)[260] and Measures on Public Participation in Environmental Impact Assessment (Measures on Public Participation) (2018)[261] have facilitated better-informed and more meaningful public participation in the government decision-making process.

2.7.3 Seeking Judicial Redress

Environmental NGOs play an increasingly important role in setting the law in motion by filing lawsuits to seek judicial redress. They are involved in two types of litigation. First, they provide legal representation to victims of pollution, using their legal expertise to assist plaintiffs battling against polluters and non-performing government agencies. Among them, the CLAPV is known for its long-term commitment and high-quality legal service to victims of pollution. Initially it focused on civil litigation against polluters, helping victims of pollution claim compensation and stop ongoing pollution. After winning a number of high-profile cases, including the Fujian Rongping case involving 1,721 pollution victims, it turned its attention to government agencies that were failing to perform their statutory duties.[262] Without the much-needed low-cost or free legal service offered by the dedicated environmental lawyers of the CLAPV, victims of pollution would likely bear the losses themselves.

Second, environmental NGOs initiate civil PIL, a type of litigation gaining momentum in China. In such cases, an NGO sues in its own name in order to protect the public interest in a sound environment. Typical remedies claimed include injunction against the polluting activity, elimination of the threat of harm, clean-up of the contamination and compensation to restore the eco-environment.[263] The ACEF took the lead in initiating environmental civil PIL during the pilot exercise period before the implementation of the EPL (2014), which formally recognized the standing of NGOs in PIL.[264] Some cases filed by the ACEF have been designated as model cases by the SPC, including the lawsuits against Jiangsu Jiangyin Harbour Container Co. in Wuxi[265] and Guiyang Dingba Paper Mill in

[259] For further discussion of public participation in the EIA process, see Chapter 4 of this book; see also Yuhong Zhao, 'Public participation in China's EIA regime: rhetoric or reality', *Journal of Environmental Law*, 22 (2010), 89–123.

[260] The MEP issued the Measures on Public Participation in Environmental Protection on 13 July 2015. The Measures came into force on 1 September 2015.

[261] The Measures on Public Participation were issued by the MEE on 16 July 2018 and came into force on 1 January 2019.

[262] Wang Canfa, 'Keynote: special functions of promoting public participation in environmental protection in aiding pollution victims', *Vermont Journal of Environmental Law*, 8 (2007), 380–92. Further discussion of the Rongping case is found in Chapter 9 of this book.

[263] For further discussion on EPIL, see Chapter 12 of this book. See also Christine Lee, '"Pollute first, control later" no more: combating environmental degradation in China through an approach based in public interest litigation and public participation', *Pacific Rim Law and Policy Journal*, 17 (2008), 795–823; and Wang Canfa, 'Chinese environmental law enforcement: current deficiencies and suggested reforms', *Vermont Journal of Environmental Law*, 8 (2006), 159–93.

[264] EPL (2014), art. 58.

[265] *Zhu Zhengmao and All-China Environment Federation* v. *Jiangsu Jiangyin Harbour Container Company* (2009), SPC Nine Model Cases on Environment and Resources (2014), case no. 5.

Qingzhen[266] to stop water pollution and clean up contamination. The ACEF has raised hopes that PIL may act as an additional channel through which green NGOs can protect the environment from pollution. However, the ACEF is a GONGO that has the legal-person status, professional legal expertise and financial resources that are not commonly found in grass-roots NGOs. The fact that the establishment of environment courts did not trigger an immediate proliferation of PIL in China[267] suggests that judicial attitudes and procedural restrictions were only part of the obstacles to initiating PIL. Second-tier NGOs, such as the CLAPV, do not have the legal-person status to sue in their own names. Most grass-roots NGOs lack the willingness or professional and financial capacity to fight legal battles against the government or enterprises.[268]

The promulgation of the revised EPL (2014) and the SPC Interpretation on Several Issues Concerning the Application of Law in Environmental Civil Public Interest Litigation (SPC Interpretation on Civil EPIL) (2015)[269] formally defined the standing of NGOs in EPILs. As a result, a small number of capable grass-roots NGOs, including the FON and China Biodiversity Conservation and Green Development Foundation (CBCGDF), have initiated high-impact PIL. China's first EPIL by a grass-roots NGO was initiated by the FON against several individuals who had engaged in illegal mining, causing serious damage to the forests around Nanping city, Fujian province on 1 January 2015, the date the EPL (2014) came into force.[270] The CBCGDF's landmark EPIL against eight polluters, demanding they clean up contamination at the Tengger Desert, and its petition to the SPC have clarified the crucially important issue of standing under article 58 of the EPL (2014).[271]

2.7.4 Promoting Access to Information

Environmental NGOs are making use of different tools to promote access to environmental information. The IPE is a small NGO established by Ma Jun, who was named by *Time* magazine as one of the 100 most influential people in 2006.[272] His book *China's Water Crisis* was a wake-up call to the Chinese government to address water pollution as a matter of urgency.[273] Ma understands the power of information and sees public access to it as an essential prerequisite to meaningful public participation. The IPE has, therefore, devoted its limited resources to promoting public access to information. It relies on

266 *All-China Environment Federation and Another* v. *Guiyang Dingba Paper Mill* (2011), SPC Nine Model Cases on Environment and Resources (2014), case no. 1.

267 See Lü Zhongmei, 'Progress and dilemma of environmental public interest litigation' in Friends of Nature and Yang Dongping (eds.), *Annual Report on Environment Development of China* (Beijing: Social Sciences Academic Press, 2009), 229–37; Lin Yanmei, 'The development of environmental public interest litigations from seven test cases' in Friends of Nature and Yang Dongping (eds.), *Annual Report on Environment Development of China* (Beijing: Social Science Academic Press (China), 2010), 272–82.

268 Huang Qi, 'Public interest litigation by Chinese NGO breaking ice', *Xinmin Weekly*, 10 August 2009.

269 The SPC Interpretation on Civil EPIL was issued on 6 January 2015 and came into force on 7 January 2015.

270 *Friends of Nature and Another* v. *Xie Zhijin and Others* (2015), SPC 10 Model Cases on Environmental Torts (2015), case no. 1. For further details, see Chapter 12 of this book.

271 *China Biodiversity Conservation and Green Development Foundation* v. *Ningxia Ruitai Science and Technology Co. and Seven Others* (2016), SPC Guiding Case No. 75 (2016); SPC 10 Model Cases of Environmental Public Interest Litigation (2017), case no. 2. For further details, see Chapter 12 of this book.

272 'The 2006 Time 100', *Time*. Ma Jun was praised for his courage and vision in raising environmental awareness in his book, *China's Water Crisis*.

273 Ma Jun, *China's Water Crisis* .

government-published data to expose polluters that are violating standards, and uses state regulations and rules on information disclosure to assess government performance and quietly demand greater transparency. The IPE has released China's Water Pollution Map, Air Pollution Map and Solid Waste Pollution Map,[274] databases providing information on environmental quality and violations by enterprises throughout China. It collects, compiles and presents the government-sourced pollution data and violation records in a user-friendly interactive database to facilitate easy public access. It empowers the general public and media to monitor and supervise polluters, thereby generating pressure to ensure polluters rectifies pollution situations.

To promote government information disclosure, the IPE has launched a project with the Natural Resources Defense Council (NRDC) to monitor government information disclosure in 113 cities. They have published annual reports – the Pollution Information Transparency Index (PITI) – since 2009. The PITI evaluates and ranks the environmental transparency of 113 municipal governments by assessing their performance under the Regulation on Government Information Disclosure (RGID)[275]and the Measures on Environmental Information Disclosure (for trial use),[276] both of which came into force on 1 May 2008. The PITI has put pressure on government to comply better with information disclosure requirements. Administrative litigation can also effectively force government into information disclosure. The case of *All-China Environment Federation* v. *Xiuwen County Environmental Protection Bureau* (2012)[277] was China's first environmental information disclosure litigation. It was initiated and won by the ACEF against the government.

All-China Environment Federation v. *Xiuwen County Environmental Protection Bureau* (2012)

On 28 October 2011, the ACEF submitted an application, by express mail, to Xiuwen County EPB for government information disclosure. It requested information on Guizhou HaoYiDuo Dairy Company (HaoYiDuo), including details of the discharge permit, the total number and locations of wastewater discharge outlets, the types and volume of effluents, wastewater discharge fees as determined by the EPB, relevant monitoring data by the EPB and records of administrative penalties. Xiuwen County EPB did not reply and did not disclose the information, later claiming this was because: (i) the ACEF had failed to provide proof of identity and failed to specify which of three HaoYiDuo production sites its request applied to, (ii) the ACEF's application was unclear as to the format in which the EPB should reply with the information, (iii) the ACEF had not told the EPB how it would receive the information from the agency and (iv) the ACEF had failed to make payment to cover the expenses incurred by the EPB for collecting, copying and posting the information.

[274] The water, air and solid waste pollution maps are available at: IPE, (n.d.). 'Air'. http://wwwen.ipe.org.cn/AirMap_fxy/AirMap.html?q=1

[275] The RGID was issued by the State Council on 5 April 2007 and came into force on 1 May 2008. It was revised on 3 April 2019, and this came into force on 15 May 2019.

[276] The Measures on Environmental Information Disclosure (for trial use) were issued by the SEPA on 11 April 2007 and came into force on 1 May 2008.

[277] *Supreme People's Court Gazette*, 1 (2013).

Qingzhen City Court (2012) found for the ACEF. It held that the ACEF had applied for information disclosure in accordance with law in terms of procedure, contents and formalities. The information requested by the ACEF had been clearly specified. Had Xiuwen County EPB thought the ACEF's application was unclear, it should, in accordance with article 21 of the RGID, have asked the ACEF to revise its request. The court ruled that Xiuwen County EPB had no legal basis on which to refuse disclosure of the information requested by the ACEF. Instead, the EPB was instructed to reply to the ACEF within ten days of the effective date of the judgment and disclose the information relating to HaoYiDuo. Xiuwen County EPB appealed.

Guiyang Municipal Intermediate Court (2012) allowed the appellant's application to withdraw its appeal. Xiuwen County EPB admitted its duty to disclose information to citizens, legal persons or any other organization and expressed willingness to perform its duty in accordance with the judgment of the Qingzhen City Court.

The important progress made by environmental NGOs has substantially improved the implementation and enforcement of environmental law in China. Each of the NGOs discussed have, over the years, made significant contributions to the development and operation of China's environmental legal regime. Together they have changed the attitudes and behaviour of government and polluters. That said, civil society remains weak in China and has not yet acquired the capacity and space to play the crucial role demanded of it if future development is to be sustainable.

3 The Environmental Protection Law

The Environmental Protection Law (EPL)[1] was first enacted in 1979 for trial implementation. In 1989, it was repealed and replaced by the EPL (1989), which was revised substantially in 2014. The EPL lays down basic environmental principles and legal mechanisms for adoption by specialized environmental legislation that addresses issues including air pollution, water pollution, noise, waste and soil contamination. This chapter focuses on the EPL (2014) and is divided into six sections. Section 3.1 introduces the legislative history of the EPL (2014), with brief references to the EPL (for trial implementation) (1979) and the EPL (1989). Section 3.2 discusses government responsibility and accountability, new and important features of the 2014 revision. Section 3.3 examines major environmental legal principles, including sustainable development, the preventative principle, the polluter-pays principle and the principle of public participation. Section 3.4 investigates China's regulatory control mechanisms for protecting and improving the environment. These range from environmental impact assessment (EIA) and total pollution control to control by permit and emergency responses to environmental incidents. Section 3.5 discusses enforcement and sanctions. Section 3.6 explores economic instruments, including pollution discharge fees (replaced by environmental tax), environmental tax, pollution liability insurance, ecological compensation and government procurement.

3.1 A HISTORICAL REVIEW OF THE EPL: 1979 TO 2014

Modern environmental lawmaking in China started in the late 1970s as the country embarked on rebuilding its legal system after the turmoil of the Cultural Revolution (1966–76).[2] The EPL (for trial implementation)(1979) is a piece of framework legislation that articulates the government position on environmental protection and on

[1] The EPL (for trial implementation) was enacted on 13 September 1979 by the 5th National People's Congress Standing Committee (NPCSC) at its 11th session. It came into force immediately. It was repealed by the EPL (1989), which was enacted on 26 December 1989 by the 7th NPCSC at its 11th session and came into force immediately. The EPL (1989) was substantially revised on 24 April 2014 by the 12th NPCSC at its 8th session. This came into force on 1 January 2015.

[2] For more discussion of the rebuilding of the Chinese legal system, see Albert Chen, *An Introduction to the Legal System*.

strategies for environmental protection work in broad terms. It reiterates article 11 of the Chinese Constitution (1978),[3] stipulating that '[t]he State protects the environment and natural resources, prevents and controls pollution and other public hazards'.[4] The EPL (for trial implementation) (1979) also states that environmental protection work must include 'overall planning, rational [geographical] layout [of zones], comprehensive utilization [of resources], waste recovery, reliance on the masses, participation by all, protecting the environment, and benefiting the people'.[5] The Law has a total of thirty-three articles in seven chapters: (i) general provisions; (ii) protection of the environment; (iii) pollution prevention; (iv) environmental protection bodies and their duties; (v) research and public education; (vi) reward and punishment and (vii) supplementary provisions. The EPL (for trial implementation) (1979) served as the basis for the first wave of environmental legislation in China, which began in the 1980s and includes the Marine Environmental Protection Law (MEPL) (1982), the Water Pollution Prevention and Control Law (WPPCL) (1984) and the Air Pollution Prevention and Control Law (APPCL) (1987).

In the early years of the development of environmental rules, the EPL (for trial implementation) (1979) was an important source of law for court adjudication of pollution cases if a specialized statute had not yet been enacted. This can be seen in cases such as *Shenzhen Shekou Environmental Monitoring Station* v. *Hong Kong Kaida Enterprise Ltd* (1984).[6] The EPL (for trial implementation) (1979) was also an important source of law used in conjunction with the WPPCL (1984) and the GPCL (1986), for example, in *Chunyang Villagers' Committee* v. *Hua'nan Gold Mine Bureau* (1988).[7]

Shenzhen Shekou Environmental Monitoring Station v. *Hong Kong Kaida Enterprise Ltd* (1984)

In 1981, Hong Kong Kaida Enterprise Ltd (Kaida) spent 16 million US dollars setting up a plastic-toy manufacturing enterprise in Shekou. It started operating in 1982, and the ensuing toxic and obnoxious odours and extreme levels of noise severely affected the lives of people working and living nearby. They approached the local government for assistance in stopping Kaida's pollution. In 1983, Shekou Environmental Monitoring Station (Monitoring Station) requested Kaida take measures to control the pollution and invited experts to make a pollution abatement plan, urging Kaida to rectify within a specified time limit. Kaida ignored the request and continued business as usual. The Monitoring Station sued, seeking remedies including: (i) abatement of noise and air pollution and (ii) payment of expenses incurred to hire experts.

Shenzhen Intermediate Court (1984) found Kaida in violation of the EPL (for trial use) (1979), notably article 6, which stipulates that 'all enterprises and other units shall prevent pollution or destruction of the environment in the siting, design, construction and production processes. An EIA should be conducted for any new, modified or expanded projects. An EIA report shall be prepared and approved by relevant environmental authorities and other departments before design starts.

[3] Article 11(3) of the Constitution (1978) provides that '[t]he State protects the environment and natural resources, prevents and controls pollution and other public hazards'. The Constitution (1978) was repealed by the Constitution (1982), which was amended in 1988, 1993, 1999, 2004 and 2018.

[4] EPL (for trial implementation) (1979), art. 1.

[5] EPL (for trial implementation) (1979), art. 4.

[6] *Supreme People's Court Gazette*, 3 (1985).

[7] *Supreme People's Court Gazette*, 4 (1988).

Pollution-control installations shall be designed, constructed and put into operation at the same time as the main projects. Pollution discharge shall be in compliance with state standards. Any unit that has caused pollution or any other hazard shall make a plan and take measures to provide treatment to control pollution based on the polluter-pays principle.' Kaida had started operations without having carried out an EIA and was emitting noise over state limits, without trying to mitigate it, and untreated obnoxious odours. It had also ignored the Monitoring Station's pollution treatment request and plan. The court held that Kaida must: (i) control the noise and odour by 31 October 1984, (ii) pay a fine of 20,000 Hong Kong dollars, (iii) pay expert consultation fees of 810 yuan and (iv) pay litigation fees of 1,740 Hong Kong dollars.

Reviewing the case from today's perspective, many questions arise, including on the nature of the litigation, the standing of the monitoring station and the remedies offered by the Shenzhen court. However, the case was adjudicated in the early 1980s when China had just embarked on its journey to rebuild the legal system. Given the absence of sophisticated legal institutions, comprehensive laws and regulations and experienced and qualified legal personnel, the court took a pragmatic approach to resolve the environmental pollution dispute by offering both civil remedies and a fine. It was a period characterized by a well-known saying of former leader Deng Xiaoping – 'crossing the river by touching stones'. The courts are refining their adjudication work through trial and error and in this way move closer to sophistication.

The case of *Chunyang Villagers' Committee* v. *Hua'nan Gold Mine Bureau* (1988)[8] was a typical case of the time, reflecting the widespread pollution disputes between polluting industrial and mining operators and farmers, the victims of pollution.

Chunyang Villagers' Committee v. _Hua'nan Gold Mine Bureau_ (1988)

In1978, Hua'nan Gold Mine Bureau built a gold-mining vessel on the upper reaches of the Liushu River in Heilongjiang province. In 1982, Hua'nan Gold Mine Bureau illegally blocked the river to alter its natural course in order to facilitate the operation of the vessel. As a result, its untreated wastewater discharge contaminated the paddy fields of the village of Chunyang, located also in Heilongjiang, but in the lower reaches of the river. The Chunyang Villagers' Committee suffered a substantial cut in its rice output due to contamination of its fields caused by the gold mining. Consequently, every year from 1982 it was forced to hire villagers to remove silt and sludge. In 1987, it sued Hua'nan Gold Mine Bureau to claim damages for compensation, including for loss of rice output and the cost of clean-ups.

Hua'nan County Court (1987) found the defendant's operation violated articles 5 and 29 of the WPPCL (1984) and article 29 of the EPL (for trial implementation) (1979). The defendant was found to bear civil liability for pollution under article 124 of the GPCL (1986) as its discharge greatly exceeded state limits, had blocked the river, contaminated the paddy fields and caused serious loss of agricultural output for four years. The court ordered Hua'nan Gold Mine Bureau to pay: (i) damages of 87,924.2 yuan to the plaintiff, which included compensation for the substantially

[8] *Supreme People's Court Gazette*, 4 (1988).

reduced rice output (18,924.2 yuan), the cost of cleaning up the paddy fields (65,472 yuan) and river (3,528 yuan) and (ii) litigation costs of 2,029 yuan. The defendant appealed.

Jiamusi Intermediate Court (1988) dismissed the appeal and upheld the lower-court decision, stating that it was based on a clear finding of facts and correct application of law.

Amending the EPL (for trial implementation) (1979) was long overdue, as it had functioned more as a guide to state policy than a sound legal instrument.[9] The EPL (1989)[10] substantially improved the regulatory pollution-control mechanisms with a much strengthened legal-liability regime. It contains forty-seven articles in six chapters on: (i) general provisions, (ii) supervision and management, (iii) protection and improvement of the environment, (iv) prevention and control of pollution, (v) legal liabilities and (vi) supplementary provisions. The EPL (1989) began the second wave of environmental legislation, which includes the amendment of existing laws, such as the MEPL (1999), the WPPCL (1996, 2008) and the APPCL (1995, 2000), and the enactment of new laws, including the Law on the Prevention and Control of Pollution by Solid Waste (SWL) (1995, 2004) and the Environmental Impact Assessment Law (EIAL) (2002).

The EPL (for trial implementation) (1979) and the EPL (1989) have witnessed China's transformation from a developing country struggling in the 1980s to feed its people and lift them out of poverty, to the world's second largest economy by the beginning of the twenty-first century.[11] The sheer size of China's population and the speed and scale of its economic growth since the 1980s have placed tremendous pressure on the environment, and environmental pollution has become China's greatest new challenge as it continues to industrialize and urbanize.[12] However, some environmental legal principles and mechanisms in the EPL (1989) had, by the beginning of the twenty-first century, become outdated, and gaps and inconsistencies had emerged between this fundamental environmental statute and new or amended specialized legislation and state policies, causing implementation and enforcement difficulties at local levels.[13] The predominant command-and-control approach to pollution could no longer effectively inhibit environmental deterioration in China.

[9] For more on China's environmental law and policy prior to the EPL (1989), see Lester Ross, *Environmental Policy in China* (Bloomington: Indiana University Press, 1988); Lester Ross and Mitchell Silk, *Environmental Law and Policy in the People's Republic of China* (London: Quorum Books, 1987).

[10] The EPL (1989) was enacted on 26 December 1989 by the 7th NPCSC at its 11th session. It came into force immediately.

[11] David Barboza, 'China passes Japan as second-largest economy', *New York Times*, 15 August 2010; *Associated Press*, 'China overtakes Japan as world's second-largest economy', *The Guardian*, 16 August 2010.

[12] For more on China's environmental management in the 1980s and 1990s, see Kristen Day (ed.), *China's Environment and the Challenge of Sustainable Development* (Armonk, NY: M. E. Sharpe, 2005); Richard Edmonds, *Patterns of China's Lost Harmony: A Survey of the Country's Environmental Degradation and Protection* (London: Routledge, 1994); Richard Edmonds (ed.), *Managing the Chinese Environment* (Oxford University Press, 1998); Richard Edmonds, 'The environment in the People's Republic of China 50 years on', *China Quarterly*, 159 (1999), 640–9.

[13] For more on the EPL (1989) and its enforcement, see William P. Alford and Yuanyuan Shen, 'Limits of the law in addressing China's environmental dilemma', *Stanford Environmental Law Journal*, 16 (1997), 125–48; Wang Canfa, 'Chinese environmental law enforcement', at 162; Srini Sitaraman, 'Regulating the belching dragon: rule of law, politics of enforcement, and pollution prevention in post-Mao industrial China', *Colorado Journal of International Environmental Law and Policy*, 18 (2007), 267–334.

Consequently, China needed more pollution-tackling tools – such as supervision by the public, and economic instruments – to supplement the conventional regulatory approach that depends solely on agency enforcement.

It was against this socio-economic context that revision of the EPL (1989) was placed on the NPCSC's five-year lawmaking plan and its annual lawmaking plan for 2011. The National People's Congress (NPC) Environment and Resources Protection Committee (ERPC) started its amendment work in January 2011 and introduced the draft to the 11th NPCSC at its 28th session in August 2012.[14] The Draft Amendment (2012), which only proposed minor changes to the EPL (1989), was then circulated to government departments and social organizations, and published on the NPC's official website for public consultation.[15] Overwhelming public dissatisfaction and criticism from NGOs, lawyers and scholars forced the NPCSC to substantially revise the draft. The NPC Law Committee produced the 2nd Draft Revision, which, introduced public participation and information disclosure and submitted it to the NPCSC in June 2013 for deliberation in the same month.[16] The 2nd Draft Revision (2013) was then published on the NPC website for a second round of public consultation.[17] Based on further public comment, the NPC Law Committee submitted, on 21 October 2013, the revised version to the NPCSC for its third reading.[18] The Law Committee then conducted a targeted consultation with local people's congresses and EPBs to produce a further revised draft for the April 2014 fourth reading by the NPCSC.[19] This time the draft bill was finally passed into law.[20] The EPL (2014) went through four readings in three years, as well as multiple consultations, including a round of public consultation after each of the first and second readings; the lengthy process was exceptional in China and serves as a good case study on public participation in the lawmaking process.[21] During the consultation period, one of the most heated debates involved provisions on public participation and, in particular, on public interest litigation (PIL). The EPL (1989) did not include PIL. The first draft of the EPL (2014) (August 2012) also did not mention PIL, and this was strongly criticized by green groups, lawyers, scholars and the general public, given the serious environmental degradation in China and the desperate need for public involvement and supervision to tackle it.[22] The second draft provided that '[the] ACEF and

14 Wang Guangtao, 'Explanation of the Draft Revision of the Environmental Protection Law of the People's Republic of China', presented on 27 August 2012 to the 11th NPCSC at its 28th session. Full text available in Xin Chunying (ed.), *Interpreting the Environmental Protection Law of the PRC* (Beijing: Law Press, 2014), 390–7.

15 Draft Amendment (2012), see Lü Zhongmei (ed.), *Environmental Protection Law of the People's Republic of China* (Beijing: China Planning Press, 2014), 238–47.

16 Submission of the NPC Law Committee on 26 June 2013, see Xin Chunying (ed.), *Interpreting the Environmental Protection Law*, at 398–403.

17 The 2nd Draft Amendment (2013), see Lü Zhongmei (ed.), *Environmental Protection Law*, at 248–57.

18 Submission of the NPC Law Committee on 21 October 2013, see Xin Chunying (ed.), *Interpreting the Environmental Protection Law*, at 404–8.

19 Submission of the NPC Law Committee on 21 April 2014, see Xin Chunying (ed.), *Interpreting the Environmental Protection Law*, at 409–14.

20 The EPL (2014) was passed on 24 April 2014 by the 12th NPCSC at its 8th session. It came into force on 1 January 2015.

21 For further discussion, see Xiao Zhu and Kaijie Wu, 'Public participation in China's environmental lawmaking: in pursuit of better environmental democracy', *Journal of Environmental Law*, 29 (2017), 389–416.

22 On 27 August 2012, Wang Guangtao, the then chairperson of the NPC's ERPC, presented the Draft Amendment (2012) to the EPL to the 11th NPCSC at its 28th session.

provincial environmental federations may initiate PIL in courts'.[23] The lawmakers intended to restrict standing to the ACEF and its provincial-level equivalents, which are GONGOs supervised by the Ministry of Environmental Protection (MEP) and provincial EPBs. This restriction triggered public outcry and consequently the draft of 21 October 2013 replaced the exclusive status of the ACEF and its provincial counterparts with a more relaxed approach that also gave standing to other NGOs. However, the NPCSC, which drafted the revisions, kept tight control of the number of NGOs that would gain standing. They did this by setting the threshold extremely high, specifying that 'national-level social organizations registered with the Ministry of Civil Affairs that have specialized in environmental protection public interest activities for at least five consecutive years with good reputation shall have standing in PIL'.[24] Though the wording changed, the number of NGOs registered at the national level is extremely small, let alone those specializing in environmental protection. A final compromise was made to expand the number of NGOs eligible to sue in EPILs by lowering the registration requirement, requiring registration only at a municipal-level civil affairs bureau and replacing the vague term 'good reputation' with the more specific requirement of 'no record of violation of law'.[25]

In addition to public participation, which is found in a new chapter on promoting transparency and supervision by the public, the EPL (2014) has also addressed other flaws and gaps in the EPL (1989). The EPL (2014) contains seventy articles in seven chapters on: (i) general provisions, (ii) supervision and management, (iii) protection and improvement of the environment, (iv) prevention and control of pollution, (v) information disclosure and public participation, (vi) legal liabilities and (vii) supplementary provisions. Compared to the command-and-control approach taken by the EPL (1989), the EPL (2014) embraces more deeply a greater number of economic instruments, such as environmental taxes, pollution liability insurance, ecological compensation and government procurement. For the first time in China's environmental lawmaking, environmental protection is treated as a 'fundamental state policy'[26] and is 'given top priority'.[27] In response to public demand, the EPL (2014) expressly stipulates government responsibilities in environmental protection and holds government officials accountable with administrative, political and legal mechanisms. It makes polluters pay and bear the true cost of pollution prevention, control, cleanup and compensation. It not only strengthens enforcement powers granted to enforcement bodies and increases sanctions in order to deter violations, but also empowers the public to supervise both polluters and the government.

The EPL (2014) came into force on 1 January 2015 and it is still too early to assess its effectiveness.[28] Initial data suggests that it is deterring violations, despite abundant diffi-

[23] 2nd Draft Amendment to the EPL. It was presented by the Laws Committee of the NPC on 26 June 2013.
[24] 3rd Draft Amendment to the EPL. It was presented by the Laws Committee of the NPC on 21 October 2013.
[25] EPL (2014), art. 58. [26] EPL (2014), art. 4(1). [27] EPL (2014), art. 5.
[28] For general comments on the EPL (2014), see Mingqing You, 'Changes and challenges of the 2014 revised Environmental Protection Law in the context of China's five fundamental transitions', *Hong Kong Law Journal*, 45 (2015), 621–49; Bo Zhang et al., 'A new Environmental Protection Law, many old problems? Challenges to environmental governance in China', *Journal of Environmental Law*, 28 (2016), 325–35.

culties and obstacles in the early stages of implementation. To guide and assist local EPBs and to promote effective and consistent implementation and enforcement, the MEP has issued administrative measures that fill out the detail of the general provisions of the EPL (2014). The MEP's measures include the Measures on Fines Calculated on a Daily Basis (2014), Measures on Seal-up and Seizure (2014), Measures on Restriction and Suspension of Production for Treatment (2014), Measures on Environmental Information Disclosure by Enterprises and Institutions (2014) and Measures on Environmental Emergency Response (2015).

3.2 GOVERNMENT RESPONSIBILITY AND ACCOUNTABILITY

One major cause of China's environmental degradation has been the failure of the government to implement and enforce the laws, regulations and policies that are designed to prevent and control industrial pollution. Typical examples include situations in which construction projects with significant adverse environmental impacts and that would not have passed environmental scrutiny routinely start construction with or without approval, projects that do not install or operate pollution treatment facilities are not properly sanctioned, polluters in serious violation of emission or discharge standards are not ordered to suspend or close down operations as required by law.[29] Local EPBs are often blamed for the weak enforcement, but political realities have stopped them from fully discharging their statutory duties to enforce the law and sanction violations.

From the late 1970s, when China shifted its focus from Mao's political struggle to economic development under Deng's leadership, local governments were encouraged towards and rewarded for fast growth in gross domestic product (GDP). Development at any cost not only brought the short-term benefits of jobs and revenue, but also highly attractive promotion opportunities for local officials with political ambitions. The system of performance appraisal of individuals and government that almost exclusively focused on GDP growth shaped the attitudes and behaviours of local governments, driving them to pursue short-term returns instead of long-term sustainable development. It is no surprise, therefore, that local governments protected investors, including heavily polluting enterprises, from the enforcement of environmental laws.[30] Local governments are in full control of the budget and staffing of local EPBs and, given the emphasis placed until recently only on economic growth, EPBs routinely operate on a tight budget compared to other bureaus. Most EPBs are too understaffed and badly equipped to conduct the routine inspections and monitoring necessary to detect violations.[31] Directors of EPBs are appointed and removed by local governments, meaning that those who stand up to pressure from local governments may lose their positions, and those who wish to keep their positions must usually yield to

[29] Wang Canfa, 'The achievement, challenges and prospects of environmental law', *Tribune of Political Science and Law*, 28:3 (2010), 106–15, at 113; Wang Canfa, 'The rapid development', at 534–5.

[30] Wang Canfa, 'The rapid development', at 533. In some cases, local governments even help polluters that lose a court case to hide assets and obstruct enforcement.

[31] Wang Canfa, 'The rapid development', at 534.

the pressure.[32] In some unfortunate but not uncommon cases, local EPBs became reluctant accomplices to illegal EIA approval of construction projects.[33] Some local EPBs have even falsified data to protect polluting enterprises.[34]

To find an effective solution to the problem of weak enforcement, one must look beyond the EPBs to the legislature, which sets out their enforcement powers, and to local governments, which are responsible for the budget and staffing of EPBs and the career development of those working in them.

3.2.1 Government Responsibility

The EPL (2014) rightly focuses on local government and expressly stipulates their roles and responsibilities in environmental protection. Environmental protection is no longer just a job for the EPBs, but is a fundamental state policy[35] that must be fully implemented by all levels of government. Local governments are responsible for the environmental quality within their own jurisdictions,[36] and this general responsibility comes with clear duties and legal liabilities.

First, the EPL (2014) requires governments at all levels to increase the budget allocated to environmental protection and improvement and to the prevention of pollution and public hazards,[37] though it does not set any target or specify the amount of the increase. Studies have found that developed countries normally spend more than 3 per cent of GDP on environmental protection.[38] In contrast, China, with the exception of Shanghai, lags behind. In 2012, China's total spending on environmental protection, including state budget allocations and private financing from financial institutions, enterprises and the general public, accounted to 1.59 per cent of GDP.[39]

Secondly, the EPL (2014) requires governments above the county level to incorporate environmental protection work into their socio-economic development plans.[40] The State Council and provincial governments must consider environmental impacts and consult stakeholders and experts when formulating economic and technology policies.[41] This does not yet amount to a statutory environmental assessment (EA) of government policy, such as that applicable to projects and plans, but is certainly an important step in that direction. For the first time in China, policymakers are expressly required by law to take environmental impact into account in their decision-making. However, this provision does not have general application to all policymaking by any level of government. It only applies to the State Council and provincial-level governments when they make economic and technology policies,[42] which are presumed to be more closely linked to the

[32] Wang Canfa, 'Rewrite environmental legal principles to contain environmental pollution accidents', *China Law*, 3 (2010), 22–6, at 25.
[33] Wang Canfa, 'The rapid development', at 534.
[34] Wang Canfa, 'Reflections on Chinese environmental law', *Tsinghua Journal of Rule of Law*, 1 (2010), 21–32, at 29.
[35] EPL (2014), art. 4. [36] EPL (2014), art. 6(2). [37] EPL (2014), art. 8.
[38] Xin Chunying (ed.), *Interpreting the Environmental Protection Law*, 30–1.
[39] 'Wu Xiaoqing: increased state fiscal input in energy conservation and environmental protection in 2014', *China Daily*, 8 March 2014.
[40] EPL (2014), art. 13(1). [41] EPL (2014), art. 14.
[42] According to Xin Chunying, 'economic and technology policies' refers to those relating to industry, agriculture, transport, urban and rural planning, energy, and marine development. Xin Chunying (ed.), *Interpreting the Environmental Protection Law*, 50.

environment and natural resources than policies in other fields, such as politics, culture and education.

Third, it is the responsibility of governments to prevent environmental deterioration. The EPL (2014) requires local governments at all levels to take effective measures to improve environmental quality in accordance with the environmental protection targets and pollution-control tasks set by the central government.[43] Local governments of key regions that do not meet state environmental quality standards must make plans to meet them, with deadlines, and take measures to meet the relevant standards in time.[44]

3.2.2 Target Responsibility System and Performance Appraisal

To reverse the 'development at any cost' mentality of local governments, the state has implemented an 'environmental protection target responsibility system'. It has also introduced a performance appraisal scheme that requires local governments at the county level and above to integrate environmental performance – their achievement of environmental targets – into the appraisal and assessment of EPBs, heads of EPBs at the same level of government, lower-level people's governments and heads of the governments.[45] Through the target responsibility system, the environmental goals and policies formulated by central government are transformed into actions at local levels from provincial to county governments. The subordinate government commits in writing to achieving the higher-level government's environmental protection or pollution abatement targets and implementing the measures it has set. The achievement of targets and implementation of measures are important elements of the performance appraisal exercise of government officials.

The air pollution control scheme is an example of this. The State Council set national and regional targets in its Action Plan on Air Pollution Prevention and Control (Air Action Plan) (2013)[46] and makes provincial governments implement the pollution-control measures necessary to achieve the targets by signing an agreement.

Air Action Plan (2013)

The State Council set a target of a cut of at least 10 per cent in concentration levels of PM_{10} in all cities by 2017 as compared to the 2012 level. For concentration levels of $PM_{2.5}$, specific abatement targets were set for three key regions: a 25 per cent cut for Beijing–Tianjin–Hebei region, a 20 per cent cut for the Yangtze River Delta region and a 15 per cent cut for the Pearl River Delta region by 2017, compared to the 2012 levels. Beijing had to reduce its annual average $PM_{2.5}$ concentration level to 60 $\mu g/m^3$ by 2017.[47]

The State Council assigned the responsibility for achieving the air pollution abatement targets to provincial governments, which then allocated abatement tasks to local governments and enterprises for them to implement. The State Council implemented an annual appraisal mechanism to evaluate

[43] EPL (2014), art. 28(1).
[44] EPL (2014), art. 28(2). 'Key regions' are areas selected by China as the focus of its efforts to tackle air pollution.
[45] EPL (2014), art. 26. For more discussion on the cadre performance appraisal system in China, see Alex L. Wang, 'The search for sustainable legitimacy'.
[46] The State Council issued the Air Action Plan on 10 September 2013 with immediate effect.
[47] Air Action Plan (2013), preamble.

the performance of each provincial-level government, with a mid-term assessment in 2015 and a final evaluation in 2017. The assessment and evaluation results were made available to the general public and were used as the basis for a performance appraisal of the individuals in charge.[48]

The MEP, on behalf of the State Council, signed an Air Pollution Abatement Target Responsibility Agreement with each of thirty-one provinces, municipalities directly under the central government and autonomous regions, which stated that they would implement the Air Action Plan (2013) and achieve the national abatement targets set by the State Council[49]

Agreement on Air Pollution Abatement Targets and Responsibilities (2014)

The specific abatement targets for provincial governments to achieve by 2017 as compared to the baseline year of 2012 are:

Air pollution abatement targets for 2017 as compared to 2012		Regulated province, autonomous region or municipality directly under central government
Annual average concentration level of $PM_{2.5}$	−25%	Beijing, Tianjin and Hebei
	−20%	Shanxi, Shandong, Shanghai, Jiangsu and Zhejiang
	−15%	Guangdong and Chongqing
	−10%	Inner Mongolia
Annual average concentration level of PM_{10}	−15%	Henan, Shaanxi, Qinghai and Xinjiang
	−12%	Gansu and Hubei
	−10%	Sichuan, Liaoning, Jilin, Hunan, Anhui and Ningxia
	−5%	Guangxi, Fujian, Jiangxi, Guizhou and Heilongjiang
	Continuous improvement	Hainan, Tibet and Yunnan

These abatement targets became binding contractual terms. Local governments were required to map out detailed plans to reduce coal consumption, eliminate outdated industrial capacity, control emissions from boilers, vehicles and construction sites, among others, and set specific goals for each year from 2014 to 2017.

3.2.3 Supervision and Accountability

Many serious pollution incidents, such as the Yancheng toxic pollution case (2008) and the Zijin water pollution case (2010), have caused grave environmental harm and heavy loss of

[48] Air Action Plan (2013), s. 27.

[49] MEP, 'MEP signs target responsibility agreement on air pollution control with 31 provinces', (press release) 7 January 2014; see also Zhang Qiulei, 'MEP signed agreement on air pollution prevention and control targets and responsibilities with 31 provincial-level governments', *China Environment News*, 8 January 2014, 1.

public and private property. They have also exposed corruption and dereliction of duty. Lack of transparency and supervision by the public aggravates the problem of corruption that can arise in connection with granting approvals, issuing permits, monitoring performance and collecting fees and fines.[50] In response to this issue, the EPL (2014) strengthens both internal and external supervision.

Internally within the administrative system, higher-level governments and EPBs should strengthen their supervision of the environmental protection work of lower-level governments and EPBs. Where any member of staff is found to be in violation of the law and is to be sanctioned, the supervisory body, a higher-level agency, recommends accordingly to the human resources or disciplinary authorities.[51] External supervision comes from multiple sources, including people's congresses, the media and the public. Under the Constitution, a people's congress and its standing committee supervise the work of the government at the same level.[52] To strengthen the role of a people's congress in the environmental field, the EPL (2014) specifically requires governments at county level and above to report annually to the same-level people's congress or its standing committee on environmental quality and progress towards the achievement of environmental protection targets. Where a severe pollution incident has occurred, the government is required to report this to the standing committee of the same-level people's congress and accept its supervision.[53] The EPL (2014) further guarantees external supervision by the public, stating that any citizen, legal person or other organization has the right to report to a higher-level supervisory body or disciplinary inspection authority any failure by local government or local EPB to perform their statutory duties.[54] In addition, media report can be a strong, quick and efficient way of attracting public attention and placing intense societal pressure on parties in violation. The EPL (2014) recognizes the important role of the media in environmental education and supervision of environmental violations.[55]

Turning to accountability, in addition to the existing administrative disciplinary sanctions[56] imposed on persons directly in charge and others directly liable, the EPL (2014) introduced a new form of accountability that applies when the violation of environmental rules by government personnel causes grave consequences. The law states that the key persons in charge at the relevant local government, EPB or other departments playing an environmental supervisory role must take the blame and resign.[57]

3.3 MAJOR ENVIRONMENTAL LEGAL PRINCIPLES

By the late 1970s, Chinese environmental law had adopted many important environmental legal principles, such as the preventative principle, which focuses on preventing harm before it occurs, and the polluter-pays principle, and had also created its own principle of coordinated development.[58] The EPL (2014) newly incorporates the most important

[50] Wang Canfa, 'Rewrite environmental legal principles', at 25. [51] EPL (2014), art. 67(1).
[52] Constitution (1982, latest amendment 2018), art. 3(3). [53] EPL (2014), art. 27.
[54] EPL (2014), art. 57(2). [55] EPL (2014), art. 9.
[56] 'Administrative disciplinary sanctions' are provided by article 56 of the Law on Civil Servants (2005). They include: warning, record of demerit, record of serious demerit, demotion, removal from post and dismissal.
[57] EPL (2014), art. 68. [58] EPL (for trial implementation) (1979), arts. 2, 5 and 6.

principle – sustainable development – and reinterprets the principles of coordinated development and public participation.[59]

3.3.1 From Coordinated Development to Sustainable Development

The principle of coordinated development has long been accepted as one of the fundamental principles in Chinese environmental law. The EPL (for trial implementation) (1979) required the State Council and its departments and local governments to coordinate environmental protection and improvement with the economic plans they made.[60] The EPL (1989) requires the integration of state environmental protection plans into socio-economic development plans. It also requires 'the State to adopt economic and technology policies and measures favourable to environmental protection so as to coordinate the work of environmental protection with economic construction and social development'.[61] The EPL (2014) places more emphasis on environmental protection and conservation of resources. It provides that '[t]he State shall adopt economic and technology policies and measures favourable for conservation of resources, protection and improvement of the environment, and harmonious interaction between man and nature so as to coordinate socio-economic development with environmental protection'.[62]

Coordinating environment and development is an immensely difficult task in practice and, unfortunately, for more than three decades, China's approach was to sacrifice the environment to economic growth. To reverse this, the EPL (2014) expressly requires 'protection first' or 'giving priority to protection',[63] and the principle of sustainable development is incorporated into its first article.[64] Sustainable development was first defined by the World Commission on Environment and Development as 'development that meets the needs of the present without compromising the ability of future generations to meet their own needs'.[65] It was incorporated into the Rio Declaration on Environment and Development (1992)[66] and has become an important environmental legal principle. China adopted the principle of sustainable development in its White Paper, *China's Agenda 21* (1994).[67]

59 For further discussion on environmental principles in China, see Yuhong Zhao, 'Environmental principles in China' in Ludwig Kramer and Emanuela Orlando (eds.), *Principles of Environmental Law* (Cheltenham: Edward Elgar, 2018), 424–36.

60 EPL (for trial implementation) (1979), art. 5.

61 EPL (1989), art. 4.

62 EPL (2014), art. 4(2).

63 EPL (2014), art. 5.

64 EPL (2014), art. 1. The Law was enacted for the purposes of protecting and improving the environment, preventing pollution and other hazards, protecting public health, building an ecological civilization and promoting sustainable socio-economic development.

65 World Commission on Environment and Development (Brundtland Commission), *Our Common Future* (Oxford University Press, 1987).

66 Rio Declaration on Environment and Development, Rio de Janeiro, 14 June 1992, *International Legal Materials*, 31 (1992), 874–80. Principle 1. provides that '[h]uman beings are at the centre of concerns for sustainable development. They are entitled to a healthy and productive life in harmony with nature'. Principle 3 further interprets 'sustainable development' by emphasizing that '[t]he right to development must be fulfilled so as to equitably meet developmental and environmental needs of present and future generations'.

67 *China's Agenda 21* was passed by the State Council on 25 March 1994 and published on 4 July 1994. It serves as a guide for the long-term planning of China's socio-economic development.

China's Agenda 21: White Paper on China's Population, Environment, and Development in the 21st Century

The State Council issued *China's Agenda 21* to fulfil its duty under the Rio Declaration on Environment and Development. *China's Agenda 21* serves as important guidance for making mid- and long-term socio-economic development plans. It covers four major areas: a general strategy for sustainable development, sustainable social development, sustainable economic development, and rational exploitation of natural resources to protect the environment.

China's Agenda 21 sets short-, mid- and long-term development goals. The short-term goals (1994–2000) dealt with the conflict inherent between development and environment, required the implementation of an emergency response mechanism and sought to prevent environmental quality from further deterioration. The mid-term goals (2000–10) focused on changing development and consumption models, undertaking sustainable development initiatives and improving the regulations governing economic and industrial policies, technology and the behaviour of the public. The long-term goals (beyond 2010) emphasize the need to control the scale and growth of China's economy and restore social and ecological systems in order to make socio-economic development sustainable, and to explore an efficient, balanced and sustainable road to modernity.

Conceptually, there is a gap between coordinated development and sustainable development. While both deal with the relationship between environment and development, sustainable development focuses more on long-term development, taking into account the needs and interests of future generations. The sustainable development principle is concerned with 'inter-generation equity'[68] and bringing about justice between our generation and future generations. It 'assumes that each generation receives a natural and cultural legacy in trust from previous generations and holds it in trust for future generations. This imposes obligations upon each generation to conserve the quality and diversity of the natural and cultural resource base for future generations and gives it certain rights to use the legacy.'[69] Inter-generation equity extends to the intra-generational context with an underlying objective of fairness in the manner of development that applies between different sectors of the current generation and between current and future generations.[70] In contrast, the concept of inter-generation equity is absent from the coordinated

[68] Inter-generation equity was addressed by the international community as early as the 1970s. The Declaration of the UN Conference on the Human Environment (1972) provides that '[t]o defend and improve the human environment for present and future generations has become an imperative goal for mankind – a goal to be pursued together with ... goals of peace and of wo rldwide economic and social development'. Principle 1 states that '[m]an ... bears a solemn responsibility to protect and improve the environment for present and future generations'. Principle 2 states '[t]he natural resources of the earth... must be safeguarded for the benefit of present and future generations through careful planning or management, as appropriate'. See Declaration of the UN Conference on the Human Environment, Stockholm, 16 June 1972. *International Legal Materials*, 11 (1972), 1416–69.

[69] Edith Brown Weiss, 'Intergenerational equity in international law', *American Society of International Law Proceedings*, 81 (1987), 126–32, at 127.

[70] Brown Weiss, 'Intergenerational equity', at 129. Brown Weiss states, '[h]ow can we expect an impoverished community to care about future generations, if it cannot even care for its own people today? In this context, principles of intergenerational equity call for wealthier countries to contribute to the costs incurred by poor countries in protecting these resources for future generations and to help them gain access to the economic

development principle, which focuses solely on the needs of the present generation for a better life through development.

3.3.2 Preventative Principle

The preventative principle promotes the prevention of environmental harm as a much-preferred alternative to remediation, because many environmental harms are irreversible and the cost of remediation and treatment tends to be higher than prevention. Evidence suggests that end-of-pipe control and treatment have failed to prevent pollution – they often transform rather than eliminate it. For example, air pollution control devices that remove sulphur and dust also generate solid waste, while wastewater treatment produces sludge. The preventative principle requires action to be taken at the source of pollution and, as far as possible, before damage is done.[71] It imposes duties on states, enterprises and individuals to take measures to avoid causing harm to the environment, and to reduce, limit and control activities that may cause or increase the risk of pollution.

The EPL (2014) provides that environmental protection must focus on prevention of pollution and comprehensively control and treat it.[72] All parties, including governments, enterprises, institutions and individuals are under a legal duty to protect the environment.[73] The governments have a crucially important role to play in regulating corporate behaviour by setting standards, monitoring performance and punishing violations in order to ensure compliance and protect environmental quality. Enterprises and institutions bear the major responsibilities to take measures to prevent and control pollution, but the lifestyles and personal choices of individuals can make a huge difference in environmental protection, as people consume energy and resources and generate waste on a daily basis. A conservation-oriented low-carbon lifestyle should be widely promoted to rein in excessive and carbon-intensive consumption.

The preventative principle is implemented through a number of mechanisms. An EIA is conducted before project construction starts or before government plans are implemented, in order to predict, analyse, prevent and mitigate potential environmental harm. The three-simultaneities requirement demands that the design, construction and operation of pollution-control facilities take place at the same time as the main project. Effective risk control and emergency response are ways of minimizing harm to people and environment: both managing risk and responding in a timely and effective manner to environmental emergencies are crucial. Prevention of pollution at source and clean production are promoted to address the limits and failures of end-of-pipe control.

3.3.3 Polluter-Pays Principle

The polluter-pays principle requires that the producer of goods should be responsible for the costs of prevention and treatment of pollution caused by the production process. This includes both costs incurred in avoiding pollution and remedial costs for damage done to

benefits from the planetary legacy. Otherwise they will be unable and unwilling to conserve resources for future generations.'

71 Philippe Sands et al. *Principles of International Environmental Law*, 4th ed. (Cambridge University Press, 2018), at 211–13.

72 EPL (2014), art. 5. 73 EPL (2014), art. 6.

the environment, people or property. It is derived from a policy recommendation of the Organization for Economic Cooperation and Development (OECD).[74]

OECD, Guiding Principles Concerning International Economic Aspects of Environmental Policies (1972)[75]

The polluter-pays principle is to be used to allocate costs of measures to prevent and control pollution, in order to encourage rational use of scarce resources and avoid distortions in international trade and investment. The principle means that the polluter bears the expense of carrying out pollution prevention and control measures decided on by public authorities to ensure that the environment is in an acceptable state. The cost of these measures will then be reflected in the cost of the goods and services that have caused the pollution in their production and/or consumption. Such measures should not be accompanied by subsidies that would create significant distortions in international trade and investment.

The EPL (2014) adopted the polluter-pays principle as a general principle and states that polluters must pay for the cost of prevention and remediation. Any enterprise, institution or other production operator that emits or discharges pollutants must take measures to prevent pollution or environmental harm caused by air pollutants, wastewater, solid waste, medical waste, dust, odour, radioactive substances, noise, vibration, light and magnetic radiation.[76] Enterprises and institutions are required to establish an 'environmental responsibility system' to designate clearly the persons in charge of pollution control and specify their responsibilities.[77] Until the environmental taxes were introduced, pollution discharge fees were collected by EPBs and earmarked for use in pollution prevention, control and treatment.[78] Whoever causes environmental harm bears liability.[79] Where harm is caused by ecological destruction, such as illegal mining or logging, or pollution, the liable party bears tort liability in accordance with the Tort Law (TL).[80] Polluters thus bear the cost of both preventative controls and remediation under the liability regimes.

3.3.4 Principle of Public Participation

The EPL (2014) not only recognizes public participation as one of the general principles of environmental protection,[81] but also provides for specific channels and mechanisms to facilitate public participation.[82] It expressly guarantees the right of access to environmental

[74] OECD, 'Recommendation on guiding principles concerning international economic aspects of environmental policies (1972)', *International Legal Materials*, 14 (1975), 236–38; OECD, 'Recommendation on the implementation of the polluter-pays principle', *International Legal Materials*, 14 (1975), 234–41.
[75] OECD, 'Recommendation on guiding principles', 237, para.4. [76] EPL (2014), art. 42(1).
[77] EPL (2014), art. 42(2). [78] EPL (2014), art. 43(1). [79] EPL (2014), art. 5.
[80] EPL (2014), art. 64. Article 15 of the TL (2009) provides for remedies such as cessation of infringement, elimination of danger, restoration of original condition and compensation for loss. In chapter VIII, it sets out special rules applicable to environmental tort.
[81] EPL (2014), art. 5. [82] EPL (2014), chapter V.

information and the right of participation and supervision by any citizen, legal person or other organization.[83] Environmental protection authorities from central to local levels are under a legal duty to disclose information and improve participatory procedures in order to facilitate public participation and supervision.[84]

So far, public participation in decision-making is mainly found in the EIA process regulated by the EIAL (2002).[85] A major breakthrough of the EPL (2014) was that it permits public access to the full text of EIA reports. Previously, under the EIAL (2002) only a summary of the EIA report had to be disclosed. The EIA approval authority is now required to disclose the full-text EIA report upon receiving it from the project proponent, except for any sections involving state or commercial secrets.[86] A project proponent preparing an EIA report[87] is required to explain the project to potentially affected parties and conduct public consultations as it prepares the report. If it fails to conduct adequate public consultation, the EIA approval authority will order it to redo this.[88]

Supervision by the general public is of crucial importance in deterring environmental violations and government inaction. The EPBs have limited staff and resources with which to conduct inspections and monitor polluting sources but, if they ally themselves with the public, whose health and well-being are directly affected by pollution, enterprises and other operators will be subject to surveillance from multiple directions at all times. The EPL (2014) provides two channels for the general public to exercise its right of supervision: one is an administrative means known as 'public report', essentially a complaint or tip-off, and the second is PIL, which was introduced by the CPL (2012) and EPL (2014), following pilot schemes in 2007. Under the system of public report, any citizen, legal person or any other organization, upon detecting environmental pollution or destruction by any unit or individual, has the right to report it to the environmental protection authorities.[89] Where they detect a failure by local government or an EPB to perform statutory duties, they have the right to report this to government authorities at a higher level or to the disciplinary authorities.[90] This public report mechanism should offer both adequate protection to whistle-blowers and timely follow-up investigation and sanction of violations.[91] It has never been easy for individuals to monitor and report environmental violations for the public good and some have paid with their personal liberty in the fight against pollution.

83 EPL (2014), art. 53(1). 84 EPL (2014), art. 53(2).

85 The EIAL was passed on 28 October 2002 by the 9th NPCSC at its 30th session. It came into force on 1 September 2003. The EIAL was amended in 2016 and 2018; see also Yuhong Zhao, 'Public participation in China's EIA regime'.

86 EPL (2014), art. 56(2).

87 Not all construction projects are required to prepare the most comprehensive and thorough EIA. Depending on the potential environmental impacts of a proposed project, a proponent may be required to prepare an EIA report, statement or simply fill out an EIA registration form. See EIAL (2002), art. 16.

88 EPL (2014), art. 56. 89 EPL (2014), art. 57(1). 90 EPL (2014), art. 57(2).

91 For further discussion on public report or complaint, see Tseming Yang and Xuehua Zhang, 'Public participation in environmental enforcement . . . with Chinese characteristics?: A comparative assessment of China's environmental complaint mechanism', *The Georgetown International Environmental Law Review*, 24 (2012), 325–66.

The Case of Wu Lihong and Lake Tai

In May 2007, a severe algae outbreak in Lake Tai (Lake Taihu) caused the suspension of the drinking water supply for half of the 2.3 million population of the city of Wuxi, Jiangsu province for more than a week. The environmental disaster resulted from excessively high levels of nitrogen and phosphorus in the lake, which came from the discharge of industrial wastewater,[92] urban sewage[93] and agricultural run-off.[94] Consequently, the quality of the water in Lake Tai fell to sub-grade V, Grade V being the lowest level as defined by the Surface Water Quality Standards, meaning that it had become unsuitable for any use.[95]

Wu Lihong, a local resident who had grown up by Lake Tai, had become an environmental activist fighting pollution at the lake since the 1990s. He took photos, collected samples and filed complaints with the environmental authorities at provincial and national levels. Since the 1990s, more than 200 polluting factories around Lake Tai had been closed down, partly due to his efforts. In 2005, he was named one of China's top ten environmentalists, having been selected by a panel of judges from the NPC and Chinese People's Political Consultative Conference (CPPCC). But this victory had come with sacrifices for the Wu family. Wu was frequently beaten by local thugs, both before and after the award, and both Wu and his wife had lost their jobs as they were seen as troublemakers by the employers. In April 2007, Wu was arrested by the local police, and in June he was prosecuted by the Yixing city procuratorate, having been charged with the criminal offences of blackmail and fraud. In August he was convicted of both offences and sentenced to three years' imprisonment for crimes he claimed he had never committed, but that had been set up by a polluting enterprise.[96]

The second form of supervision by the public is PIL.[97] The EPL (2014) provides the tool of environmental civil PIL for use against anyone who has caused environmental pollution or ecological destruction and injured the public interest.[98] It is not as widely available as the public report mechanism, because it may only be initiated by social organizations legally registered with municipal civil affairs authorities and that have specialized in environmental protection for a minimum of five consecutive years without any record of violation.[99] To facilitate the development of environmental PIL and guide the work of

[92] Thousands of industrial enterprises manufacturing chemical, steel, cement and electroplated products discharged wastewater into Lake Tai.

[93] Urban sewage was the main source of phosphorous content in Lake Tai.

[94] Agricultural runoff from farmland highly contaminated with fertilizer and pesticides contributed to nitrogen in Lake Tai.

[95] For more on the algae outbreak, see the *New York Times*, 'Choking on growth, part III', n.d. www.nytimes.com/interactive/2007/10/14/world/asia/choking_on_growth_3.html#story4.

[96] For more on Wu Lihong, see *New York Times*, 'Choking on growth, part III'.

[97] For more on PIL, see Daniel Carpenter-Gold, 'Castles made of sand: public-interest litigation and China's new Environmental Protection Law', *Harvard Environmental Law Review*, 39:1 (2015), 241–74; Sophie Zander, 'How effective a weapon is the new EPL in China's "war against pollution"?: The past triumphs and future challenges of environmental public interest litigation', *NYU Journal of International Law and Politics*, 50 (2018), 605–36; Tiantian Zhai and Yen-Chiang Chang, 'Standing of environmental public-interest litigants in China: evolution, obstacles and solutions', *Journal of Environmental Law*, 30 (2018), 369–97; Juan Chu, 'Vindicating public environmental interest: defining the role of environmental public interest litigation in China', *Ecology Law Quarterly*, 45 (2018), 485–532.

[98] EPL (2014), art. 58.

[99] EPL (2014), art. 58.

local courts, the Supreme People's Court (SPC) issued the Interpretation on Several Issues Regarding the Application of Law in Environmental Civil Public Interest Litigation (2015).[100]

In practice, however, the biggest obstacle to meaningful public participation and supervision has been lack of accurate, consistent and up-to-date information on environmental quality, the sources of emissions and discharges, and environmental emergency incidents, as well as lack of access to EIA documents, among others. This information is held by either the polluters or regulators, and the public does not have the resources, technology or physical access to monitor or collect it.[101] To enable the public to access environmental information, the EPL (2014) imposes legal duties on both polluters and regulators to monitor, collect, record and disclose accurate and reliable environmental information. Key polluting sources are required to collect data[102] and disclose information on major pollutants, means and volume of discharge and concentration levels, among others, in order to facilitate supervision by the general public.[103] Environmental authorities acquire data from their own monitoring networks and the polluters in the exercise of their regulatory or enforcement powers, and must publicize and disclose information. To facilitate supervision by the public, the MEP publishes information on national environmental quality, the monitoring data from key polluting sources and other significant environmental information. Provincial EPBs are required to publish gazettes on the state of the environment on a regular basis.[104] All EPBs at county level and above are required to disclose information on environmental quality, environmental monitoring, environmental emergency incidents, environmental permits, administrative penalty decisions and, before they were abolished, the collection and use of pollution discharge fees, among others.[105] Further, they must record in a publicly available social-credibility register any environmental violations by enterprises, institutions or other production operators and publicize the names of those in violation in a timely manner.[106]

3.4 MAJOR REGULATORY CONTROL MECHANISMS

This section examines major regulatory control mechanisms adopted by the EPL (2014) to implement environmental principles. They include EIA, which is designed to prevent or reduce potential environmental harm, the mechanism of imposing a cap and quota on total emissions and discharge of key pollutants (known as total pollution control) as a way of achieving long-term sustainable development, pollution control by permit (certain polluters must obtain permits before they may emit or discharge) to strengthen regulation and

[100] The SPC issued the Interpretation on Several Issues Regarding the Application of Law in Environmental Civil Public Interest Litigation on 6 January 2015. It came into force on 7 January 2015.

[101] For more on access to environmental information, see Kun Fang et al., 'Protecting the public's environmental right to know: developments and challenges in China's legislative system for EEID, 2007–2015', *Journal of Environmental Law*, 29 (2017), 285–315; Wu Changhua, 'Improving the legal and policy foundation for public access to environmental information in China', *Temple Journal of Science Technology and Environmental Law*, 24 (2005), 291–323; Alex L. Wang, 'Explaining environmental information disclosure in China', *Ecology Law Quarterly*, 44 (2018), 865–923.

[102] EPL (2014), art. 42(3). [103] EPL (2014), art. 55. [104] EPL (2014), art. 54(1).

[105] EPL (2014), art. 54(2). [106] EPL (2014), art. 54(3).

monitoring of individual sources, and environmental emergency response to contain pollution in a timely manner and mitigate environmental harm.

3.4.1 EIA

The EIA is an important mechanism that has been used to prevent and mitigate environmental harm since the EPL (for trial implementation) (1979).[107] The EPL (1989) further provides that '[t]he environmental impact statement on a construction project shall assess the pollution likely to be produced by the project and its impact on the environment and stipulate the preventative and remedial measures; the statement shall, after initial examination by the authorities in charge of the construction project, be submitted to the environmental authority for approval. The planning department is not permitted to endorse the construction project until after the environmental impact statement of the project is approved.'[108] The EIAL (2002) extended the application of EIA from construction projects to government development plans.[109] The EPL (2014) followed suit and offered a wider application of EIA, expanding from only covering construction projects to also development plans[110] and even the making of economic and technology policies by the departments of the State Council and provincial people's governments. That is, they must take into account the environmental impacts of the policies and consult stakeholders and experts.[111]

An EIA approval is an express precondition for implementation of development plans or construction of projects.[112] Any party in violation of the EIA requirements will be ordered to stop construction and pay a fine, and may also have to restore the site.[113] Moreover, the EIA requirement has been effectively aligned with other environmental mechanisms, such as total pollution control and the environmental target responsibility system. Consequently, provincial EPBs in administrative regions that fail to achieve the total emission quota or the environmental quality targets must suspend examination and approval of the EIA documents of proposed projects that will generate additional emissions of key pollutants.[114] To prevent the EIA process from becoming a rubber-stamp exercise and to ensure its quality, the EPL (2014) tightened control over EIA institutions by holding them accountable for the quality of the EIA documents. If any EIA institution falsifies data in the course of its work for the project proponent, causing pollution or ecological destruction, it will be held jointly liable for the environmental harm caused and for any administrative penalty and/or criminal sanction.[115]

3.4.2 Total Pollution Control

The EPL (1989) made no provision for total pollution control, instead focusing solely on the concentration levels of pollutants in the emission or discharge from sources. It was not until 1996 that the concept of 'total discharge control of key water pollutants' was introduced. The WPPCL (1996) provided that provincial governments may impose 'total discharge

[107] EPL (for trial implementation 1979), art. 6. [108] EPL (1989), art. 13(2).

[109] EIAL (2002), chapter II. For more discussion on EIA, see Yuhong Zhao, 'Assessing the environmental impact of projects'; Jing Wu et al., 'Strategic environmental assessment implementation in China: five-year review and prospects', *Environmental Impact Assessment Review*, 31 (2011), 77–84.

[110] EPL (2014), art. 19. [111] EPL (2014), art. 14. [112] EPL (2014), art. 19(2). [113] EPL (2014), art. 61.

[114] EPL (2014), art. 44(2). [115] EPL (2014), art. 65.

control' and verify the discharge abatement duties for key polluting sources if water quality is below standard, even if the effluent discharge itself complies with relevant standards.[116] Total discharge control was applied to the whole nation under the WPPCL (2008), which provides that the state implements total discharge control of key water pollutants. Provincial governments should, according to State Council provisions, abate and control the total discharge of key water pollutants within their jurisdictions and assign the abatement duties to municipal and county governments, which must allocate total discharge quotas to individual polluting sources.[117] The WPPCL (2017) further strengthens the implementation of total discharge control by aligning it with 'supervision talks' and 'suspension of EIA approval', two soft penalties used if a province fails to meet the total control target set by the central government.[118]

Total emission control of air pollution was first introduced by the APPCL (2000), but it only applied in certain circumstances. The State Council or provincial governments may designate the following as 'areas for total emission control of key air pollutants': regions not achieving the national or local air quality standards, and control zones for acid rain or sulphur dioxide (SO_2) pollution. Local governments in areas under total emission control must verify the current total emissions of enterprises and institutions, allocate total emissions quotas of key air pollutants to each and grant emissions permits. The enterprises and institutions subject to permit control must comply with the terms and conditions of the permits.[119] The APPCL (2015) extended total emission control of key air pollutants to the whole nation.[120]

Total pollution control does not apply to all pollutants, but only to key water pollutants and key air pollutants. Both the WPPCL and APPCL leave it to the State Council to designate key pollutants and set the total control targets, which are found in the five-year plans (FYPs). The first designation occurred in the 11th FYP (2006–10), which named only SO_2 and chemical oxygen demand (COD) as key pollutants and set a binding target of a 10 per cent cut in total emissions of SO_2 and total discharge of COD by 2010, compared to 2005.[121] The 12th FYP (2011–15) added nitrogen oxide (NOx) and ammonia nitrogen (NH) as key pollutants, setting 2015 abatement targets of 8 per cent for SO_2 and COD, and 10 per cent for NOx and NH, compared to 2010.[122] The 13th FYP (2016–20) continues to regulate the four key pollutants, but broadly demands deeper cuts: 15 per cent for SO_2 and NOx and 10 per cent for COD and NH by 2020, compared to 2015.[123]

The EPL (2014) has adopted the total pollution control mechanism. That is, the state implements total control of the four key pollutants. The State Council determines binding targets for cuts in key pollutants and allocates the abatement tasks to provincial people's governments.[124] The abatement tasks will ultimately be assigned to individual polluting sources through local governments. Thus, enterprises and institutions must not only comply with the national and local emission/discharge standards on concentration levels of

116 WPPCL (1996), art. 16. 117 WPPCL (2008), art. 18. 118 WPPCL (2017), art. 20.
119 APPCL (2000), art. 15. 120 APPCL (2015), art. 21. 121 11th FYP (2006–10), chapter 3.
122 12th FYP (2011–15), chapter 3. 123 13th FYP (2016–20), chapter 3.
124 EPL (2014), art. 44(1). In practice, this is carried out by the MEP on behalf of the State Council. An agreement is signed with each provincial government, setting clear total control targets, key abatement tasks and measures to be taken.

pollutants, but must also achieve the total emission/discharge quota for key pollutants.[125] In regions that fail to achieve the total emission/discharge control target for key pollutants or fail to achieve the environmental quality standards, provincial EPBs must suspend the review and approval of EIA documents for projects that will generate additional key pollutants.[126] This ability to suspend EIA approval puts real pressure on local governments and enterprises to clean up their existing pollution.

3.4.3 Pollution Control by Permit

The permit-control mechanism was introduced to implement the total pollution control of key air and water pollutants. While there had been local pilot schemes on pollution discharge permits in the cities of Tangshan, Shenyang, Hangzhou, Wuhan, Shenzhen and Yinchuan,[127] the implementation of the permit-control mechanism made slow progress due to a lack of operational guidance from higher to lower government and from government to applicant on the process of application for permits, issuance of permits, contents of permits, sanctions for violation of permits, and renewal, suspension and revocation of permits, among others.[128] The State Environmental Protection Administration (SEPA, predecessor of the MEP), started to draft the Regulation on Pollution Discharge Permits in 2004, and it was included in the State Council's annual lawmaking plan for 2007. The SEPA's draft Regulation was circulated among state departments and provincial EPBs for consultation, but strong objections from the regulated community delayed the lawmaking process.

It was the EPL (2014) that adopted the permit-control mechanism, requiring any enterprise, institution or other production operator that is subject to permit control to comply with the terms and conditions of the permits. It prohibits the discharge of pollutants without permit.[129] As the draft implementing regulation, the Regulation on Pollution Discharge Permits is taking time to reach consensus,[130] the General Office of the State Council issued the Implementation Plan on Permit Control of Pollution Discharge (Implementation Plan) (2016).[131] It urges state departments and provincial governments to build legal, technical and administrative infrastructure to make the permit-control mechanism a primary instrument for environmental management of stationary sources of pollution in China.[132] By 2020, all relevant stationary sources should have a pollution discharge permit.[133] To implement the permit-control mechanism, the MEP issued, in 2017, the Catalogue of Stationary Sources Subject to Pollution Discharge Permit Control (Catalogue), which lists sectors and processes subject to permit control.[134] In 2018, it issued

[125] EPL (2014), art. 44(1). [126] EPL (2014), art. 44(2).
[127] SEPA, Notice to Implement Pilot Schemes on Pollutant Discharge Permits (2 January 2004).
[128] For more discussion of China's discharge permit system, see Li Zhiping, 'The challenges of China's discharge permit system and effective solutions', *Temple Journal of Science, Technology & Environmental Law*, 24 (2005), 375; Wang Mingyuan, 'China's pollutant discharge permit system evolves behind its economic expansion', *Villanova Environmental Law Journal*, 19 (2008), 95–121.
[129] EPL (2014), art. 45.
[130] A draft was published on 5 November 2018 for public consultation until 6 December 2018, but a final version has not yet been agreed.
[131] The General Office of the State Council issued the Implementation Plan on 11 October 2016.
[132] Implementation Plan (2016), part I, s. 1. [133] Implementation Plan (2016), part I, s. 3.
[134] The MEP issued the Catalogue (2017) on 28 July 2017 with immediate effect. It was updated and relaced by the Catalogue (2019) on 20 December 2019.

the Measures on Permit Control of Pollution Discharge (for trial implementation) (Measures on Permit Control),[135] which regulates applications for and issuance of pollution discharge permits, the enforcement of permit conditions, and supervision and sanction of violations.[136] Each entity covered by the Catalogue (2017) must apply for and obtain a pollution discharge permit,[137] and operate in full compliance with the permit terms and conditions.[138] Discharging any pollutant without a permit is prohibited.[139]

The permit-control mechanism is by no means a standalone scheme – it must be closely aligned with EIAs and total pollution control to form an effective environmental management system. Under the EIA process, environmental scrutiny of a project is carried out prior to construction, and measures to prevent, control and mitigate environmental harm during construction and operation are proposed. The pollution-control measures proposed by the EIA documents and requested in the EIA approval decision are included in the permit as terms and conditions that must be implemented by the permit holder.[140] The permit mechanism is indispensable in implementing the system of total control of key pollutants. The total pollution abatement targets set by the central government are allocated to the provincial governments, but they are to be achieved at the level of the key polluting sources. A permit is the best tool with which to inform each polluting source of its pollution discharge quota, which may be adjusted according to the pollution-control needs of each region.[141] Further, the pollution discharge permit also provides the data basis for collecting environmental taxes and trading pollution discharge allowances.

The State Council is phasing in the application of the permit-control mechanism to all stationary sources of pollution. The starting point was to decide the scope of application of the mechanism, which was dealt with by the Catalogue (2017) and Catalogue (2019).[142] The Catalogue (2017) listed seventy-eight sectors and four industrial processes that were to be subject to permit control by 2020.[143] The Catalogue (2019) divides entities into three categories, based on their total discharge or emissions and environmental harm, and adopts three types of permit control: focused management, simplified management and management by registration. Any entity with operations in the third category is not required to apply for a permit, but must fill out a pollution discharge registration form on the permit-control platform.[144] Forty-one sectors and three processes are subject to 'focused management', while eight sectors are subject to 'simplified management', and the remaining twenty-nine sectors and one process may be subject to either depending on the technique and scale of production.[145] The distinction between focused management and simplified management is found in the MEP's Technical Guidance on the Application and Issuance of Pollution Discharge Permits (2018) and the MEE's Technical Guidance on the Environmental Management Record Keeping and Compliance Reports by Pollution Sources (2018). Simplified management applies to operations that generate and discharge relatively low levels

[135] The MEP issued the Measures on Permit Control on 10 January 2018 with immediate effect.
[136] Measures on Permit Control (2018), art. 2. [137] Measures on Permit Control (2018), art. 3.
[138] Measures on Permit Control (2018), art. 4(1). [139] Measures on Permit Control (2018), art. 4(2).
[140] Implementation Plan (2016), part II, s. 5. [141] Implementation Plan (2016), part II, s. 4.
[142] Implementation Plan (2016), part III, s. 6; Catalogue (2017).
[143] Catalogue (2017), table. The Catalogue (2019) expands the list to cover 107 sectors. It keeps the four processes, but slightly varies the names: boilers, industrial kilns, surface treatment and water treatment.
[144] Catalogue (2019), art. 2. [145] Catalogue (2019), table.

of pollution and cause less environmental harm. They do not bear as much responsibility as pollution sources subject to focused management. For example, simpified management does not require: information disclosure prior to issuance of permit, real-time monitoring of pollution discharge, total control of key pollutants or quarterly report of pollution.

The Catalogue (2017) provides a clear timetable for achieving the target of 'full coverage of permit control by 2020' set in the Implementation Plan (2016).[146] By the end of June 2017, papermaking enterprises and thermal power generators were to have obtained a pollution discharge permit. Thirteen sectors, including iron and steel, non-ferrous metals, coking, oil refining, chemicals, pharmaceuticals, pesticides, fertilizers, textiles and dyeing, tanneries, electroplating, glass, and food processing, were given an end-2017 deadline. The remaining sectors were given 2018, 2019 and 2020 deadlines. However, implementation is behind schedule. According to the MEE, inspections of eight provinces and cities – Beijing, Tianjin, Hebei, Shanxi, Jiangsu, Shandong, Henan and Shaanxi – that have taken place since March 2019 found that nearly 5,000 entities had failed to obtain permits by the relevant deadline.[147] After the relevant deadline, discharge without permit is prohibited and is subject to sanctions in the form of a fine of between 100,000 yuan and 1 million yuan. If the circumstances of the unlawful discharge are serious, sanctions will include an order to suspend operations or, with the approval of the relevant people's government, an order to close the operations.[148] Where an enterprise has been fined and ordered to rectify but has refused to rectify, it will receive further fines calculated on a daily basis, beginning the day after the rectification order was issued.[149]

3.4.4 Environmental Emergency Response

The unprecedented and intensive growth of heavily polluting industries in China since the 1980s has scaled up the production and use of toxic and hazardous chemical substances. Environmental risks have been increasing for decades, as have pollution incidents; this is causing grave ecological harm and economic loss, threatening public health and safety and social stability.[150] Sudden pollution incidents often cause fear, grief and anger and can lead to mass protests and social unrest across China.

The EPL (1989) provided a rudimentary response mechanism for environmental emergencies that imposed vague responsibilities on both polluters and governments. It required any unit that caused or threatened to cause a pollution incident to take prompt measures to prevent and control the pollution hazards, notify potentially affected units and residents, report the case to the EPB and departments concerned and accept their investigation and decision. Enterprises and institutions likely to cause severe pollution incidents if precautions are not taken were required to adopt measures for effective prevention.[151] The duty imposed on the government was even more ambiguous. If local residents' lives or property were endangered by severe environmental pollution, the relevant EPB at or above county

[146] Implementation Plan (2016), part III, s. 9.
[147] MEE, 7 January 2020, 'Responses to the press regarding the Catalogue (2019) and others'. Online article. www.mee.gov.cn/xxgk2018/xxgk/xxgk15/202001/t20200107_757941.html
[148] Measures on Permit Control (2018), art. 57. [149] Measures on Permit Control (2018), art. 59.
[150] The 12th FYP on Environmental Protection, part 1. It was issued by the State Council on 21 December 2011.
[151] EPL (1989), art. 31.

level was to report promptly to the local government, which was required to take effective measures to remove or alleviate the hazard.[152] When a chemical explosion contaminated the Songhua River in Northeast China, there was neither timely flow of information from polluter to victims, nor from local to central governments. In addition, no immediate measures were taken to contain and mitigate toxic pollution of the river. There was complete silence from the local EPB and a cover-up by the local governments.

The Case of Songhua River Contamination (2005)

On 13 November 2005, an explosion at a branch of PetroChina Co. in Jilin province killed six, injured dozens and forced tens of thousands of people out of their homes. The chemical plant was located 380 km up the Songhua River from Harbin, the provincial capital of Heilongjiang. The explosion discharged over 100 t of pollutants containing benzene, a carcinogen causing leukaemia, into the river. On 21 November 2005, Harbin Municipal Government announced that water supplies would be suspended for four days from 22 November for routine checks. It did not inform the public of the contamination, but rumours that a disaster had occurred – an earthquake was suggested – triggered immediate panic, and people rushed to buy up water and food. The Harbin Municipal Government had to reluctantly admit that same day that the Songhua River had been contaminated with chemicals. The water supply was in fact suspended for six days from 22 to 27 November, affecting four million residents.

This serious pollution incident was covered up from 13 to 21 November, more than a week. Party leaders in Jilin province withheld information about the spill and those in Heilongjiang failed to inform the public in a timely manner when they learnt of it. By the end of the day on 17 November, the SEPA had still received no report on the explosion and toxic spill. Local EPBs were absent from the scene, either silenced or excluded from the process. The toxic slick entered Russia and China attracted international criticism for its response to the environmental disaster. On 2 December 2005, Xie Zhenhua, the head of the SEPA, bowed to political pressure and resigned. Yu Li, head of the Jilin branch of PetroChina, was dismissed, but no other parties were sanctioned, including local officials in Jilin and Harbin.

In the aftermath of the Songhua River disaster, the State Council issued the National Environmental Emergency Response Plan (NEERP)[153] in 2006 to improve the capacity and effectiveness of responses to environmental emergencies, with reporting requirements imposed on relevant polluters and agencies to improve transparency and information flow. The NEERP mandates an initial report to be made within one hour of the occurrence of the

[152] EPL (1989), art. 32.

[153] The NEERP was issued by the State Council on 8 January 2006. Under section 1.3, environmental emergencies are divided into four categories. Grade I emergencies are 'especially serious environmental incidents' that kill 30 or more people or poison/injure 100 or more or cause direct economic losses of 10 million yuan or more, or other serious environmental harm; Grade II emergencies are 'serious environmental incidents' that kill between 10 and 29 people, or poison/injure between 50 and 99, or cause other environmental harm; Grade III emergencies are 'relatively serious environmental incidents' that kill 3–9 people, or poison/injure fewer than 50 or cause other environmental harm; and Grade IV emergencies are 'environmental incidents' that kill fewer than 3 people.

emergency.[154] A follow-up report is to be made as soon as the investigation has clarified the basic facts. Further, a report on the handling of the incident is requested immediately after the completion of the emergency response.[155] One year after the NEERP (2006), the Law on Emergency Response (2007)[156] was enacted to prevent and reduce the occurrence of emergencies, to control, mitigate and eliminate the harm caused by emergencies so as to protect the lives and safety of people and their property, and to maintain state security, public security, environmental safety and social order.[157]

The EPL (2014) requires people's governments of all levels, as well as relevant departments, enterprises and institutions to follow strictly the provisions of the Law on Emergency Response (2007) in controlling risk in environmental emergencies, preparing emergency response plans, taking emergency response measures and implementing post-emergency recovery.[158] It emphasizes the importance of environmental risk management and control to prevent the occurrence of environmental emergencies but, if an emergency occurs, the affected parties should be informed immediately and accurately in order to avoid chaos caused by panic, and prompt action must be taken to contain and mitigate harm. The EPL (2014) also requires governments at county level and above to establish an early warning mechanism that warns all parties potentially affected by pollution so that they can take timely measures. It also requires them to make relevant early warning work plans. Where a pollution spill may affect public health and environmental safety, the governments must issue an early warning to put everyone on alert and must activate emergency response measures.[159] Enterprises and institutions are required to prepare environmental emergency response plans and report these to EPBs for the record. Where an environmental emergency has occurred or may occur, liable and potentially liable enterprises and institutions must take immediate action to contain the impact of the pollution, inform potentially affected units and individuals and report to local EPBs and relevant bodies in a timely manner.[160] Upon completion of the emergency response, the government must immediately assess the environmental impact and loss caused by the emergency and make the results available to the public.[161]

To fully implement article 47 of the EPL (2014) on emergency response, the State Council revised the NEERP (2006) in 2014.[162] The NEERP (2014) redefines 'environmental emergency' to include triggers for a sudden deterioration of environmental quality that threatens public health and safety, or causes environmental harm or serious social impact. The

[154] NEERP (2006), s. 4.3.1. The reporting requirements apply to both polluters and regulatory agencies. They must report within one hour of the occurrence of the incident to the county government and the EPB at a higher level. Upon receiving the report, a local government must report within one hour to its supervisory body, while provincial governments must report to the State Council within one hour of receiving the report. Grade II serious environmental incidents must be reported to the provincial EPB within one hour of certification of the grade. Grade I especially serious environmental incidents must be reported to the SEPA immediately. Where Grade I or II environmental incidents occur, the SEPA must report to the State Council immediately.

[155] NEERP (2006), s. 4.3.2.

[156] The Law on Emergency Response was passed on 30 August 2007 by the 10th NPCSC at its 29th session. It came into force on 1 November 2007.

[157] Law on Emergency Response (2007), art. 1. [158] EPL (2014), art. 47(1). [159] EPL (2014), art. 47(2).

[160] EPL (2014), art. 47(3). [161] EPL (2014), art. 47(4).

[162] The State Council issued the revised NEERP (2014) on 29 December 2014 with immediate effect.

triggers are pollution discharge, natural disasters and production accidents.[163] Environmental emergencies continue to be divided into four categories (exceptionally grave, grave, relatively grave and average),[164] but the NEERP (2014) adjusts the threshold criteria for them.[165] It clarifies the responsibilities of central and local governments, placing the primary responsibility on the local governments.[166] Under the NEERP (2014), response measures include: (i) on-site pollution control, (ii) evacuation of affected people, (iii) medical rescue and assistance, (iv) emergency monitoring, (v) market supervision and control, (vi) information disclosure and dissemination of expert opinions to guide those affected and the general public; (vii) maintenance of social stability and (viii) international communication and assistance.[167] The NEERP (2014) also lists the government departments in charge of each of the above response measures.[168] Significant improvements were also made in the NEERP (2014) relating to post-emergency measures, which consist of three components: (i) timely assessment of damage and disclosure of the outcome; (ii) compulsory investigation of causes of an incident, in order to improve prevention of or response to an incident and (iii) making and implementing plans for financial assistance and resettlement of affected victims, restoration of the contaminated environment by the local governments and processing of insurance claims by insurance companies.[169] Then, in 2015, the MEP issued the Measures on Environmental Emergency Response[170] to guide local EPBs, enterprises and institutions in risk control, plan preparation, emergency response and post-emergency recovery.[171]

3.5 ENFORCEMENT: MONITORING, INSPECTION AND SANCTIONS

Effective regulatory pollution control depends on enforcement. The environmental bureaus bear the major responsibilities of monitoring and supervising polluters in order to ensure compliance, and imposing sanctions to punish and deter violations.

3.5.1 Monitoring

The EPL (2014) imposes a duty on the state to establish and improve the environmental monitoring network. The MEE is tasked with promulgating monitoring guidelines, building a monitoring network and monitoring stations, and establishing a monitoring databank for nationwide information sharing.[172] Key polluting sources are required to install and operate monitoring equipment in accordance with state provisions and monitoring guidelines,

[163] NEERP (2014), s. 1.3. [164] NEERP (2014), s. 1.5.

[165] NEERP (2014), annex I. For example, the direct economic loss of an 'exceptionally grave environmental emergency' was increased from 10 million yuan to 100 million yuan.

[166] NEERP (2014), s. 4.1. Provincial governments are in charge of response measures taken for exceptionally grave environmental emergencies and grave environmental emergencies. Municipal governments are in charge of response measures for relatively grave environmental emergencies, and county governments are in charge of responses to average environmental emergencies.

[167] NEERP (2014), s. 4.2. [168] NEERP (2014), annex II. [169] NEERP (2014), s. 5.

[170] The MEP issued the Measures on Environmental Emergency Response on 16 April 2015. The Measures came into force on 5 June 2015.

[171] MEP, Measures on Environmental Emergency Response (2015), art. 2. [172] EPL (2014), art. 17(1).

ensure normal operation of the monitoring equipment and keep raw monitoring data.[173] Tampering with or falsifying monitoring data is forbidden.[174]

3.5.2 On-Site Inspection

The EPL (2014) provides that EPBs or environmental inspection bodies delegated by environmental bureaus have the power to conduct on-site inspections of polluting enterprises, institutions or any other production operators. The party being inspected must tell the truth and provide data.[175] On-site inspection broadly covers inspection of sources of effluents and air pollutants, such as pipes or vents, of operation of the pollution-control facilities and environmental compliance by construction projects, among others. While conducting an on-site inspection, environmental enforcement officers have the power to collect samples, take photos, monitor and record, request company records and make photocopies, and consult and interview relevant staff and request information, among others. On-site inspections can be carried out by the environmental authorities at any time and without notice; they do not require prior permission from the entity subject to inspection.

3.5.3 Administrative Enforcement Measures: Seal-up and Seizure

Seal-up and seizure are new enforcement powers granted to EPBs to empower them to stop serious ongoing violations and prevent aggravation of environmental harm. Where environmental violation by any enterprise, institution or any other production operator is detected and has caused or may cause serious pollution, an EPB may seal up or seize the relevant equipment or facilities causing the pollution.[176] To fully implement article 25 of the EPL (2014) and guide the frontline enforcement officers in the exercise of such powers, the MEP issued the Measures on Seal-up and Seizure.[177] This clarifies the circumstances in which such enforcement measures may be used and lists the acts that count as 'environmental violations by enterprises, institutions or any other production operators that has caused or may cause serious pollution'.[178]

The EPBs *may* seal up and seize the polluting equipment or facilities in the following circumstances: (i) where there is illegal discharge, dumping or disposal of hazardous waste (HW) or other dangerous substances; (ii) where there is illegal discharge, dumping or disposal of pollutants in a Grade I Drinking-Water-Source Reserve (DWSR) or Core Nature Reserve; (iii) where there is illegal discharge or dumping of industrial sludge from chemical, pharmaceutical, petrochemical, printing and dyeing, electroplating, paper and tannery processes. If any of the above activities causes serious pollution, EPBs *must* seal up and seize the polluting equipment or facilities.[179] To prevent and deter intentional and malicious violations, EPBs *must* take the enforcement measures of seal-up and seizure in the following circumstances regardless of any actual pollution or harm: (i) where there is illegal discharge of pollutants by hidden pipes, seepage wells or pits and perfusion to evade regulatory supervision, where there

[173] EPL (2014), art. 42(3). [174] EPL (2014), art. 42(4). [175] EPL (2014), art. 24. [176] EPL (2014), art. 25.

[177] The MEP issued the Measures on Seal-up and Seizure on 19 December 2014. The Measures came into force on 1 January 2015.

[178] MEP, Measures on Seal-up and Seizure (2014), art. 4.

[179] MEP, Measures on Seal-up and Seizure (2014), art. 4.

is alteration or falsification of monitoring data, or where there is abnormal operation of pollution-control facilities; (ii) where there is continuing discharge in violation of law and in disregard of an administrative order to suspend production and stop discharge after an environmental emergency of a relatively grave nature, or worse.[180]

Enforcement Cases under the EPL (2014)

Guangzhou EPB[181]
On 4 January 2015, Guangzhou EPB carried out an on-site inspection without prior notice at two seriously polluting enterprises. One was a waste mineral-oil processing factory that was operating without an HW operating licence. Its collection, storage and disposal of HW had caused serious pollution. The EPB officers sealed up the operation facilities. The second enterprise was a workshop making watch cases. It was operating without the relevant environmental approvals and the emissions contained heavy metals. The EPB officers sealed up its electroplating production lines and the electricity supply cabinet.

Zhangjiagang EPB[182]
On 21 January 2015, the Zhangjiagang EPB conducted an on-site inspection at Jiangsu Zhongding Chemical Co. following a public complaint. It was found that the company had set up hidden pipes to discharge wastewater secretly. Based on its own investigation, the Zhangjiagang EPB decided to seal up the production equipment of the company – including its electricity supply cabinet, boiler and pipes – for the period from 27 January to 15 February 2015. In addition, the EPB imposed administrative penalties.

3.5.4 Sanction: Administrative Penalties and Criminal Liability

Despite having adopted the polluter-pays principle, Chinese environmental law has long failed to fully internalize the cost of externalities. Prior to the EPL (2014), legislative provisions typically capped fines at 200,000 yuan, meaning that the cost of violation was much lower than the cost of pollution prevention and control. Consequently, many polluters opted for the most cost-effective model of running their business and let society bear the cost of their pollution. In response to this irrational state of affairs, the EPL (2014) introduced three new administrative sanctions that may be used in conjunction with one another to punish environmental wrongdoing and deter violation: (i) fines imposed on a daily basis; (ii) order to restrict or suspend production and (iii) transfer of the case to a public security bureau (PSB), if administrative detention of individuals in charge, or directly liable, is a possibility.

Fines Imposed on Daily Basis

Fines must be set at the right level in order to deter violations. The EPL (2014) states that the amount of the fine will take into account the cost of installing and operating

[180] MEP, Measures on Seal-up and Seizure (2014), art. 4.
[181] 'Enforcement cases under the new Environmental Protection Law', *China Environment News*, 3 March 2015, 3, case no. 3.
[182] 'Enforcement cases', *China Environment News*, 3, case no. 4

pollution-control facilities, the direct losses caused by the violation and the illegal gains from the violation.[183] It introduced a new form of uncapped fine calculated on a daily basis, aiming to deter continuing offence and induce polluting sources to take immediate action to stop their violation. It applies in situations in which an enterprise, institution or any other production operator has already been fined for illegal emission or discharge of pollutants and has been ordered to rectify, but refuses to do so. In this situation, an EPB will impose fines calculated on a daily basis.[184] To ensure this is implemented effectively and consistently, the MEP issued the Measures on Fines Calculated on Daily Basis[185] to guide local EPBs on when to impose this fine, the legal procedure to follow and how to calculate the amount. A fine calculated on a daily basis may be imposed on a polluter only if they have already received a fine for one of the following acts and have been ordered to rectify but refuse to do so:

(i) emission or discharge of pollutants at a level exceeding national or local standards or its total control quota;
(ii) emission or discharge of pollutants that evades regulatory supervision through hidden pipes, penetration wells or pits, perfusion, alteration or falsification of monitoring data or abnormal operation of pollution-control facilities;
(iii) emission or discharge of pollutants prohibited by laws and regulations;
(iv) illegal dumping of HW and
(v) any other illegal emission or discharge.[186]

When an EPB makes its initial administrative penalty decision, including a fine, to punish environmental violation, it also issues an administrative order on rectification and requests that the polluter immediately stop the illegal acts.[187] The EPB then conducts a follow-up inspection within thirty days of the delivery of the administrative order on rectification.[188] If, upon follow-up inspection, the polluter is found to be continuing the illegal acts without rectification or it rejects or obstructs the follow-up inspection, the EPB may then impose a fine calculated on a daily basis.[189] Such fines are calculated starting from the day after the delivery of the administrative order on rectification to the date of the follow-up inspection,[190] and the daily sum is equal to the initial fine.[191] If the violation continues after the follow-up inspection, the fine continues to mount up.

Enforcement Cases under the EPL (2014)

Shandong Linyi EPB [192]

On 9 January 2015, the Shandong Linyi EPB delivered an administrative order for rectification to Hualong Thermal Power Plant on finding that its emissions of SO_2 exceeded the relevant standards.

[183] EPL (2014), art. 59(2). [184] EPL (2014), art. 59(1).
[185] The MEP issued the Measures on Fines Calculated on Daily Basis on 19 December 2014. The Measures came into force on 1 January 2015.
[186] MEP, Measures on Fines Calculated on Daily Basis (2014), art. 5.
[187] MEP, Measures on Fines Calculated on Daily Basis (2014), arts. 8 and 9.
[188] MEP, Measures on Fines Calculated on Daily Basis (2014), art. 10.
[189] MEP, Measures on Fines Calculated on Daily Basis (2014), arts. 12 and 13.
[190] EPL (2014), art. 59(1); MEP, Measures on Fines Calculated on Daily Basis (2014), art. 17.
[191] EPL (2014), art. 59(1); MEP, Measures on Fines Calculated on Daily Basis (2014), art. 19.
[192] 'Enforcement cases', *China Environment News*, 3, case no. 1.

It imposed a fine of 100,000 yuan and requested the company take measures to rectify immediately. Shandong Linyi EPB conducted the follow-up inspection on 19 January and found that the SO_2 emissions still violated the relevant standards. It imposed a further fine which was calculated on a daily basis at a rate of 100,000 yuan per day for the ten days from 10 January to 19 January 2015. The total fine amounted to 1 million yuan.

Order to Restrict or Suspend Production

The EPL (2014) replaces the EPB's power to demand rectification by a specified deadline with the power to restrict or suspend production. For polluters in violation of emission or discharge standards or the total control quota, an EPB may place restrictions on production or suspend it. In the case of a serious violation, the EPB may close the business completely, subject to government approval.[193] Previously, EPBs had no power to force polluters to stop illegal discharge immediately. The commonly used power of the EPB to order rectification by a specified deadline had inherent flaws, as polluters tended to ignore the order. Even if EPBs imposed an administrative penalty when rectification had not been completed by the deadline, the pollution had already continued for a prolonged period of time. To fully implement the new sanction on restriction or suspension of production, the MEP issued the Measures on Restriction and Suspension of Production for Treatment.[194] It clarifies the application of 'restriction of production', 'suspension of production' and 'closure' in different scenarios.

Production can be restricted at any entity in violation of emissions or discharge standards or its total control quota.[195] Restrictions on production normally last less than three months, but may be extended by a maximum three months.[196] The polluter must treat the pollution before normal production levels can resume. In contrast, if production is suspended (in cases of more serious violation and/or grave harm), this is not subject to a time limit. Resumption of production depends on the polluter treating the pollution.[197] A suspension to production ***may*** be ordered by an EPB in the following circumstances:

(i) discharge by hidden pipes, seepage wells or pits, perfusion, alteration or falsification of monitoring data, abnormal operation of pollution-control facilities, and the discharge exceeds permitted limits;
(ii) illegal emission or discharge of pollutants containing heavy metals or persistent organic pollutants (POPs), among others, that cause serious harm to both environment and public health at levels at least three times over the discharge standards;
(iii) discharge or emission of key pollutants in excess of the annual quota;
(iv) emission or discharge of pollutants that still breach standards following a previous order to restrict production;

193 EPL (2014), art. 60.
194 The MEP issued the Measures on Restriction and Suspension of Production for Treatment on 19 December 2014. The Measures came into force on 1 January 2015.
195 MEP, Measures on Restriction and Suspension of Production for Treatment (2014), art. 5.
196 MEP, Measures on Restriction and Suspension of Production for Treatment (2014), art. 15.
197 MEP, Measures on Restriction and Suspension of Production for Treatment (2014), art. 15.

(v) as a result of environmental emergency, emission or discharge of pollutants in excess of standards or the total control quota.[198]

The most draconian sanction of permanent closure penalizes parties in violation in the following circumstances: (i) illegal discharge or emission of toxic substances, including heavy metals and POPs, where the polluter has already received administrative penalties at least twice for the same violation within the past two years; (ii) where the polluter refuses to suspend production or resumes production unlawfully having been ordered to suspend production; (iii) where the same violation is detected by the follow-up inspection after the order to suspend production has been lifted. Permanent closure may only be imposed by an EPB following approval by the relevant people's government.[199]

Administrative Detention

The EPL (2014) introduced the penalty of administrative detention for individuals directly in charge and those directly liable in case of serious environmental violations, including: (i) failure to conduct an EIA and failure to stop construction as ordered; (ii) discharge without permit in violation of law and failure to stop discharge as ordered; (iii) illegal discharge through hidden pipes, seepage wells or pits, perfusion, falsification of monitoring data, or failure to operate pollution treatment facilities; (iv) production or use of pesticides and herbicides prohibited by the state and failure to rectify as ordered.[200] As administrative detention deprives a person of their freedom, it may only be imposed by a PSB, not by an administrative agency such as an environmental bureau.[201] Therefore, the EPL (2014) requests that environmental bureaus transfer cases to PSBs, which will detain the person directly in charge and others directly liable for ten to fifteen days, or five to ten days where circumstances are relatively minor.[202]

To implement article 63 of the EPL (2014) on administrative detention effectively, the Provisional Measures on Transfer of Environmental Violation Cases for Administrative Detention (2014) were issued jointly by five state departments.[203] It elaborates and subcategorizes the environmental violations under item (iii) of article 63 into: (a) secret discharge by hidden pipes, seepage wells or pits or by perfusion to evade regulatory supervision;[204] (b) alteration or falsification of monitoring data to evade regulatory supervision;[205] (c) abnormal operation of pollution-control installations.[206] As to who will be detained, 'persons directly in charge' are defined as those who profit most from the violation and who are in a position to make the decisions on managing and supervising

198 MEP, Measures on Restriction and Suspension of Production for Treatment (2014), art. 6.
199 MEP, Measures on Restriction and Suspension of Production for Treatment (2014), art. 8.
200 EPL (2014), art. 63. 201 Administrative Penalty Law (1996, amended 2009 and 2017), art. 16.
202 EPL (2014), art. 63.
203 The Provisional Measures on Transfer of Environmental Violation Cases for Administrative Detention (2014) were issued by the Ministry of Public Security (MPS), Ministry of Industry and Information Technology (MIIT), MEP, Ministry of Agriculture (MOA) and State Administration of Quality Supervision, Inspection and Quarantine (SAQSIQ) on 24 December 2014. It came into force on 1 January 2015.
204 Provisional Measures on Transfer of Environmental Violation Cases for Administrative Detention (2014), art. 5.
205 Provisional Measures on Transfer of Environmental Violation Cases for Administrative Detention (2014), art. 6.
206 Provisional Measures on Transfer of Environmental Violation Cases for Administrative Detention (2014), art. 7.

production and operation. 'Persons directly liable' are defined as frontline staff who personally discharge pollutants without treatment, dump or dispose of wastes, or alter or forge monitoring data.[207]

Enforcement Cases under the EPL (2014)

Shenzhen EPB [208]
On 17 January 2015, the Shenzhen Environmental Inspection Team conducted a night-time inspection of Shenzhen Hengjin Hardware Manufacturing Co. Ltd and found secret discharge of wastewater without treatment and in excess of the effluent discharge standards. Shenzhen EPB ordered the enterprise to suspend production and take pollution-control measures, imposed a fine of 200,000 yuan, and sealed up and seized the wastewater discharge facilities. Further, the local PSB imposed fifteen days' administrative detention on both the person directly in charge and the person directly liable.

Shandong Dongying EPB[209]
On 15 January 2015, Shandong Xianhe Pharmaceutical Co. Ltd was found to be discharging wastewater through hidden pipes. Dongying EPB imposed a fine of 100,000 yuan on the company, ordered it to suspend production and take pollution-control measures, sealed up the production equipment and facilities, and transferred two liable people to the local PSB, which then imposed administrative detention of five days on each.

It is worth noting that more than one administrative penalty may be imposed on a polluter. Further, liable parties may be investigated for criminal liabilities in the case of the most serious environmental violations,[210] and may be sanctioned under the Criminal Law (CL) (1997) and its amendments.

3.6 ECONOMIC INSTRUMENTS

A further important development of the EPL (2014) is its adoption of economic instruments, including fiscal policies, tax, pricing, government procurement, pollution liability insurance and ecological compensation, to promote and support environmental protection, energy conservation and pollution abatement.

3.6.1 Government Fiscal Support

As a matter of principle, the EPL (2014) requires all levels of government to increase the budgets they spend on environmental protection and pollution prevention, and to improve the efficiency of this spending.[211] This also has the benefit of supporting the development of environmental industries, including the manufacturing of environmental protection

[207] Provisional Measures on Transfer of Environmental Violation Cases for Administrative Detention (2014), art. 9.
[208] 'Enforcement cases', *China Environment News*, 3, case no. 7.
[209] 'Enforcement cases', *China Environment News*, 3, case no. 8.
[210] EPL (2014), art. 69.
[211] EPL (2014), art. 8.

equipment, recycling and recovery and environmental services, through fiscal policies, tax, pricing and government procurement policies and measures.[212]

Where any enterprise, institution or other production operator in compliance with relevant emissions or discharge standards achieves an additional pollution abatement, they will be rewarded by local government with financial support or favourable policies and measures on tax, pricing, government procurement, among others.[213] This creates incentives for enterprises to achieve deeper cuts to their emissions of pollutants and energy or resource consumption through technological innovations and upgrades.

China is making serious efforts to restructure its economy, currently powered by heavily polluting and energy-intensive industries, and pursue low-carbon sustainable development. The transition is painful for the enterprises that are to be relocated or phased out, but the government provides support to such entities where the change in production, the relocation or closure is carried out for environmental purposes.[214] The central government is determined to clean up industry and has earmarked budget for phasing out excess and outdated industrial capacity in the electricity, coal, iron and steel, cement, non-ferrous metals, coking, paper, tannery, printing and dyeing industries. The use of funding, in addition to supporting changes in production and technological advancements and upgrades, gives top priority to retraining, relocation and retirement packages, among others, to support employees and avoid large-scale unemployment.[215]

3.6.2 Pollution Discharge Fees and Environmental Tax

Collecting pollution discharge fees and using the fund for pollution control and treatment was an important way of making polluters pay. It was first introduced in the EPL (for trial implementation) (1979) and was then adopted by the EPL (1989), but only applied to enterprises and institutions that discharged pollutants in excess of national or local standards.[216] The EPL (2014) required all polluters to pay pollution discharge fees in line with state provisions. Fees collected were earmarked solely for use in pollution control and prevention.[217]

To implement the pollution discharge fees mechanism, the State Council issued the Regulation on the Levy and Use of Pollution Discharge Fees (Regulation on Discharge Fees) (2003),[218] supported by the Measures on the Standards for Levying Pollution Discharge Fees (2003),[219] the Measures on the Collection and Use of Pollution Discharge

[212] EPL (2014), art. 21. [213] EPL (2014), art. 22. [214] EPL (2014), art. 23.

[215] State Council, Notice to Further Strengthen the Phase-out of Outdated Industrial Capacities (2010).

[216] EPL (for trial implementation) (1979), art. 18(3); EPL (1989), art. 28. It further provides that the provisions of the WPPCL must be complied with where they are applicable. Article 24 of the WPPCL (2008) provides that enterprises, public institutions and individual industrial and commercial households that directly discharge pollutants to waterbodies must pay a pollutant discharge fee according to the category and quantity of the discharged water pollutants.

[217] EPL (2014), art. 43(1).

[218] The Regulation on Discharge Fees was issued by the State Council on 2 January 2003 and came into force on 1 July 2003.

[219] The Measures on the Standards for Levying Pollution Discharge Fees were issued by the State Planning Commission, MOF, SEPA and State Economic and Trade Commission on 28 February 2003. It came into force on 1 July 2003.

Fees (2003)[220] and the Measures on Inspection of the Work of Collecting Pollution Discharge Fees (2007).[221] Under the Regulation on Discharge Fees (2003), fees are collected from polluting sources for direct discharge of any pollutants into the environment.[222] Where an entity discharges wastewater to centralized wastewater treatment facilities, it pays a wastewater treatment fee, instead of the discharge fee.[223] Discharge fees are levied based on the type and quantity of pollutants at a rate set and adjusted by the NDRC, the Ministry of Finance (MOF) and the MEP.[224] Payment of discharge fees does not exonerate polluters from their responsibilities in pollution prevention and control or from the obligation to pay compensation for damage caused by pollution, even if they are not in breach of the standards, or any other liabilities under laws and regulations.[225]

In the same article on pollution discharge fees, article 43, the EPL (2014) provides that where an environmental tax is imposed, pollution discharge fees will cease to be collected.[226] It provides a statutory guarantee for a smooth transition from pollution discharge fees to environmental taxes in the context of China's ongoing 'fees-to-tax' reform. In 2007, the NDRC proposed using environmental taxes as tools to conserve energy and abate pollution.[227] From 2008, the MOF, State Taxation Administration and MEP worked on drafting an environmental tax law. The 12th FYP (2011–15) promoted environmental fees-to-tax reform.[228] The State Council was keen to introduce an environmental tax.[229] Consequently, the Environmental Protection Tax Law (EPTL) was adopted by the state legislature in 2016,[230] and was followed by the State Council's Regulation on the Implementation of the Environmental Protection Tax Law (Regulation on Environmental Tax) in 2017.[231] With effect from 1 January 2018, the environmental tax has completely replaced the pollution discharge fees that existed in China for nearly forty years.

Taxpayers, as defined by the EPTL (2016), are enterprises, institutions or other production operators that directly discharge taxable pollutants within the territory of China or into areas of the sea under China's jurisdiction.[232] 'Taxable pollutants' refers to air pollutants,

[220] The Measures on the Collection and Use of Pollution Discharge Fees were issued by the MOF and SEPA on 20 March 2003 and came into force on 1 July 2003.

[221] The SEPA issued the Measures on Inspection of the Work of Collecting Pollution Discharge Fees on 23 October 2007. The Measures came into force on 1 December 2007.

[222] Regulation on Discharge Fees (2003), art. 2(1).

[223] Regulation on Discharge Fees (2003), art. 2(2).

[224] Regulation on Discharge Fees (2003), art. 11.

[225] Regulation on Discharge Fees (2003), art. 12(2).

[226] EPL (2014), art. 43(2).

[227] NDRC, Comprehensive Work Plan on Energy Conservation and Emission Abatement (2007), para. 38. It was approved and issued by the State Council on 23 May 2007.

[228] 12th FYP, chapter 49, section II.

[229] State Council, Opinion on Key Tasks to Strengthen Environmental Protection (2011); 12th FYP on Environmental Protection (2010–15). In March 2015, Premier Li Keqiang presented his *Government Work Report* to the NPC; environmental tax legislation was on the work agenda for 2015. Li Keqiang, *Government Work Report* (5 March 2015). www.npc.gov.cn/npc/dbdhhy/12_3/2015-03/17/content_1930436.htm

[230] The EPTL was adopted on 25 December 2016 by the 12th NPCSC at its 25th session. It came into force on 1 January 2018. It was amended on 26 October 2018 as a result of the State Council's institutional reform in March 2018.

[231] The State Council issued the Regulation on Environmental Tax on 25 December 2017. It came into force on 1 January 2018.

[232] EPTL (2018), art. 2.

water pollutants, solid waste and noise included in the Schedule of Tax Items and Tax Rates and the Schedule of Taxable Pollutants and Equivalent Values.[233] The following circumstances do not count as direct discharge under the EPTL (2016): (i) effluent discharge to centralized wastewater treatment facilities or disposal of household waste at municipal solid waste disposal facilities; (ii) storage or disposal of solid waste at facilities or sites that comply with national and local environmental standards.[234] The following entities are exempt from the tax: (i) agricultural operators discharging taxable pollutants (excluding large-scale poultry and livestock farms); (ii) mobile sources, including vehicles, vessels and aircraft; (iii) legally constructed centralized wastewater treatment plants and municipal waste disposal facilities that discharge taxable pollutants in compliance with national and local standards; (iv) taxpayers that provide comprehensive treatment of the solid waste in compliance with national and local standards and (v) entities in other circumstances stipulated by the State Council.[235]

While the Schedule on Tax Items and Tax Rates provides a fixed nationwide rate for solid waste and noise, it gives provinces flexibility of ten times difference for taxable air and water pollutants.[236] Provincial governments may propose a rate within this range, after considering the local environmental carrying capacity, the existing pollution discharge and socio-economic and environmental development targets. The provincial government's proposal goes to the same-level people's congress standing committee for approval.[237] The transition from fees to tax was planned so as not to impose extra financial burdens onto taxpayers. Pollution discharge fees were imposed at different rates in different provinces, with the state setting a minimum and allowing provincial governments to raise rates to accommodate local pollution-control needs. In 2015, the rate in Beijing was eight to nine times the minimum rate, while in Tianjin it was five to seven times the minimum, and in Shanghai three to six and a half times the minimum.[238] The EPTL (2018) is similar, in that it continues to offer provincial governments flexibility in setting tax rates for air and water pollutants.

An important incentive exists in the form of tax reductions where taxpayers achieve, through technological innovation, deeper cuts in pollution. If a taxpayer's discharge of taxable air or water pollutants is 30 per cent below the applicable concentration standard, whether national or local, it is liable for 75 per cent of the environmental tax due. If a taxpayer's discharge of taxable air or water pollutants is 50 per cent below the applicable concentration standard, whether national or local, it pays only 50 per cent of the environmental tax due.[239]

[233] EPTL (2018), art. 3. [234] EPTL (2018), art. 4. [235] EPTL (2018), art. 12.

[236] For example, the tax rate for HW is 1,000 yuan per tonne, and for other solid waste, 25 yuan per tonne. The rates are applied consistently across China. In contrast, the tax rate for taxable air pollutants is 1.2 yuan to 12 yuan per pollution equivalent value, and 1.4 yuan to 14 yuan per pollution equivalent value for taxable water pollutants. See Schedule of Tax Items and Tax Rates.

[237] EPTL (2018), art. 6(2).

[238] Lou Jiwei, *Explanation of the Draft Bill of the Environmental Protection Tax Law* (2016). The document was presented on 29 August 2016 to the 12th NPCSC at its 22nd session by the then minister of finance, Lou Jiwei.

[239] EPTL (2018), art. 13.

Effective operation of the environmental tax regime depends on close cooperation between tax bureaus and environmental authorities in terms of data sharing regarding taxpayers' pollution discharge.

3.6.3 Trading of Pollution Discharge Allowances

'Pollution discharge allowance' refers to the types and quantities of pollutants permitted to be discharged by a polluting source upon verification by the regulatory authority. It is a market tool designed to achieve total pollution control of key pollutants.[240] Local pilot schemes had been supported by the State Council since 2007 with the target of setting up the infrastructure for paid use and trading of pollution discharge allowances by 2017. The State Council initially designated eleven provinces, autonomous regions or cities directly under the central government – Jiangsu, Zhejiang, Hubei, Hunan, Inner Mongolia, Shanxi, Shaanxi, Hebei, Henan, Tianjin and Chongqing – and encouraged others to follow suit voluntarily.[241] By the beginning of 2019, twenty-eight provinces, autonomous regions or cities under central government control had joined the pilot exercises of paid use and trading of pollution discharge allowances.[242] The pollutants traded under the pilot schemes include the key pollutants that are subject to the state's binding targets for total pollution control: SO_2, NOx, COD and ammonia nitrogen. Local governments may include additional pollutants as needed. The local pilots cover the four key pollutants, and some include extra pollutants to meet the needs of local pollution control. For instance, Shanxi, renowned for its coal mining, also includes industrial dust and smoke, both air pollutants, in the trading system. Hunan, notorious for its cadmium-contaminated rice, includes heavy metals as key pollutants. Shunde district in Guangdong province includes volatile organic compounds (VOCs) as key pollutants subject to quota control and trading.[243]

Verification of pollutant discharge allowances by local EPBs is the foundation of the pollution trading scheme. In the case of existing polluting sources, this is based on relevant laws, regulations and standards, total pollution control requirements, layout of industrial sectors and current and historical pollution discharge. In the case of new, modified or expanded projects, verification is based on relevant EIA documents. Pollution discharge allowances are to be stipulated in the pollution discharge permit. The total combined allowances of any local scheme may not go beyond the pollution cap imposed by the state.[244]

[240] State Council General Office, Guiding Opinion on Further Promoting Pilot Exercises of Paid Use and Trading of Pollution Discharge Allowances (2014), s. 1.

[241] State Council General Office, Guiding Opinion on Further Promoting Pilot Exercises of Paid Use and Trading of Pollution Discharge Allowances (2014), s. 2.

[242] Department of Economic Construction (MOF), 23 January 2019, 'Pilot exercises on paid use and trading of pollution discharge allowances making progress'. Online article. http://jjs.mof.gov.cn/gongzuodongtai/201901/t20190118_3125090.htm

[243] Department of Economic Construction (MOF), 'Pilot exercises on paid use'.

[244] State Council General Office, Guiding Opinion on Further Promoting Pilot Exercises of Paid Use and Trading of Pollution Discharge Allowances (2014), s. 4.

It is worth noting that the State Council required local governments covered by the pilot exercise to complete verification of all existing sources by the end of 2015.[245]

The state aims to promote paid use of pollution discharge allowances. That is, polluters pay to obtain pollution discharge allowances for key pollutants. In practice, flexibility is allowed for existing polluters to gradually acquire pollution discharge allowances for a fee, although new projects and modified or expanded projects must pay to obtain pollution discharge allowances.[246]

Initial allocation of the pollution discharge allowances may be by assignment at a predetermined price (for existing sources) or public auction (for new sources). The price of the allowances will be determined by the local authorities on pricing, finance and environmental protection on the basis of the cost of pollution treatment, the rarity of the environmental resources and the economic development level.[247] The revenue generated from the allocation of pollution discharge allowances belongs to the local government and is to be used for pollution prevention and control. Where the fees for the allowances are relatively high and the polluter has difficulty making payment in one go, it may arrange payment by instalment to be completed within five years. However, the minimum initial payment is 40 per cent of the total fees due.[248] To guide the local pilots, state departments have jointly issued the Provisional Measures on the Management of Revenues Generated by Assignment of Pollution Discharge Allowances (2015).[249]

3.6.4 Pollution Liability Insurance

The EPL (2014) provides that the state will encourage the purchase of environmental pollution liability insurance.[250] Pollution liability insurance covers the liability of the insured to compensate a third party who suffers personal injury or property loss caused by pollution. It also covers reasonable costs for clean-up and restoration. This economic instrument serves multiple purposes. It protects individual enterprises from bankruptcy by spreading the risk and cost of pollution across a group of polluters, offers timely compensation to victims of pollution, even if the polluter does not have the financial resources to pay, and mitigates environmental risks by incentives of reducing premiums for enterprises that enhance their environmental performance via strengthened management and risk control.

China started a voluntary pilot scheme for pollution liability insurance in 2007 under the joint leadership of the SEPA and the China Insurance Regulatory Commission (CIRC). Their Guideline on Environmental Pollution Liability Insurance (Guideline) (2007)[251] strongly encouraged provincial EPBs and insurance regulatory bodies to trial pilot schemes for

[245] State Council General Office, Guiding Opinion on Further Promoting Pilot Exercises of Paid Use and Trading of Pollution Discharge Allowances (2014), s. 4.

[246] State Council General Office, Guiding Opinion on Further Promoting Pilot Exercises of Paid Use and Trading of Pollution Discharge Allowances (2014), s. 5.

[247] State Council General Office, Guiding Opinion on Further Promoting Pilot Exercises of Paid Use and Trading of Pollution Discharge Allowances (2014), s. 6.

[248] State Council General Office, Guiding Opinion on Further Promoting Pilot Exercises of Paid Use and Trading of Pollution Discharge Allowances (2014), s. 7.

[249] The MOF, NDRC and MEP issued the Provisional Measures on the Management of Revenues Generated by Assignment of Pollution Discharge Allowances on 23 July 2015. It came into force on 1 October 2015.

[250] EPL (2014), art. 52. [251] The SEPA and CIRC issued the Guideline on 4 December 2007.

high-risk key polluting sectors and enterprises. The aim was to establish the pollution liability insurance regime nationwide by 2015.[252] The Guideline (2007) lists the following as the insured under the pilot schemes: enterprises that manufacture, operate, store, transport or use hazardous chemicals, petrochemical enterprises at high risk of pollution incident, and operators of HW. In particular, enterprises that have caused pollution incidents in recent years should be insured under the pilot schemes.[253] During the pilot stage, the insurance only covers liability for direct losses caused by a sudden pollution incident.[254]

While local pilot schemes had been carried out independently in over a dozen cities and provinces, including Hunan, Hubei, Jiangsu, Shenzhen and Shenyang, by early 2012,[255] implementing pollution liability insurance at a national level has encountered more obstacles, including lack of laws, policies, and mechanisms to support the operation of the pollution liability insurance, and resistance from both polluting enterprises and insurance companies.[256] Studies of local pilot schemes found that compulsory pollution liability insurance schemes in Wuxi and Hunan had insured a few hundred companies by mid-2011 and early 2012 respectively, while for the same period in Chongqing and Shenzhen, where voluntary pollution liability insurance models were adopted, fewer than ten companies chose to be insured.[257]

Given the low participation rate of enterprises, who see insurance premiums as an extra cost and a burden, the MEP and CIRC responded with compulsory liability insurance by issuing the Guideline on Pilot Schemes of Compulsory Environmental Pollution Liability Insurance in 2013 (New Guideline).[258] While it ***encouraged*** high-risk enterprises to purchase pollution liability insurance,[259] it expressly makes it compulsory for 'key enterprises under heavy metal pollution control' to purchase liability insurance. There are five categories of enterprise generating and discharging heavy metals and subject to the compulsory liability insurance requirement: (i) enterprises mining heavy metals, including copper, lead, zinc and nickel, among others; (ii) enterprises refining heavy metals; (iii) enterprises manufacturing lead-acid batteries; (iv) tanneries and (v) enterprises manufacturing chemical raw materials.[260] The New Guideline (2013) further clarifies the scope of coverage of the liability insurance by listing: (i) personal injury, death or loss of property suffered by a third party and caused by pollution; (ii) necessary and reasonable expenses incurred by the insured to save the life or to prevent and control property loss of the third party; (iii) necessary and reasonable expenses incurred by the insured as required by environmental

[252] Guideline (2007), part II, s. 2. [253] Guideline (2007), part III, s. 2. [254] Guideline (2007), part II, s. 1.

[255] Yan Feng et al., 'Environmental pollution liability insurance in China: compulsory or voluntary', *Journal of Cleaner Production*, 70 (2014), 211–19, at 212.

[256] Yang Zhaofei, 'Environmental pollution liability insurance: using market instrument to address environmental management difficulties', *Green Leaf*, 10 (2010), 19–28, at 26.

[257] Yan Feng et al., 'Environmental pollution liability insurance in China: compulsory or voluntary'; Yan Feng et al., 'Environmental pollution liability insurance in China: in need of strong government backing', *AMBIO: A Journal of the Human Environment*, 43:5 (2013), 1–16.

[258] The MEP and CIRC issued the New Guideline on 21 January 2013.

[259] New Guideline (2013), part II, s. 3. High-risk enterprises include: (i) oil, gas, petrochemical and chemical enterprises; (ii) enterprises that produce, store, use, trade or transport hazardous chemicals; (iii) enterprises that generate, collect, store, transport, utilize or dispose of HW and enterprises that emit dioxins; and (iv) other enterprises designated as high risk by environmental authorities.

[260] New Guideline (2013), part II, s. 1.

law to mitigate pollution and clean up the contamination and (iv) other liabilities as agreed by both the insured and the insurance company.[261]

The New Guideline (2013) uses both carrot and stick to promote pollution liability insurance. Where enterprises have purchased pollution liability insurance, they receive preferential treatment in applications to the government environmental protection fund and heavy metal pollution-control funds, and bank loans.[262] In contrast, where enterprises are required to purchase pollution liability insurance but fail to do so, they are subject to measures including: suspension of EIA approval; environmental inspection and approval of construction projects; suspension of pollution discharge permit; clean production audit (an audit required in the case of pollution- and energy-intensive enterprises[263]); environmental scrutiny in an initial public offering; and suspension of an application to the environmental protection fund or heavy metal pollution-control fund, and it may also impact negatively on their ability to obtain bank loans.[264]

The latest development is the Measures on Compulsory Liability Insurance for Environmental Pollution (draft for consultation) (Draft Measures) circulated by the MEP and CIRC in 2017.[265] This further extends the scope of enterprises subject to the compulsory liability insurance and the liabilities covered by the insurance. Those high-risk enterprises previously encouraged to purchase pollution liability insurance are now required to do so.[266] The liabilities insured not only include third-party personal injury and property loss caused by environmental emergency and pollution arising from operations,[267] but also ecological damage caused by environmental emergency, including the cost of restoring the eco-environment and compensation for loss of eco-function.[268] Under the terms of the insurance, covered costs are those arising from the necessary and reasonable emergency response and clean-up and that are incurred to prevent and mitigate personal injury, property loss or ecological damage. They include: expenses incurred by the injured, the third party, relevant government bodies and public interest organizations.[269]

3.6.5 Ecological Compensation

Ecological compensation aims to achieve environmental justice by recognizing the value of nature conservation and environmental protection and making monetary payments to those who give up opportunities for economic development in order to conserve and protect the environment. Special ecosystems or special function zones, such as DWSRs, are designated to ensure safe drinking water supply and, in these areas, development activities generating various degrees of pollution are either prohibited or restricted. People living in the designated areas are deprived of the right to development, sacrificing their individual and collective economic interests for the good of a much wider community, the ecosystem and future generations. They deserve fair compensation by the state and others who benefit from their conservation and protection efforts. To strengthen the protection of areas of ecological importance, the EPL (2014) guarantees, through the ecological compensation

[261] New Guideline (2013), part III, s. 1. [262] New Guideline (2013), part VII, s. 2.
[263] Law on Promotion of Clean Production (2012), art. 27. [264] New Guideline (2013), part VII, s. 1.
[265] The MEP and CIRC circulated the Draft Measures on 7 June 2017. [266] Draft Measures (2017), art. 5.
[267] Draft Measures (2017), art. 6(1) and (2). [268] Draft Measures (2017), art. 6(3).
[269] Draft Measures (2017), art. 6(4).

mechanism, financial support to regions that implement ecological protection.[270] The central government played an important role in establishing this mechanism and guides its implementation at local levels. Under the EPL (2014), the state will increase funding for regions of ecological protection and the relevant local governments must ensure the money is used exclusively for ecological protection and conservation.[271] Compensation should also be paid by local governments of the regions that benefit from the conservation to the local governments of regions that refrain from development. The compensation is calculated either by government-to-government consultation or market rules under the guidance of the central government.[272]

The State Council issued the Opinion on Building an Ecological Protection Compensation Mechanism (2016)[273] to guide and expand eco-compensation in seven key sectors (forests, grassland, wetland, deserts, ocean and sea, inland waters and farmland) and key regions (national nature reserves, world cultural and natural heritage sites, national scenic zones, national forest parks and geological parks), and promote horizontal regional eco-compensation between the upper and lower reaches of a river basin. The Opinion was based on years of eco-compensation pilot exercises. As early as 2005, the State Council decided to establish an ecological compensation mechanism and encouraged central and local governments to conduct pilot exercises.[274] In 2007, the SEPA issued the Guideline on Ecological Compensation Pilot Schemes,[275] which focused on eco-compensation in four areas: (i) nature reserves; (ii) important ecological function zones, such as DWSRs; (iii) exploitation of mineral resources; and (iv) river basins. The WPPCL (2008) was the first environmental statute to formally adopt the mechanism of ecological compensation. It offers financial compensation to local governments in designated DWSRs and upper reaches of rivers, lakes and reservoirs where people refrain from development activities. Payments are made by central to local governments in the designated regions.[276] By 2013, various forms of ecological compensation mechanisms had been tried and tested. The primary form is for the central government to pay directly to local governments that conserve natural resources, such as forests and grassland. For example, where local governments prohibit the raising of cattle or sheep on grassland, an annual financial subsidy is paid at the rate of 6 yuan per *mu*. Where a restriction is imposed on the use of grassland for raising cattle or sheep, an annual subsidy is paid at the rate of 1.5 yuan per *mu*. The second form of eco-compensation occurs directly between provincial governments. A provincial government that benefits from conservation pays provincial governments that make an effort to conserve and protect the ecosystem. The third form applies to mining enterprises, who must pay a certain percentage of the value of the mineral resources they exploit.[277]

[270] EPL (2014), art. 31(1). [271] EPL (2014), art. 31(2). [272] EPL (2014), art. 31(3).

[273] The State Council General Office issued the Opinion on Building an Ecological Protection Compensation Mechanism on 28 April 2016.

[274] State Council, Decision on Implementing Scientific Development and Strengthening Environmental Protection (State Council Decision) (2005), part V, s. 23.

[275] The SEPA issued the Guideline on Ecological Compensation Pilot Schemes on 24 August 2007.

[276] WPPCL (2008), art. 7.

[277] Xu Shaoshi, *Report on Establishing the Ecological Compensation Mechanism* (2013). www.pkulaw.cn. Xu Shaoshi, chairperson of the NDRC, presented the Report on 23 April 2013 to the 12th NPCSC at its 2nd session.

The Opinion consolidated the lessons learnt from the pilot schemes and pushed for a further expansion in the use of eco-compensation mechanisms to cover all key sectors and regions by 2020. It was expected that, by then, there would be multiple sources of finance and multiple forms of support to facilitate the operation of the eco-compensation mechanisms.[278]

3.6.6 Green Government Procurement

Demand-side management can create a market for a steadily growing supply of environmentally friendly products and services, and can incentivize potential investors to go low carbon and low pollution. Consumers have the power to reshape market demand for green products and services if they are willing to opt for greener lifestyles. The EPL (2014) promotes green consumption and encourages citizens, legal persons and other organizations to use environmentally friendly and recycled products to reduce waste.[279] To succeed, the government must take the lead so that the public will follow suit. As the largest consumer, government bodies and government-funded entities combined can substantially drive up demand for environmentally friendly products and services.

As early as 2002, when China enacted the Government Procurement Law,[280] there was a general requirement for government procurement to facilitate the achievement of state socio-economic development targets, including environmental protection.[281] In the same year, China enacted the Law on the Promotion of Clean Production,[282] which requires governments to give priority in their procurement to products that conserve energy, water or are recovered from waste.[283] The requirement of 'giving priority' has been implemented to various degrees in different places. To strengthen green government procurement, the State Council issued a notice in 2007 to introduce compulsory government procurement[284] of nine categories of energy- and water-saving products: air conditioners, fluorescent lamps, televisions, electric heaters, computers, printers, monitors, toilets and taps.[285] In 2008, China enacted the Law on Promotion of the Circular Economy (CEPL),[286] which also requires government procurement to prioritize energy-saving, water-saving, resource-saving, environmentally friendly and recycled products.[287]

The EPL (2014) requires government organs and government-funded bodies to give priority in their procurement and consumption decisions to environmentally friendly products, equipment and facilities that conserve energy, water or resources.[288]

[278] State Council General Office, Opinion (2016), part I, s. 3. [279] EPL (2014), art. 36(1).

[280] The Government Procurement Law was adopted on 29 June 2002 by the 9th NPCSC at its 28th session. It came into force on 1 January 2003. It was amended on 31 August 2014 by the 12th NPCSC at its 10th session.

[281] Government Procurement Law (2002), art. 9.

[282] The Law on Promotion of Clean Production was adopted on 29 June 2002 by the 9th NPCSC at its 28th session. It came into force on 1 January 2003. It was amended on 29 February 2012 by the 11th NPCSC at its 25th session.

[283] Law on Promotion of Clean Production (2002), art. 16.

[284] The State Council General Office issued the Notice on Compulsory Government Procurement of Energy-Saving Products on 30 July 2007.

[285] The MOF and NDRC issued the Notice to Adjust the List of Energy-Saving Products for Government Procurement on 5 December 2007.

[286] The CEPL was adopted on 29 August 2008 by the 11th NPCSC at its 4th session. It came into force on 1 January 2009, and was amended on 26 October 2018 by the 13th NPCSC at its 6th session.

[287] CEPL (2008), art. 47. [288] EPL (2014), art. 36(2).

Government procurement is also an important economic tool to encourage and promote the development of environmental protection industries, such as the manufacturing of environmental protection equipment, as well as recycling and recovery, and environmental services,[289] and to incentivize enterprises and other entities to achieve deeper cuts in pollution through technological innovation and advancement.[290]

[289] EPL (2014), art. 21. [290] EPL (2014), art. 22.

4

Environmental Impact Assessment

Environmental impact assessment (EIA) is a scientific and technical process that projects and assesses the potential adverse impact of any proposed development project, plan or policy through the use of environmental data, technical standards and assessment methods. An EIA is undertaken by professionally qualified engineers to ensure the EIA process is objective and science-based, and that the findings and conclusions are accurate and reliable. But EIA goes far beyond this technical process. It has become a statutory process and a decision-making tool that involves input from and supervision by the public. An effective EIA regime is based on both science and democracy in order to facilitate well-informed and sound decision-making by public authorities. In China, it was the EIA regime that introduced democratic public participation in government decision-making. The Environmental Impact Assessment Law (EIAL) (2002)[1] provides that the state 'encourages' relevant units, experts and the public to participate in the EIA process 'by proper means'.[2]

In the 1980s and 1990s, China's EIAs had only narrow applicability – to construction projects. The EIAL (2002) extended the scope of environmental assessments to include government plans and, since 2016, environmental assessment of government policies has been trialled. Over the decades, closer integration between the EIA of projects and the EA of plans, and more effective alignment of the EIA with other control mechanisms and market tools – including the three-simultaneities requirement (environmental measures proposed in an EIA document should be designed, constructed and put into operation simultaneously with the construction project itself), total pollution control, permit control, environmental tax, and trading of pollution discharge allowances – have developed.

This chapter studies the environmental assessment legal regime in China. Section 4.1 provides an overview of the development of environmental assessment in China from its beginnings as a project-based pollution-prevention instrument to a technical and statutory process that embodies

[1] The EIAL was adopted on 28 October 2002 by the 9th National People's Congress Standing Committee (NPCSC) at its 30th session. It came into effect on 1 September 2003, and was amended in 2016 and 2018.

[2] EIAL (2002), art. 5; see also EIAL (2016), art. 5 and EIAL (2018), art. 5. Part of this chapter on the early development of EIA and public participation was previously published by the author in 'Public participation in China's EIA regime: rhetoric or reality', Journal of Environmental Law, 22 (2010), 89-123, and 'Assessing the environmental impact of projects: a critique of the EIA regime in China', Natural Resources Journal, 49 (2009), 485–524.

both the preventative and participatory principles for projects and plans. Section 4.2 examines the legal instrument of project EIA, the statutory process that aims to provide a scientific basis for informed decision-making by the approval authorities. Section 4.3 discusses strategic environmental assessment (SEA), including the EA of government plans and an initial exploration of SEA on government policies. Section 4.4 focuses on public participation, an important feature of the statutory EIA process, and one that aims to improve the quality of government decision-making. Section 4.5 concludes with comment on the alignment of SEA with the EIA of projects.

4.1 ENVIRONMENTAL ASSESSMENT IN CHINA: A BRIEF HISTORY

The EIA is one of the earliest environmental legal mechanisms adopted in China to prevent and control pollution. Since the implementation of the EIAL (2002), EIA has also become a key legal instrument with which to engage the public in environment matters. Soon after the Chinese delegation returned from the Stockholm Conference on the Human Environment,[3] the State Council hosted the first national conference on environmental protection.[4] It also issued the Several Provisions on the Protection and Improvement of the Environment (draft for trial use) (1973), which adopted the preventative principle emphasizing pollution prevention.[5] In 1978, the Central Committee of the Chinese Communist Party (CCP) articulated the importance of EIA in project construction:

> The selection of a factory site shall take environmental protection and rational planning into consideration. The design profile of an engineering project must include environmental protection documents describing the environmental status prior to the construction, major environmental protection measures to be adopted, the environmental quality projected after the construction, and the environmental management system established within the enterprises.[6]

Guided by this party policy, the EIA mechanism was formally adopted in the Environmental Protection Law (for trial implementation) (EPL) (1979),[7] which required measures to prevent pollution and mitigate environmental harm to be taken at every stage of construction and operation. In planning new construction projects, redevelopment projects or extensions to existing projects, developers were required to submit EIA reports to the environmental protection authorities for examination and approval prior to the commencement of the projects.[8] In urban development and redevelopment projects, the law required the assessment of a project's

[3] The United Nations (UN) Conference on the Human Environment was held in Stockholm in June 1972. It drew international attention to the global problem of the deteriorating environment, and has facilitated the subsequent evolution of environmental law worldwide, in both developed and developing nations.

[4] Qu Geping, *Qu's Pursuit*, at 403–4.

[5] The first National Conference on Environmental Protection was held in August 1973. The State Council then issued the Several Provisions on the Protection and Improvement of the Environment on 29 August 1973, emphasizing the principle of pollution prevention in environmental protection. See also Wang Ping, 'Thirty Years of Environmental Legislation', *The People's Congress of China*, 18 (2012), 27–28.

[6] Central Committee of the CCP, Approval of the State Council's Summary Report on Environmental Protection Work (31 December 1978). See also Wang Jin, *The Principles of Chinese Environmental Law* (Beijing: Peking University Press, 2000), at 139.

[7] The EPL (for trial implementation) was enacted on 13 September 1979 by the 5th NPCSC at its 11th session. It came into force immediately.

[8] EPL (for trial implementation) (1979), art. 6.

environmental impact on industrial and residential premises, forestland and public utilities to take into account meteorological, geographical, hydrological and ecological conditions.[9] The EPL (for trial implementation) (1979) was substantially amended in 1989,[10] with the EIA mechanism reinforced for construction projects. Under the EPL (1989), EIA reports were required to predict and assess the pollution that will be caused by the construction and operation of the project, as well as the adverse impacts on the environment. The EIA reports must propose control measures to prevent and mitigate the potential harm, and should be submitted to the relevant environmental protection authorities for approval. The planning authority is only permitted to examine and approve a construction project after the project proponent has obtained the EIA approval.[11] The EIA, as an important pollution-prevention mechanism, was also incorporated into all major environmental statutes enacted in the 1980s and 1990s. Construction projects are required to conduct an EIA by the Air Pollution Prevention and Control Law (APPCL),[12] the Water Pollution Prevention and Control Law (WPPCL),[13] the Law on the Prevention and Control of Environmental Pollution by Solid Waste (SWL)[14] and the Marine Environmental Protection Law (MEPL).[15] To translate EIA from an abstract concept into a concrete tool for environmental management, administrative regulations and rules were promulgated to stipulate procedural requirements and technical standards on the EIA of construction projects. The most important of these was the Regulation on the Management of Environmental Protection of Construction Projects (EIA Regulation) (1998).[16]

However, more than two decades of practice with the EIA mechanism showed that project-based EIA was too limited in scope to effectively prevent pollution and mitigate environmental harm.[17] Decision-making at project level is guided and restricted by government plans and policies. International experience has proved that SEA better addresses the integration of environmental concerns into the government policymaking process.[18] As a formal, systematic and comprehensive process for evaluating the environmental impacts of a government policy, plan or programme and alternatives to them, SEA ensures environmental concerns are included and addressed appropriately at the earliest possible stage of decision-making on socio-economic development. In 1999, when the State Environmental Protection Administration (SEPA) started drafting the EIAL (2002), SEA was a top priority

[9] EPL (for trial implementation) (1979), art. 7.

[10] The amended EPL was enacted on 26 December 1989 by the 7th NPCSC at its 11th session. It came into force immediately.

[11] EPL (1989), art. 13.

[12] APPCL (1987), art. 11. The APPCL was enacted on 5 September 1987 by the 6th NPCSC at its 22nd session. It was amended in 1995, substantially revised in 2000 and revised again in 2015.

[13] WPPCL (1984), art. 13. The WPPCL was enacted on 11 May 1984 by the 6th NPCSC at its 5th session. It was amended in 1996, substantially revised in 2008 and amended again in 2017.

[14] SWL (1995), art. 14. The SWL was enacted on 30 October 1995 by the 8th NPCSC at its 16th session. It was amended in 2004, 2015 and 2016.

[15] MEPL (1982), arts. 43 and 47. The MEPL was enacted by the 5th NPCSC on 23 August 1982, revised in 1999 and amended in 2013, 2016 and 2017.

[16] On 29 November 1998, the EIA Regulation (1998) was issued by the State Council with immediate effect. It was revised in 2017.

[17] For more discussion on project EIA, see Yuhong Zhao, 'Assessing the environmental impact of projects', 485–524; Yan Wang et al., 'Environmental impact assessment of projects in the People's Republic of China: new law, old problems', *Environmental Impact Assessment Review*, 23 (2003), 543–79.

[18] Jane Holder, *Environmental Assessment: The Regulation of Decision Making* (Oxford University Press, 2006), at 60–5.

for inclusion. When the draft bill was submitted to the Environment and Resources Protection Committee (ERPC) of the National People's Congress (NPC) on 20 December 1999, it included proposals for an extensive application of SEA to cover government policies, plans and programmes. But after almost three years of consultation and negotiation between state departments and local governments, and a power struggle between environmental authorities and departments in charge of industrial and economic development, the scope of application of SEA was substantially narrowed down and the power of environmental authorities was restricted to a minimum in the EIAL (2002).[19] The EIAL (2002) incorporated the comprehensive legal regime of EIA for construction projects[20] and expanded EA to certain types of government plans.[21] Then, in 2009, the Regulation on Environmental Assessment of Plans (Regulation on Plan EA) (2009)[22] was issued to implement EA of plans (plan EA).

The 2016 amendment[23] to the EIAL (2002) focuses on post-approval monitoring and supervision. It also strengthens the enforcement powers of agencies and substantially increases the fines for violations. The EIAL (2016) aims to implement sustainable development, prevent adverse environmental impacts caused by plans and projects, and promote the coordination of socio-economic development with the environment.[24] An EIA includes three important components: (i) analysis, projection and assessment of the potential environmental impacts that will be caused by implementing or constructing the proposed plans and projects, (ii) measures to prevent or mitigate adverse environmental impacts and (iii) methods and mechanisms for follow-up monitoring.[25] In order for EIAs to provide a sound basis for government decision-making, the EIA process must be objective, transparent and unbiased, and must take into account all potential impacts of plans or projects on elements of the environment and on the ecosystem as a whole.[26]

The EIAL (2016) was amended again in 2018 to abolish the licensing system for EIA firms. Under EIAL (2018),[27] a proponent of a construction project may engage a professional consultancy firm to conduct the EIA and prepare EIA documents or, if the proponent possesses the technical capacity, it may do the work itself.[28] The regulatory focus has thus shifted from the body performing the EIA to quality control over the EIA documents. Construction units and professional firms are held accountable for the quality and accuracy of the EIA documents. Their violations and any sanctions are recorded and made publicly available.[29]

4.2 PROJECT EIA

The EPL (for trial implementation) (1979) provides for EIA as a mechanism to prevent and control pollution, and specialized environmental statutes followed suit. The EIA

[19] For a detailed account of the legislative history of the EIAL (2002), see Wang Jin, *A Comparative Study of Sino-Foreign EIA Mechanism*, (Beijing: Peking University Press, 2006), at 222–36.

[20] The key control mechanisms of project EIAs found in the EIA Regulation (1998) were incorporated into chapter 3 of the EIAL (2002).

[21] Chapter 2 of the EIAL (2002); see also Jing Wu et al., 'Strategic environmental assessment implementation'.

[22] The Regulation on Plan EA was issued by the State Council on 17 August 2009 and came into force on 1 October 2009.

[23] The EIAL (2002) was amended on 2 July 2016 by the 12th NPCSC at its 21st session.

[24] EIAL (2016), art. 1. [25] EIAL (2016), art. 2. [26] EIAL (2016), art. 4.

[27] The 2018 amendment was enacted on 29 December 2018 by the 13th NPCSC at its 7th session.

[28] EIAL (2018), art. 19. [29] EIAL (2018), art. 20

Regulation (1998), which was amended in 2017, set out detailed rules on EIA procedure and approval, and these formed the basis of chapter III of the EIAL (2002) and its subsequent amendments. Project proponents are required to conduct an EIA prior to construction in order to prevent and mitigate environmental harm that will be caused by the construction or operation of the proposed project. The legal regime for EIAs of projects addresses screening, which determines the type of EIA required of a given project, public participation, EIA approval, post-EIA monitoring and the legal liabilities of project proponents, government authorities and EIA firms.[30] Reforms to the EIAL (2002) in 2016 and 2018 and to the EIA Regulation (1998) in 2017 have substantially increased the cost of violations, emphasized post-approval monitoring and assessment, strengthened the link between EIA and the three-simultaneities requirement, and enhanced post-construction regulatory supervision and inspection to ensure that measures included in the EIA documents and required by the EIA authorities are implemented.

4.2.1 Types of EIA and EIA Documents

Limited resources render it unrealistic to assess all impacts of all projects. Depending on their nature, scale and location, construction projects generate varying degrees of adverse environmental impacts during construction and operation. Statutory EIA targets those adverse environmental impacts that are likely to be significant. What is 'significant' is crucial to both regulatory authorities and project proponents.[31] To address this question China divides construction projects requiring some form of EIA into three categories depending on their potential environmental impacts. Each is subject to a different EIA requirement.[32] Project proponents must prepare EIA documents according to the following:

(1) where serious environmental impacts may be caused, an ***environmental impact report*** [emphasis added] shall be prepared based on a comprehensive assessment;
(2) where slight environmental impacts may be caused, an ***environmental impact statement*** [emphasis added] shall be prepared based on an analysis or assessment of the environmental impacts that will be generated by the project and
(3) where environmental impact is so small that an environmental impact assessment is not required, an ***environmental impact registration form*** [emphasis added] shall be completed.[33]

To clarify which type of EIA document is required for a given project, the Ministry of Environmental Protection (MEP) promulgates and regularly updates the Inventory on Environmental Impact Assessment Categories of Construction Projects (Inventory).[34] The Inventory lists EIA requirements for construction projects likely to generate adverse environmental impact. Determining which type of EIA is required of a given project requires comparison of a project's nature, scale and location with the quantitative or capacity indicators set in the Inventory. The use of clearly defined thresholds may unavoidably create an incentive for project proponents to draft proposals that fall just below the

[30] For more on project EIA, see Yuhong Zhao, 'Assessing the environmental impact of projects'; Yan Wang et al., 'Environmental impact assessment of projects'.
[31] Holder, *Environmental Assessment*, at 35–7. [32] EIAL (2018), art. 16(1).
[33] EIAL (2018), art. 16(2); EIA Regulation (2017), art. 7(1).
[34] The latest version of the Inventory was issued by the MEE on 28 April 2018 with immediate effect.

TABLE 4.1 TYPES OF EIA DOCUMENTS PREPARED BY CONSTRUCTION PROJECTS

	Total number of projects	Projects requiring EIA report (%)	Projects requiring EIA statement (%)	Projects requiring EIA registration form (%)
2002	233,000	3.1	26.6	70.3
2003	278,000	2.7	26.8	70.5
2004	321,000	3.2	29.9	66.9
2005	314,000	3.6	32.8	63.6
2006	363,500	3.6	33.2	63.2
2007	278,000	5.5	42.7	51.8
2008	268,000	5.5	42.7	51.8
2009	249,000	6.4	42	51.6
2010	390,200	6.1	43.5	50.3[a]
2011	No data available			
2012	428,000	6.8	41.8	51.2%
2013	476,000	7.1	39.9	52.9%
2014	442,000	7.7	40.5	52.0%
2015	440,000	7.3	40.9	51.8%[b]

Sources: SEPA/MEP/MEE, *Environmental Statistics Yearbook.* www.mee.gov.cn/hjzl/sthjzk/sthjtjnb/

[a] Due to rounding, percentages in this table may not total 100 per cent.

[b] The *Environmental Statistics Yearbook* has been published for the years 2000 to 2015. The latest available data is for 2015 and was published in 2017.

threshold in order to avoid the most comprehensive and time-consuming EIA process, thereby causing environmental harm by reducing checks and monitoring. In practice, only a small percentage of construction projects are required to conduct the most comprehensive EIA and prepare EIA reports. EIA statements make up more than one-third of the EIA documents submitted for approval, and EIA registration forms make up just over half.

An EIA report should include a description of the project, and should identify and assess the major environmental effects and the mitigation measures necessary to control the adverse environmental impacts.[35] In contrast, there are no specific requirements on the format or contents of EIA statements or EIA registration forms.[36] Prior to the reform of 2018, both EIA reports and EIA statements had to be prepared by licensed professional EIA

[35] EIAL (2018), art. 17(1). An EIA report must include: (i) a description of the construction project; (ii) the present situation of the environment surrounding the site of the proposed construction project; (iii) analysis, forecast and assessment of the possible impacts of the construction project on the environment; (iv) environmental protection measures to be undertaken during the construction project and relevant technical and economic analysis; (v) cost-benefit analysis of the environmental impacts of the construction project; (vi) recommendations on implementing a monitoring system for the environment at the construction project and (vii) the conclusion of the EIA.

[36] EIAL (2018), art. 17(2).

firms, while EIA registration forms could be completed by the project proponents themselves, as there were few technical requirements.[37] In December 2018, the EIAL (2016) was amended and the requirement that a licensed EIA firm prepare the EIA report or statement was abolished. A project proponent may still engage a professional service provider or technical entity to prepare an EIA report or statement if it wishes, but it may also prepare these itself if it has the technical capacity to do so.[38] The focus of the EIA process and documents is the environmental analysis on the siting of projects, a forecast of the potential adverse environmental impacts, and measures to prevent and control the environmental risks.[39]

4.2.2 The EIA Approval Authorities

Construction projects that require EIA reports or statements may not start construction until EIA approval has been granted by the environmental protection authorities.[40] The EIA reports and statements are submitted to the environmental protection authorities for examination and approval.[41] The authorities complete the review and convey the decisions to the construction proponent in writing within sixty days for EIA reports, and thirty days for EIA statements.[42] An EIA registration form is submitted to the local EPB for the record.[43] The review, approval and submission for the record of the EIA documents are free of charge and the approval authorities are not permitted to charge fees.[44]

The authority to approve EIA documents is divided between the MEE and local environment bureaus.[45] That is, the EIA approval authorities lie at the national, provincial and municipal levels.[46] The MEE has exclusive authority to review the EIA documents of the following projects: '(i) special projects such as nuclear facilities and projects involving top state secrets, (ii) projects cutting across provincial boundaries and (iii) projects examined and approved by the State Council or relevant departments with delegation from the State Council'.[47] For projects not falling within these categories, provincial governments may allocate the authority to approve the project to either provincial or municipal environmental agencies, depending on local circumstances and agency capacity.[48] Where

[37] EIAL (2016), art. 20. [38] EIAL (2018), art. 19(1).

[39] MEP, Implementation Plan on EIA Reform during the 13th FYP Period (2016), part III, s. 6.

[40] EIAL (2018), art. 25; EIA Regulation (2017), art. 9(1); for more on EIA approval, see Ma Yun, 'Dynamics in central–local division of the authority of EIA approval in China', *Journal of Environmental Law* , 31 (2019), 29.

[41] EIAL (2018), art. 22(1). [42] EIAL (2018), art. 22(3).

[43] EIAL (2018), art. 22(4). Previously, under the EIAL (2002), the EIA registration form was subject to examination and approval by the environmental agency within fifteen days. This switch to 'submission for the record' in 2016 has substantially alleviated the workload and transaction costs for local EPBs and the project proponents.

[44] EIAL (2018), art. 22(5).

[45] The MEE (known as the MEP from 2008 to 2018 and the SEPA prior to 2008) is the central government's top environmental protection authority. It makes environment policies at a national level and supervises the work of local EPBs, which exist at the provincial, municipal and county level to implement and enforce environment laws and regulations. For a detailed account of Chinese environmental protection institutions, see Abigail R. Jahiel, 'The organization of environmental protection in China' in Richard Louis Edmonds (ed.), *Managing the Chinese Environment* (Oxford and New York: Oxford University Press, 2000), 33–63.

[46] MEP, Implementation Plan on EIA Reform during the 13th FYP Period (2016), part III, s. 7.

[47] EIAL (2016), art. 23(1).

[48] EIAL (2016), art. 23(2); MEP, Implementation Plan on EIA Reform during the 13th FYP Period (2016), part III, s. 6.

disputes arise between local EPBs over a construction project potentially generating environmental impacts across administrative regions, the environment bureau at the next higher level has the authority to examine and approve or reject the EIA document.[49]

An agency review of EIA documents focuses on the feasibility of the construction project in relation to the needs of the environment, the reliability of the environmental impact analysis, forecast and assessment, the effectiveness of the proposed environmental protection measures, and the scientific soundness of the EIA conclusion.[50] EIA documents will not be approved in circumstances where:

(i) the nature, location, layout and scale of the construction project contravene environmental protection laws, regulation and plans;
(ii) the construction project is located in a region that has not achieved the national or local environmental quality standards, and the environmental measures proposed by the project fail to support regional targets for the improvement of environmental quality;
(iii) the pollution-control measures proposed by the construction project fail to guarantee compliance with the national and local emission or discharge standards, or fail to prevent and control ecological destruction;
(iv) the alteration, expansion or technological upgrading project fails to propose effective measures to prevent and control pre-existing pollution and ecological destruction;
(v) the EIA reports or EIA statements use obviously inaccurate information and data, contain serious flaws or omissions, or the conclusion is unclear or unreasonable.[51]

The EIA approval authorities may engage external professional firms to conduct a technical assessment of the EIA report or statement to compensate for the authority's lack of technical capacity in the review and approval of certain projects.[52]

4.2.3 Regulation of EIA Services and Quality Control

The quality of EIA service determines the accuracy and reliability of the EIA documents, which directly affects the soundness of the EIA approval decisions. Thus, prior to 2018 reforms, the EIAL (2002) required EIA firms conducting EIAs and preparing EIA reports or statements to be licensed. Such firms were required to obtain qualification licences from the state environmental authority and provide EIA services as specified in it.[53] While the state issued and updated a list of qualified EIA firms,[54] it was not permitted to allocate a specific EIA firm to a proposed construction project.[55] Construction units were free to choose any qualified EIA firm and could do so by public tender.[56] The SEPA's Measures on Qualification Management of Construction Project Environmental Impact Assessment (2005)[57] was repealed in 2015 by the MEP, which issued substantially revised measures

[49] EIAL (2016), art. 23(3). [50] EIA Regulation (2017), art. 9(2). [51] EIA Regulation (2017), art. 11.
[52] EIA Regulation (2017), art. 9(3). [53] EIAL (2002), art. 19(1).
[54] EIAL (2002), art. 19(2). The list of qualified EIA firms can be accessed at the MEP website. Ministry of Environmental Protection (n.d.). Website. www.mep.gov.cn/zhxx/jgzn/
[55] EIAL (2002), art. 20(2). [56] EIA Regulation (2017), art. 13.
[57] The Measures on Qualification Management in Construction Project Environmental Impact Assessment (2005) were issued by the SEPA on 15 August 2005 and came into force on 1 January 2006.

under the same name (MEP Measures) to delink institutional connections between some EIA firms and EIA approval authorities.[58] The situation had put some service providers at an unfair advantage, and also created opportunities for bribery and corruption.

Under the MEP Measures (2015), the MEP was in charge of issuing, renewing and upgrading qualification licences, approving changes to licences, and adjusting the scope of EIA services a licensee was permitted to provide.[59] Regulatory supervision of EIA firms took the form of random inspection, annual check or examination during the EIA approval process.[60] The MEP organized random inspections of EIA firms, while provincial EPBs organized an annual check of EIA firms within their jurisdiction.[61] The MEP Measures (2015) imposed sanctions on firms for EIA violations. If an EIA firm produced factually incorrect EIA documents due to irresponsibility or falsification, it was downgraded or had its licence revoked, and was fined one to three times the EIA service fee it had charged the client. Individual EIA engineers directly responsible for the preparation of the EIA documents were banned from EIA work for one to three years.[62] If an EIA firm produced low-quality EIA documents, both the firm and the individuals in charge were banned from EIA work for six to twelve months.[63] If the low-quality EIA documents caused the improper siting of a project or drew a false conclusion over the impact of the project, sanctions were imposed in accordance with article 45. Sanctions included downgrading the firm, revoking its licence and a fine.[64] These administrative decisions and sanctions were recorded in the EIA institution and engineer credit archive, a publicly accessible register.[65] Despite the regulatory controls, the quality of EIA services varied. Some EIA firms chose to accommodate a client's demands instead of carrying out the EIA in an objective and professional manner. Some treated the assessment process as a formality and did not base their conclusion or recommendations on scientific evidence or technical analysis. Some even fabricated data, produced untrue descriptions of projects or concealed important evidence in the preparation of EIA documents in order to obtain agency approval.[66] The 2017 annual EIA inspection found a total of 143 EIA institutions and 256 EIA engineers were violating EIA rules. Low-quality EIA documents accounted for 90 per cent of violations by institutions and 64 per cent of violations by individuals. The MEE circulated a list, derived from the 2017 EIA inspection, of fifty-one EIA institutions and seven EIA engineers with repeat violations – two or more violations – to provincial environmental agencies for closer supervision.[67]

[58] The MEP Measures (2015) were issued on 28 September 2015 and came into force on 1 November 2015. See article 7 for the firms that were ineligible to apply for an EIA qualification licence.

[59] MEP Measures (2015), art. 12(1). [60] MEP Measures (2015), art. 30. [61] MEP Measures (2015), art. 31.

[62] MEP Measures (2015), art. 45.

[63] MEP Measures (2015), art. 36(1). A 'low-quality EIA document' contains one of the following features: (i) error in the construction-project engineering analysis or error in the use of monitoring data; (ii) omission of environmental protection target or key assessment factor; (iii) it is beyond the scope for which the EIA firm is licensed, or an error exists in the application of environmental standards; (iv) error in the methodology used for forecasting and assessing environmental impacts; (v) lack of major environmental protection measures.

[64] MEP Measures (2015), art. 36(2). [65] MEP Measures (2015), art. 39.

[66] Mei Hong, 'Problems of China's EIA law and responses', *Asia-Pacific Economic Review*, 4:July–August (2005), 93–6.

[67] MEE, Circular on 2017 Annual Inspection and Sanction of EIA Institutions and EIA Engineers (26 March 2018).

Reform to the EIA system in 2018 has, however, abolished the licensing requirement for EIA service providers.[68] Municipal environmental agencies exercise regulatory supervision over entities providing an EIA service.[69] The focus of quality control has shifted from licensing of EIA firms to the quality of the EIA documents. The proponent of a construction project is held accountable for the overall quality of the EIA, including the contents and conclusion of the EIA documents, while the technical entities hired by construction projects to provide an EIA service are accountable only for the EIA documents they produce, also including the contents and conclusion.[70] An important amendment made in the EIAL (2018) is that administrative sanctions are imposed in cases of low-quality EIA documents that contain either: (i) obviously untrue data; (ii) serious defects, omission or false statements or (iii) an incorrect or unreasonable conclusion, among others. In such cases, since 2018, fines are imposed on the construction unit and on individuals liable for the low-quality EIA: a fine of half a million to 2 million yuan is imposed on the construction unit (the legal person) and a fine of 50,000 yuan to 200,000 yuan is imposed on individuals, including legal representatives of the construction unit, senior persons in charge and those directly liable.[71] Where these quality problems are found in EIA documents prepared by technical entities that have been engaged by the construction units, the technical entity is fined an amount three to five times their EIA service fee. Where circumstances are serious, the technical entity will be prohibited from providing further EIA services.[72] In addition, the qualified EIA engineer in charge of the EIA work and key members of the team that prepared the EIA documents will be barred from working in EIA services for five years. Where a crime is committed, they will be investigated for criminal liability and prohibited from providing EIA services for life.[73]

4.2.4 Enforcement and Sanction of EIA Violations

The EIAL (2002) was groundbreaking in its promotion of pollution prevention and democratic participation in government decision-making. However, implementation and enforcement of the EIAL (2002) were less satisfactory, and EIA did not become the effective tool for sound government decision-making that it should have been. The 'EIA storm' of 2005 highlighted extensive violations of the EIAL (2002) by construction projects, including projects initiated by state-owned enterprises. Even Xie Zhenhua, head of the SEPA at the time, admitted that implementation and enforcement of EIAL (2002) was unsatisfactory.[74]

The EIA storm (2005)

On 18 January 2005, the SEPA shocked China by suspending construction work on thirty megaprojects in thirteen provinces and municipalities, because they had started construction without conducting the EIA required by the EIAL (2002). The thirty projects were worth 117.9 billion yuan; twenty-six were hydropower stations, thermal power plants and other

[68] EIAL (2018), art. 19. [69] EIAL (2018), art. 20(2). [70] EIAL (2018), art. 20(1).
[71] EIAL (2018), art. 32(1). The fines are imposed by environment agencies at or above the municipal level.
[72] EIAL (2018), art. 32(2). [73] EIAL (2018), art. 32(3).
[74] Ray Cheung, '"Toothless tiger" to pounce again', *South China Morning Post*, 16 March 2005, 7.

power-generating facilities, including three hydropower plants being constructed by the China Three Gorges Project Corp.,[75] a politically powerful state-owned enterprise at the same administrative level as the SEPA. Other big names on the list included China's three largest state-owned power companies: China Guodian Corp., Huadian Power International Corp. and Datang International Power Generation Corp. Shortly after the projects were suspended, Pan Yue, then deputy head of SEPA, said, '[m]any have treated the EIAL as a rubber stamp. What I want to say is that it isn't, and we are determined to change the conventional attitude of the people.'[76] Domestic media acclaimed the SEPA's move as a storm that would blow away longstanding obstacles to enforcement of environmental laws and regulations.[77]

It was obvious that the SEPA's enforcement action would encounter strong resistance from powerful departments in the central government. By 24 January 2005, only twenty-two of the thirty projects were complying with the suspension order.[78] A Guizhou power project owned by China Huadian Corp. resumed construction within two days of the SEPA announcement.[79] It was not until full support was given by Premier Wen Jiabao to the enforcement action that all thirty projects suspended construction on 2 February 2005.[80] However, by 19 February, the SEPA had to permit twenty-six projects to resume construction due to political pressure.[81] In this incredibly short period of time, make-up EIAs were conducted and EIA reports prepared, examined and approved, raising concerns over the quality of the assessment and validity of the approval.

It was true that EIA had been treated largely as a formality and had failed to prevent and mitigate the environmental degradation caused by construction projects. By targeting the Three Gorges hydropower projects and other power facilities at a time when China desperately needed to increase its energy generation capacity, the SEPA sent a clear message that the EIAL (2002) was to be implemented and enforced. It was time to change deep-rooted attitudes that saw EIA treated as a 'toothless tiger'.

The EIA storm revealed the common practices of going ahead with construction without conducting an EIA, or 'construction first, EIA later'. The reason for the widespread violations is simple: the cost of violation was low compared to the high cost of EIA compliance. Under the EIAL (2002), project developers starting construction without an EIA were

[75] SEPA, 'SEPA Deputy Head Pan Yue reports on the illegal construction of 30 projects and orders suspension of projects ignoring environmental impact assessment regime', (press release) no. 3, 18 January 2005; see also SEPA, *China Environment Yearbook* (2006), 279.

[76] Li Shufei and Chen Tianlu, 'The senior official that blew the "environmental protection storm" ', *Government and Law*, 6A (2005), 10–13; Shi Jiangtao, 'Watchdog flexes muscles, orders work on "illegal" projects to stop', *South China Morning Post*, 19 January 2005, 6; Shi Jiangtao, 'Wen supports crackdown on 30 unapproved projects', *South China Morning Post*, 27 January 2005, 5.

[77] Liu Yi, 'Behind the order to suspend thirty giant projects', *People's Daily*, 27 January 2005, 16; Qie Jianrong, 'Let environmental protection laws be strengthened as steel', *Legal Daily*, 31 January 2005, 1.

[78] SEPA, 'SEPA Deputy Head Pan Yue updates on the 30 illegal construction projects: most have suspended construction', (press release) no. 5, 24 January 2005.

[79] Shi Jiangtao, 'Watchdog clears the way for power plant construction to restart', *South China Morning Post*, 17 February 2005, 4.

[80] SEPA, 'SEPA Deputy Head Pan Yue: hydropower construction projects must implement EIA, all thirty projects are being rectified', (press release) no. 9, 2 February 2005; see also Qin Chuan, 'All 30 law-breaking projects building stopped', *China Daily*, 3 February 2005.

[81] 'Most postponed projects granted go-ahead for construction', *Xinhua General News Service*, 19 February 2005.

ordered by the local EPB to suspend construction and conduct a make-up EIA by a specified deadline. Failing to submit an EIA document within the stipulated time limit led to a maximum fine of 200,000 yuan.[82] A construction unit had nothing to lose by beginning construction without an EIA and submitting a make-up EIA document by the deadline. It might even have had a better chance of a swift approval since the investment was already in place and construction already in progress. A fine capped at 200,000 yuan is negligible for megaprojects involving investment of multi-million or multi-billion yuan. The low cost of violation and low risk of being sanctioned created incentives for project developers to ignore the statutory EIA requirement. The EIAL (2002) failed to deter violation.[83] Consequently, the EIAL (2016) removed the cap of 200,000 yuan on the fine for failing to submit an EIA document within a stipulated time limit, and also includes an optional sanction of restoration, meaning that the construction unit must restore the site to the state it was prior to the work it carried out. Now, if a construction unit starts construction without submitting EIA documents for approval, or prior to obtaining the EIA approval, they will be ordered to suspend construction and will be fined between 1 per cent and 5 per cent of the total project cost, depending on the circumstances of violation and degree of environmental harm. Further, EPBs may order restoration.[84] Failure to submit an EIA registration form for the record is subject to a fine of 50,000 yuan.[85]

4.2.5 Post-Approval Assessment and Follow-up Inspection

Post-approval monitoring and assessment of the environmental impact generated by construction and operation is crucial for pollution prevention and control. Where unexpected circumstances occur during construction or operation of a project that are inconsistent with the forecasts and assessments of the EIA documents, the construction units must conduct a post-approval EIA, take measures to improve pollution control and report to the EIA approval authorities for the record. In any case, the EIA approval authority has the power to order construction units to conduct post-approval EIA and take improvement measures.[86] When the project starts operating, environmental bureaus must carry out a follow-up inspection of the environmental impacts generated by the project and, where serious environmental pollution or ecological destruction is caused by the project, will investigate to determine the causes and liabilities.[87]

Reforms to the EIA process in 2016 emphasized the importance of post-approval EIA, which should be conducted for significant projects that have long-term, cumulative or uncertain environmental impacts, high environmental risks or cut across important and

[82] EIAL (2002), art. 31(1). Previously the fine was capped at 100,000 yuan under the EIA Regulation (1998), art. 24.

[83] It is estimated that the cost of environmental violation is less than 10 per cent of the cost of taking environmental measures to prevent or minimize pollution, and less than 2 per cent of the cost of environmental harm. Wang Canfa, 'Low cost of environmental violation: causes and proposal for change', *Environmental Protection*, 9 (September 2005), 32–4.

[84] EIAL (2016), art. 31(1) and (2). During the drafting of the EIAL (2002), Professor Wang Canfa proposed introducing the sanction of restoration order. However, it was not adopted by the lawmakers at that stage. Wang Canfa, 'Discussion on several issues in drafting the Chinese EIA law', *Chinese Environment News*, 9 March 2001.

[85] EIAL (2016), art. 31(3).

[86] EIAL (2016), art. 27; Regulation on Project EIA (2017), art. 19(2).

[87] EIAL (2016), art. 28.

ecologically sensitive regions. In these cases, post-approval EIA covers post-approval environmental management of the projects.[88] The regulatory focus on post-approval EIA assessment and supervision aims to ensure full implementation of the pollution-control measures proposed in the EIA documents, thereby achieving the purpose of the EIA – the prevention and mitigation of adverse environmental harm caused by construction and operation of a project.

4.2.6 Alignment with Three-Simultaneities Requirement and Permit Control

Until the reforms of 2016 and 2018, China's EIA regime focused on the preparation and approval of the EIA documents, but failed to ensure pollution-control measures were implemented effectively after EIA approval had been given. Many project proponents do not care about the environmental mitigation measures proposed in the EIA documents. Their only concern is to obtain agency approval of the EIA documents. To improve the effectiveness of EIAs in pollution prevention and mitigation and ensure they are more than a mere pass to start construction, the EIA is linked with the three-simultaneities requirement and the pollution control by permit. The alignment of the three mechanisms ensures that all the proposed pollution-control measures in the EIA documents and the additional requirements imposed by the approval agencies are in fact implemented.

Under the three-simultaneities requirement, the environmental measures proposed in an EIA document should be designed, constructed and put into operation simultaneously with the construction project itself. Unfortunately, an investigation by the SEPA prior to 2006 found that among the projects that had conducted an EIA and had received EIA approval, less than half complied with the three-simultaneities requirement.[89] Some enterprises already in operation had never installed pollution treatment facilities. Others had installed the facilities, but only ran them during site inspections in order to cut costs. The amendments of both the EIAL (2002) and the EIA Regulation (1998) shifted the regulatory focus from EIA approval to the implementation of environmental measures that had been proposed by the EIA documents and imposed by the approval agencies. The EIAL (2016) and EIA Regulation (2017) aim to ensure pollution-control measures are properly implemented by linking EIAs with the three-simultaneities requirement.[90] Throughout the stages of project design and construction, the construction units are fully responsible for implementing the pollution-control measures proposed by EIA documents or imposed by the approval authorities.[91] Upon completion of project construction, construction units must inspect their pollution-control installations and release the inspection report to the public.[92]

[88] MEP, Implementation Plan on EIA Reform during the 13th FYP Period (2016), part IV, s. 9.

[89] Bu Xuelin, 'Zhou Shengxian emphasizes Premier Wen Jiaobao's instruction to win environmental law enforcement victory at 2006 Environmental Protection Action Teleconference', *China Environment News*, 2 June 2006. Zhou Shengxian became head of the SEPA in February 2006 when Xie Zhenhua resigned over the delay in the emergency response to the Songhua River benzene spill.

[90] The three-simultaneities requirement means that a polluting source should have its pollution control installations designed, constructed and put into operation at the same time as the main project. The mechanism was written into Chinese environmental law for the first time in the EPL (for trial implementation) (1979), art. 6(1). It was then incorporated into the EPL (1989), art. 26. The three-simultaneities requirement is also found in all specialized environmental statutes.

[91] EIAL (2016), art. 26; EIA Regulation (2017), art. 16.

[92] EIA Regulation (2017), art. 17.

Constructors are encouraged to engage professional third parties to carry out the inspection and produce the inspection report.[93] A construction project may not be put into operation or use until its pollution-control installations have been inspected and passed a quality check.[94] Project operators must submit proof of compliance with the EIA and the three-simultaneities requirement before they can apply for and obtain a pollution discharge permit. All environmental protection and pollution-control measures proposed by the EIA documents and those imposed by the approval agencies are incorporated into the terms and conditions of the pollution discharge permit. Project operators, as permit holders, are legally bound by the permit while the project operates.

4.2.7 Project EIA at the Termination of Operations

Before the reforms, project EIA primarily focused on assessment prior to the construction of projects, rather than at the end of operations. An EIA has an equally important role at the stage of project decommissioning, and should be used to assess the environmental risk when a polluter shuts down or relocates. The MEP intends, by the end of the 13th FYP period, to have conducted an environmental risk assessment of key enterprises in the following sectors: non-ferrous metal refining, oil processing, chemicals, coking, electroplating and tanneries. They are prioritized because they generate and discharge pollutants including heavy metals, persistent organic pollutants (POPs), hazardous waste (HW) and carcinogens.[95]

4.3 SEA

China's environmental degradation is the direct consequence of decades of unsustainable economic growth. According to Qu Geping, chairman of the ERPC during the eighth NPC (1993–98) and ninth NPC (1998–2003), the fundamental causes of China's environmental problems are mistakes in state development policies and plans. He stated that it is impossible to tackle China's ecological and environmental problems without addressing the failure of development policies and plans.[96] Any mistakes made at the stage of making a policy or plan, such as a high concentration of heavily polluting industries in residential areas or over-exploitation of the water resources of a river basin, cannot be rectified by project EIA. Preliminary experiments with SEA had taken place in China since the 1990s. Studies of SEA carried out at the state, provincial and municipal levels include SEAs of China's automobile industry development policy, Shanxi province's coal and electricity development strategy and Changchun Economic and Technological Development Zone.[97]

93 MEP, Implementation Plan on EIA Reform during the 13th FYP Period (2016), part IV, section 9.

94 EIA Regulation (2017), art. 19(1).

95 MEP, Implementation Plan on EIA Reform during the 13th FYP Period (2016), part III, s. 7.

96 Qu Geping, *Qu's Pursuit*, 351.

97 For detailed analysis and studies of SEAs undertaken in China in the 1990s, see Che Xiuzhen et al., 'Strategic environmental assessment and its development in China', *Environmental Impact Assessment Review*, 22 (2002), 101–9; Bao Cun-kuan et al., 'Framework and operational procedure for implementing strategic environmental assessment in China', *Environmental Impact Assessment Review*, 24 (2004), 27–46; Tang Tao et al., 'Integrating environment into land-use planning through strategic environmental assessment in China: towards legal frameworks and operational procedures', *Environmental Impact Assessment Review*, 27 (2007), 243–65.

The early pilot exercises convinced the SEPA that China should formally adopt SEA to make governments consider environmental factors and consequences at the early stages of their decision-making process. While both the ERPC and SEPA had tried to expand the coverage of EIA to include not only projects, but also policies and plans in the drafting of the EIAL (2002), they encountered strong resistance from both state ministries and local governments, because their powers to make development policies and plans would have been substantially restricted by the environmental scrutiny contained in the proposed bill. There was a twenty-month impasse after the first reading of the draft bill and compromises had to be made to move the bill forward.[98] It was eventually decided that the bill would not apply to government policies.

Despite the power struggles and reluctant compromises, the EIAL (2002) did expand the scope of environmental assessment from project EIA only to include plan EA, forcing the government to take environmental factors into account at the plan-making stage. However, not all government plans are subject to the legal requirement of EA. Only development plans that are likely to cause significant adverse environmental impacts when implemented are required to conduct an EA. Plans are divided into general plans and specialized plans, each of which are subject to different types of environmental assessment.[99] General development plans include land-use plans, and plans on regional, river basin and marine development and construction, while specialized plans cover the development of industry, agriculture, animal husbandry, forestry, energy, water resources, transport, urban construction, tourism and natural resources.[100] The scope of plans subject to the statutory EA requirement will be determined by the state environmental authority and relevant departments subject to the approval of the State Council.[101] The Regulation on Plan EA (2009)[102] provides for detailed rules on the assessment, review, follow-up assessment and legal liabilities.

4.3.1 EA of General Plans

In the making of plans on land use, regional development, river basin development or marine development, state ministries and local governments (and their relevant departments) are required to conduct an EA and the plan should contain an EA chapter or statement.[103] The EA chapters or statements analyse, forecast and assess the potential environmental impacts to be caused by the implementation of a plan, and propose measures to avoid or mitigate the adverse impacts. These documents must be submitted to the

98 For more details on the difficulties encountered during the drafting of the EIAL (2002) and the expansion of the scope of EIA to include plans, as well as projects, see Qu Geping, *Qu's Pursuit*, 350–6.

99 Under articles 7 and 8 of the EIAL (2018), the type of EA and document required depends on the type of government plan. If the plan in question requires a brief and general EA, an EA chapter or statement follows (art. 7). If the plan needs a more comprehensive and in-depth EA, an EA report follows (art. 8).

100 Qu Geping, *Qu's Pursuit*, 353–4.

101 EIAL (2018), art. 9. The SEPA issued the Notice on Specific Scope of Plans Required to Prepare EA Report (for trial use) and Specific Scope of Plans Required to Prepare EA Chapter or Statement (for trial use) under article 9 of the EIAL (2002) on 6 July 2004 (Huan Fa no. 98 of 2004).

102 The Regulation on Plan EA was issued by the State Council on 17 August 2009 and came into force on 1 October 2009. See also Jing Wu et al., 'Strategic environmental assessment implementation', 77–84.

103 EIAL (2018), art. 7(1). Here 'local governments' refers to those at or above municipal level under which districts are established.

approval authority as part of the draft plan.[104] The approval authority cannot examine or approve any draft plan without the required EA chapters or statements.[105] The legislative provision is vague as to the content and environmental scrutiny required of the EA chapter or statement, leaving it to the discretion of the approval authorities in charge of development. The SEPA tried to address this legislative gap in 2006, specifying essential components to be included in the EA chapter or statement.[106] The Regulation on Plan EA (2009) adds to this by stipulating items to be included in an EA chapter or statement:

(i) the analysis, forecast and assessment of the potential environmental impacts caused by the implementation of the proposed plan shall include analysis of the carrying capacity of the environment, analysis and forecast of the adverse environmental impact, and analysis on the coordination of environmental protection and the proposed plan.
(ii) the measures to prevent and mitigate adverse environmental impact shall include policies and administrative and technological measures to prevent and mitigate potential environmental harm.[107]

The MEP is making fresh efforts to strengthen plan EA, with a focus on regional development plans. It aimed to complete SEAs on the Beijing–Tianjin–Hebei region, the Yangtze River Delta and Pearl River Delta during the 13th FYP period (2016–20) and also plans to conduct an SEA of the Yangtze River Economic Belt and of the Belt and Road Initiative, China's massive infrastructure project linking Asia, Africa and Europe.[108]

4.3.2 EA of Specialized Plans

In the making of specialized plans concerning the development of industry, agriculture, animal husbandry, forestry, energy, water resources, transport, urban construction, tourism or natural resources, departments of the State Council, local governments and their departments are required to conduct an EA before submitting the draft plans for examination and approval. They must prepare an EA report and submit it together with the draft plan to the plan approval authority,[109] which cannot examine and approve the draft plan without the EA report.[110] An EA report on a specialized plan covers: (i) analysis, forecast and assessment of the potential environmental impacts caused by the implementation of the plan; (ii) measures to prevent or mitigate the adverse environmental impacts and (iii) the conclusion of the EA.[111] The conclusion must discuss: (i) the environmental rationality and feasibility of the draft plan, (ii) the reasonableness and effectiveness of the measures proposed to

[104] EIAL (2016), art. 7(2). [105] EIAL (2016), art. 7(3).
[106] SEPA, Notice on Further Improving Environmental Impact Assessment of Plans, 25 September 2006 (Huan Ban no. 109 of 2006). Section 6 of the Notice provides that EA chapters or statements shall in principle include the following: (i) an analysis of the environmental resources factors restricting the implementation of the plan; (ii) an analysis of the coordination of the plan with the relevant policies, laws and regulations; (iii) identification, analysis and projection of the direct, indirect and cumulative adverse impacts resulting from the implementation of the plan, and assessment and evaluation of the burden of the plan on environment and resources; (iv) responses and measures to prevent and mitigate adverse environmental impact; (v) details on public participation and an explanation of whether or not public opinion was adopted; and (vi) conclusion on the environmental impact.
[107] Regulation on Plan EA (2009), art. 11(1).
[108] MEP, Implementation Plan on EIA Reform during the 13th FYP Period (2016), part II, s. 4.
[109] EIAL (2018), art. 8. [110] EIAL (2018), art. 12. [111] EIAL (2018), art. 10.

prevent and mitigate adverse environmental impact and (iii) recommendations for adjusting the draft plan.[112] The SEPA listed eight essential components to be included in the EA reports.[113]

Prior to a government approval of any specialized plan, the environmental protection authority convenes a review panel to examine the EA report. The review panel is composed of representatives of relevant departments and experts. It issues its opinion in writing.[114] The experts on the review panel are randomly selected from an expert list of the relevant profession held in a database maintained by the State Council.[115] Experts involved in the preparation of the EA report may not serve on the review panel examining the same report.[116] Experts must constitute at least half of the review panel, otherwise the panel's opinion is invalid.[117] The review panel must examine the EA report and issues its written opinion in an objective, unbiased and independent manner without any interference by the plan approval authority, the plan proponent or the environmental authority that convenes the panel.[118] The panel's opinion must discuss: (i) the accuracy of the basic information and data; (ii) the appropriateness of the assessment methods; (iii) the reliability of the analysis, forecast and assessment; (iv) the reasonableness and effectiveness of the measures on prevention and mitigation of adverse environmental impacts; (v) the reasonableness of the explanation for adopting or rejecting public opinions and (vi) the scientific soundness of the EA conclusion.[119] To be valid, the review opinion must be endorsed and signed by at least three-quarters of the members. Dissenting opinions are noted for the record.[120] Where an EA report fails to pass any one of the above six criteria, or there is any other serious flaw or omission, the review panel will issue an opinion stating that the EA report needs to be revised and re-submitted.[121] Where the review panel is of the view that the proposed plan may generate adverse environmental impact, the degree and extent of which cannot be assessed by existing knowledge and technology, or no feasible measures may be taken to

[112] Regulation on Plan EA (2009), art. 11(2).

[113] SEPA, Notice on Further Improving Environmental Impact Assessment of Plans, 25 September 2006 (Huan Ban no. 109 of 2006). Section 6 of the Notice provides that EA reports must in principle include the following: (i) a brief introduction of the plan; (ii) an analysis of the environmental resources factors restricting implementation of the plan; (iii) an analysis of the coordination of the plan with the relevant policies, laws and regulations; (iv) identification, analysis and projection of the direct, indirect and cumulative adverse impacts resulting from the implementation of the plan, and assessment and evaluation of the burden of the plan on the environment and resources; (v) responses and measures to prevent and mitigate adverse impact on the environment; (vi) details on public participation and an explanation as to whether public opinion has been adopted or rejected; (vii) a follow-up plan to assess significant adverse environmental impact; and (viii) conclusion on the environmental impact.

[114] EIAL (2018), art. 13(1). The written opinions of the examination group must record accurately the opinions of the experts, and must be signed by them. The opinions must include: (i) the rationality and accuracy of the analysis and projection of the environmental impacts of the implementation of the specialized plan; (ii) the feasibility and effectiveness of the response and the measures proposed to prevent and mitigate adverse environmental impact, and suggestions for adjustment; (iii) an evaluation of the EIA report and its conclusion and (iv) an overall evaluation of the rationality and feasibility of the specialized plan from the perspective of socio-economic and environmental sustainable development. See SEPA, Provisions on Review and Examination of the EIA Report of the Specialized Plans (2003), s. 7.

[115] EIAL (2018), art. 13(2).

[116] Regulation on Plan EA (2009), art. 18(1).

[117] Regulation on Plan EA (2009), art. 18(2).

[118] Regulation on Plan EA (2009), art. 19(1).

[119] Regulation on Plan EA (2009), art. 19(2).

[120] Regulation on Plan EA (2009), art. 19(3).

[121] Regulation on Plan EA (2009), art. 20.

prevent or mitigate the serious adverse impact to be caused by the proposed plan, the panel will refuse to endorse the EA report.[122]

The 2016 amendment of EIAL (2002) further strengthened plan EA. It stipulates that where a review panel has recommended revision, the plan proponent must revise and improve the draft plan on the basis of the conclusion of the EA report and the opinion of the review panel. The plan proponent must provide an explanation on the adoption or reasons for rejection of the EA conclusion or the review panel's opinion.[123] The plan approval authority is obliged to refer to the conclusion of the EA report and the written opinion of the review panel as the basis of its decision-making.[124] If the conclusion of the EA report or the written opinion of the review panel is not adopted in the approval process, an explanation must be noted for the record and for public inspection.[125] Relevant units, experts and the public may apply to gain access to the records.[126]

4.3.3 Follow-up Assessment

The implementation of a plan with significant environmental impacts requires the plan proponent to conduct a timely follow-up assessment during implementation and report the assessment outcome to the approval authority. Where unexpected adverse environmental impacts become obvious, the plan proponent proposes improvement measures immediately.[127] A follow-up assessment includes:[128]

(i) comparative analysis and assessment of the actual environmental impacts generated by the implementation of the plan and the projected impacts,
(ii) analysis and assessment of the effectiveness of the measures to prevent and mitigate the adverse environmental impacts of plan implementation,
(iii) public opinion on the environmental impacts caused by the implementation of the plan and
(iv) conclusion of the follow-up assessment.

Public opinion may be collected from relevant units, experts or members of the public by questionnaire, via on-site visit and interview, discussion forum or any other means.[129] Where serious adverse environmental impacts are caused by the implementation of a plan, the plan proponent must propose improvement measures in a timely manner, report to the approval authority and notify the environmental protection authority.[130] Where serious adverse environmental impacts are detected by environmental protection authorities, they must verify the impacts in a timely manner and recommend improvement measures or plan revisions to the approval authority.[131] Upon receiving a report from the plan proponent or a recommendation from the environmental protection authority, the plan approval authority organizes an investigation and discussion and, on the basis of this, improves or revises the

[122] Regulation on Plan EA (2009), art. 21. [123] EIAL (2016), art. 14(1).
[124] EIAL (2016), art. 14(2); Regulation on Plan EA (2009), art. 22(1). [125] EIAL (2016), art. 14(3).
[126] Regulation on Plan EA (2009), art. 22(2). Records involving state secrets are, however, excluded from public access.
[127] EIAL (2018), art. 15. [128] Regulation on Plan EA (2009), art. 25.
[129] Regulation on Plan EA (2009), art. 26. [130] Regulation on Plan EA (2009), art. 27.
[131] Regulation on Plan EA (2009), art. 28.

plan.[132] In a region in which plans are being implemented, if the total emission or discharge of key pollutants already exceeds national or local total control targets, examination and approval of EIAs of new projects that generate additional key pollutants will be suspended.[133]

4.3.4 Legal Liabilities of Relevant Parties

The EIAL (2018) imposes legal liabilities on relevant parties involved in the preparation and approval of government plans. Where the plan proponent, in violation of this law, fails to conduct an EA or conducts the assessment by falsifying data or other professional misconduct, causing substantial inaccuracy to the EA conclusion, the authority at the next higher level or the supervisory authority imposes administrative disciplinary sanctions on the persons in charge or others directly involved in the process.[134] Where the approval authority approves a draft plan without the required EA chapter or statement, or approves a draft specialized plan without the required EA report, the authority at the next higher level or the supervisory authority imposes administrative disciplinary sanctions on the persons in charge, or others directly involved in the process.[135] Administrative disciplinary sanctions are imposed on civil servants or government employees to punish their wrongdoing. Depending on the seriousness of the misconduct, administrative disciplinary sanctions may take the form of warning, record of a demerit, record of a serious demerit, demotion or dismissal from post and dismissal.[136]

Where experts of the review panel engage in falsification or professional misconduct in the review process, causing substantial inaccuracy to the EA of plans, they shall, by public announcement, be disqualified and removed from the database of experts.[137] Where an environmental firm in charge of the EA of plans has caused substantial inaccuracy of the EA documents by falsification or professional misconduct, it is fined the sum of one to three times the assessment fees it had charged, and may also be criminally liable.[138]

4.3.5 Implementation of Plan EA

Formidable difficulties exist at the stage of implementation and enforcement of plan EA. A general lack of support from state ministries and local governments in charge of making development plans was as expected, given that it takes time and effort to change mentality and shift focus from the speed and scale of growth to the quality and sustainability of development.[139]

The law-making on SEA had encountered strong resistance from state departments and local governments, and the provisions on plan EA were the result of compromise and are inherently flawed. The rules on EA of general plans are broad and vague, and are silent on the contents of and formalities relating to the EA chapter or statement, public involvement

[132] Regulation on Plan EA (2009), art. 29. [133] Regulation on Plan EA (2009), art. 30.

[134] EIAL (2018), art. 29; Regulation on Plan EA (2009), art. 31.

[135] EIAL (2018), art. 30; Regulation on Plan EA (2009), art. 32.

[136] The Law on Civil Servants (2005), art. 56; SEPA and Ministry of Supervision, Provisional Rule on Administrative Disciplinary Sanctions on Violation of Environmental Laws and Rules (2006).

[137] Regulation on Plan EA (2009), art. 33. [138] Regulation on Plan EA (2009), art. 34.

[139] The State Council issued the Decision on Implementing Scientific Development and Strengthening Environmental Protection (State Council Decision) on 3 December 2005. Section 8 emphasizes the need for coordinated and harmonious development that balances the needs of the economy and the environment through the EA of certain development and construction plans.

and the review and examination mechanism. Even in the case of specialized plans, which are subjected to a greater degree of statutory environmental scrutiny, environmental authorities are in an awkward and confused position. They must convene experts and representatives from relevant departments to form a review panel which will examine the EA report and issue a written opinion for the plan approval authority to consider. It is unclear, however, whether the environmental authority's role is limited to mere formation of the review panel and organization of meetings, or whether it has any further function. The resistance to any suggestion of environmental scrutiny was strong and obvious, coming from both state ministries and local governments in charge of industrial and economic development.[140]

The provision that punishes violations in the preparation or approval of a plan by imposing administrative disciplinary sanctions on individuals in charge or directly involved is very difficult to enforce. In China, the preparation and approval of development plans is a complicated process that often involves more than a few departments or administrative regions. It is seldom the work of only a few individuals. The imposition of administrative disciplinary sanctions on individuals raises the questions of fairness and feasibility in enforcement. In addition, administrative disciplinary sanctions are imposed internally by higher-level authorities. There is doubt as to how strictly authorities would enforce articles 29 and 30 of the EIAL (2018) against individuals who were acting under their supervision in the preparation and approval of government plans. The MEP is strengthening government accountability through environmental inspection. The central government inspects the work of implementation at local levels by verifying whether the EA conclusion or opinion has been implemented.[141] However, there is no statutory provision on what should be done if a government plan is prepared and approved in violation of the EIAL. The goal of plan EA is to predict, analyse and assess potential environmental harms and take measures at the earliest stage possible to prevent and mitigate adverse environmental impacts caused by the implementation of the proposed plans. Any administrative disciplinary sanctions that are in fact imposed on individuals may deter wrongdoing or neglect of duty in the future, but do not address the core issue of the defective plan. Professor Wang Canfa proposed that all government plans that violated a legal provision on the preparation and approval of EA documents should be invalidated.[142]

4.3.6 Moving Forward: EA of Government Policies

During the 13th FYP period (2016–20), the MEP has trialled the EA of policies, beginning with important policies such as policies on new-model urbanization and development restructuring. Relevant policymakers should take the lead in the assessment of the potential environmental impact and implications of the policy, with full participation by stakeholders and experts.[143] The purpose is to explore and establish a mechanism and technical framework for conducting EA of government policies.

[140] Sun Xiuyan, 'Pan Yue: Obstacles to the implementation of EIA of government plans come from conflict of interests', *People's Daily*, 8 November 2007, 10.

[141] MEP, Implementation Plan on EIA Reform during the 13th FYP Period (2016), part II, s. 5.

[142] See Wang Canfa, 'Legal issues of strategic environmental assessment', *Legal Forum*, 19:3 (2004), 13–19.

[143] MEP, Implementation Plan on EIA Reform during the 13th FYP Period (2016), part II, s. 4.

4.4 PUBLIC PARTICIPATION

The EIA regime not only provides a scientific basis and procedural framework for decision-making through the technical assessment of potential environmental impact, but also provides opportunities for stakeholders and the public to be informed and to make their voice heard in the decision-making process. 'Law contributes to these functions by demarcating the limits of discretion'[144] of the approval authorities.

4.4.1 Public Participation in Plan EA

The statutory requirement for public participation in the process of plan EA is limited. Public participation in the preparation of an EA chapter or statement for a general plan is not obligatory. Both the EIAL (2018)[145] and the Regulation on Plan EA (2009)[146] only impose a duty to consult the public if a specialized plan may generate adverse environmental impact and directly affect the rights and interests of the public in relation to the environment. Specialized plans include plans relating to industry, agriculture, animal husbandry, forestry, energy, water resources, transportation, urban construction, tourism and development of natural resources.[147]

Where a specialized plan may cause adverse environmental impacts that directly infringe upon the environmental rights and interests of the public, the plan proponent must solicit public opinion on the EA report from relevant entities, experts and members of the public by holding discussion forums, public hearings or through any other means before submitting the draft plan for examination and approval.[148] If there are serious disputes over the EA conclusion among the relevant entities, experts and the public, the plan proponent must engage in further consultation by hosting discussion forums or public hearings.[149] The plan proponent must seriously consider public opinion on the EA report and must explain why it accepts or rejects this in a document submitted with the EA report.[150] The first high-profile case of plan EA involves the hydropower development plan on the Nu River in Yunnan province.

The Nu River Hydropower Development Plan (2003)

Hydropower development on the Nu River was on the NDRC's agenda in 1999 to promote clean and renewable energy. After years of feasibility study, the Nu River Hydropower Development Plan proposed the construction of thirteen dams with an annual generation capacity of more than 100 billion kW. On 14 August 2003, the Plan was reviewed by the NDRC. SEPA raised two points of

[144] Holder, *Environmental* Assessment, at 6. [145] EIAL (2018), art. 11
[146] Regulation on Plan EA (2009), art. 13.
[147] Measures on Public Participation in Environmental Impact Assessment (Measures on Public Participation) (2018), article 2(1).
[148] EIAL (2018), art. 11(1); Regulation on Plan EA (2009), art. 13(1). An exception to the requirement for public consultation is made in the case of state secrets.
[149] Regulation on Plan EA (2009), art. 13(2).
[150] EIAL (2018), art. 11(2); Regulation on Plan EA (2009), art. 13(3).

concern: (i) the region encompassing the Nu, Lancang and Jinsha rivers, known as the Three Parallel Rivers of Yunnan, was designated by UNESCO as a World Heritage Site on 3 July 2003 due to its unique ecological value; (ii) the EIAL (2002) was to be implemented on 1 September 2003 and would require EA of government plans, including those concerning hydropower development. On 15 August 2003, local media in Yunnan province reported that the Nu River Hydropower Development Plan had been approved by the NDRC, predicting that the large-scale investment would boost the local economy. On 3 September 2003, SEPA organized a meeting to consult experts. Twenty-seven experts attended and all expressed concerns over the adverse impacts on the ecosystem, including on the World Heritage Site. In September 2003, a heated national debate began on the proposed plan and NGOs, scientists, SEPA officials, media and the public formed an alliance to campaign against the approval of the Plan.

Given the public outcry, the NDRC submitted the Plan to the State Council for a final decision. In February 2004, Premier Wen Jiabao decided to suspend it, remarking that 'with regard to this kind of large-scale hydropower development that has drawn significant public concern and attracted different views on environmental issues, we shall approach the matter with careful study before making a decision on a more scientific basis'. By November 2004, the EA Report had concluded that the Plan would generate 'limited impact' on the ecosystem, plant species, World Heritage Site, biodiversity, fish species and people. The NDRC and SEPA convened a review panel composed of fifteen experts and seventy-eight representatives from fourteen organizations. There was no public consultation and the EA report was never published. In response to an open letter of 25 August 2005 from ninety-eight environmentalists and sixty-one NGOs demanding the EA report be released to the public, the Ministry of Water Resources (MWR) and the State Secrets Bureau replied jointly that as the development of a river that crosses international borders is a state secret, the EA Report was not to be disclosed.

Public participation in the EA of the Nu River Hydropower Development Plan was blocked on the basis that it was a state secret. In the end, the Plan was scaled down to four dams from the original thirteen proposed in 2003 to control and limit environmental damage and reduce the number of residents needing to be relocated.[151]

4.4.2 Public Participation in Project EIA

Compared to plan EA, public participation in project EIA has developed into a more sophisticated statutory process with clearly defined scope, procedure and methods to ensure that the public is heard at the decision-making stage and that there are judicial remedies where a party's right of participation in the EIA process is infringed upon.[152]

Public participation is compulsory for any project that requires an EIA report.[153] This accounts for less than 10 per cent of all construction projects subject to an EIA requirement. The state encourages relevant units, experts and the public to participate in the EIA

[151] 'Nu River hydropower completes EA examination', *Wen Wei Po*, 11 January 2006.

[152] For more on public participation in the EIA process, see Yuhong Zhao, 'Public participation in China's EIA regime'; Jesse L. Moorman and Zhang Ge, 'Promoting and strengthening public participation in China's environmental impact assessment process: comparing China's EIA law and U.S. NEPA', *Vermont Journal of Environmental Law*, 8 (2007), 281–335.

[153] EIAL (2018), art. 21.

process.[154] Project proponents preparing EIA reports 'shall consult relevant institutions, experts and the public through various channels such as holding discussion forums or public hearings before submitting the report'.[155] The decision to adopt or reject public opinion is explained and attached to the EIA report submitted for approval.[156] Project proponents preparing EIA statements or EIA registration forms may be required by local regulations to consult affected units or residents. If such projects are located in residential areas and will generate nuisance, such as odour, fumes or noise that will directly interfere with people's lives, local EPBs may request that the construction units carry out public consultation. In addition, EPBs may conduct public consultation themselves during the EIA approval stage in order to solicit comments from units and residents potentially affected by the construction projects.[157]

The YuanMingYuan project dispute was addressed by the SEPA with a public hearing, the first time this had happened since the enactment of the EIAL (2002)[158] and a groundbreaking test of public engagement in China's environmental decision-making.[159]

The YuanMingYuan Hearing (2005)

The YuanMingYuan Park in the western suburb of Beijing was built during the Qing Dynasty as the Imperial Summer Palace. It was known as the 'Garden of Gardens' and the 'Versailles of the East' for its luxurious palaces and mansions combining the styles of East and West, though these were destroyed by a fire in 1860 set by British and French troops.[160] It is now a heritage park popular with both locals and tourists for its historical ruins, greenery and tranquil and vast lakes.

On 22 March 2005, a professor of ecology from Lanzhou University visited the park and by pure chance discovered an immense construction project, later known as the anti-seepage project, in the lakes. He blew the whistle and soon an article entitled 'Destruction or protection? YuanMingYuan Park is laying a waterproof membrane at the bottom of the lakes' appeared in the *People's Daily* and drew national attention.[161] There was tremendous public concern over a potential ecological disaster induced by the project, because it would artificially suspend the natural water cycle and reduce the lakes' self-cleaning capability.

SEPA ordered suspension of the controversial project,[162] blaming the Management Office of the YuanMingYuan Park (MOYP) for carrying out the project without an EIA in violation of the

[154] EIAL (2018), art. 5. [155] EIAL (2018), art. 21(1). An exception is made for projects involving state secrets.

[156] EIAL (2018), art. 21(2).

[157] SEPA, Reply on the Issue of Implementation of Public Consultation in the Environmental Impact Assessment of Construction Projects (2002).

[158] Qin Xuan, 'YuanMingYuan hearing: a suddenly emerged opportunity', *China News Weekly*, 2 January 2006, 32–4.

[159] Pan Yue, 'I care more about the YuanMingYuan hearing', *Legal Daily*, 24 September 2007, 1.

[160] The park was burnt down in 1860 by the British and French invasion troops and suffered again in 1900 by an allied army of eight foreign nations. For more discussion on the history of the YuanMingYuan Park, see Wong Young-tsu, *A Paradise Lost: The Imperial Garden Yuanming Yuan* , (Springer Singapore, 2001); Wu Boya, *The History of YuanMingYuan* (Beijing: Encyclopaedia of China Publishing, 2000); and Zhang Enyin, *A Study of the History of YuanMingYuan* (Beijing: Beijing Sports College Press, 1993).

[161] Zhao Yongxin, 'Destruction or protection? YuanMingYuan Park is laying a waterproof membrane at the bottom of the lakes', *People's Daily*, 28 March 2005, 5.

[162] SEPA, Notice on Suspending the YuanMingYuan Environmental Management Project (SEPA notice no. 101 of 2005) (1 April 2005).

EIAL[163] SEPA held a public hearing on the project, and requested that the MOYP submit an EIA report within forty days.[164] Based on a make-up EIA report prepared by Tsinghua University,[165] SEPA decided in July of the same year that the MOYP should remove the plastic membrane lining from the lakes in Qichun Garden and Changchun Garden and replace it with natural clay. It did not, however, request that the same step be taken in the Fuhai Lake for fear of a second detrimental blow to the lake's already fragile ecosystem.[166] One highlight of the YuanMingYuan controversy was that SEPA took the initiative to involve the public, in addition to experts and government bodies, at the hearing.

On 5 April 2005, SEPA announced its decision to hold a public hearing on the environmental impact of the YuanMingYuan anti-seepage project, and invited the public to register by phone.[167] More than 200 people called that day to register. The hearing was scheduled for 13 April 2005.[168] On 11 April, SEPA confirmed a list of seventy-three invitees and announced arrangements for live-streaming by *People's Net* and *Xinhua Net*, the major state news agencies.[169] On 13 April, more than 120 participants (this figure includes journalists, who were not counted in the confirmed seventy-three, while several invitees did not attend) attended the three-and-a-half hour hearing: six from the MOYP, 22 represented relevant bodies and government departments, 15 were experts, 32 were members of the public and more than 40 were members of the press. The comments made at the hearing were overwhelmingly against the MOYP decision to install a membrane to prevent water seepage.[170] Participants became emotional at times, and the head of the MOYP left in the middle of the hearing.[171]

The hearing had room for substantial improvement. First, more than half of the seventy-three participants invited by the SEPA did not represent the public: six were from the MOYP, twenty-two were from government departments, such as Haidian District Cultural

[163] Jane Cai, 'Restoration of palace lake hangs in balance', *South China Morning Post*, 5 April 2005, 5. The MOYP argued that EIA was not required for the restoration project they were undertaking, because it was not a construction project under the EIA Law. Work on the project, which was priced at 200 million yuan, started in September 2004 and was scheduled to be completed in mid-April 2005. By lining the 1.5 million m^2 of lake bed with plastic sheeting, the seepage of 9 million m^3 of water each year could be prevented. See also Vivian Wu, 'Watchdog orders halt to lake restoration', *South China Morning Post*, 1 April 2005, 8.

[164] SEPA, Notice on the Order to Conduct Make-up EIA of the YuanMingYuan Environmental Management Project within Specified Time Limit (SEPA notice no. 167 of 2005) (9 May 2005).

[165] The EIA report prepared by Tsinghua University agreed that ecological damage had been caused by the anti-seepage project, and more harm was possible, but recommended the project continue, albeit with modifications, due to the need to prevent water losses in Beijing, which suffers from a serious water shortage. See 'Evaluation report recommends continuing with controversial lake bed lining project, but with modifications', *Xinhua General News Service*, 5 July 2005.

[166] SEPA, 'SEPA requests comprehensive rectification of the YuanMingYuan anti-seepage project', (press release), 7 July 2005. See also Zhao Yongxin, 'A complete rectification of the YuanMingYuan anti-seepage project', *People's Daily*, 8 July 2005, 5; Qie Jianrong, 'Environmental impact report of the YuanMingYuan project approved', *Legal Daily*, 8 July 2005, 6.

[167] SEPA, 'SEPA announcement on environmental administrative permit hearing', (SEPA announcement no. 13 of 2005) 5 April 2005.

[168] 'The pursuit of fairness and efficiency: the YuanMingYuan environmental impact hearing in focus', *Green Leaf*, 4 (2005), 5–9.

[169] SEPA, 'SEPA notice on environmental impact hearing of the YuanMingYuan project', (SEPA notice no. 117 of 2005), 11 April 2005.

[170] Zhao Yongxin and Liu Yi, 'Five key issues of the YuanMingYuan hearing', *People's Daily*, 14 April 2005, 5. See also, 'First public hearing over environment', *China Daily*, 14 April 2005.

[171] Qin Xuan, 'YuanMingYuan hearing'.

Heritage Bureau, and fifteen were experts.[172] Second, there was no access to key project information prior to the hearing. One participant received a written submission from two fellow participants and a set of documents from the MOYP – including the Summary of YuanMingYuan Environmental Management Project – only a few minutes before the hearing started.[173] Other major documents were never disclosed. These include the Proposal on the Anti-seepage Project at East YuanMingYuan Park, the Application to Initiate the Protection and Renovation Project at YuanMingYuan Site 2003–04 and the approval decisions of the State Administration of Cultural Heritage and Beijing Municipal Administration of Cultural Heritage.[174] Without timely access to key project information, participants were unable to make well-informed comments based in science. Third, little notice of the hearing was given to attendees. SEPA announced its general invitation six days before the event and confirmed the participant list only two days before, leaving insufficient time for participants to prepare. As a result, much of the public comment at the hearing was emotional expressions of objection to the project, with little scientific evidence and few solid research findings. Fourth, participants from different backgrounds (the MOYP and from government, invited experts and members of the public who had successfully registered) were not treated equally in the seating arrangements or the time allowed for making a presentation, [175] suggesting to some that the voice of the general public was less important than others. This is detrimental to public confidence in the process and may discourage people from participating in the future. Last but not least, the hearing was too short to allow all participants to voice their concerns and have their views heard. The three and a half hours given were not enough for debating the environmental consequences of such a large-scale and complicated project that would impact significantly on a variety of stakeholders.

The YuanMingYuan hearing was a valuable trial run to help SEPA formulate rules on public participation and information disclosure.[176] The Provisional Measures on Public Participation in Environmental Impact Assessment (Provisional Measures) (2006)[177] improved the transparency of the process and ensured public access to information by imposing a duty on construction units, EIA firms and EPBs to disclose information. The effectiveness of EIA relies in significant part on an exchange of information between government, industry, environmentalists and the public.[178] Where a project is located in an environmentally sensitive region and requires an EIA report, the project proponent must disclose key project information within seven days of engaging an EIA firm.[179] Prior

[172] SEPA, 'SEPA notice on environmental impact hearing'.

[173] Zhu Xiao, 'Formulating rules of written testimony in environmental administrative permit hearing', *Academic Journal of Zhongzhou*, 4 (2005), 75–8.

[174] Li Dun, 'YuanMingYuan hearing: expose all under the sunshine', *China Newsweek*, 25 April 2005, 38–9

[175] Jiang Wenlai, 'The YuanMingYuan hearing is not perfect', *Green Leaf*, 4 (2005), 11.

[176] Qie Jianrong, 'Pan Yue: environmental authorities are ready for a lasting war [against pollution] and hope for patience and confidence from the public', *Legal Daily*, 28 February 2008, 8.

[177] On 14 February, the SEPA issued the Provisional Measures, which came into force on 18 March 2006 and were repealed by the MEE's Measures on Public Participation (2018) on 1 January 2019.

[178] Holder, *Environmental Assessment*, at 6.

[179] The construction unit must disclose the following information: '(i) the name of the project and a brief project summary, (ii) the construction unit's name and contact information, (iii) the EIA institution's name and contact information, (iv) the procedure and major items of the EIA process, (v) the major items for

to submission of the EIA report for approval, the project proponent or its EIA firm must disclose more detailed information to the public: a description of the project, a summary of the potential environmental impacts, key measures to prevent and mitigate such adverse impacts, means by which the public can access the executive summary of the EIA report and the deadline for doing so, the deadline for requesting supplementary information from the EIA firm, major issues for public comment, detailed forms and the deadline for public consultation.[180] A minimum of ten days is mandated for public consultation, during which time all information required to be disclosed must remain publicly accessible.[181] At the stage of approval, EPBs are required to disclose relevant information upon receiving an EIA report,[182] and to publicly announce its decision to approve or reject.[183]

The SEPA's Provisional Measures (2006) were repealed on 1 January 2019 and replaced by the MEE's Measures on Public Participation (2018).[184] This new document directly addresses gaps found in the Provisional Measures (2006) following implementation. The new Measures on Public Participation (2018) defines the scope of public consultation, giving priority to members of the public affected by the proposed project, but encourages construction units to also seek input from individuals, legal persons and other organizations beyond the scope of those affected by the project.[185]

Construction units bear the primary responsibility of organizing public participation in the EIA process and are held accountable for the truthfulness and outcome of the public participation data.[186] Where there is an overwhelming amount of questioning from the public on the environmental impact of a project, the construction unit must conduct further in-depth public participation in addition to the basic form of public consultation – the provision of information and an invitation to comment – already carried out.[187] Construction units must analyse the public comments collected and decide whether to adopt or reject public opinions. Reasons must be given for not adopting any particular public opinion.[188] The construction unit is required to prepare and make available a public participation note, which must include the following information: (i) the process, scope and content of public participation; (ii) how public opinion was collected, processed and analysed and (iii) whether it is adopting or rejecting public opinion, and its reasons for doing so.[189] Before a construction unit submits its EIA report for approval, it must publish online the full text of the report and the public participation note,[190] thereby facilitating public scrutiny and reducing or eliminating falsification of public consultation data. The public participation note must be attached to the EIA report submitted to environmental agencies for approval.[191]

public comment and (vi) the major channels by which the public may comment on the project.' Provisional Measures (2006), art. 8.

180 Provisional Measures (2006), art. 9.

181 Provisional Measures (2006), art. 12(2).

182 Provisional Measures (2006), art. 13(1).

183 Provisional Measures (2006), art. 13(4).

184 The MEE issued the Measures on Public Participation on 16 July 2018. They came into force on 1 January 2019.

185 Measures on Public Participation (2018), art. 5.

186 Measures on Public Participation (2018), art. 6(1).

187 Measures on Public Participation (2018), arts. 14 and 15.

188 Measures on Public Participation (2018), art. 18.

189 Measures on Public Participation (2018), art. 19(1).

190 Measures on Public Participation (2018), art. 20.

191 Measures on Public Participation (2018), art. 21.

The Measures on Public Participation (2018) provides more specific rules as to the time, means and contents of information disclosure, a duty imposed on construction units and environment agencies.[192] Within seven working days after a construction unit has selected the body that will prepare its EIA report, it must disclose certain information on its own website and to the website of at least one media outlet at the place of the proposed project or to the website of the environmental bureau. The information required is: (i) basic project information, (ii) the name of the construction unit and contact information, (iii) the name of the body preparing the EIA report, (iv) a weblink to a public opinion form and (v) the means by which the completed public opinion form may be submitted.[193] A construction unit is also required to disclose further information once the EIA report (the draft for consultation) has been completed: (i) the full text of the draft EIA report, with a weblink for the online version and a means of obtaining a hard copy; (ii) the scope of the public to be consulted; (iii) the weblink for the public opinion form; (iv) the means by which the public may comment – the public opinion form and any other means and (v) deadlines by which public comment must be received. The information must be publicly available for a minimum of ten working days,[194] and must be disclosed by three means simultaneously: continuous online disclosure for a minimum of ten working days; advertisements in at least one local newspaper on at least two occasions within ten working days; and a poster at local public venues for a minimum of ten working days.[195] In addition, the use of radio and television is encouraged, as well as new media, such as WeChat and microblogs.[196]

Last but not least, further public participation takes place at the EIA approval stage. An agency must disclose either on its official website or by other means upon receiving an EIA report: (i) the full text of the EIA report, (ii) the public participation note and (iii) the means by which the public can comment. Again, the information must be disclosed for a minimum of ten working days.[197] Before an agency makes its decision on approving or rejecting the EIA, it must disclose on its official website or by other means for a minimum of five working days: (i) the name and location of the construction project, (ii) the name of the construction unit, (iii) the name of the body preparing the EIA report, (iv) brief project information and information on key environmental impacts and environmental protection measures, (v) public participation that has been conducted by the construction unit and (vi) the means by which the public can comment.[198] Agencies must inform construction units and the affected parties of their right to a hearing.[199] During the stipulated time periods for compulsory information disclosure, the public may communicate opinions, suggestions or complaints to the EIA approval authority.[200] Agencies will review the submitted public participation notes and consider all public comments and complaints in order to decide whether construction units have conducted adequate public consultation. If an agency decides that a construction unit has not done so, it must return the EIA report to the unit for a new round of public consultation.[201]

[192] Measures on Public Participation (2018), art. 8.
[193] Measures on Public Participation (2018), art. 9(1).
[194] Measures on Public Participation (2018), art. 10.
[195] Measures on Public Participation (2018), art. 11(1).
[196] Measures on Public Participation (2018), art. 11(2).
[197] Measures on Public Participation (2018), art. 22.
[198] Measures on Public Participation (2018), art. 23(1) and (2).
[199] Measures on Public Participation (2018), art. 23(3).
[200] Measures on Public Participation (2018), art. 24.
[201] Measures on Public Participation (2018), art. 25.

4.4.3 Judicial Review to Ensure Public Participation in Project EIA

Statutory EIA not only regulates agency decision-making, but also offers an important tool with which the public can challenge agency decisions in court.[202] Environment agencies must not only publicize their EIA approval decisions on their official website, or by other means, within seven working days of making the decision, but must also inform relevant parties of their right to apply for administrative reconsideration or judicial review and the time limits for doing so.[203] Judicial review of EIA approval decisions ensures agency compliance with the legal procedural requirements, including those on public participation, which strengthens EIA as a mechanism to prevent and mitigate environmental harm. In the case of *Lu Hong and Others* v. *Xiaoshan Environmental Protection Bureau* (2013),[204] Xiaoshan EPB's EIA approval was revoked because it violated the procedural requirement of public participation in the EIA of construction projects.

Lu Hong and Others v. _Xiaoshan Environmental Protection Bureau_ (2013)

Lu Hong and others, 204 residents in total, were potentially to be affected by a road alteration and extension project. They sued Xiaoshan EPB for violating legal procedure, and sought to revoke its decision to approve the EIA.

Xiaoshan District Court (2013) found that on 20 April 2012, a joint assessment meeting was held by the EPB, the project proponent, the EIA firm and experts. The EPB had displayed a notice at its service centre from 23 April to 7 May 2012 to invite comments by phone or post. On 29 May 2012, a further assessment meeting was held by the EPB, the project proponent, the EIA firm and experts. On 28 June 2012, the project proponent submitted the EIA report to the EPB, which approved it on the same day. Article 22 of the Zhejiang Provincial Measures on Environmental Protection Management of Construction Projects expressly requires an EPB to notify the public when it receives an EIA report for approval. It must do this in a way that is publicly accessible and must give the public a minimum of seven days to comment. The public notice the EPB had displayed from 23 April to 7 May did not meet this requirement because the EIA report had not yet been submitted. The court revoked the Xiaoshan EPB's approval decision as it violated this procedural requirement.

In order to speed up the construction process, some local governments and even EPBs have chosen to skip legally required procedures to give a quick, but illegal, green-light to developers. This expedited decision-making process has often resulted in harm to the environment and infringement of the rights of those affected. Judicial review allows the public to challenge an agency decision in court and seek remedies. Xiaoshan District Court reviewed and scrutinized Xiaoshan EPB's EIA approval decision to ensure the agency had complied with the legal requirement for public participation. Complying with the legal requirements would give residents like Lu Hong access to project information and the ability to participate in the decision-making process.

[202] For more case studies, see Jin Zining, 'Environmental Impact Assessment Law in China's courts: a study of 107 judicial decisions', *Environmental Impact Assessment Review*, 55 (2015), 35–44.

[203] Measures on Public Participation (2018), art. 27.

[204] SPC 10 Important Administrative Cases on Environmental Protection (2014), case no. 4.

Even if a court upholds an agency decision, it may take extra steps to address the environmental concerns of the public, as in the case of *Zhang Xiaoyan and Others* v. *Jiangsu Environmental Protection Bureau* (2015).[205]

Zhang Xiaoyan and Others v. *Jiangsu Environmental Protection Bureau* (2015)

Zhang Xiaoyan and two others sued Jiangsu EPB, seeking revocation of its decision to approve the EIA statement of a 110 kV electricity substation proposed by Zhenjiang Power Supply Co. They argued that the proposed site was unsuitable for building a substation and that the EIA was not conducted using scientific methods. Therefore, they argued, the approval decision was unlawful.

Nanjing Intermediate Court (2015) found that Jiangsu EPB's decision to approve the EIA statement of the proposed project did comply with article 22 of the EIAL (2002) and technical guidelines, and the approval process was lawful. The plaintiffs' request to revoke the approval decision was rejected. Zhang and two others appealed.

Jiangsu High Court (2015) found that the proposed substation would form part of the city's public infrastructure and could be built in a sensitive region, such as a scenic area, a nature reserve or populated area. The pollution projected for the construction and operation phases would be well below the maximum permitted by law, the court found. The EIA approval decision was made in compliance with law, it said. The ultra-low level of magnetic radiation generated by the operation of the substation would have a limited impact and could be controlled, it added. The appeal was rejected and the lower court's decision upheld.

Although both courts focused on reviewing the legality of Jiangsu EPB's decision to approve the EIA, Jiangsu High Court took a further step in addressing the concerns of the plaintiffs. It urged the EPB to improve information disclosure by requesting the operator of the substation to monitor the level of magnetic radiation and publish real-time monitoring data that was easily accessible by the public. Without doubt, judicial review of the EIA approval decision not only safeguards public access to EIA decision-making, but also improves the overall environmental performance of both agencies and project operators.

4.5 ALIGNMENT OF SEA WITH PROJECT EIA

The EIAL (2002) addressed the relationship between plan EA and project EIA to avoid the two overlapping.[206] The 2016 amendment to the EIAL strengthened the alignment and coordination of the two in order to improve the function of plan EA. The focus was on plan EA because it happens at an earlier stage than project EIA (plans are drafted before the projects under them are built) and therefore has the crucial function of pollution control at the earliest stage. If an environmental assessment is conducted in the early stages of making sectoral, urban, river basin and regional development plans, pollution may be prevented and controlled more effectively. In practice, however, plan EA conclusions or

[205] SPC 10 Important Administrative Cases on Environmental Protection (second batch) (2016), case no. 4.
[206] EIAL (2002), art. 18.

approval decisions are not fully implemented in project construction. The 2016 amendment requires that the conclusions of plan EA are used as an important basis for project EIA.[207] Project EIA may be simplified for a construction project falling under a plan that did adopt the requirements set out by the plan EA. If an industrial park has carried out a high-quality plan EA and has clear and feasible tasks for implementation, a pilot exercise on downgrading project EIAs within that park may be carried out. Where an unexpected but significant adverse environmental impact caused by plan implementation is found during project EIA, such information must be reported to the plan-making body.[208]

By integrating environmental considerations into the decision-making process at the earliest stage possible in order to mitigate potential environmental harm caused by implementing development policies, plans and projects, China's EIA regime has expanded its application from construction projects (project EIA) to government plans (plan EA), and from specialized plans to regional plans and policies (SEA). However, for EIA to function as an effective decision-making tool and allow China to engage in more sustainable and harmonious socio-economic development, the various forms it takes at the different stages of government decision-making must be fully integrated. This will make the EIA and EA systems effective and efficient. SEA addresses regional and cross-regional environment and development issues and lays the foundation for plan EA, which then aims to improve the layout, scale and structure of industrial sectors and compiles lists of prohibited sectors and processes to control and guide the entry threshold for projects. Project EIA should then focus on environmental risk control and achievement of pollution-control targets at project level in close collaboration with other regulatory mechanisms, including total pollution control and control by permit.

[207] EIAL (2016), art. 18(3).

[208] MEP, Implementation Plan on EIA Reform during the 13th FYP Period (2016), part II, s. 5.

5

Regulation and Control of Air Pollution

Decades of large-scale and fast-paced industrialization, urbanization and population growth have caused increasingly serious air pollution in China.[1] In the early years of economic take-off from the late 1970s to the 1990s, the primary source of air pollution was coal. Coal-burning boilers and stoves were widely used in power plants, industrial factories and households, emitting sulphur dioxide (SO_2), nitrogen oxides (NOx), carbon monoxide (CO) and particulate matters.[2] Since the 1990s, more and more cities have become gigantic construction sites developing commercial and residential blocks. The economic boom led by the real-estate sector has revived heavily polluting industries, including iron and steel, cement, non-ferrous metals, ceramics and glass, all of which are powered by fossil fuels. Meanwhile, vehicles jam multi-layered highways that are expanding from downtown to the outlying suburbs. The 1990s saw an unprecedented surge of vehicles on the roads of megacities. Vehicle emissions are the main sources of NOx and volatile organic compound (VOC) pollution. Compound air pollution problems have spread from megacities to become wider regional problems as vehicle ownership continues to soar, and expands from first-tier to second- and third-tier cities. While coal burning remains the dominant source of air pollution nationwide, in the most economically advanced regions in China of Beijing–Tianjin–Hebei, the Yangtze River Delta and Pearl River Delta, four major sources of air pollution exist: coal-fired power generation, factories, vehicles and construction sites.

Both SO_2 and NOx react with water vapour and other forms of precipitation to form sulphuric acid and nitric acid and become acid rain, which kills flora and fauna, degrades soils and corrodes buildings and other structures. Exposed to solar radiation, NOx and VOCs form ozone (O_3), which poses a serious health hazard to humans as a lung irritant, and also degrades vegetation. NOx reacts with ammonia (NH_3), moisture and other atmospheric compounds to form fine particulate matters (PM_{10} and $PM_{2.5}$), which damage human health by impairing respiratory function. There is increasing evidence that fine particulates have significant adverse effects on human health, including lung cancer, irrespective of the chemical composition of the

[1] William P. Alford and Benjamin L. Liebman, 'Clean air, clear processes? The struggle over air pollution law in the People's Republic of China', *Hastings Law Journal*, 52:3 (2001), 703–37.

[2] Mao Yushi et al., *The True Cost of Coal* (Greenpeace, The China Sustainable Energy Programme and World Wide Fund for Nature, 2008), https://issuu.com/greenpeacechina/docs/the-true-cost-of-coal

pollutant. Prior to 2012, PM_{10} (particulates with a diameter of less than 10 microns) was regulated as an air pollutant in China. Development of scientific knowledge on the harmful effects of particulate matter has led to an evolution of regulatory responses and shifted the focus to smaller $PM_{2.5}$ particulates (particulates with a diameter of less than 2.5 microns).[3]

Air pollution has become a major public health concern in China.[4] According to the Beijing Municipal Health Bureau, lung cancer has increased by 60 per cent in the city over the last decade. Over the same period, there has not, however, been a notable increase in the smoking rate.[5] The worsening air pollution is believed by some experts to be the major culprit.[6] In addition to respiratory diseases and cancer, the smog also aggravates cardiovascular and cerebrovascular diseases.[7] Long-term exposure to high levels of $PM_{2.5}$ is harmful to human health, because the particulates enter deep into the lungs and bloodstream, increasing the risks of heart attack, asthma exacerbation, stroke, respiratory infection and lung cancer.[8] Nationwide, between 350,000 and 500,000 people die prematurely each year as a result of outdoor air pollution.[9] Other studies have linked the ambient air pollution in China to between 1.2 million and 1.6 million premature deaths annually.[10] In 2013, the International Agency for Research on Cancer, the specialist cancer agency of the World Health Organization (WHO), classified air pollution as carcinogenic, saying that there is 'sufficient evidence' that exposure causes lung cancer.[11] A WHO report that linked air pollution to seven million premature deaths in 2012 again sounded the alarm that air pollution is the world's largest single environmental health risk, especially in developing

[3] Ministry of Environmental Protection (MEP), Ambient Air Quality Standards (AAQS) (2012). Prior to 2012, only three air pollutants, SO_2, NOx and PM_{10}, were monitored in the assessment of ambient air quality. The new AAQS add CO, ozone and $PM_{2.5}$ as air pollutants to be monitored when assessing ambient air quality.

[4] Renjie Chen et al., 'Association of particulate air pollution with daily mortality: the China Air Pollution and Health Effects Study', *American Journal of Epidemiology*, 175:11 (2012), 1173–81; Qing Chang et al., 'Ambient air pollution and daily hospital admissions for respiratory system-related diseases in a heavy polluted city in Northeast China', *Environmental Science and Pollution Research*, 27 (2020), 10055–64.

[5] According to Mao Yu, deputy director of the Beijing Municipal Health Bureau. See Shan Juan and Wang Qian, 'Exposure to smog is severe hazard', *China Daily* , 6 December 2011.

[6] See Shan Juan and Wang Qian, 'Exposure to smog'. Shi Yuankai, vice-president of the Chinese Academy of Medical Sciences Cancer Hospital, has commented that long-term exposure to particulate matter, especially $PM_{2.5}$, is a major health hazard. Dr Zhong Nanshan, a leading respiratory expert and Fellow of the Chinese Academy of Engineering, believes that without intervention, $PM_{2.5}$ will replace smoking as the top risk factor for lung cancer.

[7] Peng Xu at al., 'Haze, air pollution, and health in China', *The Lancet*, 382:9910 (2013), 2067.

[8] Yadan Ouyang, 'The respiratory landscape in China: A focus on air pollution', *The Lancet Respiratory Medicine*, 5:1 (2017), 16-17; see also Wei-Jie Guan et al., 'Impact of air pollution on the burden of chronic respiratory diseases in China: time for urgent action', *The Lancet*, 388:10054 (2016), 1939–51.

[9] Zhu Chen et al., 'China tackles the health effects of air pollution', *The Lancet*, 382:9909 (2013), 1959–60. Zhu Chen is president of the Chinese Medical Association and a former minister of public health. The article endorsed earlier studies carried out by the World Bank, the WHO and the Chinese Academy for Environmental Planning. For more, see World Bank, *Cost of Pollution in China*; WHO, 'Country profile of environmental burden of disease: China', (Geneva: World Health Organization, 2009), www.who.int/quantifying_ehimpacts/national/countryprofile/china.pdf?ua=1; Chinese Academy for Environmental Planning, *Report of China's Environmental-Economic Accounting in 2007–2008* (Beijing: China Environmental Science Press, 2012).

[10] Edward Wong, 'Air pollution linked to 1.2 million premature deaths in China', *New York Times*, 1 April 2013; Dan Levin, 'Study links polluted air in China to 1.6 million deaths a year', *New York Times*, 13 August 2015.

[11] International Agency for Research on Cancer (WHO), 'IARC: outdoor air pollution a leading environmental cause of cancer deaths', (press release) 17 October 2013, www.iarc.fr/wp-content/uploads/2018/07/pr221_e.pdf.

countries.[12] The evidence has become a key driver for ambitious and decisive legal and regulatory action to control air pollution.

This chapter examines key regulatory mechanisms under the Air Pollution Prevention and Control Law (APPCL) (2018),[13] with reference to central government policies and plans on air pollution control, including the 12th Five-Year Plan (FYP) on Prevention and Control of Air Pollution in Key Regions (2012),[14] the Action Plan on Air Pollution Prevention and Control (Air Action Plan) (2013),[15] and the Three-Year Action Plan on Winning the Battle of Blue-Sky Protection (2018).[16] Section 5.1 introduces the history of regulatory control of air pollution under the APPCL and key plans and policies. Section 5.2 focuses on government responsibilities and agencies in charge. Section 5.3 discusses standard setting and planning as a foundation of the command-and-control approach. Section 5.4 examines key mechanisms to prevent and control air pollution. Section 5.5 addresses the major sources of air pollution and the regulations used to control them. Section 5.6 highlights the crucial importance of regional cooperation in air pollution control. Section 5.7 deals with emergency responses to heavy pollution weather. Section 5.8 examines enforcement, including monitoring, inspection and sanction, that aims to ensure compliance and deter violations.

5.1 APPCL AND GOVERNMENT PLANS

The APPCL (1987)[17] was China's first specialized statute on air pollution control, establishing the general principles and regulatory control mechanisms covering the emission of smoke and dust, particulate matters and noxious fumes. It was amended in 1995 to incorporate clean-coal initiatives, phase out heavily polluting and outdated production techniques and equipment, and strengthen pollution control in two control zones for acid rain and SO_2.[18] In the 1980s and 1990s, air pollution control had focused on coal burning and industrial installations. The APPCL (1995)[19] was revised substantially in 2000 to target air pollution control in key cities, tighten control on mobile sources including vehicles and vessels, expand control of smoke and dust in large cities, introduce total emission control, mandate emission fees and set fines for excessive emissions. Despite important progress

[12] WHO, '7 million premature deaths annually linked to air pollution', (press release) 25 March 2014. www.who.int/mediacentre/news/releases/2014/air-pollution/en/; for details, see WHO, *Burden of Disease from Household Air Pollution for 2012* (World Health Organization, n.d.). www.who.int/phe/health_topics/outdoorair/databases/FINAL_HAP_AAP_BoD_24March2014.pdf

[13] The APPCL was first enacted in 1987, and was amended in 1995 and revised in 2000 and 2015. The 2015 revision was adopted on 29 August 2015 by the 12th NPCSC at its 16th session and came into force on 1 January 2016. The APPCL (2015) was then amended in 2018 as a result of the state institutional reform. This minor amendment was restricted to changes to the names of relevant authorities. See NPCSC, Decision on the Amendment of Fifteen Laws including the Wildlife Protection Law (2018).

[14] The 12th FYP on Air Pollution Control in Key Regions (2012) was issued by the MEP, National Development and Reform Commission (NDRC) and the Ministry of Finance (MOF) on 29 October 2012, following approval from the State Council on 27 September 2012.

[15] The Air Action Plan (2013) was issued by the State Council on 10 September 2013 with immediate effect.

[16] The Three-Year Action Plan on Winning the Battle of Blue-Sky Protection was issued by the State Council on 27 June 2018.

[17] The APPCL was adopted on 5 September 1987 by the 6th NPCSC at its 22nd session.

[18] For further discussion on air pollution regulation in the early years, see Alford and Liebman, 'Clean air, clear processes?'.

[19] The APPCL (1987) was amended on 29 August 1995 by the 8th NPCSC at its 15th session.

made by the APPCL (2000),[20] the law was weak in controlling pollution at the source, total emission control of key pollutants, government implementation and enforcement, and sanction and deterrence of violations.

The 2015 revision aims to address these problems and prioritizes the improvement of overall ambient air quality (AAQ).[21] It unequivocally makes it the government's responsibility to improve air quality and imposes tight control over major sources of pollution, with strengthened measures on enforcement and sanction, information disclosure and emergency response. While the APPCL (2015) targets air pollutants, including particulate matters (PM_{10} and $PM_{2.5}$), SO_2, NOx, VOCs and NH_3, the measures taken to control air pollution will achieve the co-benefit of abatement of greenhouse gas (GHG) emissions.[22] In China, coal burning contributes to 70 per cent of smoke and dust emissions, 90 per cent of SO_2 emissions, 67 per cent of NOx emissions and 70 per cent of carbon dioxide (CO_2) emissions.[23] Controlling coal consumption will cut emissions of air pollutants and GHGs. The APPCL (2015) emphasizes the key strategies to be employed to tackle China's air pollution problem as 'pollution control at the source, planning before action, change of economic development pattern, improvement of industrial structure and layout, and adjustment of energy structure'.[24] It mandates comprehensive prevention and control measures against major sources of air pollution, including coal burning, industrial emissions, vehicles and vessels, construction and agriculture, and promotes regional collaboration to tackle air pollution.[25]

Government plans have played a crucial role in China's socio-economic development and environmental protection. The country sets FYPs on economic and social development, which lay out national development strategies, targets to be achieved and key tasks to be accomplished by the end of the five-year period. The FYP not only guides the work of central and local governments, but also sends policy signals to market players in China and to those doing business with China. The goals and measures of FYPs focused solely on socio-economic development until the 11th FYP (2006–10), which, for the first time, set binding targets for the abatement of key pollutants: a 10 per cent reduction in the total discharge of SO_2 and COD.[26] The 12th FYP (2011–15) devotes a full chapter to environmental protection and green development,[27] advocating for the development of an energy-saving and environmentally friendly society. It requires governments to abate energy and carbon intensity, prioritize the control of air pollution posing a threat to human health, expand the scope of key pollutants, tighten emission/discharge standards, establish a polluter-pays mechanism, improve the accountability regime and strengthen supervision of law enforcement.[28]

The 12th FYP on Air Pollution Prevention and Control in Key Regions (2012) was the first specialized FYP focusing on air pollution control. It covers the three key regions of

[20] The APPCL (1995) was revised on 29 April 2000 by the 9th NPCSC at its 15th session.

[21] APPCL (2015), art. 1. The APPCL aims to 'protect and improve environmental quality, prevent and control air pollution, ensure public health, promote ecological civilization and achieve socio-economic sustainable development'.

[22] APPCL (2015), art. 2(2).

[23] Yuan Jie (ed.), *Understanding APPCL*, (Beijing: China Legal Publishing House, 2015), at 7; Xin Chunying (ed.), *Interpreting APPCL* (Beijing: Law Press, 2015), at 7.

[24] APPCL (2015), art. 2(1). [25] APPCL (2015), art. 2(2). [26] 11th FYP (2006–10).

[27] 12th FYP (2011–15), chapter VI. [28] 12th FYP (2011–15), chapter VI.

Beijing–Tianjin–Hebei, the Yangtze River Delta and the Pearl River Delta, as well as ten city clusters. In total, the FYP covers 19 provinces and 117 cities. The FYP set four targets to be achieved by 2015:

(i) total emissions of SO_2 to be reduced by 12 per cent by 2015 compared to 2010, NOx by 13 per cent and industrial smoke and dust by 10 per cent, and prevention and control measures for VOCs to be in full operation;
(ii) ambient air quality to be improved with abatements of the annual average concentration of PM_{10}, SO_2, NO_2 and $PM_{2.5}$ by 10 per cent, 10 per cent, 7 per cent and 5 per cent respectively; preliminary control of O_3 and mitigation of acid rain to be achieved;
(iii) joint prevention and control mechanisms to be established to tackle regional air pollution and improve regional air quality management capacity;
(iv) a 6 per cent cut in the annual average concentration of $PM_{2.5}$ to be achieved in the regions of Beijing–Tianjin–Hebei, the Yangtze River Delta and the Pearl River Delta. This is used as an evaluation indicator in the performance appraisal exercise for each of those regions.[29]

The Air Action Plan (2013)[30] required even deeper cuts to concentration levels of $PM_{2.5}$ in the same regions: Beijing–Tianjin–Hebei was to cut by 25 per cent, the Yangtze River Delta by 20 per cent and the Pearl River Delta by 15 per cent by 2017 compared to the 2012 levels. In addition, Beijing was to achieve an annual average $PM_{2.5}$ concentration level of 60 $\mu g/m^3$ by 2017.[31] The Air Action Plan (2013) set ten specific tasks for the nation to be implemented from central to local levels:

(i) strengthen comprehensive pollution control and cut emissions of pollutants;
(ii) optimize the structuring of industry and promote industrial upgrading;
(iii) accelerate technological advancements and improve capacity for scientific innovation;
(iv) accelerate restructuring of the energy sector and increase the supply of clean energy;
(v) tighten the requirements on energy conservation and environmental protection for entry into industrial sectors and optimize the geographical layout of industry;
(vi) make use of market mechanisms and improve economic policies related to the environment;
(vii) improve the legal regime and implement supervision and management in accordance with law;
(viii) establish a regional coordination mechanism and coordinate regional environmental governance;
(ix) establish a monitoring, early warning and emergency response system to deal with heavy pollution weather;
(x) clarify the responsibilities of governments, enterprises and the public and mobilize the public to participate in environmental protection.

The APPCL (2015) adopted many important initiatives and mechanisms that had been introduced by the Air Action Plan (2013). While the binding targets on air quality improve-

[29] 12th FYP on Air Pollution Prevention and Control in Key Regions (2012), part II, s. 3.
[30] The Air Action Plan was promulgated by the State Council on 10 September 2013.
[31] Air Action Plan (2013), preamble.

ment set by the Air Action Plan (2013) were achieved in 2017, China's battle against air pollution was far from over. Compared to 2013, the monitoring data for 2017 indicated a 22.7 per cent cut in the annual mean concentration level of PM_{10} nationwide, and falls in $PM_{2.5}$ for the three key regions of Beijing–Tianjin–Hebei, the Yangtze River Delta and the Pearl River Delta of 39.6 per cent, 34.3 per cent and 27.7 per cent respectively.[32] These are significant achievements, but there remains a gap between China's air quality and the WHO guidelines. The Three-Year Action Plan on Winning the Battle of Blue-Sky Protection (2018) continues the efforts to control air pollution by focusing on key areas, including controlling coal production and consumption to reduce its contribution to the primary energy mix to 58 per cent by end-2020. Replacing coal with cleaner alternatives requires building capacity for transport and storage of natural gas and increasing consumption of renewables to 15 per cent of the primary energy mix by end-2020.[33] In addition, greater emphasis is placed on the control of air pollution by mobile sources and non-point sources. The Three-Year Action Plan on Winning the Battle of Blue-Sky Protection (2018) also aims to speed up the road-to-rail transition to develop a green transport system and substantially cut pollution by diesel vehicles.[34] It also tightens control of air pollution from open mining, construction sites, burning of crop straws and application of pesticides and fertilizers.[35]

5.2 GOVERNMENT RESPONSIBILITY AND AGENCIES IN CHARGE

The APPCL (2000) imposed duties on governments without attaching liability or supervision mechanisms with which to hold them accountable. Both the State Council and local governments were required to 'incorporate air quality protection into the socio-economic development plans, work out rational distribution of industrial layout, strengthen scientific research on the prevention and control of air pollution, and adopt preventative and remedial measures against air pollution so as to protect and improve the ambient air quality'.[36] The state was obliged to 'take measures to control and gradually abate total emission of key air pollutants nationwide',[37] and local governments were obliged to 'ensure good air quality within their own jurisdictions'.[38] There was, however, no mechanism with which to hold governments accountable for any failure to discharge these responsibilities. As a result, governments at all levels were driven by GDP growth and the pursuit of short-term economic gains, because those were the factors that counted in the assessment and appraisal of government officials and influenced career development. As a result, environmental protection became the sole responsibility of understaffed and underfunded local environmental protection bureaus (EPBs). In contrast, the APPCL (2015) aims to make governments accountable for air quality and make their environmental performance an important component of the assessment and appraisal scheme.

[32] MEE, 'Notice on the final assessment outcome of the implementation of the Air Action Plan (2018)', (notice) 17 May 2018.
[33] Three-Year Action Plan on Winning the Battle of Blue-Sky Protection (2018), part III.
[34] Three-Year Action Plan on Winning the Battle of Blue-Sky Protection (2018), part IV.
[35] Three-Year Action Plan on Winning the Battle of Blue-Sky Protection (2018), part V.
[36] APPCL (2000), art. 2. [37] APPCL (2000), art. 3(1)
[38] Local governments must plan and take measures to ensure the ambient air qualities standards are achieved. See APPCL (2000), art. 3(2).

5.2.1 Target Responsibility and Performance Appraisal

Making local governments responsible and accountable for environmental quality is the key to addressing weak implementation and enforcement of the APPCL. The Air Action Plan (2013) adopts the target responsibility mechanism,[39] and designates the MEP as coordinator of the signing of agreements between central and provincial governments. These agreements transform centrally set targets into concrete tasks to be implemented by local governments and enterprises. In 2014, the agreements on target responsibility for air pollution abatement were signed by the MEP (on behalf of the central government) and provincial governments.[40] The agreements are in fact provincial action plans that include the provincial air quality improvement targets and a list of tasks to be undertaken. The achievement of the targets and implementation of the tasks by the local governments are crucial factors to be considered in the performance appraisal of local governments and individuals.[41] The abatement targets are binding contractual terms. Local governments are required to map out detailed plans to reduce coal consumption, eliminate outdated industrial capacity, control emissions from boilers, vehicles and construction sites, among others. They were required to set specific goals for each year up to and including 2017 and, once the goals had been achieved, for the years up to and including 2020.

The APPCL (2015) makes local governments accountable for local air quality. It requires governments at county level and above to integrate air pollution control into socio-

TABLE 5.1 AIR POLLUTION ABATEMENT TARGETS SET BY THE CENTRAL GOVERNMENT

Target for 2017 compared to 2012 (%)		Province, autonomous region or centrally controlled municipality
Annual average concentration level of $PM_{2.5}$	−25	Beijing, Tianjin and Hebei
	−20	Shanxi, Shandong, Shanghai, Jiangsu and Zhejiang
	−15	Guangdong and Chongqing
	−10	Inner Mongolia
Annual average concentration level of PM_{10}	−15	Henan, Shaanxi, Qinghai and Xinjiang
	−12	Gansu and Hubei
	−10	Sichuan, Liaoning, Jilin, Hunan, Anhui and Ningxia
	−5	Guangxi, Fujian, Jiangxi, Guizhou and Heilongjiang
	Continuous improvement	Hainan, Tibet and Yunnan

Sources: MEP, 'MEP signs target responsibility agreement'.

[39] Air Action Plan (2013), part 8, s. 27.
[40] MEP, 'MEP signs target responsibility agreement on air pollution control with 31 provinces', (press release) 7 January 2014. See also Zhang Qiulei, 'MEP signed agreement'.
[41] Air Action Plan (2013), part 8, s. 27.

economic development plans and increase the fiscal budget for air pollution control.[42] Local governments are to 'make plans, take measures, control and abate emissions of air pollutants to meet the air quality standards and improve the air quality'.[43] The APPCL (2015) adopts an appraisal mechanism whereby the state environmental authority and relevant departments assess a provincial government's achievement of air quality improvement targets and implementation of key tasks. In turn, the provincial governments assess the performance of local governments. The assessment results are disclosed for public scrutiny.[44]

One further step taken by the APPCL (2015) is the new mechanism of supervision talks (known as *yuetan*), which, if necessary, follow an assessment and appraisal. Environmental authorities at provincial level and above must arrange meetings with heads of local governments and relevant officials in charge if the local government exceeds its quota for emissions of key air pollutants or fails to achieve the air quality improvement targets.[45] The supervision talks are an administrative measure through which supervisory bodies can check and improve the work of their subordinates. It was already in place in the Air Action Plan (2013), which uses it as a way for environmental authorities to meet heads of lower-level local governments and expose local pollution problems, make recommendations for control measures and supervise their implementation.[46] The APPCL (2015) requires the supervision talks[47] to be disclosed to the public in order to put pressure on local governments – a tactic of naming and shaming.

5.2.2 Agencies in Charge of Air Pollution Control

Environmental protection bodies (EPBs until 2018, now Ecology and Environmental Bureaus (EEBs) and others) at county level and above are the primary agencies in charge of regulation and control of air pollution. Other departments exercise regulatory supervision as provided for by law.[48]

The Ministry of Ecology and Environment (MEE) and its predecessors (the MEP and SEPA) set national standards for emissions and ambient air quality. It assesses the environmental performance of provincial governments in their work to achieve air quality improvement targets. The MEE works with local environmental bureaus to implement the total emission control of key air pollutants, set up a nationwide monitoring network for emissions of key polluters and AAQ, and establish regional collaboration in air pollution control. Local environmental bureaus are responsible for routine environmental enforcement, including inspecting stationary sources of pollution, inspecting vehicle emissions, inspecting vehicle emission testing firms, imposing administrative compulsory measures such as seal-up and seizure of facility, equipment or product, receiving and following up public complaints, and imposing administrative penalties for violations.

Other departments are also involved in regulating and controlling air pollution, albeit from different angles. For example, the NDRC is in charge of clean production and phasing out heavily polluting industrial operations. It issues lists of outdated techniques, equipment

[42] APPCL (2015), art. 3(1). [43] APPCL (2015), art. 3(2). [44] APPCL (2015), art. 4.
[45] APPCL (2015), art. 22. [46] Air Action Plan (2013), part 8, s. 28. [47] APPCL (2015), art. 22.
[48] APPCL (2018), art. 5.

and products that cause serious air pollution during production and sets deadlines for phasing out the use of such techniques and the production, import, sale or use of such equipment and products.[49] The state quality supervision authorities (market regulatory authorities since 2018) are another example, as they implement quality standards for products. They work with environmental bureaus to ensure that, for example, only boilers meeting the relevant environmental standards or requirements can be produced, imported, sold or used.[50] They are also responsible for recalling vehicles and non-road mobile machinery (farm and construction equipment) not meeting emissions standards due to defects in design or production.[51]

5.3 STANDARDS AND PLANS

Standards are the foundation of the regulatory control of air pollution. There are different types of standards, including ambient air quality standards (AAQS), emissions standards and product standards. Making and implementing plans ensures that measures are taken to achieve AAQS by controlling pollution at the source.

5.3.1 AAQS

The state environmental protection authority or provincial governments set AAQS to protect public health and the environment.[52] At the national level, the predecessors of the MEE issued the Ambient Air Quality Standards in 1982 and amended it in 1996, 2000 and, most recently, 2012.[53] The 2012 amendment resulted from domestic and international public pressure. On 5 December 2011, Beijing's smog was so heavy that by 3 p.m. at the city's Capital International Airport more than 200 flights had been cancelled and over 100 delayed.[54] However, the air quality that day was classed as 'lightly polluted' with an Air Quality Index (AQI) at 193, according to official data released by Beijing EPB (now Beijing EEB).[55] In contrast, the US embassy rated the air quality that day as 'hazardous'. The reason for the disparity is that China did not monitor the level of very fine particulate matter, known as $PM_{2.5}$, while the US embassy did. The clear discrepancy caused public outrage and China's outdated air quality standards, that failed to monitor $PM_{2.5}$, drew criticism for causing a serious understatement of Beijing's toxic air problem.[56] In response, China amended the AAQS (2000) and promulgated the AAQS (2012).[57]

Here, Grade I standards apply to nature reserves, scenic zones, famous sites and other special protection zones. Grade II standards apply to residential zones, combined residential and commercial zones, cultural zones, industrial zones and agricultural zones.[58]

[49] APPCL (2018), art. 27. [50] APPCL (2018), art. 40. [51] APPCL (2018), art. 58.
[52] APPCL (2018), art. 8.
[53] They are Ambient Air Quality Standards GB3095-1982, GB3095-1996, GB3095-1996 and GB3095-2012.
[54] Shan Juan and Wang Qian, 'Exposure to smog'.
[55] 'Smog in Beijing US reading beyond index EPB criticized for announcement of light pollution', *Ming Pao Daily News*, 6 December 2011, A20.
[56] 'Smog spawns environmental awareness in China', *Xinhua*, 2 December 2011.
[57] The AAQS (GB3095-2012) was issued by the MEP and the State Administration for Quality Supervision, Inspection and Quarantine (SAQSIQ) on 29 February 2012. It came into effect nationwide on 1 January 2016, but earlier in key regions.
[58] AAQS (GB3095-2012), art. 4.1.

TABLE 5.2 AMBIENT AIR QUALITY STANDARDS (2012)

Pollutant	Averaging time (duration of exposure)	Concentration limit		WHO-recommended target (published 2006)	Unit
		Grade I	Grade II		
SO_2	1 year	20	60	No target set	μg/m³
	24 hours	50	150	20	
	1 hour	150	500	(10 minutes) 500	
NO_2	1 year	40	40	40	μg/m³
	24 hours	80	80	No target set	
	1 hour	200	200	200	
CO	24 hours	4	4	No target set	mg/m³
	1 hour	10	10	No target set	
O_3	8 hours	100	160	100	μg/m³
	1 hour	160	200	No target set	
PM_{10}	1 year	40	70	20	μg/m³
	24 hours	50	150	50	
$PM_{2.5}$	1 year	15	35	10	μg/m³
	24 hours	35	75	25	

Sources: AAQS (GB3095-2012); WHO Air Quality Guideline (2006).

The AAQS (2012) had to be implemented in stages, given the varying financial and technological capacities of different regions at substantially different stages of economic development, and the varying state and impact of air pollution. China's three most economically advanced and heavily polluted regions – Beijing–Tianjin–Hebei, the Yangtze River Delta and the Pearl River Delta – as well as cities directly under the central government and provincial capitals, were required to start implementing the AAQS (2012) in 2012.[59] Implementation for the rest of China occurred incrementally up to 1 January 2016, the effective date for national implementation. This additional time was given for building infrastructure and training personnel to implement the new monitoring scheme, which covers $PM_{2.5}$.

5.3.2 Emission Standards

On the basis of the AAQS and the prevailing national economic and technological capacity, the state environmental authority and provincial governments set and update emission

59 MEP, Notice on the Implementation of the Ambient Air Quality Standards (GB3095-2012), issued on 29 February 2012.

TABLE 5.3 MAJOR EMISSION STANDARDS FOR STATIONARY SOURCES

Name	Reference number	Effective date
Air Pollutant Emission Standards for Gas Stations	GB 20952-2007	1 August 2007
Air Pollutant Emission Standards for Bulk Gasoline Terminals	GB 20950-2007	1 August 2007
Air Pollutant Emission Standards for the Coal Industry	GB 20426-2006, replacing GB 8978-1996 and GB 16297-1996	1 October 2006
Air Pollutant Emission Standards for the Cement Industry	GB 4915-2004, replacing GB 4915-1996	1 January 2005
Air Pollutant Emission Standards for Thermal Power Plants	GB 13223-2003, replacing GB13223-1996	1 January 2004
Emission Standard for Cooking Fumes	GB 18483-2001, replacing GWPB 5-2000	1 January 2002
Integrated Emission Standards for Air Pollutants	GB 16297-1996	1 January 1997
Emission Standard for Offensive and Obnoxious Odours	GB 14554-93	15 January 1994

Sources: Ministry of Ecology and Environment (n.d.). Website. www.mee.gov.cn/

standards for air pollutants.[60] At the national level, emission standards have been issued for both stationary sources and mobile sources.

One new and important development is the requirement of public consultation with experts, stakeholders and the public in setting the AAQS and emission standards.[61] Both state and provincial environmental bureaus are required to publicize the AAQS and emission standards on their websites for the public to access and download free of charge.[62] This public disclosure requirement ensures potential polluters have access to information to comply with the emission standards, ensures the public has the information it needs to supervise polluters and ensures victims of pollution have information that will help them to protect their rights and interests. The requirement for online publication on the official website does not, however, preclude the standards from being publicized elsewhere, such as in government gazettes or newspapers.

Both the AAQS and emission standards are restricted by the social, economic and technological conditions pertaining at the time of drafting,[63] but technological advancements and socio-economic development over time make it feasible to improve the standards. It is necessary to assess the implementation of the standards at regular intervals, so that they can be amended and updated in a timely manner.[64]

5.3.3 Product Standards

In addition to the AAQS and emission standards, air pollution control requires product standards, as the quality of some products, such as coal and other fuels, directly determines

[60] APPCL (2018), art. 9. [61] APPCL (2018), art. 10. [62] APPCL (2018), art. 11.
[63] APPCL (2018), art. 8 and art. 9. [64] APPCL (2018), art. 12.

TABLE 5.4 MAJOR EMISSION STANDARDS FOR MOBILE SOURCES

Name	Reference number	Effective date
Limits and Measurement Methods for Emissions from Light-Duty Vehicles (Stage VI)	GB 18352.6-2016	1 July 2020 (a) 1 July 2023 (b)
Limits and Measurement Methods for Emissions from Diesel Vehicles under Free Acceleration and Load Deceleration	GB 3847-2018, replacing GB 3847-2005 and HJ/T 241-2005	1 May 2019
Limits and Measurement Methods for Emissions from Light-Duty Vehicles (Stage V)	GB 18352.5-2013	1 January 2017
Limits and Measurement Methods for Emissions from Motorcycles on Running Mode (CHINA stage III)	GB 14622-2007, replacing GB14622-2002	1 July 2008
Limits and Measurement Methods for Emissions from Light-Duty Vehicles (Stages III, IV)	GB 18352.3-2005	1 July 2007
Limits and Measurement Methods for Exhaust Pollutants from Vehicles Equipped with Ignition Engine under Two-Speed Idle Conditions and Simple Driving Mode Conditions	GB 18285-2005	1 July 2005
Limits and Measurement Methods for Fuel Evaporative Pollutants from Heavy-Duty Vehicles Equipped with P.I Engines	GB 14763-2005	1 July 2005
Limits and Measurement Methods for Smoke from Agricultural Vehicles at Free Acceleration	GB 18322-2002	1 July 2002

Sources: Ministry of Ecology and Environment (n.d.). Website www.mee.gov.cn/

the concentration and volume of the air pollutants emitted. Controlling these products is an effective means of tackling air pollution at the source. The APPCL (2018) mandates that 'the product standards for coal, coal, petroleum coke, biomass, paint and other products containing VOCs, as well as fireworks and boilers, shall include environmental requirements'.[65] Further, it requires that 'the product standards for fuels used by vehicles, vessels and non-road mobile machinery shall meet the state requirement on air pollution control and be compatible with the emission standards of relevant vehicles, vessels and non-road mobile machinery'.[66]

In China, fuel standards have lagged behind the emission standards for vehicles. The State Council has, however, tried to improve the quality standards of fuels by requiring the State Quality Inspection Administration and State Standards Commission to promulgate, by June 2013, the Stage V Diesel Standard for Vehicles, requiring diesel to have a sulphur content below 10 ppm (parts per million), and, by end-2013, the Stage V Gasoline Standard for Vehicles, requiring diesel to have a sulphur content below 10 ppm. The Air Action Plan (2013) required that by end-2015, only Stage V diesel and petrol was supplied in key cities of the Beijing–Tianjin–Hebei region, the Yangtze River Delta and the Pearl River Delta, and

[65] APPCL (2018), art. 13(1). [66] APPCL (2018), art. 13(2).

nationwide by end-2017.[67] The Stage V diesel and gasoline standards for vehicles were issued as planned in 2013, cutting sulphur content by 80 per cent from 50 ppm to 10 ppm and requiring nationwide supply of only Stage V diesel and petrol by 1 January 2018. The state accelerated the upgrade to cleaner fuel products for vehicles and, by 1 January 2017, Stage V diesel and petrol had replaced all other diesel and petrol.[68] By 1 January 2019, the state had achieved a further nationwide upgrade to Stage VI diesel and gasoline.[69]

5.3.4 Plans for Pollution Prevention and Control, and Attainment Plans

The APPCL (2018) emphasizes the importance of government plans in air pollution prevention and control.[70] Local governments must make plans and take measures to control and abate air pollution in order to achieve the AAQS and continue to improve air quality.[71] If a city fails to achieve the AAQS, the municipal government will make an 'attainment plan' in a timely manner and take measures to achieve the AAQS by a deadline set by the State Council or provincial government.[72] Drafting the attainment plan requires consultation with stakeholders, experts and the public.[73] The attainment plan will be reviewed and amended as needed to control air pollution in that city and as economic conditions and technology develop.[74] The plan must be made publicly available and reported to the MEE for the record.[75] The implementation of the attainment plan will be supervised by both the people's congress and the public. The APPCL (2018) requires the municipal government to report its implementation of the attainment plan to the municipal people's congress or its standing committee each year, and also make the report publicly available.[76]

5.4 MECHANISMS TO PREVENT AND CONTROL AIR POLLUTION

The APPCL (2018) makes polluters pay by requiring enterprises, institutions and other production operators to take effective measures to prevent and abate air pollution, and to bear liability for damage caused.[77] While those entities bear the responsibility for controlling pollution, individuals as consumers of energy and resources also contribute to pollution. The law encourages people to adopt a low-carbon lifestyle, cutting their consumption and air pollution.[78] It adopts key mechanisms to prevent and control air

[67] Air Action Plan (2013), part I.

[68] NDRC et al., 'Announcement', (announcement no. 29 of 2016) 26 December 2016. www.ndrc.gov.cn/xxgk/zcfb/gg/201612/t20161226_961172.html. On 20 December 2016, the NDRC and seven other departments, including the Ministry of Public Security (MPS) and the MEE, announced jointly that Stage V diesel and petrol for vehicles would be available nationwide from 1 January 2017, when the sale of diesel and petrol not meeting Stage V standards would be suspended.

[69] NDRC, et al., 'Announcement', (announcement no. 16 of 2018) 29 December 2018. www.ndrc.gov.cn/xxgk/zcfb/gg/201812/t20181229_961214.html. On 29 December 2018, the NDRC and six other departments, including the MPS and the MEE, announced that Stage VI diesel and petrol for vehicles would be available nationwide from 1 January 2019, when the sale of diesel and petrol not meeting Stage VI standards would be banned. Stage VI standards further upgrade diesel and petrol by cutting emissions of CO and total hydrocarbon emissions (THC) by 50 per cent and NOx by 42 per cent, compared to Stage V diesel and petrol.

[70] APPCL (2018), art. 2(1). [71] APPCL (2018), art. 3(2). [72] APPCL (2018), art. 14(1).

[73] APPCL (2018), art. 14(2). [74] APPCL (2018), art. 17. [75] APPCL (2018), art. 15.

[76] APPCL (2018), art. 16. [77] APPCL (2018), art. 7(1). [78] APPCL (2018), art. 7(2).

pollution: environmental impact assessment (EIA), permit control, total emission control of key air pollutants, emissions trading and information disclosure and public participation.

5.4.1 EIA

The EIA is an important mechanism of regulatory control and is designed to prevent and minimize pollution at the source. An enterprise, institution or any other production operator must conduct an EIA prior to the construction of a project that will impact on AAQ. The EIA documents must be disclosed to the public.[79] The EIA mechanism is aligned with total emission control and local air quality. Where any region exceeds its total emission control quota for key air pollutants or fails to achieve the air quality improvement target, the EIA of any project that will increase the total emission of key air pollutants in that region will be suspended.[80] No new project will be approved for construction until the region has taken effective measures to clean up the existing pollution and meets the total emission control quota and air quality improvement target.

5.4.2 Emission Control by Permit

Permit control is a tailor-made regulatory mechanism applied to polluting sources on a case-by-case basis, in comparison to the standards, which apply to all. All enterprises, institutions and other production operators that emit air pollutants must comply with the relevant emission standards and total emission control quota for key air pollutants.[81] They must construct emission outlets in compliance with the law, regulations and administrative provisions.[82] However, not all enterprises, institutions and other production operators emitting air pollutants are subject to control by permit. Only four types of unit, enterprise or institution are required to obtain a permit and comply with its terms and conditions:

(i) enterprises or institutions that emit industrial air pollutants;
(ii) enterprises or institutions that emit toxic and hazardous air pollutants listed in the Catalogue under article 78;[83]
(iii) operating units of coal-burning centralized heat supply facilities and
(iv) other units subject to permit requirement by law.[84]

It should be noted that, in this case, 'units' excludes 'other operators of production' such as individual households, which are not subject to permit control under article 19.

The State Council's Implementation Plan on Permit Control of Pollution Discharge (Implementation Plan) (2016)[85] set guiding principles for national implementation of the permit scheme by 2020, with earlier implementation required by thermal power generators and the papermaking industry.[86] Enterprises subject to permit control can only discharge

[79] APPCL (2018), art. 18. [80] APPCL (2018), art. 22. [81] APPCL (2018), art. 18.
[82] APPCL (2018), art. 20. [83] This is a reference to the Catalogue on Toxic and Hazardous Air Pollutants.
[84] APPCL (2018), art. 19.
[85] The State Council issued the Implementation Plan on 10 November 2016 with immediate effect.
[86] MEP Notice on Permit Control of Thermal Power Plants and Papermaking Factories and High-Rising Emissions in Pilot Cities in Beijing–Tianjin–Hebei (2016), part I. The MEP required the issuance of permits to all thermal power plants and papermaking factories, steel and cement enterprises with high-rising emission smokestacks in Beijing, Baoding and Langfang to be completed by 30 June 2017. These enterprises were

pollution in accordance with the permit, and they are prohibited from discharging without a permit or in violation of their permit. The MEP's Provisional Measures on Pollution Discharge Permits (2016)[87] regulates applications for and the issuance of permits, as well as monitoring and supervision to ensure compliance with permit terms and conditions.

The permit-control system offers a more individualized and targeted way to regulate polluters, with the terms and conditions of the permit aligned with the EIA requirements, total emission control, emission charges or taxes, emission data collection and emissions trading. The use of permits better informs enterprises of their duties, responsibilities and potential liabilities, with better awareness promoting compliance. Information disclosure and transparency – transparency of permit application, issuance and supervision, emissions data and enforcement data – facilitate public supervision over polluters and government agencies.

5.4.3 Total Emission Control of Key Air Pollutants

Emission standards set limits on the concentration levels of air pollutants emitted from smokestacks, regardless of the cumulative total emitted. In contrast, total emission control imposes a cap on the total amount of emissions of pollutants. Total emission control was first introduced to control SO_2 in regions suffering from acid rain or at risk of acid rain, roughly 11.4 per cent of China's landmass.[88] The 2015 revision to the APPCL extends the application of total emission control nationwide by providing that '[t]he state implements total emission control on key air pollutants'.[89] Total emission control does not apply to all air pollutants listed in article 2, but only to 'key air pollutants', which are designated by the State Council as needed.[90] The targets for total emission control of key air pollutants are set at the national level by the MEP, in consultation with relevant State Council departments and in collaboration with the NDRC. Upon approval by the State Council, the targets are allocated to provincial governments for implementation at local levels.[91] Provincial governments must take measures to control and abate total emission of key air pollutants within their jurisdictions. They may also apply total emission control to any other air pollutants to tackle local problems, in addition to the key air pollutants designated by the State Council.[92]

The target set in the 11th FYP (2006–10) was China's first binding target for cutting total emissions of a key air pollutant: a 10 per cent cut in SO_2 was targeted by 2010, as compared to the 2005 level. Emissions of SO_2 were in fact cut by 14.29 per cent during the 11th FYP period.[93] The 12th FYP (2011–15) added NOx as a second key air pollutant and set binding abatement targets of 8 per cent for SO_2 and 10 per cent for NOx by 2015, as compared to the 2010 level.[94] China again overachieved and, by the end of the 12th FYP period, had cut

required to operate in full compliance with the permit requirements from 1 July 2017 and to self-monitor, disclose information, record emissions and report regularly to the authorities.

87 The Provisional Measures on Pollution Discharge Permits were issued by the MEP on 23 December 2016.

88 Xin Chunying (ed.), *Interpreting APPCL*, at 46.

89 APPCL (2015), art. 21(1).

90 The only key air pollutant during the 11th FYP period (2006–10) was SO_2. NOx was added for the 12th FYP (2011–15) and 13th FYP (2016–20) periods.

91 APPCL (2018), art. 21(2) and (3)

92 APPCL (2018), art. 21(4).

93 12th FYP (2011–15), chapter 1.

94 12th FYP (2011–15), chapter 3.

TABLE 5.5 REDUCTIONS IN EMISSIONS OF KEY AIR POLLUTANTS

FYP and time period	Key air pollutant	Abatement target (%)	Actual abatement (%)
11th FYP (2006–2010)	SO_2	−10	−14.29
12th FYP (2011–2015)	SO_2 NOx	−8 −10	−18 −18.6
13th FYP (2016–2020)	SO_2 NOx	−15 −15	Data not yet available.

Sources: 11th FYP (2006–10); 12th FYP (2011–15); 13th FYP (2016–20).

total emissions of SO_2 by 18 per cent and NOx by 18.6 per cent.[95] The state raised the abatement targets for SO_2 and NOx to 15 per cent each in the 13th FYP (2016–20).[96]

In order to achieve pollution abatement targets, both conventional end-of-pipe control methods – including desulphurization, denitrification and dust removal at power plants and large industrial boilers – and clean production, focusing on control at the source, are being aggressively adopted. Small coal-fired boilers are being closed down, outdated industrial capacity is being phased out and early retirement of yellow-label vehicles and old vehicles is being implemented.[97] Measures are being taken to phase out production techniques, equipment and products that cause serious air pollution.[98] The NDRC and relevant departments set deadlines for the phasing out and incorporate them into the Catalogue on Industrial Restructuring, a comprehensive catalogue on industrial policy.[99] Producers, importers, sellers or users must stop the production, import, sale or use of the equipment or products listed in the Catalogue by the deadline. Those who use the production techniques listed in the Catalogue must stop using such techniques by the deadline.[100]

5.4.4 Emissions Trading

Emissions trading is a market mechanism introduced by the 2015 revision. It provides for the state to implement emissions trading of key air pollutants in stages.[101] Since 2007, the State Council has designated eleven provinces, including Tianjin, Hebei and Inner Mongolia, to trial local pilot schemes on emissions trading.[102] The Air Action Plan (2013) develops and implements emissions trading to cut air pollution.[103] To operate, an emissions market requires: (i) an overall emissions cap or total emissions quota for each key air pollutant to be traded, (ii) an allocation of emissions allowances to each existing and future

95 13th FYP (2011–15), chapter 1. 96 13th FYP (2011–15), chapter 3.
97 'Yellow-label vehicles' refers to petrol vehicles of pre-National Emission Standard I and diesel vehicles not meeting National Emission Standard II.
98 APPCL (2018), art. 27(1).
99 APPCL (2018), art. 27(2). The Catalogue on Industrial Restructuring is regularly updated, most recently in 2019.
100 APPCL (2018), art. 27(3). 101 APPCL (2015), art. 21(5).
102 State Council General Office, Guiding Opinion on Further Promoting Emissions Trading (2014).
103 Air Action Plan (2013), part VI, s. 19.

polluter, (iii) trading to be regulated to ensure fairness and transparency, and (iv) active market participants.[104] By trading emissions quotas between the regulator and polluters and among polluters themselves, the cap on total emissions can be complied with in the most cost-effective manner by the market. As the state targets for abatement of key air pollutants drop, the total emissions quota also drops. The market price of emissions quotas will increase as supply drops and should incentivize polluters to innovate, upgrade existing production techniques and embrace clean production processes and clean energy.

5.4.5 Information Disclosure and Public Participation

Information disclosure and public participation are emphasized as a way of facilitating public supervision of polluters and the government, thereby strengthening enforcement of environmental laws and regulations. Information disclosure is expressly required for: appraisal results of government performance,[105] AAQS and emission standards,[106] attainment plans made by cities not meeting the AAQS,[107] reports made by governments to the same-level people's congress on the implementation of the attainment plans,[108] EIA documents of new construction projects,[109] reports on supervision talks between environmental authorities and local governments that fail to achieve total emission control targets or the AAQS,[110] inventory of key polluting sources,[111] monitoring data and source analysis of air pollution in key regions[112] and the emergency response plan for heavy pollution weather.[113]

In addition to the information disclosure mechanism that empowers the public to participate in the battle against air pollution, there is also a public complaint mechanism.[114] Public supervision and monitoring of polluters effectively support agency enforcement if public complaints are followed up by the agencies in a timely manner. The EEBs and other relevant bodies are required to provide channels such as telephone numbers and email accounts to make it easy for the public to report or complain against polluters.[115] Agencies must take immediate measures upon receiving a complaint and keep the identity of the complainant confidential. Where the complainant uses his or her real name to make the complaint, agencies must provide feedback on the outcome of the investigation. If agency investigation leads to a finding of violation, the agency must publicize the violation and pay a reward to the complainant.[116] Where a complaint is made by an employee against their employer, the employer may not retaliate in any way, including by termination or modification of the employment contract.[117] The public is encouraged to report violations to the authority by incentives of rewards and protection of whistle-blowers.

[104] Xin Chunying (ed.), *Interpreting APPCL*, at 49–50. [105] APPCL (2018), art. 4.
[106] APPCL (2018), art. 11. [107] APPCL (2018), art. 15. [108] APPCL (2018), art. 16.
[109] APPCL (2018), art. 18. [110] APPCL (2018), art. 22. [111] APPCL (2018), art. 24(2).
[112] APPCL (2018), art. 91. [113] APPCL (2018), art. 94(2).
[114] For a critique of the environmental complaint mechanism, see Tseming Yang and Xuehua Zhang, 'Public participation in environmental enforcement'.
[115] APPCL (2018), art. 31(1). [116] APPCL (2018), art. 31(2). [117] APPCL (2018), art. 31(3).

5.5 CONTROL OF KEY SOURCES OF AIR POLLUTION

China's key sources of air pollution are coal burning, industry, vehicles and vessels, construction sites and agriculture. The APPCL (2018) adopts a range of different measures to control particulate matters, SO_2, NOx, VOCs and NH_3 from these major sources.[118]

5.5.1 Production and Consumption of Coal and Other Fuels

Coal is the dirtiest fuel in terms of emissions of SO_2, NOx and particulate matters. China lacks substantial reserves of oil and natural gas, but has coal in abundance.[119] Coal has dominated China's energy structure and will continue to be a major contributor to its primary energy mix for the foreseeable future. Coal accounted for 76.2 per cent of China's primary energy mix in 1990,[120] and had fallen to 69.2 per cent by end-2010.[121] Production and consumption of coal and other fossil fuels are major sources of air pollution in China. Coal accounts for 90 per cent of China's SO_2 emissions and 70 per cent of emissions of NOx and particulate matters.[122] The State Council set a national target of a cut in coal use to 65 per cent of the primary energy mix by end-2017[123] and 58 per cent by end-2020.[124] China achieved the 2020 target ahead of schedule. By 2019, 57.7 per cent of China's primary energy mix was coal-fuelled.[125]

Two strategies are used to control air pollution caused by coal production and consumption. First, coal production and consumption is capped and cut by switching to natural gas and non-fossil fuels. Relevant State Council departments and governments at all levels take measures to improve China's energy structure by promoting the production and consumption of clean energy and reducing the share of coal in the primary energy mix. The second strategy is to promote clean and efficient use of coal in order to abate the air pollution generated in its production, consumption or processing.[126] Approximately half of China's coal consumption is used for power generation, and roughly 30 per cent by industry, including iron and steel, chemicals, petrochemicals, non-ferrous metals, construction materials, papermaking and textiles.[127] The APPCL (2018) targets the power sector by making power grids prioritize electricity generated by clean energy.[128] Despite serious efforts made by state plans to cap coal production and consumption, coal will continue to be a major source of power for decades. Advancements in technology have made clean and efficient use of coal achievable by: (i) washing coal at the production stage in order to cut its sulphur and ash content, (ii) cutting emissions through the use of advanced combustion technology and smoke and dust treatment, (iii) clean processing of coal into

[118] APPCL (2018), art. 2.

[119] China's per capita shares of oil and natural gas are 5.4 per cent and 7.5 per cent respectively of the global averages. For more details, see State Council, *China's Energy Policy 2012* (2012). www.pkulaw.cn, chapter 1.

[120] NDRC, China's National Plan on Climate Change (2007), part I, s. 3.

[121] NDRC and State Energy Bureau, 13th FYP on Energy Development (2016), chapter I.

[122] Xin Chunying (ed.), *Interpreting APPCL*, at 76.

[123] Air Action Plan (2013), part IV.

[124] 13th FYP on Energy Development (2016), chapter 2.

[125] MEE, 15 May 2020, 'The Ministry of Ecology and Environment holds a regular press conference in April'. Online article. www.mee.gov.cn/xxgk2018/xxgk/xxgk15/202005/t20200515_779537.html.

[126] APPCL (2018), art. 32.

[127] Yuan Jie (ed.), *Understanding APPCL*, at 91.

[128] APPCL (2018), art. 42.

oil and gas and (iv) using advanced technology to remove pollutants including SO_2 and NOx.[129]

The APPCL (2018) targets the source of air pollution by providing for the control of coal quality at the production stage.[130] Reducing the sulphur and ash content of coal at the production stage by washing it effectively cuts the levels of SO_2 and particulate matters emitted when coal is burnt to generate power or used in other industries. The state also restricts the mining of high-sulphur or high-ash coal and promotes coal washing. New coal mines are required to construct coal-washing facilities simultaneously with mine development to reduce the sulphur and ash content to below the prescribed limits. Existing coal mines are required to install coal-washing facilities by a deadline, unless they only produce low-sulphur and low-ash coal or meet the requirements on sulphur and ash content of power generators complying with national emission standards.[131] China prohibits the mining of coal that contains toxic or hazardous substances at levels exceeding prescribed limits. These include radioactive chemicals and arsenic.[132] Local governments have the power to suspend production or close coal mines that violate these provisions.[133] In addition to controlling domestic coal production, the APPCL (2018) also prohibits the import, sale and consumption of coal that does not meet the relevant quality standards.[134] The production, processing, storage, sale, import and consumption of coal must comply with limits on sulphur, ash and other chemicals, including radioactive substances and toxic chemicals.[135] In addition to strict control over the quality of coal for domestic consumption, the state supports research, development and application of clean-coal technology and of the exploitation of coalbed gas.[136] Coalbed gas is also known as coalbed methane; it co-exists with coal, but is much cleaner. It is a non-conventional natural gas that can be both transported and used with natural gas.[137]

Further, the APPCL (2018) provides for clean production processes to be used in coal consumption. It controls the quality of boilers and prohibits the production, import, sale and use of boilers that do not meet certain environmental requirements.[138] It requires thermal power plants and other coal-burning enterprises to adopt clean production techniques, install devices to remove dust, sulphur and nitrogen, or make other technological improvements to control emissions of pollutants.[139]

Last but not least, better urban planning can alleviate the impact of air pollution. The APPCL (2018) grants municipal governments the power to ban the sale and consumption of high-pollution fuels in certain zones and to steadily expand these zones to improve AAQ.[140]

[129] Xin Chunying (ed.), *Interpreting APPCL*, at 77. [130] APPCL (2018), art. 33.
[131] APPCL (2018), art. 33(1). [132] APPCL (2018), art. 33(2). [133] APPCL (2018), art. 102(2).
[134] APPCL (2018), art. 35(1). The NDRC and five other state departments, including the MEP, issued the Provisional Measures on Quality Control of Commercial Coal on 3 September 2014, to come into force on 1 January 2015.
[135] The Provisional Measures on Quality Control of Commercial Coal (2014), arts. 6 and 7. The sulphur content must be below 1.5 per cent for brown coal and 3 per cent for other types of coal; the ash content must be below 30 per cent for brown coal and 40 per cent for other types of coal. Where the coal is to be transported more than 600 km within China, tighter quality standards apply: the sulphur content must be below 1 per cent for brown coal and 2 per cent for other types of coal; the ash content must be below 20 per cent for brown coal and 30 per cent for other types of coal.
[136] APPCL (2018), art. 34. [137] Xin Chunying (ed.) *Interpreting APPCL* , at 84–5.
[138] APPCL (2018), art. 40. [139] APPCL (2018), art. 41. [140] APPCL (2018), art. 38(1).

The term 'high-pollution fuel' refers to raw coal, gangue, fly ash, coal slime, fuel oil (heavy oil and residue oil), combustible waste and biomass (trees, straw and sawdust, among others).[141] Further, the construction or expansion of projects consuming high-pollution fuels is prohibited in the zones. Existing projects are required to convert to natural gas, shale gas, liquefied petroleum gas, electricity or other cleaner energy before a deadline set by the municipal government.[142]

5.5.2 Industrial Emissions

Industrial production is a primary source of air pollution in China. Enterprises producing iron and steel, construction materials, non-ferrous metals, petroleum and chemicals are subject to the requirement of clean production. They must adopt clean production techniques, install devices for dust removal, desulphurization and denitration, or upgrade existing technologies to control air pollution.[143] Clean production was first endorsed officially by *China's Agenda 21* as a sustainable development strategy.[144] The legal definition of 'clean production' is found in the Law on Clean Production (2002): 'the use of improved design, clean energy and resources, advanced techniques and equipment, improved management and comprehensive treatment to reduce pollution at the source, improve efficiency in resource consumption, reduce or prevent pollution in the production, service and consumption of products, and alleviate or eliminate harm to human health and the environment'.[145] While clean production is more effective and efficient in pollution abatement compared to end-of-pipe control mechanisms, it does not completely replace other control mechanisms, including installation of devices for dust removal, desulphurization and denitration, which all work together to control pollution.

VOCs are found in a wide variety of products, such as solvent-based paints, coatings, adhesives, sealants, printing inks, organic solvents and petroleum products. When a product containing VOCs is used, VOCs are inadvertently released, not only causing air pollution by enhancing the formation of ozone and fine particulate matters, but also having direct impacts on human health, ranging from eye, nose and throat irritation to headaches, nausea and damage to the central nervous system. Some VOCs contain benzene, a known carcinogen.[146] Until 2012, when the 12th FYP on Air Pollution Control in Key Regions, was issued, VOCs were not subject to regulatory control. The APPCL (2018) expressly includes VOCs as a controlled air pollutant.[147] First, the production, import, sale and use of raw materials or products containing VOCs must comply with the relevant quality standards. The state encourages the production, import, sale and use of organic solvents with low levels of toxicity and volatility.[148] Second, where any production or service activity emits VOCs, such activity must be carried out in a hermetically sealed space. Operators must install and use pollution-prevention devices, but where that is not possible, measures must be taken to reduce emissions.[149] Third, industrial coating enterprises must use products with a low VOC content and must keep a record of their use and disposal of raw materials, and

[141] MEP, Provisions on Designation of High-Pollution Fuels (2001). [142] APPCL (2018), art. 38.
[143] APPCL (2018), art. 43. [144] State Council, *China's Agenda 21*, chapter II, para. 2.19.
[145] Law on Clean Production (2002), art. 2. [146] Yuan Jie (ed.), *Understanding APPCL*, at 124.
[147] APPCL (2018), art. 2. [148] APPCL (2018), art. 44. [149] APPCL (2018), art. 45.

the VOCs they contain, for a minimum of three years.[150] Fourth, petroleum, chemical and other enterprises that use organic solvents must take measures to maintain and repair pipes and equipment in order to reduce leaks and to recover and dispose of leaked substances in a timely manner.[151] Last, operators of oil and gas storage tanks, petrol stations, crude oil and refined oil terminals, and oil and gas tankers are required to install devices to recover VOCs.[152]

Industrial processes, such as petrochemical, chemical and coal mining, generate combustible gases. Landfill sites also emit methane and other combustible gases. It is technologically possible to recover combustible gases for the generation of energy or heat, which not only prevents emission of air pollutants, but also transforms waste into resources. The APPCL (2018) requires operators of industrial processes and landfill sites to recover combustible gases for utilization, and to take pollution-control measures where recovery is impossible.[153] If a recovery device malfunctions, operators must repair or replace them in a timely manner. While the recovery devices are not operating and combustible gases have to be emitted, operators should ensure full combustion of the gases before emission, report to local EPBs and take measures to repair or replace the recovery devices before a specified deadline.[154]

5.5.3 Emissions from Mobile Sources

Industrialization and urbanization have turned mobile sources, including vehicles, vessels, non-road mobile machinery and civil aviation, into substantial contributors to air pollution in China. The unprecedented growth of vehicles on the road in Chinese cities since the 1990s is a major cause of air pollution and also causes serious traffic congestion. To tackle air pollution caused by mobile sources, the APPCL (2018) not only regulates emission standards for vehicles and quality standards for fuels, but also requires governments to promote low-carbon transport. This entails reasonable control of the total number of conventional vehicles on the road and expansion of the public transport network.[155] Megacities such as Beijing, Shanghai and Shenzhen have already imposed caps on the annual sale of private cars, with potential buyers obtaining a purchase quota by lucky draw (in Beijing) or by auction (Shanghai). The state should, through fiscal and tax measures or government procurement, promote environmentally friendly and new-energy vehicles, vessels and non-road mobile machines to abate China's consumption of fossil fuels.[156] Municipal governments are responsible for improving road construction, thereby promoting low-carbon transport, and ensuring continuity and accessibility of bicycle lanes and pavements.[157]

The APPCL (2018) prohibits the manufacture, import or sale of any vehicle, vessel or non-road mobile machine that exceeds emission standards.[158] Manufacturers of vehicles and non-road mobile machines must conduct emissions tests and may only sell those that pass. The test results must be made public. Provincial environmental bureaus may conduct on-site inspections and take and test samples to monitor the emissions of new vehicles and

[150] APPCL (2018), art. 46. [151] APPCL (2018), art. 47(1). [152] APPCL (2018), art. 47(2).
[153] APPCL (2018), art. 49(1). [154] APPCL (2018), art. 49. [155] APPCL (2018), art. 50(1).
[156] APPCL (2018), art. 50(2). [157] APPCL (2018), art. 50(4). [158] APPCL (2018), art. 51.

non-road mobile machines.[159] Vehicles in use are subject to an annual emission test. A vehicle must pass the test in order to obtain a safety inspection label, which permits it to be used on roads, from the road traffic authority within a public security bureau (PSB).[160] Local environmental bureaus may conduct additional random testing of vehicle emissions at car parks or garages. They may also conduct additional random roadside emissions tests via remote sensors.[161] Garages must repair and maintain vehicles in order that they meet the emission standards.[162] Vehicles owners or garages are prohibited from temporarily changing emission control devices to pass the emissions test by cheating.[163] The recall and retirement schemes remove from the road vehicles that fail to meet the emission standards. Where manufacturers or importers become aware that any vehicle or non-road mobile machine is violating emission standards due to design or manufacturing defects or does not meet the durability requirements (assessed in km travelled) for environmental protection, they should recall the vehicles or non-road mobile machines. If they fail to do so, the state environmental authority and state market regulatory authority will order a recall.[164] The compulsory retirement scheme first requires vehicles that fail the emissions test to be repaired and maintained; if a vehicle still fails the test after repair, it is taken off the road. The owner must surrender the vehicle for dismantling or destruction and cancel the vehicle registration with the public security authority in charge of road traffic.[165] Older vehicles tend to be more polluting than new ones. Using Beijing as an example, 35 per cent of the vehicles in use are more than six years old and they contribute to more than 68 per cent of the total air pollutants emitted by vehicles.[166] To speed up the process of phasing out heavily polluting mobile sources, the state also encourages and supports early retirement of heavily polluting vehicles, vessels and non-road mobile machinery.[167]

The quality of fuel has a direct impact on the emissions produced by mobile sources. There are four main categories of fuel used by mobile sources in China: (i) petrol for vehicles, (ii) diesel for vehicles, (iii) regular diesel and (iv) heavy and residual oil. Regular diesel, allowed for use by vessels and non-road mobile machinery, has a higher sulphur content and is cheaper than diesel for vehicles. Heavy oil and residual oil are the cheapest and dirtiest fuels with the highest sulphur content, and can only be used by ocean-going vessels (OGVs).[168] The APPCL (2018) prohibits the production, import and sale of fuels used by vehicles, vessels and non-road mobile machines that do not meet the relevant quality standards. It prohibits the sale of regular diesel, and other fuels not for use by vehicles, to vehicles or motorcycles. It also prohibits the sale of heavy oil and residual oil to non-road mobile machinery or vessels with direct access to inland rivers and coastal waters.[169] Vessels with direct access to inland rivers and coastal waters must use regular diesel. When berthed, OGVs are required to use fuels that comply with the requirements of air pollution controls.[170] Before berthing, OGVs using heavy or residual oil must switch to regular diesel. However, the use of regular diesel to generate electricity for use on OGVs emits SO_2 and NOx. Consequently, newly constructed ports are required to install an

159 APPCL (2018), art. 52.
160 APPCL (2018), art. 53(1).
161 APPCL (2018), art. 53(2).
162 APPCL (2018), art. 55(2).
163 APPCL (2018), art. 55(3).
164 APPCL (2018), art. 58.
165 APPCL (2018), art. 60(1).
166 Xin Chunying (ed.), *Interpreting APPCL*, at 145.
167 APPCL (2018), art. 60(2).
168 Yuan Jie (ed.), *Understanding APPCL*, at 177–8.
169 APPCL (2018), art. 65.
170 APPCL (2018), art. 63(1).

onshore power supply and existing ports should retrofit with onshore power supply so that OGVs at berth have access to onshore electricity supply.[171]

5.5.4 Dust Pollution: Construction Sites and Other Sources

Dust pollution is generated mainly by four sources: (i) construction sites, (ii) road transport, (iii) storage sites, and (iv) exposed soil.[172] Local governments should play an important role in regulating construction and road transport, keeping roads clean, controlling the storage of construction materials, and reducing exposed soil by expansion of greenery, lakes, ponds, wetlands and pavements to prevent dust.[173] The work requires collaboration between the departments of housing and urban–rural construction, environmental hygiene, transport and land resources.[174] Municipal governments are responsible for cleaning roads, squares, car parks and other public places. They must use machinery powered by clean energy to reduce dust and prevent pollution.[175] It is the responsibility of the Ministry of Housing and Urban–Rural Development (MOHURD) and its local bureaus to plan, plant greenery and install permeable pavement along rivers, roads and at places with exposed soil.[176]

Proponents of construction projects, as well as contractors, bear the heavy responsibility of controlling dust from construction sites. Developers must include dust prevention in the project costs and must also contractually specify the dust prevention responsibilities of contractors. Contractors must make detailed plans for controlling dust.[177] The APPCL (2018) requires them to take dust-control measures, including setting up enclosures around the construction sites, covering exposed land, working during scheduled time periods only, spraying water to suppress dust and washing the surfaces of dusty objects and vehicles. Contractors should remove construction waste, including waste soil, from the sites in a timely manner, and must cover waste piled on site with dustproof nets.[178] To facilitate public supervision, contractors are required to post, at the construction site, information including dust-control measures, persons in charge and names of the supervisory authorities.[179] Where construction does not commence quickly, the site must be covered, and where construction does not commence within three months of obtaining the land-use rights, the site must be planted with trees or grass, or paved or covered.[180]

In addition to construction sites, road transport and storage sites are also sources of dust. The APPCL (2018) requires vehicles used to transport coal, waste, waste soil, sandstone, earth, mortar and other bulk or liquid materials to take measures to prevent leaks. To prevent dust pollution, loading and unloading should be carried out within an enclosed space or while spraying water.[181] The APPCL (2018) also mandates storage in an enclosed space for items that are likely to cause pollution: coal, gangue, coal cinder, coal ash,

[171] APPCL (2018), art. 63(2).
[172] MEP, Technical Policy on Comprehensive Prevention and Control of Fine Particulate Matters in the Air (2013).
[173] APPCL (2018), art. 68(1). [174] APPCL (2018), arts. 68(2). [175] APPCL (2018), art. 70(3).
[176] APPCL (2018), art. 71. [177] APPCL (2018), art. 69(1). [178] APPCL (2018), art. 69(3).
[179] APPCL (2018), art. 69(4). [180] APPCL (2018), art. 69(5). [181] APPCL (2018), art. 70(1) and (2).

cement, lime, plaster and sandstone. Where that is not feasible, fencing higher than the piled materials must be used to prevent dust pollution.[182]

5.5.5 Pollution from Agricultural Activities

Air pollution by agriculture is catching up with pollution from industrial and mobile sources. There are three major types of air pollution in rural China: (i) NH_3 and VOCs caused by excessive use of fertilizers and pesticides; (ii) obnoxious odours emitted from animal farms that do not dispose properly of animal waste or animal carcasses; (iii) particulate matters, SO_2 and NOx from open burning of straw and leaves. To tackle air pollution caused by these activities, local governments bear the primary responsibility for regulating, facilitating, supporting and educating farmers and rural operators to switch to environmentally friendly operations. Regulation alone will not work, because rural villagers do not always have the capacity to comply and local agencies do not have sufficient resources to monitor compliance. Control of rural air pollution relies heavily on local governments to change established village practices by providing support in the forms of finance, facilities, services and training. Local governments must promote the circular economy in rural areas and support waste collection and disposal.[183]

The excessive use of fertilizers and pesticides has severely contaminated rural China. While China consumes more than 50 million t of fertilizers and more than 1.8 million t of pesticides annually, most is wasted due to low efficiency in their application. By 2015, the efficiency rate for the use of fertilizers and pesticides was 35.2 per cent and 36.6 per cent respectively.[184] Fertilizers and pesticides contribute to air pollution through the NH_3 and VOCs they contain. The APPCL (2018) requires farmers to improve their method of application of fertilizer and use it in a scientific and rational manner,[185] and apply pesticide in accordance with state provisions.[186] It prohibits the spraying of extremely or highly toxic pesticides on trees, flowers and grass in densely populated areas.[187] Farmers, however, often lack the capacity or motivation to change their established way of operating, believing the more fertilizers and pesticides they use, the better the output and the more effective the pest control. Local governments, and especially local agriculture bureaus, must provide training and education to deliver the message that science-based use of fertilizers and pesticides is not only good for their personal health and the environment, but is also good for long-term sustainable growth of agricultural output.

Odour from animal farms is a major source of air pollution nuisance in rural China. Over 80 per cent of farms do not have proper solid waste or wastewater treatment facilities.[188] In line with the polluter-pays principle, the APPCL (2018) imposes the duties on operators of

[182] APPCL (2018), art. 72. [183] APPCL (2018), art. 73.

[184] The remainder was wasted, lost to the air, water and soil. State Council, Plan on National Agricultural Modernization (2016–2020) (2016), chapter II. The Plan set a 2020 target of a 40 per cent efficiency rate for fertilizers and pesticides.

[185] APPCL (2018), art. 74(1).

[186] APPCL (2018), art. 74(1). The Regulation on Pesticide Administration (2017) regulates the production, operation and application of pesticides. It prohibits the use of extremely or highly toxic pesticides on vegetables, fruit, teas and herbal medicines.

[187] APPCL (2018), art. 74(2). [188] Xin Chunying (ed.), *Interpreting APPCL*, at 177–8.

livestock and poultry farms to collect, store, remove and treat wastewater, animal waste and animal carcasses in a timely manner in order to prevent obnoxious odour.[189]

Open burning of crop straw and fallen leaves is a common and convenient way for farmers to dispose of large quantities in the summer and autumn. It generates dust and smoke and substantially increases the concentration of particulate matters, SO_2 and NOx. Open burning, when carried out near airports and highways, threatens aviation and road safety. The law approaches the problem in a pragmatic manner. Instead of imposing a complete ban on open burning of crop straw, which is unlikely to be achievable given the lack of easily accessible alternatives, the APPCL (2018) requires provincial governments to designate special zones in which open burning of crop straw and fallen leaves is prohibited.[190] Equally important is to provide collection, storage, treatment and disposal services so that farmers do not have to resort to open burning. The county governments are required to set up service networks for the collection, storage, transport and comprehensive utilization of straw and leaves, and to provide financial subsidies to support rural collectives, village cooperatives and enterprises offering such services.[191] Local governments must encourage and support technological innovation in order to turn crop straw and leaves into fertilizer, feedstock, energy and raw materials, among others. In particular, they must increase financial subsidies for machinery for converting crop straw into fertilizer,[192] with such machinery combining collection and utilization at the farm site, saving the cost of transport and storage.

5.5.6 Toxic and Hazardous Air Pollution

While most air pollutants, including SO_2, NOx, particulate matter (PM_{10} and $PM_{2.5}$), ozone, CO, VOCs, lead, benzene, mercury and dioxin, are harmful to human health, some are linked to an increased risk of cancer. These include arsenic, chromium VI, nickel, benzene and polynuclear aromatic hydrocarbons.[193] Heavy metal particulates are emitted into the air by combustion processes such as industrial operation, traffic, energy production and incineration of metal-containing waste (batteries and electronic equipment). These heavy metals can harm human health via complex pathways that begin in deposition in topsoil, where they are absorbed by crops that are then eaten, or by contaminating drinking water supplies. In addition to increasing the risk of cancer, lead and mercury are neurotoxins, while other heavy metals cause kidney, lung and bone problems.[194] Benzene and many aromatic organic compounds have toxic and carcinogenic effects and may alter DNA or cause birth defects. They are present in fossil fuels and are emitted by the incomplete

[189] APPCL (2018), art. 75.

[190] APPCL (2018), art. 77. According to the Measures on the Burning Ban and Comprehensive Utilization of Crop Straws (2003), a ban is imposed on the open burning of crop straw within 15 km of airports, within 2 km either side of highways and railways and within 1 km on either side of provincial main roads. Provincial governments may designate other zones, such as nature reserves, scenic areas, resorts and forests, where the ban on open burning is imposed.

[191] APPCL (2018), art. 76(2). [192] APPCL (2018), art. 76(1).

[193] WHO, *Evolution of WHO Air Quality Guidelines: Past, Present and Future*, (Copenhagen: WHO Regional Office for Europe, 2017), 15.

[194] WHO, *Health Risks of Heavy Metals from Long-Range Transboundary Air Pollution*, (Copenhagen: WHO Regional Office for Europe, 2007).

combustion of carbon-based fuels, such as coal and wood. Benzene is also widely used by the petrochemical industry to produce plastics and synthetic rubber. Persistent organic pollutants (POPs) are chemicals that are not only toxic and harmful to humans, but also remain intact in the environment for long periods, can travel long distances through air, water and soil, and accumulate in the fatty tissues of living organisms, including humans. They pass in utero and through food chains, increasing the risk of cancer, as well as neurological, reproductive and immunity problems.[195]

Toxic and hazardous air pollutants that are harmful to human health should be subject to closer monitoring and tighter regulatory control. The EPL (2014) stipulates that the state should establish and improve monitoring, survey and risk assessment systems for environment and health, encourage and support research on the impact of environmental quality on human health, and take measures to prevent and control illness caused by environmental pollution.[196] The APPCL (2018) requires state ministries in charge of environment and health to promulgate jointly a list of toxic and hazardous air pollutants and implement a risk management system.[197] Entities that emit toxic and hazardous air pollutants must manage and control the risks by: (i) establishing an environmental risk warning system, (ii) regularly monitoring the emission outlets and the environment surrounding them, (iii) assessing environmental risks and investigating hidden environmental safety issues and (iv) taking effective measures to prevent environmental risks.[198]

In relation to POPs, the APPCL (2018) requires entities that emit POPs and operators of waste incinerators to adopt techniques and processes that reduce POP emissions and to install cleaning devices to ensure the emissions meet the requisite standards.[199] China is a party to the Stockholm Convention on Persistent Organic Pollutants (Stockholm Convention),[200] which requires parties to take measures to control/restrict the trade, domestic production and use of ten 'intentionally produced' POPs[201] and reduce and eliminate the production and release of two 'unintentionally produced' by-product POPs.[202] Many intentionally produced POPs are or were used as pesticides, the best known being dichlorodiphenyltrichloroethane (DDT). Unintentionally produced by-product POPs are those that are released unintentionally and as a by-product of another process. A well-known example is dioxin, which is emitted during waste incineration, metal smelting, application of sewage sludge to land and bleaching of paper and fabric. The list of twelve POPs may be amended or added to. By 2018, sixteen new POPs had been added.[203] When the treaty was ratified in 2004, China was granted a five-year exemption, giving it time to phase out the production, sale, use, import and export of

[195] For more on POPs, see the website of the Stockholm Convention on Persistent Organic Pollutants: UN Environment Programme, Stockholm Convention, n.d., 'What are POPs?'. Online article. www.pops.int/TheConvention/ThePOPs/tabid/673/Default.aspx

[196] EPL (2014), art. 39.

[197] APPCL (2018), art. 78(1). On 23 January 2019, the MEE and State Commission on Health issued the Catalogue on Toxic and Hazardous Air Pollutants (2018) with immediate effect.

[198] APPCL (2018), art. 78(2). [199] APPCL (2018), art. 79.

[200] Stockholm Convention on Persistent Organic Pollutants, Stockholm, 22 May 2001, treaty no. 40214. *United Nations Treaty Series*, 2256, 119–404. The Stockholm Convention was adopted on 22 May 2001 and entered into force on 17 May 2004. China signed the Convention on 23 May 2001 and ratified it on 13 August 2004.

[201] Stockholm Convention, art. 3. [202] Stockholm Convention, art. 5.

[203] See UN Environment Programme, Stockholm Convention, n.d., 'The new POPs under the Stockholm Convention'. Online article. www.pops.int/TheConvention/ThePOPs/TheNewPOPs/tabid/2511/Default.aspx

POPs used as pesticides, including DDT. It set in motion plans to achieve the Convention targets of POP prevention and control in stages, and for implementation by different regions and sectors.[204] A complete ban on DDT was implemented in 2009 upon the expiry of the exemption period.[205] Dioxin, a POP released unintentionally from the incineration process, was a top priority for regulatory control by the MEP, which issued its Guiding Opinion on Strengthening Control of Pollution by Dioxin in 2010 to control the use of raw materials, techniques and processes, thereby reducing and recovering dioxin emissions.[206]

5.5.7 ODS

Ozone (O_3) is found in both the upper and lower atmosphere. Ozone in the troposphere is an air pollutant and a major contributor to smog, while ozone in the stratosphere, some 10 to 16 km above the earth's surface, forms an important layer of protection that filters out dangerous ultraviolet B radiation (UVB) from the sun and protects the environment and humans.[207] In 1974, two American atmospheric chemists, Sherwood Rowland and Mario Molina, published an article in the journal *Nature* that for the first time alerted the world to the threat of ozone depletion.[208] While they were ultimately recognized for their pioneering work on ozone depletion and their immeasurable contribution to humanity with the award of the 1995 Nobel Prize in Chemistry,[209] initial reactions to their scientific findings were less than encouraging. At the time, chlorofluorocarbons (CFCs) were seen as non-toxic, non-flammable, completely benign and ideal for a wide range of applications, including refrigerants, propellants in spray cans, solvents and blowing agents in foams.

While the US National Academy of Sciences concurred with the findings of Rowland and Molina in 1976,[210] it was not until 1985 that the image of the ozone hole over Antarctica captured public attention and support for action was mobilized.[211] The thinning of the ozone layer was caused by a range of ozone-depleting substances (ODS), including CFCs and halons. Since the 1980s, the international legal regime has targeted ODS in order to protect the ozone layer. The legal regime began with the Vienna Convention for the

[204] The National Implementation Plan for the Stockholm Convention on Persistent Organic Pollutants was approved by the State Council and submitted to the Convention Secretariat in 2007.

[205] MEP et al, 'Announcement on the ban of production, circulation, use, import and export of DDT, chlordane, mirex and HCB (2009)', (announcement) 16 April 2009. www.mee.gov.cn/gkml/hbb/bgg/200910/t20091022_174552.htm. The ban took effect on 17 May 2009.

[206] MEP et al., Guiding Opinion on Strengthening Control of Pollution by Dioxin (2010).

[207] UN Environment Programme, (2017), *A Success in the Making*, 1. Online report. https://unep.ch/ozone/Publications/MP_A_Success_in_the_making-E.pdf.

[208] Mario Molina and Sherwood Rowland, 'Stratospheric sink for chlorofluoromethanes: chlorine atom-catalysed destruction of ozone', *Nature*, 249 (1974), 810–12.

[209] By 1995, the year they were awarded the Nobel Prize in Chemistry, Professor Sherwood Rowland had retired from the University of California, Irvine and Professor Mario Molina was at the Massachusetts Institute of Technology.

[210] UN Environment Programme, *Achievements in Stratospheric Ozone Protection: Progress Report 1987–2007*. Online report. https://unep.ch/ozone/Publications/MP_Acheivements-E.pdf, at 21.

[211] In 1985, British Antarctic Survey scientists published results showing a steep decline in the levels of ozone over the Halley research station since the 1970s, particularly during the austral spring, and the existence of the ozone hole was revealed. Since then, the extent of the ozone hole has been monitored continuously using both ground- and satellite-based techniques. For more, see British Antarctic Survey, n.d., 'Ozone'. Online article. www.bas.ac.uk/about/antarctica/geography/ozone/

Protection of the Ozone Layer (Vienna Convention) (1985),[212] and was followed by the Montreal Protocol on Substances that Deplete the Ozone Layer (Montreal Protocol) (1987),[213] and subsequent amendments.

China, as a party to the Vienna Convention (1985), the Montreal Protocol (1987) and subsequent amendments, submitted its National Plan on Gradually Phasing Out Ozone-Depleting Substances in 1993, which was substantially amended in 1999. The State Council issued the Regulation on the Administration of Ozone-Depleting Substances (Regulation on ODS) (2010),[214] followed by the Inventory on Ozone-Depleting Substances (2010) to provide better control over the production, sale, consumption, import and export of ODS in China.[215] The state is required to provide support for the production and consumption of ODS substitutes in order to phase out ODS production and use.[216] It must adopt total control and quota management over the production, consumption, import and export of ODS, with detailed measures issued by the State Council.[217] Anyone who produces or consumes ODS must obtain a production or consumption quota permit, although there are limited exceptions for consumers.[218] Producers and consumers of ODS must apply to the MEE by 31 October each year for the annual quota permit to be used the year after.[219] The MEE is required to review the application and decide, by 20 December, whether to issue the permit, as well as the quota to be allocated, taking into account the total annual quota for production and consumption nationwide and an individual applicant's record of production or consumption.[220] Where there is a need to adjust the production or consumption quota, parties apply to the MEE for approval.[221] The production of ODS must comply strictly with the terms and conditions prescribed in the permit.[222] It is prohibited to produce ODS without permit.[223] Those holding consumption permits must strictly comply with the terms and conditions.[224] With the exception of uses exempt under article 10 from the permit requirement, using ODS without a permit is prohibited.[225] The Regulation on ODS also controls the sale of ODS. Parties selling ODS must report for the record to the MEE, which publishes a list of ODS sellers.[226] The sale or purchase of ODS is only permitted among the parties that can lawfully produce, sell and consume ODS under the Regulation on ODS.[227]

[212] Vienna Convention for the Protection of the Ozone Layer, Vienna, 22 March 1985, *International Legal Materials*, 26 (1987), 1516–40.

[213] Montreal Protocol on Substances that Deplete the Ozone Layer, Montreal, 16 September 1987, *International Legal Materials*, 26 (1987), 1541–61.

[214] The Regulation on ODS was issued by the State Council on 8 April 2010. It came into force on 1 June 2010 and was amended in 2018.

[215] The Inventory on Ozone-Depleting Substances was issued by the MEP, NDRC and the Ministry of Industry and Information Technology (MIIT) on 27 September 2010 with immediate effect.

[216] APPCL (2018), art. 85(1). [217] APPCL (2018), art. 85(2).

[218] Regulation on ODS (2018), art. 10. Exemptions are given to the following: (i) the use of ODS for maintenance of cooling devices, cooling systems or fire-extinguishing systems by maintenance entities; (ii) the use of small amounts of ODS by a lab for experimental analysis; (iii) the use of ODS by entry and exit inspection and quarantine authorities for quarantine of harmful organisms and (iv) other circumstances determined by the MEP.

[219] Regulation on ODS (2018), art. 12(1). [220] Regulation on ODS (2018), art. 12(2).

[221] Regulation on ODS (2018), art. 14. [222] Regulation on ODS (2018), art. 15(1).

[223] Regulation on ODS (2018), art. 15(2). [224] Regulation on ODS (2018), art. 16(1).

[225] Regulation on ODS (2018), art. 16(2). [226] Regulation on ODS (2018), art. 17.

[227] Regulation on ODS (2018), art. 18.

China started controlling the import and export of ODS in the late 1990s by issuing the Measures on the Management of Import and Export of Ozone-Depleting Substances (1999)[228] and Provisions to Enhance Control of the Import and Export of Ozone-Depleting Substances (2000),[229] both of which were replaced by the Administrative Measures on the Import and Export of Ozone-Depleting Substances (2014).[230] The control of ODS is based on a Catalogue on Controlled Ozone-Depleting Substances for Import and Export.[231] Anyone who imports or exports ODS included in the Catalogue must apply for a quota and obtain the import or export approval form.[232] The import and export approval form is valid for a maximum of ninety days.[233]

5.5.8 Other Activities Causing Air Pollution

In addition to regulating the major sources of air pollution discussed above, the APPCL (2018) also controls activities that emit an obnoxious odour, oil fumes, dust and organic air pollutants by targeting catering and cooking, open burning, fireworks, dry-cleaning and vehicle repair and maintenance.

Obnoxious odour is a persistent and lingering smell that is unpleasant and disturbing to human beings. Obnoxious odours are generated by different sources, such as: (i) agricultural sources (including from waste from animal farms or muck-spreading); (ii) industrial sources (including from solvents and other chemicals); (iii) municipal infrastructure (including from sewage and drainage systems)[234] and (iv) open burning of certain materials, including rubber, plastics, leather and garbage.[235] The APPCL (2018) requires entities that discharge offensive and obnoxious odour to choose operation sites scientifically, build reasonable protection zones and install devices or take measures to prevent emission.[236] In densely populated areas and other areas that need special protection, there is a prohibition on burning asphalt, rubber, plastics, leather, rubbish or any other materials that generate toxic or hazardous smoke and obnoxious odour.[237]

Cooking fumes from kitchens contain $PM_{2.5}$, VOCs and odour that is both a nuisance and a lung cancer risk. In Beijing, complaints against cooking fumes account for 20 per cent to 30 per cent of environmental complaints.[238] The APPCL (2018) requires caterers to install devices to remove oil fumes or take other measures to ensure compliance with emission standards and prevent any nuisance being caused to residents nearby.[239] It is prohibited to

[228] The Measures on the Management of Import and Export of Ozone-Depleting Substances were issued by the SEPA, Ministry of Foreign Trade and Economic Cooperation (MOFTEC) and State Customs Administration on 3 December 1999.

[229] The Provisions to Enhance Control of the Import and Export of Ozone-Depleting Substances were issued by the SEPA, MOFTEC and State Customs Administration on 13 April 2000.

[230] The Administrative Measures on the Import and Export of Ozone-Depleting Substances were issued by the MEP, Ministry of Commerce and State Customs Administration on 27 January 2014. It came into force on 1 March 2014 and was amended by the MEP on 22 August 2019.

[231] Regulation on ODS (2018), art. 22(1). By 2019, six batches of the Catalogue on Controlled Ozone-Depleting Substances for Import and Export had been issued by the MEP, Ministry of Commerce and State Customs Administration: first batch (2000), second batch (2001), third batch (2004), fourth batch (2006), fifth batch (2009) and sixth batch (2012).

[232] Regulation on ODS (2018), art. 22(2). [233] Regulation on ODS (2018), art. 23(2).

[234] Xin Chunying (ed.), *Interpreting APPCL*, at 186. [235] Xin Chunying (ed.), *Interpreting APPCL*, at 191.

[236] APPCL (2018), art. 80. [237] APPCL (2018), art. 82(1).

[238] Xin Chunying (ed.), *Interpreting APPCL*, at 188. [239] APPCL (2018), art. 81(1).

construct new catering projects or modify or expand existing catering projects in residential buildings, mixed commercial and residential buildings without separate chimneys, or on a floor adjacent to a residential section of mixed commercial and residential buildings.[240] No one may barbecue or provide sites for barbecue in an open area where barbecuing is banned by local government.[241] In Beijing, outdoor barbecuing is banned in streets, lanes, squares, residential premises, public green spaces and any other public places of urban areas and near suburbs.[242] Local governments in the far suburbs are required to designate areas where outdoor barbecuing is prohibited.[243]

Fireworks contribute to substantial increases of SO_2, NOx and $PM_{2.5}$ levels during the first fifteen days of Lunar New Year. According to the MEP, the $PM_{2.5}$ level soared from 75 μg/m^3 to 647 μg/m^3 in Beijing within four hours on the eve of Lunar New Year 2017.[244] On Lunar New Year 2016, the $PM_{2.5}$ level had reached 699 μg/m^3, also because of fireworks.[245] The constant bangs and pops of fireworks are believed to scare away evil spirits and bring good luck and prosperity. The APPCL (2018) aims to prevent low-quality high-polluting fireworks from entering the market by prohibiting any units or individuals from producing, selling or setting off fireworks or firecrackers that do not meet the relevant quality standards. In addition, setting off fireworks or firecrackers is banned in certain areas and during certain time periods.[246] In Beijing, restrictions have been imposed since 2005 on fireworks within the fifth ring road. Initially, fireworks were only allowed from 7 a.m. to midnight on the eve of Lunar New Year and from the 2nd to 15th of the first lunar month.[247] However, rising concern over air quality after years of severe pollution led to public support for a firework ban in the city. In a public survey conducted by the Beijing government in late 2017, 82.9 per cent of people said they would not set off fireworks in the future.[248] In December 2017, the Beijing legislature amended the local regulation on fireworks and imposed a ban within the fifth ring road, allowing fireworks only in specified suburban areas beyond this and at specific times.[249]

5.6 REGIONAL COOPERATION IN AIR POLLUTION CONTROL

The implementation and enforcement of environmental law has traditionally been based around administrative jurisdictions. That is, the central government sets targets and

[240] APPCL (2018), art. 81(2). [241] APPCL (2018), art. 81(3).

[242] The Beijing Provision on the Ban on Outdoor Barbecue was promulgated on 25 September 2000 and revised on 23 November 2007 and 12 February 2018. 'Urban areas' refers to the six districts in central Beijing: Dongcheng, Xicheng, Chaoyang, Haidian, Fengtai and Shijingshan. 'Near suburbs' refers to six districts: Tongzhou, Daxing, Fangshan, Mentougou, Changping and Shunying.

[243] Beijing Government, Clean Air Action Plan (2013–17). 'Far suburbs' of Beijing refers to four districts: Pinggu, Huairou, Miyun and Yanqing.

[244] Data released by the MEP at: http://www.mee.gov.cn/gkml/sthjbgw/qt/201701/t20170128_395322.htm.

[245] Data released by the MEP at: http://www.mee.gov.cn/gkml/sthjbgw/qt/201701/t20170126_395308_wh.htm.

[246] APPCL (2018), art. 82(2).

[247] Beijing Provisions on Fireworks Safety Management (2005). It was amended in 2017 to impose a complete ban on fireworks within the fifth ring road.

[248] 'Beijing bans fireworks within fifth ring road, good law in response to public opinion', *New Beijing News*, 2 December 2017.

[249] The Beijing Provisions on Fireworks Safety Management (2005) were amended on 1 December 2017.

allocates targets and tasks to provincial governments for implementation. Measures taken and effectiveness in implementation vary from province to province. Air pollution, however, does not stop at provincial boundaries. In the case of Beijing, the capital city has been blanketed in heavy smog each winter for years, but nearly a quarter of the air pollutants come from nearby cities and provinces, including Tianjin and Hebei.[250] Experience shows that effective air pollution control requires regional collaboration. Beijing was able to host the Summer Olympics in August 2008 and the APEC Summit in November 2014 under clear blue skies, due to the concerted efforts of its neighbouring provinces, including Tianjin, Hebei, Shandong, Shanxi and Inner Mongolia.[251] Drastic measures were taken to reduce emissions from all sources by suspending industrial operations, restricting vehicle use, tightening control of construction sites, banning crop-straw burning and ensuring frequent inspections and enforcement by local EPBs and the police. Regional cooperation in air pollution control was promoted by the MEP and the State Council in the Guiding Opinion on Air Pollution Cooperation to Improve Regional Air Quality (2010), the 12th FYP on Air Pollution Prevention and Control in Key Regions (2012) and the Air Action Plan (2013). Regional cooperation for air pollution control is now a legal mechanism to be implemented in key regions. Provincial governments in key regions must cooperate and coordinate, within the region, their efforts and resources in order to implement unified plans, standards, monitoring and enforcement to improve air quality in the region.[252]

5.6.1 Designation of Key Regions

The key regions for air pollution control are designated by the state environmental authority subject to approval by the State Council and taking into account the main function of the region, the regional air quality and the transmission and dispersion of the air pollutants.[253] In the 12th FYP on Air Pollution Prevention and Control in Key Regions (2012),[254] the State Council approved the designation of key regions for air pollution control: 117 cities in 19 provinces, with a total area of more than 132 km^2, covering the three regions of Beijing–Tianjin–Hebei, the Yangtze River Delta and the Pearl River Delta, and ten city clusters.[255] While the key regions account for 14 per cent of China's land mass, they support nearly 48 per cent of the population, account for 71 per cent of the national GDP, consume 52 per cent of the coal, account for 48 per cent of SO_2 emissions, 51 per cent of NOx emissions, 42 per cent of particulate matter emissions and 50 per cent of VOC

[250] In Tianjin and Hebei, there are many cement, steel and petrochemical plants and oil refineries that burn a total of 350 million t of coal per year. About 24.5 per cent of the $PM_{2.5}$ in Beijing comes from those plants. See 'Experts explore Beijing's air pollution', *China Daily*, 11 June 2012.

[251] Jim Yardley, 'China announces more pollution controls', *New York Times*, 1 August 2008; Mimi Lau, 'How leaders and an army of staff turned Beijing's grey into APEC blue', *South China Morning Post* , 18 November 2014.

[252] APPCL (2018), art. 86.

[253] APPCL (2018), art. 86(1).

[254] The 12th FYP on Air Pollution Control in Key Regions (2012) was issued by the MEP, NDRC and the Ministry of Finance (MOF) on 29 October 2012, following approval from the State Council on 27 September 2012.

[255] A list of cities in the key regions can be found in the Appendix to the 12th FYP on Air Pollution Control in Key Regions (2012). They include thirteen cities in the Beijing–Tianjin–Hebei region, twenty-five cities in the Yangtze River Delta, nine cities in the Pearl River Delta, and others in the ten city clusters in the provinces of Liaoning, Shandong, Hubei, Hunan, Sichuan, Fujian, Shanxi, Shaanxi and Gansu, as well as the city of Chongqing, Ningxia Autonomous Region and Xinjiang Autonomous Region.

emissions.[256] The key regions are required to implement tighter controls by setting more stringent standards, because they are more economically advanced and more pollution intensive compared to the national average. To strengthen further the control on particulate matters, the Air Action Plan (2013) also places great emphasis on the key regions of Beijing–Tianjin–Hebei, the Yangtze River Delta and the Pearl River Delta. It set special reduction targets for $PM_{2.5}$ concentration levels of 25 per cent, 20 per cent and 15 per cent respectively for the key regions to be achieved by end-2017, compared to a baseline year of 2012.[257]

5.6.2 Collaboration within the Key Regions

Provincial governments within a key region are required to meet regularly and take joint action to achieve the joint targets on pollution prevention and control, in accordance with unified regional planning, standards, monitoring and pollution-control measures. The state environmental authority is required to strengthen its guidance and supervision in order to promote regional collaboration.[258] In principle, joint meetings are convened once every year, but may be convened at any time as needed to address important issues.[259]

The state environmental authority and the relevant state departments should work with provincial governments to make action plans on pollution control for key regions, in accordance with regional socio-economic development and the carrying capacity of the atmosphere. By setting control targets, improving the regional economic structure, coordinating transport management, promoting clean energy and proposing key pollution-control tasks and measures, the regional action plans aim to improve regional air quality.[260] The MEP, NDRC and other departments issued the Detailed Implementation Plan of the Action Plan on Air Pollution Prevention and Control for Beijing–Tianjin–Hebei and Surrounding Areas (Detailed Implementation Plan) (2013) to specify tasks and targets to be accomplished in stages.[261] It applies to six provincial-level administrative regions: Beijing, Tianjin, Hebei, Shanxi, Shandong and Inner Mongolia. Targets for abatement of the concentration level of $PM_{2.5}$ by end-2017 as compared to the 2012 level were set and achieved: a 25 per cent cut in Beijing, Tianjin and Hebei, 20 per cent in Shanxi and Shandong and 10 per cent in Inner Mongolia. In addition, Beijing was required to achieve an annual average concentration of 60 $\mu g/m^3$ by 2017, which it achieved.[262] It was required to phase out small coal-burning boilers in stages, strictly control the number of vehicles registered, ensure a supply of high-quality gasoline and diesel (Stage V) by end-2015, restrict road use of yellow-label vehicles by end-2014 and phase out all yellow-label vehicles by end-2015, eliminate outdated industrial capacity and upgrade or close 1,200 heavily polluting enterprises by end-2017. A cap on coal consumption was imposed on Beijing, Tianjin, Hebei and Shandong, and Beijing was required to substantially lower the percentage of coal in its energy mix to below

[256] 12th FYP on Air Pollution Control in Key Regions (2012), 15–16.
[257] Air Action Plan (2013), preamble.
[258] APPCL (2018), art. 86(2).
[259] Yuan Jie (ed.), *Understanding APPCL*, at 236; Xin Chunying (ed.), *Interpreting APPCL*, at 203.
[260] APPCL (2018), art. 87.
[261] The Detailed Implementation Plan was issued by the MEP, NDRC, MIIT, Ministry of Finance, MOHURD and National Energy Administration on 17 September 2013.
[262] Detailed Implementation Plan (2013), part I on major targets; Air Action Plan (2013), preamble.

10 per cent by end-2017, with 90 per cent of energy consumed being cleaner energy, such as electricity and natural gas.[263] Beijing achieved the coal consumption reductions and the phasing out of heavily polluting vehicles. By end-2017, coal accounted for 5.7 per cent of total energy consumption, while 1.7 million old and polluting vehicles were phased out from 2013 to 2017.[264]

In key regions, which are more economically advanced than other regions, mobile sources tend to be a major contributor to air pollution. The APPCL (2018) not only requires provincial governments in the key regions to implement more stringent emission standards for vehicles, but also requires them to apply the same emission testing methods and emission limits against all vehicles in use.[265] They must provide high-quality fuel that allows a vehicle to meet emission standards.[266] Regional collaboration to tackle air pollution requires closer cooperation in environmental monitoring and information sharing among provinces. The state environmental authority should establish regional data-sharing mechanisms to facilitate access to information on air quality and emissions from sources, to analyse air pollution sources and changing trends and to make the information publicly accessible.[267]

Regional collaboration is also seen in the closer cooperation taking place in enforcement to tackle local protectionism. The state environmental authority works with provincial governments in the key regions to organize joint enforcement, cross-border enforcement and exchange enforcement within the key regions in order to control air pollution.[268] Joint enforcement refers to enforcement actions taken jointly by local environmental bureaus and other departments, such as local police, with their counterparts in other regions, or with supervisory bodies at higher levels. Cross-border enforcement allows local environmental bureaus to enforce law in another administrative jurisdiction within the same key region, as well as their own. Exchange enforcement refers to the practice whereby local environmental bureaus enforce law only in each other's jurisdiction within the key region. These mechanisms aim to tackle local protectionism and prevent undue influence and pressure being placed on environmental bureaus by local governments.[269] Joint enforcement has been successfully tested to tackle the problem of weak enforcement by local EPBs. In 2013, the MEP and MPS issued the Opinion on Strengthening Cooperation in Law Enforcement between Environmental Protection and Public Security Departments.[270] Joint enforcement actions have been carried out by local EPBs and PSBs against key polluting sources with a track record of intentional violations that cause or are likely to cause serious environmental harm.[271]

[263] Detailed Implementation Plan (2013), part II on key tasks.
[264] UNEP, *A Review of 20 Years' Air Pollution Control in Beijing* (United Nations Environment Programme, 2019), chapter 4.
[265] APPCL (2018), art. 88. [266] APPCL (2018), art. 88. [267] APPCL (2018), art. 91.
[268] APPCL (2018), art. 92. [269] Xin Chunying (ed.), *Interpreting APPCL*, at 215.
[270] The Opinion on Strengthening Cooperation in Law Enforcement between Environmental Protection and Public Security Departments was issued by the MEP and MPS on 4 November 2013 with immediate effect.
[271] For more discussion on joint enforcement, see Yuhong Zhao, 'Innovative measures to improve environmental law enforcement in China', *China–EU Law Journal*, 4 (2015), 155–72.

5.6.3 Tighter Control of Air Pollution in the Key Regions

Tighter control measures are imposed in the key regions to improve environmental protection and energy consumption[272] with the aim of promoting a low-carbon green industry to replace highly polluting and energy-intensive industrial operations. In key regions, provincial governments are required to implement more stringent vehicle emission standards than elsewhere[273] in order to cut pollution from mobile sources.

The 12th FYP on Air Pollution Prevention and Control in Key Regions (2012) sets targets for both total emission control and AAQ improvement. For total emission targets, the FYP targets for key regions are more ambitious than the national targets. For AAQ, there is no national target for a reduction in pollution concentration levels, but the FYP sets targets for key regions to reduce their annual average concentration levels of major air pollutants. The FYP further required the three key regions of Beijing–Tianjin–Hebei, the Yangtze River Delta and Pearl River Delta to reduce $PM_{2.5}$ concentration by 6 per cent by end-2015, a binding target for provincial governments in these regions.[274]

In order for key regions to achieve the abatement targets in Table 5.6 and Table 5.7, the FYP allocates individual abatement targets to governments of provinces and provincial-level cities depending on, among others, the economic activities and environmental carrying capacities of the province. Table 5.8 contains examples of select cities and provinces that were allocated the abatement targets:[275]

The Air Action Plan (2013) was issued to tackle air pollution by particulate matter, with a special focus on the three regions of Beijing–Tianjin–Hebei, the Yangtze River Delta and the Pearl River Delta. It sets a 10 per cent target for reducing the urban concentration of PM_{10} nationwide by end-2017 as compared to 2012, and cutting the concentration of $PM_{2.5}$ in Beijing–Tianjin–Hebei by 25 per cent, the Yangtze River Delta by 20 per cent and Pearl River Delta by 15 per cent. A specific target was set for Beijing: the annual average concentration of $PM_{2.5}$ must remain at or below 60 $\mu g/m^3$.[276]

TABLE 5.6 TOTAL EMISSIONS ABATEMENT TARGETS FOR 2015

	SO_2 (%)	NOx (%)	Industrial smoke and soot (%)
National target	−8	−10	No target set
Key-region target	−12	−13	−10

Sources: 12th FYP on Air Pollution Control in Key Regions (2012), part II, s. 3.

In order to cap total coal consumption, the APPCL (2018) requires key regions to abate coal consumption from existing sources by an amount equal to or more than the coal consumption projected for any new, modified or expanded coal-burning projects.[277] Such

[272] APPCL (2018), art. 88(1). [273] APPCL (2018), art. 88(2).
[274] 12th FYP on Air Pollution Control in Key Regions (2012), Part II, sec.3.
[275] 12th FYP on Air Pollution Control in Key Regions (2012), Part II, sec.3.
[276] Air Action Plan (2013), preamble. [277] APPCL (2018), art. 90.

TABLE 5.7 KEY-REGION 2015 ABATEMENT TARGETS FOR ANNUAL AVERAGE CONCENTRATION LEVELS

	SO_2 (%)	NO_2 (%)	PM_{10} (%)	$PM_{2.5}$ (%)
National target	No target set	No target set	No target set	No target set
Key-region targets	−10	−7	−10	−5 −6 (Beijing–Tianjin–Hebei, Yangtze River Delta and Pearl River Delta.

Sources: 12th FYP on Air Pollution Control in Key Regions (2012), part II, s. 3.

TABLE 5.8 CITY/PROVINCE 2015 ABATEMENT TARGETS FOR ANNUAL AVERAGE CONCENTRATION LEVELS

	SO_2 (%)	NO_2 (%)	PM_{10} (%)	$PM_{2.5}$ (%)
Beijing	−10	−7	−15	−15
Tianjin	−8	−9	−12	−6
Hebei	−11	−7	−12	−6
Shanghai	−11	−9	−10	−6
Jiangsu	−12	−10	−14	−7
Zhejiang	−11	−10	−10	−5
Guangdong	−12	−9	−8	−5

Sources: 12th FYP on Air Pollution Control in Key Regions (2012), Part II, sec.3.

abatement of coal consumption from existing sources will be achieved mainly by phasing out low-efficiency, high-energy-consuming, high-pollution industrial projects, by improving energy efficiency and conservation through technological innovations and upgrades and by switching from coal to gas or coal to electricity.

5.6.4 EIA Consultation on Plans and Projects

The EIA is also an important pollution-control mechanism in tackling regional air pollution problem. The APPCL (2018) emphasizes the requirement of consultation where a plan or project has regional impact beyond a provincial jurisdiction or autonomous region. In the case of plans for industrial parks, development zones or regional development of sectors that may cause serious air pollution to a key region, an EIA must be conducted. Those drafting the plan must consult relevant provincial governments and departments.[278] In the case of construction projects proposed in a key region and that may cause serious impact on

[278] APPCL (2018), art. 89(1).

the air quality of any neighbouring province, project proponents must notify the potentially affected provinces in a timely manner and consult with them.[279] Comments and feedback from the consultation, and their adoption or otherwise by the plan or project proponent, are a basis for the EIA review and examination conducted by environmental authorities during the EIA approval process.[280]

5.7 EMERGENCY RESPONSE TO HEAVY POLLUTION WEATHER

Emergency response to heavy pollution weather aims to alleviate the impact of heavy pollution on public health by giving an early warning of it and a timely response to it, in order to prevent continuing deterioration of the AAQ. The EPL (2014) requires governments to establish a pollution monitoring and warning mechanism, prepare emergency response plans and, where pollution is likely to affect public health and the safety of the environment, issue a timely warning and activate emergency response measures.[281] Under the APPCL (2018), the state must establish a heavy-pollution-weather monitoring and early warning system.[282] The state environmental authority works with the meteorological authority and provincial governments in key regions to establish a regional heavy-pollution-weather monitoring and early warning mechanism and implement a unified system of early warning threat levels. Where heavy pollution weather is likely to occur in a key region, the provincial governments of that region must be informed in a timely manner.[283] Provincial and municipal environmental bureaus work with meteorological departments to establish heavy-pollution-weather monitoring and early warning mechanisms within provinces and cities.[284] Heavy pollution weather is defined by reference to the AQI.

5.7.1 AQI

Under the Technical Regulation on Ambient Air Quality Index (for trial use) (2012),[285] the AQI uses a scale from zero to 500 to indicate AAQ and is derived from the concentration levels of major air pollutants, including SO_2, NO_2, PM_{10}, $PM_{2.5}$, CO and O_3.[286] An AQI reading above 200 indicates heavy pollution weather.[287] To inform the public in a straightforward manner on the health impacts corresponding to an AQI reading, the index is divided into six grades, each represented by a colour.

5.7.2 Emergency Response Plans

Local governments at county level and above are required to include heavy pollution weather in their emergency response management system.[288] Provincial, municipal and county governments in areas where heavy pollution weather is likely must prepare a heavy-pollution-weather emergency response plan, report it to environmental authorities at a

279 APPCL (2018), art. 89(2).
280 APPCL (2018), art. 89(3).
281 EPL (2014), art. 47.
282 APPCL (2018), art. 93(1).
283 APPCL (2018), art. 93(2).
284 APPCL (2018), art. 93(3).
285 The Technical Regulation on Ambient Air Quality Index (for trial use) (HJ633-2012) was issued by the MEP on 29 February 2012.
286 Technical Regulation on Ambient Air Quality Index (for trial use) (HJ633-2012), s. 4.1.
287 Technical Regulation on Ambient Air Quality Index (for trial use) (HJ633-2012), s. 4.3.
288 APPCL (2018), art. 94(1).

TABLE 5.9 AQI AND AAQ

AQI	Grade	AAQ	Colour	Health impact
0–50	I	Good	Green	No pollution impact
51–100	II	Fair	Yellow	Minor impact on sensitive population
101–150	III	Lightly polluted	Orange	Increasing impact on sensitive population, allergic reaction from healthy population
151–200	IV	Moderately polluted	Red	Intensifying impact on sensitive population, may have impact on cardiac and respiratory systems of healthy population
201–300	V	Heavily polluted	Purple	Obvious deterioration in cardiac and lung-disease patients, impacts on healthy population
>300	VI	Severely polluted	Maroon	Intensifying symptoms on healthy population and development of disease

Sources: Technical Regulation on Ambient Air Quality Index (for trial use) (HJ633-2012).

higher level and ensure it is publicly available.[289] The essential elements of an emergency response plan are details of: government bodies in charge of the emergency response and their duties; how heavy pollution weather is monitored and the early warning given; the emergency response; reflection and assessment of the emergency response; and guaranteed personnel and finances for the emergency response measures.[290] Governments are responsible for timely post-emergency assessment of the response and, based on the outcome of the assessment, for revising and improving the emergency response plans.[291] Assessment is an indispensable part of the process, allowing governments to reflect on the emergency response operation, identify gaps and make improvements.

5.7.3 Forecast and Early Warning

The APPCL (2018) requires provincial and municipal environmental bureaus to work with meteorological departments to forecast air quality. If heavy pollution weather is likely, they should report to the same-level governments in a timely manner. Based on the forecast for heavy pollution weather, the provincial and municipal governments decide on the grade of early warning and issue it in a timely manner. The grade of early warning is adjusted and updated as needed, as circumstances change.[292] The Emergency Response Law (2007) divides early warnings into grades I to IV, depending on the degree of emergency and the potential scale and gravity of the harm to be caused, with grades represented by colours (red, orange, yellow and blue).[293] Under the Beijing Heavy-Pollution-Weather Emergency

[289] APPCL (2018), art. 94(2).
[290] MEP, Guidance on Preparing Heavy-Pollution-Weather Emergency Response Plan (2013).
[291] APPCL (2018), art. 96(2). [292] APPCL (2018), art. 95(1).
[293] The Emergency Response Law (2007), art. 42.

TABLE 5.10 EARLY WARNINGS FOR HEAVY POLLUTION WEATHER IN BEIJING

Grade	Colour	Conditions
I	Red	• AQI > 200 for four days or more and AQI > 300 for two days or more; • AQI > 500 for one day or more
II	Orange	AQI > 200 for three days and AQI >300 at any time
III	Yellow	AQI > 200 for two days or more, but does not reach 300
IV	Blue	AQI > 200 for one day and does not reach 300

Sources: Beijing Municipal Heavy-Pollution-Weather Emergency Response Plan (2016).

Response Plan (2016),[294] early warnings escalate from blue (Grade IV), yellow (Grade III), orange (Grade II) to red (Grade I), depending on the impact and duration of the air pollution projected.[295]

Once the early warning has been issued, relevant governments and departments should inform the public and advise them of health protection measures, transport issues and other social and economic activities through television, radio, internet and text messages.[296]

5.7.4 Emergency Response

Following an early warning of heavy pollution weather, a local government at county level or above should activate its emergency response plan and take measures as needed based on the grade of the warning. It may: order enterprises to suspend or restrict production, restrict the use of vehicles on the road, ban fireworks and firecrackers, suspend earthwork at construction sites and demolition work, ban outdoor barbecues, suspend outdoor activities at kindergartens and schools and organize the operation of artificial interference with the weather system.[297] In the case of Beijing, a range of advisory and compulsory measures are provided in the Heavy-Pollution-Weather Emergency Response Plan (2016) to alleviate the heavy pollution.[298] For example, a red warning triggers compulsory measures, including the suspension of construction work, removal of vehicles from the road, suspension or restriction of operations at designated enterprises, a ban on fireworks and barbecues and reduction of local power generation.[299]

5.8 ENFORCEMENT: MONITORING, INSPECTION AND SANCTION

The command-and-control regulatory approach to air pollution relies on effective enforcement to ensure compliance with emission standards and achievement of air quality

[294] The Beijing Municipal Heavy-Pollution-Weather Emergency Response Plan (2016) was issued on 12 November 2016. It came into force on 15 December 2016.
[295] Beijing Municipal Heavy-Pollution-Weather Emergency Response Plan (2016), part I.
[296] APPCL (2018), art. 95(2). [297] APPCL (2018), art. 96(1).
[298] Beijing Municipal Heavy-Pollution-Weather Emergency Response Plan (2016), part II.
[299] Beijing Municipal Heavy-Pollution-Weather Emergency Response Plan (2016), part II, s. 4.

objectives. Routine and regular monitoring (via the monitoring network and on-site inspections) of AAQ and emissions from specific sources generates data that can be used by regulators and the public to supervise potential polluters. Inspection is an indispensable way for regulators to gain access to an operator's premises in order to inspect, observe, collect evidence and record the operations, with a focus on the pollution-control facilities. Where an ongoing violation may cause serious pollution, administrative compulsory measures may be imposed requiring the seizure or seal-up of an operation's tools, instruments, equipment and facilities. Local environmental bureaus have the power to impose sanctions to punish violation and deter non-compliance.

5.8.1 Monitoring

Accurate and reliable data is the basis of environmental enforcement and requires both sophisticated monitoring networks and scientific methods to be used during the collection and processing of data on air quality and pollution emission. However, monitoring has been a weak link in air pollution control in China. Prior to the issuance of the Ambient Air Quality Standards (2012), monitoring of air quality had covered three pollutants only: SO_2, NO_2 and PM_{10}. When data showed declining PM_{10} concentration levels from 1998 to 2010, official 2011 reports for Beijing announced an improvement in air quality and 274 'blue-sky days'. However, the monitoring data failed to reflect air pollution by $PM_{2.5}$, which are very fine particulates that float in the air longer than PM_{10}, penetrate deeper into the lungs than PM_{10} and are also more toxic. Worse still, protective measures, such as the wearing of face masks, are of little help due to the size of $PM_{2.5}$. To improve the quality of data monitoring, the APPCL (2018) requires the state environmental authority to issue technical guidelines on monitoring and assessment of AAQ and emission of air pollutants, organize the construction and management of monitoring networks nationwide to cover both AAQ and emissions from polluting sources, and publicize data on national AAQ.[300] Local environmental bureaus are in charge of the construction and management of monitoring networks for both AAQ and emissions from polluting sources, and also engage in monitoring work and publicize data on local AAQ.[301]

In addition to monitoring by the state, the APPCL (2018) imposes a duty of monitoring on polluters. Entities that emit industrial air pollutants or toxic and hazardous air pollutants must monitor their emissions and keep a record of the monitoring data. Further, entities designated as a 'key polluting unit' (KPU) are required to install and operate automatic monitoring devices connected to the supervisory monitoring system of local environmental bureaus, so that real-time monitoring data on emissions is transmitted to the agencies. The KPUs are responsible for the normal operation of monitoring devices and are required to disclose emissions data to the public.[302] The KPUs are held accountable for the accuracy of emissions data produced by the automatic monitoring devices, and environmental bureaus must engage in timely investigation upon finding abnormal transmission of emissions data.[303] Local environmental bureaus have the power to inspect the automatic monitoring

300 APPCL (2018), art. 23(1). 301 APPCL (2018), art. 23(2). 302 APPCL (2018), art. 24(1).
303 APPCL (2018), art. 25.

devices, collect evidence and conduct tests, among others.[304] It is the responsibility of municipal environmental bureaus to designate KPUs in accordance with the MEP's Provisions on the List of Key Polluting Units (for trial use) (MEP Provisions) (2017), taking into account the local environmental carrying capacity for air pollution, total emissions control targets, and types, quantity and concentration levels of the air pollutants emitted by the polluting sources. A list of KPUs must be disclosed to the public.[305] The MEP Provisions (2017)[306] set clear criteria for the designation of KPUs for different categories of water, air, soil and noise pollution, among others. In the case of air pollution, the list of KPUs should include the following:

(i) entities emitting SO_2, NOx, smoke, soot and VOCs above the limits set by the municipal environmental bureau;
(ii) large- and medium-sized enterprises in the following sectors: thermal power generation, heat and power generation, cement, iron and steel, non-ferrous metal refining, oil refining, coking, ceramics, glass, chemicals, pharmaceuticals, coal chemicals, paint and printing, among others;
(iii) units subject to permit control of their pollution discharge;
(iv) entities emitting toxic and hazardous air pollutants, and operators of solid waste incinerators;
(v) entities obliged to take pollution-control measures to achieve local government targets for air pollution and
(vi) enterprises on a warning list, enterprises on a pollution blacklist, or entities that have caused relatively grave environmental pollution emergencies in the past three years or have been reprimanded by EPBs, but have not completed pollution treatment and rectification work.[307]

The KPUs are subject to closer environmental scrutiny by both regulators and the public. They must invest in the installation, operation and maintenance of automatic monitoring devices and ensure the real-time transmission of emissions data to the supervisory monitoring network of local environmental bureaus.

5.8.2 On-Site Inspection

Local environmental bureaus, or an environmental inspection team to which a bureau has delegated its power of inspection, and any other bodies that perform environmental enforcement are expressly granted the power to conduct on-site inspections at polluting sources. The entities being inspected are required to cooperate by reporting truthfully and providing necessary documents.[308] More specific powers that may be exercised when conducting an on-site inspection include:

(i) entry of premises to observe and collect samples, monitoring, taking photos and videoing, recording conversations and producing a written record of the inspection;

[304] Measures on On-Site Inspection of Automatic Monitoring Devices of Polluting Sources (2012).
[305] APPCL (2018), art. 24(2). [306] The MEP Provisions were issued by the MEP on 25 November 2017.
[307] MEP Provisions (2017), art. 6. [308] APPCL (2018), art. 29.

(ii) inspecting and photocopying relevant documents;
(iii) meeting and questioning relevant staff to request explanation or relevant documents;
(iv) ordering violations to stop or be rectified;
(v) imposing administrative sanction in a summary procedure and
(vi) take other measures as provided by law.[309]

An on-site inspection must be conducted by a minimum of two persons, who must produce identity documentation showing their right to conduct the environmental inspection and explain their law enforcement activities.[310] The on-site inspection looks at emission of pollutants, operation of pollution-control facilities and devices and compliance with permit conditions, among others.[311] Where needed, on-site inspection also covers the operation of monitoring devices installed and maintained by the polluters.[312]

In practice, however, obstruction of inspection is common and inspection teams often fail to gain entry to premises for timely inspection and detection of violations. A case involving the Suzhou Industrial Park EPB is only the tip of the iceberg. In *Montaplast Automotive System (Suzhou Industrial Park) Co. Ltd* v. *Suzhou Industrial Park Environmental Protection Bureau* (2014),[313] Suzhou Industrial Park EPB was denied entry for an on-site inspection and consequently imposed an administrative penalty on Morsbach Automotive System (Morsbach). Morsbach sued the agency, demanding it revoke its penalty decision.

Montaplast Automotive System (Suzhou Industrial Park) Co. Ltd v. *Suzhou Industrial Park Environmental Protection Bureau* (2014)

On receiving a public complaint of an obnoxious odour generated by enterprises near a residential area, the Suzhou Industrial Park EPB began on-site inspections of fifty-eight enterprises, including Morsbach, on 30 September 2013. The environmental inspection officers arrived at Morsbach's operations, but were denied entry by a company security guard, because they had not made an appointment. The officers called 110 for police assistance. At the request of the police and the inspection team, the security guard called the person in charge of environmental protection at the company, but continued to refuse entry to the inspectors. In the end, no inspection was conducted on 30 September. The Suzhou Industrial Park EPB decided that Morsbach had violated the APPCL (2000) by denying entry for on-site inspection and imposed an administrative penalty, a fine of 40,000 yuan. Morsbach sued the Suzhou Industrial Park EPB, demanding revocation of the administrative penalty.

Gusu District Court (2014) held that on-site inspection by an EPB is both a power granted by law and a statutory duty of environmental enforcement imposed by law. Morsbach should not obstruct environmental enforcement by denial of entry. In accordance with the APPCL (2000), any party that

309 Measures on Environmental Supervision (2012), art. 13(1).
310 Measures on Environmental Supervision (2012), art. 13(2).
311 Measures on Environmental Supervision (2012), art. 6.
312 APPCL (2018), art. 25. Where the monitoring data transmitted to the EPB by the KPS appears to be abnormal, the EPB must investigate in a timely manner. Such investigation includes on-site inspection of the monitoring devices installed by the KPS.
313 SPC 10 Important Environmental Administrative Cases (2014), case no. 8.

denies on-site inspection will be ordered by the EPB to stop its unlawful acts (in this case, the denial of entry), rectify by a specified deadline (in this case, grant entry to the inspectors) and will be given a warning or fined up to 50,000 yuan. Morsbach had refused the on-site inspection and did not take any remedial measures to rectify this. The fine had been imposed properly and within the range stipulated by law. The plaintiff's claim was dismissed.

In this case, the court upheld the EPB's decision and confirmed that the administrative sanction was proper and lawful. The case was decided in 2014, before the APPCL was revised in 2015. Under the APPCL (2000), the fine for obstruction of environmental enforcement was capped at 50,000 yuan.[314] To deter such violation by potential polluters and facilitate timely on-site inspection, the APPCL (2015) substantially increased the fine to between 20,000 yuan and 200,000 yuan.[315]

5.8.3 Administrative Compulsory Measures

Administrative compulsory measures may be taken by agencies in order to stop a violation, preserve evidence and prevent or mitigate harm. The measures include temporary restriction of a citizen's freedom or temporary control of the property of the citizen, legal person or any other organization.[316] The EPL (2014) grants the power of seal-up and seizure to environmental enforcement bodies.[317] The APPCL (2018) specifies the circumstances in which compulsory administrative measures, including seal-up and seizure, may be taken and the bodies with the power to impose them. First, only environmental bureaus at county level and above and other agencies with relevant duties to regulate and supervise air pollution have the power to impose administrative compulsory measures, including seal-up and seizure of a facility, equipment or products.[318] Such power may not be delegated by the responsible agencies to other bodies.[319] Second, the subjects of seal-up and seizure can include pollution-causing production facilities, equipment or products relating to the violations. Property irrelevant to the violations in question, such as personal belongings or other production facilities not related to the violation, may not be sealed up or seized.[320] Third, the compulsory measures may be used only when an entity's emission in violation of law has caused or is likely to cause serious air pollution, or relevant evidence may be destroyed or concealed by the polluter.[321] Last, administrative compulsory measures may only be used as temporary measures and are subject to specified time limits. Seal-up or seizure can be used for a maximum of thirty days. An extension of thirty days is possible in complicated cases, subject to approval by the head of the administrative agency.[322]

5.8.4 Administrative Sanctions

Administrative sanctions are widely used to punish environmental violations, and include warnings, fines, orders to suspend production to address pollution, orders to suspend or

[314] APPCL (2000), art. 46(2). [315] APPCL (2015), art. 98.
[316] Administrative Compulsion Law (2011), art. 2. [317] EPL (2014), art. 25. [318] APPCL (2018), art. 30.
[319] Administrative Compulsion Law (2011), art. 17. [320] Administrative Compulsion Law (2011), art. 23.
[321] APPCL (2018), art. 30. [322] Administrative Compulsion Law, art. 25.

permanently close a business, suspension or revocation of permits, confiscation of illegal gains or unlawful property[323] and administrative detention.[324] Environmental bureaus may impose most of those sanctions, except administrative detention, which may only be imposed by PSBs.[325]

Fines are a commonly used administrative sanction to punish environmental violation. If the fine is set at the right level, it can deter violation because it will be cheaper for a potential polluter to comply with the law. There are four types of fines calculated in different ways. For the first, an agency can exercise its discretion on the level of the fine within a specified range, depending on the circumstances of the violation. For example, anyone obstructing or delaying entry for on-site inspection or producing falsified data or records during inspection will be fined between 20,000 yuan and 200,000 yuan.[326] Emission of a pollutant without a permit, emission in violation of emission standards, emission in excess of the total control quota or emission by evading regulatory supervision are subject to fines of 100,000 yuan to 1 million yuan.[327] The second type of fine is directly linked to the value of goods being produced, imported, sold or consumed, where this is prohibited by law. There is no cap on the level of the fine, which is determined by the value of the goods. For example, the sale of coal and petroleum coke that does not meet relevant quality standards, the production or sale of raw materials or products containing VOCs and not meeting relevant standards or requirements and the production or sale of fuels not meeting relevant standards are subject to fines in the amount of one to three times the value of the goods, and raw materials, products and illegal gains will be confiscated.[328] The third type of fine is also uncapped, and is calculated by reference to the actual harm caused by a violation. For example, if a violation causes an average (Grade IV) or relatively serious (Grade III) air pollution emergency, the parties liable will be fined one to three times the direct economic loss; where grave (Grade II) or extremely grave (Grade I) emergencies are caused, the parties liable will be fined three to five times the direct economic loss.[329] The fourth type of fine was introduced by the EPL (2014) to tackle the problem of continuing violations. It is imposed on parties in violation who refuse to rectify with measures to control pollution. The APPCL (2018) provides that parties in violation of the law in six circumstances that have been fined and ordered to rectify, but refuse to take pollution-control measures, are subject to fines calculated on a daily basis. The six circumstances are: (i) emission without permit, (ii) emission in violation of emission standards, (iii) emission in violation of the total control quota, (iv) emission by evading regulatory supervision, (v) failure to take dust-control measures at a construction site, (vi) failure to take dust-control measures at a storage site.[330]

[323] The term 'unlawful property' refers to unlawfully gained property, property used for unlawful acts, and items that are expressly prohibited by Chinese laws and regulations. See NPC, 18 April 2002, 'What is unlawful property?'. Online article. www.npc.gov.cn/npc/c2385/200204/bc7a4d5a84ec410583fd3d921f98a98e.shtml

[324] MEP, Provisions on Environmental Administrative Sanction (2010), art. 10.

[325] MEP, Provisions on Environmental Administrative Sanction (2010), art. 16.

[326] APPCL (2018), art. 98.

[327] APPCL (2018), art. 99.

[328] APPCL (2018), art. 103.

[329] APPCL (2018), art. 122. See also the Measures on Environmental Emergency Response (2015) and National Plan on Environmental Emergency Response (2014).

[330] APPCL (2018), art. 123.

In addition to fines, confiscation of illegal gains is another administrative sanction that aims to eliminate any profits made from violations. For example, the production, import and sale of vehicles that do not meet the emission standards are subject to sanctions of confiscation of illegal gains, confiscation of vehicles in violation, and fines.[331] Further, environmental bureaus have the power to order production to be restricted or suspended to allow pollution treatment to take place, where parties are found in violation of law in four circumstances: (i) emission of a pollutant without a permit, (ii) emission of a pollutant in violation of emission standards, (iii) emission of a key air pollutant in violation of the total control quota and (iv) emission of a pollutant by evading regulatory supervision. In serious circumstances, administrative sanctions in the form of suspension or permanent closure of the operation or business may be imposed, upon approval by the local government.[332]

5.8.5 Case Transfer for Criminal Sanction

While administrative sanctions serve as a major form of punishment for environmental violation under the APPCL (2018), they do not substitute criminal sanctions. If any violation constitutes a crime, the liable parties will be investigated and prosecuted for criminal liabilities according to law.[333] Environmental offences are sanctioned under the Criminal Law.

[331] APPCL (2018), arts. 109 and 110. [332] APPCL (2018), art. 99. [333] APPCL (2018), art. 127.

6

Regulation and Control of Water Pollution

China's water resources are among the worst polluted and most severely degraded in the world.[1] More than 200 million people do not have access to safe drinking water in China,[2] and thousands of incidents of social unrest related to water pollution take place every year.[3] Serious contamination of both surface water and groundwater is revealed by official data.

Surface water is divided into five grades from I to V (excellent, good, moderate, poor, very poor) determined by levels of pollutants.[4] Official statistics show that more than 67 per cent of the surface water in China is of grades I to III, but approximately one-third is of Grade IV or worse, which is not safe for skin contact and is only suitable for industrial use. Nearly 10 per cent of China's surface water does not meet Grade V criteria.[5] This is referred to as 'sub-Grade V water' and is not safe for any use. Among China's ten major river basins, only those in Southwest and Northwest China were found to have water quality rated primarily grades I to III. Major stretches of the Yellow, Liao and Huai rivers are rated as grades IV and V, while the Hai River is mostly Grade V. This water quality data taken from China's major rivers may understate the severity of surface water pollution, as small tributaries feeding the main river systems tend to be more contaminated due to their reduced dilution capacity and the poorer regulatory control of industrial wastewater discharged to tributaries in rural areas.[6]

Groundwater accounts for one-third of total water use across the domestic, agricultural and industrial sectors in China, and approximately two-thirds of cities use groundwater as a major water supply. Contamination of groundwater is alarming. Groundwater is divided into five grades from I to V (very good, good, average, poor and very poor).[7] In 2018, of the

[1] For more on water pollution in China, see Ma Jun, *China's Water Crisis*; Elizabeth Economy, *The River Runs Black: The Environmental Challenge to China's Future* (Ithaca, NY: Cornell University Press, 2004).

[2] Dongmei Han et al, 'Deep challenges for China's war on water pollution', *Environmental Pollution*, 218 (2016), 1222–33; Tao Tao and Kunlun Xin, 'A sustainable plan for China's drinking water', *Nature*, 511 (2014), 527–8.

[3] Natasha Gilbert, 'Green protests on the rise in China', *Nature*, 488 (2012), 261–2.

[4] Environmental Quality Standards for Surface Water (GB3838-2002). The Standards was first issued in 1983 and was revised in 1988 and 1999.

[5] MEP, *2016 China Environment Gazette*, 5.

[6] Dongmei Han et al., 'Deep challenges for China's war', at 1223.

[7] Standard for Groundwater Quality (GB/T 14848-2017), s. 4.1.

10,168 monitoring wells, 70.7% were Grade IV (poor) and 15.5% were Grade V (very poor).[8] In 2019, of the 10,168 monitoring wells, 66.9% were Grade IV (poor) and 18.8% were Grade V (very poor).[9] The main pollutants exceeding the safe levels were three types of nitrogen, as well as phenol, heavy metals and chemical oxygen demand (COD).[10] Researchers found that groundwater contamination had increased in an alarming manner between 2000 and 2014.[11] On the North China Plain, the most seriously affected and densely populated area in China, only 22.1 per cent of shallow groundwater and 26.4 per cent of deep groundwater is safe for drinking (grades I to III).[12] Widespread contamination, at depths greater than 100 m, of deep semi-confined and confined aquifers is much more concerning than contamination of surface water or shallow groundwater because remediation is costly, technically challenging and likely to be of limited effectiveness.

Water pollution not only causes acute waterborne diseases, including hepatitis, cholera and diarrhoea, but also exposes people to carcinogens, putting them at risk of illness, in particular liver, gastric and oesophageal cancers. This has led to the emergence of 'cancer villages',[13] where the incidence of cancer morbidity or mortality is significantly higher than the national average.[14] China's first cancer village was documented in 1954, but by the end of 2011 the number had risen to 351, which included 186 that emerged between 2000 and 2009, years that are now known as China's decade of cancer.[15] North China, characterized by intensive agriculture and heavy industry, is also where cancer villages are most densely distributed.[16] It was not until 2013, however, that Chinese authorities admitted the existence of cancer villages.[17] Studies have found that cancer villages tend to cluster along the major rivers and their tributaries, especially in rural areas. High concentrations of cancer villages can be found in the Hai River Basin, the mid-low Yellow River Basin, the Huai River Basin, the mid-low Yangtze River Basin and the Pearl River Delta. These regions have easy access to water resources, labour and transportation, all at low cost, and had become prime locations for the quick growth of a wide range of heavily polluting industries. In addition, state support in the 1980s for village

[8] MEE, *2018 China Ecology and Environment Gazette*, at 33–4.

[9] MEE, *2019 China Ecology and Environment Gazette*, at 32.

[10] COD is a measurement of the oxygen required to oxidize soluble and particulate organic matter in water. A higher COD number means a greater amount of organic pollutants in effluent discharge, causing a reduction of dissolved oxygen in rivers and lakes, and threatening the health and safety of aquatic animals and plants. China imposes maximum COD limits for wastewater discharge through the Integrated Wastewater Discharge Standard (GB 8978-1996) and the Discharge Standard of Pollutants for Municipal Wastewater Treatment Plant (GB 18918-2002). For ease of communication with the public and the regulated, however, COD is often referred to as a water pollutant in environmental law and policy. For example, COD is one of four key pollutants subject to total discharge abatement targets under China's FYPs and is a key pollutant covered by the discharge permit control mechanism and one of the water pollutants for the calculation of environmental tax.

[11] Dongmei Han et al., 'Deep challenges for China's war', at 1225. Groundwater rated grades IV and V rose from 37 per cent in 2000 to 55.1 per cent in 2011 and 61.5 per cent in 2014.

[12] Dongmei Han et al., 'Deep challenges for China's war', at 1225.

[13] Gong Shengsheng and Zhang Tao, 'Temporal–spatial distribution changes of cancer villages in China', *China Population Resources and Environment*, 23 (2013), 156–64; Gonghuan Yang and Dafang Zhuang (eds.) *Atlas of the Huai River Basin Water Environment: Digestive Cancer Mortality* (Dordrecht: Springer Netherlands, 2014).

[14] Lee Liu, 'Made in China'.

[15] Gong Shengsheng and Zhang Tao, 'Temporal-spatial distribution'.

[16] Dongmei Han et al., 'Deep challenges for China's war', at 1229.

[17] 'China's environmental ministry acknowledges', *Science*.

and township enterprises that were small in scale and poorly equipped and managed seriously aggravated water pollution in rural areas.[18]

This chapter critically examines China's regulatory control of water pollution. Section 6.1 briefly introduces the Water Pollution Prevention and Control Law (WPPCL) and the Action Plan on Prevention and Control of Water Pollution (Water Action Plan) (2015). Section 6.2 focuses on government responsibilities and the agencies in charge. Section 6.3 discusses the crucially important planning and standard setting as the foundation of the command-and-control approach to water pollution. Section 6.4 examines key mechanisms to prevent and control pollution. Section 6.5 discusses how major sources of water pollution are addressed with different types of regulatory control instruments. Section 6.6 highlights the importance of drinking water safety to protect public health. Section 6.7 deals with emergency responses to water pollution incidents in order to control and mitigate environmental harm. Section 6.8 examines enforcement and sanctions that aim to ensure compliance and deter violations. Section 6.9 briefly discusses civil liabilities for water pollution under the WPPCL (2017), with further investigation and case studies in Chapter 9.

6.1 THE WPPCL: FROM 1984 TO 2017

Specialised legislation on water pollution control started with the WPPCL (1984) in the first wave of lawmaking after the end of the Cultural Revolution (1966–76).[19] It preceded environmental legislation on air pollution and waste management due to the profound importance of water quality and its impact on human health. The WPPCL was substantially revised to address water pollution that, since the 1980s, had been seriously aggravated by industrialization at an unprecedented scale and speed.[20] The WPPCL (2008) made significant improvements to regulatory control and legal liabilities, establishing mechanisms to protect drinking water safety and promote ecological compensation.[21] In 2015, amending the WPPCL (2008) was placed on the agenda of the five-year lawmaking plan of the 12th NPCSC.[22]

[18] Yonglong Lu et al., 'Impacts of soil and water pollution on food safety and health risks in China', *Environment International*, 77 (2015), 5–15, at 10.

[19] The WPPCL was enacted on 11 May 1984 by the 6th National People's Congress Standing Committee (NPCSC) at its 5th session.

[20] The WPPCL (1984) was amended on 15 May 1996 by the 8th NPCSC at its 19th session. It was revised on 28 February 2008 by the 10th NPCSC at its 32nd session, and further amended on 27 June 2017 by the 12th NPCSC at its 28th session. This latter amendment came into force on 1 January 2018. For more on the regulation of water pollution in the early years, see W. Scott Railton, 'The rhetoric and reality of water quality protection in China', *Pacific Rim Law & Policy Journal*, 7 (1998), 859–88; Zunxuan 'Digger' Chen, 'Tackling China's water pollution problem: a legal and institutional perspective from Taihu Lake water pollution control', *Temple Journal of Science Technology and Environmental Law*, 24 (2005), 325–50; Zachary Tyler, 'Transboundary water pollution in China: an analysis of the failure of the legal framework to protect downstream jurisdictions', *Columbia Journal of Asian Law*, 19 (2006), 572–613.

[21] For more, see Dawn Winalski, 'Cleaner water in China? The implications of the amendments to China's Law on the Prevention and Control of Water Pollution', *Journal of Environmental Law and Litigation*, 24 (2009), 181–201; Hong Lan et al., 'Water pollution and regulatory cooperation in China', *Cornell International Law Journal*, 44 (2011), 349–83.

[22] The 12th NPCSC Lawmaking Plan was issued on 30 October 2013 and amended in 2015. The WPPCL was on the 2013 and 2015 lists.

Meanwhile, the State Council issued the Water Action Plan (2015)[23] to tackle serious water contamination and continuing deterioration of the water quality of rivers, lakes and groundwater. It set national targets for 2020 and 2030 on the improvement of water quality. By end-2020, 70 per cent of surface water in the seven major river basins must have achieved water quality of grades I to III, a maximum of 15 per cent of groundwater monitoring wells are permitted to have water quality of Grade V, and 93 per cent of drinking water sources must have water quality of Grade III or better. By end-2030, 75 per cent of surface water in the seven major river basins must have achieved water quality of grades I to III, and 95 per cent of drinking water sources must have water quality of Grade III or better.[24] To achieve the targets, the Water Action Plan (2015) mandates ten key tasks to be implemented by governments of all levels, from central to local:

(i) comprehensive control of pollutant discharge,
(ii) promotion of economic restructuring and upgrading,
(iii) enhanced conservation and protection of water resources,
(iv) strengthened support for science and technology,
(v) full use of market mechanisms,
(vi) tightened environmental enforcement and supervision,
(vii) strengthened water environmental management,
(viii) full guarantee of water ecosystem safety,
(ix) clarification and implementation of the responsibilities of relevant parties,
(x) improvement of public participation and supervision.

Many policy instruments in the Water Action Plan (2015) were adopted by the 2017 amendment to the WPPCL.[25] The WPPCL (2017) aims to protect and improve the environment, prevent and control water pollution, ensure drinking water safety, protect public health and promote sustainable socio-economic development.[26] The WPPCL (2017) applies to both surface water (rivers, lakes, canals, irrigation channels and reservoirs) and groundwater,[27] but not marine water, which is protected by the Marine Environmental Protection Law (MEPL).[28] Water pollution control in China adheres to the preventative principle, combining prevention and control with restoration, and using a comprehensive range of legal, economic, technological and administrative tools. To prevent, control and mitigate water pollution and ecological destruction, the WPPCL (2017) gives top priority to the protection of sources of drinking water, strictly controls industrial pollution, municipal wastewater and agricultural non-point sources, and promotes construction of ecological projects, such as those designed to protect and restore wetland.[29]

[23] The Water Action Plan (2015) was issued by the State Council on 2 April 2015 with immediate effect.
[24] Water Action Plan (2015), preamble.
[25] The draft amendment was submitted to the NPCSC for its first reading on December 2016. The amendment was adopted on 27 June 2017 by the 12th NPCSC at its 28th session.
[26] WPPCL (2017), art. 1. [27] WPPCL (2017), art. 2(1).
[28] WPPCL (2017), art. 2(2). The MEPL was enacted on 23 August 1982 by the 5th NPCSC at its 24th session. It was substantially revised on 25 December 1999 by the 9th NPCSC at its 13th session and was amended on 28 December 2013 by the 12th NPCSC at its 6th session. It was revised again in 2016 and 2017.
[29] WPPCL (2017), art. 3.

6.2 GOVERNMENT RESPONSIBILITY AND AGENCIES IN CHARGE

The WPPCL (2017) takes the conventional command-and-control regulatory approach, whereby the central government makes plans to be implemented by local governments, and sets standards the local agencies must enforce. Governments and agencies at all levels play a crucial role in regulating and supervising corporate behaviour to ensure compliance and punish violations. Local governments at county level and above are required to integrate protection of the water environment into their socio-economic development plans.[30] The WPPCL (2017) makes it clear that local governments are accountable for the local water quality and must take measures to prevent and control water pollution.[31] The Water Action Plan (2015) requires local governments to issue local action plans on water pollution control, setting key tasks and annual targets for each river basin, administrative district and industrial sector. Local governments must increase the amount budgeted for pollution-control initiatives in both urban and rural regions, and improve regulation and enforcement to ensure tasks are fully implemented and targets achieved.[32]

6.2.1 Target Responsibility and Performance Appraisal

To hold local governments accountable for water quality, the WPPCL (2017) provides for a target responsibility mechanism and takes into account the achievement of targets when appraising the performance of local governments and the persons in charge.[33] The State Council and all provincial governments enter into target responsibility agreements, which set specific pollution abatement targets and key tasks. The State Council conducts an annual assessment on the implementation of local action plans. The assessment results are disclosed to the public and are used as a basis for performance appraisal.[34] Where a provincial government is found in the annual assessment to have failed to achieve targets or implement tasks, the persons in charge attend supervision talks with the state environmental authority, which makes recommendations on tackling the failures and supervises progress. Further, environmental impact assessment (EIA) approval is suspended for the relevant regions and enterprises,[35] a form of economic punishment as no new development project may be approved during the suspension period.

The performance appraisal system is used by superiors to assess officials and can impact significantly on an individual's career development: those who meet the targets are rewarded with promotions and bonuses and are publicly praised by their superiors, while those who fail to meet them are likely to face demotion, a reduction in salary and public censure.[36] In the past, environmental protection was a secondary concern for officials, as it was economic development that brought the concrete benefits of career advancement, political stature, financial reward (to both individuals and local offices resulting from increased tax revenues) and wider local support as a result of better job opportunities and

[30] WPPCL (2017), art. 4(1). [31] WPPCL (2017), art. 4(2). [32] Water Action Plan (2015), part IX, s. 29.
[33] WPPCL (2017), art. 6. [34] Water Action Plan (2015), part IX, s. 32.
[35] Water Action Plan (2015), part IX, s. 32.
[36] For more, see Xin Qiu and Honglin Li, 'China's environmental super ministry'; Carl Minzner, 'Riots and cover-ups: counterproductive control of local agents in China', *University of Pennsylvania Journal of International Law*, 31 (2009), 53–123.

improved living standards. Local governments had no incentive to finance or provide staff for local environmental bureaus to ensure effective enforcement. Some even offered to protect polluting industries from environmental scrutiny or sanctions. By expressly linking the appraisal system to environmental performance, the law makes local governments accountable for local water quality and forces heads of local governments to give political and financial support to local environmental bureaus to ensure they are able to enforce the laws effectively. The mechanism aims to deter local governments from pursuing GDP growth at the cost of environment, but it is, however, subject to manipulation by self-interested officials. Some may falsify data, allowing them to pass the assessment without making any real effort to control pollution. To ensure data accuracy, the foundation of the mechanism, it is crucial to conduct frequent monitoring and verification of the data reported by local governments and severely penalize data falsification. Other officials may invest government resources in programmes that generate short-term improvement, rather than long-term sustainable development. Due to the rotation system used for civil servants and the relatively short tenure of each term, self-interested officials feel that projects generating short-term improvements are more beneficial for them. Since water pollution of rivers, lakes and ponds naturally cuts across administrative jurisdictions, a fundamental weakness of the performance appraisal mechanism is found when needing to address regional water pollution covering multiple jurisdictions.[37] Effective water pollution control cannot be achieved with control measures implemented solely within the territory of artificially created administrative units, such as counties, cities and provinces.

6.2.2 Regional Cooperation and the River Basin Approach

To address the problem of cross-jurisdiction water pollution involving multiple administrative jurisdictions, the WPPCL (2017) has taken a river basin approach to strengthen regional cooperation. It requires the state environmental authority to work with the Ministry of Water Resources (MWR) and relevant provincial governments to set up regional coordination mechanisms for key rivers and lakes to improve protection of the aquatic environment.[38] The Water Action Plan (2015) emphasizes the importance of cross-department and cross-jurisdiction cooperation and promotes joint monitoring, joint enforcement, collaborative emergency response and information sharing.[39] A river basin is a naturally formed, relatively independent and complete hydrological unit that covers the land drained by a river and its tributaries, including watersheds, confluences, the source of a river and its mouth where it flows into the sea or an ocean.[40] All the streams, rivers and lakes in the river basin are highly interconnected, which requires an integrated approach to effective management against pollution.

[37] For further discussion, see Wyatt F. Golding, 'Incentives for change: China's cadre system applied to water quality', *Pacific Rim Law & Policy Journal*, 20 (2011), 399–428.

[38] WPPCL (2017), art. 28. Here, coordination specifically refers to unified planning, unified standard setting, unified monitoring and unified implementation of pollution-control measures.

[39] Water Action Plan (2015), part VI, s. 19.

[40] Lu Hao et al. (eds.), *Understanding the Law on Prevention and Control of Water Pollution* (Beijing: China Legal Publishing House, 2017), 95; see also Xia Yu, 'Transboundary water pollution management: lessons learned from river basin management in China, Europe and the Netherlands', *Utrecht Law Review*, 7 (2011), 188–203.

The WPPCL (2017) makes it the responsibility of state and provincial environmental authorities to specify the environmental protection requirements needed for any river basin depending on its ecological functions, to conduct monitoring and assessment of the carrying capacity of river basins and implement an early warning mechanism.[41] Based on the needs of the ecological functions of the river basin, local governments must initiate and organize the conservation and restoration of rivers, lakes and wetlands and construct eco-environmental projects, including artificial wetlands, water-source-preservation forests and vegetation buffer zones. They must take measures to provide treatment and clean up contaminated 'black and odorous waters' to improve the overall carrying capacity of the watersheds.[42] Any development activities must ensure the preservation of the ecological function of the river basin and guard against the erosion of the 'ecological conservation red line'.[43]

One of China's earliest trials of the river basin approach was at Lake Tai. The trial brought in the provinces of Jiangsu and Zhejiang, in which the lake is located, and the city of Shanghai on the banks of the Huangpu River, which is fed by the lake. In 2001, SEPA took the lead and local EPBs within the Lake Tai river basin worked with relevant departments, including those of water resources and fisheries, to set up a joint-meeting mechanism on pollution control. Soon, similar mechanisms were also established for the Songhua, Liao and Hai river basins. After a decade of testing, the river basin approach was embedded in China with the creation of river basin management bureaus, the making of plans for controlling water pollution in river basins, and formulating targets and measures applicable to particular water courses.[44] In 2011, the State Council issued the Regulation on the Management of Lake Tai River Basin, which sets up the Lake Tai River Basin Management Organ under the MWR.[45] In 2012, the State Council approved the Plan on Water Pollution Prevention and Control at Key River Basins (2011–15),[46] which covers ten key river basins: those of the Songhua, Huai, Hai, Liao rivers, the upper and middle reaches of the Yellow River, lakes Tai, Chao and Dian, and the Three Gorges and Danjiangkou reservoirs and their upper reaches.[47] A second Plan on Water Pollution Prevention and Control at Key River Basins (2016–20) covers the Yangtze, Yellow, Pearl, Songhua, Huai, Hai and Liao river basins, rivers in Zhejiang and Fujian provinces and rivers in Southwest and Northwest China.[48] For the water management of river basins, the MWR has established special commissions that cut across local administrative jurisdictions,[49] thereby enhancing China's capacity for integrated management of water resources. Nonetheless,

[41] WPPCL (2017), art. 29(1). [42] WPPCL (2017), art. 29(2).

[43] WPPCL (2017), art. 29(3). The concept of the 'ecological conservation red line' was first formally adopted by environmental law in the EPL (2014). Article 29(1) stipulates that the state must designate ecological conservation red lines in key ecological zones and sensitive or vulnerable eco-environments and exercise strict protection and conservation of these areas.

[44] Lu Hao et al (eds.) Understanding the Law, at 95–96.

[45] State Council, Regulation on the Management of Lake Tai River Basin (2011), art. 5.

[46] The Plan on Water Pollution Prevention and Control at Key River Basins (2011–15) was issued by the MEP, NDRC, Ministry of Finance (MOF) and MWR on 16 May 2012. It came into force with immediate effect.

[47] Plan on Water Pollution Prevention and Control at Key River Basins (2011–15), chapter I, part 1. This plan was issued by the MEP, NDRC and MWR on 12 October 2017.

[48] MEP, NDRC, MOF and MWR, Plan on Water Pollution Prevention and Control at Key River Basins (2011–15), chapter 1, part 1.

[49] Water Law (2002), art. 12.

there remains a lack of coordination and cooperation between these commissions and local environmental bureaus in water pollution control.

6.2.3 Agencies in Charge of Water Pollution Control

Many government departments are involved in the regulatory control of water pollution. While environmental bureaus at county level and above supervise and manage the prevention and control of water pollution,[50] other agencies are involved in managing different sources of water pollution. To protect waters from pollution, environmental protection authorities have the following main duties: (i) making plans to prevent and control water pollution in river basins; (ii) setting water quality standards and effluent discharge standards; (iii) taking the lead in setting up a monitoring system, with the state environmental authority promulgating guidelines on water environment monitoring, releasing data on water quality and working with relevant departments to establish a monitoring network and plan the location of monitoring stations, while provincial environmental authorities monitor and assess the environmental carrying capacity of river basins and issue warnings; (iv) reviewing for approval or rejection the EIA documents of construction projects that will discharge wastewater directly or indirectly into the surface water; (v) managing the permit-control system for entities that discharge industrial or clinical wastewater directly into surface water or for other parties subject to permit control; (vi) in the case of the state environmental authority, working with provincial governments to establish coordination mechanisms to protect the water in the basins of major rivers and lakes; (vii) conducting routine environmental enforcement, including on-site inspections, ordering rectification, monitoring discharge from wastewater treatment facilities, reporting water pollution incidents as required by law and imposing sanctions to punish violations.

Maritime administrative authorities are in charge of the supervision and control of pollution caused by vessels.[51] The Maritime Safety Administration (MSA) has offices along China's coastline and major rivers, such as the Yangtze and Yellow rivers. The offices on the coast are directly led by the MSA, while branches along rivers are affiliated with local governments.

The WPPCL also tasks other bodies with performing their regulatory roles to prevent and control water pollution; these bodies are: departments in charge of water resources, state land and resources, public health, construction, agriculture and fisheries, as well as commissions on the protection of water resources at major rivers basins.[52] For example, the Ministry of Housing and Urban–Rural Development (MOHURD) and its local departments are in charge of municipal water supply, construction of wastewater treatment plants and drainage. The capacity of the wastewater treatment system has a direct impact on the wastewater discharged into rivers, lakes and ultimately the sea. Prior to China's institutional reform of 2018, the MWR and its local departments were in charge of flood control, drought relief, licensing water collection from rivers and lakes, among others, resolving transboundary water conflicts and protecting water resources. The 2018 reform

[50] WPPCL (2017), art. 9(1). The state environmental authority and its local bureaus are in charge of controlling pollution, monitoring water quality, monitoring wastewater discharge and EIA.

[51] WPPCL (2017), art. 9(2). [52] WPPCL (2017), art. 9(3).

shifted certain responsibilities from the MWR to the MEE: regional planning of water function, setting up wastewater discharge outlets and protecting water in river basins.[53] The MWR now focuses more on the management and utilization of water resources. The Ministry of Land and Resources (MLR) and its local departments had been in charge of monitoring and protecting groundwater resources. However, the 2018 reform replaced the MLR with a new Ministry of Natural Resources (MNR) and shifted monitoring and protecting groundwater from the MLR to the MEE.[54] The Ministry of Agriculture (MOA) and its local departments were previously in charge of control of non-point sources of agricultural pollution, management of fisheries and wildlife conservation. The 2018 reform shifted control of all rural non-point source pollution from the MOA to the MEE.[55]

6.2.4 The River Chief System

Some local pilot schemes included a trial of a 'river chief' system, in which local party and government leaders also organize and coordinate work to control water pollution and protect and restore water ecosystems. Local trials of the river chief system were soon formalized in the binding Opinion on the Promotion of River Chief System (2016), which targeted the establishment of the river chief system nationwide by the end of 2018.[56] The river chief system tries to enhance environmental governance by building better coordination among the agencies in charge of environmental protection, agriculture, water resources, housing and construction. To improve the governance of the water environment and formalize the responsibility of local governments in water pollution control and treatment, the WPPCL (2017) provided for the river chief system at provincial, city, county and township levels, stipulating in more detail its role in leading, coordinating and supervising the work on protecting water resources, managing land use of river banks, preventing and controlling water pollution, and water environment governance.[57]

6.3 STANDARDS AND PLANS

Standards and plans form the crucial basis of the command-and-control approach to pollution control. The governments make plans, set targets for water pollution control and formulate water quality and effluent discharge standards in order to protect public health and the water environment. The WPPCL (2017) provides that discharge of wastewater must not exceed national or local effluent discharge standards or the total discharge

[53] NPC, Decision of the 1st session of the 13th NPC on State Council Institutional Reform (2018), part I, s. 2. On 17 March 2018, the 13th National People's Congress (NPC) at its 1st session approved the State Council's Institutional Reform Proposal by issuing the Decision with immediate effect.

[54] NPC, Decision on State Council's Institutional Reform Proposal (17 March 2018), part I, s. 2.

[55] NPC, Decision on State Council's Institutional Reform Proposal (17 March 2018), part I, s. 2.

[56] The Opinion on the Promotion of River Chief System (2016) was issued by the Chinese Communist Party (CCP) Central Committee and the State Council in December 2016. The river chief system was established by June 2018.

[57] WPPCL (2017), art. 5.

quota for key water pollutants (KWPs).[58] The state environmental authority and provincial governments set standards[59] and amend them in a timely manner to accommodate the changing needs of water pollution control, in accordance with national and local economic and technological capacities.[60]

6.3.1 Water Quality Standards

Water quality standards (WQS) mandate the maximum permitted concentration level of pollutants to ensure safe use of water for a specific function, such as drinking water, irrigation, fishery or recreational or industrial use. The state environmental authority sets national WQS.[61] Provincial governments may set local standards for pollutants not specified in the national WQS and must report to the state environmental authority for the record.[62]

China has issued WQS for surface water, marine water and groundwater. Further, WQS have also been issued for different water functions, fisheries, irrigation and drinking water. Some, however, were outdated after three decades of socio-economic development and technological advancement. Consequently, the MEP initiated public consultation in 2009 to amend and consolidate some of the standards in order to address the problems of inconsistency and overlap among the WQS for surface water, groundwater, irrigation and fisheries.[63]

TABLE 6.1 MAJOR WQS

	Reference number	Date of issue	Effective date
Environmental Quality Standards for Surface Water	GB 3838-2002	28 April 2002	1 June 2002
Sea Water Quality Standards	GB 3097-1997	3 December 1997	1 July 1998
Standards for Groundwater Quality	GB/T 14848-2017 (replacing GB/T 14848-1993)	14 October 2017	1 May 2018
Water Quality Standards for Drinking Water Sources	CJ 3020-93	5 August 1993	5 August 1993
Water Quality Standards for Drinking Water Quality	GB 5749-2006 (replacing GB 5749-1985)	29 December 2006	1 July 2007
Water Quality Standards for Farmland Irrigation	GB 5084-2005 (replacing GB 5084-1992)	21 July 2005	1 November 2006
Water Quality Standards for Fisheries	GB 11607-89	12 August 1989	1 March 1990

Sources: www.mee.gov.cn/

[58] WPPCL (2017), art. 10. [59] WPPCL (2017), arts. 12 and 14. [60] WPPCL (2017), art. 15.
[61] WPPCL (2017), art. 12(1). [62] WPPCL (2017), art. 12(2).
[63] MEP, Notice on Consultation to Amend the Surface Water Quality Standards (17 July 2009). For more details, see: www.mep.gov.cn/gkml/hbb/bgth/200910/t20091022_175025.htm.

The Environmental Quality Standards for Surface Water (GB3838-2002) applies to inland waters, including rivers, lakes, and reservoirs. It sets the maximum levels of pollutants for five categories of water use:

Grade I: water flowing through state nature reserves;
Grade II: drinking-water-source reserve (DWSR) (I); conservation area for rare aquatic species; area for fish spawning;
Grade III: DWSR (II); conservation area for common aquatic species; area for swimming;
Grade IV: industrial water supply; recreational use other than swimming (for example, boating, fishing);
Grade V: cooling water for industry; irrigation; ordinary landscape.

Grades I to III represent good water quality that is safe for human consumption and as a habitat for aquatic species and fish spawning. Grades IV and V are of poor water quality that is unsafe for skin contact, but can be used for industrial purposes. The use of Grade V water for irrigation proved to be a serious mistake, as contaminated farmland and poisoned agricultural produce has posed a risk to food safety and human health. Official data released annually by the MEP and MEE revealed serious water contamination of China's major river basins. Overall, only two-thirds of surface water is of grades I to III. More than one-third is poor quality, meaning grades IV and V and sub-Grade V, while nearly 10 per cent is sub-Grade V, meaning it is not safe for any use.

The data in Table 6.2 covers ten major river basins, with rivers in Southwest and Northwest China less contaminated than the Yangtze, Yellow, Pearl, Songhua, Hai, Huai and Liao rivers. The Water Action Plan (2015) set a target for 70 per cent of samples taken from each of those seven major river basins to achieve grades I to III by 2020 and, by 2030, 75 per cent.[64] By 2017, less than half of the samples taken at the Hai, Huai and Liao rivers were of grades I to III, and less than 60 per cent of those taken at the Yellow River were of grades I to III.[65]

According to China's Standard for Groundwater Quality,[66] there are five categories of groundwater, each with different uses:[67]

Grade I (very good): low levels of chemicals detected, suitable for any use;
Grade II (good): relatively low levels of chemicals detected, suitable for any use;
Grade III (average): medium levels of chemicals detected, suitable for centralized drinking water supply and industrial and agricultural use;
Grade IV (poor): relatively high levels of chemicals detected, suitable for agricultural and certain industrial use, may be used for drinking water supply subject to proper treatment;
Grade V (very poor): high levels of chemicals detected, not suitable for drinking water supply, may be used for other purpose.

[64] Water Action Plan (2015), Key Targets. [65] MEP, *2017 China Ecology and Environment Gazette*, at 18.
[66] The Standard for Groundwater Quality (GB/T 14848-2017, replacing GB/T 14848-1993) was issued by the State Administration for Quality Supervision, Inspection and Quarantine (SAQSIQ) and the State Standardization Commission on 14 October 2017. It came into force on 1 May 2018.
[67] Standard for Groundwater Quality (GB/T 14848-2017), s. 4.1.

TABLE 6.2 WATER QUALITY OF MAJOR RIVER BASINS IN CHINA

<table>
<tr><th></th><th>Grade I (%)</th><th>Grade II (%)</th><th>Grade III (%)</th><th>Grade IV (%)</th><th>Grade V (%)</th><th>Sub-Grade V (%)</th></tr>
<tr><td>2011</td><td colspan="3">61[a]</td><td colspan="2">25.3</td><td>13.7</td></tr>
<tr><td>2012</td><td colspan="3">68.9</td><td colspan="2">20.9</td><td>10.2</td></tr>
<tr><td>2013</td><td colspan="3">71.7</td><td colspan="2">19.3</td><td>9.0</td></tr>
<tr><td>2014</td><td>2.8</td><td>36.9</td><td>31.5</td><td>15.0</td><td>4.8</td><td>9.0</td></tr>
<tr><td>2015</td><td>2.8</td><td>31.4</td><td>30.3</td><td>21.1</td><td>5.6</td><td>8.8</td></tr>
<tr><td>2016</td><td>2.4</td><td>37.5</td><td>27.9</td><td>16.8</td><td>6.9</td><td>8.6[b]</td></tr>
<tr><td>2017</td><td>2.2</td><td>36.7</td><td>32.9</td><td>14.6</td><td>5.2</td><td>8.4</td></tr>
<tr><td>2018</td><td>5.0</td><td>43</td><td>26.3</td><td>14.4</td><td>4.5</td><td>6.9</td></tr>
</table>

Sources: MEP, *2011 China Environment Gazette – 2016 China Environment Gazette*; MEE, *2017 China Ecology and Environment Gazette;* MEE, *2018 China Ecology and Environment Gazette.* Prior to 2011, the data covered seven major basins – the Yangtze, Yellow, Pearl, Songhua, Huai, Hai and Liao river basins. Since 2011, the data has included river basins in Zhejiang and Fujian provinces and in Southwest China and Northwest China. To enable data to be compared accurately, 2011 is used as the baseline year.

[a] Data for individual grades in 2011, 2012 and 2013 is unavailable.

[b] Due to rounding, percentages in this table may not total 100 per cent.

TABLE 6.3 GROUNDWATER QUALITY

<table>
<tr><th></th><th>Number of monitoring wells</th><th>Grade I Very good (%)</th><th>Grade II Good (%)</th><th>Grade III Average (%)</th><th>Grade IV Poor (%)</th><th>Grade V Very poor (%)</th></tr>
<tr><td rowspan="2">2010</td><td rowspan="2">4,110</td><td rowspan="2">10.2</td><td rowspan="2">27.6</td><td rowspan="2">5</td><td>40.4</td><td>16.8</td></tr>
<tr><td colspan="2">57.2</td></tr>
<tr><td rowspan="2">2015</td><td rowspan="2">5,118</td><td rowspan="2">9.1</td><td rowspan="2">25</td><td rowspan="2">4.6</td><td>42.5</td><td>18.8</td></tr>
<tr><td colspan="2">61.3</td></tr>
<tr><td rowspan="2">2016</td><td rowspan="2">6,124</td><td rowspan="2">10.1</td><td rowspan="2">25.4</td><td rowspan="2">4.4</td><td>45.4</td><td>14.7</td></tr>
<tr><td colspan="2">60.1</td></tr>
<tr><td rowspan="2">2017</td><td rowspan="2">5,100</td><td rowspan="2">8.8</td><td rowspan="2">23.1</td><td rowspan="2">1.5</td><td>51.8</td><td>14.8</td></tr>
<tr><td colspan="2">66.6</td></tr>
<tr><td rowspan="2">2018</td><td rowspan="2">10,168</td><td rowspan="2">1.9</td><td rowspan="2">9.0</td><td rowspan="2">2.9</td><td>70.7</td><td>15.5</td></tr>
<tr><td colspan="2">86.2</td></tr>
</table>

Sources: MEP, *2010 China Environment Gazette – 2016 China Environment Gazette*; MEE, *2017 China Ecology and Environment Gazette;* MEE, *2018 China Ecology and Environment Gazette.*

In 2010, the MEP started to publish more detailed data on groundwater quality in its annual gazette. Table 6.3 shows deterioration of groundwater quality, with 57 per cent of groundwater sources classed as 'poor' and 'very poor' in 2010, rising to 86.2 per cent in 2018.

6.3.2 Effluent Discharge Standards

In order to achieve and maintain adherence to the WQS, the state environmental authority sets national effluent discharge standards that are economically and technologically feasible.[68] Provincial governments may set local effluent discharge standards for pollutants not specified in the national standards. If a pollutant is already specified in the national standards, provincial governments may set a more stringent local standard. All local standards must be reported to the state environmental authority for the record.[69] Where local effluent standards are issued, they must be implemented and enforced.[70]

In addition to the standards in Table 6.4, there are sector-specific discharge standards, including for the papermaking, shipbuilding, textile printing and dyeing, and iron and steel industries. Operators of projects in sectors with sector-specific discharge standards must comply with those, instead of the Integrated Wastewater Discharge Standard (GB 8978-1996).

6.3.3 WPPCP

Water pollution prevention and control plans (WPPCPs) are made either for river basins or administrative regions. There are four main types of WPPCP: (i) river basin WPPCP for key rivers and lakes designated by the state, made by the state environmental authority, NDRC and provincial governments, and reported to the State Council for approval;[71] (ii) river basin WPPCP for other rivers and lakes cutting across provinces, made by relevant provincial environmental bureaus, endorsed by provincial governments and reported to the State Council for approval;[72] (iii) river basin WPPCP for rivers and lakes within

TABLE 6.4 MAJOR STANDARDS FOR EFFLUENT DISCHARGE

Name	Reference number	Date of issue	Effective date
Integrated Wastewater Discharge Standard	GB 8978-1996 (replacing GB 8978-88)	4 October 1996	1 January 1998
Discharge Standard of Pollutants for Municipal Wastewater Treatment Plant	GB 18918-2002	24 December 2002	1 July 2003
Wastewater Quality Standards for Discharge to Municipal Sewers	CJ 343-2010 (replacing CJ 3082-1999)	29 July 2010	1 January 2011
Discharge Standards for Water Pollutants from Ships	GB 3552-2018 (replacing GB3552-83)	16 January 2018	1 July 2018

Sources: www.mee.gov.cn/

[68] WPPCL (2017), art. 14(1). [69] WPPCL (2017), art. 14(2). [70] WPPCL (2017), art. 14(3).
[71] WPPCL (2017), art. 16(1). [72] WPPCL (2017), art. 16(2).

provinces and cutting across counties, made by provincial environmental bureaus, approved by provincial governments and reported to the State Council for the record[73] and (iv) local WPPCP, made by local governments in accordance with the approved river basin WPPCP.[74] A river basin WPPCP is implemented by local plans that set clear targets, tasks and measures. Any amendment to an approved river basin WPPCP or local plan requires approval by the original approval authority.[75] A local government that is found during its appraisal to have failed in the implementation of a plan is penalized by having to suspend EIA approvals, and the heads of the governments must attend supervision talks.[76] The State Council has approved WPPCPs including the Key River Basin WPPCP (2011–15), the Key River Basin WPPCP (2016–20) and the National Plan on Groundwater Pollution Prevention and Control (2011–2020).

6.3.4 Attainment Plans

If a municipal or county government fails to achieve the water quality improvement targets set by the relevant WPPCP, it is required to make an attainment plan that specifies pollution-control measures to be taken, and take measures to achieve the water quality objectives by a specified deadline.[77] Attainment plans must be reported to the next-higher-level government for the record and disclosed to the public.[78] The Water Action Plan (2015) requires the attainment plans to be released to the public on a regular basis from 2016.[79] The WPPCL (2017) further enhances external supervision over the implementation of the attainment plans by requiring municipal and county governments to report annually to the same-level people's congress, or its standing committee, on local environmental quality, the achievement of environmental protection targets and implementation of the water quality attainment plan.[80] The report must be released to the public[81] to facilitate public access to information and public supervision over government environmental performance.

6.4 MECHANISMS TO PREVENT AND CONTROL WATER POLLUTION

The WPPCL (2017) uses a wide range of legal mechanisms to prevent and control water pollution. There is increasing alignment between the EIA system, the three-simultaneities requirement, permit control and total discharge control, advancing China's progress towards full implementation of the preventative principle.

6.4.1 EIA and the Three-Simultaneities Requirement

An EIA is required for all new construction projects and for expansion or reconstruction projects discharging wastewater directly or indirectly into waterbodies.[82] Before building, modifying or expanding outlets discharging into a river or lake, a construction unit must obtain consent from relevant water administration departments or river basin administration authorities. Where a project affects navigation or fishery waters, environmental

[73] WPPCL (2017), art. 16(3). [74] WPPCL (2017), art. 16(5). [75] WPPCL (2017), art. 16(4).

[76] Chen Changzhi, *Report of the NPCSC Inspection Team on the Implementation of the WPPCL* (2015). www pkulaw.cn. On 27 August 2015, Chen Changzhi, vice chairman of the 12th NPCSC, presented the report to the 12th NPCSC at its 16th session.

[77] WPPCL (2017), art. 17(1). [78] WPPCL (2017), art. 17(2). [79] Water Action Plan (2015), part VII, s. 20.

[80] WPPCL (2017), art. 18. [81] WPPCL (2017), art. 18. [82] WPPCL (2017), art. 19(1).

bureaus must consult the relevant transport or fishery departments when they review EIA documents during the approval process.[83] Facilities to control water pollution must be designed, constructed and put into operation simultaneously with the main projects. They must meet the technical requirements specified in the EIA documents.[84]

In a region where the discharge of a KWP exceeds the total quota set by the government, or if a region fails to achieve the water quality improvement objectives, the environmental bureau suspends the review and approval of EIA documents for any project that will discharge additional KWPs.[85] This means no project may be approved until the region reduces its total discharge of KWPs to a level below the discharge quota.

6.4.2 Total Discharge Control of Key Water Pollutants

Effluent discharge standards control the concentration levels of pollutants discharged by point sources. The focus is on the pollutant concentration level instead of the total amount of pollutants discharged. An operator may dilute its discharge in order to comply with effluent standards. However, where a large number of operators discharge wastewater that complies with the effluent discharge standards, they may still overload the carrying capacity of the receiving water bodies and cause serious environmental damage. It is therefore necessary to impose a cap on the total discharge of KWPs to prevent degradation of the water quality. The WPPCL (2017) has adopted the 'double control' of both effluent discharge standards and total discharge quota for KWPs.[86]

The total discharge quota applies to KWPs.[87] Each quota is designated by the state environmental authority in consultation with provincial governments and relevant departments of the State Council. The state environmental authority and the NDRC put forward the proposal on KWP designation to the State Council for approval.[88] During the 11th five-year plan (FYP) period (2005–10), COD was the sole KWP. Since the beginning of the 12th FYP period in 2011, ammonia nitrogen (NH) has also been added as a KWP. Provincial governments must abate and control total discharge of KWPs within their jurisdictions.[89] Provincial governments may designate additional KWPs for abatement and control of the total discharge on the basis of local water quality and the need for pollution control,[90] though in practice they follow the State Council's designation. The Water Action Plan (2015) has as an objective the inclusion of further water pollutants as KWPs, such as nitrogen, phosphorus and heavy metals, and also aims to cover industrial, municipal, agricultural and mobile pollution sources.[91] Where a region (a county, city or province) discharges effluents in excess of the total control quota or fails to achieve its WPPCP water quality improvement objective, the administrative head of the region must attend supervision talks with provincial or state environmental authorities. All EIA review and approval must be suspended for the region, pending rectification. Details of the supervision talks must be released for public scrutiny.[92]

83 WPPCL (2017), art. 19(2).
84 WPPCL (2017), art. 19(3).
85 WPPCL (2017), art. 20(5).
86 WPPCL (2017), art. 10.
87 WPPCL (2017), art. 20(1).
88 WPPCL (2017), art. 20(2).
89 WPPCL (2017), art. 20(3).
90 WPPCL (2017), art. 20(4).
91 Water Action Plan (2015), part VII, s. 21.
92 WPPCL (2017), art. 20(5).

6.4.3 Pollution Discharge Permits

The state has imposed a permit-control system for effluent discharge. Any enterprise, institution or other production operator that, directly or indirectly, discharges industrial or clinical wastewater to surface waters must obtain a pollution discharge permit.[93] Industrial or clinical wastewater may not be discharged, whether directly or indirectly, to surface waters without a permit or in violation of the terms and conditions of a permit.[94] The permit-control system also applies to wastewater treatment plants.[95] The discharge permits must clearly specify the types of permitted pollutants, the concentration, the total permitted discharge and the destination of the wastewater.[96] Permit control is thus effectively aligned with the principle of double control, targeting both the total discharge quota and effluent discharge standards.

The Water Action Plan (2015) set a timetable for phased implementation of permit controls. By the end of 2015, all 'key polluting sources under state control' and sources covered by the emissions trading pilot areas were required to obtain pollution discharge permits; all other sources were required to obtain permits by the end of 2017, by which time a nationwide permit management data platform was to have been established by the MEP.[97] In 2016, the State Council issued the Implementation Plan on Permit Control of Pollution Discharge,[98] which aims at full coverage of all stationary sources with issuance of permits, operation of the national permit management platform and alignment of all environmental management tools, such as EIA, with the permit-control mechanism by end-2020.

6.4.4 Preservation and Restoration of the Water Ecosystem

China's water crisis is the result of heavy discharge of wastewater and excessive exploitation of water resources, both of which have caused serious water shortage and intensified the deterioration in water quality. The destruction of forests and wetlands, which preserve soil and purify water, has left rivers and lakes without natural protection. Recognizing a close connection between the quality and quantity of water resources, the WPPCL (2017) requires relevant state departments and local governments to ensure reasonable water volumes in rivers and reasonable water levels of lakes, reservoirs and groundwater aquifers before permitting the exploitation, utilization and diversion of water resources.[99]

Equally as important as pollution control is the preservation and restoration of the water ecosystem. It is important to ensure that human activities do not burden river basins beyond their carrying capacity. The WPPCL (2017) requires state and provincial environmental authorities to conduct monitoring and assessment of the environmental and resource carrying capacities of river basins based on their ecological functions, and issue warnings if human exploitation of water resources means that the basin is reaching its carrying capacity.[100] Local governments are required to organize works to protect and

[93] WPPCL (2017), art. 21(1). [94] WPPCL (2017), art. 21(2). [95] WPPCL (2017), art. 21(1).
[96] WPPCL (2017), art. 21(1).
[97] Water Action Plan (2015), part VII, s. 23. The platform was launched on 1 January 2017.
[98] The Implementation Plan on Permit Control of Pollution Discharge was issued by the general office of the State Council in November 2016.
[99] WPPCL (2017), art. 27. [100] WPPCL (2017), art. 29(1).

restore rivers, lakes and wetlands, construct projects that treat and conserve the eco-environment, including man-made wetlands, forests to preserve water sources and buffer green-belts along rivers and lakes, and clean up contaminated 'black and odorous' waters in order to improve the carrying capacity of river basins.[101] All development activities must be accompanied by measures that will ensure the preservation of the ecological functions of river basins and strictly guard the red line of ecological protection.[102]

6.5 CONTROL OF KEY SOURCES OF WATER POLLUTION

Major sources of water pollution include the discharge of municipal and industrial wastewater and agricultural run-off. Illegal industrial discharge often involves discharge to bodies of surface water through unmonitored discharge points or via secret disposal wells or hidden pipes. Agricultural non-point sources include overuse of fertilizers and pesticides and improper disposal of human and animal waste in rural regions.[103] Shallow aquifers are vulnerable to pollution by surface activities. A recent switch in the predominant recharge source for groundwater from the natural infiltration of rainfall and surface water to return-flow from agricultural irrigation has had a significant adverse impact on groundwater quality. The switch is due to a combination of extensive dam building in mountainous areas that has prevented natural flooding over groundwater recharge areas, and intensive over-irrigation in agriculture. Irrigation return-flow tends to be high in salt, nitrate and agricultural chemicals.[104] Deep aquifers are no longer isolated from polluting surface activities as a result of the boom in groundwater abstraction over the last four decades. Millions of wells have been drilled across the nation, with many drawing water from multiple aquifers; this has created a large number of potential conduits between shallow and deep aquifers and risks of cross-contamination of deep aquifers.[105] The WPPCL (2017) provides regulatory control over toxic and hazardous discharge, activities posing risks to surface and ground waters, industrial discharge, municipal wastewater, agricultural run-off and discharge by vessels.

6.5.1 Control of Toxic and Hazardous Discharge

Toxic and hazardous substances pose high risks to both the water environment and human health. They are subject to tight and special control, without which they mix with other types of discharge and enter wastewater treatment facilities that do not have the technological capacity to provide detoxification treatment. This can result in discharge in violation of state standards and/or damage to treatment facilities. To address the problem, the WPPCL (2017) requires state ministries in charge of environmental protection and public health to work together to issue a 'list of toxic and hazardous water pollutants' that harm human health and the environment, and implement risk management and control.[106] Any

[101] WPPCL (2017), art. 29(2). [102] WPPCL (2017), art. 29(3).

[103] MEP, National Plan on Groundwater Pollution Prevention and Control (2011–2020). China's average per unit area application of fertilizer and pesticide on farmland are 2.8 times and 3 times the world average respectively.

[104] Dongmei Han et al., 'Deep challenges for China's war', at 1228–9.

[105] Dongmei Han et al., 'Deep challenges for China's war', at 1229. [106] WPPCL (2017), art. 32(1).

entities discharging a toxic and hazardous pollutant on the list must monitor at and around the discharge outlets, assess environmental risks and take measures to prevent and eliminate potential environmental harm.[107]

The WPPCL (2017) prohibits the discharge of oil, acid or alkaline solutions[108] or highly toxic wastewater to surface waters, and prohibits the washing of vehicles and containers used for storing oil or hazardous pollutants in the waters.[109] It also prohibits the dumping of radioactive waste or the discharge of wastewater containing medium to high levels of radioactive substances.[110] While discharging wastewater containing a low level of radioactive substance is permitted, the discharge is subject to state regulation and standards under the Radioactive Pollution Prevention and Control Law.[111]

In addition, the law requires heated wastewater to be properly treated before discharge,[112] and wastewater containing pathogens to be disinfected before discharge.[113] Heated wastewater is generated by thermal power plants, nuclear power plants, non-ferrous metal refineries and petrochemical plants, among others, during cooling. Discharging heated wastewater not only affects the health of aquatic species, but also intensifies the toxicity of cyanides and heavy metals. Thus the WPPCL (2017) requires proper treatment, including cooling, before discharge, so that discharge to rivers or lakes does not increase the water temperature by more than 1 °C,[114] and discharge to the sea does not increase the water temperature by more than 1 °C in summer or 2 °C in other seasons.[115] Wastewater containing pathogens mainly refers to, but is not limited to, clinical wastewater. Municipal sewage and industrial wastewater may also contain bacteria and viruses, causing illness and endangering public health.

6.5.2 Control of Activities Posing Risks to Water Quality

Other activities in addition to effluent discharge into waterbodies may potentially contaminate surface water and/or groundwater and are thus subject to control under the WPPCL. To prevent surface water pollution, the WPPCL (2017) prohibits the depositing or dumping of industrial solid waste (ISW), municipal waste or other waste into surface waters.[116] It also prohibits the piling or storing of solid waste or other pollutants on beaches or sloping banks below the high-water mark of rivers, lakes, canals, irrigation channels and reservoirs.[117] Here, 'solid waste' includes ISW, municipal waste and hazardous waste

[107] WPPCL (2017), art. 32(2).
[108] Integrated Wastewater Discharge Standard (GB 8978-1996). Acid or alkaline solutions are solutions outside a pH range of 6 to 9.
[109] WPPCL (2017), art. 33. 'Hazardous pollutant' is defined by art. 102 of the WPPCL to be a pollutant that, once absorbed directly or indirectly by animal, plant or human, is capable of causing illness, behavioural abnormality, gene mutation, physical malfunction, deformation or death. These are mainly heavy metals, including mercury, chromium, cadmium and lead, and organic chemicals, such as phenol, chlorine, phosphorus and ethene.
[110] WPPCL (2017), art. 34(1).
[111] The Radioactive Pollution Prevention and Control Law was passed on 28 June 2003 by the 10th NPCSC at its 3rd session.
[112] WPPCL (2017), art. 35.
[113] WPPCL (2017), art. 36.
[114] Surface Water Environmental Quality Standard (GB 3838-2002).
[115] Sea Water Quality Standard (GB 3097-1997).
[116] WPPCL (2017), art. 37(1).
[117] WPPCL (2017), art. 38.

(HW). 'Other pollutants' refers to pollutants in the form of gas or liquid that are stored in containers.

To prevent groundwater pollution, the WPPCL (2017) not only prohibits the depositing or dumping of soluble and highly toxic waste containing mercury, cadmium, arsenic, chromium, lead, cyanide or yellow phosphorus into surface waters, but also bans the burying of these substances underground.[118] In addition, it requires sites used to store soluble toxic waste to be waterproof, leakproof and non-permeable[119] to prevent contamination of soil and groundwater. Further, the WPPCL (2017) prohibits the transmission or storage of hazardous wastewater, sewage containing pathogens, and other wastes in any ditch, pit or pond without measures to prevent seepage.[120] Last but not least, special duties are imposed on certain high-risk sectors that, by nature of their operations, tend to threaten groundwater safety. Thus, chemical manufacturers, and operators or managers of industrial zones, mining exploration areas, tailing reservoirs, HW disposal sites and landfills, among others, are required to take measures to prevent seepage and to construct wells to monitor groundwater quality and prevent groundwater contamination.[121] Petrol stations are required to use double-layer oil tanks or take other measures to prevent leakage and must conduct monitoring in order to prevent groundwater pollution.[122]

The WPPCL (2017) prohibits activities that enable regulatory monitoring to be evaded. Such evasions cause severe harm to the environment as unchecked effluent discharge is often several times over the state limits, both in terms of quantity and concentration. In line with the EPL (2014)[123] and the Water Action Plan (2015),[124] the WPPCL (2017) expressly prohibits: (i) discharge of wastewater into seepage well, pit, fissure or karst cave; (ii) discharge of wastewater through hidden pipes; (iii) falsification of monitoring data and (iv) abnormal operation of wastewater treatment facilities.[125]

6.5.3 Control of Industrial Discharge

Discharge of untreated industrial effluents has been a major source of water pollution in China, especially since the economic take-off in the 1980s. Based on the polluter-pays principle, the WPPCL (2017) imposes a duty on industrial enterprises to take effective measures to collect and treat industrial effluent before it is discharged. Toxic and hazardous wastewater must be collected and treated separately to prevent water pollution.[126] However, the rules are not always adhered to, due to the limited financial and technological capacities of some operators, especially small and medium-sized enterprises. A more efficient and effective approach to industrial wastewater treatment is to use centralized treatment facilities operated by industrial parks that have been planned and developed by state and provincial governments. Such centralized treatment facilities would adopt advanced technology and sound environmental management. The NPCSC recommended that where new industrial parks are to be built or existing industrial parks upgraded, centralized treatment facilities for wastewater and solid waste should be planned

[118] WPPCL (2017), art. 37(2). [119] WPPCL (2017), art. 37(3). [120] WPPCL (2017), art. 40(3).
[121] WPPCL (2017), art. 40(1). [122] WPPCL (2017), art. 40(2). [123] EPL (2014), art. 42(4).
[124] Water Action Plan (2015), part VI, s. 18. [125] WPPCL (2017), art. 39. [126] WPPCL (2017), art. 45(1).

at the same time.[127] Following the recommendation, both the Water Action Plan (2015)[128] and the WPPCL (2017) require zones in which industry is concentrated, including industrial parks, to construct centralized wastewater treatment facilities, install automatic monitoring equipment that is connected to the local regulatory monitoring network of the environmental bureaus, and ensure the monitoring devices function normally.[129] Generators of wastewater are required to provide pre-treatment before discharging industrial wastewater to the centralized treatment facilities.[130] This ensures that the centralized treatment facilities can function as they should and that treatment before discharge is effective.

While end-of-pipe control is essential to prevent the discharge of untreated industrial wastewater, it only eliminates pollutants to a certain level. In contrast, pollution prevention is a more effective and efficient approach, and involves rational planning of industry to take into account the impact on the environment, resources and long-term sustainability, the phasing out of outdated techniques and equipment, banning new heavily polluting projects and promoting clean production. Governments must take the lead in promoting industrial upgrades and clean production. The WPPCL (2017) requires State Council departments and local governments to ensure rational spatial and geographical layout of industry through planning, force polluting enterprises to invest in technological innovations, take comprehensive pollution-control measures, improve wastewater recycling and reuse and abate effluent discharge.[131] The requirement for rational industrial layout demands the consideration of environmental carrying capacity and the resources available for the operation of industrial projects in any given region, as well as the impact on the health and well-being of the population. All existing heavily polluting enterprises in the iron and steel, non-ferrous metal, papermaking, printing and dyeing, pharmaceutical and chemical sectors in the more established areas of cities are to be relocated or closed down in an orderly manner.[132] Enterprises must adopt clean production techniques that improve their efficiency in using raw materials and reduce their effluent discharge, and must strengthen management in order to abate their generation of wastewater.[133] The Water Action Plan (2015) targets ten industrial sectors for compulsory clean production upgrade: papermaking, coking, nitrogen fertilizer, non-ferrous metals, printing and dyeing, the processing of agricultural products, pharmaceutical, tannery, pesticides and electroplating. Any new, alteration or expansion projects in the above sectors may not increase the sector's total discharge of KWPs.[134] This means that existing wastewater discharge from the sector has to be abated to create a quota before new projects, or alterations or expansion of existing projects, can be approved.

To implement clean production, the state phases out production techniques and equipment that cause serious water pollution.[135] The NDRC and relevant departments of the State

[127] Chen Changzhi, *Report of the NPCSC Inspection Team on the Implementation of the WPPCL.* Approximately 50 per cent of chemical and petrochemical enterprises and more than 60 per cent of printing and dyeing enterprises operate in industrial parks.

[128] Water Action Plan (2015), part I, s. 1. The Water Action Plan sets two deadlines for construction of centralized wastewater treatment facilities with automatic monitoring devices: end-2016 for Beijing–Tianjin–Hebei, the Yangtze River Delta and Pearl River Delta, and end-2017 for the rest of China.

[129] WPPCL (2017), art. 45(2). [130] WPPCL (2017), art. 45(3). [131] WPPCL (2017), art. 44.

[132] Water Action Plan (2015), part II, s. 6. [133] WPPCL (2017), art. 48.

[134] Water Action Plan (2015), part I, s. 1(2). [135] WPPCL (2017), art. 46(1).

Council issue and update a catalogue of industrial techniques that cause serious water pollution, setting deadlines by which their use must be phased out, and catalogues of equipment causing serious water pollution, setting deadlines by which their production, sale, import and use must be phased out.[136] The equipment thus phased out may not be transferred to others for use.[137] Producers, sellers, importers or users must, within the prescribed time limit, stop producing, selling, importing or using any equipment listed in the catalogue of equipment to be phased out. Anyone using a production process listed in the catalogue as one to be phased out must stop using it within the prescribed time limit.[138]

Clean production, as promoted by government and implemented by enterprises, requires finances, technology and human resources to upgrade equipment, techniques and environmental management. Small-scale industrial projects (in sectors including paper-making, tannery, printing and dyeing, dyestuff and coking) that are operated by township or village enterprises or individual households are the most polluting, given the large numbers in operation and their lack of pollution-control measures and the capacity to upgrade to clean production. The Water Action Plan (2015) set a deadline of end-2016 for eliminating small-scale and heavily polluting enterprises in ten sectors.[139] The WPPCL (2017) prohibits the construction of new small-scale projects that contravene state industrial development policies and cause serious water pollution, including in the sectors of papermaking, tannery, printing and dyeing, dyestuff, coking, electroplating, pesticides, asbestos, cement, glass, iron and steel, thermal power generation and the refining of arsenic, mercury, oil and sulphur.[140]

6.5.4 Control of Municipal Wastewater

Urbanization and population growth has substantially increased water consumption and municipal wastewater discharge. The low treatment rate makes it another major source of water pollution. The treatment rate in cities rose from 77.5 per cent in 2010 to 91.9 per cent in 2015, and from 60.1 per cent to 85 per cent in county towns over the same period. However, this does not cover China's vast number of rural towns, for which the treatment rate was below 20 per cent in 2010.[141]

To control pollution by municipal wastewater, centralized treatment is crucial. Governments from central to local levels play a crucial role in planning and constructing wastewater treatment infrastructure, and in supervising the operation and maintenance of treatment facilities and connection pipes. The WPPCL (2017) requires centralized treatment of municipal wastewater,[142] and makes it the responsibility of local governments to use public finances or raise funds by other means to construct wastewater treatment facilities and pipes to enhance local capacity for wastewater collection and treatment.[143] The

[136] WPPCL (2017), art. 46(2). [137] WPPCL (2017), art. 46(4). [138] WPPCL (2017), art. 46(3).

[139] Water Action Plan (2015), part I, s. 1(1). The sectors are: papermaking, tannery, printing and dyeing, dyestuff, coking, electroplating, pesticides and the refining of sulphur, arsenic and oil.

[140] WPPCL (2017), art. 47. The WPPCL (2017) specifies duties, liabilities and sanctions in greater detail than the state industrial development policies.

[141] The 2015 figure for rural towns is unavailable. State Council, 12th FYP on the Construction of Wastewater Treatment, Recycling and Reuse Facilities (2012); NDRC and MOHURD, 13th FYP on the Construction of Wastewater Treatment, Recycling and Reuse Facilities (2016).

[142] WPPCL (2017), art. 49(1). [143] WPPCL (2017), art. 49(2).

MOHURD, together with the NDRC and MEE, is required to make national plans for the construction of municipal wastewater treatment facilities. Local governments are required to organize local construction bureaus, development and reform commissions, environmental bureaus and water resources bureaus to make local plans. Local construction bureaus are in charge of both constructing the infrastructure and supervising its operation.[144] The Water Action Plan (2015) set targets to be achieved by end-2020: maintaining the municipal wastewater treatment rate at 85 per cent in county towns and increasing it to 95 per cent in cities.[145] The three most economically advanced regions of Beijing–Tianjin–Hebei, the Yangtze River Delta and Pearl River Delta were required to achieve the targets by end-2019.[146]

Operators of wastewater treatment facilities charge a fee for the service. The fees collected may only be used for the construction and operation of wastewater treatment facilities and the disposal of sludge generated by the treatment process.[147] The NDRC, MOF and MOHURD are required to set the fee at a level that fully covers the costs of wastewater treatment and safe disposal of sludge.[148] Wastewater discharged by the treatment facilities is subject to both the effluent discharge standards and total discharge control,[149] and must be covered by a discharge permit.[150] Operators of the treatment facilities must comply with relevant discharge standards, the total control quota and permit conditions.[151] Local environmental bureaus supervise and inspect the concentration levels and total discharge of KWPs.[152] To ensure the wastewater treatment facilities function properly and are able to treat the waste effectively, the WPPCL (2017) requires discharge to wastewater treatment facilities to meet the relevant effluent discharge standards.[153]

Treating wastewater generates sludge in semi-solid and solid forms[154] that must be disposed of safely to prevent secondary pollution. Random dumping of sludge on farmland has caused serious site contamination and has threatened food safety. The Water Action Plan (2015) expressly bans the dumping of untreated sludge on farmland and targets a 90 per cent treatment rate for both semi-solid and solid sludge by end-2020 in prefecture-level cities.[155] Under the WPPCL (2017), operators of wastewater treatment facilities and sludge disposal entities have a duty of safe treatment and disposal of sludge, meeting relevant state standards and recording the collection, transport, storage and treatment of sludge and its final destination.[156] They must take measures to control pollution by sludge from the point at which it is generated, through storage, transportation and treatment, to its eventual disposal by incineration, landfill or composting.

[144] WPPCL (2017), art. 49(3).
[145] Although the 85 per cent rate was achieved for county towns in 2015, China's fast-moving urbanization means that governments cannot rest on their laurels, but must continue to act if those levels are to be maintained.
[146] Water Action Plan (2015), part I, s. 2(1).
[147] WPPCL (2017), art. 49(4).
[148] Water Action Plan (2015), part V, s. 14(2).
[149] WPPCL (2017), art. 10.
[150] WPPCL (2017), art. 21.
[151] WPPCL (2017), art. 50(2).
[152] WPPCL (2017), art. 50(3).
[153] WPPCL (2017), art. 50(1). Under the Integrated Wastewater Discharge Standard (GB8978-1996), different effluent standards are set for discharge to wastewater treatment facilities, to inland waters and to the sea.
[154] WPPCL (2017), art. 102(4).
[155] Water Action Plan (2015), part I, s. 2(3).
[156] WPPCL (2017), art. 51.

6.5.5 Control of Water Pollution in Rural Areas

Water pollution in rural China presents a dire picture due to long-term neglect by state regulation. According to the first national survey of polluting sources, rural sources contribute to 43.7 percent of the total discharge of COD, 57.2 per cent of the total discharge of nitrogen and 67.4 per cent of the total discharge of phosphorus.[157] There is a serious lack of infrastructure for the collection and treatment of solid waste and wastewater in rural China. At the end of 2015, 40 per cent of villages did not have any solid waste collection and treatment facilities, and 82 per cent did not have wastewater treatment plants.[158] The overall wastewater treatment rate in rural China was 1 per cent in 2006, 6 per cent in 2010 and nearly 10 per cent in 2014.[159] Most household waste and wastewater is disposed of without any treatment, contaminating land and water and threatening the safety of drinking water. In addition, there has been exponential growth of pollution caused by mining and smelting, pesticides and fertilizers, irrigation with sewage, sludge reuse, livestock farms and rural households. Contamination of farmland continues to threaten food safety in China. Among all types of pollutants surveyed, heavy metals pose the highest risk to human health.[160] The Water Action Plan (2015) urges the acceleration of comprehensive environmental treatment in rural China to control pollution from all sources and improve wastewater treatment.[161] Building infrastructure requires government action, but the WPPCL (2017) only provides a general requirement for the state to support the construction of facilities for wastewater and solid waste treatment in rural regions, promoting centralized treatment as a state goal.[162] It is the responsibility of local governments to coordinate and plan the construction of treatment facilities for wastewater and solid waste, and ensure their proper operation.[163] Municipal wastewater treatment facilities or services may be extended to cover rural regions.[164]

New infrastructure is also needed for the collection, treatment and use of animal waste and wastewater from livestock farms. China has seen rapid growth in animal husbandry, a pillar of the rural economy. Solid waste and wastewater from intensive livestock and poultry production have become major sources of pollution in rural areas.[165] Treatment before discharge or disposal has been lacking. While the WPPCL (2017) includes a general requirement for the state to 'support' the construction of treatment facilities at livestock and poultry farms to enable the comprehensive use or treatment of animal waste and wastewater,[166] it also requires county and township governments to organize door-to-door collection of animal waste and wastewater – which will be taken for centralized treatment – from individual households engaging in livestock and poultry farming.[167] Operators of livestock farms must ensure proper operation of their treatment facilities and comply with

[157] MEP et al., *Gazette on the First National Survey of Polluting Sources* (National Bureau of Statistics, 2010). The survey was conducted by the MEP, National Bureau of Statistics and MOA.

[158] Lu Hao et al. (eds.), *Understanding the Law*, at 161.

[159] Lu Hao et al. (eds.), *Understanding the Law*, at 164.

[160] MEP and MLR, *National Soil Pollution Survey Report*, 17 April 2014. www.mee.gov.cn/gkml/sthjbgw/qt/201404/W020140417558995804588.pdf

[161] Water Action Plan (2015), part I, s. 3. [162] WPPCL (2017), art. 52(1). [163] WPPCL (2017), art. 52(2).

[164] Water Action Plan (2015), part I, s. 3(4). [165] Yonglong Lu et al., 'Impacts of soil', at 6.

[166] WPPCL (2017), art. 56(1). [167] WPPCL (2017), art. 56(3).

the effluent discharge standards to prevent water contamination.[168] The Water Action Plan (2015) requires the designation of special zones where livestock and poultry farms are prohibited.[169] Existing livestock and poultry farms in the designated zones were to be closed or relocated by end-2017. The three most economically advanced regions of Beijing–Tianjin–Hebei, the Yangtze River Delta and Pearl River Delta were required to accomplish the task by end-2016.[170] By the end of 2017, a total of 92,000 zones had been designated in 26 provinces for a ban on livestock and poultry farming.[171]

In addition to the need for new infrastructure, there is a real urgency to control pollution from agricultural run-off that contains residues of fertilizers and pesticides, and pollution caused by aquatic farms. Farming in China consumes much greater than average amounts of fertilizers, pesticides and drugs, and in a less efficient way.[172] China's arable land accounts for 7 per cent of the world's total, yet China is responsible for one-seventh of the world's total pesticide consumption. China is the world's largest fertilizer producer and ranks fourth in fertilizer consumption. In contrast to the high consumption is the low efficiency rate; only 30 to 40 per cent of fertilizer and pesticides applied is actually used.[173] Excessive amounts of chemical residues end up in the soil, washed into surface waterbodies by rainwater and permeating to underground aquifers. As a non-point source, agricultural run-off cannot rely on the end-of-pipe control applied to point sources. The only solution is to target the source and process, meaning the quality of fertilizers and pesticides used and how they are applied by farmers, including quantity, frequency and means of application. First, the WPPCL (2017) requires standards to be set for the quality and application of fertilizers and pesticides and that these standards meet the needs of water protection.[174] Second, it requires safe use of pesticides in accordance with state regulations and standards[175] and tight control over the transportation and storage of pesticides, as well as safe disposal of expired pesticides to prevent water pollution.[176] Third, the WPPCL (2017) imposes a duty on the agricultural authorities of local governments to provide training and guidance for farmers on scientific and rational use of fertilizers and pesticides, to promote the technique of testing soil before applying fertilizer and the use of highly efficient low-toxicity and low-residue pesticides, and to control excessive use of fertilizers and pesticides in order to prevent water pollution.[177] The Water Action Plan (2015) aims to improve fertilizer efficiency to more than 40 per cent by end-2020 through widely promoting scientific techniques in fertilizer application.[178]

Aquaculture is increasingly a contributor to water pollution. Some farmers not only overburden the carrying capacity of the waters, but also overuse fish feed and drugs in their pursuit of fast growth. The excess feed and drugs create water pollution, and the waste

[168] WPPCL (2017), art. 56(2). [169] Water Action Plan (2015), part I, s. 3(1).
[170] Water Action Plan (2015), part I, s. 3(1).
[171] Li Ganjie, *Report of the State Council on 2017 Environmental Status and Achievement of Environmental Targets* (2018). The report was presented by Li Ganjie, minister of ecology and environment, on 25 April 2018 to the 13th NPCSC at its 2nd session.
[172] MEP, National Groundwater Pollution Prevention and Control Plan (2011).
[173] Lu Hao et al. (eds.), *Understanding the Law*, at 167. [174] WPPCL (2017), art. 53.
[175] WPPCL (2017), art. 54(1). [176] WPPCL (2017), art. 54(2). [177] WPPCL (2017), art. 55.
[178] Water Action Plan (2015), part I, s. 3(2).

generated by overcrowded and dead fish further contaminates the water. The WPPCL (2017) requires farmers to protect the ecological environment of waters by scientific determination of the appropriate breeding density and reasonable use of feed and drugs.[179] Both the State Council and the state agricultural authority have issued regulations, provisions, standards and guidelines on the production and application of feedstuff, aquaculture safety, application of fish feed and drugs.

Last, irrigation with sewage is causing extensive farmland contamination and threatening food safety and public health, as toxic and hazardous pollutants enter the food chains of crops, vegetables and fruits. Widespread substandard mining and smelting operations generate large quantities of heavy metals that are discharged without treatment and then contaminate farmland through sewage irrigation, particularly in southern China where mineral resources are abundant.[180] China has irrigated with untreated sewage since the 1950s to alleviate a serious shortage of water available for agricultural use. An official survey in the 1980s found 86 per cent of the area receiving sewage irrigation used sewage that did not meet the standards for irrigation water quality, and 65 per cent of sewage irrigation area was contaminated with heavy metals, including mercury, lead and cadmium.[181] A more recent survey found that thirty-nine of fifty-five sewage irrigation areas were contaminated by toxins, including cadmium and arsenic.[182] In addition to the general requirement that irrigation water must meet the Water Quality Standards for Farmland Irrigation (GB 5084-2005) to prevent contamination of soil, groundwater and agricultural produce,[183] the WPPCL (2017) prohibits the discharge of industrial effluent and sewage from hospitals and clinics to irrigation canals. Any party discharging municipal wastewater, wastewater from livestock and poultry farms or wastewater from plants that process agricultural products to irrigation canals must ensure that the water at the nearest points from which water is drawn meets the Water Quality Standards for Farmland Irrigation (GB 5084-2005).[184]

6.5.6 Control of Vessel-Generated Pollution

China's economic growth and its expansion in global trade have made vessel-generated water pollution an increasing concern. Vessels, whether for shipping or fishing purposes, generate solid waste and wastewater during operation and while under way. In addition to sewage, vessels generate wastewater containing oil and chemicals, and carry ballast water containing pathogens and alien aquatic species.

To control the discharge of untreated solid waste and wastewater from vessels, the WPPCL (2017) strictly prohibits the dumping of garbage or discharge of waste oil or oil residue from vessels.[185] In the case of wastewater containing oil or sewage generated by vessels, the WPPCL (2017) does not ban discharge completely, but requires compliance with vessel discharge standards. Ocean-going vessels (OGVs) must comply with discharge standards set for inland waters when they are in port or in inland waters.[186] Where a vessel

179 WPPCL (2017), art. 57.
180 Yonglong Lu et al., 'Impacts of soil'.
181 Yonglong Lu et al., 'Impacts of soil', at 6.
182 MEP and MLR, *National Soil Pollution Survey Report.*
183 WPPCL (2017), art. 58(1).
184 WPPCL (2017), art. 58(2).
185 WPPCL (2017), art. 59(2) and (3).
186 WPPCL (2017), art. 59(1).

carries oil or toxic substances, it must take effective measures to prevent spill or leakage and ensure that no cargo falls into the water, causing contamination.[187]

Vessels normally carry ballast water to ensure safe and efficient operation throughout a voyage. Ballast water reduces stress on the hull, provides transverse stability, improves propulsion and manoeuvrability and compensates for changes in the weight of the load carried. However, ballast water always contains bacteria, microbes, small invertebrates, eggs, cysts and larvae of various species. The discharge of ballast water at the destination leaves these in the host environment, potentially causing an invasion of alien species that may outcompete native species. China is a party to the International Maritime Organization's ballast water convention,[188] which aims to halt the spread of invasive aquatic species that may cause ecological catastrophes, a loss of biodiversity and substantial economic damage. The WPPCL (2017) requires international vessels entering China's inland waters to treat the ballast water or take other measures to remove or render harmless all aquatic organisms and pathogens prior to its discharge.[189]

All vessels are required to install pollution-control devices and hold relevant licences and documents relating to water pollution control.[190] They must discharge in full compliance with the operation procedures stipulated by the maritime authority and record the discharge in the log book.[191] While it is the responsibility of the vessel owner and operator to prevent and control pollution (based on the polluter-pays principle), on-board treatment is of limited effect due to space restrictions and difficulties in disposing of sludge. A better approach is to pass vessel-generated solid waste and wastewater to facilities on land for treatment and disposal. It is thus necessary to ensure that ports, docks, loading and unloading stations and shipyards have infrastructure to receive, transport, treat and dispose of vessel-generated solid waste and wastewater. The WPPCL (2017) requires local governments to coordinate the planning and construction of facilities for the collection, transfer, treatment and disposal of vessel-generated pollution.[192] Ports, docks, loading and unloading stations and shipyards must have adequate facilities to accept vessel-generated solid waste and wastewater for treatment. Operators that collect waste or clean vessels that carry oil or toxic and hazardous substances must have the capacity and qualifications to handle the waste.[193]

[187] WPPCL (2017), art. 59(4).

[188] International Convention for the Control and Management of Ship's Ballast Water and Sediments, London, 13 February 2004. https://treaties.un.org/doc/Publication/UNTS/No%20Volume/55544/Part/I-55544-080000028053b465.pdf. The Convention was adopted by the International Maritime Organization in 2004 and entered into force on 8 September 2017. The Convention requires ships to manage their ballast water to remove, render harmless or avoid the uptake or discharge of aquatic organisms and pathogens within ballast water and sediments. All ships engaged in international trade must manage their ballast water and sediments to certain standards, according to a ship-specific ballast-water management plan. All ships also have to carry a ballast-water record book and an International Ballast Water Management Certificate. Most ships will need to install an on-board system to treat ballast water and eliminate unwanted organisms.

[189] WPPCL (2017), art. 59(5). The Water Action Plan (2015) requires international vessels navigating in the waters of China to either carry out ballast-water exchange before entering a port or install ballast-water management equipment on board to eliminate harmful aquatic organisms and pathogens. See Water Action Plan (2015), part I, s. 4(1).

[190] WPPCL (2017), art. 60(1). [191] WPPCL (2017), art. 60. [192] WPPCL (2017), art. 61(1).

[193] WPPCL (2017), art. 61(2). The Water Action Plan (2015) set deadlines for ports, docks, loading and unloading stations and shipyards to have infrastructure to receive, transfer, treat and dispose of vessel-generated waste and wastewater: by end-2017 for coastal facilities and end-2020 for inland rivers. See Water Action Plan (2015), part I, s. 4(2).

Where vessels or other operators engage in activities posing pollution risks, they must take effective measures to prevent pollution. Both maritime and fishery authorities supervise and monitor the operation of vessels and relevant parties in order to prevent pollution.[194] In the case of vessel-to-vessel transfer of bulk toxic liquids, vessel operators must compile a work plan, take measures to ensure safety and prevent pollution and seek approval from the local maritime authorities.[195]

Vessels are dismantled and recycled at the end of their service lives. Ships may contain hazardous substances, such as asbestos, heavy metals, hydrocarbons and ozone-depleting substances, meaning that shipbreaking poses risks to both human health and the environment. The old-fashioned and low-cost shipbreaking on the beach discharges toxic substances without collection or treatment. China has promoted green shipbreaking since the 1990s.[196] The WPPCL (2017) expressly prohibits vessel dismantling on beaches in order to prevent toxic contamination of beaches and waters.[197]

6.6 SAFETY OF DRNKING WATER

The threat to the safety of drinking water is a serious water pollution issue deserving immediate attention and action.[198] In 2015, an NPCSC inspection report found that in only 84.5 per cent of the 329 cities inspected did drinking water sources used for central water supply meet the relevant WQS. Drinking water supply in rural areas is left without any protection, monitoring or supervision. Serious groundwater contamination is found in many parts of China.[199] To address China's drinking water crisis, both the WPPCL (2017) and the Water Action Plan (2015) provide for regulatory control to ensure drinking water safety from source to tap, covering risk assessment and control, monitoring and inspection of water quality at DWSRs, water suppliers and the taps of end-consumers. They further strengthen rules on emergency response, information disclosure and building water supply infrastructure, in order to ensure the safety of drinking water. In addition, specialized plans on drinking water safety have been issued: the National Plan on the Protection of Drinking-Water-Source Reserves in Cities (2008–2020) (Plan on DWSRs) (2008–2020),[200] the National Plan to Ensure Drinking Water Hygiene and Safety in Cities (2011–2020)[201] and the 12th FYP on Safe Drinking Water Projects in Rural China (2011-15).[202]

[194] WPPCL (2017), art. 62(1). [195] WPPCL (2017), art. 62(2).

[196] The NDRC issued the General Standards on Green Shipbreaking (2005) and issued the Opinion on Regulating the Development of the Shipbreaking Industry (2009) jointly with other ministries, including the Ministry of Commerce (MOC), Ministry of Industry and Information Technology (MIIT), MOF, MEP, Ministry of Transport, MOA and the General Administration of Customs (GAC) to phase out shipbreaking on the beach.

[197] WPPCL (2017), art. 62(3).

[198] In 2015, the NPCSC formed an inspection and supervision team to examine the implementation of the WPPCL (2008). It produced the *Report of the NPCSC Inspection Team on the Implementation of the WPPCL*, which was presented to the 12th NPCSC by Chen Changzhi.

[199] Chen Changzhi, *Report of the NPCSC Inspection Team on the Implementation of the WPPCL.*

[200] The Plan on DWSRs was issued by the MEP, NDRC, MOHURD, MWR and Ministry of Health on 11 June 2010

[201] The National Plan to Ensure Drinking Water Hygiene and Safety in Cities (2011–2020) was issued by the MOH, NDRC, MEP, MOHURD and MWR on 30 December 2011. It came into force with immediate effect.

[202] The 12th FYP on Safe Drinking Water Projects in Rural China (2011–15) was issued by the NDRC, MWR, MOH and MEP upon approval by the State Council on 21 March 2012.

6.6.1 DWSRs

The state has adopted a DWSR system under which Grade I and Grade II DWSRs are designated for special protection, and projects and activities that carry a risk of water contamination are prohibited or restricted. Quasi-reserves may be designated as buffer zones for enhanced protection of drinking water sources.[203] A DWSR is proposed by the municipal or county government and approved by the provincial government. Where a DWSR cuts across municipal or county boundaries, the designation is made jointly and in consultation with the relevant municipal or county governments and submitted to the provincial government for approval. In case of dispute or lack of consensus, the provincial environmental bureau proposes the designation of the DWSR in collaboration with provincial bureaus in charge of water resources, land and resources, health and construction, and submits it to the provincial government for approval.[204] Where a DWSR cuts across provincial boundaries, the designation is made by relevant provincial governments in consultation with the river basin management authority. In case of dispute or lack of consensus, the state environmental authority proposes the designation in collaboration with ministries in charge of water resources, public health and construction, and submits it to the State Council for approval.[205] Both the State Council and provincial governments may adjust the area designated as a DWSR to ensure the safety of the drinking water supply. Local governments must install clear signs at the boundary of a DWSR and must warn that certain activities are prohibited.[206] The WPPCL (2017) prohibits the construction of wastewater discharge outlets in DWSRs.[207] The ban applies to both Grade I and Grade II DWSRs.

Within the boundaries of a Grade I DWSR, there is a prohibition on constructing new projects or altering or expanding existing projects unrelated to water supply facilities or water source protection. Local governments must order existing projects unrelated to water supply facilities or water source protection to be demolished or closed down.[208] Activities such as cage breeding of aquatic species, tourism, swimming, fishing or any activity that may contaminate drinking water is prohibited in a Grade I DWSR.[209] The Plan on DWSRs (2008–2020) requires fences to be built around some Grade I DWSRs, with signs indicating the boundary of the DWSR and the measures taken to prevent pollution at the points at which water is drawn.[210] It aims to eliminate all existing sources of pollution within Grade I DWSRs by demolishing buildings, shutting down discharge outlets and relocating residents, farms and rubbish dumps.[211]

In Grade II DWSRs, there is a prohibition on constructing new projects and altering or expanding existing projects that discharge pollutants. Where existing projects discharge pollutants, local governments must order them to be demolished or closed down.[212] Anyone

[203] WPPCL (2017), art. 63(1). [204] WPPCL (2017), art. 63(2). [205] WPPCL (2017), art. 63(3).

[206] WPPCL (2017), art. 63(4). Detailed rules on the designation of DWSRs and protection measures are provided by the Measures on Pollution Prevention and Control at Drinking-Water-Source Reserves (1989), which was issued by the National Environmental Protection Agency (NEPA, predecessor of the MEP), Ministry of Health, Ministry of Construction, MWR and Ministry of Geology and Minerals (now part of the MLR) on 10 July 1989 with immediate effect.

[207] WPPCL (2017), art. 64. [208] WPPCL (2017), art. 65(1). [209] WPPCL (2017), art. 65(2).

[210] Plan on DWSRs (2008–2020), art. 15(1). [211] Plan on DWSRs (2008–2020), art. 15(2).

[212] WPPCL (2017), art. 66(1).

conducting cage breeding, tourism or other activities must take measures to prevent contamination of the drinking water.[213] The Plan on DWSRs (2008–2020) targets both point sources and non-point sources located in Grade II DWSRs. Pollution from point sources can be resolved by shutting down or relocating discharge outlets or enterprises.[214] To tackle pollution from the non-point sources of agriculture, households, livestock farming and water transport within the Grade II DWSR, the Plan on DWSRs (2008–2020) proposes measures to control use of fertilizer and pesticides, turn waste into resources, provide central collection and transfer of waste and ban livestock farming and water transport.[215]

Limited control is imposed on quasi-DWSRs. At quasi-DWSRs, there is a prohibition on constructing new projects or expanding projects that are likely to cause serious water pollution. In the case of alteration of an existing project, there can be no increase in the total effluent discharge.[216] The State Council and provincial governments have the power to impose further restrictions to prohibit or limit the use of fertilizers, pesticides and detergents containing phosphorus, and to curb planting or breeding activities.[217]

6.6.2 Protection of Groundwater

Groundwater is a major source of drinking water supply in northern China,[218] and groundwater contamination by heavy metals, organic pollutants and carcinogens continues to pose a serious threat to public health.[219] The sources of contamination include leaking sewage pipes, landfill leachate, petrol stations, industrial-waste dump sites, petrochemical operations and discharge of untreated industrial wastewater to wells, pits or fissures, as well as farming activities including the overuse of fertilizers and pesticides, and irrigating with sewage.[220]

The WPPCL (2017) prohibits the discharge of wastewater to seepage wells, pits, fissures or karst caves, or through hidden pipes.[221] In order to prevent contamination of groundwater by high-risk operators, the WPPCL (2017) requires operators and managers of chemical production enterprises and industrial zones, mining zones, tailings ponds, HW disposal facilities and landfills to take measures to prevent seepage of wastewater and to install monitoring devices at underground aquifers.[222] Operators of petrol stations are required to use double-layer underground oil tanks or construct an anti-seepage pond to avoid contaminating groundwater.[223] Ditches or pits without anti-seepage measures may not be used to transmit or store sewage containing pathogens or toxic wastewater.[224] When engaging in activities such as constructing underground engineering facilities or underground exploitation and mining, measures must be taken to prevent groundwater contamination.[225] Abandoned underground mines, boreholes and wells must be sealed or restored.[226] The exploitation of each layer of a multi-layer groundwater source must be carried out separately if there is great disparity in the water quality of the layers. Where groundwater is already contaminated, each layer must be

213 WPPCL (2017), art. 66(2). 214 Plan on DWSRs (2008–2020), art. 15(3).
215 Plan on DWSRs (2008–2020), art. 15(4). 216 WPPCL (2017), art. 67. 217 WPPCL (2017), art. 73.
218 Plan on DWSRs (2008–2020), art. 1.
219 National Plan on Groundwater Pollution Prevention and Control (2011–2020), part 1.
220 National Plan on Groundwater Pollution Prevention and Control (2011–2020), part 1.
221 WPPCL (2017), art. 39. 222 WPPCL (2017), art. 40(1). 223 WPPCL (2017), art. 40(2).
224 WPPCL (2017), art. 40(3). 225 WPPCL (2017), art. 42(1). 226 WPPCL (2017), art. 42(2).

extracted separately.[227] Where groundwater sources are artificially recharged, this must not cause the water quality to deteriorate.[228]

The Water Action Plan (2015) requires regular survey and assessment of the water quality at groundwater aquifers that are sources for centralized water supply. Anti-seepage measures must be taken on the sites of petrochemical production, storage and sales, industrial parks, mining sites, landfills and petrol stations. High-risk and seriously contaminated groundwater aquifers in regions such as Beijing–Tianjin–Hebei must be disclosed to the public and clean-up and restoration carried out.[229] Measures are also in place to prevent and control over-exploitation of groundwater. Wells built without approval in an area served by a centralized drinking water supply network will be shut down. In north China, where over-exploitation of groundwater is a serious problem, the industrial, agricultural and service sectors are not allowed to abstract extra groundwater over the 2015 extraction level. By the end of 2017, relevant departments must have designated the zones subject to a ban or restriction on groundwater exploitation.[230]

6.6.3 Ecological Compensation

The legal protection for the safety of drinking water, together with the DWSR mechanism, imposes a ban or restriction on industrial and economic activities in designated areas. This affects the livelihoods of local people, who sacrifice their opportunities for economic development and an improved standard of living to conserve and protect water resources. Ecological compensation is based on the principles of fairness and user pays. The WPPCL (2017) requires the state to establish an ecological compensation regime to make payments to people living in the DWSRs and the upper reaches of rivers, lakes and reservoirs.[231]

6.6.4 Local Governments

Local governments have wide-ranging responsibilities to ensure the safety of drinking water. First, they must take engineering measures or build wetlands and water-source-preservation forests in quasi-DWSRs to ensure water is safe for human consumption.[232] Quasi-DWSRs are set up as needed outside Grade II DWSRs to protect the DWSR water quality.[233] To enhance the ecological function of a quasi-DWSR in maintaining the water quality and quantity of a DWSR, local governments are required to build and conserve wetlands and forests within the quasi-DWSR and take other measures to ensure the water quality at DWSRs meets state standards.

Second, local governments are held accountable for the safety of drinking water. They must assess, manage and control risks that endanger the safety of drinking water. The water supply from source to tap involves private entities and many different government

[227] WPPCL (2017), art. 41. [228] WPPCL (2017), art. 43. [229] Water Action Plan (2015), part VIII, s. 24(3).

[230] Water Action Plan (2015), part III, s. 8(2). This was achieved, according to the MEE. See Li Ganjie, *Report of the State Council on 2017 Environmental Status and Achievement of Environmental Targets.*

[231] WPPCL (2017), art. 8. [232] WPPCL (2017), art. 68.

[233] WPPCL (2017), art. 67. While quasi-DWSRs are not subject to the ban or restrictions imposed on DWSRs, the WPPCL (2017) prohibits the construction of new projects that will cause serious water pollution or the expansion of existing projects that cause serious water pollution, and any alteration of a project that will increase the pollution load.

bureaus[234] and, therefore, it requires leadership, supervision and coordination from local governments. They must organize and conduct risk investigation and assessment at DWSRs, groundwater aquifers and at areas surrounding the water supply companies, and take measures to prevent and control pollution risks.[235] Where there is an imminent threat to the safety of drinking water, environmental bureaus must order the relevant entities or production operators to stop discharging effluent and notify water supply entities and relevant agencies in charge of water supply, public health and water resources.[236]

Third, local governments play a major role in building infrastructure that will ensure the safety of drinking water. In cities with single-source water supply, municipal governments must construct an emergency or spare water supply source. If possible, local governments should develop regional water supply networks.[237] The construction of emergency or spare water supply sources should be completed by end-2020 or earlier.[238] The emergency or spare water sources may be surface water, groundwater, water from other regions or from regional networks, but they must be sources different to and separate from the regular water supply and not subject to the same risks. In addition, local governments must arrange sources of drinking water supply in rural areas. Where possible, urban water supply networks should be extended to rural areas to develop a centralized water supply system for rural China.[239] There is an urgent need to improve the protection of drinking water sources and the testing of water quality in rural regions in order to address the safety risks involved in taking untreated drinking water from scattered and unmanaged small-scale sources.

Last, information disclosure is a major responsibility of the local governments, who must monitor and assess the water quality at DWSRs, water supply companies and consumer taps. The data must be published on at least a quarterly basis.[240] Public access to this crucial information, which directly affects people's health and safety, facilitates supervision and improves governance. The Water Action Plan (2015) sets a clear schedule for the local governments to disclose monitoring data to the public. Municipal governments were required to disclose drinking water monitoring data on a quarterly basis from the beginning of 2016, and all governments at county level and above were required to release quarterly data from the beginning of 2018.[241]

6.6.5 Suppliers of Drinking Water

Water suppliers play a crucial role in ensuring the safety of drinking water from source to tap. They collect water from DWSRs, treat it and deliver it to consumers whose health and safety depends on its quality. The WPPCL (2017) makes water suppliers accountable for the quality of the drinking water. The water they supply must meet the relevant state standards,

[234] This includes environmental bureaus and water resources bureaus in charge of water quality at the source, housing and construction bureaus in charge of water suppliers and water supply networks, and health bureaus in charge of the safety of tap water.

[235] WPPCL (2017), art. 69(1). [236] WPPCL (2017), art. 69(2). [237] WPPCL (2017), art. 70(1).

[238] Water Action Plan (2015), part VIII, s.24(2). [239] WPPCL (2017), art. 70(2).

[240] WPPCL (2017), art. 72.

[241] Water Action Plan (2015), part VIII, s.24(1). Unfortunately not all governments have disclosed the data; see Li Zhanshu, *NPCSC Inspection Report on Implementation of the WPPCL* (2019). www pkulaw.cn. The report was presented on 23 August 2019 by Li Zhanshu, chairman of the NPCSC, to the 13th NPCSC at its 12th session.

including the Hygiene Standard for Drinking Water (GB5749-2006). Suppliers must ensure the water supply system is operating safely and is reliable.[242] In addition, they must test and monitor the quality of water at the water collection points and at the point it exits the water supply company. If a supplier detects substandard water at either a collection or supply point, it must take timely measures and immediately report to its supervisory agency, which in turn must notify the relevant environmental bureau, health bureau and water resources bureau.[243] The water quality at the collection point must comply with the Water Quality Standard for Drinking Water Sources (CJ3020-93), while water at the supply point must comply with the Hygiene Standard for Drinking Water (GB5749-2006). Where any risk to water safety is detected or a pollution incident has occurred, water suppliers and relevant government bureaus must take emergency response measures.

6.7 WATER POLLUTION INCIDENTS AND EMERGENCY RESPONSE

After decades of intensive economic growth and large-scale industrialization at an unprecedented speed, China faced a high risk of pollution incidents. The 2005 pollution incident at the Songhua River not only forced the head of the SEPA to resign, but also served as a wake-up call that immediate action was needed to strengthen China's emergency response mechanism.

Songhua River Toxic Spill (2005)[244]

On 13 November 2005, an explosion occurred at the Jilin branch of PetroChina Co. Firefighters used water to contain the heavy smoke and dust, but it was estimated that 100 t of benzene, nitrobenzene and other toxic substances spilt into the Songhua River, located 500 m from the factory. By 24 November, the toxic contaminants had arrived in Harbin, the provincial capital of Heilongjiang. The city had suspended its water supply on 22 November, causing serious economic losses and inconvenience for the residents.

Both the Jilin branch of PetroChina Co. and the local Jilin government were slow in communicating information. Whether this was due to a lack of ability in emergency response or an intentional cover-up, people affected by the suspension of water supplies lacked information and panicked. Without an emergency response plan in place and without the necessary preparation and training, firefighters used a large amount of water on the explosion sites and discharged toxic water directly to the Songhua River, causing severe secondary pollution.

The environmental disaster caused by the Jilin branch of PetroChina Co. was only the tip of the iceberg. Of China's 7,555 large-scale heavily polluting chemical projects, 81 per cent are located by rivers, in densely populated areas and other environmentally sensitive zones.

[242] WPPCL (2017), art. 71(2). [243] WPPCL (2017), art. 71(1).

[244] For more discussion of the case, see Wang Jin et al., 'Reflections from the transboundary pollution of Songhua River' in Michael Faure and Song Ying (eds.) *China and International Environmental Liability: Legal Remedies for Transboundary Pollution* (Cheltenham and Northampton, MA: Edward Elgar, 2008), 273–90; Wang Canfa et al., 'Pondering over the incident of Songhua River pollution from the perspective of environmental law' in Faure and Song (eds.), *China and International Environmental* Liability, 291–314; Song Ying, 'International legal aspects of the Songhua River incident' in Faure and Song (eds.), *China and International Environmental Liability*, 315–32.

Further, 45 per cent of the 7,555 are assessed to be very high-risk sources of pollution.[245] They operate by rivers for easy access to water, but pose a high risk of pollution to nearby rivers and the health and safety of local residents.

The lesson learned from the Songhua River toxic contamination was the crucial importance of risk management and emergency response. The State Council issued the National Environmental Emergency Response Plan (2006) (NEERP),[246] which was followed by the Law on Emergency Response (2007)[247] to put in place working mechanisms for effective prevention, timely response and recovery in order to minimize and contain harm caused by emergencies. The MEP also issued the Measures on Environmental Emergency Response (2015)[248] to implement the Law on Emergency Response (2007), the EPL (2014) and NEERP (2014) and to prevent, control, mitigate and eliminate any harm caused by environmental emergencies and protect the health and safety of the public, the environment and public and private property.[249]

The WPPCL (2017) makes it the joint responsibility of both governments and polluters to prevent and control harm caused by pollution incidents. Governments of all levels, relevant agencies and entities likely to cause pollution incidents are required to follow strictly the Law on Emergency Response (2007), to be prepared for water pollution emergencies, respond to emergencies in a timely manner and follow up with recovery work.[250] The Water Action Plan (2015) clarifies governments' responsibilities in making and improving response plans for water pollution emergencies by specifying the parties in charge and clarifying the procedures for warning, forecast, response, recovery and timely disclosure of relevant information.[251]

An enterprise or institution likely to cause water pollution incidents must have an emergency response plan in place, make good preparations and carry out routine drills.[252] Entities that manufacture or store hazardous chemicals must take measures to prevent the discharge of potentially toxic untreated wastewater generated in an emergency response.[253] To prevent and mitigate water pollution caused by vessels, the Water Action Plan (2015) requires operators of ports, docks or loading and unloading stations to prepare emergency response plans in case a pollution incident occurs during the reception, transfer, treatment or disposal of vessel-generated waste or wastewater contaminated by oil or chemicals.[254] Where a water pollution incident is caused or likely to be caused, liable enterprises or institutions must immediately activate emergency response plans, take emergency response measures, including isolation of polluting sources, to prevent toxic pollutants from entering surface waterbodies directly or indirectly, and report to the local government or environmental bureau, which must immediately report to the same-level government and notify relevant

[245] Lu Hao et al. (eds.), *Understanding the Law*, at 226.

[246] The National Environmental Emergency Response Plan was issued by the State Council on 24 January 2006. It came into force with immediate effect. It was revised and re-issued on 29 December 2014. The revision came into force with immediate effect.

[247] The Law on Emergency Response was enacted on 30 August 2007 by the Standing Committee of the 10th NPC at its 29th session. The law came into force on 1 November 2007.

[248] The Measures on Environmental Emergency Response were issued by the MEP on 16 April 2015 and came into force on 5 June 2015.

[249] Measures on Environmental Emergency Response (2015), art. 1.

[250] WPPCL (2017), art. 76.

[251] Water Action Plan (2015), part VII, s. 22(2).

[252] WPPCL (2017), art. 77(1).

[253] WPPCL (2017), art. 77(2).

[254] Water Action Plan (2015), part I, s. 4(2).

departments.[255] Where an entity causes a fishery pollution incident, or a water pollution incident is caused by its fishery vessel, the entity must report to the local fishery bureau for investigation and punishment. An incident caused by a vessel other than a fishery vessel must be reported to the local maritime bureau for investigation and punishment.[256]

To prevent and control any water pollution incident that threatens drinking water safety, the WPPCL (2017) requires municipal and county governments to organize the preparation of emergency response plans for drinking water safety.[257] The water supplier uses the municipal or county plan as the basis for the action plan it must make, which is submitted to the municipal or county government for the record; the supplier must also conduct regular drills.[258] Where a water pollution incident occurs at a DWSR, or any other emergency incident occurs that may affect the safety of drinking water, water suppliers must take immediate emergency response measures, report to the municipal or county governments and inform the public. The relevant government must take effective measures to ensure the safety of drinking water.[259]

6.8 ENFORCEMENT: MONITORING, INSPECTION AND SANCTION

Weak enforcement has long been blamed for China's environmental degradation. To strengthen enforcement, the WPPCL (2017) grants powers in clear terms to local agencies and facilitates their exercise of power by punishing those who obstruct enforcement.

6.8.1 Monitoring

Monitoring is a crucial link in the control of water pollution. There are two types of monitoring under the WPPCL (2017): self-monitoring and regulatory monitoring. Self-monitoring is conducted by operators or polluters to monitor and record both volume and concentration of wastewater discharged from their pipes. Regulatory monitoring is conducted by regulatory agencies on both the water quality and effluent discharge.

Self-monitoring is required of entities that are subject to permit control. They must monitor their effluent discharge and keep records of the raw monitoring data.[260] Further, entities designated as key polluting units (KPUs) are required to install and maintain automatic effluent monitoring equipment and connect this to the environmental bureau's monitoring network in order to transmit real-time data on effluent discharge. They must ensure the proper operation of the monitoring devices.[261] Municipal environmental bureaus must issue a list of KPUs, taking into account the environmental carrying capacity of the region, the total discharge quota and the specific type, quantity and concentration of the pollutants discharged from each KPU.[262] To ensure data accuracy and prevent falsification, the WPPCL holds entities conducting self-monitoring accountable for the truthfulness and accuracy of the monitoring data,[263] and imposes a duty on the environmental bureau to investigate if it detects any abnormality in data transmitted from a KPU.[264]

255 WPPCL (2017), art. 78(1).
256 WPPCL (2017), art. 78(2).
257 WPPCL (2017), art. 79(1).
258 WPPCL (2017), art. 79(2).
259 WPPCL (2017), art. 79(3).
260 WPPCL (2017), art. 23(1).
261 WPPCL (2017), art. 23(1).
262 WPPCL (2017), art. 23(2).
263 WPPCL (2017), art. 24(1).
264 WPPCL (2017), art. 24(2).

Regulatory monitoring of ambient water quality has, for a long time, been conducted separately by both environmental protection authorities and water resources management authorities. They build their own water monitoring system and release monitoring data on the water quality of major rivers and lakes that is sometimes contradictory, causing confusion and wasting public resources. The Water Action Plan (2015) places great emphasis on collaboration and uniformity in monitoring and enforcement – that is, collaboration among different departments, different regions and different river basins to implement joint monitoring, enforcement, emergency responses and information sharing[265] – and uniformity in the planning of monitoring stations and networks.[266] Where a specialized water resources authority has been established for a state-designated key river or lake, it must monitor the quality of water crossing provincial boundaries and report the monitoring data to state authorities in charge of environment and water resources.[267] The WPPCL (2017) aimed to achieve uniformity and consistency of monitoring data for water quality by requiring the state environmental authority to issue technical guidelines on environmental monitoring methods, and publish uniform national water quality data, both of which it has done. As required by the WPPCL (2017), the state environmental authority worked with the MWR to design and organize monitoring networks, make uniform plans for the establishment of the monitoring stations and set up mechanisms for sharing monitoring data.[268]

Regulatory monitoring of end-of-pipe effluent discharge acts as a check on the self-monitoring carried out by the polluting entities. To facilitate monitoring by the regulatory agencies, the WPPCL (2017) requires enterprises, institutions and any other production operator to set up wastewater discharge outlets in accordance with laws, administrative regulations and provisions of the state environmental authority. Where the receiving waters are rivers or lakes, the enterprises, institutions and other production operators must also comply with relevant provisions issued by the MWR.[269]

6.8.2 Inspection

Local environmental bureaus and environmental supervision bodies have the power to inspect the premises of polluters within their jurisdiction. The operators being inspected must truthfully report relevant information and provide necessary records to the authority, which must keep commercial secrets obtained during the inspection strictly confidential.[270] The Water Action Plan (2015) requires environmental bureaus to inspect all industrial enterprises one by one and issue yellow warnings to those violating discharge standards or the total discharge quota. An enterprise in violation will be ordered to restrict or suspend production and take measures to control pollution. If an enterprise that has received a yellow warning still fails to meet the discharge requirements after treatment and rectification, it will receive a red warning and will be ordered to stop operating and permanently close the business. In addition, environmental bureaus must conduct random inspections of polluting enterprises without prior notice as a routine practice and must publicise the inspection reports.[271] The Water Action Plan (2015)

[265] Water Action Plan (2015), part 6, s. 19(1). [266] Water Action Plan (2015), part 6, s. 19(2).
[267] WPPCL (2017), art. 26. [268] WPPCL (2017), art. 25. [269] WPPCL (2017), art. 22
[270] WPPCL (2017), art. 30. [271] Water Action Plan (2015), part VI, s. 18(1).

specifically targets intentional and malicious violations, including discharge of toxic and hazardous wastewater or effluent containing pathogens via hidden pipes or into wells, pits and karst caves, as well as falsification of monitoring data and abnormal operation of wastewater treatment facilities.[272] The Water Action Plan (2015) requires environmental bureaus and the police to cooperate more closely in environmental enforcement in order to punish and deter violations more effectively.[273]

6.8.3 Administrative Sanctions

Violations are detected by inspection and monitoring, and must be followed by proper sanctions to punish and deter such violations. Under the WPPCL (2017), administrative sanctions are imposed by the government or administrative agencies, including environmental bureaus, the police, maritime and fishery administrative authorities. Decision-making on administrative sanctions is regulated by the Administrative Penalty Law[274] and subject to judicial review. Major environmental violations that are punished under the WPPCL (2017) by administrative sanctions are: agency inaction, violations relating to inspection and monitoring, unlawful discharge, unlawful toxic discharge and relevant activities, violation against clean production and state industrial policies, violation by vessels, violation endangering drinking water safety and violation causing water pollution incidents.

Agency Inaction

There is a wide range of public bodies in charge of different aspects of water pollution control and management, including environmental bureaus, maritime authorities and agencies in charge of water resources, land resources, public health, construction, agriculture and fisheries.[274] If any public body fails to grant a permit or approval in accordance with law, or fails to investigate or sanction an environmental violation upon discovering it or upon receipt of a public complaint of violation, or fails to perform any other statutory duty, the person in charge and the person directly liable will receive an administrative disciplinary sanction.[275] Typical inaction includes failure to issue a pollution discharge permit, failure to make a decision on EIA documents and failure to take proper action against an environmental violation. The Water Action Plan (2015) emphasizes the critical importance of supervision over all levels of environmental enforcement. It required a national environmental supervision mechanism to be established to monitor the performance of local governments and environmental bureaus to ensure effective environmental enforcement.[276]

Violations Relating to Inspection and Monitoring

Through on-site inspections and monitoring discharge, agencies can observe operations, review records, take samples and collect data in relation to wastewater discharge, allowing

[272] Water Action Plan (2015), part VI, s. 18(3).

[273] Water Action Plan (2015), part VI, s. 18(2). Innovative joint enforcement by EPBs and the police has been tested to sanction and deter intentional and malicious violations causing grave harm and loss to both the environment and public health.

[274] The Administrative Penalty Law was enacted on 17 March 1996 by the 8th NPC at its 4th session. It was amended on 27 August 2009 by the 11th NPCSC at its 10th session, and was amended again in 2017.

[274] WPPCL (2017), art. 9. [275] WPPCL (2017), art. 80. [276] Water Action Plan (2015), part VI, s. 18(2).

them to assess an operator's performance, ensure compliance and punish violations. Any acts that aim to interfere with agency inspection and monitoring are subject to sanctions under the WPPCL (2017). Any individual or operator who refuses inspection and supervision by an environmental bureau or any other agency, or falsifies data or records will be ordered to rectify and will be fined 20,000 yuan to 200,000 yuan.[277] Where a polluter fails to perform its monitoring duties, including: (i) self-monitoring the wastewater discharge and recording raw data; (ii) installing automatic monitoring devices with a connection to the environmental bureau's supervisory monitoring network, normal operation of the monitoring system and (iii) monitoring of toxic and hazardous wastewater discharge outlets and surrounding areas and disclosure of monitoring data, it will be ordered to rectify by a specified deadline and will be fined 20,000 yuan to 200,000 yuan. If it fails to rectify by the deadline, it will be ordered to suspend production while it rectifies the failure.[278]

Unlawful Discharge

With regard to four types of unlawful discharge, local environmental bureaus may order the parties in violation to rectify, or to restrict or suspend production to provide treatment, and impose a fine of 100,000 yuan to 1 million yuan: (i) discharge without permit; (ii) discharge in violation of discharge standards or the total discharge quota; (iii) evasion of supervision by discharge to seepage wells, pits, fissures or karst caves, via hidden pipes, through falsifying monitoring data or abnormal operation of wastewater treatment facilities and (iv) discharge to central wastewater treatment facilities without treatment.[279] Where circumstances are serious, a party in violation may be ordered to suspend or permanently close its business. This, however, requires the approval of the local people's government.[280] Shutting down a factory has an impact far greater than a temporary suspension of operations to allow for rectification to take place. A particular concern is the potentially large number of laid-off workers who must find alternative employment quickly if social instability is to be avoided.

Unlawful Toxic Discharge and Relevant Activities

If any party engages in toxic discharge or certain other activities, it will be ordered by local environmental bureaus to stop the unlawful act and take measures to clean up the toxic contamination and eliminate pollution before a specified deadline. It will also be fined. If the party fails to do as instructed, the environmental bureau must designate a capable third party to provide the treatment at the polluter's expense.[281] The amount of the fine varies depending on the nature of the effluent and the potential and actual environmental harm. A fine of 20,000 yuan to 200,000 yuan is imposed for engaging in the acts of:[282]

(i) rinsing vehicles or containers used for storage of oil or toxic pollutants in surface waterbodies;
(ii) discharge or dumping of industrial waste, MSW or other waste into surface waterbodies, or piling or storing solid waste on sloping banks below the high-water mark of rivers, lakes, canals, drains and reservoirs;

[277] WPPCL (2017), art. 81. [278] WPPCL (2017), art. 82. [279] WPPCL (2017), art. 83.
[280] WPPCL (2017), art. 83. [281] WPPCL (2017), art. 85(1). [282] WPPCL (2017), art. 85(2).

(iii) discharge of low-level radioactive wastewater, heated wastewater or sewage containing pathogens in violation of state provisions or standards;
(iv) failure to take anti-seepage measures or failure to install a groundwater monitoring well with which to conduct monitoring;
(v) failure to use a double-layer underground oil tank at a petrol station or take other measures to prevent leakage, or failure to conduct monitoring to prevent leaks.

A fine of 100,000 yuan to 1 million yuan is imposed for engaging in acts that are potentially more harmful to the environment:[283]

(i) discharge of wastewater containing oil, acid or alkali to surface waterbodies;
(ii) discharge of highly toxic wastewater to surface waterbodies, or deposit or dumping into surface waterbodies or directly burying underground highly toxic waste containing mercury, cadmium, arsenic, chromium, lead, cyanide or yellow phosphorus;
(iii) discharge of high-level or medium-level radioactive wastewater or dumping of radiative waste to surface waterbodies;
(iv) failure to take anti-seepage measures or other measures to prevent pollution; use of drains, pits or pools without anti-seepage or anti-leakage protection to transmit or store toxic wastewater, sewage containing pathogens or other waste.

If the circumstances are serious, the parties in violation will be ordered, following local government approval, to suspend their operations or permanently close.[284]

Violation of Clean Production and State Industrial Policies

To promote clean production and phase out pollution-intensive equipment and techniques and small-scale pollution-intensive plants, the WPPCL (2017) imposes sanctions, including suspension and permanent closure of business operation, against those in violation. Anyone who produces, sells, imports or uses equipment listed in the NDRC Catalogue of Prohibited Equipment, or uses a production technique listed in the NDRC Catalogue of Prohibited Techniques, will be ordered by the local economic development commission to stop doing so and will be fined between 50,000 yuan and 200,000 yuan. Where circumstances are serious, the local commission will recommend that local governments suspend or close the operations.[285] In the case of small-scale pollution-intensive plants that are constructed in violation of state industrial policies, the WPPCL (2017) requires city or county governments to shut them down.[286]

Violation by Vessels

To prevent pollution by vessels under way, the WPPCL (2017) requires vessels to: (i) install pollution prevention and control devices or equipment, (ii) hold a pollution prevention permit or document[287] and (iii) follow the rules of procedure for discharge and recording discharge in the log book.[288] Any vessel in violation of requirements (i) and (ii) will be

[283] WPPCL (2017), art. 85(2). [284] WPPCL (2017), art. 85(2). [285] WPPCL (2017), art. 86.
[286] WPPCL (2017), art. 87. Such projects may exist in a variety of sectors: papermaking, tannery, printing and dyeing, dyestuff, coking, electroplating, pesticides, asbestos, cement, glass, iron and steel, thermal power generation, refining of sulphur, arsenic, mercury and oil, and other projects causing serious water pollution.
[287] WPPCL (2017), art. 60(1). [288] WPPCL (2017), art. 60(2).

ordered by maritime or fishery authorities to rectify by a specified deadline and will be fined between 2,000 yuan and 20,000 yuan. Failure to rectify by the deadline results in the vessel being prevented from moving on.[289] Any vessel violating the third requirement will be ordered to rectify and will be fined between 2,000 yuan and 20,000 yuan.[290]

Where violation by vessels causes pollution or the threat of pollution, heavier penalties are imposed by maritime or fishery authorities. A fine of 10,000 yuan to 100,000 yuan is imposed on acts that entail a high degree of risk to the environment:[291]

(i) dumping or discharging vessel-generated waste or waste oil to surface waterbodies;
(ii) transferring bulk liquid cargo from one vessel to another without prior approval by a maritime authority, where the nature and state of the cargo pose a high risk of pollution;
(iii) vessels and relevant operators engaging in activities that entail pollution risks without taking preventative measures;
(iv) shipbreaking on the beach and
(v) discharging of ballast water in violation of relevant provisions by international vessels entering inland waters.

Where any of the above acts cause water pollution, the party liable will be fined between 20,000 yuan and 200,000 yuan and ordered to clean up the contamination and eliminate pollution by a specified deadline. If the liable party fails to do so, the relevant authority will designate a qualified third party to carry out treatment at the polluter's expense.[292]

Violation Endangering Drinking Water Safety

To ensure the safety of drinking water, the WPPCL strictly controls sources of pollution in DWSRs and imposes a duty on water supply companies to ensure drinking water safety. First, any person setting up a wastewater discharge outlet in a DWSR will be ordered by the local government to dismantle it within a specified time limit and will be fined between 100,000 yuan and 500,000 yuan. If the party in violation fails to dismantle the outlet, it will be dismantled by a third party at the expense of the party in violation, which will also be fined between 500,000 yuan and 1 million yuan, and may be ordered to suspend operations to clean up and restore the site.[293] Second, for violations relating to the construction, alteration or expansion of projects a local environmental bureau will order the unlawful act to stop, will impose a fine of 100,000 yuan to 500,000 yuan and will order the project to be dismantled or closed permanently, given the approval of the local government. Such violations are: [294]

(i) construction, alteration or expansion of projects in a Grade I DWSR that are unrelated to water supply or to the protection of water sources;
(ii) construction, alteration or expansion of projects in a Grade II DWSR that discharge pollutants or

[289] WPPCL (2017), art. 89(1). [290] WPPCL (2017), art. 89(2). [291] WPPCL (2007), art.90.
[292] WPPCL (2017), art. 90. [293] WPPCL (2017), art. 84(1). [294] WPPCL (2017), art. 91(1).

(iii) construction or expansion of projects in a quasi-DWSR causing serious water pollution, or alteration of projects in a quasi-DWSR that increases the total discharge of pollutants.

Third, where any person engages in activities such as cage breeding or organizes tourism, fishing or any other activity in a Grade I DWSR that may contaminate drinking water, they will be ordered to stop the unlawful act and will be fined 20,000 yuan to 100,000 yuan. In the case of individuals swimming, fishing or engaging in any other activities in a Grade I DWSR that may contaminate drinking water, they will be ordered to stop the unlawful act and will be fined up to 500 yuan.[295]

Water suppliers play a critically important role in ensuring the safety of drinking water. They must guarantee the safe and reliable operation of the water supply system and must supply water in full compliance with the Standards for Drinking Water Quality (GB 5749-2006).[296] Where the water supplied fails to meet state standards, the water supplier will be ordered to rectify and will be fined 20,000 yuan to 200,000 yuan. Where circumstances are serious and if the local government approves, the party in violation may be ordered to suspend its operations and take the measures necessary to bring it into compliance. Individuals directly in charge or others directly liable will be sanctioned.[297] It is the agency in charge of housing and urban and rural construction, under the MOHURD, and not the environmental bureau, that exercises regulatory supervision of water suppliers.

Violation Causing Water Pollution Incidents

Water pollution incidents often cause grave environmental harm resulting in heavy losses of public and private property and human casualties. The WPPCL (2017) adopts the emergency response mechanism to prevent water pollution incidents and to ensure a timely response so that pollution can be contained and its impact mitigated. Where any enterprise or institution fails to prepare an emergency response plan for water pollution as required by law, fails to activate its emergency response plan in a timely manner or fails to implement the responses detailed in the plan, the local environmental bureau will order the enterprise or institution to rectify its error and, in serious circumstances, will impose a fine of 20,000 yuan to 100,000 yuan.[298]

Where any entity has caused a water pollution incident in violation of the WPPCL (2017), it is liable for compensation, and administrative sanctions will also be imposed.[299] In the case of 'average' or 'relatively serious' water pollution incidents, a fine equivalent to 20 per cent of the direct economic loss is imposed. Where a pollution incident is classed as 'serious' or 'extraordinarily serious', a fine equivalent to 30 per cent of the direct economic loss is imposed.[300] In addition to fines, liable parties will be ordered to clean up the pollution and restore the site by a specified deadline. Failure to do so results in third-party treatment at the expense of the liable

[295] WPPCL (2017), art. 91(2).

[296] The Standards for Drinking Water Quality (GB 5749-2006) is a revision of the 1985 version. It was issued by the Ministry of Health and the Standardization Administration on 29 December 2006, and came into force on 1 July 2007.

[297] WPPCL (2017), art. 92. [298] WPPCL (2017), art. 93. [299] WPPCL (2017), art. 94.

[300] WPPCL (2017), art. 94(2). Water pollution incidents as a form of environmental emergency are divided into four categories, depending on the scale and harm caused. For more details, see the Law on Emergency Response (2007) and the State Council's National Plan on Environmental Emergency Response (2014).

parties. In the case of a serious or extraordinarily serious water pollution incident, the liable parties may be ordered to permanently close the business, given the approval of the local government.[301] In case of a pollution incident caused to fishery waters or by a fishery vessel, sanctions are imposed by the fishery authorities. If a pollution incident is caused by another vessel, sanctions are imposed by the maritime authorities.[302]

To further deter violation and promote compliance, the WPPCL (2017) imposes sanctions on individuals, in addition to legal persons. Individuals directly in charge and others directly liable for the water pollution incident may be fined up to half the total income earned by the person or entity in the previous year. In case of intentional and malicious violations under article 63 of the EPL (2014), administrative detention may be imposed on individuals for up to fifteen days, depending on the seriousness of the case.[303]

In conclusion, administrative agencies in China have wide-ranging powers to impose a variety of penalties to punish and deter violations. It is worth noting that in addition to the commonly used sanctions of a fine, order to rectify, order to restrict or suspend production to take treatment measures, order to suspend or permanently close a business operation and administrative detention of persons in charge and persons directly liable, the WPPCL (2017) has incorporated a new form of fine, which is calculated on a daily basis. Where any enterprise, institution or other production operator in violation has been fined and ordered to rectify, the agency imposing the fine must conduct a follow-up inspection to ensure rectification has taken place. If the violation is found not to have been rectified, or the parties refuse or obstruct the follow-up inspection, a local agency will impose a fine calculated on a daily basis in accordance with the EPL.[304] This aims to address the problem of the low cost of violation and the consequent failure or delay in rectification. The fines calculated on a daily basis are potentially higher than the previous form of fine and should deter inaction by parties in violation.

6.8.4 Criminal Sanction

Administrative sanctions imposed on environmental violations under the WPPCL (2017) do not replace potential criminal liabilities of violators. Where any violation of the WPPCL (2017) constitutes a crime, the liable parties will be investigated and prosecuted for criminal sanctions under the Criminal Law (CL).[305] This is illustrated by the case of *Zijin Mining Group Ltd and Others* (2011),[306] a high-profile water pollution incident that caused grave environmental harm to the Ting River in Fujian province.

301 WPPCL (2017), art. 94(1).

302 WPPCL (2017), art. 94(3).

303 WPPCL (2017), art. 94(1). Article 63 of the EPL (2014) provides for the following acts: (i) construction starts without an EIA, ordered to suspend but refuses to suspend; (ii) discharge without permit, ordered to stop discharge but refuses to stop; (iii) unlawful discharge through hidden pipes, seepage wells and pits, among others; falsifying monitoring data, or tampering with a pollution treatment facility to evade supervision and (iv) production or use of pesticide banned by the state, ordered to rectify but refuses to rectify. In any of these circumstances, the local environmental bureau must transfer the case to the local police, which will impose the administrative sanction of detention of ten to fifteen days on those individuals directly in charge and others directly liable. Where circumstances are relatively minor, detention of five to ten days is imposed.

304 WPPCL (2017), art. 95; EPL (2014), art. 59.

305 WPPCL (2017), art. 101. For instance, the crime of environmental pollution under article 338 of the CL, and the crime of dereliction of environmental duties under article 408 of the CL.

306 SPC Four Model Cases on Environmental Crimes (2013), case no. 1.

Zijin Mining Group Ltd and Others (2011)

On 3 and 16 July 2010, Zijin Mining Group Ltd's Fujian plant (Zijin Ltd) experienced accidental leaks of 9,100 m^3 of acidic wastewater containing copper. This caused serious contamination of the Ting River. The direct economic loss was 31,877,000 yuan. Fujian Provincial EPB imposed a fine of 9,563,130 yuan on Zijin Ltd and ordered it to mend the leak, eliminate contamination and clean up the river.[307] The EPB also fined two key persons responsible for the pollution incident: Chen Jinghe, chairman of the board of directors, was fined 705,997 yuan, and Zou Laichang, deputy president of Zijin Ltd, was fined 449,768 yuan. Given the very grave consequences of the water pollution incident, the case was transferred to the public security bureau (PSB) for an investigation into potential criminal liabilities. Zijin Ltd and five persons in charge or directly responsible for the leaks were prosecuted by Xinluo District Procuratorate under article 338 of the CL (1997) for the crime of causing a serious environmental pollution incident.

Xinluo District Court (2011) found that the defendants had intentionally connected the wastewater collection tank with the storm-water drain, creating the risk that industrial wastewater would be discharged via the drainage system to the Ting River. In July 2010, the discharge of a large volume of acidic wastewater containing copper through the storm-water drain into the Ting River had unduly interrupted the lives of residents and had harmed the livelihoods of farmers using the Ting River for aquaculture, the court said. The court convicted both the company and five individuals for the crime of causing a serious pollution incident under article 338 of the CL (1997). Zijin Ltd was fined 30 million yuan. Individuals in charge were penalized:

(i) Chen Jiahong (vice president of Zijin Mining) was sentenced to three years' imprisonment and fined 200,000 yuan;
(ii) Huang Fucai (head of the environmental protection and safety division of Zijin Mountain Gold/Copper Mining) was sentenced to three and a half years' imprisonment and fined 200,000 yuan.

Individuals directly liable for the leaks received heavier criminal sanctions:

(i) Lin Wenxian (head of Copper Factory at Zijin Mountain) was sentenced to four years' imprisonment and fined 300,000 yuan;
(ii) Wang Yong (deputy head of Copper Factory at Zijin Mountain) was sentenced to four years' imprisonment and fined 300,000 yuan; and
(iii) Liu Shengyuan (head of the environmental division of Copper Factory) was sentenced to four and a half years' imprisonment and fined 300,000 yuan. All defendants appealed.

Longyan Intermediate Court (2011) upheld the lower court's decision with regard to the fine imposed on Zijin Ltd and the fines imposed on the individuals. It did, however, consider the good attitudes of the five individuals and efforts they had made to contain and mitigate harm after the pollution incident, reducing the custodial sentencing for each:

(i) Chen Jiahong was sentenced to three years' imprisonment suspended for three years;
(ii) Huang Fucai was sentenced to three years' imprisonment suspended for five years;
(iii) Lin Wenxian, Wang Yong and Liu Shengyuan each had their imprisonment reduced by one year.

[307] The fine of 9.56 million yuan was the largest environmental fine imposed by any EPB. It was calculated at 30 per cent of the direct economic loss, under the WPPCL (2008), art. 83.

Here, the administrative sanctions imposed by the provincial EPB were not substitutes for the criminal penalties imposed by the courts following a further investigation by the police and prosecution by the local procuratorate.

6.9 CIVIL LIABILITIES

The WPPCL (2017) takes a slightly different approach from other environmental statutes by stipulating civil liabilities in greater detail. Where polluters cause harm to the environment leading to property loss or personal injury, the victims have the right to claim compensation from the polluters and demand that the harm be eliminated.[308] It is commonly known as 'no-fault liability', and does not require proof of fault or violation by polluters for them to be held liable for the environmental harm caused by the pollution. It is in line with the rule of no-fault liability for environmental torts under the Tort Law (TL) (2009).[309] However, a polluter does not bear tort liability for the environmental harm caused by its wastewater discharge under two circumstances. One is when the pollution discharge is triggered by a *force majeure* incident,[310] which commonly refers to an unforeseeable, unavoidable and insurmountable natural or human disaster, such as earthquake, flooding or war. However, there is a proviso to the rule of *force majeure*: where the law makes the polluter liable despite *force majeure*, the polluter will be liable. For instance, *force majeure* does not exempt one's civil liability for the harm caused by pollution emanating from nuclear operations. The second circumstance under which a polluter is exempt from civil liability is where the harm caused by water pollution is intentionally caused by the victim. If the harm is caused by the victim's serious negligence, the polluter's liability for compensation is mitigated, instead of exempted.[311] Where the harm caused by the water pollution is the fault of a third party, the polluter still bears the liability for compensation, but has the right to seek indemnity from the third party.[312] In other words, the third-party fault that triggered the pollution and caused harm does not exempt the polluter from its liability. To alleviate the burden on victims of pollution who wish to seek remedies, they may sue either the polluter or the third party, whichever is easier.[313]

A water pollution dispute involving liability for compensation and calculation of the amount of damages to be paid may be resolved by mediation facilitated by an EPB, or maritime or fishery authority. If mediation fails, parties may resort to court to settle the dispute. Parties may also settle disputes by litigation without first going to mediation.[314] The administrative mediation conducted by agencies is often seen as a more efficient and less costly alternative to litigation in settling environmental disputes.[315] Agencies not only have the legal and technical expertise, but also have monitoring data and enforcement records, enabling them to play the role of facilitator effectively and help the parties to negotiate and reach agreement. The mediation has to be voluntarily accepted by both parties, and the final settlement

[308] WPPCL (2017), art. 96(1).
[309] Article 65 of the TL (2009) states that where pollution has caused harm, polluters bear tort liability.
[310] WPPCL (2017), art. 96(2). [311] WPPCL (2017), art. 96(3). [312] WPPCL (2017), art. 96(4).
[313] WPPCL (2017), art. 96(4). [314] WPPCL (2017), art. 97.
[315] For more, see Yuhong Zhao, 'Mediation of environmental disputes', *Journal of Comparative Law*, 10 (2016), 237–53; Yuhong Zhao, 'Environmental dispute resolution in China', *Journal of Environmental Law*, 16 (2004), 157–92.

agreement should reflect the free will of both. Agencies do not make any administrative decisions in the process and therefore the contents of the settlement agreement are not subject to administrative or judicial review. The WPPCL (2017) makes it clear that mediation is not compulsory and parties are free to resort to courts for dispute settlement.

The conventional rule of burden of proof requires the plaintiff to present evidence to the court to establish the causal link between the defendant's acts and the plaintiff's injury. However, due to the complex and technical nature of the process by which pollution impacts on the environment, and often a lack of information on the part of the pollution victims, the WPPCL (2017) reverses the burden of proof from plaintiff to defendant to facilitate access to remedies and justice for victims of pollution. The polluter bears the burden of proof regarding circumstances on exemption of liabilities, as well as the absence of a causal link between its discharge and the damage suffered by victims.[316] Victims still need to provide evidence to prove that pollution occurred and that loss or injury was suffered if they are to establish a prima facie case in court, which often requires monitoring data and test results, both of which can be difficult to obtain. To address the difficulty of collecting evidence, the WPPCL (2017) provides that parties disputing compensation liabilities and the amount of damage caused by water pollution may rely on environmental monitoring bodies to provide monitoring data. The monitoring stations must provide the relevant data as requested.[317] Environmental data is often the basis for lawmaking and policymaking, law enforcement by agencies and adjudication by courts. The accuracy and reliability of data directly affects the soundness, effectiveness and justice of all decision-making. The EPL (2014) requires monitoring institutions to use monitoring equipment and devices that comply with the relevant state standards and to follow strictly the technical guidelines on monitoring. Both the monitoring bodies and individuals in charge are held accountable for the truthfulness and accuracy of the monitoring data.[318] Data accuracy and access to data are of equal importance; without these, victims of pollution cannot establish a prima facie case in court as they attempt to seek remedies.

The WPPCL (2017) also promotes access to legal assistance by victims of pollution. It specifically requires the state to encourage law firms and lawyers to provide legal assistance to victims of water pollution,[319] and that EPBs and relevant social organizations may support victims of pollution who are engaged in litigation.[320] Such support may take the form of advice, referring lawyers or paying litigation costs.

[316] WPPCL (2017), art. 98. [317] WPPCL (2017), art. 100. [318] EPL (2014), art. 17(3).
[319] WPPCL (2017), art. 99(3). [320] WPPCL (2017), art. 99(2).

7

Waste Management

China's economic growth has increased its waste generation at unprecedented speed and scale. It surpassed the United States as the world's largest generator of municipal solid waste (MSW) in 2004.[1] In line with the speed of urbanization and GDP growth in China, the country's generation of MSW is growing at a faster rate than anywhere else in the world.[2] In contrast to this huge growth in waste, there was a complete lack of comprehensive and effective waste management until the mid-1990s, when the Law on the Prevention and Control of Pollution by Solid Waste (SWL)[3] was enacted to regulate waste management.

The SWL aims to prevent and control pollution caused by solid waste, safeguard human health, maintain ecological safety (protecting ecosystems, which sustain all life on earth) and promote sustainable socio-economic development.[4] 'Solid waste' refers to articles and substances in solid or semi-solid state, or taking the form of a gas stored in a container, that are generated during production, consumption or other activities and have lost their original value, or to those discarded or abandoned even though they have not completely lost their value, and to any other articles and substances subject to the regulatory control of solid waste laws and regulations.[5] The Law approaches industrial solid waste (ISW), MSW and hazardous waste (HW) with different regulatory mechanisms. ISW refers to waste or by-products from industrial processes. This can include scrap metal, slag and mine tailings. MSW is generated from urban households and by service providers, including shops, restaurants, hotels, hospitals and other public facilities. It can be divided further into different waste streams, including kitchen waste, clinical waste, electrical and electronic waste, construction waste, packaging waste and animal waste. HW refers to waste that is either included in the National Catalogue of Hazardous Waste (HW Catalogue) or is identified as hazardous according to the criteria and methods of

[1] World Bank, *Waste Management in China: Issues and Recommendations* (Washington, DC: World Bank Group, 2005), at 5.

[2] World Bank, *What a Waste: A Global Review of Solid Waste Management* (Washington, DC: World Bank Group, 2012), at x.

[3] The SWL was passed on 30 October 1995 by the 8th NPCSC at its 16th session. It was substantially revised on 29 December 2004 by the 10th NPCSC at its 13th session. Minor amendments were made on 29 June 2013, 24 April 2015 and 7 November 2016.

[4] SWL (2016), art. 1. [5] SWL (2016), art. 88(1).

identification.[6] While the safe treatment and disposal of both ISW and HW are the responsibilities of the waste generator, it is the local governments that bear the responsibility for managing MSW, in order to ensure that urban environments are hygienic and public health is protected.

The sheer amount of waste generated in China is daunting. By 2016, the annual generation of ISW had reached 3.3 billion t, the annual generation of MSW in large and medium-sized cities 200 million t and the annual generation of HW 40 million t. That does not include 1.8 billion t of construction waste, 1.35 million t of clinical waste, 4 billion t of animal waste and 1 billion t of crop straws. In addition, historically accumulated ISW had reached 60 billion t to 70 billion t, which was stockpiled on and off the premises of waste generators.[7] In sharp contrast to the enormous amount of waste is China's low disposal capacity. By the end of 2016, centralized HW disposal capacity had increased to 64.71 million t per year, but only 16.29 million t of HW had actually reached the centralized HW disposal facilities.[8] This was less than half of the HW generated that year. In 2015, approximately 1.99 billion t of ISW had been recovered for utilization, which was 65 per cent of the ISW generated that year.[9] Safe disposal of MSW reached 96.6 per cent in cities in 2016,[10] but that figure excludes rural villages and the vast suburban areas on the outskirts of cities. In rural China, only 43 per cent of villages provide for the collection and transport of household waste. Nearly 40 per cent of animal waste in villages is not treated for safe disposal.[11] Illegal dumping and disposal of waste has not only created rubbish dumps surrounding cities, towns and villages, but also poses a serious threat to the health and safety of the environment and people. Even Beijing, China's capital, had a waste problem, having been surrounded by approximately 500 illegal and polluting garbage dumps until attention was drawn to the issue by a documentary.[12] Without environmentally sound management, solid waste contaminates the environment, transmits diseases, harms animals that consume waste unknowingly and increases the risk to human health via exposure to and consumption of contaminated water and agricultural products.

Waste management involves the collection, transport, storage, recovery and disposal of waste. Waste is a complicated issue as it is potentially harmful to both the environment and human health if dumped and disposed of without pollution-control measures. However, some waste, such as paper, glass and plastics, may be recycled or recovered to become a resource that can be used for other purposes. It is this dual nature of waste as environmental harm and potentially valuable resource that has led to the development of the waste management hierarchy, which encourages waste prevention at the source and recycling

[6] The first HW Catalogue was issued by the NEPA, State Economic and Trade Commission, Foreign Economic and Trade Commission and Ministry of Public Security (MPS) on 1 April 1998. It was updated in 2008 and was reissued by the Ministry of Environmental Protection (MEP) and National Development and Reform Commission (NDRC) on 6 June 2008. The current HW Catalogue was reissued by the MEP, NDRC and MPS on 14 June 2016.

[7] Zhang Dejiang, *Inspection Report on the Implementation of the Solid Waste Law*.

[8] Zhang Dejiang, *Inspection Report on the Implementation of the Solid Waste Law*.

[9] Zhang Dejiang, *Inspection Report on the Implementation of the Solid Waste Law*.

[10] Zhang Dejiang, *Inspection Report on the Implementation of the Solid Waste Law*.

[11] Zhang Dejiang, *Inspection Report on the Implementation of the Solid Waste Law*.

[12] Stefan Landsberger, *Beijing Garbage: A City Besieged by Waste* (Amsterdam University Press, 2019), at 160–1; Liu Qin, 'Film: how China became the world's rubbish dump', *China Dialogue*, 1 May 2014.

and recovery to divert as much waste as possible before final disposal by incineration and landfill. This chapter is divided into six sections. Section 7.1 introduces key principles of waste management, including waste hierarchy, lifecycle management, the proximity principle and the polluter-pays principle. Section 7.2 examines the key roles of government agencies in setting standards, monitoring performance and sanctioning violations. Sections 7.3, 7.4 and 7.5 analyse the unique regulatory approaches to pollution control taken for ISW, MSW and HW. Section 7.6 focuses on waste imports and China's changing strategy.

7.1 IMPORTANT PRINCIPLES OF WASTE MANAGEMENT

In addition to basic environmental legal principles, such as the polluter-pays principle, waste management law and policy has developed its own special principles, including waste management hierarchy, lifecycle management and the proximity principle, to prevent and control pollution by waste.

7.1.1 The Waste Management Hierarchy

The waste management hierarchy gives top priority to waste prevention and reduction, followed by reuse, recycling and recovery to reduce the amount of waste that must be disposed of. Sound waste management should fully apply the waste hierarchy to, first and foremost, reduce waste generation and sort waste into different types at the source. Waste metal, paper, glass and plastics, among others, that cannot be prevented, reduced or reused should be recycled. Waste that cannot be recycled may be recovered, for instance by bacteriological decomposition, allowing a substance derived from the waste to be used. Implementation of the waste management hierarchy extends the lifetime of landfills, recovers valuable resources and raw materials for industry, and reduces the extraction of non-renewable resources. The SWL (2016) emphasizes by order of importance: (i) waste reduction; (ii) reuse, recycling and recovery and (iii) safe treatment and disposal.[13] It requires relevant departments of the State Council, as well as local governments and their departments, to take into account the need for waste reduction, reuse and recycling, and safe treatment and disposal of waste as they formulate plans on urban and rural construction, land use, regional development and industrial development.[14] However, no specific targets have been set for waste reduction (for example, a maximum daily per capita waste generation) or waste diversion (for example, recycling and recovery rates). Targets or a cap, however, are needed if the rate of growth of waste generation is to be controlled below the rate of GDP growth.

Top priority is given to waste reduction at the source, which means reducing the quantity and toxicity of the waste generated during production and consumption. The SWL (2016) requires the state to issue standards to prevent excessive packaging.[15] It requires municipal governments to cut MSW generation by improving the fuel mix of cities and switching to cleaner energies,[16] and by arranging the supply of cleaned and trimmed vegetables into

[13] SWL (2016), art. 3(1). [14] SWL (2016), art. 4(2). [15] SWL (2016), art. 18(1).
[16] SWL (2016), art. 43(1).

cities.[17] It requires enterprises and institutions to act rationally when they select and use raw materials, energy and other resources, and to adopt advanced production techniques and equipment that will reduce the quantity and toxicity of ISW generated by production or operation processes.[18] Waste disposal fees are imposed on generators of HW, including those generating industrial HW and clinical waste.[19] More aggressive public education campaigns are needed to encourage individuals to cut the waste they produce. Next, reuse, recycling and recovery can substantially cut the quantity of waste that ends up in landfill or is incinerated. Often, items that are considered waste can in fact be utilized as resources. To those generating the waste, it has lost its original value, but for others it may be a useful resource, whether through reuse or recovery.[20] The SWL (2016) requires the state to adopt economic and technological policies and measures favourable to the comprehensive utilization of solid waste, enabling solid waste to be recovered fully and utilized rationally.[21] At the bottom of the hierarchy is safe disposal by incineration or landfill, which is of crucial importance to prevent air, water and soil pollution. Despite progress in technology and waste management, there are still types of waste that cannot be prevented, reused, recycled or recovered. To achieve safe disposal of such waste, the state supports the use of centralized disposal facilities and fosters the development of waste disposal service providers.[22] To prevent waste disposal projects from contaminating air, water or soil, the SWL (2016) prohibits the construction of centralized industrial waste storage and disposal facilities or MSW landfills in areas requiring special protection, including different types of nature reserves, drinking-water-source reserves (DWSRs) and basic farmland protection zones.[23]

7.1.2 Lifecycle Management or EPR

Lifecycle management, also known as extended producer responsibility (EPR), seeks to reduce waste at the source of production, instead of focusing on waste at the point at which it is discarded. Recovery targets are set for materials in certain waste streams, such as packaging waste, waste electrical and electronic equipment and used vehicles, and obligations are imposed on producers of relevant products to achieve the targets. The producers of those products are responsible for achieving the target for waste recovery and for ensuring products are designed in an ecologically sound manner to minimize waste generation.

China has been slow in adopting lifecycle management to prevent waste at the source, though an EPR scheme was proposed by the Law on Promotion of the Circular Economy

[17] SWL (2016), art. 43(2). [18] SWL (2016), art. 31.

[19] The NDRC, State Environmental Protection Administration (SEPA), Ministry of Health, Ministry of Finance (MOF) and Ministry of Construction jointly issued the Notice on Implementation of Hazardous Waste Disposal Fees to Promote Hazardous Waste Disposal Industry (2003) on 18 November 2003. Provincial price bureaus determine the principles behind HW disposal fees and the methods for collecting them, while municipal price bureaus set the rate.

[20] 'Reuse' refers to any operation by which products or components that are not waste are used again for the same purpose for which they were conceived. 'Recovery' results in waste serving a useful function for the original waste generator or in the wider economy. It includes 'recycling', by which waste materials are reprocessed into products, materials or substances, whether for the original purpose or others.

[21] SWL (2016), art. 3(2). [22] SWL (2016), art. 3(3). [23] SWL (2016), art. 22.

(CEPL) as early as 2008.[24] The EPR scheme in the CEPL sought to make manufacturers of products and packaging that are covered by the Catalogue of Articles Subject to Compulsory Recycling bear primary responsibility for recycling, reuse and disposal of used products and packaging.[25] Where producers entrust retailers or other bodies with collecting used products and packaging for recycling, or hire waste disposal operators to reuse or dispose of the used products and packaging, those parties must perform their duties under relevant laws, regulations and the contracts signed with the producer to collect, recycle, reuse and dispose of used products and packaging.[26] Consumers also bear a responsibility: they must deliver used products and packaging that are subject to compulsory recycling to the relevant parties for recycling.[27] The SWL (2016) briefly addresses the issue of pollution by excessive packaging.[28] For waste recycling and recovery, the SWL also refers to the Catalogue of Articles Subject to Compulsory Recycling, which should detail products and packaging materials that are subject to compulsory recycling; enterprises manufacturing, selling or importing those products and materials are responsible for collecting, recycling and disposing of them.[29] However, this Catalogue has never been issued.

It was not until 2016 that the State Council issued the Plan on Implementation of the Extended Producer Responsibility Scheme (Plan on EPR),[30] formally implementing the EPR scheme laid down in the CEPL and extending a producer's responsibility from waste control during production only to waste control for the full life cycle of a product, meaning design, circulation, consumption, reuse, recycling and final disposal. A producer's major responsibilities under the Plan on EPR (2016) are: eco-design, the use of recycled resources, reusing and recycling waste and discarded products, and information disclosure.[31] This means that, at the design stage, a producer must take into account not only the function and quality of a product, but also the toxicity of the raw materials used to make it, the pollution and waste generated while producing and consuming it, its recyclability and recoverability once the purpose for which it was made has been exhausted, and the environmental impact of its eventual disposal.

The Plan on EPR (2016) initially covers producers of four categories of products that were selected based on the size of their market share, the environmental harm they can cause, and the value of resource recovery. The four categories are: electrical and electronic products (EEPs), vehicles, lead-acid batteries and paper-based drinks packaging.[32] The Plan on EPR (2016) contains clear targets: producers of those products must achieve an average 40 per cent reuse, recycling and recovery rate by end-2020, and 50 per cent by end-2025.[33] Further, the Plan on EPR (2016) designates certain cities to take the lead in carrying out pilot exercises: Beijing for reuse and recycling of waste EEPs, Shenzhen for reuse and recycling of batteries used in electrical vehicles, and Shanghai for reuse and recycling of lead-acid batteries.[34]

[24] The CEPL was passed on 29 August 2008 by the 11th NPCSC at its 4th session and came into force on 1 January 2009. The CEPL (2008) was amended in 2018 after the state institutional reform of all levels of government.
[25] CEPL (2018), art. 15(1). The Catalogue should be issued by the NDRC. [26] CEPL (2018), art. 15(2).
[27] CEPL (2018), art. 15(3). [28] SWL (2016), art. 18(1). [29] SWL (2016), art. 18(2).
[30] The State Council issued the Plan on EPR on 25 December 2016. [31] Plan on EPR (2016), part II.
[32] Plan on EPR (2016), part III. [33] Plan on EPR (2016), part I, s. 3. [34] Plan on EPR (2016), part III.

Of the four categories of products, China has more experience with waste EEPs, following three-year pilot exercises that were initiated in 2015 under the Work Plan on a Pilot Exercise of Extended Producer Responsibility on Electrical and Electronic Products (Work Plan on EEP Pilots).[35] According to the Work Plan on EEP Pilots (2015), China was the largest generator of waste EEPs in the world in 2015, and remained so in 2020.[36] It was estimated in 2015 that more than 200 million major EEPs were discarded annually in China, weighing over 5 million t.[37] The pilot exercises covered household electrical products (televisions, refrigerators, washing machines and air conditioners), computers and office electrical products (printers and photocopiers), communications and electronic products, lighting products and batteries. China's leading manufacturers of these products participated in the trials. They include Sichuan Changhong Electrical Co. Ltd (televisions, refrigerators, air conditioners and mobile phones), Zhuhai Gree Electrical Co. Ltd (air conditioners, refrigerators and mobile phones), Hisense Corp Ltd (televisions, air conditioners, refrigerators, washing machines), Legend Co. Ltd (computers, notebook computers and mobile phones), Huawei Co. Ltd (mobile phones and tablets). As producers, they were required to establish collection networks – via their own sales, repair and maintenance channels – to collect the used products for recycling and recovery, or to entrust a third party to do so. Prior to the implementation of EPR, producers and importers of EEP were only 'encouraged' to collect waste EEP for recycling,[38] though they were required to pay a fee to the special e-waste disposal fund to support the recycling industry.[39]

7.1.3 Proximity Principle

The proximity principle requires that waste disposal occurs at one of the nearest appropriate installations by means of the most appropriate methods and technologies. This lowers the risk of pollution by waste while being transported.

Chinese waste law imposes control and restrictions over both domestic and international cross-border movement of waste. Movement of solid waste across provincial borders for storage or disposal requires approval from the provincial EPB at the place of origin. The EPB will not approve this unless it obtains consent from the provincial EPB of the destination province. No transfer may be carried out without these approvals.[40] This regulatory control only applies if the solid waste is transferred for storage or disposal; transfer for other purposes, such as recycling, recovery or utilization, does not require EPB approval, leaving a potential loophole.

Moving HW is subject to tighter control and supervision. The SWL (2016) requires all parties involved, including generators, transporters and recipients of HW, to complete an

[35] The Work Plan on EEP Pilots was issued by the Ministry of Industry and Information Technology (MIIT), MOF, Ministry of Commerce (MOC) and Ministry of Science and Technology on 29 June 2015.

[36] Vanessa Forti et al., *The Global E-waste Monitor 2020: Quantities, Flows, and the Circular Economy Potential* (Bonn, Geneva and Rotterdam: United Nations University/United Nations Institute for Training and Research, 2020). http://ewastemonitor.info/, at 75.

[37] Work Plan on EEP Pilots (2015), part I. Here, 'major' refers to controlled products that cannot be dumped or mixed with household waste.

[38] Regulation on the Recycling and Disposal of Waste Electrical and Electronic Products (2009), art. 11.

[39] Regulation on the Recycling and Disposal of Waste Electrical and Electronic Products (2009), art. 7.

[40] SWL (2016), art. 23.

'HW transfer registration form' (see Section 7.5.5). Any movement of HW across a provincial border, regardless of the purpose, must apply to the provincial EPB in the provinces of origin and designation for permission, and must consult with them in order to receive their consent.[41] The legal requirement of consultation with the provincial EPB of the destination province is a critical mechanism allowing for prior assessment of the safe disposal capacity of the destination province. Where the transfer of HW involves more administrative regions than the cities of origin and destination, the municipal EPB of the place of origin must notify all municipal EPBs of places of transit in a timely manner.[42] This ensures that the transport of HW is supervised continuously from generator to final destination.

7.1.4 Polluter-Pays Principle

China implements the polluter-pays principle,[43] meaning that the cost of waste management is borne by the waste generator. Manufacturers, sellers, importers and users of products are responsible for the prevention and control of pollution caused by the waste they generate.[44] Generators of solid waste are obliged to adopt measures to prevent and reduce pollution by waste.[45] All waste operators – entities and individuals that collect, store, transport, utilize or dispose of solid waste – must prevent pollution by taking measures to prevent solid waste from scattering, producing run-off or leaking.[46] No entity or individual may dump solid waste into rivers, lakes, canals, ditches or reservoirs, nor may they pile solid waste on river banks or slopes below the high-water line.[47] Generators of waste and all waste operators involved in any stage of the process, from collection to final disposal, are treated as potential polluters who must pay to prevent pollution and remedy any harm caused by it. This cradle-to-grave approach ensures waste is handled safely by all parties in the waste management chain, including generators of waste and those who collect, transport, store, utilize, treat and dispose of it.

Under the polluter-pays principle, enterprises and institutions must take measures to prevent and control pollution by waste generated by production and other activities. Operators of livestock farms are required to collect, store, utilize and dispose of animal waste to prevent environmental pollution.[48] Generators of ISW waste are required to construct storage facilities or sites for safe and sorted storage of waste, or take measures for its safe disposal.[49] They must either treat, store and dispose of the waste themselves, or pay centralized facilities to treat and dispose of it. Constructors are required to collect construction waste in a timely manner and utilize or dispose of the waste as required by environmental hygiene authorities.[50] In addition, service providers such as operators of public transport[51] and airports, harbours, stations, parks and shops are responsible for collecting waste generated by customers.[52]

The polluter-pays principle also applies to individuals, who must pay for household waste to be collected, treated and disposed of, according to a scheme for MSW disposal that was

[41] SWL (2016), art. 59(1). [42] SWL (2016), art. 59(2). [43] SWL (2016), art. 5(1).
[44] SWL (2016), art. 5(2). [45] SWL (2016), art. 16. [46] SWL (2016), art. 17(1).
[47] SWL (2016), art. 17(2). [48] SWL (2016), art. 20(1). [49] SWL (2016), art. 33. [50] SWL (2016), art. 46.
[51] SWL (2016), art. 47. [52] SWL (2016), art. 48.

introduced in 2002.[53] Provincial governments have phased in the scheme by assessing local conditions and capacity. The fees are set by the municipal government to cover the cost of collection, transport and disposal, as well as a reasonable profit for the operators.[54] The phase-in has been slow, and fees are low. Using Beijing as an example, since 1999, each household has been charged 30 yuan per year for waste collection and disposal, while non-residential generators of MSW were charged 25 yuan per t[55] It was not until 2013 that the fees for collection and disposal of non-residential MSW were substantially increased in Beijing (though the fees for residential sources of MSW remained unchanged). General waste from workplaces is charged at 300 yuan per t, and restaurant and canteen waste 100 yuan per t. In the case of construction and demolition waste, collection is charged at 6 yuan per t within 6 km and 1 yuan per t for each further kilometre, with the disposal fee at 30 yuan per t.[56] The increase in the MSW collection and disposal fees intended to make polluters pay for the cost of waste disposal in landfill and incinerators, with the price encouraging waste reduction and recovery, in order to reduce the amount of waste for disposal.

7.2 GOVERNMENT RESPONSIBILITY AND AGENCIES IN CHARGE

Effective prevention and control of pollution by waste requires the joint efforts of government, industry and community. The government at all levels is responsible for promoting the key tenets of this – waste reduction and prevention at the source, waste recovery and recycling, and safe disposal of waste – by formulating policies, plans and standards to guide industry and the public. Local governments and agencies supervise the construction and operation of waste disposal infrastructure and collection services. They also monitor performance and punish violation.

Broadly, the state promotes clean production and the circular economy by targeting waste reduction, waste recovery and the safe disposal of waste.[57] It makes economic and technological policies, takes measures to achieve full recovery and rational utilization of solid waste,[58] and supports the use of centralized facilities for safe disposal of waste to prevent pollution.[59] More specifically, the SWL (2016) requires local governments to incorporate the work on prevention and control of pollution by waste into their socio-economic development plans and take measures to prevent pollution by waste.[60] Relevant departments of the State Council, as well as local governments and relevant local agencies, are required to take into account waste reduction (volume and toxicity) and waste recovery for utilization and safe disposal when formulating plans for urban and rural construction,

[53] In 2002, the NDRC, MOF, Ministry of Construction and SEPA issued the Notice on Implementing Municipal Solid Waste Disposal Fees to Foster the Waste Disposal Industry (Notice on MSW Disposal Fees).

[54] Notice on MSW Disposal Fees (2002), part II.

[55] Beijing Price Bureau and Beijing Finance Bureau, Notice on Adjustment of Waste Collection and Waste Disposal Fees (1999).

[56] Beijing Development and Reform Commission and Beijing Urban Management Commission, Notice on Adjustment of Waste Disposal Fees for Non-Residential MSW (2013). The Notice came into force on 1 January 2014.

[57] SWL (2016), art. 3(1). [58] SWL (2016), art. 3(2). [59] SWL (2016), art. 3(3). [60] SWL (2016), art. 4(1).

land use, regional development, industrial development, among others.[61] All levels of governments are responsible for public education to raise awareness of the problem of pollution by waste and for promoting environmentally friendly production models and lifestyles.[62] The state encourages units and individuals to buy and use reusable products and products made from recycled materials.[63]

7.2.1 Regulatory Agencies in Charge

The regulatory control of waste management involves many government bodies at both national and local levels. They have different roles to play, from making plans and policies and setting standards to monitoring and enforcement. The state ministries and local bureaus in charge of environmental protection and construction are the key agencies responsible for waste management, with the former focusing on environmental protection and pollution control, and the latter on the planning, construction, operation and supervision of waste collection services and disposal facilities such as sanitary landfills, transfer stations (including waste sorting facilities), compost plants and incinerators.

Ministry of Ecology and Environment, and Local Bureaus

Among all the regulatory bodies involved, the Ministry of Ecology and Environment (MEE) exercises administration and supervision of control of pollution by solid waste.[64] Local environmental bureaus exercise equivalent powers within their own administrative jurisdictions.[65] The MEE and local bureaus are in charge of: (i) setting environmental protection standards for ISW storage and disposal facilities and sites, and setting technical standards and guidance on environmental monitoring; (ii) receiving information from producers of ISW on the nature of their waste; (iii) review and approval of HW operation licence; (iv) issuing permits for waste imports; (v) reviewing and approving HW exports under the terms of the Basel Convention;[66] (vi) imposing administrative penalty on entities in violation and (vii) setting environmental protection standards for MSW disposal facilities and sites.[67]

MOHURD and Local Environmental Hygiene Bureaus

The state authority in charge of construction, the Ministry of Housing and Urban–Rural Development (MOHURD), and the environmental hygiene departments of governments at county level and above are in charge of the supervision and administration of clearing up, collecting, storing, transporting and disposing of MSW.[68] The MOHURD supervises and guides the work of urban environmental hygiene by setting environmental hygiene standards for MSW disposal facilities and sites. Initially, municipal environmental hygiene

[61] SWL (2016), art. 4(2). [62] SWL (2016), art. 6(2). [63] SWL (2016), art. 7. [64] SWL (2016), art. 10(1).
[65] SWL (2016), art. 10(2).
[66] Basel Convention on the Control of Transboundary Movements of Hazardous Wastes and their Disposal, Basel, 22 March 1989, treaty no. 28911. *United Nations Treaty Series*, 1673, 57–336.
[67] Huang Jianchu et al. (eds.), *Interpreting the Solid Waste Law* (Beijing: Law Press, 2005).
[68] SWL (2016), art. 10(3). The State Council, in the Regulation on Urban Appearance and Environmental Hygiene (1992), delegated the power to the then Ministry of Construction (the predecessor of MOHURD) to administer the work of urban environmental hygiene at the national level, with provincial departments of construction and municipal departments of environmental hygiene managing the work within their jurisdictions.

departments or their affiliated bodies were in charge of cleaning, collection, storage, transport and disposal of MSW, construction and operation of MSW transfer and disposal sites and facilities, as well as the construction of municipal waste transfer and disposal sites and facilities, and the operation of those facilities.[69] This institutional design for MSW management has proved inefficient and incapable of handling the exponential growth in MSW since the 1990s. Reforms have shifted the role of municipal environmental hygiene departments from that of service provider to regulator in charge of planning and supervision over waste operation.[70] This has opened up the waste collection, transport and disposal service to the private sector.

National Development and Reform Commission and Others

Other relevant departments involved in waste management include: (i) the NDRC and its local counterparts, which together are in charge of promoting clean production and the circular economy as it relates to waste reduction, recycling and recovery. The NDRC issues catalogues of outdated industrial processes and equipment that generate highly polluting ISW and must be phased out; (ii) the National Health Commission works with the MEE to set standards for clinical waste treatment and disposal, supervises and inspects the treatment and disposal, and conducts inspection and emergency responses if needed; (iii) government departments in charge of foreign trade, customs, quality supervision, inspection and quarantine exercise control over waste imports and (iv) railway, transport and aviation departments are in charge of waste management related to services provided by trains, vessels and airplanes.

7.2.2 Setting Standards

The MEE, in collaboration with relevant departments of the State Council, formulates national technical standards on the prevention and control of pollution by solid waste pursuant to national environmental quality standards and economic and technological feasibility.[71] There are three main categories of standards issued for waste management. The first category covers pollution-control standards for incineration, landfill and storage:

- Standard for Pollution Control on the Municipal Solid Waste Incineration (GB 18485-2014, replacing GB 18485-2001)[72]
- Standard for Pollution Control on the Landfill Site of Municipal Solid Waste (GB 16889-2008, replacing GB 16889-1997)[73]

[69] Huang Jianchu et al. (eds.), *Interpreting*.

[70] See National Planning Commission, MOF, Ministry of Construction and SEPA, Notice on MSW Disposal Fees (2002); Ministry of Construction, Provisions on MSW Management (2007).

[71] SWL (2016), art. 11.

[72] It sets standards for the siting and technical requirements of municipal waste incinerators, the waste to be incinerated, operation of the plant and its emissions, as well as monitoring, operation and supervision.

[73] It applies to pollution control and supervision of the construction, operation and post-operation maintenance of municipal waste landfills. Some standards also apply to the construction and operation of municipal waste transfer stations. Standards are set for siting, design and construction of the landfill facilities, the requirements for waste accepted, and the operation, closure, maintenance and monitoring to prevent pollution.

- Pollution-Control Standard for Hazardous Wastes Incineration (GB 18484-2001, replacing GWKB 2-1999)[74]
- Standard for Pollution Control on Hazardous Waste Storage (GB 18597-2001)[75]
- Standard for Pollution Control on the Hazardous Waste Landfill (GB 18598-2019)[76]
- Standards for Pollution Control on the Storage and Disposal Site for General Industrial Solid Wastes (GB 18599-2001).[77]

The second category relates to testing, measurement and determination of HW. Examples are:

- Technical Specifications on Identification for Hazardous Waste (HJ/T 298-2007)
- Identification Standards for Hazardous Wastes: General Specifications (GB 5085.7-2007)
- Identification Standards for Hazardous Wastes: Identification for Corrosivity (GB 5085.1-2007, replacing GB 5085.1-1996)
- Identification Standards for Hazardous Wastes: Screening Test for Acute Toxicity (GB 5085.2-2007, replacing GB 5085.2-1996)
- Identification Standards for Hazardous Wastes: Identification for Extraction Toxicity (GB 5085.3-2007, replacing GB 5085.3-1996)
- Identification Standards for Hazardous Wastes Part 5: Identification for Ignitability (GB 5085.4-2007)
- Identification Standards for Hazardous Wastes: Identification for Reactivity (GB 5085.5-2007)
- Identification Standards for Hazardous Wastes: Identification for Toxic Substance Content (GB 5085.6-2007)

The third category includes standards on the methods of monitoring and testing solid waste. Examples are:

- Solid Waste: Determination of Hexavalent Chromium: by Alkaline Digestion/Flame Atomic Absorption Spectrophotometric (HJ 687-2014)[78]
- Solid Waste: Determination of Volatile Organic Compounds: Headspace/Gas Chromatography/Mass Method (HJ 643-2013)[79]
- Technical Guideline of Monitoring on Dioxins Emission from Hazardous Waste (including Medical Waste) Incinerators (HJ/T 365-2007)[80]

[74] It sets standards for preventing pollution from centralized incinerators and requires heat recovery where technologically feasible.

[75] It covers general requirements on HW storage, setting standards for HW packing, and for the siting, design, operation, monitoring and closure of HW storage facilities, and necessary safety measures.

[76] It sets standards for the construction and operation of HW landfills in order to prevent pollution, including threshold requirements for waste to be accepted, and the siting, design, construction, operation, closure and monitoring of the facilities.

[77] It sets standards for the siting, design, operation, closure and monitoring of ISW storage and disposal facilities, and for pollution control at those facilities.

[78] It sets the methods for testing hexavalent chromium in solid waste.

[79] It sets the methods for testing for VOCs in solid waste.

[80] It sets the standards for monitoring emissions of dioxins from HW and medical waste incinerators, including technical requirements on the determination of monitoring points, sampling devices, analysis methods, quality control, data processing, expression of results and monitoring reports.

It is of crucial importance that uniform methods are used at all monitoring stations so that the data collected is accurate and can be relied upon.

7.2.3 Monitoring and Information Disclosure

The state environmental authority is responsible for establishing a system for monitoring pollution by solid waste, formulating uniform monitoring standards and, in conjunction with relevant departments, setting up a monitoring network.[81] Accurate and reliable environmental monitoring is essential for effective regulation and enforcement. Environmental bureaus of large and medium-sized cities are required to regularly release information on solid waste, including the types and quantity generated and collected and the methods of disposal.[82] Large and medium-sized cities generate more solid waste due to their larger population and more active industrial and commercial sectors.[83] The compulsory requirement for information on waste generation to be disclosed promotes public access to information and improves awareness of the waste problem and its consequences. This not only encourages the public to reduce their waste and sort it for recycling, but also empowers people to monitor and supervise the waste management performance of polluters and government.

SEPA stipulated the specific information to be disclosed, and the time and means by which to do so, interpreting the general statutory disclosure requirement.[84] It requires municipal environmental bureaus to release solid waste information annually by 5 June through local media, including newspapers, television, specialized media and government websites.[85] They must disclose: (i) local plans for the prevention and control of pollution by ISW, HW, clinical waste and MSW, the current state of waste management, existing problems and proposed solutions; (ii) the total amount of ISW and HW generated, utilized, stored and disposed of, the total amount of clinical waste generated and disposed of and the means of disposal, the total amount of MSW generated or collected, the means of disposal and the amount disposed of; (iii) a list of holders of HW operation permits issued by environmental bureaus.[86] A city may choose to release further information if it has the ability to do so. This optional disclosure covers information on: the top five types of ISW and HW by quantity generated; the top five types of ISW and HW by quantity of generation and waste type; construction waste; restaurant and kitchen waste; disposal facilities for MSW, HW and clinical waste, including operators, disposal capacity, type of operation, location, significant technologies employed and measures to prevent pollution; movement of HW, including types of waste, quantity and purpose of movement (disposal, storage or

[81] SWL (2016), art. 12(1). [82] SWL (2016), art. 12(2).

[83] In China, cities are defined by the size of their population, though the definitions have changed at times. Under the now-repealed Urban Planning Law (1989), a 'large' city had a population of more than half a million, while a 'medium-sized' city had a population of 200,000 to 500,000. Under the State Council Notice to Adjust the Criteria for the Size of Cities (2014), a large city now has a population of one to five million, and a medium-sized city half a million to one million. China now also has megacities with populations of five million to ten million and 'super' cities with populations of more than ten million.

[84] The SEPA issued the Guidance on Solid Waste Information Disclosure by Large and Medium-Sized Cities (SEPA Guidance) on 10 July 2006.

[85] SEPA Guidance (2006), s. 3 and s. 4. [86] SEPA Guidance (2006), sec. 6(1).

utilization); the plans made by HW operators on emergency response and risk control and prevention.[87]

7.2.4 On-Site Inspections

Local environmental bureaus and relevant departments[88] have the statutory power to conduct on-site inspections to prevent and control pollution by solid waste. An entity being inspected is required to make accurate report and provide the information required by the authority.[89] The inspection bodies may monitor the operations, collect samples and consult or make photocopies of any documents or records relating to pollution by solid waste.[90] On-site inspections are an important enforcement power, allowing the local enforcement officers to enter the premises of enterprises and institutions to check waste generation and pollution-control measures. It is a statutory power expressly granted by law, and exercising it does not require the consent of the parties to be inspected, nor prior notice to be given to them. According to the SWL (2016), no entity may refuse entry or inspection, and entities must cooperate by accurately reporting the quantity of waste, the types, flow direction, utilization, storage and method and quantity of disposal. Entities being inspected are required to provide relevant documents – such as a licence, permit, records of production, waste generation and operation of pollution-control facilities, monitoring data and incident records – when requested by inspection officers.

7.2.5 Administrative Sanctions

The SWL (2016) sets out a wide range of administrative sanctions to punish violations by both polluters and agencies. Where any agency fails to perform a statutory duty, for example a duty related to the issuance of permits or sanctioning a violation, it will be ordered to rectify (perform the duty) by the same-level people's government or the supervisory body at a higher level. Persons in charge or others directly responsible will receive administrative disciplinary sanctions.[91] A fine is the most common sanction for a polluter found to be violating the law, and this is imposed at the same time as an order to stop the violation and take measures to rectify it by a specified deadline.[92] If any person is found to be collecting, storing, utilizing or disposing of HW without a permit or in violation of permit conditions, it will be ordered to stop the violation, the illegal gains will be confiscated, and it may be fined up to three times the illegal gains or have its HW operation permit revoked.[93] Where solid waste has caused serious environmental contamination or a pollution incident, the liable parties may be ordered by the local government to suspend operations and/or permanently close the business.[94]

None of the administrative sanctions exempt the liable parties from potential criminal liabilities under the Criminal Law (CL). Agency staff may be investigated and prosecuted for

[87] SEPA Guidance (2006), s. 6(2) and (3).

[88] Relevant departments are administrative departments in charge of construction, environmental hygiene, health, transport, railways and aviation, among others. See Huang Jianchu et al. (eds.), *Interpreting*.

[89] SWL (2016), art. 15(1). [90] SWL (2016), art. 15(2). [91] SWL (2016), art. 67.

[92] For example, SWL (2016), art. 68 on the handling of ISW; art. 74 on the handling of MSW; and art. 75 on the handling of HW.

[93] SWL (2016), art. 77. [94] SWL (2016), arts. 81 and 82.

failing to perform their statutory duties.[95] Any person who, by evading customs supervision, transports solid waste into the territory of China, may be investigated for criminal liability.[96] Any person who, in violation of law, collects, stores, utilizes or disposes of HW and causes serious environmental pollution will be investigated for criminal liability.[97] Toxic contamination of water and soil by chromium waste that occurred in Qujing, Yunnan province is only the tip of the iceberg. As a result of limited waste treatment capacity, the high cost of safe disposal, and lackadaisical agency supervision, pollution caused by waste is a serious problem for China.

Qujing Toxic Contamination (2011)

From April to June 2011, 5,222 t of chromium waste was dumped by three truck drivers along roads and hills surrounding the Chachong Reservoir, located within the administrative area of Qujing city, Yunnan province. Heavy rainfall in June washed the toxic waste into the reservoir and contaminated water and soil nearby. Seventy-seven goats and cattle died after drinking contaminated water. The drivers were local villagers contracted by Luliang Chemical Co. (Luliang Chemical) to take the waste to the purchaser, Sanli Fuel Co., a treatment plant in Guizhou province. However, to save transport costs they did not take it to the plant.[98] Further investigation confirmed excessive levels of hexavalent chromium (Cr^{6+}) in local waters including the Nanpan River, a tributary of the Pearl River.[99]

Further, Luliang Chemical, located by the Nanpan River, had stockpiled 288,400 t of chromium waste on its site since 1989, of which 148,000 t had not been treated.[100] The cancer village of Xinglong was located 2 km away, with a population of approximately 3,000. From 2002 to 2011, fourteen villagers had been diagnosed with cancer, eleven of whom had died, according to government data. In 2011, villagers claimed that, since 2002, at least thirty villagers had suffered from cancer caused by chromium-contaminated water and soil.[101]

Luliang County EPB and Luliang county government ordered Luliang Chemical to suspend production and imposed a fine of 300,000 yuan. They also ordered Luliang Chemical to remove the 5,222 t of chromium waste dumped illegally in Qujing and clean the contaminated sites. Luliang Chemical was further ordered to treat, by end-2012, the 148,000 t of chromium waste it had stockpiled at its premises near the Nanpan River.[102] The MEP suspended review and approval of the environmental impact assessment (EIA) of new projects in Qujing until the waste had been cleaned up and properly treated and disposed of.[103]

95 SWL (2016), art. 67. 96 SWL (2016), art. 78(2). 97 SWL (2016), art. 83.

98 Yan Jie, 'Illegal dumping pollutes water', *China Daily*, 15 August 2011; Yan Jie, 'Plant stored toxic waste, endangering residents', *China Daily*, 17 August 2018; Yang Jian, 'Top team in cancer scare probe', *Shanghai Daily*, 19 August 2011.

99 Stephen Chen and Ada Lee, 'Lab tests confirm Yunnan toxic spill', *South China Morning Post*, 31 August 2011.

100 Fiona Tam, 'Yunnan plant'. 101 Yang Jian, '"Cancer village" blames'.

102 'Qujing city government report on chromium waste pollution incident at press conference', *Yunnan Daily*, 5 September 2011.

103 Li Jing, 'Pollution scandal brings halt to projects', *China Daily*, 2 September 2011.

Qilin District Procuratorate prosecuted seven individuals for the crime of causing environmental pollution under article 338 of the CL: the three villagers Wu Xinghuai, Liu Xingshui and Wang Pingkun, who had approached Luliang Chemical in April 2011 to collect chromium waste; Zuo Xianglin, Luliang Chemical's deputy general manager and Tang Zaiyang, its general manager, who had agreed to let them handle the waste without checking their HW operation permit and without complying with rules and procedures on HW movement; Yuan Ke, general manager of Sanli Fuel Co.; and Dai Muchang, who had introduced Liu to Yuan. Wu, Liu and Wang were paid 260,000 yuan to collect chromium waste and take it to Guizhou. However, they transported approximately 60 t to Guizhou and dumped the remainder close to the Chachong Reservoir, located in Qujing's Qilin district. The serious toxic contamination caused direct economic losses amounting to 4.22 million yuan.

Qilin District Court (2012) found all seven defendants guilty under article 338 of the CL. Wu, Liu and Wang were each imprisoned for four years and fined 50,000 yuan; Zuo was imprisoned for three and half years and fined 40,000 yuan; Yuan and Dai were sentenced to three years' imprisonment suspended for four years and fined 30,000 yuan; Tang was sentenced to three year's imprisonment suspended for three years and fined 30,000 yuan. All illegal gains were confiscated.[104]

Chromium and chromium salts are widely used to tan leather, make ceramics and glass and produce chrome alloy and chromium metal, as well as being used in chrome plating and for corrosion control.[105] China is the world's largest producer and consumer of chromium and has been home to more than seventy factories producing chromium at one time or another since 1958. The number of chromium producers peaked at fifty-two in 1992 and had dropped to twenty-five by 2003. In 2003 alone, China's chromium production reached 238,000 t and consumption 231,000 t.[106] Due to the outdated technology and techniques applied in the production process, each tonne of chromium produced yields 3 t to 5 t of chromium waste, most of which is dumped. From 1958 to 2005, more than 2 million t of chromium had been produced, generating more than 6 million t of waste, of which only 2 million t had been treated. That is, more than 4 million t of chromium waste was stockpiled on and off factory premises or dumped at landfills and unofficial sites, posing high risks of water and soil contamination and endangering ecosystems and human health.[107] The Cr^{6+} found in the waste is highly toxic and causes kidney and liver damage. It is a carcinogen according to the World Health Organization (WHO), which recommends a maximum limit of 0.05 mg/l for drinking water.[108] Laboratory testing in the aftermath of the Qujing toxic contamination found that the level of Cr^{6+} had reached 0.204 mg/l at the middle of the Nanpan River in Qujing, double the national standard. Water samples from a spring near the Luliang Chemical factory

[104] Zi Min, 'Seven penalized for the crime of environmental pollution', *China Environment News*, 22 May 2012.

[105] WHO, *Chromium in Drinking Water* (Geneva: World Health Organization, 2003), at 1.

[106] Comprehensive Treatment Plan on Chromium Waste Contamination (2005), chapter I. The Plan was issued by the NDRC and SEPA.

[107] Comprehensive Treatment Plan on Chromium Waste Contamination (2005), chapter I.

[108] WHO, *Chromium in Drinking Water*, at 6; WHO, *Guidelines for Drinking-Water Quality: Fourth Edition Incorporating the First Addendum* (World Health Organization, 2017), at 178, 340.

contained 24.25 mg/l, and the soil samples had chromium levels 162 times higher than the national standard.[109]

The central government was already aware of the severe risk posed by chromium waste and had issued the binding Comprehensive Treatment Plan on Chromium Waste Contamination (2005),[110] aiming to achieve safe disposal of the waste by end-2010 with subsidies from the central government. However, local implementation was behind schedule and it was not until 2012 that the MEP was able to report that 6.7 million t of historical chromium waste had been safely disposed of.[111] Most of this waste had been stockpiled for ten to twenty years, and some for as long as fifty years. Chromium waste had contaminated approximately 5 km^2 of land and a total of 15 million m^3 of soil.[112]

To further address the contamination caused by Luliang Chemical, Friends of Nature (FON) and Chongqing Green Volunteers Association initiated an environmental public interest litigation (EPIL) at Qujing Intermediate People's Court on 20 September 2011, seeking an injunction to stop Luliang Chemical illegally dumping or stockpiling untreated chromium waste both on and off its premises, to force it to clean up the contamination and to pay ecological compensation of 10 million yuan.[113] The court accepted the case in October 2011 and conducted pre-trial exchange of evidence in May 2012.[114] The court then facilitated mediation, and both sides signed a settlement agreement in late 2012. However, by April 2013, Luliang Chemical had changed its mind and refused to sign the court-prepared mediation report, which would have had the binding force of a judgment. The failure of mediation returned the dispute to court adjudication, pending an assessment by a qualified third party of the environmental damage.

The dispute was finally settled by mediation in August 2020.[115] Considering the clean-up and remediation work conducted by Luliang Chemical from 2011 to 2019, the FON agreed to lower its claim from 10 million yuan to 3.08 million yuan, covering the cost of continuing remediation, monitoring and assessment. Luliang agreed further to pay 1.32 million yuan to cover reasonable costs incurred by the two NGOs in relation to the litigation. The agreement also stipulated detailed arrangements for future remediation of the contaminated sites and monitoring by the NGOs.[116]

7.3 ISW

Industrial production generates ISW.[117] It is a major source of water and soil contamination in China. While the polluter-pays principle requires generators to bear the primary

[109] Stephen Chen and Ada Lee, 'Lab tests'.
[110] The NDRC and SEPA issued the Comprehensive Treatment Plan on Chromium Waste Contamination (2005) to promote safe treatment and disposal of chromium waste.
[111] MEP, *2012 China Environment Gazette*, at 32.
[112] MEP, NDRC, MIIT and Ministry of Health, 12th FYP on Prevention and Control of Pollution by Toxic and Hazardous Waste (2012), part I.
[113] Qie Jianrong, 'Environmental organizations sued for 10 million yuan of compensation caused by chromium waste in Qujing, Yunnan', *Legal Daily*, 20 September 2011.
[114] Liu Baijun, 'Trial of environmental public interest litigation on Yunnan chromium waste pollution starts soon', *Legal Net*, 23 May 2012.
[115] Friends of Nature and Chongqing Green Volunteer League v. Yunnan Luliang Chemical Industry and Another (Yunnan Qujing Intermediate Court, 3 August 2020).
[116] Chen Yuanyuan, 'Nine years to conclude a case: Qujing chromium case settled by mediation', *China Environment News*, 11 August 2020.
[117] SWL (2016), art. 88(2).

responsibility of pollution prevention and control, governments play an indispensable role in promoting clean production and the circular economy in order to reduce waste at the source and protect both the environment and public health.

7.3.1 Government-Led Clean Production

The SWL (2016) requires the state environmental protection authority to work with the NDRC and others to issue technology policies designed to prevent pollution by solid waste, and promote the use of advanced production techniques and equipment.[118] Here, 'advanced production techniques and equipment' means: (i) advanced techniques and equipment for controlling pollution during the treatment and disposal of ISW and (ii) clean production processes and equipment that reduce waste at the source. State authorities may promote advanced production techniques and equipment by releasing guidance on industrial development, issuing catalogues on state-encouraged industrial sectors and on comprehensive use of resources through reuse, recycling and recovery.[119] The NDRC is in charge of supporting research, development and application of production techniques and equipment that reduce the quantity and toxicity of waste generated, and phasing out heavily polluting industrial techniques and equipment that generate solid waste, thereby causing serious environmental harm, by issuing catalogues on outdated production techniques and equipment.[120] The catalogues have legal force. Producers, sellers, importers or users must stop producing, selling, importing or using the equipment listed in the catalogue by the deadline specified by the state. Users of the production techniques listed in the catalogue must stop the use as required.[121] Phased-out equipment may not be transferred to another party for use.[122] Local governments are required to formulate programmes to prevent and control environmental pollution by ISW, and to promote advanced production techniques and equipment in order to reduce the quantity and toxicity of ISW.[123]

7.3.2 Waste Generators' Responsibilities

Generators of industrial waste bear the primary responsibility of preventing and reducing waste generation at the source, of reusing, recycling and recovering waste as far as possible, and ensuring it is treated safely and disposed of in an environmentally sound manner. Waste prevention starts before the operation of a project that will generate ISW. Proponents of certain projects are required to conduct an EIA. These are: (i) projects that will generate solid waste and (ii) projects for storage, utilization and disposal of solid waste.[124] An EIA identifies, projects and assesses the potential adverse impacts of a proposed project and formulates measures to prevent, control and minimize the potential harm. The EIA mechanism works jointly with the three-simultaneities requirement, meaning that the pollution prevention and control measures proposed in the EIA documents must be designed, built and put into operation simultaneously with the main project. The main project cannot start operating until the environmental protection facilities have been inspected and

[118] SWL (2016), art. 27. [119] Huang Jianchu et al. (eds.), *Interpreting*. [120] SWL (2016), art. 28(1).
[121] SWL (2016), art. 28(2).
[122] SWL (2016), art. 28(3). 'Transfer' broadly covers any transaction, including sale, lease and donation.
[123] SWL (2016), art. 29. [124] SWL (2016), art. 13.

approved.[125] Further, facilities or sites that prevent and control environmental pollution by ISW may not be closed, idled or dismantled without prior approval. The SWL (2016) requires generators of industrial waste to establish and improve their internal responsibility system for pollution prevention and take pollution-control measures.[126] The internal responsibility system clearly allocates pollution-control duties to specific individuals and divisions.

Waste generators are required to implement clean production and a circular economy: they must reduce the volume and toxicity of the ISW they generate by rationally selecting and using raw materials, energy and other resources, and adopting advanced production processes and equipment.[127] They must use the ISW they produce as far as possible. Where waste utilization is not possible at the time of generation, generators must build facilities or sites for the safe and sorted storage or disposal of the waste.[128] 'Utilization' refers to recovery of substances from waste for use as source materials or fuels.[129] 'Storage' refers to temporary placement of solid waste at a specified facility or site.[130] 'Disposal' refers to activities conducted to reduce the quantity or volume of the solid waste, abate or eliminate the toxicity of the waste through incineration or other methods that change its physical, chemical or biological characteristics, and activities conducted to put solid waste ultimately in landfills that meet the requirements of environmental protection.[131] The construction of facilities or sites for storing or disposing of ISW must comply with national standards on environmental protection.[132]

Where generators of ISW are to terminate operations, they must, in advance, take measures at the waste storage and disposal facilities and sites to prevent and control pollution. Proper disposal of ISW must be carried out to prevent environmental pollution.[133] If the legal-person status of an entity generating ISW has been altered, the new entity must dispose of the waste safely and take measures to ensure safe operation of the waste storage and disposal facilities and sites. Where the parties concerned have reached agreement otherwise prior to the alteration, such agreements prevail. However, no agreement may exempt the obligations of the parties concerned to prevent and control pollution.[134] If an entity terminated its operation prior to the implementation of this requirement, the local government pays for the safe disposal of untreated ISW and the waste storage and disposal facilities and sites. However, if the land-use rights of the said entity have been transferred to another party, the transferee must pay for such waste disposal. Where the parties concerned have reached agreement otherwise, such agreement prevails, except that the duty of both parties to prevent and control pollution cannot be exempted.[135]

To facilitate state regulation and public supervision, waste generators must provide information about the types, quantity, flow direction, storage and disposal of ISW to local

[125] SWL (2016), art. 14. [126] SWL (2016), art. 30. [127] SWL (2016), art. 31. [128] SWL (2016), art. 33(1)
[129] SWL (2016), art. 88(7). [130] SWL (2016), art. 88(5). [131] SWL (2016), art. 88(6).
[132] SWL (2016), art. 33(2). The SEPA issued the Pollution Control Standard for the Storage and Disposal Sites of General Industrial Solid Waste (GB 18599-2001) to provide technical standards on the siting, design, operation, monitoring and closure of ISW storage and disposal facilities and sites, and the safety measures to be employed at such facilities and sites.
[133] SWL (2016), art. 35(1). [134] SWL (2016), art. 35(2). [135] SWL (2016), art. 35(3).

environmental bureaus, and must make timely report in case of any significant change.[136] Waste registration is valuable in that it informs both the authorities and the public of the generation, movement and disposal of ISW.

7.4 MSW

Daily life, and the services provided to cater to it, generate MSW. The definition of MSW also includes any solid waste that is treated as MSW by relevant laws and regulations.[137] It broadly includes household waste from residential premises and waste generated by restaurants, hotels, shops, transport and even hospitals.[138] Initially, clinical waste was managed as MSW and did not receive any extra treatment. It was not until the SARS outbreak in 2003 that public attention was drawn to this issue, because the amount of highly toxic and hazardous clinical waste dumped with MSW in landfills suddenly increased. A special control mechanism was then implemented. Since China's economic take-off, the composition of household waste has changed significantly, with a surge in electrical and electronic waste, including televisions, computers, refrigerators, washing machines, air conditioners, mobile phones, batteries, fluorescent light bulbs and light tubes. These items have made MSW increasingly flammable and toxic, as they contain heavy metals and chemicals. The exponential growth in construction and demolition waste, the result of China's massive urbanization and property market boom, has meant that landfill sites have reached capacity faster than expected. The rise of online shopping and mobile phone apps for food deliveries have triggered unprecedented growth in packaging waste, namely cardboard boxes, as well as plastic bags, and disposable meal boxes and cutlery.

To protect the environment and public health, governments bear the primary responsibility for ensuring adequate disposal installations and reliable collection services for the timely collection and safe disposal of MSW. Unfortunately, by the 1990s, less than 2 per cent of MSW produced each year had been disposed of safely, while the rest was dumped or buried.[139] Following a drive from the central government, the safe disposal rate rose to 34.8 per cent in 2005, 63.5 per cent in 2010[140] and 90.2 per cent in 2015.[141] The clearing up, collection, transportation and disposal of MSW are regulated in order to protect the environment and ensure environmental hygiene.[142] Local governments are responsible for building infrastructure and providing services to deal with MSW, while the public plays a crucial role in waste reduction and waste sorting. If the public fulfils its role, this facilitates waste recycling and recovery, improves the composition of waste that is incinerated and consequently the efficiency of the incineration, and reduces the amount of waste that ends up in landfill. The private sector is indispensable, providing waste collection and recycling services, and operating waste disposal facilities.

[136] SWL (2016), art. 32. [137] SWL (2016), art. 88(3). [138] Huang Jianchu et al. (eds.), *Interpreting.*
[139] Huang Jianchu et al. (eds.), *Interpreting.*
[140] State Council, 12th FYP on the Construction of Safe Disposal Facilities for Municipal Solid Waste (2012).
[141] State Council, 13th FYP on the Construction of Safe Disposal Facilities for Municipal Solid Waste (2016).
[142] SWL (2016), art. 41.

7.4.1 Building Infrastructure

The SWL (2016) requires governments at or above the county level to plan and coordinate the construction of facilities for the collection, transportation and disposal of municipal and rural solid waste, increase the percentage of waste that can be utilized or safely disposed of, support the development of the waste collection and disposal industry, and steadily establish and improve waste disposal services to prevent and control pollution by MSW.[143] While it is beyond the capacity of governments to build and operate all waste disposal facilities, they play a crucial role in planning infrastructure and supervising operations in order to ensure the disposal capacity is adequate and that waste is safely disposed of. The state introduced MSW disposal fees in 2002 for implementation by provincial governments. Both residential and non-residential generators of MSW are made to bear the cost of collecting, transporting and disposing of it, in order to foster private-sector involvement in waste disposal.[144]

In response to the low rate of safe disposal of MSW, which was only 34.8 per cent nationwide in 2005,[145] the central government issued FYPs on the construction of MSW disposal facilities. These plans were designed to mobilize local governments and the private sector to build waste disposal infrastructure to accommodate the increasing need for it, which was driven by urbanization and population growth in cities and towns. The 11th FYP (2006–10) set a national target of an annual 60 per cent for the safe disposal of MSW in all cities by the end of 2010.[146] The target was overshot, and 63.5 per cent of MSW was safely disposed of in 2010.[147] A new national safe-disposal target of 80 per cent was set for 2015,[148] which again was overshot when 90.2 per cent of MSW was safely disposed of in 2015.[149]

Facilities and sites for MSW disposal, and the process of constructing them, must comply with standards for environmental protection and environmental hygiene.[150] Landfill and incineration remain two major forms of disposal for MSW. Since 2005, the percentage of MSW that is disposed of by incineration has been increasing, while the amount of MSW disposed of in landfill rose for several years, but had fallen by 2015, due to the limited amount of land available for landfill sites.[151] It is projected that, by 2020, incineration will account for 54 per cent of safe disposal, while landfill will have dropped to 43 per cent.[152] Most cities in China are no longer able to cope with the unlimited expansion of landfills.

143 SWL (2016), art. 38.
144 NDRC, MOF, Ministry of Construction and SEPA, Notice on Municipal Solid Waste Disposal Fees (2002).
145 State Council, 12th FYP on the Construction of Safe Disposal Facilities for Municipal Solid Waste (2012).
146 State Council, 11th FYP on the Construction of Municipal Solid Waste Disposal Facilities (2007), part III.
147 State Council, 12th FYP on the Construction of Safe Disposal Facilities for Municipal Solid Waste (2012), preamble.
148 State Council, Opinion on Further Improving the Work of Municipal Solid Waste Disposal (2011), part II, s. 3.
149 State Council, 13th FYP on the Construction of Safe Disposal Facilities for Municipal Solid Waste (2016), preamble.
150 SWL (2016), art. 44.
151 State Council, 11th FYP on the Construction of MSW Disposal Facilities (2007), part I; State Council, 12th FYP on the Construction of MSW Disposal Facilities (2012), annex 3; State Council, 13th FYP on the Construction of MSW Disposal Facilities (2016), annex 3.
152 State Council, 13th FYP on the Construction of MSW Disposal Facilities (2016), annex 3.

TABLE 7.1 NATIONAL SAFE DISPOSAL OF MSW (INCINERATION AND LANDFILL)

	Landfill (%)	Incineration (%)	Compost and other (%)
2005	76.3	12.1	11.6
2010	77	20	3
2015	66	31	3
2020 (projected)	43	54	3

Sources: 11th FYP on the Construction of MSW Disposal Facilities (2007), part I; 12th FYP on the Construction of MSW Disposal Facilities (2012), annex 3; 13th FYP on the Construction of MSW Disposal Facilities (2016), annex 3.

However, incinerators in China face strong opposition from the public.[153] The first anti-incinerator public campaign occurred in 2006 in the Haidian district of Beijing. After years of petitioning and protests activists were finally able to persuade the local government to drop its original plan and relocate the project.

Public Protests against the Beijing Liulitun Incinerator (2006–11)[154]

Liulitun is a community of 30,000 people in the district of Haidian, located in north-west Beijing. It is home to several schools and residential estates. In August 2006, news spread on an online residents forum that an incinerator was planned for Liulitun. Residents wrote letters of protest to the Beijing municipal government, but received no response.

In December 2006, the Haidian district government confirmed that construction of the proposed incinerator would start in March 2007 and the district's existing landfill would close in 2010. Residents were angry and, on 22 December, launched a protest, using the media to express their grievances. From 1 to 3 January, they also hosted an exhibition in the community to illustrate the adverse impacts of the proposed incinerator, soliciting support from more residents from nearby estates. On 17 January 2007, the Haidian district government invited representatives of the residents to attend a meeting to discuss the project. Government officials and invited environmental scientists tried but failed to convince the residents attending of the safety of incinerators. Further rounds of petitions and protests occurred from January to April 2007, including a petition to the SEPA. On 10 May 2007, the Beijing municipal government announced that construction would be postponed. However, after the 2008 Summer Olympics, the Liulitun incinerator was again on the government's agenda. Further rounds of petitions and protests ensued from October 2008, including a petition with 10,000 signatures that was sent to all relevant agencies in February 2009. The protests finally ended in January 2011, when the Haidian district government formally announced the relocation of the proposed incineration project to Sujiatuo, a less populated community.

[153] Johnson, 'The health factor'.

[154] For detailed discussion, see Natalie W.M. Wong, 'Environmental protests and NIMBY activism: local politics and waste management in Beijing and Guangzhou', *China Information*, 30:2 (2016), 143–64; Johnson, 'The health factor'.

The success story of the public campaign against the Liulitun incinerator was then replicated in many other cities in China, including in Panyu in Guangdong province.

***Public Campaign against Panyu Waste-to-Energy Incinerator* (2009–13)**[155]

In 2000, Panyu county in Guangdong province was upgraded administratively to become a district of Guangzhou city. Unsustainable production and consumption in the Pearl River Delta region since China's economic take-off in the 1980s had generated so much waste that landfills were quickly being filled. In 2002, the Panyu district government started to look for a site for a waste-to-energy incinerator. In 2006, it chose the town of Dashi. Both the Guangzhou Development and Reform Commission and Guangzhou Urban Planning Bureau approved the Panyu district government's proposal.

The proposed site in Dashi was close to a densely populated residential area, home to more than 300,000 people. The residents were unaware of the incinerator plan until September 2009, when they immediately started a public campaign that included petition letters and street protests. Some activists were detained by the police. The Panyu district government hosted a press conference to explain why Dashi was the preferred site, and invited four experts to confirm that waste incineration would not cause pollution or health problems. The public remained unconvinced. The conflict was covered by national media,[156] and triggered a public debate on waste incineration.

In November 2009, the Guangzhou municipal government announced that the incinerator would not be constructed if it failed to pass the EIA and was opposed by a majority of residents. One month later, the Panyu district government formally postponed construction of the planned incinerator in order to reconsider the location. In 2012, it proposed three options in order of preference: Dagang, Dongyong and Dashi. The public was consulted during the EIA process and, in May 2013, Guangzhou EPB approved the project's EIA report for construction of the incinerator in Dagang. Residents obtained financial compensation and an entire village nearby was relocated.

In these cases, and in many others, disputes were settled after years of delay by relocating the proposed projects. However, moving pollution from one site to another does not resolve the fundamental problem of the environmental and health risks associated with incinerators.

7.4.2 Waste Reduction, Waste Sorting and Waste Collection

Waste reduction is given top priority in the waste management hierarchy. Every effort should be made to reduce waste generation at the source and, through reuse, recycling and recovery, divert as much waste from being disposed of in landfill or by incineration. To reduce the volume of MSW, the SWL (2016) requires municipal governments to make plans

[155] For detailed discussion, see Yanwei Li et al., 'Government responses to environmental conflicts in urban China: the case of the Panyu waste incineration power plant in Guangzhou', *Journal of Cleaner Production*, 134 (2016), 354–61; Natalie W.M. Wong, 'Environmental protests'.

[156] Luo Aihua, 'People's will more important: Panyu residents say no to incinerator', *People's Net*, 2 November 2009.

to improve the fuel mix of their municipality by replacing coal with coal gas, liquefied petroleum gas or other cleaner energy.[157] This will substantially reduce the amount of coal-ash waste generated by coal consumption. Relevant departments of municipal governments must arrange for the supply of cleaned and trimmed vegetables to cities and towns to reduce kitchen waste.[158]

Sorting waste is an essential step in any successful waste management programme that follows the waste hierarchy principle. It can significantly increase the diversion of waste away from landfill and incineration, improve the quality of compost and recyclables, and optimize the incineration process. At present, waste sorting is regulated by provincial governments and is implemented according to each province's own timeline. Strict waste sorting and maintaining the separation of different types of waste at all stages from collection and transport to treatment and disposal requires public participation at the household level. As people become accustomed to sorting their waste, they gain a better understanding of the environmental harm and risks to human health caused by solid waste. They then become more willing to change their consumption habits and are able to reduce the amount of waste they generate, by consuming less and more wisely, choosing recyclable products or products made from recycled materials. Sorted waste is more expensive to collect and transport, and successful waste sorting depends on the support, participation and compliance of all members of the community. The revenue gained from selling recyclables is not sufficient, however, to offset these higher costs. It takes government resources and commitment to gain support from households for waste sorting and from all relevant operators to ensure that waste is sorted at all stages.

Local environmental hygiene departments are in charge of cleaning up, collecting, transporting and disposing of MSW. They may contract the service to eligible third parties by tender or any other means,[159] in which case, they supervise the waste collection and disposal. The involvement of a mix of public and private services in the collection, transfer and disposal of waste improves the quality of services and reduces the cost. In order to prevent pollution, the cleaning up, collection, transfer and disposal of MSW must comply with state provisions on environmental protection and environmental hygiene management.[160] Further, MSW must be collected and transported in a timely manner. Sorting of waste should be introduced in stages depending on the capacity of a province, allowing different types of MSW to be collected and transported separately, thereby promoting waste recovery and recycling, and preventing as much waste as possible from entering landfill or incinerator.[161] While the government and waste operators are in charge of waste collection, public participation and support are crucial for sorting and collecting waste. The SWL (2016) requires all individuals and entities to place MSW at designated sites as required by the environmental hygiene departments, and refrain from the indiscriminate dumping, scattering or piling up of waste.[162]

Further, entities such as construction companies, developers, operators of public transport and other public facilities must collect waste generated at their site and provide waste bins. Construction companies must clear and transport their construction waste in a timely manner for recovery or safe disposal in accordance with the provisions of the

[157] SWL (2016), art. 43(1). [158] SWL (2016), art. 43(2). [159] SWL (2016), art. 39.
[160] SWL (2016), art. 41. [161] SWL (2016), art. 42. [162] SWL (2016), art. 40.

environmental hygiene department.[163] Operators of public transport, such as trains, buses and ships, must clean up and collect the solid waste generated during service.[164] Entities engaged in urban development and redevelopment, and development of residential premises, as well as operators of facilities and sites accessible by the public, including airports, harbours, stations, parks and shops, must provide waste collection facilities in accordance with the state provisions on environmental hygiene.[165]

7.4.3 Waste Reuse, Recycling and Recovery

The state encourages entities and individuals to purchase and use recycled and reusable products.[166] The State Council is required to release a catalogue for products and packaging materials that must be recycled so that enterprises that manufacture, sell or import any of the listed products or materials are aware of their obligations to collect them for recycling.[167] However, this has not yet happened. The implementation of compulsory recycling is seriously overdue, but the delayed catalogue, as well as ways to control excessive packaging, have been on the government's agenda.[168] Municipal governments must coordinate and plan a collection network to promote the reuse, recycling and recovery of MSW.[169] It should be noted, however, that substances recovered from MSW may only be used in accordance with state provisions and cannot be used in products if this would endanger human health.[170]

Recycling is an important component of the waste management system. Much of the MSW, such as paper, plastics, glass and metals, can be recycled. The cost of sorting and transporting recycled materials is compared with the value of the material as a feedstock for local industry to determine whether materials should be recycled. The government should formulate policies and measures to attract private investment in waste recycling and recovery, foster private recycling and recovery facilities, and promote technological innovation. While the State Council has issued regulations to promote recycling, recovery and disposal of e-waste and vehicles,[171] it needs to do more. For instance, making it compulsory for the government to procure recycled or recyclable products would send a clear signal to investors and business operators of a strong and stable source of demand for such products.

In China, recycling occurs via two routes. The first route is the formal system for collection of MSW, which is operated or supervised by the environmental hygiene departments of local governments. Collection service providers may choose to sort out the recyclables and sell them to recycling operators. The second route is operated by informal waste pickers who often come from rural areas neighbouring the city. They make a living by picking recyclables, such as metals, glass, paper and plastics, from landfills located on the outskirts of cities. Working at these contaminated environments of mixed MSW without protection exposes them to the risks recorded by photographer Wang Jiuliang in his documentary *Beijing*

[163] SWL (2016), art. 46. [164] SWL (2016), art. 47 [165] SWL (2016), art. 48. [166] SWL (2016), art. 7.

[167] SWL (2016), art. 18(2).

[168] State Council, Circular Economy Development Strategy and Short-Term Action Plan (2013), chapter 8.

[169] SWL (2016), art. 43(3). [170] SWL (2016), art. 45.

[171] See State Council, Provisions on Recycling of End-of-Life Vehicles (2001); State Council, Regulation on the Recovery and Disposal of Waste Electrical and Electronic Products (2009).

Besieged by Garbage.[172] China's current recycling rates are lower than most other countries, and much of its current recycling system is adversely affected by the import of low-cost waste from high-income countries. The recycling sector needs to be professionalized and formalized if it is to capitalize on the opportunities of China's market economy. A World Bank report of 2005 projected tenfold growth of China's recycling industry by 2030.[173]

7.4.4 Safe Disposal

Safe disposal of waste by incineration or in landfill is at the bottom of the waste management hierarchy and should be a last-resort destination for MSW that cannot be reused, recycled or recovered. Until the 1980s, open dumping of waste was common practice in China. By 2005, the national rate for safe disposal of MSW was only 34.8 per cent.[174] Incineration technology was introduced to China in the late 1980s and developed rapidly in the 1990s.[175] As discussed in Section 7.4.1 on infrastructure building, incinerators are promoted by the governments of cities with limited land resources.

Landfill

Landfill is essential for any solid waste management system, providing space for the final disposal of the residual substances from treatment facilities, such as ash from incinerators. The life of a landfill can be extended by aggressive implementation of waste recycling and resource recovery. In many Chinese cities, landfill is no longer a viable option due to fast population growth and limited available land. Worse still, landfills are a major source of serious water and soil contamination.[176] The documentary *Beijing Besieged by Garbage*, produced by photographer Wang Jiuliang, presented Beijing as a capital city surrounded by approximately 500 waste dumps.[177] It drew public attention to the grave environmental and health risks posed by improperly managed landfills. While the Beijing municipal government responded by immediately closing the illegal sites and investing in 'sanitary' landfills, much more needs to be done to improve the operation of landfills in China.

Poorly operated landfills have caused serious contamination of land and water. To control and reduce the environmental and public health risks, a World Bank study identified five problems to be addressed as a matter of urgency: (i) the presence of waste pickers, (ii) flawed design of the landfill slopes, (iii) inadequate collection and treatment of leachate,

[172] Landsberger, *Beijing Garbage*, at 160–1; Liu Qin, 'Film: how China became'; Christy Choi, 'Documentary maker captures mounting waste from Chinese population boom', *South China Morning Post*, 5 December 2013.

[173] World Bank, *Waste Management in China*, at 45.

[174] State Council, 12th FYP on the Construction of Safe Disposal Facilities for Municipal Solid Waste (2012).

[175] Dongliang Zhang, et al, 'Waste-to-energy in China: key challenges and opportunities', *Energies*, 8 (2015), 14182–96. China's first incinerator was Shenzhen Qingshui River MSW Incineration Plant, which was constructed in 1988.

[176] Groundwater contamination is found near landfills in most provinces in China, and is especially serious in East China, which is home to much older landfills than West China. Leakage of leachate, a complex mixture of pollutants containing high levels of chemical oxygen demand (COD), ammonia nitrogen (NH) and other toxic substances, is common. See Zhiyong Han et al., 'A review of groundwater contamination near municipal solid waste landfill sites in China', *Science of the Total Environment*, 569–70 (2016), 1255–64.

[177] Landsberger, *Beijing Garbage*, at 160–1; Liu Qin, 'Film: how China became'; Christy Choi, 'Documentary maker captures mounting waste'.

(iv) inadequate compaction and covering of waste and (v) lack of landfill gas collection.[178] Landfills generate odour and air pollution, directly affecting the life and health of people living nearby. This results in public opposition to landfills and makes it more difficult to plan and construct new sites. Closed illegal sites continue to impact public health, environmental quality and land values. It is crucial for governments to clean up such sites as soon as is practicable in order to control and mitigate water and soil contamination.

Incineration

Incineration has the advantage of significantly reducing waste volumes, energy recovery and complete disinfection. Since 2000, there has been increasing reliance on incineration for the disposal of waste. Between 2005 and 2015, the percentage of waste disposed of by incineration rose from 12.1 per cent to 31 per cent.[179] It is projected to reach 54 per cent by end-2020, with a target of 60 per cent set for the highly populated and economically advanced eastern region of China.[180] The central government has enacted incentives to encourage investment in incinerators, including value-added tax (VAT) refunds, prioritization for commercial bank loans, state subsidies (2 per cent) for loan interest, and a subsidized electricity price. Municipal governments are encouraged to expand their incineration capacity to address the lack of land resources for landfill.

Incinerators typically generate emissions of dioxin, furans and mercury, which must be controlled. Burning waste also results in fly ash and bottom ash, both of which require treatment and safe disposal at landfill. Substandard incineration facilities and techniques have not only triggered pollution incidents, but have also intensified not-in-my-backyard (NIMBY) campaigns against incinerators. Studies have found that concerns surrounding environmental pollution are the number one reason behind public campaigns against incinerators.[181] The cases of the Liulitun and Panyu incinerator projects highlight first the failure of local governments to communicate effectively with the affected residents, and then their attempts to educate the public on the safety of incineration at meetings with representatives. Local governments must take anti-incinerator campaigns seriously, and must address public opposition by engaging the public early in the decision-making process, thereby building mutual trust and the confidence of local communities.

To further alleviate public concerns, governments and operators of incinerators must control toxic air pollution effectively, improve the efficiency of energy recovery, strengthen environmental monitoring, supervision and enforcement, and ensure public access to accurate and reliable monitoring data in a timely manner. First, the low efficiency in energy recovery in China's incinerators is caused mainly by the nature of the waste that goes into the furnace, a high proportion of which is organic matter and material with a high moisture content. This results from poor waste sorting at the stage of collection and

[178] World Bank, *Waste Management in China*, at 30.

[179] State Council, 11th FYP on the Construction of MSW Disposal Facilities (2007), part I; State Council, 13th FYP on the Construction of MSW Disposal Facilities (2016), annex 3.

[180] State Council, 13th FYP on the Construction of MSW Disposal Facilities (2016), part I, s. 3; annex 3.

[181] Youliang Huang et al., 'Public acceptance of waste incineration power plants in China: comparative case studies', *Habitat International*, 47 (2015), 11–19.

recycling. Aggressive measures have been taken by some municipal governments to require waste sorting at source in order to improve the heat value of the waste for incineration.[182] Pre-treatment can further address the high moisture content of the MSW. Second, while incineration cuts the volume of waste significantly, residues remain in the form of bottom and fly ash. Bottom ash may be used as a building material after it has been stabilized. Fly ash, which contains dioxin and heavy metals, must be controlled.[183] Strict environmental compliance by operators of incinerators and effective supervision and monitoring by regulatory agencies are crucial to control pollution and alleviate public concerns. Third, full disclosure of information by governments and incinerators is the basis of building the trust of local communities. Lack of access to information intensifies public concern and unfounded panic. Last, even if incinerators do operate in full compliance with relevant environmental standards, they may still cause nuisance and an adverse environmental impact. Local communities should be compensated fairly and this could take the form of job opportunities, leisure facilities such as green parks, indoor swimming pools, gyms and free parking, and discounted heating and electricity.[184] These benefits could, to certain extent, ease local resistance to such nuisance projects.

7.5 HW

Waste defined as hazardous is a special category of solid waste that is either listed in the HW Catalogue or is identified as hazardous according to the criteria and methods of identification prescribed by the state environmental authority.[185] Tighter control is exercised over HW to ensure its traceability, while extra caution must be taken by generators of HW and all operators dealing with it in order to prevent and manage the high risks to humans and environment. The state environmental authority works with relevant departments of the State Council to formulate the HW Catalogue and sets uniform criteria and methods for identifying HW and uniform labels for HW facilities and containers.[186] The HW Catalogue (2016) lists: solid and liquid wastes demonstrating one or more of the hazardous characteristics of corrosivity, toxicity, ignitability, reactivity and infectivity; and wastes that are potentially hazardous and may cause harm to the environment and human health and must be subject to control as HW.[187] Chemical substances included in the Directory of Hazardous Chemical Substances are also treated as HW when discarded.[188]

In addition, clinical waste is also classed as HW.[189] It was not until the SARS outbreak in 2003 that China realized it had a lack of capacity for the safe disposal of clinical waste. As a

[182] Shanghai leads the way in implementing compulsory sorting of MSW by enacting the Shanghai Regulation on Management of Municipal Solid Waste (2019). It came into force on 1 July 2019.

[183] Jinglan Hong et al., 'Intensification of municipal solid waste disposal in China', *Renewable and Sustainable Energy Reviews*, 69 (2017), 168–76; Yan Wang et al., 'Atmospheric emissions of typical toxic heavy metals from open burning of municipal solid waste in China', *Atmospheric Environment*, 152 (2017), 6–15.

[184] Zhao Xin-gang et al., 'Technology, cost, a performance of waste-to-energy incineration industry in China', *Renewable and Sustainable Energy Reviews*, 55 (2016), 115–30.

[185] SWL (2016), art. 88(4).

[186] SWL (2016), art. 51. MEP, NDRC and Ministry of Public Security (MPS), HW Catalogue (2016). It replaced the HW Catalogue (2008) that was issued by the MEP and NDRC.

[187] HW Catalogue (2016), art. 2. [188] HW Catalogue (2016), art. 4. [189] HW Catalogue (2016), art. 3.

consequence of this, China issued the Regulation on the Control of Clinical Waste (2003)[190] and the National Plan on the Construction of Disposal Facilities for Hazardous Waste and Clinical Waste (Construction Plan) (2004).[191] The regulation and control of clinical waste is undertaken by two state ministries: the state health authority and its subordinate health bureaus supervise generators of clinical waste, while the state environmental authority and local environmental agencies supervise operators of clinical waste disposal facilities. The health and environmental authorities collaborate on supervision of the collection, transport, storage and disposal of clinical waste; the former focus on disease control and safe handling of clinical waste by hospitals and clinics, and the latter focus on pollution prevention and safe disposal at facilities accepting clinical waste for disposal.[192]

7.5.1 Compulsory Labelling

The SWL (2016) requires the use of identification labels on HW containers and packages, as well as at the facilities and sites used to collect, store, transport and treat such waste.[193] The label alerts anyone coming into contact with such a container or package, or visiting a facility or site, to act with caution in order to prevent and control the risk of toxic contamination.

7.5.2 Governments: Infrastructure Planning and Construction

The state environmental authority works with the NDRC to formulate, for approval by the State Council, national plans on the construction of centralized HW disposal facilities and sites.[194] Local governments are responsible for organizing the construction of centralized HW disposal facilities or sites in accordance with the plan.[195] In January 2004, the SEPA (predecessor of the MEP and the MEE) and the NDRC issued the Construction Plan.[196] The State Council, in its approval of the Construction Plan (2004), required provincial governments to implement it and ensure safe storage and disposal of HW, clinical waste and radioactive waste by 2005.[197] By the beginning of this century, a small percentage of China's HW had either been treated in a rudimentary manner or disposed of in landfill or by incineration, with little thought given to environmental protection. More than 26 million t of HW had been stored on or off the premises of the HW generators from 1996 to 2002, occupying land and posing a serious risk to the environment and human health.[198] The Qujing environmental catastrophe is only the tip of the iceberg of China's problem of HW disposal, which has caused toxic contamination of land and water.

190 The State Council issued the Regulation on the Control of Clinical Waste on 16 June 2003 and revised it on 1 August 2011.

191 The SEPA and NDRC issued the Construction Plan on 19 January 2004, following State Council approval on 19 December 2003.

192 Regulation on Clinical Waste (2011), art. 5.

193 SWL (2016), art. 52.

194 SWL (2016), art. 54(1).

195 SWL (2016), art. 54(2).

196 SEPA and NDRC, Construction Plan (2004). The Construction Plan was issued on 19 January 2004 with immediate effect.

197 State Council, Approval of the National Plan on the Construction of Disposal Facilities for Hazardous Waste and Medical Waste (2003). State Council approval was granted on 19 December 2003.

198 Construction Plan (2004), chapter I.

According to the Construction Plan (2004), a national disposal centre is to be built to treat and dispose of persistent organic pollutants (POPs) and other special HW. Each province is required to construct a central HW disposal facility for the treatment and disposal of HW generated by households, teaching and research institutions and enterprises generating small quantities of HW. Generators of large quantities of HW are required to install their own waste treatment and disposal facilities, and clinical waste disposal facilities were to be built in each city. However, by early 2020, one-quarter of cities did not have central disposal facilities for clinical waste.[199] Provincial governments plan the location and construction of HW landfill for final disposal of ash and soot from incineration and sludge from clinical wastewater treatment. The overall emphasis is on sorting waste that may be utilized, as well as incineration and safe disposal in landfill.[200] The Construction Plan (2004) set the specific targets of building 31 comprehensive HW disposal facilities and 300 clinical waste disposal facilities nationwide by end-2006.[201]

7.5.3 HW Generators: Management Plan, Registration and Disposal

Generators of HW are required to prepare a management plan for dealing with HW,[202] and report it to local environmental bureaus for the record.[203] The management plan must describe the measures that will be taken to reduce the volume and toxicity of the HW, and details of its storage, utilization and disposal.[204] Each generator of HW must inform the local environmental bureau of the type of HW generated, the quantity, flow direction, storage and means of disposal.[205] A generator must make timely report if there is substantial change to the management plan or to the information that has been given to the bureau.[206] Generators must dispose of their HW in compliance with state provisions and are prohibited from dumping or stockpiling waste on- or off-site without approval. An HW generator that fails to dispose of HW properly will be ordered by its local environmental bureau to dispose of the waste within a specified time limit. If it fails to do so, the local agency will designate a third party to dispose of the waste at the waste generator's expense.[207] Disposing of HW at a landfill site is a violation of state provisions and an HW disposal fee will be charged.[208] The fees thus collected may only be used to prevent and control pollution and may not be appropriated for any other purpose.[209]

7.5.4 HW Operators: Permit Control

Due to the high level of risks posed by the mishandling of HW, the SWL (2016) imposes permit control on operators engaged in collecting, storing, utilizing and disposing of HW. Entities engaged in collecting, storing or disposing of HW must apply to their local environmental bureau for a permit to operate. Entities engaged in HW recovery for

[199] Chen Yu, 'Alleviating pressure on clinical waste disposal facilities', *Science and Technology Daily*, 30 April 2020, 5.
[200] Construction Plan (2004), chapter II.
[201] Construction Plan (2004), chapter III.
[202] SWL (2016), art. 53(1).
[203] SWL (2016), art. 53(2).
[204] SWL (2016), art. 53(2).
[205] SWL (2016), art. 53(1).
[206] SWL (2016), art. 53(3).
[207] SWL (2016), art. 55.
[208] SWL (2016), art. 56(1). The specific measures for levying the HW disposal fee are formulated by the State Council.
[209] SWL (2016), art. 56(2).

utilization must apply instead to the state or provincial environmental authority for a permit to operate.[210] In 2014, the MEP delegated the authority to approve HW operation permits to provincial EPBs.[211] The SWL (2016) prohibits the collection, storage, utilization or disposal of HW without an operation permit or in violation of the terms and conditions of the permit.[212] To tighten permit control on HW operations, the SWL (2016) also prohibits any individual or entity from supplying HW to any person not possessing an HW operation permit allowing the collection, storage, utilization or disposal of HW.[213] The case of *Yunguang Chemical* (2012)[214] involved the illegal disposal of HW. The court imposed criminal sanctions not only on the party disposing of the HW without a permit, but also on the party that provided the HW.

Yunguang Chemical (2012)

Yunguang Chemical, an HW disposal company with an operation permit, agreed to dispose of HW for Changfeng Chemical. Jiang Yunchuan, the legal representative of Yunguang Chemical, assigned the task of disposal to Xia Yong, an employee. Xia passed the HW to Zhang Bibin, a contractor, for disposal, without checking whether the latter had an HW operation permit. Zhang did not possess an HW operation permit. He was assisted by two others, Zhou Gang and Hu Xuehui, and they dumped more than 28 t of HW and more than 75 t of toxic sludge on a hillside, causing serious pollution. The total cost of clean-up, transportation and proper disposal of the waste was 918,315 yuan.

Sichuan Xingwen County Court (2012) found Yunguang Chemical had violated the SWL by entrusting the HW to Zhang, who did not have a permit, thereby causing serious pollution. The court convicted both Yunguang Chemical and relevant individuals for the crime of environmental pollution, imposing criminal sanctions. Yunguang Chemical was fined 500,000 yuan. Xia was sentenced to two years' imprisonment and fined 20,000 yuan. Zhang was sentenced to one and a half years' imprisonment and was fined 20,000 yuan. The other three defendants Jiang, Zhou and Hu were given suspended sentences.

It was later expressly stipulated by the SPC and SPP Interpretation on the Application of Laws in Adjudicating Environmental Criminal Cases (2013, revised 2016) (SPC and SPP Interpretation) that 'anyone who entrusts a party, knowing that the latter has no HW operation permit or operates beyond the scope of the permit, to collect, store, utilize or dispose of HW and serious pollution is caused, commits the crime of environmental pollution'.[215]

The State Council implemented the permit-control mechanism by issuing the Measures on Permit Control over Hazardous Waste Operations (Measures on HW Permit Control).[216] There are two types of HW operation permit: a comprehensive permit allowing the holder to

210 SWL (2016), art. 57(1).
211 MEP, Notice on Delegation of Approval Authority over Operation Permit for Toxic and Hazardous Waste Operation (2014).
212 SWL (2016), art. 57(2). 213 SWL (2016), art. 57(3).
214 SPC, Four Model Cases on Environmental Crimes (2013), case no. 3.
215 SPC and SPP Interpretation (2013, revised 2016), art. 7.
216 State Council, Measures on HW Permit Control (2004, revised 2013 and 2016).

collect, store and dispose of any HW, with five years' validity, and the collection permit, which is valid for three years and allows the holder to collect waste mineral oil generated from vehicle repairs and maintenance, and waste cadmium and nickel batteries from household waste.[217] Applications for the comprehensive permit are subject to higher thresholds for requirements on personnel, transport vehicles, packaging, facilities and equipment for temporary storage, waste disposal facility and equipment, technology, techniques and emergency response, among others.[218] In contrast, applications for the collection permit are only subject to requirements regarding transport vehicles, packaging, facilities and equipment for temporary storage, and emergency response.[219] Holders of a collection permit may not keep HW for more than ninety days, the limit for temporary storage.[220]

Local environmental bureaus at different levels issue the HW operation permits.[221] County bureaus issue HW collection permits.[222] Municipal bureaus issue permits to operators of facilities for the disposal of clinical waste.[223] Provincial bureaus issue permits for all other types of HW operation.[224] These environmental bureaus exercise supervision over permit holders by both paper review and on-site inspection. Results of the supervision and inspection are to be recorded and made publicly accessible.[225] Permit holders must regularly report to an environmental bureau. They must also record the operation accurately, including the type, source and destination of HW collected, stored and disposed of, and any pollution incidents. They must keep the records for a minimum of ten years. Operation records for HW landfills must be kept for all time. Where an operator ceases operation, the records must be transferred to the local environmental bureau.[226]

It should be noted that the collection and storage of HW are both subject to a compulsory sorting requirement. The SWL (2016) prohibits the mixed collection, storage, transport and disposal of types of HW that are not compatible with each other and have not been treated for safe disposal in a mixed manner.[227] The SWL (2016) also prohibits HW from being stored with non-HW.[228] Storage of HW is meant to be temporary and may not last more than one year. Any extension is subject to approval by the environmental bureau that issued the operation permit.[229] To prevent secondary contamination, the SWL (2016) requires that any site, facility, equipment, container and packaging material, among others, used to collect, store, transport or dispose of HW must be decontaminated before being used for any other purpose.[230] Further, the decommissioning cost for key centralized HW disposal facilities and sites should be budgeted for in the investment or operation costs.[231]

7.5.5 Movement of HW

The SWL (2016) imposes strict controls on the movement of HW by requiring parties involved in HW generation, transportation, storage, treatment or disposal to complete an

[217] Measures on HW Permit Control (2016), arts. 3 and 13(1).
[218] Measures on HW Permit Control (2016), art. 5.
[219] Measures on HW Permit Control (2016), art. 6.
[220] Measures on HW Permit Control (2016), art. 20.
[221] Measures on HW Permit Control (2016), art. 7(1).
[222] Measures on HW Permit Control (2016), art. 7(3).
[223] Measures on HW Permit Control (2016), art. 7(2).
[224] Measures on HW Permit Control (2016), art. 7(4).
[225] Measures on HW Permit Control (2016), art. 17.
[226] Measures on HW Permit Control (2016), art. 18.
[227] SWL (2016), art. 58(1).
[228] SWL (2016), art. 58(3).
[229] SWL (2016), art. 58(2).
[230] SWL (2016), art. 61.
[231] SWL (2016), art. 65.

HW transfer registration form. Movement across provincial borders is subject to the requirement of application, consultation, consent and approval from provincial environmental bureaus at the place of origin and destination. The party handling HW applies for approval to the provincial bureau at the place of origin, which will not grant approval unless it, upon consultation, obtains consent from the provincial bureau at the place of destination. The movement of HW is prohibited without such approval.[232] The legal requirement of consultation with the environmental bureau at the place of destination to seek their consent is a necessary mechanism to assess the capacity for safe disposal. Where movement of HW involves more administrative regions than the cities of origin and destination, the municipal EPB of the place of origin is required to notify all municipal environmental bureaus of the transit cities in a timely manner.[233] This ensures that all movement of HW from the place in which it is generated until its eventual disposal is supervised. Carriers of HW must take measures to prevent and control pollution and observe state regulations on transportation of hazardous goods. Passengers and HW may not be carried in the same vehicle.[234]

7.5.6 HW Emergency Response

Entities that generate, collect, store, transport, utilize and dispose of HW must take measures to prevent pollution incidents, must prepare an emergency response plan and report it to the local environmental bureau for the record. Environmental bureaus must inspect the emergency response preparations.[235] Where a pollution incident or other emergency causes serious environmental harm by HW, the entities liable must take immediate measures to eliminate or mitigate the environmental harm, promptly inform potentially affected entities and residents, report to local environmental bureaus and relevant departments, and accept a government investigation and any settlement decisions.[236] Where serious pollution has been or is likely to be caused by HW, threatening the lives and property of residents, the local environmental bureau must immediately report to the people's government of the same level and the supervisory environmental authority at the next-higher level. The people's government must take effective measures to eliminate or mitigate the harm, including issuing an order to suspend operations where necessary.[237]

7.6 WASTE IMPORTS

Transboundary movement of waste is often motivated by the desire to reduce the cost of waste disposal and avoid potential environmental liabilities at the place of origin. From the late 1970s to the mid-1990s, when China enacted the SWL (1995), the country was a popular destination for waste generated in developed countries in Asia, Europe and North America. As much of the imported waste could not be recovered for use as raw materials, they ended up in landfills, storage sites or were dumped indiscriminately across China, causing serious contamination of land and water. China began to regulate waste imports in 1995 and the rules have been tightened since then. The Measures on the Import of Solid

[232] SWL (2016), art. 59(1). [233] SWL (2016), art. 59(2). [234] SWL (2016), art. 60.
[235] SWL (2016), art. 62. [236] SWL (2016), art. 63. [237] SWL (2016), art. 64.

Waste (2011) (Measures on Waste Import)[238] regulates waste imports in order to prevent pollution caused by imported waste.[239] 'Solid waste import' refers to any movement of solid waste into China from outside its territory.[240] The regulatory control on waste import applies equally to waste from Hong Kong, Macau and Taiwan,[241] despite the fact that they are treated as part of China under the Hong Kong SAR Basic Law,[242] Macau SAR Basic Law[243] and Chinese Constitution.[244]

While China has banned the importing of waste for dumping, storage or disposal by landfill or incineration since 1995, it does permit the importing of waste that will be used as a raw material and waste for recovery and utilization. This is due to the shortage of resources that China has experienced since its economic take-off in the late 1970s. Thus, solid waste is divided into three categories: waste that is banned from being imported, waste that is subject to import restrictions and waste for which importing is permitted. The SWL (2016) requires the state environmental authority to work with the MOC, NDRC, the State Customs Administration and the SAQSIQ to issue and update the national catalogues on the three categories.[245]

7.6.1 Banned Imports

Considering China's limited capacity for safe disposal of solid waste, the SWL (2016) banned the shipment of solid waste into China from outside its territory for dumping, storage or disposal via incineration or landfill.[246] It prohibits the importing of solid waste that cannot be used as a raw material or solid waste that cannot be recovered for safe utilization.[247] It also prohibits the importing of solid waste included in the National Catalogue of Waste Prohibited for Import, which forms one part of the National Catalogue on Waste Import.[248] Under the National Catalogue on Waste Import (2014),[249] waste that is banned from being imported includes animal waste, mineral waste, clinical waste, MSW, waste leather, waste rubber including waste tyres, particular types of waste paper such as wallpaper, waste textiles including second-hand clothes, waste glasses such as broken glasses, certain designated waste metals, waste batteries, waste electrical and electronic equipment and waste asbestos.[250]

The Measures on Waste Import (2011) expressly prohibits the importing of HW, the importing of solid waste for heat recovery, the importing of solid waste of the types that are

[238] SWL (2016), art. 25(5). Five departments of the State Council, the MEP, MOC, NDRC, State Customs Administration and the SAQSIQ, devised administrative measures on the control of waste imports. Together, they issued the Measures on Waste Import on 8 April 2011, which came into force on 1 August 2011.

[239] Measures on Waste Import (2011), art. 1.

[240] Measures on Waste Import (2011), art. 2(2).

[241] Measures on Waste Import (2011), art. 54.

[242] The Basic Law of the Hong Kong Special Administrative Region of the People's Republic of China (1990), preamble and art. 1.

[243] The Basic Law of the Macau Special Administrative Region of the People's Republic of China (1993), preamble and art. 1.

[244] Constitution (2004), preamble.

[245] SWL (2016), art. 25(2).

[246] SWL (2016), art. 24.

[247] SWL (2016), art. 25(1).

[248] SWL (2016), art. 25(3). The Catalogue was published on 30 December 2014.

[249] The MEP, MOC, NDRC, State Customs Administration and State Administration for Quality Supervision, Inspection and Quarantine (SAQSIQ) issued the National Catalogue on Waste Import on 30 December 2014. It came into force on 1 January 2015.

[250] National Catalogue on Waste Import (2014), annex I, National Catalogue on Waste Prohibited for Import.

generated domestically and stored in large quantities without being recovered for utilization, and the importing of solid waste not yet subject, in China, to compulsory environmental protection standards or technical guidance.[251] The SWL (2016) also prohibits HW from transiting through the territory of China.[252] While using China for transit means the shipment of HW will not remain in China permanently, the very nature of HW creates tremendous environmental risks during transportation, and any spill or leakage may cause irreversible harm to the environment and to human health and safety. This provision is also consistent with the Basel Convention, to which China is a party.

7.6.2 Restricted and Permitted Imports

Solid waste that can be used as a raw material is divided into two categories: 'restricted import' and 'permitted import',[253] based on the intensity of the pollution created during the process of recovery for utilization. Under the National Catalogue on Waste Import (2014), 'waste restricted for import' includes waste plastics, waste paper, waste textile raw materials such as waste cotton and synthetic fabrics, waste vehicle parts and waste vessels.[254] 'Waste permitted for import' contains only two categories: waste wood and waste metals.[255] Importing solid waste that is listed in the Catalogue of Waste Restricted for Import requires the prospective importer to apply to the state environmental authority, which will consider the application in collaboration with the MOC.[256] The import of solid waste listed in the Catalogue of Waste Permitted for Import does not require prior agency approval.

Imported solid waste will be inspected by the authority for quality supervision, inspection and quarantine.[257] If the imported waste is found to be in violation of relevant environmental protection standards or technical guidance, the quarantine authority must immediately inform the customs authority and the provincial environmental bureau of the province in which the border control point is located. The bureau will then inform the provincial bureau of the province in which the waste utilization enterprise is located and the state environmental authority.[258] The customs authority will order the waste to be returned to its place of origin by the importer or carrier within a specified time limit. Neither the importer nor the carrier may abandon the waste.[259]

7.6.3 The Import Ban of 2017

China is determined to ban foreign rubbish, stop waste smuggling and improve the regulatory control of solid waste imports.[260] The changes to the waste importing rules have been phased in according to waste type and the availability of domestic substitutes. The 2017 amendment of the National Catalogue on Waste Import increased the categories of waste that may not be imported, adding waste plastics from households, unsorted waste

[251] Measures on Waste Import (2011), art. 8. [252] SWL (2016), art. 66. [253] SWL (2016), art. 25(1).

[254] National Catalogue on Waste Importing (2014), annex II, National Catalogue on Waste Restricted for Import for Use as Raw Materials.

[255] National Catalogue on Waste Importing (2014), annex III, National Catalogue on Waste Automatically Permitted for Import for Use as Raw Materials.

[256] SWL (2016), art. 25(3). [257] SWL (2016), art. 25(4). [258] Measures on Waste Import (2011), art. 26.

[259] Measures on Waste Import (2011), art. 29.

[260] State Council, Implementation Plan on the Ban of Foreign Garbage to Promote Reform of Waste Import Control System (2017).

paper, waste textiles and vanadium slag, all of which China had imported for recovery and recycling for decades.[261] The ban on this first tranche of wastes came into force on 31 December 2017. A second ban came into force on 31 December 2018. It applies to: waste hardware, ships for scrapping, waste automobile parts, smelter slag, and waste plastics from industrial sources. A third ban came into force on 31 December 2019, applying to: scrap stainless steel waste, scrap titanium waste and scrap wood waste.[262]

Until the 2020 amendment of the SWL, China's waste management had focused primarily on waste collection and disposal, aiming to provide waste collection for all urban areas and expand the service to rural regions. China is building infrastructure, including landfills and incinerators, for the safe disposal of waste, and efforts are being made to improve the performance of waste disposal facilities. There is an urgency, however, to move up in the waste management hierarchy and give top priority to waste reduction, recycling and recovery. Solid waste management should achieve a reduction in waste by reshaping production and consumption. Charging user fees, disposal fees or waste collection fees based on volume or weight provides a direct incentive for those generating waste to reduce their waste volumes. Charging industrial, commercial and institutional waste generators fees sends a clear signal on the cost of operation and can lead to behavioural change. While it may take time for the general public to refuse overconsumption and shift to a green lifestyle, public education and awareness campaigns can speed up the process of change. Compulsory waste sorting by households is the indispensable first step to boost recycling and recovery and reduce the amount of waste that is incinerated or disposed of in landfill. Residents' participation in household waste sorting also directs them towards a new lifestyle in which waste reduction is key. China must de-link economic growth from resource consumption and waste generation by working towards a circular economy, an economic model that reduces resource use and the impact of human activity on the environment. In a circular economy, the value of products and materials is maintained for as long as possible. Resource use is minimized, as is waste, and, when a product reaches the end of its life, it is repurposed to create further value.

[261] The Announcement on the National Catalogue of Waste Import was issued by the MEP, MOC, NDRC, the General Administration of Customs and the SAQSIQ on 10 August 2017.

[262] The Announcement on Adjustment of the National Catalogue on Waste Import was issued by the MEE, the MOC, NDRC and the General Administration of Customs on 13 April 2018.

8

Soil Contamination

Soil contamination is caused by current and historical activities, including industrial and mining operations, waste disposal and agriculture. For decades this issue has been neglected by Chinese environmental regulation, because toxic substances in the soil are invisible and have a long period of latency before harm is detected. Soil contamination was believed to be a problem only in rural areas, with pollution caused by excessive use of fertilizers and pesticides (dichlorodiphenyltrichloroethane (DDT) and hexachlorocyclohexane (HCH)) in agricultural fields, and a lack of household waste disposal facilities.[1] Farmland contamination was further aggravated in the 1980s and 1990s by an increase in industrial and mining operations, which released heavy metals including lead, mercury and cadmium, among others. For these reasons, China's initial response to soil contamination was narrow and focused on rural areas. The first Soil Environmental Quality Standard (1995)[2] applied solely to agricultural land and covered only eight heavy metals (cadmium, mercury, arsenic, copper, lead, chromium, zinc and nickel) and two organic compounds (DDT and HCH). Toxic contaminants in the soil may be absorbed by crops grown on the contaminated farmland, thereby entering the food chain.

It was not until the beginning of the twenty-first century that soil contamination in both rural and urban China caught public attention.[3] Media exposure of lead poisoning and cadmium-tainted rice set off the alarm for food safety in China.[4] Nitrogen from fertilizers can cause blood disorders in infants that result in brain damage or death, while cadmium affects liver function and bone health and lead is especially harmful to children's behavioural and cognitive development.[5] Soil pollution clearly poisons more than China's farmland.[6]

[1] State Council, *Environmental Protection in China (1996–2005)*; see also the 10th FYP (2001–05) on Environmental Protection and 11th FYP (2006–10) on Environmental Protection; Yang Meng, 'The damaging truth'; Patton, 'China farm pollution worsens'.

[2] The Soil Environmental Quality Standard (GB15618–1995) was recently replaced by the Soil Environmental Quality Risk Control Standard for Soil Contamination of Agricultural Land (GB15618–2018).

[3] 'The bad earth: the most neglected threat to public health in China is toxic soil', *The Economist*, 8 June 2017.

[4] Xinhua, 'Pollutants, pesticides'; LaFraniere, 'Lead poisoning in China'; Liu Hongqiao, 'The polluted legacy'; Chen Huamian et al., 'Heavy metal pollution'; Gong Jing, 'Toxic rice'.

[5] Drenguis, 'Reap what you sow'.

[6] Li Jing, 'Soil pollution poisons more'.

The urbanization that has taken place since the 1990s has been characterized by the relocation of industry from city centres to the outskirts, as well as property development and infrastructure building, which together have exposed the hidden risks of contaminated sites that were previously used for industrial operations.[7] China's large-scale relocation of industry was driven primarily by the growth of the urban population and increasing demand for residential premises and office buildings. The relocation was partly also a response to the increasing pollution-related disputes between urban residents and industrial operators. The former industrial sites became a limited source of land for redevelopment into residential or commercial premises supported by subway networks. In April 2004, at the Hongshi site, three construction workers were poisoned while working on Beijing's SongJiaZhuang subway station. This was the first time that public attention had been drawn to serious historical contamination left behind by industrial operators, in this case a pesticide factory and subsequently Beijing Hongshi Paint Co.[8] In July 2006, six road construction workers fainted as they dug at a site in Guoxiang, an area near the southern ring road in the city of Suzhou. The site had been contaminated by a chemical factory that had since been relocated. In February 2007, a construction worker at a property development site in Heshan, in the Hanyang district of Wuhan city, was poisoned and rushed to hospital for emergency treatment. As more workers fell ill on the site, which had been contaminated by the relocated Wuhan Pesticide Factory, construction had to be suspended.[9] These seemingly isolated cases are only the tip of the iceberg in China.

While these cases highlight the acute poisoning of construction workers caused by sudden exposure to exceptionally high levels of toxins accumulated in the soil, more cases of land contamination cause harm quietly in a chronic manner to humans, property and the environment. People with long-term exposure by direct skin contact and/or consumption of contaminated water and food are also at high risk of harm from land contamination. In December 2015, nearly 500 students at Changzhou Foreign Language School fell ill after moving to the new campus in September of the same year. They suffered headaches, skin rashes and from December 2015 to early 2016 some were even diagnosed with lymphoma and leukaemia. The Changlong toxic site was located less than 100 m from the school campus.[10]

In addition, the National Soil Pollution Survey (2005–13) painted an extremely bleak picture to the public and to policymakers of the extent of China's land contamination. The extent and degree of soil contamination first exposed by isolated incidents of contaminated

[7] Zhao Yuhong, 'Land contamination in urban China'; Jian Xie and Fasheng Li, *Overview of the Current Situation.* In China's efforts to transform and upgrade the economy from one dependent on the secondary industrial sector to one focused on the tertiary services sector, the relocation of industry away from city centres and residential zones has exposed the issue of land contamination. The relocation of hundreds of old industrial facilities from Beijing to the city outskirts left behind 8 million m^2 of contaminated brownfield land in need of redevelopment.

[8] Zhao Yuhong, 'Land contamination in urban China'; 'Hidden toxic sites', *Caijing*; 'Toxic site clean-up', *Jinghua Times*; Liu Wei, 'Beijing: after the subway workers'; Liu Yang, 'Soil at the site'; Pan Hongtao, 'Relocation of chemical enterprises'.

[9] Luo Jingyun and Zhou Hui, 'Lack of information disclosure'; Zhang Yanchun et al., 'Wuhan Heshan "toxic site"'; Zhou Hui, 'Wuhan toxic site'; Jeffery and Xiaobo Zhao, 'Developing a national contaminated land liability scheme'.

[10] Li Jing, 'Hundreds of pupils'; 'School campus 100 meters', *Xinhua News.*

food, toxic poisoning and then by systematic national soil pollution survey, confirmed the real threat posed to the health and safety of humans and the environment. Soil contamination demanded immediate and effective legal and regulatory responses to prevent new contamination and to clean up historically contaminated sites. In response to this need, the State Council issued the Action Plan on Prevention and Control of Soil Pollution (Soil Action Plan) (2016)[11] and the National People's Congress Standing Committee (NPCSC) enacted the Soil Pollution Prevention and Control Law (2018) (SPPCL).[12] This chapter focuses on the key regulatory mechanisms found in the SPPCL (2018) for preventing new contamination and cleaning up contaminated land, with reference to state policies and plans on soil pollution control, including the Soil Action Plan (2016). Section 8.1 introduces China's first National Soil Pollution Survey (2005–13), which provided the basic data and preliminary understanding of land contamination needed for the state to deliver government plans and a legislative regime. Section 8.2 focuses on government responsibilities and agencies in charge. Section 8.3 discusses standards, survey and monitoring as a crucial basis for regulatory control of land contamination. Section 8.4 examines key mechanisms used to protect land from pollution. Section 8.5 addresses risk control and remediation of contaminated land, including farmland and land for development. Section 8.6 discusses information disclosure and public supervision.

8.1 NATIONAL SOIL POLLUTION SURVEY, STATE PLANS AND LAWMAKING

The first regulatory instrument to highlight the urgency of soil pollution control was the Decision on Implementing Scientific Development and Strengthening Environmental Protection (State Council Decision) (2005).[13] It stipulates key measures to be taken, including the National Soil Pollution Survey, comprehensive treatment of contaminated farmland, control of pollution from pesticides, fertilizers and agricultural films (plastic membranes used as mulch),[14] and risk control and remediation of sites from which polluting enterprises have been relocated.[15] While these are general declarations of the state's position, not detailed mechanisms, the State Council Decision (2005) started the process of government action and regulation on soil contamination, which now includes the National Soil Pollution Survey (2005–13), the Soil Action Plan (2016) and the SPPCL (2018).

8.1.1 The First National Soil Pollution Survey (2005–2013)

The first National Soil Pollution Survey, led and coordinated by the Ministry of Environmental Protection (MEP) and the Ministry of Land Resources (MLR), was conducted from April 2005 to December 2013. The survey covered approximately 6.3 million km^2, including all China's farmland, and part of its forestland, grasslands, unutilized land and

[11] The Soil Action Plan (2016) was issued by the State Council on 28 May 2016 and came into force immediately. It is also known as the Ten Provisions on Soil Pollution, following the Ten Provisions on Air Pollution (2013) and the Ten Provisions on Water Pollution (2015).

[12] The SPPCL (2018) was passed on 31 August 2018 by the 13th NPCSC at its 5th session. It came into force on 1 January 2019.

[13] The State Council Decision was issued on 3 December 2005.

[14] State Council Decision (2005), part IV, s. 14.

[15] State Council Decision (2005), part IV, s. 12.

land for development. The MEP and MLR issued a brief report entitled *National Soil Pollution Survey Report*, which painted a very bleak picture of the serious soil contamination that existed in China.[16] It started with a general statement that '[t]he overall national soil environmental quality does not allow us to be optimistic. Soil pollution in some regions is quite severe. Soil environmental quality of the farmland is of great concern. Soil pollution at the sites historically used by industrial or mining operators are particularly problematic.'[17] Such a pessimistic tone is rarely seen in the opening statement of a government report. From the limited data released,[18] we gain a general understanding of the nature, type, distribution, causes, extent and degree of soil pollution in China. Overall, 16.1 per cent of the total number of monitoring points were in violation of soil environmental quality standards.[19] A closer look at the contamination of different types of land reveals that 19.4 per cent of farmland, 10 per cent of forestland and grassland and 11.4 per cent of unutilized land was in violation of the relevant standards.[20] Of 55 farms irrigated with sewage, 39 were contaminated. Of the 1,378 monitoring points tested on the 55 farms, violations of standards were found at 26.4 per cent.[21] More serious pollution is found at and near the following sites:[22]

(i) heavily polluting industrial operators: at the 690 heavily polluting enterprises surveyed (ferrous metal, non-ferrous metal, tannery, papermaking, petrochemical, coal chemical, pharmaceutical, plastic, mineral production, metal production and electricity, among others), 36.3 per cent of the 5,846 monitoring points were in violation.

(ii) abandoned industrial sites: at the 81 sites that had been used by chemical, mining or refinery operators, 34.9 per cent of the 775 monitoring points were in violation.

(iii) industrial parks: at the 146 industrial parks surveyed, 29.4 per cent of the 2,523 monitoring points were in violation.

(iv) waste disposal sites: at the 188 solid waste disposal sites surveyed, 21.3 per cent of the 1,351 monitoring points were in violation.

(v) oilfields: at the 13 oilfields surveyed, 23.6 per cent of the 494 monitoring points were in violation.

(vi) mining zones: at the 70 mining zones surveyed, 33.4 per cent of the 1,672 monitoring points were in violation.

16 MEP and MLR, *National Soil Pollution Survey Report*.

17 MEP and MLR, *National Soil Pollution Survey Report*, part I.

18 The government refused to release a full detailed report and raw survey data to the public, presumably in order to avoid public concern over the seriousness of rural and urban soil contamination in China. Requests from the public for disclosure of the survey data was rejected on the basis that the data was a state secret. Li Jing, 'Report on mainland China's soil pollution'; see also discussion on government data control in Itakura, 'Current issues'.

19 MEP and MLR, *National Soil Pollution Survey Report* , part I. The standards referred to by the *National Soil Pollution Survey Report* include the Soil Environmental Quality Standard (GB15618–1995), Environmental Quality Evaluation Standards for Farmland of Edible Agricultural Products (HJ/T 332-2006) and Environmental Quality Evaluation Standards for Farmland of Greenhouse Vegetable Production (HJ/T 333-2006).

20 MEP and MLR, *National Soil Pollution Survey Report*, part III.

21 MEP and MLR, *National Soil Pollution Survey Report*, part IV(7).

22 MEP and MLR, *National Soil Pollution Survey Report*, part IV.

Key pollutants in the soil can be divided into inorganic and organic pollutants. Eight major inorganic pollutants found in the soil are cadmium, mercury, arsenic, copper, lead, chromium, zinc and nickel, while major organic pollutants are HCH, DDT and polycyclic aromatic hydrocarbon.[23] The more severe soil contamination is found in the south of China as compared to the north. Southern China and Southwest China suffer from large areas of contamination by heavy metals, including cadmium, mercury, arsenic and lead. The Pearl River Delta, the Yangtze River Delta and the former industrial base in Northeast China have particularly serious soil pollution compared to other regions.[24]

The first national survey ended up with the release of only a very brief report containing limited data; the fact that the authorities refused full disclosure of the survey results, claiming that the results were a state secret, indicates that soil contamination in China is indeed a significant threat to both public health and food safety.[25] Soil contamination directly affects the growth and quality of agricultural products. It not only reduces agricultural output, but also increases health risks where pollutants are absorbed by plants and enter the food chain. There have been incidents of cadmium-tainted rice from Hunan province causing serious health concerns.[26] Where contaminated land is redeveloped for residential, commercial or industrial purposes, people living or working on the premises are subject to health risks from exposure to toxic and hazardous pollutants in the soil by ingestion, inhalation or skin contact. The Changzhou Foreign Language School case highlights the public health risk posed by sites left toxic by industrial operators.[27] Soil pollution affects the growth and reproduction of all plants, animals and microorganisms in the soil, causes loss of normal biological function of the soil and potential contamination of surface water, groundwater and the atmosphere. The *National Soil Pollution Survey Report* points to major sources of pollution: pollution discharge by industrial and mining operations, piling of mineral waste and hazardous waste (HW) on land, emissions from vehicles and agricultural activities such as sewage irrigation, overuse of fertilizers, pesticides and agricultural films, and livestock breeding. The survey results have convinced all stakeholders of the urgency of regulating and controlling soil pollution, if further deterioration of the soil is to be prevented.

8.1.2 The Recent Work Arrangement on Soil Environmental Protection and Comprehensive Treatment (2013)

As the National Soil Pollution Survey came to an end, the State Council issued the Recent Work Arrangement on Soil Environmental Protection and Comprehensive Treatment (Recent Work Arrangement)(2013) to address China's dire soil contamination.[28] It set short-term targets: 80 per cent of farmland was to meet the national soil quality standards by 2015, no further soil deterioration related to contamination was to occur, and farmland

[23] MEP and MLR, *National Soil Pollution Survey Report*, part II.

[24] MEP and MLR, *National Soil Pollution Survey Report* , part I.

[25] Christina Larson, 'Soil pollution is a state secret in China', Bloomberg Business Week, 25 February 2013; Jonathan Watts, 'The clean-up begins on China's dirty secret: soil pollution', *The Guardian*, 12 June 2012.

[26] A high concentration of cadmium in the soil of rice paddies results from long-term mining of non-ferrous metals, and from refineries discharging waste and wastewater containing heavy metals, including cadmium.

[27] Li Jing, 'Hundreds of pupils'; 'School campus 100 meters', *Xinhua News*.

[28] The Recent Work Arrangement was issued by the State Council on 23 January 2013.

and drinking-water-source reserves (DWSRs) were to be strictly protected from pollution. The Recent Work Arrangement (2013) was brief, but laid down basic environmental principles to be adhered to in cases of soil contamination[29] and key tasks[30] to be undertaken to address the soil contamination. The principles and tasks were adopted by the Soil Action Plan (2016) and the SPPCL (2018).

8.1.3 The 13th Five-Year Plan (2016–2020)

The State Council's 13th Five-Year Plan on Socio-Economic Development (2016–20) (13th FYP)[31] stipulates that measures must be taken to prevent and control soil pollution, to prioritize protection of farmland to ensure the quality of soil and safety, and to strengthen the environmental monitoring of soil on development land (land due to be developed).[32] Key projects of soil pollution control contained in the 13th FYP include: more frequent soil pollution investigation; 100 pilot remediation projects each for contaminated farmland and development land; six demonstration zones for sharing good practice in soil pollution control; remediation of contaminated sites following the relocation of chemical enterprises; remediation of 10 million *mu* of contaminated farmland and risk control at 40 million *mu* of contaminated farmland; treatment of heavy metal contamination at the Xiang Jiang River basin.[33]

8.1.4 Soil Action Plan (2016)

The State Council issued the legally binding Soil Action Plan (2016) to address, as a matter of urgency, the serious problem of soil pollution. It aimed to improve soil environmental quality, ensure the safety of agricultural products, protect the human environment and promote long-term sustainable use of soil by setting short- and medium-term goals.[34] It set out ten key tasks:

(i) conduct regular soil contamination survey and investigation to assess soil environmental quality across China;

[29] These include the polluter-pays and the investor-pays principles. Under the first principle, polluters must pay for the clean-up of the contaminated sites. The second principle covers situations where the polluters cannot be identified or do not have the capacity to pay. In such cases, potential investors in the land redevelopment bear the cost of site remediation. See Recent Work Arrangement (2013), part III, s. 2.

[30] The approaches taken include: (i) prioritizing the prevention of new contamination by targeting source control; (ii) designating priority protection zones that cover farmland and DWSRs; (iii) applying risk control measures over the use of contaminated sites, including farmland and development land; (iv) conducting site clean-up and remediation in select areas and regions; (v) improving the environmental monitoring capacity of soil quality; and (vi) speeding up the soil environmental protection project implementation. See Recent Work Arrangement (2013), part II.

[31] The 13th FYP (2016–20) was issued on 16 March 2016 by the 12th NPC at its 4th session.

[32] 13th FYP (2016–20), part X on 'Speeding up the improvement of the eco-environment', chapter 44 on 'Strengthening environmental governance'. The measures to be taken are determined by land-use type and degree of contamination.

[33] 13th FYP (2016–20), part X on 'Speeding up the improvement of the eco-environment', chapter 44 on 'Strengthening environmental governance'.

[34] According to the Soil Action Plan (2016), national soil pollution should be preliminarily contained by end-2020 and the safety of farmland and development land basically guaranteed. The safe-use rate of contaminated arable land should be around 90 per cent and the safe-use rate of contaminated development land should be above 90 per cent. By end-2030, soil environmental quality should have been improved nationwide to ensure the safety of both farmland and development land. The safe-use rate of contaminated arable and development land should have reached above 95 per cent. See Soil Action Plan (2016), preamble.

(ii) promulgate legislation, standards and regulations to control soil pollution;
(iii) adopt classified management of farmland with measures to ensure the environmental safety of agricultural produce;
(iv) implement threshold management over development land to prevent human health risks;
(v) strengthen protection of uncontaminated land and prevent more sites from being contaminated;
(vi) enhance regulatory control of polluting sources to prevent soil pollution;
(vii) conduct pollution treatment and remediation to improve regional soil environmental quality;
(viii) improve research and development and support the environmental protection industry;
(ix) develop a government-led governance system to protect soil;
(x) strengthen the environmental performance appraisal mechanism and strictly implement the accountability mechanisms.

The Soil Action Plan (2016) is significant because it initiated China's soil pollution regulatory control in five key areas: (i) it demanded in-depth surveying of soil pollution to produce solid data on the location, size and distribution of contaminated agricultural land and the impact on agricultural produce, and data on the distribution of contaminated sites on land used by key sectors and enterprises and the environmental risks; (ii) it required the making and revising of laws, regulations, rules, measures and standards on the prevention and control of soil pollution; (iii) it set general targets for implementing pilot schemes and demonstration projects for treatment and remediation to establish a technical system for soil pollution prevention and control, which includes pollution prevention at source, risk control, treatment, remediation and regulatory supervision; (iv) it clarified the responsibilities of liable parties and regulates service providers that engage in treatment and remediation of contaminated land and (v) it improved information disclosure and public education in order to establish a control regime for soil pollution that is led by the government, implemented by enterprises, involves the public, and is supervised and monitored by the public.

8.1.5 SPPCL (2018)

The SPPCL (2018) was placed on the lawmaking agenda in 2013 by the 12th NPCSC.[35] It took five years to draft and pass the SPPCL (2018), which came into force in 2019.[36] The SPPCL (2018) aims to protect and improve the ecological environment, prevent soil pollution, protect the health of the public, promote sustainable use of land resources and foster the ecological civilization to achieve sustainable socio-economic development.[37] 'Soil pollution' is defined as 'a phenomenon where human activities have caused certain substances to enter the surface of the earth, triggering chemical, physical, biological and other

[35] Lawmaking Plan of the 12th NPCSC, 30 October 2013. According to the Plan, the SPPCL was listed as Category I legislation, meaning that it was ready for deliberation by the 12th NPCSC.
[36] The SPPCL (2018) was passed on 31 August 2018 by the 13th NPCSC at its 5th session. It came into force on 1 January 2019.
[37] SPPCL (2018), art. 1.

changes that affect the function and effective use of soil, endangering public health and damaging the ecological environment'.[38] The basic principles of soil pollution prevention and control include: an emphasis on prevention, priority given to protection, classified management, risk control, the polluter-pays principle and public participation.[39] Instead of focusing on clean-up of historically contaminated land, the SPPCL (2018) prioritizes pollution prevention and the protection of uncontaminated land.

8.2 GOVERNMENT RESPONSIBILITY AND AGENCIES IN CHARGE

The governance system for soil environmental protection under the SPPCL (2018) is led by the government, participated in by enterprises and the public, and supervised by the public. The central government makes law and policy, sets standards and guidelines and coordinates among different departments and regions. The provincial governments are in charge of implementation to achieve the soil protection targets allocated by the central government. Municipal and county governments are responsible for carrying out the soil survey, investigating and monitoring any contamination, and risk assessment, risk control and remediation, among others.[40] The Ministry of Environment and Ecology (MEE) is responsible for overall supervision and regulation of the prevention of soil pollution. Other departments including the Ministry of Agriculture and Rural Affairs (MARA), Ministry of Natural Resources (MNR), Ministry of Housing and Urban–Rural Development (MOHURD) and the Forestry and Grassland Bureau (FGB) provide supervision and management.[41] Local bureaus of these bodies, as well as environmental bureaus, perform similar functions within local jurisdictions.[42]

Local governments at all levels bear primary responsibility within their jurisdictions for the prevention of soil pollution and the safe use of land.[43] They are required to implement the Soil Action Plan (2016) by making local work plans with key tasks and targets. Provincial governments must submit their work plans to the State Council for the record.[44] Local governments at county level and above must incorporate soil pollution prevention and control into their socio-economic development plans and environmental protection plans.[45] Environmental bureaus at municipal level and above are required to work with relevant bureaus in charge of agriculture and rural affairs, natural resources, housing and urban and rural development, forestry and grassland to compile 'soil pollution prevention and control plans' (SPPCPs) in accordance with environmental protection plans, land functions and the results of the land contamination survey and monitoring. An SPPCP is issued for implementation once it has been approved by the people's government at the same level as the bureau that drafted it.[46]

Governments of all levels are supervised by the same-level people's congress. In a government's annual report on environmental status to the same-level people's congress or its standing committee, it is required to include soil pollution prevention and control and

[38] SPPCL (2018), art. 2. [39] SPPCL (2018), art. 3. [40] Soil Action Plan (2016), part IV, s. 28.
[41] SPPCL (2018), art. 7(1). [42] SPPCL (2018), art. 7(2). [43] SPPCL (2018), art. 5(1).
[44] Soil Action Plan (2016), part X, s. 32. [45] SPPCL (2018), art. 11(1). [46] SPPCL (2018), art. 11(2).

its progress towards achieving environmental targets.[47] Within the government, the target responsibility regime and the performance appraisal mechanism now cover prevention and control of soil pollution. This means that the achievement of targets, or otherwise, for soil pollution control is taken into account in the annual performance assessment of departments and individuals.[48] The State Council signs agreements with provincial governments to allocate national targets to each province. It has conducted assessments of different provinces in different years between 2016 and 2020 on progress in implementation of key tasks. A review of the implementation of the Soil Action Plan (2016) by provincial governments was due in 2020 to assess their performance in achieving the targets. The outcome of the assessment will be an important consideration in the performance appraisal of both the local administration and individuals.[49] A provincial government that fails in its annual review will be ordered to rectify the situation by a specified deadline, and, until the deadline is reached, environmental impact assessment (EIA) reviews are suspended. If rectification is not completed by the deadline, the EIA suspension continues and the heads of the provincial governments and relevant agencies must attend supervision talks with the MEE.[50] Provincial environmental bureaus will arrange to meet heads of municipal governments and relevant departments for talks if those governments and departments have failed to tackle serious soil contamination. The bureaus will request that the government or department takes timely and effective measures to rectify the situation. Information on the supervision talks and the rectification measures is disclosed to the public.[51]

8.3 STANDARDS, SURVEY AND MONITORING

The MEE and other ministries set standards on soil quality and standards targeting sources of soil pollution, as well as technical standards on site investigation, monitoring, risk assessment and remediation, among others. Surveying and monitoring are carried out by local bureaus under the leadership of ministries.

8.3.1 Standards

Prior to the Soil Action Plan (2016) and the SPPCL (2018), there had been very few standards on soil environmental management, and those that existed were either outdated or of narrow application.[52] The SPPCL (2018) grants standard-setting powers to the MEE and provincial governments and also stipulates the standard-setting process, which must include expert review and public consultation, and follow-up review and updating of the standard. The MEE is required to issue risk control standards for national land contamination based on the state of the land contamination, the risk to public health, ecological risk, scientific and technological capacity, and land use.[53] Provincial governments may set local standards for items that are not regulated by national standards, or may set standards that are tighter than national standards. Local standards must be reported to the MEE for the

[47] SPPCL (2018), art. 75. [48] SPPCL (2018), art. 5(2). [49] Soil Action Plan (2016), part X, s. 35.
[50] Soil Action Plan (2016), part X, s. 35. [51] SPPCL (2018), art. 76.
[52] For example, the Soil Environmental Quality Standard (GB15618–1995) covers agricultural land, pastures, forestland and nature reserves, but not development land in China's vast urban areas.
[53] SPPCL (2018), art. 12(1).

record.[54] The land contamination risk control standards are compulsory standards.[55] The setting of standards must involve expert review, and consultation with relevant government departments, trade associations, enterprises and institutions, and the public.[56] Implementation of the standards will be regularly assessed, and they should be amended as needed.[57] The MEE and provincial environmental bureaus must publish the standards on their websites for public access and free download.[58]

Soil quality standards indicate the desired quality of the soil for the particular land use. Without them it would be difficult to determine whether soil is contaminated, whether it is in need of treatment and remediation, and what the targets of remediation should be. In June 2018, the MEE issued two sets of soil environmental quality standards (for trial use): one for agricultural land and the other for development land. The Soil Environmental Quality: Risk Control Standard for Soil Contamination of Agricultural Land (for trial use) (GB15618-2018)[59] aims to protect the environmental quality of agricultural land, manage and control the risks of soil contamination of agricultural land, ensure the safety of agricultural products, ensure the normal growth of crops and protect the ecological environment of the land. The Soil Environmental Quality: Risk Control Standard for Soil Contamination of Development Land (for trial use) (GB36600-2018)[60] aims to strengthen environmental regulation of soil on development land, manage and control the risks of contaminated sites and their impacts on human health, and ensure the safety of the human environment.

In addition to quality standards for agricultural and development land, technical standards or guidance on monitoring, survey, investigation, risk control and remediation are of crucial importance to ensure the accuracy and reliability of monitoring data and assessment reports, and the quality and effectiveness of risk control and remediation. Examples are:

- Technical Guidance on Environmental Site Investigation (HJ 25.1-2014)
- Technical Guidance on Environmental Site Monitoring (HJ 25.2-2014)
- Technical Guidance on Risk Assessment of Contaminated Sites (HJ 25.3-2014)
- Technical Guidance on Remediation of Contaminated Sites (HJ 25.4-2014)

Standards targeting sources of soil pollution should be formulated or revised to give priority to prevention. There is an urgent need to make or revise quality standards for agricultural films, pesticide packaging and the maximum permitted levels of toxic and hazardous substances in fertilizers, feedstuffs and irrigation water. Agricultural films have become a major source of farmland contamination. As agricultural films are ultra-thin (0.008 mm $\pm$ 0.003 mm), it is difficult and costly to recover them from soil for recycling. In 2013 alone, more than 1 million t of agricultural films were dumped as waste plastics.[61]

[54] SPPCL (2018), art. 12(2). [55] SPPCL (2018), art. 12(3). [56] SPPCL (2018), art. 13(1).
[57] SPPCL (2018), art. 13(2). [58] SPPCL (2018), art. 13(3).
[59] The Soil Environmental Quality: Risk Control Standard for Soil Contamination of Agricultural Land (for trial use) (GB15618-2018) was issued on 22 June 2018. It came into force on 1 August 2018. It replaced the Soil Environmental Quality Standard (GB15618-1995).
[60] The Soil Environmental Quality: Risk Control Standard for Soil Contamination of Development Land (for trial use) (GB36600-2018) was issued on 22 June 2018. It came into force on 1 August 2018.
[61] MEP, 31 May 2016, 'MEP answers reporters' questions'. Online article. www.mee.gov.cn/gkml/sthjbgw/qt/201605/t20160531_352670.htm

There is an urgent need for new standards on durability and biodegradability of agricultural films in order to prevent farmland from being contaminated by plastics.

8.3.2 Survey

The first National Soil Pollution Survey (2005–13) covered 6.3 million km^2 of land in rural and urban China. Smaller-scale surveys conducted by the MLR between 1999 and 2014 covered 1.5 million km^2 of land, including nearly 1.4 billion *mu* of farmland, by 2014. A heavy metal contamination survey conducted in 2012 by the Ministry of Agriculture (MOA) covered 1.6 billion *mu* of farmland used for major agricultural production.[62] These surveys have provided the data for a preliminary understanding of China's soil pollution, but they were conducted over a long period of time using different methods and standards. More accurate and reliable data on the current status of soil pollution is needed if regulation to prevent and control soil pollution and to conduct proper remediation of contaminated sites is to be effective.

To ensure data is accurate and updated in a timely manner, a national survey of soil environmental quality and soil contamination will be conducted every ten years.[63] The State Council leads the national soil pollution survey. The MEE is required to work with bodies in charge of agriculture and rural affairs, natural resources, housing and urban and rural development, forestry and grassland to conduct the national survey at least once every ten years.[64] Further investigations may be carried out as needed by state departments or local governments at a municipal level and above.[65] In-depth survey is needed to acquire authoritative, consistent and accurate data. Considering the time, and financial and human resources needed to conduct an in-depth survey of soil pollution, the Soil Action Plan (2016) takes the practical approach of focusing on agricultural land and land used by 'key polluting sectors and enterprises' in the early stages of its implementation. By end-2018, the surveying of agricultural land should have been completed, thereby giving a deeper understanding of the scope and distribution of soil contamination of agricultural land and the impact on the quality of agricultural products. By end-2020, the state should have a sound understanding of the distribution of contaminated sites used by key polluting sectors and enterprises and the associated risks, and should have made plans for in-depth investigation of contamination and developed technical rules.[66]

8.3.3 Monitoring

Historically, environmental monitoring of soil was conducted by three different departments – environmental protection, land resources and agriculture – for different purposes. They set up their own monitoring stations, used different methods and collected data at different intervals. By 2018, the MEE had set up 38,880 monitoring stations, while the MARA had established 40,061 and the MNR 1,000, forming a national monitoring network.[67]

[62] MEP, 31 May 2016, 'MEP answers'. [63] Soil Action Plan (2016), part I, s. 1; SPPCL (2018), art. 14(1).
[64] SPPCL (2018), art. 14(1). [65] SPPCL (2018), art. 14(2). [66] Soil Action Plan (2016), part I, s. 1.
[67] MEE, 16 November 2018, 'MEE answers reporters' questions regarding the work plan on monitoring of agriculture land by national soil environmental monitoring network'. Online article. www.mee.gov.cn/xxgk2018/xxgk/xxgk15/201811/t20181116_674167.html

The SPPCL (2018) aims to consolidate soil environmental monitoring systems to achieve data consistency, accuracy and reliability, and to promote data sharing to allow regulation and enforcement to be improved. It requires the state to establish a land contamination monitoring system, with the MEE in charge of issuing monitoring guidelines.[68] A national monitoring network will be established by the MEE, in collaboration with state ministries in charge of agriculture and rural affairs, natural resources, housing and urban and rural development, water resources, public health, and forestry and grassland. They must jointly plan the siting of monitoring stations.[69] This general monitoring must focus on: (i) key heavy metal pollutants, including cadmium, mercury, arsenic, lead and chromium, and organic pollutants, including polycyclic aromatic hydrocarbon and petroleum hydrocarbon; (ii) key sectors, including the mining of non-ferrous metals, the smelting of non-ferrous metals, oil exploitation, oil processing, chemicals, coking, electroplating and tanneries; (iii) major grain-producing counties and urban developed areas.[70]

In addition to general monitoring led by the central government, local governments are required to conduct focused monitoring of agricultural and development land.[71] Local agencies in charge of agriculture and rural affairs, and forestry and grassland are required to work with agencies in charge of environment and natural resources to conduct focused monitoring of certain sites used for agricultural purposes. These are: (i) sites producing crops that are contaminated by excessive levels of pollutants; (ii) sites that are irrigated by sewage or have, in the past, been so irrigated; (iii) sites previously used as animal farms or for storage or landfill of solid wastes; (iv) sites previously used for mining or at which grave or severe pollution incidents have taken place; (v) sites in the vicinity of facilities for the production, storage, utilization or disposal of toxic and hazardous substances and (vi) any other sites as determined by the state ministries in charge of agriculture and rural affairs, forestry and grassland, the MEE and MNR.[72] Local environmental bureaus are required to work with agencies in charge of natural resources to conduct focused monitoring of certain sites to be used for development. These are: (i) sites previously used for the production, utilization, storage, recycling or disposal of toxic and hazardous substances; (ii) sites previously used for storage or landfill of solid waste; (iii) sites at which grave or severe pollution incidents have occurred and (iv) any other sites as determined by the MEE and MNR.[73]

One of the aims of the Soil Action Plan (2016) was to establish a national platform for environmental data on soil by end-2018. The platform, which was launched by the MEE on 26 December 2018,[74] was to provide updated information and a scientific basis enabling departments (of environmental protection, land resources, agriculture and public health) to develop effective regulation and make sound decisions.[75] With the assistance of advancements in technology, the general and focused monitoring data is to be updated and transmitted to the national soil environmental data platform.[76] The sharing of monitoring

[68] SPPCL (2018), art. 15(1). [69] SPPCL (2018), art. 15(2). [70] Soil Action Plan (2016), part II, s. 6.
[71] SPPCL (2018), arts. 16 and 17. [72] SPPCL (2018), art. 16. [73] SPPCL (2018), art. 17.
[74] Liu Xiaoxing, 'National soil environmental data platform launched', *China Environment News*, 27 December 2018.
[75] Soil Action Plan (2016), part I, s. 3. [76] SPPCL (2018), art. 82.

data among different government departments will improve enforcement, standard setting and policymaking.

8.4 PROTECTION OF LAND FROM CONTAMINATION: SOURCE CONTROL

The SPPCL (2018) gives top priority to preventing new pollution and aims to protect uncontaminated land to ensure its continued safe use, both for agricultural production and for urban development. It requires the state to strengthen protection of uncontaminated land.[77] Local governments at all levels must prioritize the protection of uncontaminated farmland, forestland, grasslands and DWSRs.[78] All levels of governments must strengthen the protection of national parks and other nature reserves in order to maintain their ecological function.[79] Unused land must be protected from pollution and ecological destruction.[80] Local agencies must strengthen their environmental enforcement against the illegal discharge or dumping of toxic and hazardous substances in deserts and on shoals, saline and alkaline land and marshland.[81] In addition to using EIA as an instrument to prevent and mitigate adverse environmental impacts, the SPPCL (2018) focuses on key sources of soil pollution, including industrial operations, mining, waste disposal and agriculture.

8.4.1 Prevention at Source by EIA and Planning

The EIA mechanism is an important instrument for preventing and mitigating environmental harm that may be caused by proposed plans and projects. An EIA is required of plans involving land use and construction projects that may cause land contamination. Relevant EIA documents must include an assessment of adverse impacts on the land and measures to prevent such impacts.[82] The EIA operates in tandem with the three-simultaneities requirement to prevent new contamination of soil on development land. This means a proponent of a construction project must conduct the EIA and propose measures to prevent and control soil pollution, following which the design, construction and operation of the pollution-control facilities must occur simultaneously with the main project.[83]

Planning the location and distribution of industrial enterprises and nuisance projects in a scientific manner has a direct positive impact on soil environmental quality and the health and safety of other land users. Local governments must implement land-use and urban and rural development plans, and strictly apply their requirements on the geographical distribution of industries and enterprises. Constructing new projects that may cause land contamination, and modifying or expanding existing projects that may do so, is prohibited in the vicinity of residential premises, schools, hospitals, nursing homes and residential care homes for the elderly, among others.[84] The Soil Action Plan (2016) specifically prohibits the construction of new non-ferrous metal smelters and coking plants in the above areas, and requests relocation or permanent closure of existing enterprises that cause serious soil contamination. Special care is required in the planning and siting of nuisance projects,

[77] SPPCL (2018), art. 31(1). [78] SPPCL (2018), art. 31(2). [79] SPPCL (2018), art. 31(3).
[80] SPPCL (2018), art. 31(4). [81] Soil Action Plan (2016), part V, s. 15. [82] SPPCL (2018), art. 18.
[83] Soil Action Plan (2016), part V, s. 16. [84] SPPCL (2018), art. 32.

including facilities and sites for waste disposal and recycling and livestock farming, in order to prevent and control soil contamination.[85]

8.4.2 Industry

Based on the polluter-pays principle, any unit or individual involved in the production, utilization, storage, transport, recycling, disposal or discharge of toxic and hazardous substances must take measures to prevent leakage, run-off or dispersal in order to avoid land contamination.[86] A catalogue of toxic and hazardous substances is to be issued and regularly updated by the MEE and the National Health Commission to impose tight control and prevent soil contamination.[87] As an interim measure before the catalogue is issued, 'toxic and hazardous substances' subject to tighter control refers to substances included in the following: Catalogue of Toxic and Hazardous Water Pollutants (first batch) (issued 2019), Catalogue of Toxic and Hazardous Air Pollutants (2018) (issued 2019), Catalogue of Toxic and Hazardous Waste (revised 2016), Soil Pollution Risk Control Standards for Development Land (issued 2018) and Catalogue of Chemicals under Priority Control (first batch) (issued 2017).[88]

Local environmental bureaus issue a list of key entities that are under special control because they discharge toxic and hazardous substances. This special control is designed to prevent soil contamination. The list is to be released to the public and is subject to timely revision.[89] These key entities have legal duties to: (i) strictly control their toxic discharge and report annually to local environmental bureaus; (ii) screen for hidden soil-contamination risks and prevent leakage, run-off or dispersal of toxic and hazardous substances and (iii) conduct self-monitoring and report monitoring data to the local environmental bureaus.[90] These legal duties must be expressly stipulated in the pollution discharge permits.[91] The key entities are accountable for the accuracy of the self-monitoring data. Where environmental bureaus detect abnormal data, they must investigate in a timely manner.[92] In addition, the bureaus must inspect the soil surrounding the sites of key entities on a regular basis.[93]

The dismantling of facilities, equipment, buildings and structures is part of the process of relocation or closure of enterprises for urban development. The dismantling poses a high risk of causing soil contamination if carried out improperly. Key entities are required to make plans, including emergency response measures, to prevent soil pollution occurring during the process of dismantling any facility, equipment, building or structure, and submit them to local environmental bureaus and industry and information bureaus for the record before the work begins.[94] Enterprises in the sectors of non-ferrous metal smelting, oil processing, chemicals, coking, electroplating and tannery are specifically required to plan

[85] Soil Action Plan (2016), part V, s. 17.

[86] SPPCL (2018), art. 19.

[87] SPPCL (2018), art. 20. The MEE and National Health Commission must screen the toxic and hazardous substances in the soil and, based on their impact and harm to human health and the ecological environment, must issue and revise the catalogue.

[88] Measures on the Management of Soil Environment of Industrial and Mining Land (for trial use) (2018), art. 20.

[89] SPPCL (2018), art. 21(1).

[90] SPPCL (2018), art. 21(2).

[91] SPPCL (2018), art. 21(3).

[92] SPPCL (2018), art. 21(4).

[93] SPPCL (2018), art. 21(5).

[94] SPPCL (2018), art. 22(2).

for the safe disposal of residual pollutants in order to prevent soil contamination, and such plans must be reported to local agencies for the record before dismantling starts.[95]

8.4.3 Mining

Mining is another major source of soil contamination in China,[96] and deserves closer supervision and monitoring by the regulatory agencies. The cadmium-tainted rice in Hunan province painted a bleak picture of rice paddies contaminated by industrial and mining operations. In February 2013, *Southern Daily*, the newspaper of the Guangdong branch of the Chinese Communist Party (CCP), reported that 10 thousand t of cadmium-tainted rice had entered the food chain in Guangdong.[97] In May 2013, Guangdong Provincial Food Safety Commission announced that of thirty-one batches of cadmium-contaminated rice the province had received, fourteen came from Hunan, four from Guangdong, four from Jiangxi and two from Guangxi. The origins of the remaining batches were unknown. In the same month, Guangzhou Food and Drug Regulatory Bureau announced that of eighteen batches of rice and rice products tested, eight had cadmium levels that violated state standards and, of those, six came from Hunan province.[98] Hunan is famous for its rice output. By 2012, its annual rice production ranked number four among all provinces, accounting for more than 11 per cent of national rice production.[99] Hunan is also known for its rich resources of non-ferrous metals, including lead and zinc. Mining non-ferrous metals generates tailings and wastewater, both of which contain cadmium, contaminating the soil and irrigation water of rice paddies. In addition, heavy metal smelters discharge cadmium in air emissions and sludge, both of which further contaminate the paddies.

Cadmium Poisoning and Cadmium Contamination in Hunan

In the summer of 2009, the autopsy reports of two people from the village of Shuangqiao in the city of Liuyang, Hunan province showed that their urinary cadmium levels significantly exceeded the national permitted maximum. Both had worked at the heavily polluting Xianghe Chemical Factory and experienced occupational exposure to cadmium. Another 571 people from the same village were found to have urinary cadmium levels in excess of the national permitted maximum, and 208 were diagnosed with cadmium poisoning. Most of those with cadmium poisoning had not worked at chemical factories, but had been exposed to cadmium-contaminated farmland, drinking water and rice. Another cadmium-contaminated village, Xinma in the city of Zhuzhou, Hunan province is located 50 km from Shuangqiao. In March 2008, a six-year-old girl, Liu Bingjie, was certified by the local hospital to have died of chronic cadmium poisoning after two years of treatment.[100]

[95] Soil Action Plan (2016), part VI, s. 18.
[96] MEP and MLR, *National Soil Pollution Survey Report*.
[97] Cheng Xi, 'Tainted rice from Hunan to be on the dining tables in Guangdong', *Southern Daily*, 27 February 2013.
[98] Zheng Dao, 'Rescue rice', *Caixin New Century Weekly*, 27 May 2013; see also He Guangwei, 'Special report: the legacy of Hunan's polluted soils', *China Dialogue*, 7 July 2014.
[99] Zheng Dao, 'Rescue rice'.
[100] Liu Hongqiao, 'The coming of cadmium epidemic', *Caixin New Century Weekly*, 3 June 2013.

Researchers from the Chinese Academy of Sciences and other universities collected rice samples from a hundred rice paddies located near the mines throughout Hunan province. They found that 65 per cent of the samples exceeded the cadmium limit set by the National Authority on Public Health. They further found that contaminated rice had entered local markets and the national food-supply network.[101] Cadmium, a by-product of lead and zinc mining, is a heavy metal that accumulates in the body and causes kidney failure and bone lesions. It is carcinogenic and is one of the ten chemicals that pose the greatest danger to public health, according to the World Health Organization (WHO).[102]

The SPPCL (2018) requires supervision over mining operations to be strengthened and pollution discharge to comply with relevant standards and the total control quota.[103] Since 2017, provinces engaging in intensive mining – Inner Mongolia, Jiangxi, Henan, Hubei, Hunan, Guangdong, Guangxi, Sichuan, Guizhou, Yunnan, Shaanxi, Gansu and Xinjiang – have been required to implement additional discharge limits for key pollutants.[104] Entities operating or managing tailings ponds must take measures to prevent soil contamination and control the risks posed by the ponds. Where a tailings pond poses danger or risks, the operator and manager of the pond must regularly inspect and assess the soil contamination at the sites.[105] Local governments must ensure full treatment of abandoned tailings ponds by taking measures to eliminate safety risks and risks of contamination.[106]

8.4.4 Waste Disposal

Wastewater treatment and solid waste disposal are potential sources of land contamination. The SPPCL (2018) requires constructors and operators of treatment and disposal facilities to take measures to prevent soil contamination.[107] Local environmental bureaus must regularly inspect the soil surrounding the sites of relevant facilities. Where monitoring data suggests pollutants in the soil exceed the relevant standards, local agencies must instruct the operators to address the pollution problem.[108] Local governments are required to coordinate, plan and construct treatment and disposal facilities for wastewater and solid waste from household sources, and ensure their proper operation to prevent soil contamination.[109] At sites used to stockpile industrial and mining waste, measures must be taken to prevent soil being contaminated by dispersal, run-off or leakage of waste. Enterprises engaging in the recycling of electrical and electronic waste, waste tyres and waste plastics must install and operate waste control facilities to prevent soil and groundwater pollution.[110]

[101] Paul N. Williams, 'Occurrence and partitioning of cadmium, arsenic and lead in mine impacted paddy rice: Hunan, China', *Environmental Science and Technology*, 43 (2009), 637–42.

[102] WHO, *Action Is Needed on Chemicals of Major Public Health Concern* (Geneva: World Health Organisation, 2010). www.who.int/ipcs/features/10chemicals_en.pdf?ua=1

[103] SPPCL (2018), art. 23(1). [104] Soil Action Plan (2016), part VI, s. 18. [105] SPPCL (2018), art. 23(2).

[106] Soil Action Plan (2016), art VI, s. 18. [107] SPPCL (2018), art. 25(1). [108] SPPCL (2018), art. 25(2).

[109] SPPCL (2018), art. 25(3). [110] Soil Action Plan (2016), part VI, s. 18.

8.4.5 Agriculture

Agricultural activities cause rural land contamination in China via four major routes: (i) overuse of pesticides and fertilizers, leaving chemical residues in the soil; (ii) use of agricultural films and disposal of pesticide packaging on agricultural land; (iii) irrigation with industrial wastewater and the dumping of sludge (usually from wastewater treatment plants) on farmland and (iv) overuse of veterinary drugs and feed additives in livestock breeding and improper disposal of animal waste. Central and local government agencies must regulate and control these activities in order to prevent contamination and protect vulnerable rural ecosystems.

Fertilizers and Pesticides

High agricultural yields require plenty of nutrition. Chinese farmers rely on fertilizers to boost nutrients in the soil. China is the world's largest fertilizer producer and consumes around one-third of the world's total, though it only has 10 per cent of the world's arable land.[111] Fertilizers and pesticides are routinely overused in pursuit of larger harvests, but excess use causes soil and water pollution. Soil pollution reduces soil productivity, which in turn requires more fertilizers and pesticides to be applied. Farmers enter a vicious cycle, believing that yields will drop and plagues of insects appear without chemicals. The excess fertilizers and pesticides stay in the soil and are carried into rivers and lakes, causing soil and water pollution and increasing risks to food safety.

To tackle the problem of abuse of fertilizers and pesticides, the Soil Action Plan (2016) set 2020 targets for zero growth in total consumption of fertilizers and pesticides for major crops, and an improvement in the efficiency rates to above 40 per cent.[112] The SPPCL (2018) requires central and local governments to work together to change farmers' attitudes and practice. The state ministries in charge of agriculture and rural affairs, and forestry and grassland, must make plans and improve standards and measures to strengthen guidance on the application of pesticides and fertilizers on agricultural land, impose total amount control and restrict the use of agricultural films.[113] The MARA is required to strengthen the regime for registration of pesticides and fertilizers by producers, and assess the impacts of pesticides and fertilizers on the soil.[114] New standards for agricultural inputs, including pesticides, veterinary drugs, fertilizers, feedstuffs and agricultural films, the packaging materials of agricultural inputs and the quality of water used for irrigation must ensure soil contamination is prevented.[115]

Local agencies in charge of agriculture and rural affairs, forestry and grassland are responsible for creating and conducting awareness campaigns and technical training to guide farmers to engage in safe and rational use of agricultural inputs and control the total consumption of pesticides, veterinary drugs and fertilizer.[116] Local agencies in charge of agriculture and rural affairs are required to encourage farmers to take measures such as crop rotation and fallowing (leaving some land unseeded for a growing season) to help

[111] MEE, Division of Law and Standards, *Handbook on the Interpretation and Application of SPPCL* (Beijing: Law Press, 2018), at 82.

[112] Soil Action Plan (2016), part VI, s. 19.

[113] SPPCL (2018), art. 26(1).

[114] SPPCL (2018), art. 26(2).

[115] SPPCL (2018), art. 26(3).

[116] SPPCL (2018), art. 27(1).

prevent soil pollution. They should support farmers in adopting soil maintenance and cultivation measures to improve soil quality and fertility, and in the construction of treatment and utilization facilities for livestock waste.[117] To prevent soil pollution, the state supports farmers with funding, education and training to encourage them to apply low-toxicity, low-residue pesticides and to use more advanced spraying technologies, use organic and high-efficiency fertilizers, apply mixed fertilizers based on the results of soil testing, use biological prevention and control of plant diseases and pests and use biodegradable agricultural film, among others.[118]

Packaging Waste and Agricultural Films

Packaging waste is a direct by-product of China's high level of consumption of pesticides and fertilizer. It is estimated that more than 3.2 billion pesticide packets – weighing more than 100,000 t – are discarded annually by Chinese farmers in surface waterbodies or the field. Pesticide residues in these packets account for 2 per cent to 5 per cent of the total weight of pesticides used.[119] Packaging is usually made from non-biodegradable plastic, and residues pollute water and soil, threatening human and animal health. To prevent soil from being polluted by packaging waste and agricultural films, the waste needs to be collected for proper disposal. The Soil Action Plan (2016) set a target for provinces that use large amounts of agricultural films, including Hebei, Liaoning, Shandong, Henan, Gansu and Xinjiang, to implement full recovery and recycling of agricultural films by end-2020.[120] The SPPCL (2018) prohibits the manufacture, sale or use of agricultural inputs expressly prohibited by the state.[121] Manufacturers, sellers and users of agricultural inputs have a general duty to collect packaging waste and agricultural films in a timely manner, and pass pesticide packaging to qualified bodies for safe treatment.[122] The state must provide financial and technological support to encourage units and individuals to recycle packaging waste and agricultural film.[123]

Sewage Irrigation and Sludge Dumping

Agricultural water use accounts for 70 per cent of the total water use in China. Due to a serious water shortage across China, and particularly in farming and industrial regions, farmland is irrigated with wastewater that meets the Water Quality Standard for Irrigation (GB 5084-2005). If wastewater or sludge contains heavy metals or other toxic and hazardous substances in excess of state limits it may not be discharged onto farmland. Further, any dredged sediments, tailings or slag that may cause soil pollution may not be dumped on farmland.[124] Water used for irrigation must meet the Water Quality Standard for Irrigation in order to prevent contamination of soil, groundwater and agricultural products. Local environmental bureaus are required to work with local agencies in charge

[117] SPPCL (2018), art. 27(2). [118] SPPCL (2018), art. 29.

[119] Shuqin Jin et al., 'Mitigating land pollution through pesticide packages: the case of a collection scheme in rural China', *Science of the Total Environment*, 622–3 (2018), 502–9, at 503; Yan Huiqi, *Pesticide Law and Compliance Decision Making: A Case Study of Chinese Farmers* (Springer Singapore, 2017).

[120] Soil Action Plan (2016), part VI, s. 19. [121] SPPCL (2018), art. 30(1). [122] SPPCL (2018), art. 30(2).

[123] SPPCL (2018), art. 30(3). [124] SPPCL (2018), art. 28(1).

of agriculture and rural affairs and water resources to tighten control on irrigation water quality and to monitor and inspect the irrigation water.[125]

Livestock Breeding and Animal Waste

Animal waste, such as pig and chicken manure, presents another risk to soil if applied to farmland, because pig and chicken fodder may contain antibiotics, hormones and other chemicals. The production and consumption of veterinary drugs and feed additives must be strictly controlled to achieve a reduction of the total use.[126] Animal waste must be treated for comprehensive utilization.[127] By end-2020, more than 75 per cent of the large-scale livestock and poultry farms must have installed waste treatment facilities.[128] Local agencies are required to strengthen their supervision of the collection, storage, utilization and disposal of livestock waste in order to prevent soil pollution.[129]

8.5 CONTAMINATED SITES: RISK CONTROL AND REMEDIATION

In addition to regulating the prevention of pollution, the SPPCL (2018) also provides a legal response to contaminated agricultural and development land. There are general provisions on the response process that apply to both agricultural and development land, as well as more specific provisions for each type. The critical issues of determination of liable parties and clean-up funding remain the biggest challenge.

8.5.1 The Process of Response

Ideally, contaminated sites should be cleaned to ensure safe use for any purpose. However, site clean-up and remediation are complicated and expensive. Given the extent and degree of soil contamination in China, and the current financial and technological capacities of the public and private sectors, it is not feasible to request clean-up of all contaminated land in rural and urban areas. The SPPCL (2018) takes a pragmatic approach based on risk assessment and risk control to determine whether and to what extent remediation is required, taking into account the future use of the land. Contaminated agricultural and development land is subject to different mechanisms to ensure the safety of crops and the built environment. If land is contaminated, risk control and remediation measures must be taken by liable parties, and in general they include steps such as: (i) site investigation for soil pollution; (ii) risk assessment of the soil pollution; (iii) risk control or remediation; (iv) assessment of the effects of risk control or remediation and (v) follow-up assessment and management.[130]

Site Investigation for Soil Pollution

Site investigation aims to accurately assess the extent and degree of contamination. A report must be prepared upon completion of the investigation.[131] The soil pollution site investigation report must include basic information on the relevant sites, such as location,

[125] SPPCL (2018), art. 28(3). [126] Soil Action Plan (2016), part VI, s. 19.
[127] Soil Action Plan (2016), part VI, s. 19. [128] Soil Action Plan (2016), part VI, s. 19.
[129] SPPCL (2018), art. 28(2). [130] SPPCL (2018), art. 35. [131] SPPCL (2018), art. 36(1).

size and current use, and whether the pollutants in the soil exceed the relevant standards for soil pollution risk management and control. If the level of a pollutant exceeds the limit, the report must specify the types of pollution it has caused, the sources of the pollution and whether groundwater has been contaminated by pollutants in the soil.[132] Where development land is found to have pollutants above 'risk screening values' for soil contamination, a detailed investigation is required, in accordance with the Technical Guidance on Environmental Site Investigation (HJ25.1-2014) and Technical Guidance on Environmental Site Monitoring (HJ25.2-2014). If detailed investigation finds that the level of pollutants is at or below 'risk intervention values', a risk assessment must be conducted under the Technical Guidance on Risk Assessment of Contaminated Sites (HJ25.3-2014). If the level of pollutants is above the 'risk intervention value', measures must be taken to control risk or remediate the site.[133]

Risk Assessment

Soil contamination poses risks to the health and safety of humans and the environment. Contamination of agricultural land directly affects the quality of crops and reduces output. The toxic pollutants in the soil may be absorbed by and accumulate in produce, increasing risk to food safety and public health. Contamination of development land endangers the human environment. Toxins in the land may endanger the health of those who are exposed to it via ingestion, inhalation or skin contact. Soil contamination poses risks to the safety of the eco-environment. It affects the normal ecological functioning of soil and impairs the growth of animals, plants and microorganisms. Toxic pollutants in the soil also contaminate surface water, groundwater and the air. These risks need to be assessed and controlled. Risk assessment focuses on health risks and ecological risks arising from soil contamination and assesses the possibilities of human injury, disease, death or ecological damage being caused. A report is to be prepared upon completion of the soil pollution risk assessment.[134] The soil pollution risk assessment report must include information on: (i) the key pollutants, including concentration levels; (ii) the extent of the contamination of land and groundwater; (iii) the risk to the safety of produce and public health, and ecological risk and (iv) targets and basic requirements of risk control and remediation.[135]

Risk Control or Remediation

Risk control refers to measures taken to manage and control risks emanating from soil pollution in order to prevent harm to human beings. It is a low-cost alternative to site remediation that controls and reduces the risks to people by managing their exposure, and that of animals and plants, to the soil pollution. Risk control at contaminated agricultural land includes the use of alternative farming techniques to manage the pollution pathway and exposure in order to lower the risks of contamination, the return of farmland to forest or grassland, and the designation of special zones in which growing crops is forbidden, so

[132] SPPCL (2018), art. 36(2).

[133] The Soil Environmental Quality: Risk Control Standard for Soil Contamination of Development Land (for trial use) (GB36600-2018), art. 5.3.

[134] SPPCL (2018), art. 37(1). [135] SPPCL (2018), art. 37(2).

as to ensure the safe use of farmland and the safety of produce. Risk control at contaminated development land includes installing warning signs to inform the public of the danger, containing the contamination and preventing it from spreading, stopping people from entering or interfering with the site, and strictly controlling the land use to prevent risks emanating from its development.

Site remediation or clean-up refers to the use of biological, physical or chemical measures to migrate, absorb, degrade or transform pollutants in the soil and lower the concentration and toxicity of pollutants. Remediation reduces the risk and harm posed by soil pollution and restores the ecological function of the soil, but it is a lengthy, costly and complex process.[136] Soil remediation relies on technology and qualified professional service providers. The research and development of soil remediation technology, predominantly government driven, started in China during the 10th FYP period (2001–05). More government support was provided by special funding for heavy metal pollution prevention and control during the 12th FYP period (2011–15). In 2010, a dozen enterprises provided soil pollution treatment and remediation services, rising to approximately 1,000 in 2016, with staffing levels increasing from 2,000 to nearly 10,000 over the same period.[137]

Risk control and remediation should take a scientific and reasonable approach that is suited to local circumstances, correctly focused and effective in controlling or eliminating risk.[138] Any risk control or remediation must not cause new contamination to the site.[139] Prior to risk control and remediation, local agencies may request parties liable for the soil contamination or parties with land-use rights to remove the sources of pollution and to prevent it from proliferating.[140] Pollution generated during risk control and remediation, including wastewater, air pollutants and solid waste, must be treated and disposed of in compliance with relevant state provisions and standards.[141] Where solid waste is generated by risk control or remediation, or dismantled facilities, equipment, buildings or other structures are themselves HW, they must be disposed of in accordance with relevant state provisions and standards on HW.[142]

During remediation work, notices must be installed to inform the public of the nature of the site and project, and of the environmental protection measures being undertaken.[143] In principle, risk control and remediation should be carried out on site. Measures should be taken to prevent secondary pollution from being caused by excavating and stockpiling contaminated soil.[144] Where remediation work involves transporting the contaminated soil to another site, the remediation operator must prepare a transport plan that includes the time and means of transport, the route to be taken, the quantity of soil, the destination and the method for final disposal, and must submit the plan to local environmental bureaus at the place of origin and of destination.[145] Where the contaminated soil to be transported is

[136] The cost of remediation varies depending on the type and degree of pollution and the remediation technology applied. For example, the cost of remediation of agricultural land can range from several thousand yuan per *mu* to tens of thousands of yuan per *mu*, while the cost of remediation of contaminated sites due to be developed can range from several hundred yuan per m^3 to several thousand yuan per m^3. See MEP, 31 May 2016, 'MEP answers'.

[137] See MEP, 31 May 2016, 'MEP answers'. [138] SPPCL (2018), art. 38(1). [139] SPPCL (2018), art. 38(2).

[140] SPPCL (2018), art. 39. [141] SPPCL (2018), art. 40(1). [142] SPPCL (2018), art. 40(2).

[143] SPPCL (2018), art. 40(3). [144] Soil Action Plan (2016), part VII, s. 23. [145] SPPCL (2018), art. 41(1).

classed as HW, it must be disposed of in compliance with relevant state provisions and standards.[146]

Follow-up Assessment and Management

A report assessing the effect of risk control work and remediation must be prepared once the work and remediation have taken place.[147] The assessment report should focus on whether the risk control and remediation targets set in the soil pollution risk assessment report have been achieved.[148] Where follow-up risk management is needed, for example to address latent risks, parties liable for the soil contamination are responsible for the management.[149]

8.5.2 Contaminated Agricultural Land

The term 'agricultural land' refers to farmland, orchards, tea plantations and pasture.[150] Priority is given to farmland for risk control and remediation. The SPPCL (2018) adopts a system of management of contaminated agricultural land whereby land is divided into three categories depending on the level of contamination. Each category of land has different permitted uses and different applicable measures. This helps to ensure that risk control is affordable.

Risk Control: Classified Management

The SPPCL (2018) does not require clean-up of all contaminated agricultural land. Instead, agricultural land is divided into three categories for the purposes of protection and risk control to ensure the safety and normal growth of crops. The categories are: (i) land for priority protection; (ii) safe use and (iii) strict control.[151] Here, the relevant standard is the Soil Environmental Quality: Risk Control Standard for Soil Contamination of Agricultural Land (for trial use) (GB15618-2018), which sets risk screening values and risk intervention values for soil contamination of agricultural land by reference to levels of major toxic substances, including cadmium, mercury, arsenic, lead and chromium.

The first category is known as 'priority protection'. Where the levels of toxins are at or below the risk screening values, the agricultural land is treated as posing low risk to crop safety, the normal growth of crops and the soil eco-environment, and the risk may be ignored.[152] Agricultural land with very low-level contamination, which poses negligible risk to human health, is offered priority protection by local governments and is classed as 'perpetual basic farmland'. The construction of new projects on land designated as a perpetual-basic-farmland concentration zone is prohibited if the construction may cause soil pollution. Existing projects that may cause soil pollution must be shut down and dismantled by a specified deadline.[153] The State Council has stipulated the principle that

[146] SPPCL (2018), art. 41(2). [147] SPPCL (2018), art. 42(1). [148] SPPCL (2018), art. 42(2).

[149] SPPCL (2018), art. 42(3).

[150] The Soil Environmental Quality: Risk Control Standard for Soil Contamination of Agricultural Land (for trial use) (GB15618-2018), art. 3.1.

[151] SPPCL (2018), art. 49.

[152] The Soil Environmental Quality: Risk Control Standard for Soil Contamination of Agricultural Land (for trial use) (GB15618–2018), art. 3.4.

[153] SPPCL (2018), art. 50.

the total area of perpetual basic farmland may not decrease, and that its soil quality is not permitted to decline. If either the total area or the soil quality declines in any county, provincial governments will issue a warning to the county government and take measures such as suspension of EIA review and approval to restrict local development.[154]

The second category is known as 'safe use'. Where the levels of toxins are above the risk screening values, the agricultural land may pose risk to crop safety, the normal growth of crops and the soil eco-environment. Safe-use measures must be taken to strengthen environmental monitoring and inspection of the soil and monitoring of the quality of the produce.[155] Local agencies in charge of agriculture and rural affairs, and forestry and grassland are required to make a safe-use plan for each area of safe-use agricultural land, based on existing types of major crops and farming practices.[156] Safe-use plans must include: (i) agronomic control to be used to lower the risks of crops ; (ii) regular inspection and assessment of both soil environmental quality and quality of produce; (iii) technical guidance and training of farmers, rural collectives and other agricultural production operators and (iv) additional risk control measures.[157] The State Council set a target of designating 40 million *mu* of lightly and moderately contaminated farmland as safe-use agricultural land by end-2020.[158]

The third category is known as 'strict control'. Where the levels of toxins are above risk intervention values, the agricultural land poses high risk and the produce fails to meet food safety standards. Strict control measures must be taken.[159] Local agencies in charge of agriculture and rural affairs, and forestry and grassland must take the following risk control measures: (i) designation of special zones in which specified crops are prohibited, with the designation subject to approval by the local government; (ii) regular assessment of both soil and produce; (iii) technical guidance and training of farmers, rural collectives and other agricultural production operators and (iv) additional risk control measures.[160] Designating a zone as one in which growing certain crops is prohibited is a power granted to local agriculture agencies to ensure the safety of produce. These local agencies must monitor the toxic and hazardous substances in the air, water and soil and decide which, if any, crops may be grown on the farmland. They may also propose that the local government bans the growing of all crops at the contaminated farmland.[161] The State Council in its Recent Work Arrangement (2013) formally adopted the approach of cutting off pathways by which contamination can enter the food chain by instructing local governments to designate seriously contaminated farmland as zones in which agricultural production is prohibited.[162] Governments of all levels must provide policy incentives to support any party to take risk

[154] Soil Action Plan (2016), part III, s. 8.

[155] The Soil Environmental Quality: Risk Control Standard for Soil Contamination of Agricultural Land (for trial use) (GB15618–2018), art. 3.4.

[156] SPPCL (2018), art. 53(1).

[157] SPPCL (2018), art. 53(2). See also the Soil Environmental Quality: Risk Control Standard for Soil Contamination of Agricultural Land (for trial use) (GB15618–2018), art. 6.2.

[158] Soil Action Plan (2016), part III, s. 9.

[159] Soil Environmental Quality: Risk Control Standard for Soil Contamination of Agricultural Land (for trial use) (GB15618–2018), art. 3.5.

[160] SPPCL (2018), art. 54(1).

[161] The Law on the Quality and Safety of Agricultural Products (2018), art. 15.

[162] Recent Work Arrangement (2013), part II, s. 3.

control measures at agricultural land that is subject to strict control. The measures to be supported include adjusting or changing the crops to be grown, returning farmland to forest or grassland ('grain for green'), returning farmland to wetland, employing crop rotation and leaving land fallow, employing livestock rotation and leaving pasture land fallow.[163] By end-2020, 20 million *mu* of seriously contaminated farmland will have completed farming restructuring or grain-for-green transformation.[164]

For safe-use and strict-control agricultural land, if the soil pollution has impacted or may impact on the safety of groundwater or drinking water sources, local environmental bureaus must work with agencies in charge of agriculture and rural affairs, and forestry and grassland to make plans on pollution prevention and control, and act on the plan.[165] Parties liable for the contamination of safe-use and strict-control agricultural land are required to take risk control measures in accordance with state provisions and the requirements of the soil pollution risk assessment report. They must also report regularly to local agencies in charge of agriculture and rural affairs, and forestry and grassland.[166]

Remediation

Where the agricultural land has produced crops with pollution levels in excess of relevant standards and remediation is needed, parties liable for the soil contamination must prepare remediation plans, report to local agencies in charge of agriculture and rural affairs, and forestry and grassland for the record, and implement the plans. Remediation work must prioritize biological remediation measures that do not have any adverse impact on agricultural production or soil productivity. The site remediation plan must include provision for groundwater pollution control.[167] Remediation must also prevent or reduce pollution from entering crops in order to ensure their safety.[168] Rural collectives and their members and other agricultural production operators are under a duty to assist in the implementation of measures for risk control and remediation.[169] Upon completion of the risk control or remediation work, parties liable for the soil pollution are required to hire a third party to assess the effects of the work, and must submit the assessment reports to local agencies in charge of agriculture and rural affairs, and forestry and grassland for the record.[170]

The State Council has required provinces with large areas of contaminated farmland, including Jiangxi, Hubei, Hunan, Guangdong, Guangxi, Sichuan, Guizhou and Yunnan, to take the lead in treatment and remediation of contaminated sites. Other provinces must follow suit. By end-2020, the government expects 10 million *mu* of farmland to have completed treatment and remediation of contamination.[171]

[163] SPPCL (2018), art. 54(2). See also the Soil Environmental Quality: Risk Control Standard for Soil Contamination of Agricultural Land (for trial use) (GB15618–2018), art. 6.3.
[164] Soil Action Plan (2016), part III, s. 10.
[165] SPPCL (2018), art. 55.
[166] SPPCL (2018), art. 56.
[167] SPPCL (2018), art. 57(1).
[168] SPPCL (2018), art. 57(2).
[169] SPPCL (2018), art. 57(4).
[170] SPPCL (2018), art. 57(3).
[171] Soil Action Plan (2016), part VII, s. 23.

8.5.3 Contaminated Development Land

Development land refers to land used for the construction of buildings or structures, including urban and rural land used for residential premises and public facilities, land for industrial and mining operations, land for transport and hydropower infrastructure, land for tourism and for military facilities, among others.[172] For the purposes of risk control and management, development land is divided into two types. Type I includes land to be used for residential premises, primary and secondary schools, medical services, social welfare facilities, community parks and children's playgrounds, among others. Type II includes land to be used for industrial operations, logistics storage, commercial services, roads and transport networks, public facilities, public services, green areas and public squares.[173]

The risks emerging from contaminated development land are the adverse impacts on human health that result from long-term exposure to toxic or carcinogenic pollutants in the soil for the people living or working there.[174] The Soil Environmental Quality: Risk Control Standard for Soil Contamination of Development Land (for trial use) (GB36600-2018) sets both risk screening values and risk intervention values for soil contamination at development land. The values are set for pollutants including heavy metals, inorganic chemicals, volatile organic compounds (VOCs) and semi-VOCs. Where the level of a pollutant in development land is at or below the risk screening value, the risk to human health is low and may be ignored. Where the level reaches the risk screening value, there may be risk to human health and further investigation and risk assessment must be conducted to determine the scope of contamination and the level of risk.[175] Where the level of pollutant reaches the risk intervention value, there is an unacceptable level of risk to human health, and measures must be taken to control risk or remediate.[176] It should be noted that a different set of risk screening values and risk intervention values is stipulated for each of the two development-land types, offering different levels of protection. Type I development land tolerates lower levels of pollutants than Type II, as the former tends to be occupied by more vulnerable elements of the population (for example, children, elderly and the ill), who may stay longer at the Type I premises and would therefore have a longer period of exposure.

Site Investigation and Risk Assessment

The Soil Action Plan (2016) requires that, where governments plan to reclaim land-use rights held by tanneries, non-ferrous metals smelters and oil processing, chemical, coking and electroplating enterprises and change the land use to development of residential or commercial premises, schools, medical services and housing for the elderly, among others,

[172] Soil Environmental Quality: Risk Control Standard for Soil Contamination of Development Land (for trial use) (GB36600-2018), art. 3.1.

[173] Soil Environmental Quality: Risk Control Standard for Soil Contamination of Development Land (for trial use) (GB36600-2018), art. 4.1.

[174] Soil Environmental Quality: Risk Control Standard for Soil Contamination of Development Land (for trial use) (GB36600-2018), art. 3.2.

[175] Soil Environmental Quality: Risk Control Standard for Soil Contamination of Development Land (for trial use) (GB36600-2018), art. 3.4.

[176] Soil Environmental Quality: Risk Control Standard for Soil Contamination of Development Land (for trial use) (GB36600-2018), art. 3.5.

the enterprise must assess the soil quality prior to surrendering the land-use rights. Where land-use rights have already been reclaimed by a local government, the government must arrange the assessment of the site. Where seriously contaminated agricultural land is to be used for urban development, the local governments must arrange the assessment of the contamination. The results of the assessment must be reported to local environmental protection, urban planning and land resources agencies for the record.[177] The SPPCL (2018) requires 'key entities of soil pollution' with land-use rights to conduct a site investigation prior to a change in land use from production and operation, or prior to the surrender or transfer of land-use rights.[178] The site contamination investigation report must be submitted to the local authority in charge of real property registration and reported to the local environmental bureau for the record.[179]

The Catalogue System

The state uses a catalogue system for the risk control and remediation of contaminated development land.[180] A Catalogue on Risk Control and Remediation of Contaminated Development Land is prepared by each provincial ecology and environment bureau in collaboration with the natural resources bureau, is disclosed to the public and updated in a timely manner.[181] Contaminated sites included in the Catalogue may not be developed for use as residential, public management or public service premises.[182] A provincial bureau's decision to include a contaminated site in the Catalogue is based on a risk assessment report conducted either by parties liable for the contamination or parties with land-use rights, and the Catalogue must be reported regularly to the MEE.[183] Where the risk control and remediation work has been completed, and the site is assessed to have achieved the risk control and remediation targets set by the soil pollution risk assessment report, parties liable for the pollution or parties with land-use rights may apply to the bureau for the site to be removed from the Catalogue.[184] The removal decision is based on third-party assessment of the results of the risk control and remediation, which is disclosed to the public and reported to the MEE.[185]

Risk Control of Contaminated Sites

For the contaminated sites included in the Catalogue, parties liable for the soil contamination must take measures to manage and control risk, and report these to the local environmental bureau. Such risk control must include measures to prevent and control

[177] Soil Action Plan (2016), part IV, s. 12.

[178] Key entities of soil pollution are operators designated by the state environmental authority based on the nature of their operation. The entities are involved in the production, use or storage of toxic and hazardous substances.

[179] SPPCL (2018), art. 67.

[180] SPPCL (2018), art. 58(1).

[181] SPPCL (2018), art. 58(2).

[182] SPPCL (2018), art. 61(2). 'Public management or public service' is a category of land use that covers land use for schools, hospitals, welfare services, sports stadiums and parks, among others.

[183] SPPCL (2018), art. 61(1). Risk assessment is conducted on development land that has been found by the soil pollution investigation report to contain pollutants at levels that violate the risk control standards for soil pollution.

[184] SPPCL (2018), art. 66(1).

[185] SPPCL (2018), art. 66(2).

[186] SPPCL (2018), art. 62.

[187] SPPCL (2018), art. 63.

groundwater contamination.[186] Local environmental bureaus may also take risk control measures over the contaminated sites contained in the Catalogue, including designating quarantine zones around them and monitoring soil and groundwater.[187] Local governments must install signs and issue announcements to inform the public of key information on the contaminated sites, and must, over the period of risk control, monitor the soil, surface water, groundwater and air quality. If the contamination spreads, the liable parties must take timely measures to isolate the pollutants, or stop them spreading from the contaminated site.[188]

Remediation of Contaminated Sites

Remediation of contaminated sites must prioritize those to be used for the development of residential premises, commercial buildings, schools, hospitals and housing for the elderly.[189] Liable parties must prepare a remediation plan, report it to the local environmental bureau for the record and implement it. The remediation plan must include prevention and control of groundwater pollution.[190] Remediation targets must be set in accordance with the Technical Guidance on Risk Assessment of Contaminated Sites (HJ25.3-2014) and Technical Guidance on Remediation of Contaminated Sites (HJ25.4-2014), and the pollutant levels must be below the risk intervention values for soil contamination of development land.[191] Where the land-use rights have already been reclaimed by the local government, and the party liable for the soil pollution is the former holder of the land-use rights, the local government is responsible for organizing the risk control and remediation work.[192] Upon completion of the risk control or remediation work, the parties liable for the soil pollution must hire a third party to assess the effects of the risk control or remediation. The assessment report is submitted for the record to local agencies in charge of agriculture and rural affairs, and forestry and grassland.[193]

Prior to the SPPCL (2018), liabilities for soil pollution were stipulated by provisions in other statutes and by administrative measures. The SWL (2016) provides that entities generating industrial solid waste (ISW) must, before terminating operations, take preventative measures to control pollution at the facilities and at sites used to store and treat waste.[194] The MEP and SEPA issued measures to address prevention and clean-up of land contamination following the relocation of industry. Local governments have taken different approaches to the clean-up of contaminated land. Some undertake the remediation work themselves and pass the clean-up cost to the land transferee, others require the land transferee to remediate the site under their supervision. Either way, the cost of site remediation is borne by the developer of the land instead of the polluter. The Hongshi site in Beijing is an example in which the government expressly required, in the bidding documents, that developers remediate the contaminated site to the satisfaction of the environmental authority before redeveloping it.

[188] Soil Action Plan (2016), part IV, s. 12. [189] Soil Action Plan (2016), part VII, s. 23.
[190] SPPCL (2018), art. 64.
[191] Soil Environmental Quality: Risk Control Standard for Soil Contamination of Development Land (for trial use) (GB36600-2018), art. 5.3.6.
[192] SPPCL (2018), art. 68. [193] SPPCL (2018), art. 65. [194] SWL, art. 35.

Beijing's Hongshi Site

In April 2004, three construction workers at Beijing's SongJiaZhuang subway station were poisoned by obnoxious gas as they excavated to 3 m underground. When they reached 5 m underground, one started to vomit. All were rushed to hospital for emergency treatment. This was the first time that the public in China had become aware of toxic sites. An initial assessment of the site found high levels of DDT and HCH in the soil. The site had previously been used by a pesticide factory (established in the 1970s) and by Beijing Hongshi Paint Factory until November 2005 when its land-use rights were reclaimed by the Beijing municipal government under the industry-relocation plan.[195]

The Hongshi site was eventually designated for the development of fixed-price housing and was auctioned in 2007. All parties interested in bidding were informed of the site contamination and were required to submit site remediation proposals for approval by the Beijing EPB. Beijing Vanke, one of China's biggest property developers, acquired the land-use rights of the Hongshi site for 590 million yuan, far above Beijing Municipal Land Reserve Centre's initial asking price of 352 million yuan. The first task for Beijing Vanke was the 100-million-yuan removal of the contaminated soil for safe disposal by incineration – as recommended by the Soil Research Institute of the Chinese Academy of Sciences – to the satisfaction of Beijing EPB.[196]

The toxic poisoning of the subway construction workers in Beijing forced the SEPA to investigate and address historical contamination. It issued the Circular on Earnestly Accomplishing Pollution Prevention Work in the Enterprise Relocation Process (SEPA Circular) (2004),[197] requesting industrial enterprises and laboratories generating HW, and bodies generating or disposing of HW, to hire qualified environmental monitoring firms to conduct site assessment and prepare a site contamination report. The report must detail the types of pollutants and the extent and degree of soil and groundwater contamination that will be present when operations are terminated and the land use changes. The site assessment report must be submitted to the provincial EPB for examination. An environmental remediation plan must be prepared based on the assessment report and must be implemented under the supervision of local EPBs when the operations are terminated.[198] In principle, it is the responsibility of the entities that have operated on the site and caused contamination to clean up and restore the soil.[199] In practice, however, it is not always feasible to make the polluter pay. Former industrial operators may either cease to exist or may not have the financial capacity to pay. In contrast, the potential land transferees and property developers

[195] Zhao Yuhong, 'Land contamination in urban China'; 'Hidden toxic sites', *Caijing*; 'Toxic site clean-up', *Jinghua Times*; Liu Wei, 'Beijing: after the subway workers'; Liu Yang, 'Soil at the site'; Pan Hongtao, 'Relocation of chemical enterprises'.

[196] Wang Weimin, 'Beijing land bureau responds to query over toxic site transfer', *China Real Property News*, 20 August 2007; Liu Yuxin, 'Big developers bid for second batch of two limits housing sites', *Beijing Daily*, 12 July 2007; Xu Huiying, 'Vanke won the second batch of two limits housing bids in Beijing', *First Financial Daily*, 27 July 2007.

[197] The SEPA Circular was issued on 1 June 2004. www.mee.gov.cn/gkml/zj/bgt/200910/t20091022_173879.htm

[198] SEPA Circular (2004), art. 1. [199] SEPA Circular (2004), art. 3

[200] Michael G. Faure and Liu Jing, 'Compensation for environmental damage in China: theory and practice', *Pace Environmental Law Review*, 31 (2014), 226–309.

are more able to bear the high cost of site remediation.[200] The Beijing Hongshi site is an example of the common practice in China's first-tier cities, such as Beijing, Shanghai, Guangzhou and Shenzhen, where the property markets promise lucrative returns.

In less-developed cities, such as Wuhan in central China, property developers are less willing or able to bear the cost of site clean-up, as seen in the legal dispute over the Heshan toxic site in Wuhan.[201]

The Heshan Site in Wuhan (2006–2014)

In 2006, the 242-*mu* Heshan site in the centre of Wuhan was sold by the Wuhan Land Reserve Centre to Sanjiang Aerospace Property Co. (Sanjiang), a local property developer, for 405.5 million yuan. Soon after construction started in early 2007, many workers fell ill and showed symptoms of toxic poisoning. By February 2007, Sanjiang had become aware of the seriousness of the extent and degree of toxic contamination at the site.

The site had been occupied by Wuhan Pesticide Factory, which was established in 1959 and manufactured herbicides and pesticides. From the 1960s to early 1980s, the factory had routinely buried toxic waste underground. Numerous leakages had caused further contamination with DDT and HCH. From 1985, the company experienced several restructurings, and each year suffered a loss. By August 1991, the factory was operating at an annual loss of more than 30 million yuan. It went into bankruptcy in 1994. The land-use right was then reclaimed by Wuhan Land Reserve Centre. In May 2005, the site was listed for auction without any information on soil contamination.

In early 2007, Sanjiang suspended construction and requested cancellation of the transaction. After nearly four years of litigation, the parties reached a settlement agreement. In 2010, Sanjiang returned the site to Wuhan Land Reserve Centre for a refund of 405.5 million yuan and was paid compensation of 120 million yuan.

Next, Wuhan EPB inspected the site several times and found that more than 70 per cent of soil was contaminated with organic pollutants, including DDT and HCH. Contamination reached 9 m underground. The local government earmarked 232 million yuan for the site remediation and started the work in May 2011. It took more than three years to complete the remediation, and the final cost was more than 280 million yuan. Thanks to the continuing boom in China's property market in first- and second-tier cities, Wuhan Land Reserve Centre was able, in December 2014, to transfer the land-use right to Shanghai Huiye Enterprise Ltd at the initial asking price of 1.44 billion yuan.

In the cases of Hongshi (Beijing) and Heshan (Wuhan), the polluters causing the land contamination had either ceased to exist or did not have the capacity to pay. However, contaminated sites must be cleaned up before they can be redeveloped safely for use as commercial or residential premises, and therefore the government or transferee of the land-use rights takes the remediation measures. In some cases, central and local governments must jointly foot the bill.

[201] Luo Jingyun and Zhou Hui, 'Lack of information disclosure'; Zhang Yanchun et al., 'Wuhan Heshan 'toxic site' cleaned up at high cost', *People's Daily*, 4 January 2013, 1; Zhou Hui, 'Wuhan toxic site'; Jeffery and Xiaobo Zhao, 'Developing a national contaminated land liability scheme'.

Qiaokou's Most Toxic Site (2012)[202]

Qiaokou is one of seven districts in the centre of Wuhan that together had hosted 99 of the 127 chemical factories located within the third ring road of the city. As a result of the relocation of industry away from Wuhan city centre, a total of 4,118 *mu* of industrial land in Qiaokou was, between 2008 and 2015, returned to the government. More than 30 per cent of the land (1,260 *mu*) was contaminated, according to Wuhan EPB. The most toxic of the sites had formerly been used by Wuhan Dye Factory and four other chemical factories. The site was more than 200 *mu* in size and the cost of remediation was estimated at 188 million yuan. In 2012, the NDRC chose the site for a pilot project on treatment and remediation of land contaminated by heavy metals. It allocated 56.4 million yuan of central government budget to the project, and the remainder had to come from local government and enterprises.

The SPPCL (2018) continued the practical approach of making polluters, developers and governments all potentially liable for the risk control or remediation of contaminated land. Based on the polluter-pays principle, parties liable for causing the soil pollution must take measures to carry out risk control or remediation of the contaminated site.[203] They are liable for the expenses incurred for soil pollution investigation, risk assessment, risk control and remediation, for the assessment of the outcome of the risk control and remediation, and follow-up management.[204] Where a liable party has changed its legal status, the entity or individual who has inherited the rights and duties of the polluter is treated as the liable party with a duty to conduct and bear the cost of risk control or remediation of the contaminated site.[205] Where it is impossible to ascertain the polluter of a site, the SPPCL (2018) states that the party possessing the land-use right over the contaminated site must conduct risk control and remediation.[206] Where needed, local governments and local agencies may also organize the implementation of risk control and remediation work.[207]

A few days before the SPPCL (2018) came into force on 1 January 2019, Jiangsu Provincial High Court delivered its judgment regarding the Changlong toxic site in *Friends of Nature and China Biodiversity Conservation and Green Development Foundation* v. *Changlong Chemical and Others* (2018).[208]

Friends of Nature and China Biodiversity Conservation and Green Development Foundation v. Changlong Chemical and Others (2018)

In December 2015, nearly 500 students of Changzhou Foreign Language School fell ill after moving to a new campus in September of the same year. Less than 100 m to the north of the school campus was the Changlong toxic site, which was being treated for contamination. The remediation work

[202] Luo Jingyun and Zhou Hui, 'Lack of information disclosure'.
[203] SPPCL (2018), art. 45(1); Soil Action Plan (2016), part VII, s. 21.
[204] SPPCL (2018), art. 46.
[205] SPPCL (2018), art. 47; Soil Action Plan (2016), part VII, s. 21.
[206] SPPCL (2018), art. 45(1).
[207] SPPCL (2018), art. 45(2).
[208] Judgments of both courts can be accessed at Peking University Legal Information Network (n.d.). Website. www.pkulaw.cn.

had been organized by the local government. The site had been occupied by three chemical factories – Changlong, Changyu and Huada – since the late 1970s. All were relocated in 2008 and 2009 and the land-use rights had been surrendered to the Changzhou Xinbei Land Reserve Centre.

Serious contamination of the soil and groundwater had been discovered in 2011 when Changzhou Xinbei District Government planned to allow residential development of the site. Site investigation found intolerable risks that rendered remediation essential before redevelopment for any other purpose could start. In 2013, risk assessment and risk control were carried out and remediation plans were made. Remediation work started in March 2014. Nearly 95 per cent of the contaminated soil had been excavated and removed from the site by December 2015, when a large number of students developed itchy skin and nausea, and some were diagnosed with lymphoma and leukaemia. Excavation work was suspended. At the beginning of 2016, the local government announced that the Changlong site would be used as a green space for the public, not for property development, and revised the site remediation plan. To avoid further secondary pollution from the release of toxins, the toxic soil was to be capped and sealed by clay on site, rather than being excavated and removed.

Friends of Nature (FON) and the China Biodiversity Conservation and Green Development Foundation (CBCGDF) sued Changlong, Changyu and Huada, seeking remedies including: (i) elimination of pollution to the soil and groundwater at and around the Changlong site; (ii) agreement that the polluters would pay for the 370-million-yuan remediation; (iii) a public apology for the site contamination, to be made via national, provincial and municipal media; (iv) compensation to the plaintiffs to cover the cost of litigation, the fees for investigation, testing, appraisal and drafting the remediation plan, the fees charged by lawyers and experts, and the fee charged by the court for accepting the case, among others. The defendants denied liability on the ground that they had surrendered the land-use rights to the local government years before the contamination was discovered in 2011, and that the government-organized site remediation had been underway since 2013.

Changzhou Intermediate Court (2017) rejected the plaintiffs' claims and ordered them to pay the 1,891,900-yuan fee charged by the court for accepting the case.[209] The Changlong land-use right were reclaimed by the government in 2009. Prior to this litigation, the Changzhou government and Xinbei district government had already started site remediation following site investigation and risk assessment, making it practically impossible to ask three defendants to take over. Further, the defendants did not have land-use rights enabling them to access or control the site. In addition, the plaintiffs had failed to prove the extent and percentage of the liability of the three defendants and their predecessors, all of which had jointly caused site contamination since the 1970s. The plaintiffs appealed.

Jiangsu High Court (2018) overturned the first-instance judgment and clarified important issues on legal liabilities for site contamination. The three respondents had polluted the soil and groundwater through their industrial operations and toxic waste disposal at the Changlong site.

[209] Court acceptance fees are charged in accordance with the Measures on Payment of Litigation Fees (2006). Where a plaintiff claims monetary payment in cases of property dispute, fees are charged under article 13(1) and are calculated based on the claim amount. For example, 50 yuan is charged for claims up to 10,000 yuan, 2.5 per cent of the claim amount is charged for claims of 10,000 yuan to 100,000 yuan and 2.0 per cent of the claim amount is charged on claims of 100,000 yuan to 200,000 yuan. Changzhou Intermediate Court calculated the court fees for accepting the case based on the plaintiffs' claim for projected site remediation costs of 370 million yuan. Under article 29(1), the party who loses the case must pay the litigation fees.

The court noted that the polluter-pays principle requires polluters to bear the cost of pollution, meaning that Changlong, Changyu and Huada, as polluters, are liable parties for site clean-up. The fact that they no longer held the land-use rights did not exempt them from their liabilities as polluters. The court found that it would be undesirable to order the three respondents to initiate site remediation since the government-organized remediation by a third party was already underway. The court also said that it was impossible to order payment of remediation expenses since the process was ongoing, and therefore this case should not count as a monetary claim for the purposes of calculating the court acceptance fees. The local governments did, however, have the right to recover the cost of remediation from the three polluters in due course, the court held. The court ordered Changlong, Changyu and Huada to issue public apologies via national media and pay 230,000 yuan to each appellant to cover their litigation costs, including lawyers' fees and travel expenses. The court acceptance fees were revised to 100 yuan for the first-instance trial and 100 yuan for the appeal.[210] The fees were to be paid by the three companies.

Although the case was tried and decided before the SPPCL (2018) came into force, it is an important test case for the application of the polluter-pays principle in the clean-up of contaminated sites. Changlong, Changyu and Huada were chemical factories identified as former occupiers and operators that had caused toxic contamination of the site. Unlike the Hongshi site in Beijing or Heshan in Wuhan, the Changlong site was not an 'orphan site' for which the polluters could not be ascertained or no longer existed. Jiangsu High Court clarified that the polluters were liable financially for the remediation of the Changlong toxic site, even though the government-organized clean-up work was already underway.

8.6 INFORMATION DISCLOSURE AND PUBLIC SUPERVISION

Public supervision over governments and liable parties promotes effective regulation of land contamination. Public participation is dependent on information transparency. However, transparency of information on soil pollution is seriously lacking in China. Without an express stipulation on information disclosure, governments and liable parties would keep land contamination information confidential as many residential neighbourhoods and villages are built on or near toxic sites. Disclosure of information could lead to compensation claims by injured residents, depreciation of property values and a shrinking market for agricultural produce from that area. Even the National Soil Pollution Survey (2005–13) was conducted under strict confidentiality and the government's reluctant disclosure of only a limited amount of survey information was highly controversial.

[210] The court fee for accepting the case was revised by Jiangsu High Court to 100 yuan, because the plaintiffs' request was that the defendants remedy the soil and water contamination. This was not a monetary claim, meaning that the fee should have been calculated by reference to article 13(2) of the Measures on Payment of Litigation Fees (2006), which sets the fee per case at 50 yuan to 100 yuan.

The 'State Secret' Controversy (2013)

As the first National Soil Pollution Survey (2005–13) came to an end, it was difficult for the media to obtain any information on survey findings. Government agencies remained silent and each member of the survey team had been required to sign a non-disclosure agreement upon joining. They were prohibited from disclosing data to anyone other than the state agencies in charge of the survey.[211]

On 30 January 2013, Dong Zhengwei, a Beijing lawyer, applied to the MEP requesting disclosure of the survey methods and soil pollution data under the Regulation on Government Information Disclosure (RGID).[212] The MEP, in a reply dated 20 February 2013, refused to disclose the information requested by Dong, excusing itself on the grounds that the survey was a state secret, an exception to information disclosure requirements permitted by article 14 of the RGID.[213] Dong applied to the MEP for administrative review of its decision not to disclose the information. On 5 May 2013, the MEP delivered its decision. It upheld its previous decision to withhold the information and explained why it was treated as a state secret. The MEP said that preliminary and incomplete survey data was still being analysed, and it had been temporarily classified as a state secret in order to avoid any adverse effect from disclosure of inaccurate or incomplete data. It added that the environmental information would ultimately be disclosed by the state.[214]

Although Dong Zhengwei failed to obtain the soil pollution data from the MEP, his request for information disclosure and the ensuing media reports put tremendous pressure on the government to release the survey results, which eventually happened a year later.[215]

The SPPCL (2018) improves information transparency by imposing a duty of disclosure on governments and polluters. The public have the right to access information on the soil environmental quality and soil contamination of agricultural land and development land that impacts their health, safety or well-being.[216] Environmental bureaus must disclose information on soil contamination and existing and proposed measures of prevention and control.[217] The MEE is required to issue information on the national soil environment, while each provincial environmental bureau publish such information for its province. Where key soil environmental information relates to agricultural land used to cultivate crops for human consumption, timely notice of the information must be conveyed to agencies in charge of agriculture and rural affairs, public health and food safety.[218] A national soil environmental information platform is under construction, and is designed for timely uploading of all relevant reports, including soil contamination survey reports, monitoring reports, investigation reports, risk assessment reports and reports assessing the outcome of

[211] Luo Jingyun and Zhou Hui, 'Lack of information disclosure'.

[212] The RGID was issued by the State Council on 5 April 2007 and came into force on 1 May 2008. It aims to promote government transparency by imposing legal duties on the government to disclose information, both on its own initiative and upon request by a member of the public.

[213] RGID (2007), art. 14. Qie Jianrong, 'MEP refused disclosure on basis of state secret', *Legal Daily*, 25 February 2013.

[214] Qie Jianrong, 'MEP replied to lawyer that soil pollution data will be disclosed', *Legal Daily*, 8 May 2013; Zhang Yuan, 'MEP lawful in treating soil pollution data as state secret', *New Beijing News*, 9 May 2013.

[215] The MEP and MLR issued the *Report on National Soil Pollution Survey* on 17 April 2014.

[216] SPPCL (2018), art. 81(3). [217] SPPCL (2018), art. 81(1). [218] SPPCL (2018), art. 81(2).

risk control and remediation.[219] In addition, key polluters within designated industrial sectors must disclose the pollutants they emit, the means by which they are discharged, the concentration levels and the total amount of discharge, and information on the installation and operation of pollution-control facilities, such as the treatment capacity.[220]

In addition, information on the quality of services provided by firms that produce reports on soil pollution survey and investigation, risk assessment and evaluation of outcomes of risk control and remediation, and information on those who conduct remediation work, has a direct impact on the effectiveness of measures taken to control soil pollution. Therefore, the SPPCL (2018) requires provincial environmental agencies to establish records of violations of law by units and individuals providing such environmental services, register violations and upload the records to the National Credit Information Sharing Platform and the National Enterprise Credit Information Disclosure System for easy public access.[221]

Public participation in and supervision of the work of soil pollution prevention and control is crucial.[222] Everyone has the right to report acts that contaminate land to agencies in charge of ecology and environment.[223] The agencies must publicly announce the means by which such acts can be reported and must facilitate the filing of reports.[224] The public can report environmental violations by calling the 12369 hotline, by post, by email and online at government websites and WeChat platforms.[225] If an agency receives a report, it must follow it up in a timely manner and must keep the identity of the informant confidential. To encourage public supervision, an informant is rewarded upon verification of the case by an agency.[226] Where an informant files a report against their employer, the SPPCL (2018) protects the whistle-blower by prohibiting the employer from retaliating with the dismissal of the employee, variation of the employment contract or any other means.[227] The media also exercises a crucial supervisory role over acts causing soil pollution. Any unit or individual subject to media scrutiny for an act causing soil pollution is prohibited from retaliating in any way.[228]

Soil contamination in China will remain one of the biggest environmental challenges for the foreseeable future. Substantial resources are required to fund the clean-up and remediation of contaminated sites and liable parties do not realistically have the financial capacity to bear the cost in all cases. There must be other sources of funding to supplement the polluter-pays regime. The SPPCL (2018), in line with the Soil Action Plan (2016), proposed a special fund to be earmarked for the prevention and control of soil pollution.[229] The resources are mainly used for the prevention and control of contamination of agricultural land, and risk control and remediation of orphan contaminated sites, where liable parties and parties previously holding land-use rights cannot be ascertained.[230] In the case

[219] SPPCL (2018), art. 82; Soil Action Plan (2016), part IX, s. 30. The platform was launched on 26 December 2018. See MEE, 26 December 2018, 'National soil environmental information platform launched online'. Online article. www.mee.gov.cn/xxgk2018/xxgk/xxgk15/201812/t20181226_686129.html

[220] Soil Action Plan (2016), part IX, s. 30. [221] SPPCL (2018), art. 80. [222] SPPCL (2018), art. 81(3).

[223] SPPCL (2018), art. 84(1). [224] SPPCL (2018), art. 84(2). [225] Soil Action Plan (2016), part IX, s. 30.

[226] SPPCL (2018), art. 84(3). [227] SPPCL (2018), art. 84(4). [228] SPPCL (2018), art. 83.

[229] The Measures on Management of the Soil Pollution Prevention and Control Fund were issued by the Ministry of Finance (MOF), MEE, MARA, MNR, MOHURD and SFGA on 17 January 2020.

[230] SPPCL (2018), art. 71(1). Under the Soil Action Plan (2016), the central government establishes the special fund by consolidating the existing special fund on prevention and control of pollution caused by heavy metals. See Soil Action Plan (2016), part IX, s. 28.

of contamination that occurred before the implementation of the SPPCL (2018), if the liable parties cannot be ascertained, then the parties holding land-use rights may apply to the special fund for money to carry out soil pollution risk control and remediation.[231] However, public finances alone cannot sustain the fund, given the high cost of clean-up and the amount of contaminated land. A possible solution could be to force all key entities of soil pollution to contribute to the fund. The charge is imposed in line with the polluter-pays principle. The state is required to introduce measures, including fiscal, tax, pricing and financial measures and policies, favourable to the prevention and control of soil pollution in order to attract private investment to the sector.[232] For example, the state encourages financial institutions to increase loans to risk control and remediation projects at contaminated sites, and encourages financial institutions to investigate site contamination when approving mortgages for land-use rights.[233] Tax reduction or exemption is offered to entities conducting risk control and remediation of contaminated sites.[234] Effective control and prevention of new contamination on one hand and efficient risk control and remediation on the other are both crucial for the protection of the soil environment and public health.

[231] SPPCL (2018), art. 71(2). [232] SPPCL (2018), art. 69. [233] SPPCL (2018), art. 72.
[234] SPPCL (2018), art. 73.

9

Environmental Tort

Pollution and pollution-triggered disputes have increasingly affected people's lives in China since economic reform and industrialization began in the 1980s. Rural villagers blame air, water and soil pollution for the death of fish, shrimp, tadpoles, livestock, crops and fruit trees, among others. Studies of cancer villages have drawn a link between pollution and illness.[1] Urban residents complain about air pollution, noise nuisance and light pollution harming their health and well-being. While most environmental disputes are resolved by mediation,[2] with victims of pollution aware of the tremendous difficulties involved in seeking remedies by litigation,[3] courts are the crucial last resort for China's most aggrieved victims of pollution seeking remedies and justice unavailable by other means.[4] Despite the obstacles they encounter in collecting evidence, assessing damage, getting their case accepted by the courts and having the judgment enforced, parties seeking judicial redress are shaping and reforming the rules and practice of environmental tort law in China.

This chapter examines environmental tort liabilities with a focus on the special rules and doctrines developed since the 1980s, including no-fault liability, burden of proof, joint liability, remedies, judicial mediation and class action. Key sources of civil law and civil procedure include the General Rules of Civil Law (GRCL) (2017),[5] the General Principles of

1 Lora-Wainwright, 'An anthropology'; Lee Liu, 'Made in China'; Helen Gao, 'Chinese government admits existence of cancer villages', *Lancet Oncology*, 14 (2013), 284; Anna Lora-Wainwright and Ajiang Chen, 'China's cancer villages: contested evidence and the politics of pollution' in Merrill Singer (ed.), *A Companion to the Anthropology of Environmental Health* (Chichester: Wiley Blackwell, 2016), 396–416.

2 For more discussion on environmental dispute resolution, see Yuhong Zhao, 'Environmental dispute resolution'; Yuhong Zhao, 'Mediation of'.

3 For more, see Adam Briggs, 'China's pollution victims: still seeking a dependable remedy', *Georgetown International Environmental Law Review*, 18 (2006), 305–33; Joseph McMullin, 'Do Chinese environmental laws work? A study of litigation as a response to the problem of fishery pollution in China', *UCLA Pacific Basin Law Journal*, 26 (2009), 142–83; Adam Moser and Tseming Yang, 'Environmental tort litigation in China', *Environmental Law Reporter*, 41 (2011), 10895; Rachel E. Stern, 'From dispute to decision: suing polluters in China', *The China Quarterly*, 206 (2011), 294–312.

4 One of the best examples of an aggrieved victim is Yu Mingda, the plaintiff in the well-known Pinghu tadpole case (2009), who spent fifteen years seeking justice. His case went through three levels of court before reaching the Supreme People's Court (SPC). For more details, see *Pinghu Normal Farm Special Aquatic Farm* v. *Jiaxing Buyun Dye and Chemical Co. and Others* (2009), discussed later in this chapter.

5 The GRCL was enacted on 15 March 2017 by the 12th National People's Congress (NPC) at its 5th session. It came into force on 1 October 2017.

Civil Law (GPCL) (1986),[6] the Tort Law (TL) (2009)[7] and the Civil Procedure Law (CPL) (2017).[8] Environmental statutes, including the Environmental Protection Law (EPL) (2014),[9] the Air Pollution Prevention and Control Law (APPCL) (2018),[10] the Water Pollution Prevention and Control Law (WPPCL) (2017)[11] and the Law on Prevention and Control of Pollution by Solid Waste (SWL) (2016),[12] are important legal authorities in addressing pollution issues. In addition to legislation, the SPC has issued judicial interpretations, including the Opinion on Several Issues in the Application of the Civil Procedure Law (1992),[13] Several Provisions on Evidence for Civil Litigation (2001)[14] and the Interpretation on the Application of Laws in Adjudicating Environmental Tort Cases (SPC Interpretation) (2015)[15] to guide the adjudication of environmental tort cases.

This chapter is divided into six sections. Section 9.1 discusses the development of no-fault liability as an exception to the conventional rule of fault-based liability under Chinese civil law. Section 9.2 examines proof of causation and the shift of the burden of proof from plaintiff to defendant. Section 9.3 investigates forms of liability where multiple tortfeasors jointly or separately cause pollution. Section 9.4 discusses class actions involving a large number of plaintiffs in China. Section 9.5 analyses the remedies offered to victims of pollution. Section 9.6 discusses judicial mediation as a preferred option for settling pollution disputes in court.

9.1 NO-FAULT LIABILITY

In China, civil liability is conventionally based on fault. Under the GPCL (1986), '[a]ny person who pollutes the environment and causes damage to others ***in violation of state provisions*** [emphasis added] for environmental protection and pollution prevention shall

[6] The GPCL was enacted on 12 April 1986 by the 6th NPC at its 4th session. It came into force on 1 January 1987, and was amended on 27 August 2009.

[7] The TL was enacted on 26 December 2009 by the 11th National People's Congress Standing Committee (NPCSC) at its 12th session. It came into force on 1 July 2010.

[8] The CPL was enacted on 9 April 1991 by the 7th NPC at its 4th session. It was amended on 28 October 2007 by the 10th NPCSC at its 30th session and again on 31 August 2012 by the 11th NPCSC at its 28th session. On 27 June 2017, it was amended for the third time by the 12th NPCSC at its 28th session.

[9] The EPL was enacted on 26 December 1989 by the 7th NPCSC at its 11th session. It came into force immediately. The EPL (1989) was substantially revised on 24 April 2014 by the 12th NPCSC at its 8th session, to come into force on 1 January 2015.

[10] The APPCL was enacted on 5 September 1987 by the 6th NPCSC at its 22nd session. It was amended on 29 August 1995 by the 8th NPCSC at its 15th session. It was then revised on 29 April 2000 by the 9th NPCSC at its 15th session, and revised again on 29 August 2015 by the 12th NPCSC at its 16th session, to come into force on 1 January 2016. It was amended again in 2018.

[11] The WPPCL was enacted on 11 May 1984 by the 6th NPCSC at its 5th session. It was amended on 15 May 1996 by the 8th NPCSC at its 19th session and revised on 28 February 2008 by the 10th NPCSC at its 32nd session. It was amended again on 27 June 2017 by the 12th NPCSC at its 28th session, to come into force on 1 January 2018.

[12] The SWL was enacted on 30 October 1995 by the 8th NPCSC at its 16th session, was revised substantially on 29 December 2004 by the 10th NPCSC at its 13th session. Minor amendments were made on 29 June 2013, 24 April 2015 and 7 November 2016.

[13] The SPC issued the Opinion on Several Issues in the Application of the Civil Procedure Law (1992) on 14 July 1992.

[14] The SPC issued the Several Provisions on Evidence for Civil Litigation (2001) on 21 December 2001.

[15] The SPC issued the SPC Interpretation (2015) on 6 January 2015.

bear civil liability in accordance with the law'.[16] Courts interpreted the article as requiring violation of relevant environmental provisions and standards in the determination of polluters' civil liability. That is, polluters were not held liable for compensation if they had complied with provisions and standards.

Environmental legislation of the 1980s took a different path and adopted no-fault liability in order to make polluters pay. Under the EPL (1989), 'anyone who has caused environmental pollution shall eliminate harm and compensate the unit or individual that suffers direct losses'.[17] A polluter was exempted from its civil liability only if the environmental damage was ***solely*** caused by irresistible natural disasters that could not be avoided even by taking reasonable measures promptly.[18] Specialized environmental statutes followed suit, making polluters liable for direct losses caused by pollution.[19] The departure of environmental statutes from the conventional rules of fault-based civil liability aimed to improve victims' access to judicial remedies by making polluters pay.

In practice, some courts applied fault-based liability under the GPCL (1986) and others no-fault liability under the environmental statutes. Inconsistent adjudication practice has existed for many years. In theory, the conflict of laws was addressed by the Law on Legislation (2000), which provides that 'where conflicts exist among the laws, administrative regulations, local regulations... enacted ***by the same body*** [emphasis added], special provisions shall prevail over general provisions and new provisions shall prevail over old provisions'.[20] As environmental statutes are newer than the GPCL (1986) and 'special' in terms of addressing torts caused by pollution, they prevail over relevant provisions of the GPCL (1986). This view has been challenged by some on the basis that article 83 of the Law on Legislation applies to legal instruments enacted 'by the same body', and the GPCL (1986) and environmental statues were not enacted by the same body. The former was enacted by the NPC and the latter by the NPCSC. There remains no consensus as to whether the NPC and the NPCSC should be treated as the same body.

No-fault liability for environmental tort was unequivocally affirmed by the TL (2009).[21] It stipulates that '[w]here any harm is caused by environmental pollution, the polluter shall bear tort liability'.[22] That is, polluters bear civil liability for the loss or injury suffered by victims of pollution, even in the absence of fault or any violation of state provisions. If the fault of a third party triggers pollution and causes harm, the victim may claim civil remedies against either the polluter or the third party.[23] The TL (2009) has made a significant contribution to the better protection of victims of pollution by holding polluters liable under articles 65 and 68. The EPL (2014) makes reference to the TL (2009) for civil liability by providing that '[w]here harm is caused by pollution or ecological destruction, responsible

16 GPCL (1986), art. 124. 17 EPL (1989), art. 41(1). 18 EPL (1989), art. 41(3).

19 For instance, article 62 of the APPCL (2000) provides that any party or any legal or natural person that has caused air pollution is liable to eliminate the hazard and compensate the units or individuals for their direct losses; articles 84 and 85 of the SWL (2004) provide that entities and individuals suffering damage caused by solid waste pollution have the right to claim compensation and that those whose solid waste contaminates the environment must eliminate the danger, compensate losses and take restoration measures; article 85 of the WPPCL (2008) provides that anyone whose rights and interests are damaged by a water pollution incident may request that the polluter eliminate the harm and compensate their losses.

20 Law on Legislation (2000), art. 83. 21 TL (2009), chapter 8. 22 TL (2009), art. 65.

23 TL (2009), art. 68.

parties shall bear liability in accordance with the Tort Law'.[24] Other statutes, including the APPCL (2018)[25] and SPPCL (2018),[26] follow the line taken by the EPL (2014) on civil liability, by referring generally to bearing tort liability according to law.

Even if pollution is caused by pure accident without any fault or violation of law by the polluter, the polluter is still liable for the damage caused by pollution, as in the case of *Chongqing Yanjing Village Group 1* v. *Lichao Transport, Puyang Transport and Others* (2011)[27] where the carrier of toxic substances was held liable for the harm caused by a spill. Puyang Transport was held liable as the carrier in actual control of the polluting sources, despite the fact that the traffic accident was the fault of the driver of another vehicle.

Chongqing Yanjing Village Group 1 v. *Lichao Transport, Puyang Transport and Others* (2011)

On 6 July 2010, a traffic accident was caused by the fault of the driver of a vehicle registered under Lichao Transport and Guangcheng Transport. The vehicle crashed into a container truck owned by Puyang Transport that was carrying monomethylamine solution. The accident caused 5.34 t of the chemical to spill. This seriously contaminated the farmland and fish pond of Yanjing Village Group 1, who sued Lichao Transport, Guangcheng Transport, Puyang Transport and others seeking compensation of 7,500 yuan.

Changshou District Court (2011) found the defendants liable under article 68 of the TL (2009), which states that where any harm is caused by pollution due to the fault of a third party, the victim may claim compensation from either the polluter or the third party. The court said that after compensating the victim, the polluter is entitled to claim reimbursement from the third party at fault. Puyang Transport, as carrier of the chemical substances, was in physical control of the polluting source that caused the environmental harm. It was liable to pay compensation to the plaintiff, but also had the right to claim against the defendants who were liable for the traffic accident.

To further clarify the rule of no-fault liability in environmental tort and ensure that it is applied consistently by the courts, the SPC issued the SPC Interpretation (2015). This restates and paraphrases article 65 of the TL (2009) in a more straightforward manner: 'Regardless of the fault of the polluter, where pollution has caused damage, the polluter shall bear tort liability. Where a polluter claims no liability on the basis that its discharge is in compliance with national or local standards, people's courts shall not support such a claim.'[28] The SPC has thus reemphasized that 'discharge in compliance with state standards' does not exempt one's civil liabilities for environmental harm caused. As for circumstances where a polluter's liability is exempted or mitigated, reference is to be made to specialized environmental statutes, in the absence of which the TL (2009) applies.[29] With regard to

[24] EPL (2014), art. 64.

[25] APPCL (2018), art. 125. Any party causing damage by its emission of air pollutants bears tort liability according to law.

[26] SPPCL (2018), art. 96(1). Where soil pollution has caused personal injury or property loss, polluters bear tort liability according to law.

[27] SPC Nine Model Cases on Environment and Resources (2014), case no. 4.

[28] SPC Interpretation (2015), art. 1(1).

[29] SPC Interpretation (2015), art. 1(2).

situations where the fault of a third party triggers pollution, a polluter is not permitted to claim exemption or mitigation of liability based on the fact of the third-party fault, and courts are not permitted to accept such a claim.[30] It is hoped that the SPC Interpretation (2015) will eradicate any uncertainty or ambiguity in the application of law, ensure consistency and improve the quality of adjudication in environmental tort cases.

9.2 CAUSATION AND BURDEN OF PROOF

Tort liability hinges on the proof of causation, meaning the causal link between a polluter's act of pollution and a victim's injury or loss. The general rule of civil procedure requires the party who makes the claim to provide evidence to support it.[31] In environmental tort litigation, the defendant's act, the plaintiff's loss or injury and the causal link between the two need to be proved. Victims of pollution face unique challenges to prove causation as they lack access to pollution data, professional expertise and financial resources. Applying the conventional rule on the burden of proof would deny victims' access to judicial remedies. To directly address the substantial power imbalance between victims and polluters, special rules have been developed to alleviate the heavy burden on victims of pollution and shift it to the polluters, given that they enjoy greater access to data, knowledge of production processes and financial resources.

9.2.1 Reversal of the Burden of Proof

Soon after the enactment of the CPL (1991), the SPC expressly reversed the burden of proof in environment tort litigation by the SPC Opinion on Several Issues in the Application of Civil Procedure Law (1992). It provides that 'a party who makes a claim in litigation bears the burden of proof. However, in tort litigations such as pollution compensation litigation, the defendant bears the burden of proof if he denies the infringement as claimed by the plaintiff.'[32] The rule was reaffirmed in Several Provisions on Evidence for Civil Litigation (2001), which stipulates that 'in pollution compensation lawsuits, the polluter bears the burden of proof with respect to causes for exemption of liability and lack of causal link between the polluter's acts and the harmful result'.[33] Since then, environmental statutes have also addressed the issue of burden of proof. The SWL (2004) provides that in pollution compensation litigation, the defendant bears the burden of proving they fall within a statutory exemption and of disproving causation between the defendant's act and the harmful consequences.[34] Similarly, the WPPCL (2008) stated that 'in litigation for damage caused by a water pollution incident, the party discharging pollutants shall bear the burden of proof on legally prescribed exemptions or the non-existence of the causal link between its act and the harmful consequences'.[35] The TL (2009) unequivocally stipulates the rule on the burden of proof. It states that in an environmental pollution dispute, the polluter bears

[30] SPC Interpretation (2015), art. 5(3). [31] CPL (2017), art. 64(1).
[32] SPC Opinion on Several Issues in the Application of the Civil Procedure Law (1992), art. 74.
[33] SPC Several Provisions on Evidence for Civil Litigation (2001), art. 4(3). [34] SWL (2004), art. 86.
[35] WPPCL (2008), art. 87.

the burden of proving the legally provided circumstances for exemption or mitigation of its liability or the lack of causation between its act and the harmful consequences.[36]

9.2.2 The Gap between Law and Practice

From 1992 to 2009, the legal rules on the burden of proof of causation in environmental tort have been stipulated with increasing clarity by legislation and judicial interpretation. However, there remains a substantial gap between law and practice.[37] Many courts continue to require the plaintiffs to prove causation, practically a mission impossible for most victims of pollution.

The Pinghu tadpole case (2009)[38] is particularly striking, as the dispute lasted fifteen years and went through four levels of Chinese court; this was exceptional given the procedural rule of 'two trials conclude a case'.[39] The case involved erroneous application by three levels of court of the rule on the burden of proof of causation in environmental tort cases. It highlights the difficulties experienced by victims of pollution in obtaining judicial remedies.

***Pinghu Normal Farm Special Aquatic Farm* v. *Jiaxing Buyun Dye & Chemical Co. and Others* (2009)**

Pinghu Aquatic Farm was set up in 1991 to raise American frogs. It was 6 km downstream from five dye and chemical enterprises in Buyun county, Zhejiang province. In April 1994, Yu Mingda, head and founder of the aquatic farm, became aware that the tadpoles were dying. He immediately approached local bureaus for assistance, but failed to stop the defendants from discharging wastewater. By October 1994, more than 2.7 million tadpoles had died, resulting in direct economic losses of 483,000 yuan. In December 1995, Yu sued all five polluting enterprises, seeking compensation and an injunction to stop the infringement and eliminate harm.

Pinghu City Court (1997) found that the five defendants had discharged wastewater without treatment in serious violation of national standards. The plaintiff had suffered economic loss from the death of the tadpoles. However, existing evidence failed to prove that the tadpoles had been killed by water pollution – there was a lack of a causal link between the plaintiff's loss and the defendants' discharge. The plaintiff's claim was rejected. Yu petitioned Pinghu Procuratorate and, in June 1998, the procuratorate filed a protest with Jiaxing Intermediate Court.

Jiaxing Intermediate Court (1998) reviewed the case and concluded that there was a lack of certainty as to the cause of death and the total amount of the loss. The aquatic farm had failed to provide scientific evidence to certify the cause of death of the tadpoles, the court said. The court

[36] TL (2009), art. 66.

[37] Moser and Tseming Yang, 'Environmental tort litigation'; van Rooij, 'The people vs. pollution'; Rachel E. Stern, 'On the frontlines: making decisions in Chinese civil environmental lawsuits', *Law & Policy*, 32 (2010), 79–103; Fan Yang et al, 'Adjudicating environmental tort cases in China: burden of proof, causation, and insights from 513 court decisions', *Asia Pacific Journal of Environmental Law*, 21 (2018), 171–89.

[38] *Pinghu Normal Farm Special Aquatic Farm* v. *Jiaxing Buyun Dye and Chemical Co. and Others* (2009): the judgment is available at www.pkulaw.cn. For a detailed account of the litigation, see Yang Sujuan, 'Water pollution compensation: the Zhejiang Pinghu tadpole case', in Wang Canfa and Feng Jia (eds.), *China's Environmental Litigation*, 156–71.

[39] CPL (2017), art. 10.

was unable to conclude that there was a causal link between the unlawful discharge by the five enterprises and the loss suffered by the aquatic farm. The protest was dismissed and the first-instance judgment upheld. Yu continued to petition his case. In March 2001, Zhejiang Provincial Procuratorate filed a protest with Zhejiang High Court on the basis of 'error in finding of facts and application of law'.

Zhejiang High Court (2001) confirmed the finding of facts of lower courts, that five enterprises had discharged wastewater in violation of state standards and caused water contamination and that Yu had lost all his tadpoles in 1994. Yu had not, however, produced forensic evidence to prove cause of death of the tadpoles, the court found. The lower court's decision was upheld.

Yu continued to petition. From 2002 to 2005, one sympathetic NPC deputy from Zhejiang province requested every year at the annual NPC/Chinese People's Political Consultative Conference (CPPCC) meetings in Beijing that the SPC and the Supreme People's Procuratorate (SPP) review the case. In December 2005, the SPC decided to accept the case for retrial.

The SPC (2009) attempted mediation at its first hearing in May 2006, but failed. It proceeded to adjudication and held that the lower courts' finding of facts and application of law were incorrect. The SPC overturned the judgment of Zhejiang High Court, clarifying that polluters must prove that their acts have not caused the loss suffered by the victims in pollution compensation litigation. The five polluting enterprises had failed to prove a lack of causal link between their polluting acts and the loss suffered by the aquatic farm, it found. Since it was not possible to differentiate each polluter's contribution to the damage caused, they were held jointly and equally liable for the total loss of 483,000 yuan plus interest. Each polluter was liable for 96,600 yuan plus interest, but each bore joint and several liability to the victim for the total amount.

In June 2009, payment of more than 930,000 yuan (including interest) was made to Yu Mingda, who had spent fifteen years on his legal battle against polluters. His long journey from local city court to the supreme court illustrates local courts' erroneous application of the rule on burden of proof, despite clearly stipulated rules in laws and judicial interpretations.

9.2.3 The SPC's Further Clarification on the Burden of Proof

To address the widespread misapplication of law on causation and burden of proof, the SPC issued the SPC Interpretation (2015) to list in explicit terms exactly what must be proven by plaintiff and defendant respectively. A plaintiff must establish a prima facie case by presenting evidence to prove the following:[40]

(i) the defendant has discharged/emitted pollutants;
(ii) the plaintiff has suffered damage and
(iii) there is relevance between the defendant's pollution and the plaintiff's damage.[41]

[40] SPC Interpretation (2015), art. 6.

[41] The SPC Interpretation (2015) does not further define 'relevance'. According to Justice Shen Deyong of the SPC, the threshold for 'relevance' is low, simply requiring proof of 'possibility of a causal link', rather than proof that a link is more probable than not. Plaintiffs may rely on reports from local EPBs, appraisal/assessment reports from professional bodies, academic studies and expert opinions, among others, to

Once a prima facie case has been established by the plaintiff, the burden is shifted to the defendant polluter to establish to the satisfaction of the court one of the following in order to prove lack of causation:[42]

(i) the pollutants discharged by the defendant cannot possibly cause the damage suffered by the plaintiff;
(ii) the potentially damage-causing pollutants discharged by the defendant had not reached the site of the damage at the time the damage was caused;
(iii) the damage claimed by the plaintiff occurred prior to the discharge of the relevant pollutants by the defendant or
(iv) any other circumstances that prove a lack of causal link between the defendant's polluting acts and the plaintiff's damage.

The provisions of the SPC Interpretation (2015) were based on years of adjudication practice, including *Qu Zhongquan* v. *Shandong Fuhai Co.* (2015).[43] The case came to the SPC for clarification of whether the victim plaintiff had established a prima facie case and what the defendant polluter needed to prove to show lack of causation.

Qu Zhongquan v. *Shandong Fuhai Co.* (2015)

Qu Zhongquan, a farmer, had been growing cherry trees since 1995. Shandong Fuhai Co. (Fuhai), an aluminium producer adjacent to Qu's cherry orchard, started operations in 2001. Qu sued Fuhai in April 2009, seeking remedies to stop the defendant's emission of air pollutants and compensation of 5.01 million yuan for the loss of cherries and cherry trees.

Yantai Intermediate Court (2013) accepted the case. Qu provided the following evidence: (i) a notarized on-site inspection report recording an obnoxious smell, which became stronger closer to the defendant's factory, smoke being emitted from the defendant's site and an absence of other industrial operators nearby, as well as the facts that most cherry trees were not bearing fruit, that trees that did bear fruit were producing small and abnormally shaped cherries, that some trees had died and others had withered leaves; (ii) a test report by Yantai Agricultural Products Quality Inspection and Testing Centre that proved there was an excessive level of fluoride on leaves; (iii) an appraisal report by the court-appointed Laboratory of Shandong Agricultural Academy, which proved the existence of fluoride on cherry leaves, and the closer to the defendant's site, the higher the level of fluoride content; (iv) reference books and other resources indicating that aluminium production generates pollutants, including fluoride, sulphur and carbon monoxide; (v) SEPA standards on air pollutant limits and the protection of agricultural products, which confirm that cherries are sensitive to fluoride and (vi) assessment reports by Yantai Muping Fruit Trees Development Centre and Yantai Judicial Appraisal Institute on Price quantifying Qu's total economic loss, based on the estimated reduction in his cherry yield. Fuhai failed to prove lack of causation. The court held Fuhai liable and ordered it to stop emitting fluoride and to pay 1.84 million yuan in compensation to Qu for his loss of cherries and cherry trees. Both parties appealed.

establish a possibility of causation. See Shen Deyong (ed.), *Understanding and Applying SPC's Judicial Interpretation on Environmental Tort Liability Disputes* (Beijing: People's Court Press, 2016), at 93–5.

[42] SPC Interpretation (2015), art. 7. [43] SPC 10 Model Cases on Environmental Torts (2015), case no. 4.

Shandong High Court (2014) upheld the first-instance judgment on the injunction against further fluoride emissions, but increased the amount of compensation to 2.24 million yuan. Fuhai petitioned the SPC to retry the case, arguing that there was a lack of causation. Fuhai stated that there was no causal link between its emissions and Qu's loss of cherries and cherry trees. Qu's losses could have been caused by abnormal weather conditions, Fuhai claimed.

The SPC (2015) reviewed the case and ruled that Qu's evidence had established that: (i) Fuhai had emitted pollutants containing fluoride; (ii) Qu had suffered loss of cherries and cherry trees and (iii) there was relevance between Fuhai's pollution and Qu's loss. Qu had discharged his burden of proof to establish the prima facie case. According to article 66 of the TL (2009), a polluter bears the burden of proof to show that there are circumstances that mitigate its liability or exempt it from liability, or a lack of causal link between its acts and the victim's loss. Fuhai presented its environmental impact assessment (EIA) reports, as well as monitoring reports for the fluoride emissions that did not cover the time span relevant to the dispute. Even if its operation and emissions were in compliance with state provisions and standards, it still bore civil liability if damage was caused, the court said. Fuhai had failed to prove a lack of causation between its emission and Qu's loss. The lower courts had taken into account the extreme weather and had mitigated Fuhai's liability to 70 per cent of Qu's total loss, which was proper and which it supported, the SPC said. It dismissed Fuhai's petition and upheld the decision of Shandong High Court.

In this case, Qu proved: (i) the existence of the defendant's fluoride emissions by producing an on-site inspection report, a testing report by a body of its own choice and an appraisal report by a court-appointed body agreed by both parties and (ii) the loss, calculated based on the assessment reports. The proof of relevance clearly has a lower threshold than that of causation. The courts were satisfied by evidence from reference books and the national standards that aluminium production generates fluoride and cherries are sensitive to fluoride. Nonetheless, a plaintiff's tasks of collecting evidence of pollution and producing proof of damage can be a huge challenge, if not impossible.

Evidence of pollution includes photos and videos of pollution, for example, dead fish in toxic-looking waters, dying trees and plants set in landscapes devastated by heavy dark smoke from chimneys. The more reliable evidence is government reports and monitoring records, which are treated as authoritative by courts. Local environmental bureaus are the primary sources of pollution data, while local agricultural and fishery bureaus may also be helpful in providing on-site inspection reports or records of pollution. Studies have found that the competence and efficiency of local agencies varies. Some offer efficient assistance, while others are less responsive.[44] Timely support and assistance from local agencies for plaintiff victims of pollution can effectively alleviate their burden, as in *Liang Zhaonan* v. *China Resources Cement Holdings Ltd* (2014),[45] the events of which took place in Guangxi autonomous region.

[44] Stern, 'From dispute to decision', at 302; van Rooij, 'The people vs. pollution', at 65–7.
[45] SPC 10 Model Cases on Environmental Torts (2015), case no. 7.

Liang Zhaonan v. *China Resources Cement Holdings Ltd* (2014)

Liang Zhaonan had operated a fish farm at Xiazou Reservoir since 1993. On 5 October 2011, the water in the reservoir turned yellow and muddy and the fish started to die. Liang reported to the local agency in charge of aquaculture and animal husbandry. The agency immediately formed a joint investigation team with Shangsi County Environmental Monitoring Brigade and the township government. They visited the site on the same day Liang approached them, and found many dead fish were floating on the surface of the yellow and muddy water of the reservoir. China Resources Cement Holdings Ltd (CRC) stood 50m from the reservoir and had a drain connected to it. Cement powder and coal soot were washed into the drain from the defendant's site by heavy rainfall. Shangsi County Fishery Management Station produced an inspection report on 6 October, stating that 'CRC is located about 50 m from the reservoir, with a drain connected to the latter. On-site inspection found rainwater in the drain directly discharged to the reservoir.' By 7 October, all fish in the reservoir were dead. Liang sued CRC for compensation of his loss of fish caused by its discharge of cement powder and coal soot.

Shangsi County Court (2013) appointed a qualified appraisal body to assess Liang's economic loss. The body calculated the loss at 112,500 yuan in total. Liang paid the appraisal fee of 5,625 yuan. The court found CRC liable under articles 65 and 66 of the TL (2009) and ordered CRC to pay Liang 118,125 yuan to cover compensation for his loss of fish and the appraisal fees. CRC appealed, claiming that Liang had not proved the causal link between the discharge and his loss, and insisting that the cement powder and coal soot rinsed from its site and discharged to the reservoir was incapable of killing all the fish. It further claimed that the heavy rainfall brought by a strong typhoon was a *force majeure* incident.

Guangxi Fangchenggang Intermediate Court (2014) found the lower court's finding of facts and application of law correct and proper. The inspection reports of the joint investigation team and the local fishery management station had recorded CRC's discharge of cement powder and coal soot from its site through the drain to the reservoir and the fish killed by the contaminated water. These reports established a prima facie case of CRC's pollution and its relevance to Liang's loss. CRC failed to provide any solid evidence to prove absence of causal link as required by article 66 of the TL (2009). The court found that CRC's claim of *force majeure* did not stand as a typhoon warning had been given, allowing sufficient time for CRC to take measures to prevent the discharge by moving cement and other materials by the drain to indoor or other sites for storage. The court dismissed CRC's appeal and upheld the decision of the lower court.

In this case, the timely response and on-site inspection by local agencies upon Liang's report of reservoir contamination were of critical importance, enabling Liang to obtain evidence of the defendant's pollution. Agency reports and inspection records of an incident are commonly accepted by court as evidence to prove the defendant's pollution, the plaintiff's loss and relevance between the two.

Proof of damage requires a plaintiff to quantify the economic loss linked to the pollution. Judges tend to rely heavily on the appraisal reports produced by a government institution or qualified professional body appointed by the court. The reports may assess the extent of damage, causation between pollution and loss, or both.[46] They are treated as science-based,

[46] Fan Yang et al., 'Adjudicating environmental tort', at 183–4.

objective and unbiased by the courts, and judicial decisions rarely deviate from their conclusions. However, researchers have expressed concern over the quality and objectivity of some appraisal reports, questioning the competence and professionalism of some appraisal bodies,[47] or fearing undue influence may have been imposed by polluters to the disadvantage of pollution victims.[48] Not all appraisal reports are accurate and reliable, especially in cases involving new types of environmental torts. In *Ni Xulong* v. *Dandong Haiyanghong Wind Power Co.* (2013),[49] Liaoning High Court examined the qualification of the appraisal body and dismissed its report.

Ni Xulong v. *Dandong Haiyanghong Wind Power Co.* (2013)

Ni Xulong had farmed soft-shell turtles since 1993 and had expanded his business in 1995 and 1997. In March 2000, Dandong Haiyanghong Wind Power Co. (Haiyanghong) installed large-scale wind turbines nearby with one set placed only 100 m from the south-east boundary of the turtle farm and another set placed 400 m to 500 m from its north-west boundary. In September 2000, large numbers of the soft-shell turtles died. Ni hired Liaoning Freshwater Fishery Environmental Monitoring Station to assess the impact of Haiyanghong's wind-power generation on the turtle farm. The assessment report concluded that the noise and the changing light and shade of the wind turbines had disturbed the quiet environment enjoyed by the soft-shell turtles. The impact was significant in April and May, the reproduction and growth period for turtles. Ni hired Dandong Guoxin Asset Evaluation Co. (Guoxin) to quantify his economic losses. The appraisal report concluded that Ni's total loss was 1,637,966 yuan, covering 1,508,400 yuan for the loss of the turtles and 129,566 yuan for relocation of the farm. Ni sued Haiyanghong to claim damages.

Donggang City Court (2010) entrusted Fishery Eco-monitoring Centre to assess the impact of the defendant's wind-power generation on the turtles. Following a site inspection, the Centre concluded in a report that the noise, electromagnetic radiation and the turning blades would not have affected the survival or growth of the soft-shell turtles. In response, Ni produced a reference letter from the Resources and Environment Division of the Fishery Bureau of the Ministry of Agriculture (MOA) stating that the assessment of the impact of wind turbines on the turtle farm was beyond the scope of services the Centre was qualified to provide, which were the investigation and certification of fishery pollution incidents. The court sought clarification from the Fishery Bureau of the MOA on two questions: (i) whether the Centre was qualified to investigate and certify fishery pollution incidents and (ii) whether the Centre was qualified to assess the death of the soft-shell turtles. The Fishery Bureau replied that it had issued the Centre with a qualification certificate allowing it to investigate and certify fishery pollution incidents. The Court accepted the Centre's certification report and rejected Ni's claim of damages. Ni appealed.

Dandong Intermediate Court (2010) dismissed the appeal and upheld the decision of the lower court. Ni petitioned for retrial.

Liaoning High Court (2013) applied article 4 of the SPC's Several Provisions on Evidence for Civil Litigation (2001), which states that in environmental tort caused by pollution, the tortfeasor bears

[47] Stern, 'From dispute to decision', at 304.
[48] Moser and Tseming Yang, 'Environmental tort litigation', at 10899.
[49] SPC 10 Model Criminal, Civil and Administrative Cases on Environment and Resources (2017), case no. 5.

the burden to prove that circumstances exist that allow for its liability to be exempted or a lack of causal link between its acts and the loss or injury suffered by the victim. Ni had suffered loss of turtles. The operation of the wind turbines generates noise, electromagnetic radiation and changing light and shade that are potential sources of pollution, for which reason the Liaoning Provisional Measures on Wind-Power Generation and Eco-protection requires a protection distance of 500 m between turbines and any objects sensitive to noise and changing light and shade. In this case, one set of turbines was only 100 m from the turtle farm. The appraisal report that had concluded there was no impact on the survival or growth of turtles was produced by a body qualified for investigation and certification of fishery pollution incidents, meaning pollution of fishery waters. The court found that the body was not qualified to assess the impact of wind turbine operation on turtles, and therefore dismissed the report. Haiyanghong had failed to prove lack of causation and was found to bear civil liability. Considering all relevant circumstances, Haiyanghong was held liable for 80 per cent of Ni's loss of soft-shell turtles. The court overturned the judgments of the lower courts and ordered Haiyanghong to pay Ni 1,310,327.8 yuan (80 per cent of 1,637,966 yuan) in compensation.

Given the complex and technical nature of environmental tort, professional appraisal reports provide an important basis for a court's decision on causation and liability, but they should not be treated as exclusive evidence or a substitute for a court's own judgment.

9.3 THE LEGAL LIABILITY OF MULTIPLE TORTFEASORS

An environmental tort is often committed by multiple tortfeasors. There are two possible scenarios. Under the first, multiple parties collaborate to carry out the acts of pollution; for example, an operator without a hazardous waste (HW) operation permit may illegally dispose of toxic waste, causing severe water and soil contamination. The liable parties are the generator of the HW and all involved in its collection, transportation and disposal. Under the second scenario, multiple tortfeasors separately engage in activities that all contribute to the pollution; for example, several factories operate along a river and all discharge wastewater to it, causing pollution. In the former scenario, multiple tortfeasors bear joint and several liabilities.[50] In the latter scenario, if the act of each party is sufficient to cause all the harm, then each tortfeasor bears joint and several liability.[51] If the act of each party would not on its own have caused all the harm, each tortfeasor bears liability for a fair portion of the total loss based on its contribution. If it is difficult or impossible to determine each tortfeasor's contribution to the harm, then each shall bear an equal share of the liability.[52]

9.3.1 Multiple Parties Jointly Committing a Tort

The TL (2009) provides that where two or more persons jointly infringe upon another person's rights and cause that person damage, they bear joint and several liability.[53] The

[50] TL (2009), art. 8; SPC Interpretation (2015), art. 2.
[51] TL (2009), art. 11; SPC Interpretation (2015), art. 3(1).
[52] TL (2009), art. 12; SPC Interpretation (2015), art. 3(2).
[53] GPCL (1986), art. 130; TL (2009), art. 8.

injured party has the right to seek remedies against any or all of them.[54] In the context of environmental tort, where two or more parties jointly undertake activities that cause pollution and harm, they bear joint and several liability for the damage suffered by the victims of the pollution.[55] Each tortfeasor is potentially 100 per cent liable to victims of pollution for the harm jointly caused by all tortfeasors. The concept of joint and several liability substantially increases the chance that victims of pollution will be able to obtain remedies through tort litigation.

Among tortfeasors that bear joint and several liability, there is a mechanism to apportion liability among themselves by reference to each party's contribution to the harm. Where it is difficult to determine the liability of each party, they must bear equal shares of the liability.[56] If any party has paid more than its share to the injured party, it has the right to recover the money from other joint tortfeasors.[57] In environmental tort, a party's contribution to the harm is determined by factors including the type and volume of the pollution discharge.[58] In judicial practice, courts consider types of pollutants, the volume of discharge or emission, the toxicity, whether the discharge or emission is conducted with or without a permit, and whether the discharge or emission is in violation of state discharge or emission standards or the total control quota.[59]

In the case of *Shanghai Songjiang Yexie Township Government* v. *Jiang Rongxiang and Others* (2012),[60] in which defendant Jiang Rongxiang instructed Dong Shengzhen, his employee and driver, to collect and discharge waste acid from three companies in violation of law, the court decided the legal liabilities of the five parties in accordance with the TL (2009).[61]

Shanghai Songjiang Yexie Township Government v. *Jiang Rongxiang and Others* (2012)

Haomeng Bicycle Co. (Haomeng), Rixin Co. (Rixin) and Jiayu Chemical Co. (Jiayu) contracted Jiang Rongxiang to dispose of waste acid generated from their production processes, knowing that Jiang had no HW operation permit. In February and March 2011, Jiang instructed his employee and driver Dong Shengzhen to collect six trucks of waste acid (four from Haomeng, one each from Rixin and Jiayu) and discharge them into a rainwater catchment basin 100 m south of Hongxian River. The waste acid flowed from the basin into the storm drain and then into the river, causing serious damage to the river, soil and vegetation. Yexie Township Government took immediate action to clean up and restore the contaminated river at a cost of 887,266 yuan. It sued Jiang, Dong, Haomeng, Rixin and Jiayu for compensation of expenses incurred.

Songjiang District Court (2012) found that the plaintiff had been vested with a duty to manage Hongxian River. It had performed its duty to clean up the river and mitigate harm at the cost of liable parties, the court found. Waste acid is classed as HW under the SWL, the collection, transport, storage and disposal of which requires an HW operation permit, it noted. Jiang, who did not have

[54] TL (2009), art. 13. [55] SPC Interpretation (2015), art. 2. [56] TL (2009), art. 14(1).
[57] TL (2009), art. 14(2). [58] TL (2009), art. 67. [59] SPC Interpretation (2015), art. 4.
[60] SPC Nine Model Cases on Environment and Resources (2014), case no. 3.
[61] TL (2009), arts. 65, 66 and 67.

such a permit, collected waste acid from three enterprises for a profit and instructed Dong to collect and dispose of the waste acid in a manner that caused serious contamination and environmental damage, it added. Jiang and Dong were held jointly liable for the harm caused. Haomeng, Rixin and Jiayu generate waste acid and should have been registered with the local EPB, should have completed HW transfer forms and entrusted the waste acid to licensed operators for disposal, as required by the SWL, the court said. It noted that neither Haomeng, Rixin or Jiayu had complied with the HW control requirements. They were held jointly liable with Jiang in accordance with their individual contributions to the illegal disposal: 65 per cent of the waste came from Haomeng, 20 per cent from Jiayu and 15 per cent from Rixin. The court held that in accordance with articles 65, 66 and 67 of the TL (2009): (i) Jiang should pay 887,266 yuan to Yexie Township Government to compensate it for the economic loss it incurred in cleaning and restoring the contaminated river; (ii) Dong bore joint and several liability with Jiang; (iii) Jiayu bore joint liability with Jiang for 20 per cent of the damage; (iv) Haomeng bore joint liability with Jiang for 65 per cent of the damage and (v) Rixin bore joint liability with Jiang for 15 per cent of the damage.

In this case, Jiang and Dong jointly committed the environment tort by engaging in the illegal collection and dumping of HW, causing severe contamination of the environment and high clean-up costs for the plaintiff. Jiang and Dong bore joint and several liability. The three waste generators facilitated Jiang's illegal disposal of the HW and were held jointly liable with Jiang, with the liability of each commensurate with its contribution to the tort. On a separate note, the five defendants had also received administrative and criminal sanctions prior to this civil trial. The three companies had received fines, while Jiang and Dong were arrested, prosecuted and convicted for the crime of environmental pollution. Both received prison sentences.

9.3.2 Separately Committing Tort

Environmental torts are often committed by parties separately without a meeting of minds. Under the TL (2009), if two or more persons commit torts separately, but cause the same harm, the tortfeasors bear respective liabilities where each party's liability can be determined. Where it is difficult to determine each tortfeasor's liability, then each bears an equal share of the liability.[62] Where the separate polluting acts of two or more polluters cause the same harm, and neither act is sufficient to cause all the harm, and the victims of pollution seek remedies against polluters under article 12 of the TL (2009), the courts will apportion the respective liabilities of each party.[63]

In the case of *Zhou Hang* v. *Mingxiang Logistics Co. and Suiyu Highway Co.* (2014),[64] the carrier of the pollutants was held liable despite its lack of fault or violation of law. The highway company was liable for its failure to mitigate the contamination caused by the oil spill.

[62] TL (2009), art. 12. [63] SPC Interpretation (2015), art. 3(2).
[64] SPC 10 Model Cases on Environmental Torts (2015), case no. 8.

Zhou Hang v. *Mingxiang Logistics Co. and Suiyu Highway Co.* (2014)

On 20 February 2012, a traffic accident caused a serious oil leakage from an oil tanker owned by Mingxiang Logistics Co. (Mingxiang) on a road managed by Suiyu Highway Co. (Suiyu). The driver of the oil tanker was not at fault or in violation for the traffic accident. The leaked oil contaminated more than 1 km of the highway, but Suiyu Highway did not take immediate action to contain the oil spill. As a result, the oil ran downhill into a drain and then into a fish pond managed by Zhou Hang. Zhou suffered heavy losses and sued both companies for compensation.

Yubei District Court held Mingxiang, as carrier and polluter, liable for 70 per cent of Zhou's losses. Suiyu was liable for 30 per cent for its failure to mitigate and control the impact of the oil spill. Mingxiang and Suiyu appealed.

Chongqing No. 1 Intermediate Court (2014) upheld the lower court's decision. Mingxiang petitioned Chongqing High Court for a retrial, claiming there was no fault on the part of its driver and the accident was unexpected and unforeseeable.

Chongqing High Court (2014) rejected the petition and upheld the second-instance judgment. It emphasized that no-fault liability applied in environmental tort. Even though the driver was not at fault, he had been in control of the oil, the polluting source, at the time of the traffic accident. As he was an employee of Mingxiang, and was working for his employer at the time of the spill, the employer was held liable for the environmental damage.

In this case, Mingxiang Logistics was found to bear the primary liability (70 per cent) as carrier of the oil, the polluter in control of the polluting source. Suiyu Highway was found to bear secondary liability (30 per cent) for its failure to take immediate action to contain and mitigate pollution.

It should be noted that parties separately committing a tort may still bear joint and several liability for the harm caused. The TL (2009) provides that where two or more parties separately commit torts and each party's tort is capable of causing the total loss, liable parties bear joint and several liability.[65] Where the separate polluting acts of two or more polluters have caused the same harm, and each act is sufficient to cause all the harm, victims may seek remedies against polluters under article 11 of the TL (2009), and the courts will hold defendants jointly and severally liable.[66] In the Pinghu tadpole case,[67] by the time the SPC reopened the case nearly fifteen years after the torts were committed, it was impossible to differentiate the individual contribution of each defendant enterprise to the damage caused. The SPC held the five polluters jointly and severally liable to Yu Mingda for his total loss of 483,000 yuan plus interest. Internally among the five liable parties, each bore 20 per cent of the liability.

A number of factors are considered in the determination of each party's liability for an environmental tort committed by multiple parties separately. Types of pollutants and

[65] TL (2009), art. 11. [66] SPC Interpretation (2015), art. 3(1).

[67] *Pinghu Normal Farm Special Aquatic Farm* v. *Jiaxing Buyun Dye and Chemical Co. and Others* (2009): the judgment is available at www.pkulaw.cn. For a detailed account of the litigation, see Yang Sujuan, 'Water pollution compensation'.

quantity of discharge are crucial under the TL (2009),[68] as they directly determine the toxicity and impact of the pollution. The SPC's judicial interpretation clearly stipulates a list of factors for consideration: 'types, quantity and toxicity of the pollutants discharged, whether the polluter holds valid discharge permits, whether the discharge was in violation of national or local discharge standards, and whether the discharge exceeds the total discharge quota for key pollutants'.[69] A violation of national or local standards has substantial impact on the apportionment of liabilities among multiple polluters, even though compliance does not exempt a party's civil liability for pollution. This differential treatment is not only fair to operators investing in pollution control and treatment in order to comply with laws and regulations, but also incentivizes compliance by significantly increasing the potential cost of violation.

Tianjin High Court adopted this approach in the case of *Qian'an Paper Factory and Others* v. *Sun Youli and Others* (2003).[70] The court carefully addressed the liabilities of multiple tortfeasors: it held that tortfeasors in violation of standards were jointly and severally liable, thereby safeguarding the victims' rights to remedies; it fairly apportioned the liability to be borne by the tortfeasor who did comply with standards and excluded it from joint and several liability.

Qian'an Paper Factory and Others v. *Sun Youli and Others* (2003)

Sun Youli and seventeen farmers from Laoting county, Hebei province operated aquatic farms in the Luan River estuary. In October 2000, all their fish and shellfish were killed overnight when highly toxic industrial wastewater was discharged into the Luan River. In May 2001, they sued nine paper factories and chemical plants discharging wastewater to the Luan River, seeking a court injunction to stop the defendants from discharging wastewater to the Luan River, and compensation in the amount of 20 million yuan.

Tianjin Maritime Court (2002) accepted the plaintiffs' evidence as proof of their economic loss. Of the nine defendants discharging wastewater, Qian'an Chemical Plant was the only one that had complied with standards, the court found, adding that the discharges from eight companies had violated national standards. Applying no-fault liability for the environmental tort, the court found all defendants liable as they had failed to prove a lack of causal link between the discharge and the loss suffered by the victims. The court ordered the defendants to immediately stop discharging wastewater to the Luan River and to eliminate the danger of pollution to the aquatic farms. It held that all nine defendants bore joint and several liability to the plaintiffs for a total of 13,659,700 yuan as damages for the loss of fish and shellfish. The defendants appealed.

Tianjin High Court (2003) disagreed with the Maritime Court on liabilities and calculation of damages. On the issue of liability, the court held that Qian'an Chemical Plant's wastewater discharge had complied with national standards. It was liable for the harm caused to the plaintiffs, but its liability was different from the eight who had discharged wastewater in violation of the law, the court found. The plaintiffs were also at fault for choosing to set up aquatic farms near the estuary of Luan River, which is well known for its decades-long contamination by industrial effluents, it said. One of the defendants was a 100-year old factory. The plaintiffs had assumed risk

[68] TL (2009), art. 67. [69] SPC Interpretation (2015), art. 4.
[70] SPC 10 Model Cases on Maritime Trials (2014), case no. 8.

having established the farms near the pollution and therefore had to bear part of the liability, the court said. The court found that the farmers would not be able to sell their aquatic products at retail price, which had been used by the lower court as the basis of its damages calculation. Instead, it found that the loss should be calculated on the basis of the wholesale price (i.e. 70 per cent of the retail price), reducing the total loss to 9,561,790 yuan. Sun Youli and others, who had approached the pollution and had therefore assumed risk, were held to bear 2,868,540 yuan of the loss. The defendants were found liable for the remaining 6,693,250 yuan. Qian'an Chemical Plant was liable to pay 140,000 yuan, and did not bear joint and several liability with the other eight polluters, who were held jointly and severally liable for 6,553,250 yuan of compensation.

Tianjin High Court adopted the principle of 'respective liability' to apportion fairly the tort liabilities of tortfeasor in violation and tortfeasor in compliance. It sent a clear message that polluters in violation should face higher costs for their pollution. Meanwhile, joint and several liability offers victims of pollution a better chance of obtaining compensation by giving them access to those with deeper pockets. The court's approach was innovative at the time and has been formally adopted by both law and judicial interpretation as a binding rule of environmental adjudication.

In cases where the discharges of all defendants are in compliance with relevant standards, but still cause pollution and harm the lawful rights and interests of others, courts hold defendants liable based on no-fault liability and then apportion individual liability based on the quantity and nature of their respective discharge. This occurred in the case of *Nie Sheng and 148 Other Households* v. *Tian'an Coal Co. Fifth Mine and Two Others* (2011)[71] in Henan province.

Nie Sheng and 148 Other Households v. *Tian'an Coal Co. Fifth Mine and Two Others* (2011)

Since June 2003, the wells in the village of Xinzhuang had been contaminated and the water was not safe for human consumption. Nie Sheng and members of 148 other rural households had to travel a long distance to collect water from other villages. They sued three defendants – Fifth Mine, Sixth Mine and Central Hospital – for causing groundwater contamination by discharging industrial and clinical wastewater. The plaintiffs claimed compensation for loss of wages in the amount of 2.12 million yuan.

Xinhua District Court (2010) accepted the case and calculated the total loss of wages to be 441,431 yuan. It found that part of the contamination was caused by household sewage, meaning that the plaintiffs had contributed to the contamination. The court held the three defendants jointly liable for 76 per cent of the total loss suffered by the plaintiffs, which was 335,488 yuan. The plaintiffs and defendants appealed.

Pingdingshan Intermediate Court (2011) agreed with the lower court on the calculation of loss of wages and on its application of articles 65 and 66 of the TL (2009) in holding the defendants

[71] SPC Nine Model Cases on Environment and Resources (2014), case no. 2.

liable based on no-fault liability. The court disagreed on the apportionment of liabilities among the three defendants. Based on an appraisal report and considering all factors, including the nature and volume of discharge by each defendant, the court found the three defendants jointly and severally liable for 40 per cent of the loss, or 176,572 yuan, while Fifth Mine and Sixth Mine were jointly and severally liable for 36 per cent of the loss, or 158,915 yuan.[72]

The second-instance court carefully considered the different contribution of each defendant and apportioned liability among them as fairly as possible, based on the nature and volume of their discharges.

9.4 CLASS ACTION

Environmental torts often involve more than one pollution victim. Class action is an efficient and effective option by which victims claim compensation from polluters. Class action was introduced by the CPL (1991).[73] Where one party to litigation is a significant number of people, they may elect a representative to sue on their behalf. The acts of the representative in the litigation are legally valid for and upon all those represented. However, any modification or waiver of the claims or any acceptance of the other party's request to reach a compromise requires the prior consent of the persons being represented.[74] The best-known class action, *Zhang Changjian and Others* v. *Rongping Chemical Plant* (2005),[75] also involves the largest number of plaintiffs in the history of Chinese environmental law. Zhang represented more than 1,700 villagers in tort litigation against a chemical factory to claim compensation and demand clean-up of the solid waste.

Zhang Changjian and Others v. *Rongping Chemical Plant* (2005)

Rongping Chemical Plant (Rongping), Asia's largest manufacturer of potassium chlorate, was built in the village of Xiping (in Pingnan county, Ningde city, Fujian province) in 1992 and started operations in 1995. In 1998, its production doubled. Major pollutants from the plant included hexavalent chromium (Cr^{6+}) in the wastewater and industrial solid waste, and chlorine in the air emissions. Villagers suffered greatly and blamed the industrial pollution: bamboo and fruit trees turned yellow and died, fish and shrimp disappeared from the river, and people fell ill

[72] The 1-yuan difference between the value of the liabilities in the Xinhua District Court judgment and the Pingdingshan Intermediate Court judgment is due to rounding.

[73] Class action or representative litigation was introduced by article 54 of the CPL (1991). The CPL was amended in 2007, 2012 and 2017. The content of the article remains unchanged, but it became article 53 in the CPL (2012) and the CPL (2017).

[74] CPL (1991), art. 54; CPL (2007), art. 54; CPL (2012), art. 53; CPL (2017), art. 53.

[75] SPC Nine Model Cases on Environment and Resources (2014), case no. 6. For a detailed account of the litigation, see Zhang Jingjing, 'The environmental tort case sued by 1,721 villagers of Fujian Pingnan against Rongping Chemical Company Ltd' in Wang Canfa and Feng Jia (eds.) *China's Environmental Litigation*, 68–81; see also Stern, 'From dispute to decision'.

with headaches, chest pain, skin rashes and cancer. Zhang Changjian, a village doctor, kept a record of villagers who died of cancer: one between 1990 and 1994, four from 1995 to 1998, and 17 from 1999 to 2001. Disputes between Rongping and the villagers were settled by administrative mediation facilitated by the local EPB in 2001 and 2002. Rongping accepted liability and paid 434,415.20 yuan in compensation, but continued to pollute. Zhang and 1,721 villagers sued, seeking remedies including: (i) a court order to stop the infringement; (ii) clean-up of the toxic waste stockpiled on and off the factory premises; (iii) compensation of 10.33 million yuan for loss of property and physical injury and 3.2 million yuan for emotional distress.

Ningde Intermediate Court (2005) ruled that Rongping's proof that its emissions had complied with relevant laws was not relevant to the issue of causation. The causal link was presumed to be established.[76] The court held Rongping liable and ordered it to: (i) immediately stop the infringement; (ii) pay 249,763 yuan as compensation for the loss of fruit trees, bamboo and crops; (iii) clean up the industrial solid waste stockpiled on and near the factory premises. The court rejected claims for damages for physical injury and emotional distress. Zhang and others appealed with legal assistance from the Centre for Legal Assistance to Pollution Victims (CLAPV) of the China University of Politics and Law (CUPL).

Fujian High Court (2005) agreed with the lower court and re-emphasized the special rules on the burden of proof of causation and no-fault liability in environmental tort.[77] Rongping's evidence and expert testimony on its proper pollution-control facilities, its first-class production machinery, its emission and discharge of three waste types (air pollutants, wastewater and solid waste) in compliance and the absence of pollution incidents did not prove lack of causation, the court said. Rongping had failed to prove that there was no causal link between its discharge and the loss suffered by the plaintiffs. The court upheld the first-instance judgment on Rongping's liability and the injunction order of cessation of infringement, but revised the other two remedies: (i) the amount of compensation for the loss of fruit trees, bamboo and crops increased from 249,763 yuan to 684,178.2 yuan; (ii) Rongping was order to clean up and properly dispose of the ISW on and off the site, in the river and the soil, within one year. The claims of damages for physical injury and emotional distress were rejected.

Another high-profile case involves ninety-seven rural households engaged in aquatic farming suing two factories: *Shandong Linshu Jinyimeng Paper Co. and Another* v. *Xie Yinli and 96 Others* (2002).[78]

[76] As evidence of the defendant's pollution, the plaintiffs presented photos of heavy smoke from the plant's chimneys and proof of illness and property loss that had occurred since operations began at Rongping, the only major factory in the county. The plaintiffs established a possible link between pollution and injury, and the burden was shifted to the defendant to prove lack of causation. Rongping failed to prove this with its argument that its emissions were in compliance.

[77] SPC Several Provisions on Evidence for Civil Litigation (2001). In pollution compensation litigation, the polluter bears the burden of proof and must introduce evidence to prove there is no causal link between its act and the harm.

[78] The judgment is available at www.pkulaw.cn. The case is one of the fifty-one most influential cases in the sixty-five-year history of the SPC. See SPC, '51 cases influencing China over 65 years of SPC', *People's Court News*, 25 November 2014. Details of the case are discussed in Liu Xiang, 'Shilianghe 97 households of aquatic farming suing two polluters in Shandong for compensation' in Wang Canfa and Feng Jia (eds.), *China's Environmental Litigation*, 172–88.

***Shandong Linshu Jinyimeng Paper Co. and Another* v. *Xie Yinli and 96 Others* (2002)**

Shilianghe is the largest reservoir in Jiangsu province and had, since 1997, been used by local farmers to breed fish in net cages. A serious incident occurred in September 1999 in which wastewater containing high levels of chemical oxygen demand (COD) was discharged into the reservoir by Shandong Linshu Jinyimeng Paper Co. (Jinyimeng) and Linshu Chemical Co. (Linshu Chemical) of Shandong province, killing large amounts of fish and causing serious losses to the ninety-seven rural households engaged in aquatic farming. The same occurred again in June 2000. The victims sued Jinyimeng Paper and Linshu Chemical, seeking an injunction and claiming damages of 5,652,000 yuan, which included 5.604 million yuan as compensation for the loss of fish and 48,000 yuan for the cost of investigating the incident and appraising the losses.

Lianyungang Intermediate Court (2001) accepted the investigation and appraisal report produced by Huangbo Marine Monitoring Station. The report concluded that the COD levels in the wastewater discharge into the reservoir by Jinyimeng and Linshu Chemical over state concentration limits had suffocated large numbers of fish. It assessed the value of the lost fish at 5.604 million yuan. The two companies had failed to prove there was no causal link between their discharges and the fish deaths, or any circumstances that would exempt them from liability or mitigate their liability. The court held both companies jointly and severally liable for the loss suffered by the ninety-seven households and ordered the two companies to: (i) stop the infringement by effluent discharge into the reservoir; (ii) pay 5.6 million yuan as compensation for the fish losses and 48,000 yuan to cover the pollution investigation and appraisal expenses.

Jiangsu High Court (2002) upheld the first-instance judgment and ordered Jinyimeng and Linshu Chemical to make payment within thirty days.

This is a case involving cross-provincial border pollution, in which the enforcement of judgment proved difficult. Although the ninety-seven households won the legal battle at both courts in Jiangsu province in 2001 and 2002, the two Shandong companies refused to pay and went into bankruptcy. It was not until the enforcement division of the SPC intervened that the ninety-seven households finally received, in May 2004, payment of 5.6 million yuan. In the end, however, the payment was made by the Shandong provincial government.[79]

9.5 REMEDIES

Remedies for tort take a variety of different forms, including 'cessation of infringement, removal of obstruction, elimination of danger, return of property, restoration to the original condition, compensation for loss, offer of apology, elimination of negative effects and rehabilitation of reputation'.[80] Where environmental tort is concerned, courts may offer victims one or more of the remedies including 'cessation of infringement, removal of

[79] SPC, '51 cases'. The case is discussed in Liu Xiang, 'Shilianghe 97 households'. The payment was made by the provincial government because the two companies were bankrupt. However, the government may also have been swayed by the fact that it had failed to enforce environmental laws and regulations against the polluters.

[80] GPCL (1986), art. 134; TL (2009), art. 15; GRCL (2017), art. 179.

obstruction, elimination of danger, restoration to original condition, offer of apology and compensation for loss'.[81]

9.5.1 Injunction

Where a tort injures or endangers another's personal safety or the safety of another's property, the victim may seek the judicial remedies of cessation of infringement, removal of obstruction and elimination of danger.[82] An injunction order from a court halts an ongoing infringement, removes an obstruction that is preventing a victim exercising their rights, and eliminates danger. It is an effective remedy to stop pollution and mitigate and control environmental harm, and is always claimed by victims of ongoing pollution, as in the case of *Lu Yaodong* v. *Yongda Co.* (2004),[83] which concerned light pollution in Shanghai.

Lu Yaodong v. *Yongda Co.* (2004)

Yongda Co., an auto dealer, installed three lamp posts outside its showroom. The lights were on every day between 7 p.m. and 5 a.m. Lu Yaodong was disturbed by the lighting, which he found extremely bright. He could not sleep at night and developed insomnia, anxiety and loss of concentration. Lu sued Yongda for its light pollution, alleging that it violated the Shanghai Provisions on Decorative Lighting. He sought remedies including: (i) cessation of infringement and elimination of harm; (ii) a public apology and (iii) compensation of 1,000 yuan, which he reduced to 1 yuan during the trial. Yongda insisted that the lamp posts, which were located on its own premises, had caused neither light pollution nor actual harm to the plaintiff.

Pudong District Court (2004) found that the defendant's lamps were at the same height as the plaintiff's balcony, which was only 20 m away with no barrier between the two. The dazzling light from 7 p.m. to 5 a.m., which had changed the dark night environment needed for rest and sleep, amounted to light pollution under the Shanghai Provisions, the court found. The plaintiff presented photos as evidence of the light pollution. His claim that he suffered from insomnia and anxiety as a result of the light pollution conformed to empirical evidence on the impact of such pollution. The defendant failed to prove there was no causal link between its light pollution and the plaintiff's insomnia, anxiety and loss of concentration. The court held Yongda liable and ordered it to stop using the lamps at night in order to prevent the light pollution. It rejected Lu's other claims. No compensation was awarded since Lu had not proved he had suffered monetary loss. No offer of public apology was awarded as Lu has not suffered any adverse social impact; his reputation or dignity had not been harmed.

9.5.2 Restoration to the Original Condition

Restoration to the original condition in the context of environmental tort refers to a clean-up of the contaminated site or restoration, where possible, of the destroyed eco-environment, for example, a forest. If restoration at the original site is impossible, a

[81] SPC Interpretation (2015), art. 13. For more, see Stern, 'On the frontlines'. [82] TL (2009), art. 21.
[83] *Supreme People's Court Gazette*, 5 (2005). www.pkulaw.cn

substitute site may be used. In the case of *Zhang Changjian and Others* v. *Rongping Chemical Plant* (2005),[84] the plaintiffs requested the contamination be cleaned up, in addition to requesting the remedies of cessation of infringement and compensation. Fujian High Court ordered the restoration and, further, set a deadline of one year in order to mitigate and control the harm caused by the toxic waste contamination.

The SPC, in the SPC Interpretation (2015), developed the remedy of restoration in order to ensure restoration actually occurs, and occurs in a timely manner. Where a plaintiff seeks the remedy of restoration to the original condition, the court may order the defendant to undertake restoration, while simultaneously determining the cost of restoration that must be paid by the defendant if it defaults on the restoration.[85] If the defendant fails to perform its duty of restoration by the date stipulated in the judgment, the court will order a third party to carry out the restoration and will order the defendant to pay for it.[86]

9.5.3 Compensation for Loss

Both sudden environmental pollution incidents and accumulated long-term pollution discharge can harm the environment and the ecosystem, and this may result in personal injury or the loss of property. Compensation for loss is an important civil remedy provided by the GPCL (1986), TL (2009), GRCL (2017) and the SPC's judicial interpretations. A court will support a claim by a plaintiff for compensation for loss of property, personal injury and reasonable expenses incurred to contain and eliminate pollution.[87] In case of an environmental emergency, where the plaintiff has taken immediate action to contain, mitigate and clean up the contamination caused by the defendant's pollution, the plaintiff will be compensated for relevant expenses incurred, as in the case of *Shanghai Songjiang Yexie Township Government* v. *Jiang Rongxiang and Others* (2012).[88]

Damages for Loss of Property

Compensation for loss of property is calculated based on the market price for that property at the time the harm was caused.[89] The victims in pollution cases bear the burden to prove and quantify their loss caused by pollution in order to seek compensation in court. They often approach local agencies, including environmental bureaus, and agricultural and fishery bureaus, for assistance in recording the pollution and damage. These records or reports by local agencies, together with other monitoring data, are evidence that can be used to establish a prima facie case.[90] Since the calculation of loss and damages is often disputed by plaintiff and defendant, courts often designate judicial appraisal bodies to

[84] SPC Nine Model Cases on Environment and Resources (2014), case no. 6. For a detailed account of the litigation, see Zhang Jingjing, 'The environmental tort case'; see also Stern, 'From dispute to decision'.
[85] SPC Interpretation (2015), art. 14(1). [86] SPC Interpretation (2015), art. 14(2).
[87] SPC Interpretation (2015), art. 15.
[88] SPC Nine Model Cases on Environment and Resources (2014), case no. 3. [89] TL (2009), art. 19.
[90] Before accepting a case, most courts require substantial evidence from the plaintiff as to the harm and the source of harm, and prima facie proof of a causal link. For more discussion, see Moser and Tseming Yang, 'Environmental tort litigation'.

assess and certify damages. Given the complexity of the technical methods and procedures of assessment and appraisal, many judges lack the professional knowledge to synthesize science and legal liability. As a result, courts give great deference to appraisal reports produced by the judicial appraisal bodies.[91] However, appraisal fees can be prohibitively high, often beyond the means of victims of pollution, as in the case of *Wu Guojin* v. *China Railway Fifth Bureau Group and CRFB Road and Bridge Co.* (2015).[92]

Wu Guojin v. *China Railway Fifth Bureau Group and CRFB Road and Bridge Co.* (2015)

Wu Guojin had operated a chicken farm in Guiyang, Guizhou province since 2010. From October 2013 to May 2014, the two defendants had carried out road construction 20 m to 30 m away from Wu's farm. During the construction period, a large number of chickens died and eggs were either soft or abnormally shaped. Three experts invited by Wu to the farm in March 2014 concluded that the chicken deaths had been caused by extreme stress resulting from sudden explosions and prolonged exposure to high levels of construction noise. Wu sued both defendants for compensation of more than 1.5 million yuan.

Qingzhen City Court (2014) found that the defendants' construction noise had caused damage to Wu. The defendants accepted liability to pay compensation, but disagreed with the plaintiff on the amount. The court, however, did not request the plaintiff to provide an appraisal report, which was common practice and would have made the court's work easier, but took an alternative route. It relied on experts to provide data and calculation formulas and, with reference to the livestock breeding handbook, ordered the defendants to pay 355,940 yuan in compensation. Both Wu and the two construction firms appealed, challenging the court's use of data and the calculation method.

Guiyang Intermediate Court (2015) agreed with the first-instance court in the finding of facts and held both tortfeasors liable under articles 65 and 66 of the TL (2009) for Wu's loss caused by the construction noise. Based on expert testimony, the court concluded that Wu's loss not only included his loss of the chickens killed by the construction noise, which was to be calculated by reference to the costs involved in breeding them, but also included his loss of profits from the reduction in the number of eggs produced, given the reduced number of chickens. The two tortfeasors were ordered to pay 458,576 yuan in compensation to Wu.

In this case, the two courts in Guizhou province alleviated the heavy burden on Wu to produce an appraisal report of his losses by accepting all relevant evidence presented by experts and in the livestock breeding handbook to work out the basic data and calculation formula, thereby enabling it to assess the loss suffered by Wu.

In other cases, however, judicial appraisal of damage may be practically impossible if it is required years after the infringement. The case of *Ni Xulong* v. *Dandong Haiyanghong Wind Power Co.* (2013)[93] is such an example. Both first- and second-instance courts had failed to

[91] Appraisals by a certified and court-appointed entity typically serve as the key evidence regarding damages and causation. See Alex L. Wang, 'The role of law in environmental protection in China: recent developments', *Vermont Journal of Environmental Law*, 8 (2007), 195–223.

[92] SPC 10 Model Cases on Environmental Torts (2015), case no. 9.

[93] SPC 10 Model Criminal, Civil and Administrative Cases on Environment and Resources (2017), case no. 5.

reverse the burden of proof from plaintiff to defendant and denied remedies to Ni Xulong because Ni was unable to prove causation. It was years later that Liaoning High Court, at a retrial requested by Ni, correctly applied the rule on burden of proof and held Haiyanghong liable. However, it was unrealistic to appoint a judicial appraisal body to assess Ni's loss of turtles. Liaoning High Court accepted the assessment report that had been produced immediately after the death of the turtles by Guoxin, a company hired by Ni. The report concluded that Ni had suffered economic loss of 1,508,400 yuan for the death of turtles and would incur costs of 129,566 yuan for relocating his business. Ni claimed damages of 1,637,966 yuan. Guoxin staff attended the retrial and answered questions posed by the court and Haiyanghong. Liaoning High Court then set the total damages at 1,310,327 yuan, approximately 80 per cent of Ni's claim, based on the assessment report and taking all relevant factors into consideration.

Damages for Personal Injury or Death

Compensation for personal injury or death includes medical expenses, loss of income, living subsidies if the victim is disabled, funeral expenses if the victim dies and, where necessary, the living expenses of dependents of the deceased and other expenses.[94] Additional items include nursing fees, travel costs and other reasonable expenses incurred for treatment and recovery.[95] Environmental pollution has caused serious harm to human health and well-being, but compensation for illness, injury or death is rarely offered by courts.[96] A plaintiff's claim of compensation for illness or death caused by the defendant's polluting activities has been denied in most cases, with *Zhang Changjian and Others* v. *Rongping Chemical Plant* (2005) just one example.[97] In the lawsuit involving more than 1,700 victims of pollution, their claim of compensation for illness and death was rejected by the courts at both first and second instances. In contrast, victims are more likely to obtain compensation where the harm is an acute injury to health, as in the case of *Liu Lu and 406 Others* v. *A Chemical Factory* (2001), the events of which took place in Hangzhou, the Zhejiang provincial capital.[98]

Liu Lu and 406 Others v. *A Chemical Factory* (2001)

On the morning of 4 April 2001, toxic chemicals leaked from the defendant's illegal operation. The leak seriously affected pupils attending school nearby. Liu Lu and 406 other pupils experienced headaches, dizziness, nausea, stomach aches and coughing. Local government bureaus in charge of environmental protection, public health and education jointly investigated the incident, ordered the chemical factory to suspend its operations and sent the pupils to hospital for check-up and

[94] GPCL (1986), art. 119. [95] TL (2009), art. 16.

[96] One study found that only 13.8 per cent of environmental tort cases from 1991 to 2015 involved health complaints and about half of the claims were accepted by courts, with very small amounts of compensation awarded. See Heng Li, 'Legislation and adjudication of tort liability in environmental pollution: an empirical study based on health-related cases in China', *Hong Kong Law Journal*, 46 (2016), 961–90.

[97] SPC Nine Model Cases on Environment and Resources (2014), case no. 6. For a detailed account of the litigation, see Zhang Jingjing, 'The environmental tort case'.

[98] Details of the case are found in Lü Zhongmei (ed.), *Comments on Environmental Cases* (Beijing: Higher Education Press, 2006), chapter 8, at 163–84.

treatment. By 12 April, experts from both Hangzhou city and Zhejiang provincial centres for disease control had concluded that the illness suffered by the pupils was caused by styrene leaking from the chemical factory on 4 April. The city government decided that the chemical factory should bear the cost of the check-ups, treatment and hospitalization of all 407 pupils. By the time the case came to court, the chemical factory had paid in full the medical costs of more than 130,000 yuan. Liu Lu and 406 others sued to claim damages amounting to 7.66 million yuan as compensation for physical injuries, property loss and emotional distress.

Hangzhou Intermediate Court (2001) accepted the case and found the defendant's styrene leak had caused serious air pollution and injured the health of the 407 plaintiffs. The defendant was found liable under article 124 of the GPCL (1986) and article 41 of the EPL (1989) for the environmental tort. The court noted, however, that the defendant had already fully compensated the plaintiffs' physical injuries and relevant loss of property in accordance with the administrative decision. For the serious interference with the life and schooling of the 407 pupils, the defendant was, significantly, ordered to pay damages for emotional distress at the rate of 500 yuan per person (203,500 yuan in total), in accordance with article 8(2), article 9(3) and article 10(1) of the SPC Interpretation on Several Issues in Determining Emotional Damages in Tort (2001).

In this case, 407 pupils were acutely poisoned by the toxic release of chemicals. The chemical factory not only paid all the medical expenses for diagnosis, treatment and hospitalization, but also compensated the victims for their emotional distress.

Damages for Emotional Distress

While the GPCL (1986) does not specify emotional damages as an item that may be compensated, the TL (2009) provides for 'damages for emotional distress' where infringement has inflicted serious mental distress on the victim of tort.[99] The SPC's judicial interpretation expressly stipulates that where a natural person claims damages for distress caused by infringement of their right to life or right to health, courts must accept the case, provided a prima facie case is established.[100] Damages for emotional distress have been offered to victims of noise pollution, which is a common cause of environmental disputes between neighbours in both rural and urban China. Such compensation is payment for the pain, suffering and emotional distress caused, and is awarded in addition to the remedy of cessation of infringement. The case of *Jiang Jianbo* v. *Jing Jun* (2012)[101] is a typical example.

Jiang Jianbo v. *Jing Jun* (2012)

Jing Jun had leased a house with a courtyard since 2009. He set up a steel-processing operation in the courtyard, which was adjacent to Jiang's house. The extreme noise of the steel cutting seriously disturbed Jiang, who approached the villagers' committee and the local EPB for assistance, but to

[99] TL (2009), art. 22.
[100] SPC Interpretation on Several Issues in Determining Emotional Damages in Tort (2001), art. 1.
[101] SPC Nine Model Cases on Environment and Resources (2014), case no. 7.

no avail. Jiang sued Jing, seeking the remedies of cessation of infringement, removal of obstruction and 8,000 yuan in damages for emotional distress.

Midong District Court ordered Jing to stop the infringement immediately and remove the obstruction by relocating the steel-cutting operation away from the courtyard adjacent to Jiang's home. In addition, Jing was ordered to pay 2,000 yuan for the emotional distress caused. Jing appealed.

Urumqi Intermediate Court (2012) considered the noise level and duration of the steel processing, the proximity between Jing's operation and Jiang's home and the commonly known impact of noise on human health. It accepted Jiang's claim that he had suffered serious mental distress as a result of loss of sleep caused by the noise. Jing had failed to prove that the noise generated by his operation had not harmed Jiang's health. The court upheld the first-instance judgment and dismissed the appeal.

Noise nuisance is the top environmental complaint in urban China. In the case of *Yuan Kewei* v. *Guangzhou Jiafu Property Development Co.* (2015),[102] Yuan was disturbed by noise generated by a lift in a residential building in Guangzhou and sued the property developer.

Yuan Kewei v. *Guangzhou Jiafu Property Development Co.* (2015)

Yuan purchased a flat in a residential building that had been developed by Jiafu Property Development Co. (Jiafu). The flat was adjacent to the lift and the night-time noise level was tested and found to exceed the noise limits for residential and public buildings. Yuan sued Jiafu, seeking the remedies of abatement of noise and compensation for loss and emotional distress.

Yuexiu District Court (2014) found that the lift noise exceeded the relevant state standards for residential and public buildings. It also found that the defendant had failed to prove any circumstances that would exempt it from liability or mitigate its liability. The court held Jiafu liable for the noise pollution caused by the lift and ordered it to take measures to improve the soundproofing and abate the noise level within sixty days. It ordered that failure to do so by the deadline would entitle Yuan to compensation at the rate of 100 yuan per day. It also ordered Jiafu to pay, within three days, 1,500 yuan as compensation for the cost of the noise testing and assessment fee and 10,000 yuan for the emotional distress caused. Jiafu appealed.

Guangzhou Intermediate Court (2015) dismissed the appeal and upheld the first-instance decision.

Calculating damages for emotional distress is never an easy task. Courts determine the level by taking into account the following factors: (i) the degree of fault of the tortfeasor; (ii) the means and circumstances of the infringement, and the acts of infringement themselves; (iii) the consequences of the infringement; (iv) any profits made by the tortfeasor; (v) the financial capacity of the tortfeasor and (vi) the average local living costs.[103] Based on these factors, one should not be surprised by the disparity in the amounts awarded to Jiang and

[102] SPC 10 Model Cases on Environmental Torts (2015), case no. 6.

[103] SPC Interpretation on Several Issues in Determining Emotional Damages in Tort (2001), art. 10.

Yuan: in the case of Jiang, 2,000 yuan for the emotional distress caused by the noise of steel cutting in Xinjiang, and for Yuan, 10,000 yuan for the emotional distress caused by the noise of a lift in Guangzhou. In addition to the degree of fault and the impact on the victim, the tortfeasor's ability to pay and the local living costs also contributed to the five-times difference in the amount of damages for emotional distress in the two cases.

Denial of compensation for physical injury, illness and death caused by chronic pollution has left most victims of pollution without judicial remedies. The problems of cancer villages and lead poisoning have been settled by local governments with payment made from public finances.[104] Courts seldom offer the full amount of the compensation claimed by plaintiffs. Judges find a variety of reasons to lower the compensation, considering factors including a defendant's ability to pay, a plaintiff's failure to mitigate and a plaintiff's assumption of risk by approaching the pollution. It is a pragmatic approach adopted by the courts to achieve compromise between the parties in dispute, so that defendants are more willing to pay.

9.6 JUDICIAL MEDIATION

Most environmental disputes are settled by administrative mediation facilitated by the local environmental bureaus. Litigation remains a last resort for most victims of pollution.[105] Even at the litigation stage, it is still possible for the disputing parties to settle by judicial mediation. Chinese courts always attempt mediation prior to adjudication to settle civil disputes. Empirical evidence shows that defendants are more willing to perform duties agreed at mediation than those imposed by court judgment. The mediation rate in Chinese courts ranges from 30 per cent at the beginning of the twenty-first century to more than 60 per cent a decade later.[106] The court-prepared mediation report has the same legally binding force of a judgment.[107] In the case of *Zhu Zhengmao and All-China Environment Federation* v. *Jiangsu Jiangyin Harbour Container Co.* (2009),[108] Wuxi Intermediate Court actively encouraged the parties to settle disputes and reach agreement on remedies in a timely manner via mediation, which it also facilitated. The agreed remedies included cessation of infringement, elimination of danger and restoration to the original condition. One highlight of the mediation report is that the defendant was required to make post-mediation reporting to the court of its performance, as evidenced by monitoring reports from the local environmental bureau.

[104] See Heng Li, 'Legislation and adjudication', at 984.

[105] Victims of pollution often cannot afford the expensive and time-consuming litigation, do not have the ability or experience to collect evidence in a timely manner, and cannot afford the professional services of lawyers and appraisal institutions. For more on mediation of environmental disputes, see Yuhong Zhao, 'Environmental dispute resolution'; and Yuhong Zhao, 'Mediation of'.

[106] Yedan Li et al., 'Understanding China's court mediation surge: insights from a local court', *Law & Social Inquiry*, 43:1 (2018), 58–81. According to the authors' field study, trial judges are required to reach a mediation rate of 40 per cent to 45 per cent of the cases they handle.

[107] CPL (2017), art. 234. Before the CPL (2017), the applicable articles were: CPL (2012), art. 234; CPL (2007), art. 211; CPL (1991), art. 215. A mediation report prepared by the court is to be enforced in the same manner as the judgment or decision of the court.

[108] SPC Nine Model Cases on Environment and Resources (2014), case no. 5.

The case of *Li Caineng* v. *Hainan Haishi Co.* (2014)[109] is another good example of the timely settlement of a dispute by judicial mediation in Haikou, the capital of Hainan province, resulting in lower costs for the plaintiff.

Li Caineng v. *Hainan Haishi Co.* (2014)

In 2010, Hainan Haishi Co. (Haishi) leased a piece of land adjacent to Li Caineng's goat pen and built a brick factory without the required approvals. The factory emitted cement soot, boiler steam, smoke and noise, causing serious damage to Li's health and property. The damage to his property included miscarriages suffered by pregnant goats, loss of tree leaves and grass for grazing, and contamination of his well. Li sued Haishi for 53,000 yuan in compensation.

Qiongshan District Court (2014) accepted the case and sent the presiding judge to collect evidence at the defendant's premises. The court also requested the local EPB and the Land Bureau to provide relevant records, which proved that Haishi had not conducted an EIA before constructing the plant and bringing it into operation, and that using the land for making bricks was illegal and had caused pollution. The court facilitated mediation and explained the laws and regulations to both parties, who then reached the settlement agreement voluntarily. Haishi agreed to pay 53,000 yuan to Li as compensation and made the payment upon signing the court-prepared mediation report.

Mediation can provide timely settlement of disputes, alleviating the undue pressure and stress on the plaintiff of a costly appraisal and time-consuming litigation. It is dependent on the active engagement of the court and its professional skills in bringing disputing parties to an agreement. *Li Caineng* v. *Hainan Haishi Co.* (2014) was an exceptional case in that the plaintiff was compensated for the full amount he had claimed. The court also issued advice to the local EPB on follow-up monitoring and supervision of the defendant's pollution-control measures.

The law of environmental tort offers remedies to victims of pollution, whose access to judicial redress and full compensation continues to be impeded by both legal and non-legal factors.[110] They must overcome tremendous difficulties involved in timely collection of evidence of pollution and in professional assessment and appraisal of losses caused by the pollution. Even if a victim overcomes all the legal hurdles and wins a court case, full compensation for loss of property, not to mention compensation for injury to life and health, is unlikely. Timely collection of evidence of pollution very much depends on how local agencies respond to a victim's request for assistance, and is crucial as courts treat government records or reports of a pollution incident as authoritative and comprehensive proof of a prima facie case of pollution, loss and relevance between a defendant's polluting act and a plaintiff's loss. Where local agencies refuse to assist or delay in assisting, a victim of pollution has to pay an appraisal body, which not only costs the victim money (agencies

[109] SPC 10 Model Cases on Environmental Torts (2015), case no. 10.

[110] For more case studies, see Fan Yang et al., 'Adjudicating environmental tort'; Heng Li, 'Legislation and adjudication'; van Rooij, 'The people vs. pollution'.

do not charge for their assistance), but also runs the risk of being discredited by the court. A victim's recourse to justice can also be impeded by local protectionism. In pursuit of GDP growth, local governments offer special privileges to major enterprises that contribute significantly to local revenues and job creation. Agencies and courts are under the control of local governments both financially and administratively. The case of *Zhang Changjian and Others* v. *Rongping Chemical Plant* (2005) highlighted the strong influence and protection enjoyed by Rongping. The low level of compensation (249,763 yuan) ordered by the first-instance court was more than doubled (to 684,178 yuan) by Fujian High Court, which is not directly linked to the economic interests of the region. It is hoped that recent reforms to environmental law, which now holds local governments accountable for local environmental quality, and the national priority on environmental protection and the construction of an ecological civilization will eliminate the once-pervasive influence of local protectionism over pollution. This would give victims of pollution improved access to the judicial remedies offered by environmental tort law.

10

Judicial Review

Chinese environmental law is dominated by the command-and-control approach. Regulatory agencies, including environmental bureaus, as well as departments of natural resources, urban and rural construction, public health and border control play crucial functions in the prevention and control of pollution. They set standards, monitor performance and impose sanctions to punish and deter violations that harm the environment. Their acts or omissions directly determine the effectiveness of implementation and enforcement of environmental law and, consequently, also determine environmental quality and the sustainability of long-term development. Through judicial review, courts can ensure agencies perform their statutory duties in compliance with law. Effective judicial review improves the quality of agency decisions and promotes good governance in pollution prevention and control, ecological conservation and rational use of natural resources for long-term sustainable development.

Judicial review is commonly known as administrative litigation in China, and has a much shorter history than civil and criminal law. The Administrative Litigation Law (ALL) (1989)[1] was not enacted until a decade after the first initiatives to rebuild China's legal system in the post-Mao period.[2] The ALL (1989) was hailed as groundbreaking, because it recognized that private parties had the right to sue the government, challenging administrative decisions that adversely affected their rights or interests.[3] It expressly gives courts the power to uphold, revoke and revise agency decisions, and to compel an agency to act if it has failed to do so.[4] While the ALL (1989) laid down the legal foundation for protection against unlawful agency acts or omissions, and the emergence of non-governmental organizations (NGOs) since the mid-1990s has made it possible for individuals to obtain free or low-cost

[1] The ALL was adopted on 4 April 1989 by the 7th National People's Congress (NPC) at its 2nd session. It came into force on 1 October 1990. The ALL was amended by the 12th NPC Standing Committee (NPCSC) at its 11th session in 2014 and its 28th session in 2017.

[2] Pitman Potter (ed.), *Domestic Law Reforms in Post-Mao China* (Armonk, NY and London: M.E. Sharpe, 1994); Stanley Lubman, *China's Legal Reforms* (Oxford University Press, 1996).

[3] Susan Finder, 'Like throwing an egg against a stone? Administrative litigation in the People's Republic of China', *Journal of Chinese Law*, 3 (1989), 1–28.

[4] ALL (1989), art. 54.

professional legal assistance,[5] private parties still face tremendous obstacles in gaining access to the courts. There is a huge gap between the expected outcomes of the ALL (1989) and reality.[6] The law was amended in 2014 and 2017 to relax the statutory requirement on standing and expand the scope of judicial review. The Supreme People's Court (SPC) issued ten important administrative cases on environmental protection in 2014 and again in 2016 to guide adjudication work in environmental administrative litigation.[7] This chapter is divided into four sections. Section 10.1 examines the issue of standing and statutory developments that have liberalized the formerly restrictive rules. Section 10.2 focuses on the scope of judicial review; that is, which agency acts or omissions are subject to judicial scrutiny. Section 10.3 discusses the remedies the courts may grant in administrative litigation cases. Section 10.4 reviews the challenges in the implementation of administrative litigation in China and measures taken to counter local protectionism.

10.1 STANDING

An applicant seeking judicial review of agency acts or omissions must first overcome the legal hurdle of standing. This was a major obstacle in environmental administrative cases prior to the 2014 amendment to the ALL.

The ALL (1989) provided that 'where any citizen, legal person or other organization considers that a concrete act of an administrative organ or its personnel has infringed their lawful rights or interests, they shall have a right to sue in court'.[8] It further stipulated that 'plaintiffs in administrative litigation shall be citizens, legal persons or other organizations who consider their lawful rights and interests are infringed by the concrete administrative acts'.[9] 'Consider' is a vague and flexible term that is difficult to apply in judicial practice. Consequently, the SPC addressed the issue of standing in its Interpretation on the Application of the Administrative Litigation Law (SPC Interpretation on the ALL) (2000)[10] by stating that a plaintiff should have a 'legal interest' in the concrete administrative act.[11] In practice, most courts took a very narrow approach to standing by accepting cases filed by applicants directly subject to the administrative decisions and able to demonstrate that the agency had infringed their rights and interests.

[5] For example, the Center for Legal Assistance to Pollution Victims (CLAPV) set up by Professor Wang Canfa at the China University of Political Science and Law (CUPL) offers legal assistance to victims of pollution in bringing their case to court. See Yuhong Zhao, 'Environmental NGOs and sustainable development'.

[6] He Haibo, 'Litigations without a ruling: the predicament of administrative law in China', *Tsinghua China Law Review*, 3 (2011), 257–81; Minxin Pei, 'Citizens v. mandarins: administrative litigation in China', *The China Quarterly*, 152 (1997), 832–62; Xixin Wang, 'Administrative procedure reforms in China's rule of law context', *Columbia Journal of Asian Law*, 12 (1998), 251–77; Xixin Wang, 'Between dreams and the reality: making of the Administrative Procedure Act in China', *Journal of Korean Law*, 7 (2007), 157–82; Kevin J. O'Brien and Lianjiang Li, 'Suing the local state: administrative litigation in rural China', *The China Journal*, 51 (2004), 75–96.

[7] SPC 10 Important Administrative Cases on Environmental Protection (2014); SPC 10 Important Administrative Cases on Environmental Protection (second batch) (2016).

[8] ALL (1989), art. 2. [9] ALL (1989), art. 41(1).

[10] The SPC Interpretation on the ALL (2000) was issued on 8 March 2000, and came into force on 10 March 2000. Following amendments in 2014 and 2017, the SPC Interpretation on the ALL was reissued in 2015 and 2018.

[11] SPC Interpretation on the ALL (2000), art. 12.

The first administrative litigation concerning a breach of the Environmental Impact Assessment Law (EIAL) (2002)[12] was filed by two villagers with legal assistance from the CLAPV. Their application for judicial review of an environmental impact assessment (EIA) approval decision issued by Dingzhou Environmental Protection Bureau (EPB) was rejected by both Dingzhou City Court and Baoding Intermediate Court in Hebei province in 2005 for lack of standing.[13] Dingzhou EPB had approved the EIA statement of a heavily polluting project that would dispose of 500 t of waste – waste photographic paper and sludge from a wastewater treatment plant – by open burning to recover 2 t of silver annually. The two applicants lived 150 m away from the project, which emitted excessive toxic and hazardous air pollutants without any pollution-control measures. They sued Dingzhou EPB, trying to have the EIA approval revoked, but were dismissed by both courts for lack of standing. The courts held that they were not parties 'subject to' the agency's decision and had not suffered any injury directly caused by the agency's administrative acts. Having failed to obtain judicial redress, the CLAPV filed complaints to the State Environmental Protection Administration (SEPA), which concluded in a circular that the proponent of the hazardous waste (HW) disposal project should, according to the Inventory on Classified Management of Environmental Protection of Construction Projects,[14] have prepared an EIA report based on a comprehensive technical assessment of the project, instead of a brief EIA statement.[15] It sanctioned the liable EIA institution by suspending its licence to practise for six months from 1 December 2005 to 31 May 2006.[16] However, neither the courts nor the SEPA clarified the legal liability of Dingzhou EPB for approving the EIA statement in violation of the EIAL (2002). The case of Dingzhou EPB was typical of mainstream court practice in China for years. Others who tried to seek judicial review of EIA approval decisions were, before the 2014 reforms of the ALL, mostly rejected by the courts.[17]

The narrow approach to standing created obstacles for the public and for victims wishing to use administrative litigation to monitor and rectify agency decisions. Nevertheless, there were exceptional cases in which parties affected by, but not directly subject to, an agency's decision successfully launched legal battles to revoke the unlawful administrative decisions. The case of *Shen Xixian and 181 Others* v. *Beijing Urban Planning Commission* (2003)[18] is an early example.

[12] The EIAL (2002) was enacted on 28 October 2002 by the 9th NPCSC at its 30th session. It came into force on 1 September 2003. The EIAL was amended on 2 July 2016 by the 12th NPCSC at its 21st session, and was amended again in 2018.

[13] Judgment of Hebei Baoding Intermediate Court (21 November 2005) (on file with author); see also Qie Jianrong, 'Law compliance more costly than violation: five major problems in implementing the EIA Law', *Legal Daily*, 19 September 2005.

[14] The classified management is provided for in the EIAL (2002), art. 16.

[15] SEPA Office, Circular on the EIA Work Conducted by the China Metallurgy Geologic Examination Engineering Administration's Geophysics Survey Institute (Huanban no. 135, 9 December 2005).

[16] SEPA Office, Circular on the EIA Work Conducted by the China Metallurgy Geologic Examination Engineering Administration's Geophysics Survey Institute (Huanban no. 135, 9 December 2005).

[17] Jin Wang, 'Environmental public interest litigation: when will it flourish in China?', *Journal of Korean Law*, 7 (2007), 217–28.

[18] *Supreme People's Court Gazette*, 3 (2004).

Shen Xixian and 181 Others v. *Beijing Urban Planning Commission* (2003)

Shen Xixian and 181 residents each represented a household living in residential buildings numbers four and six, located close to a proposed animal laboratory. They sued Beijing Urban Planning Commission, seeking judicial review and revocation of the Commission's approval of the construction of the laboratory, in order to eliminate potential harm to human health. On 10 December 2001, the defendant had issued a planning permit for the project to the two proponents, the Food Safety Institute and the Health and Safety Institute, allowing them to build the laboratory only 19.06 m away from building number six.

Xicheng District Court (2003) held that article 13 of the EPL (1989) required construction projects to prepare EIA documents. A planning authority was not permitted to approve the construction of a project before the EPB had approved the EIA documents, it said. On 10 December 2001, the defendant approved the construction of the animal lab and issued the planning permit, long before the EPB approved the EIA on 21 February 2002, it noted. In addition, the Provisions on Management of Animal Testing issued by the Ministry of Health requires a minimum 20-m-wide isolation zone around a laboratory to protect the public. The distance between the proposed laboratory and residential building number six was only 19.06 m. The defendant's issuance of the construction permit violated the law and was therefore revoked. Beijing Urban Planning Commission appealed.

Beijing No.1 Intermediate Court (2003) accepted the case, but received an application from the appellant to withdraw its appeal soon after the first hearing. The court approved the withdrawal application.

In this case, the Beijing courts took a wider view of the rules, accepting that the plaintiffs had standing. Even though they were not directly subject to the agency decision to approve the project, they were allowed to sue because their rights and interests in health and safety had been infringed.

The different approaches to standing have resulted in uncertainty as to whether an applicant for judicial review may have their case heard. Without express statutory provisions on the right of public access to judicial review, many whose rights have been adversely affected by agency decisions are left without redress. Professor Wang Canfa proposed that an enforceable right of access to judicial review be written into the EIAL (2002) as a check on administrative acts and omission,[19] but this was not accepted. Others echoed his proposal to relax the restrictions on standing.[20] Turning Chinese courts into an effective check on agency behaviour has been an arduous, but not impossible, task.

The implementation of the EIAL (2002) and the promotion of public participation in the EIA process motivated more people potentially affected by EIA approval decisions to challenge them in court.[21] Consequently, an urgent need arose to reform the restrictive

[19] Wang Canfa, 'Discussion on several issues'; see also Qie Jianrong, 'EIA law still young: does it need big surgery?', *Legal Daily*, 5 September 2006. Professor Wang Canfa, a leading environmental law scholar, is best known for the CLAPV, the legal assistance organization he established at the CUPL.

[20] Jin Wang, 'Environmental public interest litigation', at 226–7.

[21] For more on EIA litigation, see Jin Zining, 'Environmental Impact Assessment Law in China's courts: a study of 107 judicial decisions', *Environmental Impact Assessment Review*, 55 (2015), 35–44.

rules on standing. The reform would enhance judicial review of environmental agency decisions by allowing those potentially affected to play a more effective role in monitoring and supervising agency decisions on development projects. Article 41(1) of the ALL (1989) was amended in 2014 to address the issue of standing.[22] It was reworded to 'the plaintiff shall be a citizen, a legal person or any other organization as provided for under article 25 of this Law'.[23] Article 25(1) provides that 'any party ***subject to*** [emphasis added] the administrative act, or any citizen, legal person or other organization ***with an interest in*** [emphasis added] the administrative act shall have the right to initiate the administrative litigation'.[24] This clarifies and expands the standing to citizen, legal person or other organization not 'subject to' but 'with an interest' in the administrative act.[25] Such persons may also be adversely affected by an agency decision.

The liberal approach to standing had gained momentum prior to the 2014 reform. Of the twenty important environmental administrative cases promulgated by the SPC in 2014 and 2016, five involved judicial review of EIA decisions and all were brought by parties potentially affected by the agency decisions, rather than directly subject to the agency decisions. The cases are: *Lu Hong and others* v. *Xiaoshan Environmental Protection Bureau* (2013),[26] *Xia Chunguan and others* v. *Dongtai Environmental Protection Bureau* (2014),[27] *Zhengwen Garden Homeowners' Committee and Another* v. *Shanghai Environmental Protection Bureau* (2013),[28] *Zhang Xiaoyan and Others* v. *Jiangsu Environmental Protection Bureau* (2015),[29] and *Zhou Kun and Zhang Wenbo* v. *Ministry of Environmental Protection* (2014).[30] In fact, EIA approval decisions have become one of the major types of administrative acts to be subjected to judicial review. The plaintiffs in these cases were either residents potentially adversely affected by the agency decisions or organizations, such as homeowners' committees, representing residents in the protection of their rights and interests. All plaintiffs proved the existence of sufficient interest in the administrative act to the satisfaction of the courts and were able to challenge the agency decisions.

Lu Hong and Others v. *Xiaoshan Environmental Protection Bureau* (2013)

Lu Hong and others, a total of 204 residents potentially affected by a road alteration and extension project, sued Xiaoshan EPB for violating legal procedure and sought to revoke the EIA approval of the project. On 20 April 2012, a joint assessment meeting was held by Xiaoshan EPB, the project proponent, the EIA firm and experts. The EPB placed a notice at its service centre from 23 April to 7 May 2012, inviting comments by phone or by post. On 29 May 2012, a further assessment

[22] Article 41(1) of the ALL (1989) provided only a vague definition of standing. It stated that 'the plaintiff shall be a citizen, a legal person or any other organization whose lawful rights or interests have been infringed upon by a concrete administrative act'.

[23] ALL (2014), art. 49. [24] ALL (2017), art. 25(1). [25] ALL (2014), art. 25(1).

[26] SPC 10 Important Administrative Cases on Environmental Protection (2014), case no. 4.

[27] SPC 10 Important Administrative Cases on Environmental Protection (2014), case no. 9.

[28] SPC 10 Important Administrative Cases on Environmental Protection (2014), case no. 10.

[29] SPC 10 Important Administrative Cases on Environmental Protection (second batch) (2016), case no. 4.

[30] SPC 10 Important Administrative Cases on Environmental Protection (second batch) (2016), case no. 8.

meeting was held by the EPB, the project proponent, the EIA firm and experts. On 28 June 2012, the project proponent submitted the EIA report to the EPB, which approved it on the same day.

Xiaoshan District Court (2013) held that Xiaoshan EPB's approval decision was made in violation of a procedural requirement. Under article 22 of Zhejiang Provincial Measures on Environmental Protection Management of Construction Projects, the EPB must, on receiving an EIA report for approval, inform the public in an easily accessible manner and invite comments for a minimum of seven days. The defendant EPB's public notice from 23 April to 7 May did not satisfy this requirement as the EIA report had not been submitted at that point. Xiaoshan EPB's approval of the EIA was revoked.

In *Lu Hong and Others* v. *Xiaoshan Environmental Protection Bureau* (2013), the local EPB violated the procedural requirement of public participation by approving the EIA report on the same day it was submitted. In order to speed up the construction process, many local governments, and even EPBs, chose to skip legally required procedures. The expedited process often results in harm to the environment and infringement of the rights and interests of potential victims of pollution. Through administrative litigation, the affected individuals in this case obtained judicial remedies from Xiaoshan District Court, which revoked the agency decision. The court played a crucial role where the agency decision did not fully comply with a legal requirement on public participation, ensuring that Lu Hong and 203 other residents would in the future have access to project information and that their right of participation in the decision-making process would be respected.

In *Zhengwen Garden Homeowners' Committee and Another* v. *Shanghai Environmental Protection Bureau* (2013),[31] the committee sued the EPB on behalf of a group of homeowners. It requested revocation of the EIA approval of a proposed power transmission and distribution project.

Zhengwen Garden Homeowners' Committee and Another v. *Shanghai Environmental Protection Bureau* (2013)

Zhengwen Garden Homeowners' Committee and another sued Shanghai EPB, requesting the court to revoke the EPB's approval of the EIA report of a 500 kV Hongyang power transmission and distribution project. The project proponent was Shanghai Power Co., owned by the State Grid. The plaintiffs claimed that a high-voltage electricity substation should not be constructed near residential premises. Shanghai EPB had failed to consider the impact of the project on the health of residents nearby and its approval decision was unlawful. They applied to the Ministry of Environmental Protection (MEP) for administrative reconsideration, which upheld Shanghai EPB's approval decision.

Upon receiving the EIA report for the proposed Hongyang project on 25 June 2012, Shanghai EPB published the information online. On the same day, it hired Shanghai Academy of Environmental Sciences to conduct a technical review of the EIA report. The technical review report,

[31] SPC 10 Important Administrative Cases on Environmental Protection (2014), case no. 10.

produced on 5 July, concluded that the EIA report had been conducted in compliance with technical guidelines and standards and that the EIA report's conclusion was reliable in general. Shanghai EPB hosted an expert consultation meeting on 17 July. The experts confirmed that the EPB's response to public concerns complied with relevant provisions, and that the project would meet relevant environmental standards and would not have significant adverse impact on the residents nearby. On 6 August, Shanghai EPB published online its proposed approval of the EIA report, which was later found by the court to have met all legal and technical requirements. On 22 October, the EPB granted the formal approval. The plaintiffs claimed that the EPB had replaced the public hearings or forums with the expert consultation meeting. They also said that the project proponent had failed to meet all public participation requirements during the EIA process.

Huangpu District Court (2013) found that Shanghai EPB had complied with relevant procedural requirements on information disclosure and public participation. The court said that, in accordance with the Provisional Measures on Public Participation in Environmental Impact Assessment, consulting experts during the approval process counted as public participation. As to public participation in the preparation of the EIA report, there was evidence that a questionnaire survey had been conducted, and the EIA report documented reasons for adopting or rejecting public comments. It held that both the preparation and approval of the EIA report complied with relevant laws and regulations. The court dismissed the plaintiffs' claim and upheld the agency decision. The plaintiffs appealed.

Shanghai No.2 Intermediate Court (2013) dismissed the appeal and upheld the decision of the lower court.

While judicial review of agency decisions ensures redress where decisions are not made in compliance with the law, courts usually focus on the procedure of the decision-making rather than on substantive environmental issues. As long as the EIA firm preparing the EIA documents and the decision-making of the approval agency comply with the relevant legal requirements, including public participation, courts do not second-guess agency decisions on technical issues. Courts view agencies as the appropriate arbiter of technical issues.

10.2 SCOPE OF JUDICIAL REVIEW

In administrative litigation, courts are required to review the legality of agency acts.[32] Judicial review aims to ensure that agencies not only perform their statutory duties as required by law in a timely manner, but also make decisions in full compliance with the law. Effective judicial review promotes good governance by checking and reshaping agency behaviour. The ALL (2017) lists the administrative acts or omissions that are subject to judicial review:[33]

(i) administrative penalty decisions, including administrative detention, suspension or revocation of permit or licence, order to suspend production or business, confiscation of illegal gains, confiscation of unlawful property, fines and warning;

[32] ALL (2017), art. 6. [33] ALL (2017), art. 12.

(ii) administrative compulsory measures, such as restriction of freedom of the person, and seal-up and seizure of property or freezing of assets;
(iii) agency decisions relating to applications for permits, and agency failure to make a permit decision within the time limit;
(iv) agency decisions on the ownership of or right to use natural resources, including land, minerals, water, forests, mountains, grassland, uncultivated land, tidal flats and sea areas;
(v) agency decisions on government acquisition or use of property or relevant compensation;
(vi) agency refusal to perform its statutory duty to protect the personal or property rights of a person, or agency failure to respond to a request for such rights to be protected;
......
(xii) other agency acts that infringe upon the legal rights and interests of a person.

Courts are not permitted to review four categories of agency acts: (i) acts of national defence or foreign affairs; (ii) administrative regulations and rules, or agency decisions or orders with general binding power; (iii) agency decisions on rewards and penalties for employees, and appointment or removal of employees and (iv) agency acts that are final as provided by law.[34]

As illustrated by Tables 10.1 and 10.2, administrative cases on environment and resources have concentrated on three major types of agency act or omission: (i) administrative penalty decisions; (ii) agency failure to perform statutory duties and (iii) agency EIA approval decisions.

10.2.1 Administrative Penalty Decisions

In China, administrative agencies have wide-ranging power to impose sanctions on parties in violation of law. The exercise of such power is regulated by the Administrative Penalty Law (APL) in general,[35] while administrative penalties for specific environmental violations are stipulated by environmental statutes. The APL (2017) regulates the creation and implementation of administrative penalties.[36] Administrative penalty decisions made without legal basis or in violation of legal procedure are void.[37] Any citizen, legal person or other organization subject to an administrative penalty decision has the right to seek judicial review of the decision.[38] There are six main types of administrative penalty: (i) warning; (ii) fine; (iii) confiscation of illegal gains, confiscation of unlawful property; (iv) order to suspend production or business; (v) suspension or revocation of permits or licence and (vi) administrative detention.[39] The environmental bureaus and relevant agencies have the power to impose the administrative penalties listed above, except for administrative detention, which may only be imposed by public security bureaus (PSBs).[40] Agency use of the

[34] ALL (2017), art. 13.
[35] The APL was first enacted on 17 March 1996 by the 8th NPC at its 4th session. It came into force on 1 October 1996, and was amended in 2009 and 2017.
[36] APL (2017), art. 2. [37] APL (2017), art. 3(2). [38] APL (2017), art. 6(1). [39] APL (2017), art. 8.
[40] Article 16 of the APL (2017) provides that only PSBs may impose an administrative penalty that restricts personal freedom.

TABLE 10.1 TEN IMPORTANT ADMINISTRATIVE CASES ON ENVIRONMENTAL PROTECTION (2014)

	Plaintiff	Defendant	Agency act subject to judicial review
1	Foshan Scien Co.	Shunde District EPB	Administrative penalty decision
2	Dynamic Bar	Liangzhou District EPB	Order to rectify
3	Haili Golf Co.	State Oceanic Administration	Administrative penalty decision
4	Lu Hong and Others	Xiaoshan District EPB	EIA approval decision
5	Junning Factory	Jin'an District EPB	Administrative penalty decision
6	Su Yaohua	Boluo County Government	Decision to designate areas in which livestock farming is prohibited
7	Hongsheng Co.	Jinjiang City EPB	Administrative penalty decision
8	Montaplast Co.	Suzhou Industrial Park EPB	Administrative penalty decision
9	Xia Chunguan and Others	Dongtai EPB	EIA approval decision
10	Zhengwen Garden Homeowners' Committee and Another	Shanghai EPB	EIA approval decision

Sources: SPC, Ten Important Administrative Cases on Environmental Protection (2014).

TABLE 10.2 TEN FURTHER IMPORTANT ADMINISTRATIVE CASES ON ENVIRONMENTAL PROTECTION (2ND BATCH) (2016)

	Plaintiff	Defendant	Agency act subject to judicial review
1	Wu Yi	Jiangsu EPB	Failure to perform statutory duty
2	Putie Steel Co.	Qingdao City EPB	Administrative penalty decision
3	A'ke Disi Co.	Weihai City EPB	Administrative penalty decision
4	Zhang Xiaoyan and Others	Jiangsu EPB	EIA approval decision
5	Bishan Pig Farm	Linxiang City EPB	Administrative penalty decision
6	Jinhai Household Co.	Fengxian District City Management Bureau	Administrative penalty decision
7	Qinhui Cement Co.	Fengxian District Government	Decision to permanently close
8	Zhou Kun and Zhang Wenbo	MEP	EIA approval decision
9	Liu Desheng	Jiaozhou City EPB	Administrative penalty decision
10	Jinping County Procuratorate	Jinping County EPB	Failure to perform statutory duty

Sources: SPC, Ten Important Administrative Cases on Environmental Protection (second batch) (2016)

power to impose administrative penalties is, however, subject to the legal controls of the APL (2017) and environmental statutes.

Seeking judicial review of administrative penalty decisions imposed by local EPBs is common in China. Half of the twenty important environmental administrative cases issued by the SPC in 2014 and 2016 belong to this category.[41] Two model environmental administrative cases issued by the SPC in 2017 involved the review of administrative penalties.[42] Judicial review of administrative penalties imposed by agencies has focused on the legality of the decision and whether it complied with procedural requirements. The case of *Sound Water Co.* v. *Hainan Danzhou Environmental Protection Bureau* (2016)[43] in Hainan province is an example of this.

***Sound Water Co.* v. *Hainan Danzhou Environmental Protection Bureau* (2016)**

Hainan Danzhou EPB imposed an administrative penalty on Sound Water Co. based on a monitoring report produced by Hainan Environmental Monitoring Centre. The report showed that Sound Water Co. had discharged wastewater in violation of law. The EPB issued a fine of 177,719 yuan. Sound Water Co. sued, requesting the administrative penalty be revoked.

Danzhou City Court (2015) found that Danzhou EPB had failed to provide evidence that samples had been taken in compliance with legal and technical procedural requirements. This cast doubt on the accuracy and reliability of the monitoring report and on its use as a basis for imposing sanctions. The fine was revoked. Danzhou EPB appealed.

Hainan No.2 Intermediate Court (2016) agreed with the decision of the first-instance court that there was no proof that the monitoring report was based on samples collected legitimately, and that it should not have been used by Danzhou EPB as key evidence on which to make its administrative penalty decision. The EPB had not investigated further, nor had it produced other evidence to support its decision. Danzhou EPB's appeal was dismissed.

The court's revocation of the administrative penalty, a fine in this case, emphasizes the importance of ensuring there is a sound legal basis for administrative penalty decisions, and that environmental enforcement is carried out in a lawful manner and is based on solid and legally obtained evidence. Violation of procedures for collecting samples affects the accuracy and integrity of data. Such data must not form the basis of an agency's administrative penalty decision.

Where a court upholds an agency's administrative penalty decision, it interprets and clarifies the relevant statutory provisions, as in *Chen Delong* v. *Chenghua Environmental Protection Bureau* (2014),[44] the events of which took place in Chengdu, the provincial capital of Sichuan.

[41] See SPC 10 Important Administrative Cases on Environmental Protection (2014), and SPC 10 Important Administrative Cases on Environmental Protection (second batch) (2016).

[42] The SPC issued 10 Model Criminal, Civil and Administrative Cases on Environment and Resources on 22 June 2017.

[43] SPC 10 Model Criminal, Civil and Administrative Cases on Environment and Resources (2017), case no. 9.

[44] SPC 10 Model Criminal, Civil and Administrative Cases on Environment and Resources (2017), case no. 10.

***Chen Delong* v. *Chenghua Environmental Protection Bureau* (2014)**

Chen Delong was the sole owner of Delong Processing Factory and had processed glass since March 2011. An on-site inspection by Chenghua District EPB in November 2012 found hidden pipes used for the secret discharge of wastewater from the factory. In December 2012, the EPB issued its decision, stating that Chen was in violation of article 22(2) of the WPPCL (2008), which prohibits hidden pipes being used to evade environmental monitoring. Under article 75(2) of the WPPCL (2008), the EPB ordered the hidden pipes to be immediately dismantled and imposed a fine of 100,000 yuan. Chen sued Chenghua EPB, requesting the administrative penalty decision be revoked.

Chenghua District Court (2014) accepted the case. Chen presented a monitoring report dated May 2012 and conducted by Chenghua District Environmental Monitoring Station. The report stated that the wastewater discharged by Delong Processing Factory complied with relevant discharge standards. The court, however, held that article 22(2) prohibits secret discharge by hidden pipes that enable the user to evade environmental monitoring and supervision. Whether the effluent discharged is in compliance with the discharge standards is irrelevant, it said. It upheld the administrative penalty decision made by Chenghua EPB and dismissed Chen's claim. Chen appealed.

Chengdu No.2 Intermediate Court (2014) agreed with the first-instance court and stressed that Chen had been sanctioned for secret discharge by hidden pipes in violation of article 22 of the WPPCL (2008). Whether the discharge complies with state limits is irrelevant, it said. It added that the EPB is permitted to exercise its discretion in determining the amount of the fine (depending on the circumstances of the violation) within a range of 20,000 yuan to 100,000 yuan, as specified by article 75 of the WPPCL (2008). The appeal was dismissed and the decision of the lower court upheld.

By reviewing the administrative penalty decision of the local EPB, the court confirmed that secret discharge by hidden pipes to evade environmental monitoring and supervision is in itself a serious violation and is subject to administrative sanctions, regardless of the consequences (actual or potential environmental harm) or whether the discharge complied with standards.

10.2.2 Failure to Perform Statutory Duty

In many cases, environmental harm is aggravated by agency inaction. Agency failure to detect and sanction environmental violations has encouraged repeated and continuing violation by polluters, who maximize their financial gains by externalizing the cost of pollution onto victims and the society. Administrative litigation offers a tool with which to supervise agencies and ensure they perform their statutory duties. In *Wu Yi* v. *Jiangsu Environmental Protection Bureau* (2015),[45] an agency's failure to regulate and control noise pollution resulted in adverse impact on residents, including the person applying for judicial review.

[45] SPC 10 Important Administrative Cases on Environmental Protection (second batch) (2016), case no. 1.

Wu Yi v. *Jiangsu Environmental Protection Bureau* (2015)

Wu Yi used Jiangsu province's online platform for reporting environmental violations to complain about noise from the Yanjiang Highway, which was located only 18 m from his home. The environmental noise was 70 dB during the day and more than 60 dB at night, causing serious adverse impact to his health. Wu asked Jiangsu EPB to perform its statutory duty to control and prevent the noise nuisance. Jiangsu EPB passed Wu's complaint to Wuxi EPB, which passed it to Jiangyin EPB. Jiangyin EPB told Wu that his complaint on noise nuisance had already been handled by the Jiangyin court and that his complaint to the EPB would not be accepted. Wu disagreed and sued Jiangsu EPB for failing to perform its statutory duty to prevent and control noise nuisance.

Nanjing Intermediate Court (2015) found that the section of the Yanjiang Highway in question had been inspected and approved by Jiangsu EPB. At the time of inspection, Jiangsu EPB had detected noise levels that violated relevant standards at night, the court said. The defendant had a statutory duty to prevent and control noise pollution, but, by passing the matter to Wuxi EPB, had failed to perform its duty. The court ruled in favour of Wu and held that Jiangsu EPB's failure to perform its statutory duty was unlawful. It ordered the defendant to perform its duty within thirty days from the effective date of the judgment.

As early as 2012, the All-China Environment Federation (ACEF) won China's first litigation on environmental information disclosure against a local EPB that had failed to disclose information. The case, the events of which occurred in Guizhou province, is *All-China Environment Federation* v. *Xiuwen Environmental Protection Bureau* (2012).[46]

All-China Environment Federation v. *Xiuwen Environmental Protection Bureau* (2012)

The ACEF sued Xiuwen EPB for failing to perform its statutory duty of information disclosure under the Regulation on Government Information Disclosure (RGID). The ACEF requested that the court order the defendant to disclose the information. On 28 October 2011, the ACEF had submitted to Xiuwen EPB, by express mail, an application requesting disclosure of information regarding Guizhou HaoYiDuo Dairy Co. Ltd. In particular, the ACEF requested information on the company's discharge permit, the number and locations of wastewater discharge outlets, the types and volume of effluents, the wastewater discharge fees determined by the EPB and paid by the dairy, relevant EPB monitoring data and records of any administrative penalties that had been imposed on the dairy. Xiuwen EPB did not reply and did not disclose the requested information. On 24 November 2011, the ACEF wrote to Guiyang EPB, asking it to urge Xiuwen EPB, its subordinate, to disclose the information. No responses were received from either EPB by the end of the fifteen-day limit. Xiuwen EPB claimed that it had not replied or disclosed the information because the ACEF's application was unclear as to the information requested, the format of the information and the

[46] *Supreme People's Court Gazette*, 1 (2013). For more details, see Qie Jianrong, 'China's first environmental information disclosure public interest litigation won by the public', *Legal Daily*, 6 April 2012; and Liu Xiaoxing, 'China's first environmental information disclosure public interest litigation won by the public: information disclosure relies on judicial redress?', *China Environment News*, 15 February 2012.

means of obtaining the information. It said the request was also unclear as the dairy company had several operation sites. Further, Xiuwen EPB said it had not received proof of identity (a copy of registration documents) from the ACEF, that the ACEF had not used the application form provided by the EPB and had not paid fees to cover expenses that would be incurred by the agency in collecting, copying and posting the information.

Qingzhen City Court (2012) held for the ACEF. It stated that: (i) the ACEF had applied for information disclosure in accordance with law regarding procedure, content and formalities, and the information requested by the ACEF had been clearly specified; (ii) had the defendant thought the ACEF's application was unclear, it should, in accordance with article 21 of the RGID, have told the ACEF to revise its request; (iii) Xiuwen EPB had no legal basis to refuse to disclose information requested by the ACEF, and therefore it must disclose the information within ten days. Xiuwen EPB appealed.[47]

Guiyang Intermediate Court (2012) allowed the appeal and then approved Xiuwen EPB's application to withdraw the appeal.

At appeal, Xiuwen EPB accepted it had a duty to disclose information to the public, legal persons or any other organizations and said it was willing to perform its duty in accordance with the first-instance judgment.

10.2.3 EIA Approval Decisions

Judicial review is playing an increasingly important role in the EIA regime in China.[48] Of twenty important environmental administrative cases issued by the SPC in two batches in 2014 and 2016, five involved judicial review of EIA decisions and were brought by parties potentially affected by an agency decision, rather than by parties subject to an agency decision.[49] Judicial review of agency decisions on EIA approval should strengthen the role of EIA as an effective tool to prevent and mitigate environmental harm.

In *Zhou Kun and Zhang Wenbo* v. *Ministry of Environmental Protection* (2014),[50] the court reviewed the agency's EIA approval of a high-speed rail project, focusing on the procedural legality of the MEP's decision-making.

Zhou Kun and Zhang Wenbo v. *Ministry of Environmental Protection* (2014)

Zhou Kun and Zhang Wenbo sued the MEP over its approval of the EIA report of the Beijing–Shenyang High-Speed Railway project. Zhou and Zhang lived near the project and were affected by noise and vibration. They sued, requesting that the MEP's approval be revoked on the grounds that the EIA report was flawed.

[47] Zhao Yinan, 'Court backs environmental group', *China Daily*, 20 January 2012; and Liu, 'China's first environmental information disclosure'.

[48] For more cases studies of judicial review of EIA decisions, see Jin Zining, 'Environmental Impact Assessment Law in China's courts'.

[49] See Section 10.1 of this chapter for a list of the cases.

[50] SPC 10 Important Administrative Cases on Environmental Protection (second batch) (2016), case no. 8.

Beijing No.1 Intermediate Court (2014) found that the constructor of the project and the firm that carried out the EIA had posted an announcement of the project and the EIA being undertaken, advertised in newspapers and online and solicited public comment. The EIA report had been prepared, as required, in compliance with the Technical Guidance on Environmental Impact Assessment, it said. Upon receiving the EIA report, the MEP had announced the relevant project information on its website and had hosted a public hearing to collect feedback. The court found that the MEP's EIA approval process was in full compliance with the legal requirements and that its EIA approval decision was neither unlawful nor improper. The court upheld the agency decision and rejected the request to revoke the EIA approval.

Without doubt, judicial review of EIA approval decisions provides an additional check on agency behaviour. Crucially, courts are improving the quality of the EIA process and, with public input, are changing agency behaviour to ensure environmental considerations are integrated within the decision-making process. This strengthens EIA as a regulatory tool to prevent potential environmental harm.

10.3 OUTCOME OF JUDICIAL REVIEW

Chinese courts have the power to review and uphold, revoke, compel or revise agency decisions under the ALL (2017). Courts uphold administrative acts that are based on solid evidence, correct application of law and regulation and in compliance with legal procedural rules.[51] Where unlawful agency acts or omissions are found, courts offer a range of remedies: they may revoke an administrative decision,[52] compel an agency to act[53] or revise an administrative decision.[54]

10.3.1 Upholding Administrative Decisions

A court judgment to uphold an administrative decision made by government or an agency can strengthen environmental regulation and enforcement, as occurred in *Shanghai Qinhui Cement Co.* v. *Fengxian District Government* (2016).[55]

Shanghai Qinhui Cement Co. v. _Fengxian District Government_ (2016)

Qinhui Cement Co. (Qinhui) was founded in 2006 to produce, process and sell cement. It was located close to the upper reaches of the Huangpu River in Shanghai. In 2010, the site of the operations was included in a Grade II drinking-water-source reserve (DWSR). In 2015, Fengxian District Government decided, in accordance with article 59(1) of the WPPCL (2008), to permanently close Qinhui, because it was generating dust and soot inside the Grade II DWSR. Qinhui sued, requesting the court to revoke the government decision to close the factory.

[51] ALL (2017), art. 69. [52] ALL (2017), art. 70. [53] ALL (2017), art. 72. [54] ALL (2017), art. 77.
[55] SPC 10 Important Administrative Cases on Environmental Protection (second batch) (2016), case no. 7.

Shanghai No.1 Intermediate Court (2015) found that the plaintiff's cement production generated pollution and was subject to article 59(1) of the WPPCL (2008), which requires local government to shut down existing projects that discharge pollution in Grade II DWSRs. The defendant's decision was based on a clear finding of facts and correct application of law, the court said. The plaintiff's application was dismissed. Qinhui appealed.

Shanghai High Court (2016) found that the dust and soot generated by Qinhui impacted on the water quality at the Grade II DWSR. It held that there was a legal basis for Fengxian District Government to permanently close the plant, and dismissed the appeal.

It is worth noting that when Chinese courts do uphold administrative decisions, they often take extra steps in order to address the grievances and concerns of the plaintiffs, as Guangdong High Court did in *Su Yaohua* v. *Guangdong Boluo County Government* (2014).[56]

Su Yaohua v. *Guangdong Boluo County Government* (2014)

Su Yaohua had operated a pig farm since 2006 and had all the necessary documents and permissions: a tax registration certificate, a pollution discharge permit and a business licence for an individual industrial and commercial household. In March 2012, Boluo County Government issued a public notice that it was designating an area of land in which livestock farming would be banned. It required existing farms to relocate and clean up their site by 30 June 2012. Su's pig farm was in the designated area and he sued, requesting the court revoke Boluo County Government's notice of March 2012.

Huizhou Intermediate Court (2013) held that the Guangdong Provincial Environmental Protection Regulation granted Boluo County Government the power to designate areas in which livestock farming was prohibited, in order to protect the environment. The administrative decision was made in accordance with law and was upheld by the court. Su appealed.

Guangdong High Court (2014) dismissed the appeal and upheld the first-instance judgment. It explained that the river near the designated area was connected to the DWSR, and thus the county government has the power under the Guangdong Provincial Environmental Protection Regulation to prohibit livestock farming in order to prevent water pollution and protect the public interest in the environment.

In this case, Guangdong High Court reviewed the legality of the local government's decision and upheld it. It balanced the public interest in environmental protection with Su's private business interest, the pig farm, which had operated lawfully prior to the notice of March 2012. The court said that his lawful interest must be protected and that if acting in the public interest required the government to revoke his permit or licence, the government should pay fair compensation.[57] The court advised Su to seek administrative compensation

[56] SPC 10 Important Administrative Cases on Environmental Protection (2014), case no. 6.

separately.[58] A similar approach was taken by Jiangsu High Court in the case of *Zhang Xiaoyan and Others* v. *Jiangsu Environmental Protection Bureau* (2015).[59]

***Zhang Xiaoyan and Others* v. *Jiangsu Environmental Protection Bureau* (2015)**

Zhang Xiaoyan and two others sued Jiangsu EPB, seeking revocation of the EPB's decision to approve the EIA statement of a 110 kV electricity substation. The project proponent was Zhenjiang Power Supply Co. They argued that the proposed site was unsuitable for building a substation and that the EIA was not conducted using scientific methods, making the approval decision unlawful.

Nanjing Intermediate Court (2015) found that Jiangsu EPB's decision to approve the EIA statement of the proposed project had been made in accordance with article 22 of the EIAL (2002) and relevant technical guidance. The approval process was lawful. The plaintiffs' request that the approval decision be revoked was rejected. Zhang and two others appealed.

Jiangsu High Court (2015) dismissed the appeal and upheld the first-instance judgment. It found that the substation, as part of the city's public infrastructure, could be built, where proper, in sensitive regions such as scenic areas, nature reserves and populated areas. The projected pollution during construction and operation was well below the maximum level permitted by law, it noted. Further, it said that the ultra-low level of magnetic radiation to be generated by the substation would have only a slight impact and could be controlled. The court held that the EIA approval decision was made in compliance with law.

In addition to reviewing the legality of Jiangsu EPB's EIA approval, Jiangsu High Court took extra steps to address the plaintiffs' concerns. It urged Jiangsu EPB to ensure information disclosure by requesting the substation operator to monitor the level of magnetic radiation and disclose real-time monitoring data to the public.[60]

10.3.2 Revoking Agency Decisions

Courts have the power to entirely or partially revoke an unlawful agency act in the following circumstances:[61] (i) where key evidence is lacking; (ii) where law or regulation has been applied erroneously; (iii) where the act violates legal procedure; (iv) where the act is ultra vires; (v) where the agency has abused its power or (vi) the act is patently inappropriate. By revoking an agency decision made in violation of law, the courts protect the rights and interests of parties injured by the unlawful administrative acts. In *Lu Hong and others* v. *Xiaoshan Environmental Protection Bureau* (2013),[62] Xiaoshan District Court revoked the EIA approval decision of Xiaoshan EPB because the EPB had violated the legal procedures designed to protect the plaintiffs' rights of access to information and participation in the EIA decision-making process. In *Xia Chunguan and others* v. *Dongtai Environmental Protection Bureau* (2014),[63] the courts in Jiangsu province revoked

[58] SPC 10 Important Administrative Cases on Environmental Protection (2014), case no. 6.
[59] SPC 10 Important Administrative Cases on Environmental Protection (second batch) (2016), case no. 4.
[60] SPC 10 Important Administrative Cases on Environmental Protection (second batch) (2016), case no. 4.
[61] ALL (2017), art. 70.
[62] SPC 10 Important Administrative Cases on Environmental Protection (2014), case no. 4.
[63] SPC 10 Important Administrative Cases on Environmental Protection (2014), case no. 9.

Dongtai EPB's EIA approval because it had violated procedure requirements of public participation under the Administrative Licence Law (2003).

Xia Chunguan and Others v. *Dongtai Environmental Protection Bureau* (2014)

Xia Chunguan and three others were residents of building number nineteen. They sued Dongtai EPB, requesting that the court revoke the EPB's decision to approve the EIA statement of a proposed public bathhouse. The bathhouse was to be constructed between buildings number seventeen and nineteen. The plaintiffs had not been consulted and no hearing or discussion forum was held prior to the EPB's approval decision.

Dongtai City Court (2013) revoked Dongtai EPB's EIA approval decision because it had violated legal procedures. The court found that although the defendant had the power to examine and approve the EIA statement of construction projects within its jurisdiction, it had not complied with the procedural requirements for granting the approval. Article 47 of the Administrative Licence Law (2003) requires an administrative agency to notify the applicant and relevant parties of their right to a hearing prior to making the decision, if the applicant's licence application has a significant impact on the interests of others, the court noted. Xia and three others lived next to the site proposed for the bathhouse and potentially would have been significantly affected by humidity, heat and noise. The court found that granting EIA approval to the project directly impacted the 'significant interest' of Xia and three others, who were entitled to a hearing prior to the decision. Dongtai EPB appealed.

Yancheng Intermediate Court (2014) dismissed the appeal and upheld the first-instance judgment. It confirmed that the examination and approval of EIA documents for construction projects is an act of administrative licence and must comply with the Administrative Licence Law (2003), which sets out detailed procedural requirements for an agency to follow in the decision-making process. The court also agreed that Xia and three others, as neighbours directly adjacent to the proposed public bathhouse, did have significant interest in the approval of the project. The court held that the EPB should have informed them that, before the decision was made, they had the right to comment and object, and were also entitled to a hearing. Dongtai EPB had failed to notify Xia and three others of their right to a hearing and therefore the approval had been granted in violation of the procedural requirement, the court found.

Judicial review is an effective instrument with which courts can supervise agencies and ensure lawful environmental enforcement, including of monitoring and sanctions. If an agency's administrative penalty decision is not based on solid and accurate evidence of violation, a court revokes the decision in order to protect the rights and interest of the regulated. In *Sound Water Co.* v. *Hainan Danzhou Environmental Protection Bureau* (2016),[64] the court revoked the administrative penalty decision because key evidence was missing. The judgment emphasizes the importance of legally collected evidence, including monitoring reports and pollution data, as the legal basis for an administrative penalty decision. The monitoring process, including sample collection, must comply strictly with legal requirements and technical guidance.[65] Hainan Danzhou EPB had failed to provide

[64] SPC 10 Model Criminal, Civil and Administrative Cases on Environment and Resources (2017), case no. 9.

[65] MEP, Measures on Environmental Administrative Sanction (2010), art. 34. The article stipulates procedures for on-site inspections. If samples are taken during the inspection, the process of sample collection must be photographed, filmed or recorded by other means.

records of its collecting of samples or any other evidence to prove that the collecting complied with law. As a result, the monitoring report based on the samples could not be used as key evidence to impose an administrative penalty on Sound Water Co. The court's decision in this case has far-reaching impact on environmental agencies in the enforcement of law and the sanction of polluters in violation.

10.3.3 Compelling Agencies to Act

If an agency is sued for failing to perform a statutory duty, the court must order the defendant to perform the relevant duty by a specified deadline.[66] In *All-China Environment Federation* v. *Xiuwen Environmental Protection Bureau* (2012),[67] Qingzhen City Court found that Xiuwen EPB had failed to perform its statutory duty of information disclosure. The court ordered it to disclose the information within ten days of the effective date of the judgment. Similarly, in the case of *Wu Yi* v. *Jiangsu Environmental Protection Bureau* (2015),[68] Nanjing Intermediate Court found that Jiangsu EPB had failed to perform its statutory duty to prevent and control noise generated by a highway project. The court ordered it to perform its duty within thirty days of the effective date of the judgment.

10.3.4 Revising Agency Decisions

If an administrative penalty decision is patently inappropriate, or an agency's calculation of the amount of a payment is erroneous, a court may decide to modify the agency decision.[69] However, a court may not increase a plaintiff's obligation or adversely affect a plaintiff's rights or interests.[70] In practice, courts tend to defer to agency discretion as long as the administrative penalty decisions or other decisions are made in accordance with legal procedure and the amount of payment is within the range stipulated by relevant laws and regulations.[71]

10.3.5 Court Declaration of Illegal Act by Agency

In many cases in which an agency is sued for an unlawful act or for failing to perform a statutory duty, the agency rectifies and performs the statutory duties during the trial. If that happens, the plaintiff may either withdraw the lawsuit or amend the claim to request a court declaration that the agency's act or omission was unlawful. The court will then decide whether or not the agency's act or omission was unlawful.[72] In the case of *All-China Environment Federation* v. *Qingzhen Municipal Bureau of Land and Resources* (2009),[73] the defendant performed its duty to revoke a lease and reclaim land after being sued by the

[66] ALL (2017), art. 72. [67] *Supreme People's Court Gazette*, 1 (2013).
[68] SPC 10 Important Administrative Cases on Environmental Protection (second batch) (2016), case no. 1.
[69] ALL (2017), art. 77(1). [70] ALL (2017), art. 77(2).
[71] In each of the ten administrative cases involving administrative penalty decisions, the court upheld the agency decision on the amount of the fine and on other sanctions. See SPC 10 Important Administrative Cases on Environmental Protection (2014), case nos. 1, 3, 5, 7 and 8; SPC 10 Important Administrative Cases on Environmental Protection (second batch) (2016), case nos. 2, 3, 5, 6 and 9.
[72] ALL (2017), art. 74.
[73] See Chapter 12 of this book for further discussion of the case. Ma Yong, 'Social organizations making an impact by promoting environmental public interest litigations' in Zeng Xiaodong and Chang Jiwen (eds.), *Environmental Law in China*, vol. A, (Beijing: Law Press China, 2009), 67–73.

ACEF for an unlawful omission. During the trial, the agency performed the duty as requested by the ACEF and the NGO decided to withdraw the lawsuit.

Procuratorates, however, take the other approach. Instead of withdrawing a lawsuit, procuratorates amend their claims and request the court to confirm that the agency's act or omission was unlawful. In the case of *Fujian Qingliu People's Procuratorate* v. *Qingliu Environmental Protection Bureau* (2016),[74] despite Qingliu EPB's rectification during trial (it imposed administrative sanctions on Liu – suspension of operation and a fine – and ordered confiscated e-waste to be disposed of safely by a qualified third party), Qingliu County Procuratorate still requested a court decision that the defendant's handling of e-waste was unlawful. Similarly, in the case of *Guizhou Jinping County Procuratorate* v. *Jinping Environmental Protection Bureau* (2015),[75] the defendant had issued a rectification order to two stone-processing enterprises, but had failed to conduct follow-up monitoring to stop the violation from continuing. During the trial, on 31 December 2015, the local government shut down all illegal operations, including the two enterprises in question. Guizhou Jinping County Procuratorate nevertheless requested the court to decide whether Jinping EPB's failure to perform its statutory duty of environmental supervision from 5 August 2014 to 31 December 2015 was unlawful. A court decision that an agency's act or omission was unlawful puts pressure on the agency, because it has an adverse impact on its performance appraisal and that of individuals in charge.

10.4 CHALLENGES IN ADMINISTRATIVE LITIGATION IN CHINA

Administrative litigation was introduced in China by the ALL (1989), but tremendous difficulties have been encountered in its implementation, though these difficulties have eased somewhat in recent years. Judicial review has achieved limited success in checking and restraining decision-making by administrative organs. Local courts are often unable or unwilling to engage in judicial scrutiny of the administrative acts of local governments or agencies. Administrative litigation in China is characterized by low success rates for plaintiffs, high rates of appeal, high petition rates (indicating that aggrieved parties are dissatisfied with the final court decisions), low adjudication rates at courts of first instance (indicating that many cases are withdrawn by plaintiffs), and low rates of retrial or reversal of judgment ordered by appellate courts, all of which contribute to low public satisfaction.[76]

10.4.1 Low Win Rates, High Rates of Appeal and Petition

The win rates for plaintiffs in courts of first instance remain low, decreasing from 30 per cent in the 1990s to below 10 per cent in 2012. First-instance courts delivered judgments against defendants in only 12.07 per cent of cases in 2009, 11.18 per cent in 2010, 9.89 per

[74] SPP 8th Batch of Guiding Cases (2016), case no. 31. See Chapter 12 of this book for further discussion of the case.

[75] SPC 10 Important Administrative Cases on Environmental Protection (second batch) (2016), case no. 10. See Chapter 12 of this book for further discussion of the case. See also SPP 8th Batch of Guiding Cases (2016), case no. 32.

[76] Jiang Bixin, 'Reform of China's administrative adjudication', *Administrative Law Studies*, 4 (2013), 3–11, at 3–5.

cent in 2011 and 9.87 per cent in 2012.[77] Another empirical study found that between 1990 and 1995 plaintiffs had a 15 per cent to 21 per cent chance of obtaining a favourable ruling either revoking or modifying an agency decision at a court of first instance.[78] The extremely low win rates for plaintiffs result in high appeal rates and high petition rates. In 2012, the appeal rate for administrative cases was 70 per cent, in contrast to 11 per cent for criminal cases and 28 per cent for civil cases. In the same year, the petition rate for administrative cases was 8 per cent, while civil and criminal cases each had a petition rate of 1 per cent.[79] Consequently, large numbers of administrative disputes between individuals and local governments that should have been resolved by administrative litigation ended up as 'letters and visits' public complaints.[80] People have no confidence in the ability of local courts to adjudicate in their favour against local governments. Instead, the aggrieved parties bring their disputes to higher-level governments or to people's congresses, travelling long distances to Beijing to complain about the acts of local governments, and sometimes even resorting to violence to express their anger and despair.[81] The SPC has admitted that the failure of administrative litigation has resulted in an increased number of petitions, public protests and violence, all of which undermine social stability.[82]

10.4.2 High Withdrawal Rates

Subject to court approval, a plaintiff may apply to withdraw a case at any time before judgment is delivered.[83] The case is concluded once the court approves the withdrawal application. A very high percentage of administrative cases are withdrawn by plaintiffs before judgment is given; the percentage is abnormally high compared to civil and commercial cases.[84] The withdrawal rate had been increasing steadily, rising from 36 per cent in 1990 to 51 per cent in 1995.[85] It is understandable for a plaintiff to withdraw a case after a defendant has rectified or has performed its statutory duty as requested. However, in less than half of withdrawal cases did the withdrawal occur after the defendant had rectified its administrative act or omission.[86] The remaining cases of withdrawal – above 50 per cent each year from 1994 to 2010 – are puzzling, as the plaintiff has gained nothing.[87] An empirical study of nearly 200 withdrawal cases found that in only one out of five did the plaintiff withdraw voluntarily, while the remainder involved coercion by either the defendant, the court or both.[88] Defendants are strongly motivated to pressurise plaintiffs to drop a case. Even though the defendant faces a low risk of losing in court, there is a negative

77 Jiang Bixin, 'Reform of China's administrative adjudication', at 4.
78 Minxin Pei, 'Citizens v. mandarinsMinxin ', at 841–2.
79 Jiang Bixin, 'Reform of China's administrative adjudication', 3–11, at 4–5.
80 Public complaint via letters and visits is a mechanism allowing any aggrieved member of the public to file a complaint to a government office either by letter or by visiting in person.
81 Jiang Bixin, 'Reform of China's administrative adjudication', at 3–4.
82 SPC Opinion on the Legal Protection of Parties' Rights to Sue in Administrative Litigations (2009).
83 ALL (1989), art. 51; ALL (2017), art. 62.
84 Michael Palmer, 'Controlling the State? Mediation in administrative litigation in the People's Republic of China', *Transnational Law & Contemporary Problems*, 16 (2006), 165–87, at 182.
85 Minxin Pei, 'Citizens v. mandarins', at 842.
86 Minxin Pei, 'Citizens v. mandarins', at 843. In 1994 and 1995, 38 per cent and 45 per cent respectively of all withdrawal cases were withdrawn after defendant agencies rectified administrative actions or omissions.
87 He Haibo, 'Litigations without a ruling', at 264.
88 Palmer, 'Controlling the State?', at 184.

impact, which is not merely about losing face. Media exposure and public outcry could, in serious circumstances, undermine agency authority and the careers of the officials in charge.[89] Courts also prefer it if a case is settled and withdrawn by the plaintiff. Local courts are tightly controlled by local governments and impartiality is difficult to attain. It can be difficult for a court to revoke a government decision. However, a court cannot always favour the defendant as aggrieved and determined plaintiffs would appeal and petition to higher-level courts, or bring their complaints through extra-judicial channels to higher-level governments.[90] Caught between pressure from local governments and the risk of social unrest, courts resort to persuading parties to end the adjudication without a ruling.[91] Withdrawals by the plaintiff not only leave plaintiffs without legal protection of their rights and interests, but also defeats the value of judicial review in promoting good governance and the rule of law.

10.4.3 Impact of Judgments on Agency Behaviour

Ideally, a court ruling on the legality of an agency act or omission, especially a finding against the agency, will ensure that the agency rectifies its behaviour and promotes good governance. There has been limited study of the impact of administrative litigation judgments on agency behaviour in China. A small-scale analysis of fourteen cases in Hubei province revealed if and how judicial review had achieved its goal of restraining administrative behaviour.[92] It found that only in half of the fourteen cases had the judgments led to long-term changes in agency practice. In each of those seven cases, the officials in charge had knowledge of law and they agreed with the court judgment over their agency's flawed practice.[93] Losing a lawsuit clearly did not necessarily cause an agency to change its illegal behaviour. The study uncovered an absence of concern over potential future legal challenges.[94]

10.4.4 Responses to Local Protectionism

Interference by local party committee or local government contributes to the overwhelmingly high rate of cases lost by plaintiffs.[95] Local courts are tightly controlled by local governments on issues ranging from personnel to budget, and this external pressure and interference means they are not free to adjudicate impartially in administrative cases.

Empirical studies find that higher-level courts are more likely to find in favour of a plaintiff as they are more detached from the influence of local protectionism. A plaintiff in administrative litigation has a better chance of being heard by a judge who is able to ignore pressure from a defendant agency if the case is heard in a higher-level court.[96] Apart from the higher-level court's relative insulation from the local agency involved in the

[89] Minxin Pei, 'Citizens v. mandarins', at 844.
[90] Minxin Pei, 'Citizens v. mandarins', at 844–5.
[91] He Haibo, 'Litigations without a ruling'.
[92] Xuehua Zhang and Leonard Ortolano, 'Judicial review of environmental administrative decisions: has it changed the behavior of government agencies?', *The China Journal*, 64 (2010), 97–119.
[93] Xuehua Zhang and Ortolano, 'Judicial review', at 99.
[94] Xuehua Zhang and Ortolano, 'Judicial review', at 116–17.
[95] Jiang Bixin, 'Improvement of the administrative litigation system from a macroscopic perspective', *Frontiers of Law in China*, 9 (2014), 1–30, at 6.
[96] O'Brien and Lianjiang Li, 'Suing the local state', at 86.

administrative litigation, the judge may be better qualified professionally, which may also contribute to a less-biased approach.[97]

To address local protectionism and eliminate interference by the local government, courts have initiated reforms on jurisdiction of administrative cases: the reforms include centralized jurisdiction, designated jurisdiction and upgraded jurisdiction.[98] 'Centralized jurisdiction' refers to a cross-region administrative court system set up by provincial high courts, subject to approval by the SPC.[99] In 2013, the SPC decided to introduce a pilot exercise for centralized jurisdiction in which each provincial high court was required to designate one or two intermediate courts and two or three basic-level courts to exercise jurisdiction over all administrative cases within that province.[100] The purpose of this was to ensure that the designated courts were geographically distant from the influence of the defendants. Under 'designated jurisdiction', a higher court designates a court in another geographical region to exercise jurisdiction.[101] Again, this offers better protection of the plaintiffs in administrative litigation. Where a citizen, legal person or organization considers that a case of major importance is complicated or is not suitable for the local court, they may apply for a higher court to designate a different court to hear the case. 'Upgraded jurisdiction' strengthens the power of higher courts to hear cases of lower courts or to designate other courts to exercise jurisdiction, in order to eliminate local government intervention in local-court adjudication. Under upgraded jurisdiction, higher courts have the power to act as courts of first instance for administrative cases over which lower courts have jurisdiction.[102] In addition, a first-instance court with jurisdiction may, if it deems it necessary, apply to a higher court to move the case up or designate another court for adjudication.[103] It is a challenge to exercise judicial review independently and without interference in a country without separation of powers.

Judicial review aims to make agencies adhere to their statutory mandates, including implementation and enforcement of environmental law. It is a mechanism that courts may use to check, supervise and rectify the unlawful acts or omissions of administrative bodies. It allows courts to ensure agencies perform their statutory duties, that they do so in full compliance with law, and do not abuse their powers. There are limits, however, to the ability of judicial review to achieve sound environmental decision-making; a court's role is limited to examining the legality of administrative acts.[104] Courts are aware of the scope of their judicial power and always defer to agency discretion on technical issues, given the expertise and technical knowledge of agencies in administrative decisions. Courts do not make their own evaluation of the public good or deliver judgment on the social and economic benefits of a decision. These are matters of policy and the preserve of administrative agencies. Even if an agency decision is revoked or a duty is enforced, it does not

[97] Minxin Pei, 'Citizens v. mandarins', at 847. [98] Jiang Bixin, 'Improvement of the', at 10.
[99] ALL (2017), art. 18(2).
[100] SPC Notice on Pilot Exercise of Centralized Jurisdiction over Administrative Cases (2013). Implementation by provincial high courts is ongoing: Guangdong implemented in 2015, Yunnan in 2016 and Henan, Shandong, Fujian and Guangxi in 2019. www.pkulaw.cn
[101] SPC Provisions on Jurisdictions over Administrative Cases (2008). [102] ALL (2017), art. 24(1).
[103] ALL (2017), art. 24(2). [104] ALL (2017), art. 6.

necessarily follow that the final decision of the administrative body will be to the liking of the applicants for judicial review.

Thirty years since the ALL (1989) came into force, administrative litigation in China has not fully achieved the goal of checking and rectifying agency abuse of power or violation of law, due to the limited independence of the judiciary and the political-legal constraints it operates under. Nonetheless, judicial reforms on standing and jurisdiction are having a positive impact and are strengthening the capacity of the judiciary to check agency decisions, thereby improving environmental governance.

11

Environmental Crimes

Criminal law aims to punish and deter socially unacceptable behaviour. In the past, environmental pollution was accepted as a way of life because industrial operators contribute to the economy and improve people's living standards. However, things have changed. Growing environmental awareness and a fundamental change in the public's attitude towards pollution have shaped the development of environmental criminal law, both in legislation and in judicial practice. As more pollution incidents, such as lead poisoning[1] and cancer villages,[2] are exposed, people gain a deeper understanding of the devastating environmental impacts of pollution and the serious threat to human health. While pollution is an unavoidable consequence of industrialization, urbanization and socio-economic development, a distinction is drawn between 'acceptable' pollution that occurs during routine operations and is in compliance with state provisions and 'unacceptable' pollution that violates law and was caused either intentionally or negligently to maximize financial gains. The harm caused by 'unacceptable' pollution will be punished either by administrative penalty or criminal sanction, depending on the seriousness of the circumstances.

The shift in public perception on environment and pollution has had a clear impact on the development of environmental criminal law. 'Environmental crime' refers to all criminal offences endangering the environment. In a very broad sense, such a crime is any act or

1 'Over half of Chinese children suffering from lead poisoning, experts advocate legislation', *China News Net*, 31 March 2005. www.chinanews.com/news/2005/2005-03-31/26/557546.shtml; Yang Yan, 'Over one hundred children suspected of lead poisoning in Shaanxi Fengxiang', *People's Daily*, 11 August 2009, 6; Yang Yan, 'Dongling smelter main cause for lead poisoning in Fengxiang', *People's Daily*, 16 August 2009, 2; *Xinhua News Agency*, 'Shaanxi Fengxiang lead poisoning: 615 children confirmed blood lead levels exceed state standard', 14 August 2009. www.gov.cn/jrzg/2009-08/14/content_1391538.htm; 'Lead pollution: whose fault?', *CCTV*, 9 July 2011. http://news.cntv.cn/china/20110710/100502.shtml.

2 Cancer villages appeared in China from the 1990s, mainly in the eastern and central part of the country. See Zhang Yingying, 'The shadow over rural China', *China Dialogue*, 10 February 2011. www.chinadialogue.net/article/show/single/ch/4098-The-shadow-over-rural-China. The Ministry of Environmental Protection (MEP), in its 12th Five-Year Plan on the Prevention and Control of Environmental Risk of Chemicals (2013), admitted the grave health and environmental impacts resulting from the production and use of chemicals, and also admitted to the existence of cancer villages in China.

omission that violates law , causes or is capable of causing grave environmental harm and is subject to criminal sanctions. Criminalizing environmental wrongdoing contributes to the legal implementation of the preventative principle and the polluter-pays principle. Environmental criminal law not only sanctions wrongdoers, but also aims to deter individuals and the general population from committing environmental offences. Certainly, the ability of law to deter crime depends on the risk of being sanctioned and the nature and impact of the sanction. This chapter examines how environmental crimes are defined, prosecuted and sanctioned in order to protect the environment and public health.

Chinese law confines provisions on criminal liability to the Criminal Law (CL)[3] to maintain consistency and prevent disparities in the construction and sanction of different environmental crimes under different statutes.[4] Thus, the Environmental Protection Law (EPL)[5] and all specialized environmental statutes typically provide a general reference to criminal liability for the most serious environmental violations without specifying elements of the crime or punishment in detail. They provide that 'anyone who violates this law and commits a crime shall bear criminal liability in accordance with relevant law'.[6] Here 'relevant law' refers to the CL, its amendments and related judicial interpretations by the Supreme People's Court (SPC) and the Supreme People's Procuratorate (SPP). Legislation on environmental crimes has progressed steadily in the years since the enactment of the CL (1979), which was substantially revised in 1997.[7] Two important amendments followed: CL Amendment IV (2002) addresses the smuggling of waste and CL Amendment VIII (2011) addresses the crime of environmental pollution.

This chapter is divided into five sections. Section 11.1 introduces the early development of environmental criminal law under the CL (1979). Section 11.2 examines the more sophisticated and focused approach taken by the CL (1997) to environmental crimes, investigating the crime of causing a serious pollution incident, crimes relating to cross-border movement of waste and the crime of environmental dereliction of duty. Section 11.3 focuses on the crime of waste smuggling under the CL Amendment IV (2002). Section 11.4 analyses the crime of environmental pollution under the CL Amendment VIII (2011). Section 11.5 discusses key issues of criminal law as applied to environmental crimes, including legal and natural persons, fault-based liability, defences, multiple parties jointly committing crimes and sanctions balancing severe punishment with leniency. The chapter

[3] The CL was first enacted on 1 July 1979 by the 5th National People's Congress (NPC) at its 2nd session, and was revised on 14 March 1997 by the 8th NPC at its 5th session. The CL (1997) has been amended ten times, most recently in 2017.

[4] Shizhou Wang, 'Environmental crime and environmental criminal law in the People's Republic of China', *European Journal of Crime, Criminal Law and Criminal Justice*, 12 (2004), 150–65, at 156.

[5] The EPL was first enacted as the EPL (for trial use) in 1979. The EPL was enacted on 26 December 1989 by the 7th National People's Congress Standing Committee (NPCSC) at its 11th session. It was revised on 24 April 2014 by the 12th NPCSC at its 8th session, and the new version came into force on 1 January 2015.

[6] EPL (2014), art. 69; Air Pollution Prevention and Control Law (APPCL) (2015), art. 127; Water Pollution Prevention and Control Law (WPPCL) (2017) art. 101; Law on the Prevention and Control of Pollution by Solid Waste (SWL) (2016), arts. 67, 78 and 83; and the Soil Pollution Prevention and Control Law (SPPCL) (2018), art. 98.

[7] For more, see Cai Dingjian, 'China's major reform in criminal law', *Columbia Journal of Asian Law*, 11 (1997), 213–18.

concludes with discussion of criminal sanctions as part of the command-and-control regulatory approach.

11.1 THE CL (1979): PROVISIONS RELEVANT TO THE ENVIRONMENT

The CL (1979) was enacted as China prepared to embark on economic reform and reconstruction of its legal system. Awareness of pollution and environmentally damaging behaviours was low. The CL (1979) contained several provisions imposing sanctions on acts or omissions that cause environmental degradation. As illustrated by Table 11.1, these criminal acts or omissions fell into three categories: crimes that endanger public security,[8] crimes that undermine the socialist economic order,[9] and crimes involving dereliction of duty.[10] Despite the fragmented approach taken by the CL (1979) to environmental crimes, it did communicate a message that harming the environment, human health and public or private property is morally and socially unacceptable.

Environmental statutes of the 1980s and early 1990s mostly made reference to articles 115 and article 187 of the CL (1979) when applying criminal sanctions. For instance, both the WPPCL (1984) and WPPCL (1996) provide that 'anyone who, in violation of this law, causes a serious water pollution incident resulting in heavy losses of public or private property or human casualties, shall be investigated for criminal liabilities by reference to the CL (1979), article 115 or article 187'.[11] The SWL (1995) provides that 'anyone who, in violation of this law, collects, stores or disposes of hazardous waste and causes a serious environmental pollution incident resulting in heavy losses of public or private property or human casualties, shall be investigated for criminal liabilities by reference to the CL (1979), article 115 or article 187'.[12] The SWL (1995) also provides that 'where a unit commits the above crime, it shall be fined. Individuals in charge or others directly responsible shall also be criminally liable.'[13]

Zhang Changlin (1979),[14] the first environmental criminal case prosecuted under the CL (1979), was tried in the city of Suzhou.

[8] CL (1979), part II on 'Specific provisions', chapter II on 'Crimes endangering public security'. Articles 105, 106 and 115 are the most relevant.

[9] CL (1979), part II on 'Specific provisions', chapter III on 'Crimes undermining the socialist economic order'. In particular, articles 128, 129 and 130 impose criminal sanctions for illegal logging, illegal fishing and illegal hunting.

[10] CL (1979), part II on 'Specific provisions', chapter VIII on 'Crimes of dereliction of duty'. In particular, article 187 covers various circumstances, including environmental damage caused by dereliction of duty by state personnel.

[11] WPPCL (1984), art. 43; WPPCL (1996), art. 57.

[12] SWL (1995), art. 72(1).

[13] SWL (1995), art. 72(2).

[14] *Zhang Changlin* (1979), criminal judgment no. 26 (1979) of Jiangsu Suzhou Intermediate Court. See Xiang Lili, 'The first environmental case: story of the Grand Canal 29 years ago', *The Beijing News*, 24 February 2008; see also Ross and Silk, *Environmental Law and Policy*, at 250–1; Yang Chunxi et al., 'China's treatment of crimes against the environment: using criminal sanctions to fight environmental degradation in the PRC', *Journal of Chinese Law*, 8 (1994), 145–84, at 180; Jeffrey M. Bellamy, 'Putting the boss behind bars: using criminal sanctions against executives who pollute: what China could learn from the United States', *Indiana International and Comparative Law Review*, 13 (2003), 579–604, at 599–601.

TABLE 11.1 PROVISIONS OF THE CL (1979) RELEVANT TO ENVIRONMENTAL CRIMES

Type of crime	Provisions
Crimes that endanger public security (part II, chapter II)	Article 105: Whoever sets a fire, breaches a dike, causes an explosion or uses other dangerous means to sabotage a factory, mine, oilfield, harbour, river, water source, warehouse, dwelling, forest, farm, threshing ground, pasture, important pipeline, public building or other public or private property and thereby endangers public security shall be sentenced to fixed-term imprisonment of three to ten years if serious consequences have not yet resulted. Article 106: Whoever sets a fire, breaches a dike, causes an explosion, spreads poison or uses other dangerous means to cause serious human injury or death or heavy loss of public or private property shall be sentenced to a fixed term of not less than ten years' imprisonment, life imprisonment or death. Whoever negligently commits the crime mentioned in the preceding paragraph shall be sentenced to fixed-term imprisonment of up to seven years or criminal detention.[a] Article 115: Whoever violates the regulations on the control of explosive, inflammable, radioactive, poisonous or corrosive substances and thereby causes a serious incident during the production, storage, transportation or use of the relevant substances shall be sentenced to fixed-term imprisonment of up to three years or criminal detention if the consequences are serious; if the consequences are especially serious, the offender shall be sentenced to fixed-term imprisonment of three to seven years.
Crimes that undermine the socialist economic order (part II, chapter III)	Article 128: Whoever, in violation of the laws and regulations on forestry protection, engages in illegal logging or destruction of forest or other woodland, and if the circumstances are serious, shall be sentenced to fixed-term imprisonment of up to three years, or criminal detention or a fine. Article 129: Whoever, in violation of the laws and regulations on the protection of aquatic resources, engages in fishing in an area where fishing is prohibited, or during a period in which fishing is prohibited or by means that are prohibited, and if the circumstances are serious, shall be sentenced to fixed-term imprisonment of up to two years, or criminal detention or a fine. Article 130: Whoever, in violation of game laws and regulations, engages in hunting in a game reserve, during a period in which hunting is prohibited or by means that are prohibited, thereby damaging rare birds, beasts or other wild animals, and if the circumstances are serious, shall be sentenced to fixed-term imprisonment of up to two years, or criminal detention or a fine.
Crimes involving dereliction of duty (part II, chapter VIII)	Article 187: Any state personnel who, as a result of neglect of duty, causes heavy loss of public property or damages the interests of the state and the people, shall be sentenced to fixed-term imprisonment of up to five years or criminal detention.

Sources: CL (1979).

[a] 'Criminal detention' is a more lenient form of punishment (one to six months). 'Fixed-term imprisonment' sentences are between six months and fifteen years.

Zhang Changlin (1979)

On 12 September 1979, Zhang Changlin, an employee of Renmin Chemical Plant in Suzhou, switched on a valve to divert liquid cyanide from a 150-t storage tank to an 8-t measurement tank just before 4 p.m. He forgot to switch off the valve when he left the factory at around 8 p.m. When his fellow workers returned to the factory at around 7 a.m. on 13 September 1979, they found that the liquid cyanide had overflowed from the measurement tank and had been released via a sewer into the Beijing–Hangzhou Grand Canal. Zhang had negligently left the valve on for more than 15 hours and 28 t of liquid cyanide had been released into the Beijing–Hangzhou Grand Canal. The concentration level of the cyanide within 300 m of the factory was 47 mg/l, 940 times above the national standard for surface water.

Immediate emergency action was taken by Suzhou Environmental Protection Office, which warned the public not to use water from the Grand Canal for any purpose, including drinking, cooking and irrigation. Zhang was detained by the police on 18 September and arrested on 21 September.[15] He was then prosecuted under article 115 of the CL (1979).

Suzhou Intermediate Court (1979) found that due to Zhang's negligence, the release of more than 28 t of highly toxic liquid cyanide to the Beijing–Hangzhou Grand Canal had caused serious losses to fisheries and had created a grave public hazard, as well as causing a loss of more than 34,800 yuan to Renmin Chemical Plant. Zhang was convicted and sentenced to two years' imprisonment under article 115 of the CL (1979) and article 32 of the EPL (for trial implementation) (1979).

In *Cao Baozhang* (1992),[16] another case of serious water pollution by cyanide waste, Shanghai Intermediate Court convicted Cao Baozhang for the crime of depositing poisons under article 106(1) of the CL (1979). It imposed the death penalty with a two-year suspension.

Cao Baozhang (1992)

In January 1989, Cao, operator of Xiangyang Chemical Factory in a village in Jiangsu province, signed a contract with Shanghai Saw Factory to treat and dispose of the latter's HW, which contained cyanide. Cao did this despite knowing that his small village factory had no capacity for safe treatment of cyanide waste. According to the contract, Xiangyang Chemical Factory was

[15] In China, a public security bureau (PSB) makes the decision to detain a suspect, while the subsequent 'arrest' requires the formal approval of the People's Procuratorate. Under the Criminal Procedure Law (1979), a PSB may detain a person for criminal investigation, but must interrogate the detainee within 24 hours. The PSB must release the person immediately if, based on the interrogation, it finds that the person should not have been detained (art. 44). If a PSB decides then to arrest the detainee, it must apply to a people's procuratorate within three days of detention for approval of arrest. In special circumstances, the three-day limit may be extended by one to four days (art. 48).

[16] *Cao Baozhang* (1992) was not formally reported by the court and hence this summary is based on scholarly discussion of the case. See Xie Zhenhua, *Typical Cases and Enforcement Guide of Chinese Environmental Law* (Beijing: China Environmental Science Press, 1994), at 66–8; Yu Haisong, *Practice and Interpretation of Crimes Against Environment and Resources* (Beijing: Law Press, 2017), at 127.

required to collect 10 t of cyanide waste each month from January 1989 and treat it in accordance with environmental provisions in order to prevent secondary pollution.

From January 1989 to August 1991, Cao's employees collected a total of 294 t of cyanide waste, but they did not treat it. At Cao's instruction, the HW had been dumped into the river on the way back from collecting it in Shanghai. In August 1991, large quantities of dead fish were found in the river and the water supplier found that the cyanide level was eighteen times over the national limit. Water supply to five townships was suspended for two days. Nineteen factories had to suspend operations, costing them an estimated 740,000 yuan in lost profits. They also lost more than 400,000 yuan in fish and other fishery resources. Further investigation by the Jiading County Environmental Protection Bureau (EPB) found that Xiangyang Chemical Factory's toxic dumping had created seven water pollution incidents during the two years, causing direct economic losses of more than 2.1 million yuan and serious harm to both the environment and public health. Cao had made a profit of more than 73,000 yuan.

Shanghai Intermediate Court (1992) convicted Cao under article 106(1) of the CL (1979) for the crime of depositing a poison and imposed the death penalty with a two-year suspension. Other parties involved were imposed prison sentences.

While both cases involved serious water pollution by cyanide, a toxic substance, and caused grave loss, Zhang was convicted under article 115 and received a two-year imprisonment, while Cao was sentenced to the death penalty with a two-year suspension under article 106. The Shanghai court found that Cao had intentionally instructed two employees to dump the highly toxic cyanide waste into the river. Cao had knowledge of the toxicity of the cyanide waste and nonetheless instructed his employees to dump 10 t of such waste each month for more than two years. He should have foreseen the grave harm and threat caused by large quantities of toxic waste, 294 t in total. Cao's mental state meets the *mens rea* requirement of article 106(1). In contrast, Zhang was sanctioned under article 115 as he had caused a serious toxic release of wastewater by his negligence.

11.2 THE CL (1997): AN INTEGRATED APPROACH TO ENVIRONMENTAL CRIMES

After nearly two decades of an exploratory and fragmented approach to environmental criminal law, important progress was made by the CL (1997).[17] It adopted a more focused treatment of environmental crimes in section 6 (entitled 'Crimes against the protection of environment and resources')[18] of chapter VI on 'Crimes obstructing the administration of public order'. The section covers the crime of causing a serious environmental pollution incident,[19] waste-related crimes including the crime of illegal dumping, deposit or disposal of imported solid waste, the crime of illegal importing of solid waste and the crime of waste smuggling,[20] and crimes against natural resources, including illegal fishing, hunting,

[17] The CL (1979) was substantially revised on 14 March 1997 by the 8th NPC at its 5th session. The 1997 revision came into force on 1 October 1997.

[18] CL (1997), chapter VI, section 6, covering articles 338–46.

[19] CL (1997), art. 338.

[20] CL (1997), art. 339.

TABLE 11.2 PROVISIONS OF THE CL (1997) ON ENVIRONMENTAL CRIMES (EXCLUDING CRIMES AGAINST NATURAL RESOURCES)

Crime	Provision
Causing a serious pollution incident	Article 338: Whoever releases, dumps or disposes of radioactive waste, waste containing pathogens of a contagious disease, toxic substances or other dangerous waste onto land, into water or the atmosphere in violation of state stipulations, causing a major environmental pollution incident resulting in heavy loss of public or private property or grave consequences in terms of human casualties or personal injuries shall be sentenced to fixed-term imprisonment of up to three years or criminal detention, and may be fined concurrently or exclusively. In especially serious circumstances, the liable party shall be sentenced to fixed-term imprisonment of three to seven years and fined.
Illegal disposal of imported waste	Article 339(1): Those who dump, store or process solid waste from abroad in China in violation of state regulations shall be sentenced to fixed-term imprisonment of up to five years or criminal detention, and shall be fined. Those who cause serious environmental pollution and heavy loss of public or private property or serious threat to human health shall be sentenced to fixed-term imprisonment of five to ten years and fined. In especially serious circumstances, the liable party shall be sentenced to fixed-term imprisonment of more than ten years and fined.
Illegal import of solid waste	Article 339(2): Those who import solid waste as a raw material without state approval and cause a serious environmental pollution incident, leading to heavy loss of public or private property or serious threat to human health shall be sentenced to fixed-term imprisonment of up to five years or criminal detention and fined. In especially serious circumstances, the liable party shall be sentenced to fixed-term imprisonment of five to ten years and fined.
Waste smuggling	Article 339(3): Those who import solid waste described as raw material but which cannot be used as raw material are to be punished in accordance with the provisions of Article 155 of this Law. Article 155: The following shall be offences of smuggling and punished according to the relevant provisions under this Section: ...... (3) those who ship solid waste into China by evading customs supervision. Article 153: Those who commit a crime under Article 155 of this Law shall be fined an amount based on the amount of tax evaded by the smuggling.
Environmental dereliction of duty	Article 408: State personnel in charge of environmental protection and supervision, whose serious irresponsibility has resulted in serious consequences, including severe environmental pollution that causes heavy loss of public or private property or human casualties, shall be sentenced to fixed-term imprisonment of up to three years or criminal detention.

Sources: CL (1997).

mining and logging.[21] The crime of waste smuggling was amended by the CL Amendment IV (2002), and the crime of causing a serious environmental pollution incident was amended by the CL Amendment VIII (2011).

[21] CL (1997), arts. 340–5.

11.2.1 The Crime of Causing a Serious Pollution Incident

Yang Junwu (1998),[22] the first case successfully prosecuted for the crime of causing a serious pollution incident under the CL (1997), involved discharge of toxic wastewater from Yang Junwu's paper factory in Shanxi province in North China.[23] Arguably, both the factory, known as Tianma Paper Factory, and Yang should have been held criminally liable under the CL (1997), which provides that 'where a unit commits any of the crimes under articles 338 to 345, it shall be fined, and the persons who are directly in charge and others directly responsible for the offence shall be punished respectively'.[24] However, the prosecution did not pursue corporate criminal liability, which had only just been introduced by the CL (1997). Previously, under the CL (1979), only a natural person could bear criminal liability. In *Li Jian and Others* (2005), a more serious water pollution incident was caused by Sichuan Chemical Group at the Tuo River, and only key responsible persons were prosecuted.

Li Jian and Others (2005)

From February to April 2004, serious water pollution affected the Tuo River, resulting in the suspension of the water supply to one million people in five cities in Sichuan province. Industry had to stop operating, agriculture suffered heavy losses, and more than 15 million yuan of losses were caused to fisheries. Jinjiang District Procuratorate estimated the direct economic losses came to 219 million yuan, and prosecuted three individuals from Sichuan Chemical Group who had either been in charge or were responsible for the crime of causing a serious pollution incident. They were: Li Jian, general manager; Wu Guixin, deputy manager for production safety and environmental protection; and He Liguang, head of the environmental safety division.

Jinjiang District Court (2005) found that the chemical company had started trial operations without EPB approval. Technical problems at the plant had resulted in the toxic discharge of ammonia nitrogen (NH) at excessive levels of more than 1,000 mg/l (the national standard was 60 mg/l), the court said. The discharge had caused particularly serious pollution of the Tuo River, it said. All three defendants were convicted for the crime of causing a serious pollution incident under article 338 of the CL (1997) and sentenced: (i) Li was sentenced to imprisonment of three years with a three-year suspension and was fined 20,000 yuan; (ii) Wu was sentenced to four years' imprisonment and fined 30,000 yuan; (iii) He was sentenced to five years' imprisonment and fined 40,000 yuan. All defendants appealed.

Chengdu Intermediate Court (2005) dismissed the appeal and upheld the first-instance judgment.

Sichuan Chemical Group was not prosecuted for criminal liability under article 338 of the CL (1997), but only received an administrative penalty from Sichuan Provincial EPB in the form of a fine of 1 million yuan. It offered to pay 11 million yuan of compensation to victims of the Tuo River contamination.

[22] *Supreme People's Court Gazette*, 2 (1999). The judgment is available at www.pkulaw.cn. See Chapter 2 of this book for full details of the case.

[23] CL (1997), art. 346.

[24] *Li Jian and Others* (2005) is available at www.pkulaw.cn.

The CL (1997) made important progress on environmental crimes, but criminal prosecution, conviction and sanction of parties in violation was rare. From 1998 to 2006, fewer than ten cases concerning the crime of causing a serious pollution incident were concluded annually in China. The numbers are unreasonably low given the number of serious or grave environmental pollution incidents reported by official sources during the same period.[25] Obstacles, namely a lack of clearly defined criteria for prosecution and conviction, prevented the police, the procuratorates and the courts from putting article 338 to full use. To address this, the SPC issued the Interpretation on the Application of Law in Adjudicating Environmental Criminal Cases (SPC Interpretation on Environmental Crime) (2006).[26] It set specific threshold criteria for conviction and sentencing in order to guide adjudication and promote consistency among courts of different levels and in different geographical regions. 'Heavy loss of public or private property' is defined as:

(i) loss of public or private property amounting to more than 300,000 yuan;
(ii) loss of basic function of, or permanent destruction of, more than 5 *mu* of basic farmland, shelter forestland or special-purpose forestland or more than 10 *mu* of agricultural land, or more than 20 *mu* of other land or
(iii) death of 50 m^3 of forest or other woods, or more than 2,500 young trees.[27]

'Serious human casualties and serious impact on human health' refers to:

(i) one or more deaths, or serious injury to three or more persons, or slight injury to ten or more persons, or serious injury to one or more persons and slight injury to five or more persons;
(ii) occurrence or prevalence of infectious diseases, or poisoning that creates a Grade III public health incident under the State Emergency Response Plan to Public Health Incidents and causes serious harm to human health or
(iii) other circumstances.[28]

'Especially serious consequences' refers to:

(i) loss of public or private property amounting to more than 1 million yuan;
(ii) water source pollution and human evacuation that creates an environmental emergency of Grade II or worse under the State Emergency Response Plan to Environmental Incidents;
(iii) loss of basic function or permanent destruction of more than 15 *mu* of farmland, shelter forestland or special-purpose forestland, or more than 30 *mu* of agricultural land, or more than 60 *mu* of other land;
(iv) destruction of more than 150 m^3 of forests or other woods or more than 7,500 young trees;

[25] Yu Haisong, *Practice and Interpretation*, at 23.
[26] The SPC Interpretation on Environmental Crime (2006) was issued by the SPC on 21 July 2006 and came into force on 28 July 2006. It was repealed by the Interpretation on the Application of Laws in Adjudicating Environmental Criminal Cases (SPC and SPP Interpretation) (2013).
[27] SPC Interpretation on Environmental Crime (2006), art. 1.
[28] SPC Interpretation on Environmental Crime (2006), art. 2.

(v) three or more deaths, or serious injury of ten or more persons, or slight injury of thirty or more persons, or serious injury of three or more persons and slight injury of ten or more persons;
(vi) occurrence or prevalence of infectious disease that creates a public health incident of Grade II or worse under the State Emergency Response Plan to Public Health Incidents or
(vii) other circumstances.[29]

The calculation of 'loss of public or private property' includes both the actual value of the damage or loss of property directly resulting from pollution, as well as expenses incurred in taking the necessary measures to control and eliminate the pollution.[30]

The SPC Interpretation on Environmental Crime (2006) reemphasized that 'where a unit commits crimes under article 338 or article 339, it shall be convicted and sanctioned in accordance with both the CL and this Interpretation'.[31] From 2007 to 2012, more than ten cases involving the crime of causing a serious pollution incident were heard annually.[32] Due to the SPC Interpretation on Environmental Crime (2006), it has become common for courts to penalize both the legal person and the natural person in charge or directly responsible for the crimes committed by an entity, as in *Chengjiang Jinye Co. and Others* (2009).[33]

Chengjiang Jinye Co. and Others (2009)

From 2005 to 2008, Chengjiang Jinye Co. (Jinye) discharged untreated wastewater containing arsenic to a pond on its premises and dumped solid waste containing arsenic outside the factory without taking measures to prevent spreading or permeation of the toxic substances. In the rainy season, the wastewater overflowed from the pond, washed through the site and entered the YangZongHai Lake. The water quality of the lake dropped from Grade II to sub-Grade V and water supply to 26,000 people was suspended. The contamination caused direct loss of public and private property of more than 1 million yuan.

Chengjiang County Court (2009) found that the toxic discharge and disposal by Jinye had caused serious arsenic contamination of YangZongHai Lake. Both Jinye and individuals in charge or directly liable were convicted of the crime of causing a serious pollution incident. Jinye was fined 16 million yuan. Li Dahong, chairman of the board of directors, was sentenced to four years' imprisonment and fined 300,000 yuan. Li Yaohong, general manager, was sentenced to three years' imprisonment and fined 150,000 yuan. Jin Dadong, head of production, was sentenced to three years' imprisonment and fined 150,000 yuan. All defendants appealed.

Yuxi Intermediate Court (2009) dismissed the appeal and upheld the first-instance judgment.

In *Zijin Mining Group Ltd and Others* (2011),[34] the courts in Fujian province convicted and sanctioned both the legal person and individuals in charge or directly responsible for

29 SPC Interpretation on Environmental Crime (2006), art. 3.
30 SPC Interpretation on Environmental Crime (2006), art. 4.
31 SPC Interpretation on Environmental Crime (2006), art. 5.
32 Yu Haisong, *Practice and Interpretation*, at 24.
33 SPC Four Model Cases on Environmental Crimes (2013), case no. 2.
34 SPC Four Model Cases on Environmental Crimes (2013), case no. 1. See Chapter 6 of this book for details of the case.

the serious pollution of the Ting River. Zijin was fined 30 million yuan. Individuals directly in charge were penalized with both imprisonment and fines.

The SPC Interpretation on Environmental Crime (2006) promoted better use of criminal sanctions to punish and deter serious violations of law by corporate entities. It achieved this by introducing a unified approach to conviction and sentencing with quantitative threshold requirements.

11.2.2 Waste-Related Crimes

Article 339 of the CL (1997) provides for three waste-related crimes: (i) the crime of illegal disposal of imported waste;[35] (ii) the crime of illegal importing of waste;[36] and (iii) the crime of waste smuggling.[37] Before the CL (1997) came into force on 1 October 1997, waste smuggling had been prosecuted under the NPCSC's Supplementary Provisions on Punishing the Crime of Smuggling (1988).[38] *William Ping Chen* (1997)[39] is one such case.

William Ping Chen (1997)

From July to December 1995, Chen imported sixteen containers that were described as containing 'waste paper' and 'mixed paper' from the USA. He did not have an important permit for any of the containers, which were stopped by the Shanghai customs authority. In May 1996, Shanghai EPB and the Commodity Inspection Authority opened the containers and found municipal and medical waste, the import of which was banned. Chen was arrested in June 1996 and prosecuted by Shanghai No.1 Procuratorate for the crime of waste smuggling.

Shanghai No.1 Intermediate Court found that Chen had faked the consignees and filed false declarations to the customs authority to import 238 t of banned waste. It found that Chen had violated article 4(1)(i) of the NPCSC's Supplementary Provisions on Punishing the Crime of Smuggling (1988). Although Chen was a US citizen, he had committed the crime in China and was subject to the jurisdiction of Chinese law under article 3 of the CL (1997). Chen was convicted of the crime of waste smuggling, sentenced to ten years' imprisonment, fined 500,000 yuan and expelled from China. Chen appealed.

Shanghai High Court dismissed the appeal and upheld the first-instance judgment, which was supported by clear facts, sufficient evidence, correct application of law, proper sentencing and a lawful adjudication procedure.

Under the CL (1997), anyone transporting solid waste into the territory of China from abroad by evading customs supervision has committed the crime of smuggling.[40] The crime of waste smuggling was sanctioned by reference to the total amount of evaded customs duties. Where the amount was more than 500,000 yuan, the liable party was sentenced to

[35] CL (1997), art. 339(1). [36] CL (1997), art. 339(2).

[37] CL (1997), art. 339(3). It was amended by the CL Amendment IV (2002).

[38] The Supplementary Provisions on Punishing the Crime of Smuggling were issued by the NPCSC on 21 January 1988 with immediate effect. It was repealed on 1 October 1997 when the CL (1997) came into force.

[39] *Supreme People's Court Gazette*, 1 (1997). The judgment is available at www.pkulaw.cn.

[40] CL (1997), art. 155(3).

imprisonment of more than ten years or life imprisonment and fined one to five times the amount of the evaded customs duties or ordered confiscation of property.[41] In the case of *Wu Shengli* (2000),[42] the offender was prosecuted and convicted under article 155(3) of the CL (1997).

Wu Shengli (2000)

On 29 August 1999, Wu Shengli arrived at Hong Kong's Yau Ma Tei ferry terminal in a boat, the *Jinhua 268*, to collect used electrical appliances. On 15 September 1999, once the *Jinhua 268* had re-entered Guangdong province, it was stopped by the Huidong county border-check team. A total of 31 t of used electrical appliances were found on the boat, including 220 televisions with 29-inch screens, 704 televisions with 25-inch screens, 540 televisions with 14-inch screens, 728 video recorders and 30 radios and cassette recorders. The total evaded duties amounted to 534,093 yuan. Wu was prosecuted by Huizhou City Procuratorate for the crime of waste smuggling.

Huizhou Intermediate Court (2000) held that Wu had, in violation of law, evaded customs supervision to transport solid waste into the territory of China. The court convicted Wu for the crime of waste smuggling under article 155(3) of the CL (1997), sentencing him to ten years' imprisonment and fining him 540,000 yuan. The e-waste and the *Jinhua 268* were confiscated.

While Wu Shengli was penalized for smuggling e-waste into China, it has proven difficult to assess the amount of evaded customs duties on waste that is banned from being imported. This problem was resolved by the CL Amendment IV (2002).

11.2.3 The Crime of Environmental Dereliction of Duty

Many serious pollution incidents have resulted from agency failure in environmental enforcement. While there are deep-rooted systemic and institutional reasons for weak enforcement and lack of capacity of local EPBs, some administrative omission does involve misconduct and violation by EPB officers. The serious contamination of the Ting River by Zijin Co. in Fujian province in 2010 is only the tip of the iceberg of widespread dereliction of duty in environmental supervision and enforcement. Some EPB officers not only fail to perform their statutory duties, but also accept bribes from enterprises in exchange for favours and privileges.

Under article 408 of CL (1997), a procuratorate may investigate and prosecute state personnel where serious pollution incidents have caused heavy loss of public or private property or human casualties. More specific rules were provided by the SPP in its Provisions on Standards for Accepting Cases Involving the Crimes of Dereliction of Duties and Infringement of Rights (SPP Provisions) (2006).[43] On the crime of environmental dereliction of duty, it provides that a procuratorate must investigate for prosecution if the pollution incident has caused any of the following:[44]

[41] CL (1997), art. 153(1). [42] *Wu Shengli* (2000). The judgment is available at www.pkulaw.cn.

[43] The SPP Provisions (2006) were issued by the SPP on 26 July 2006 and came into force immediately.

[44] SPP Provisions (2006), art. 19.

(i) one or more death, or serious injury of three or more, or serious injury of two and slight injury of four or more, or serious injury of one and slight injury of seven or more, or slight injury of ten or more;
(ii) serious poisoning of thirty or more;
(iii) direct loss of private property of 150,000 yuan or more, or both direct loss of less than 150,000 yuan and indirect loss of more than 750,000 yuan;
(iv) direct loss of public property or property of legal persons or other organizations of 300,000 yuan or more, or both direct loss of less than 300,000 yuan and indirect loss of more than 1.5 million yuan;
(v) combined direct loss of (iii) and (iv) of more than 300,000 yuan, or combined indirect loss of (iii) and (iv) of more than 1.5 million yuan;
(vi) serious destruction of basic farmland, protection forestland or special-use forestland of 10 *mu* or more, or arable land other than basic farmland of 50 *mu* or more, or any other land of 70 *mu* or more;
(vii) serious pollution of surface water or groundwater serving as sources of drinking water supply;
(viii) serious loss of public or private property or human casualties in any other circumstances.

The serious water pollution of the Tuo River in Sichuan and the Ting River in Fujian led to the prosecution of local EPB officers for the crime of environmental dereliction of duty. They were convicted and sanctioned for their failure to perform environmental monitoring, inspection and enforcement. *Song Shiying and Others* (2005)[45] was tried after the serious water pollution incident at the Tuo River in 2004.

Song Shiying and Others (2005)

In the aftermath of the contamination of the Tuo River, Jinjiang District Procuratorate prosecuted, in December 2004, three EPB officers for committing the crime of environmental dereliction of duty. Song Shiying was deputy head of QingBaiJiang District EPB and was in charge of environmental monitoring, inspection and pollution control. He had failed to act when informed on 23 February 2004 by a wastewater treatment plant of the high level of ammonia (NH_3) in the water. On receiving the monitoring data on 27 February, Song assigned staff to carry out monitoring and inspection at Sichuan Chemical Group. However, he failed to follow up and report to the head of the EPB on the monitoring data and inspection results. Zhang Ming, head of QingBaiJiang District Environmental Monitoring Station, had been assigned the task of monitoring on 27 February, and instructed his staff to collect monitoring data. He received the written monitoring report on 1 March, but did not immediately report to the head of the QingBaiJiang District EPB. Zhang Shan, director of QingBaiJiang District Environmental Inspection Centre, was assigned the task of investigation and on-site inspection on 27 February, but did not inspect the site until 1 March. Chengdu Intermediate Court assigned the case to Jinjiang District Court.

[45] *Song Shiying and Others* (2005). The judgment is available at www.pkulaw.cn.

Jinjiang District Court (2005) found that all three defendants failed to perform their statutory duties of environmental supervision and enforcement. Their seriously irresponsible behaviour failed to mitigate the pollution incident in an effective and timely manner, causing heavy losses to public and private property. The defendants were convicted under article 408 of CL (1997) for the crime of environmental dereliction of duty and sentenced accordingly: (i) Song was sentenced to imprisonment of two years and six months; (ii) Zhang Ming was sentenced to imprisonment of two years and six months and (iii) Zhang Shan was sentenced to imprisonment of one year and six months, with two years' suspension.

The serious water pollution incident caused by Zijin Co. in Fujian province in the summer of 2010 also led to the criminal prosecution and conviction of EPB officers in the case of *Chen Jun'an and Lan Yong* (2011).[46]

Chen Jun'an and Lan Yong (2011)

From January 2004 to July 2010, Chen Jun'an, head of Shanghang County EPB, and Lan Yong, deputy head of the same EPB, failed to perform their statutory duties of environmental supervision and enforcement. Their irresponsibility resulted in their failure to prevent the illegal acts of Zijin Co.

Wuping County Court (2011) convicted Chen for the crimes of corruption, accepting a bribe, environmental dereliction of duty and misappropriation of state assets. Chen was sentenced to imprisonment of nineteen years and six months, fined 10,000 yuan and his private property of 160,000 yuan and all illegal gains were confiscated. Lan was convicted for the crimes of corruption, accepting a bribe and environmental dereliction of duty. He was sentenced to nine years' imprisonment and his private property of 10,000 yuan and all illegal gains were confiscated. The defendants appealed.

Longyan Intermediate Court (2011) dismissed the appeal and upheld the first-instance judgment.

It should be noted that the scope of application of article 408 goes beyond civil servants or agency officers as strictly defined. The NPCSC's Interpretation on the Subject for the Crime of Dereliction of Duty (2002) provides that the following categories of persons may be criminally liable for the crime of dereliction of duty under the CL (1997) when they exercise power on behalf of the state: (i) any person who performs a public service in an organization that exercises state administrative power according to laws and regulations; (ii) any person who performs a public service in an organization that is entrusted by a state organ to exercise the power on its behalf and (iii) any person who is not formally classed as state personnel, but performs a public service within a state organ. In *Cui Jianguo* (2010),[47] an employee of the state institution was convicted and sanctioned for the crime of environmental dereliction of duty under article 408.

46 SPP 15 Model Cases on Crimes against the Ecological Environment (2014), case no. 10.
47 SPP 2nd Batch of Guiding Cases (2012), case no. 4.

Cui Jianguo (2010)

Cui Jianguo was head of team number two of the environmental supervision division of the Yancheng city government. Biaoxin Chemical Co. (Biaoxin) was a key polluting unit in Yancheng. It directly discharged untreated toxic wastewater into a river, upstream of several points from which water companies collected drinking water. While conducting an on-site inspection, Cui had observed many times that untreated wastewater was being discharged directly into the river, but he did not report this to the head of the environmental supervision division. A local campaign to check key chemical companies took place in December 2008, but even at this point Cui did not organize inspection and monitoring of Biaoxin. On 18 February 2009, Cui paid a routine visit to the company and completed an on-site inspection record without actually checking the operations. In the same month, serious toxic contamination of the river caused water supplies to be suspended for more than 66 hours, affecting 200,000 residents. Direct economic losses reached 5.43 million yuan. From 2006 to 2008, Cui had accepted a total of 7,800 yuan from Hu Wenbiao, the legal representative of Biaoxin.

Funing County Court (2009) found that Cui was seriously irresponsible in performing his duty of environmental inspection and supervision. He was convicted of the crime of environmental dereliction of duty under article 408 of the CL (1997) and sentenced to two years' imprisonment. Cui appealed, claiming that his role was inspection only, not supervision or enforcement.

Yancheng Intermediate Court (2010) dismissed the appeal. It further clarified that Cui, as an employee of a state institution to which the state had delegated the power of environmental supervision, could be held criminally liable under article 408 of CL (1997). In accordance with the NPCSC's Interpretation on the Subject for the Crime of Dereliction of Duty (2002), Cui was held criminally liable for environmental dereliction of duty.

It remains common practice for local EPBs to entrust the power of environmental inspection and supervision to state institutions, such as the environmental supervision team in the *Cui Jianguo* case. In 2012, the SPP issued the case as a guiding case due to its significance in clarifying the application of criminal liability for environmental dereliction of duty to Cui, who was not a state employee of the EPB, but only an employee of the environmental supervision team. By reference to the NPCSC's 2002 interpretation, Yancheng Intermediate Court held Cui liable under article 408 of the CL (1997), as he had been entrusted by the local EPB to exercise the power of inspection and supervision on behalf of the state.

11.3 CL AMENDMENT IV (2002): THE CRIME OF WASTE SMUGGLING

Prior to the CL Amendment IV (2002), the sanctioning of an offender convicted under article 339(3) and article 155 of CL (1997) for the crime of waste smuggling was calculated by reference to the total amount of evaded customs duties. However, waste is different to goods. It was nearly impossible to calculate the amount of evaded customs duties on waste that was imported in contravention of rules prohibiting or restricting such imports. This problem was addressed by the CL Amendment IV (2002).[48] Article 339(3) of the CL was

[48] CL Amendment IV (2002).

revised to provide that anyone importing solid waste that cannot be used as a raw material, or waste in the state of liquid or gas that cannot be used as raw materials will be convicted and punished under article 152 (2) and (3).[49] Article 155(3) of the CL (1997) was removed and article 152 was amended as follows:

> (2) Anyone transporting solid waste or waste in the state of liquid or gas into China by evading supervision and control of customs authorities is liable to fixed-term imprisonment of up to five years and/or a fine where circumstances are serious; where circumstances are especially serious, the liable party shall be sentenced to fixed-term imprisonment of more than five years and fined.[50]
>
> (3) Where an entity commits the above crime, it shall be fined. Individuals directly in charge or others directly liable shall be sanctioned as above.[51]

In 2006, the SPC further clarified the application of law in smuggling cases.[52] In relation to article 152(2), it defines 'serious circumstances' and 'especially serious circumstances' by reference to the quantity of waste, its nature and the harmful consequences.

> Article 6: Anyone who, by evading customs control, smuggles any waste that is banned by the State from being imported, or the imports of which are restricted by the State, shall be convicted of waste smuggling and sentenced to imprisonment of up to five years and/or fined if the circumstances fall into one of the following categories, which are treated as 'serious circumstances' under article 152(2) of the Criminal Law:
>
> (1) the smuggling of 1 to 5 tonnes of hazardous waste that is prohibited from being imported;
>
> (2) the smuggling of 5 to 25 tonnes of non-hazardous waste that is prohibited from being imported;
>
> (3) the smuggling, without a permit, of 20 to 100 tonnes of waste restricted by the State only for use as raw material or
>
> (4) the smuggling of any waste that is prohibited from being imported and that causes a serious pollution incident.[53]
>
> Article 7: Any one of the following circumstances shall be treated as 'especially serious' under article 152(2) of the Criminal Law, and the liable party shall be sentenced to imprisonment of five years or more and fined concurrently:
>
> (1) the quantity of smuggled waste exceeds the quantitative range prescribed in article 6;
>
> (2) the quantity reaches the quantitative range prescribed in article 6 and a serious pollution incident has been caused or

[49] CL (2002), art. 339(3). [50] CL (2002), art. 152(2) [51] CL (2002), art. 152(3).

[52] The SPC Interpretation on the Application of Law in Smuggling Cases (II) (2006) was repealed by the SPC and SPP Interpretation on the Application of Law in Smuggling Cases (SPC and SPP Interpretation on Smuggling) (2014).

[53] SPC Interpretation on the Application of Law in Smuggling Cases (II) (2006), art. 6.

(3) the quantity does not reach the quantitative range prescribed in article 6, but a serious pollution incident has been caused with especially serious consequences.[54]

The CL Amendment IV (2002) and the SPC Interpretation on the Application of Law in Smuggling Cases (II) (2006) have made it easier to prosecute and convict liable parties for the crime of waste smuggling. First, the concept of 'waste' has been broadened from 'solid waste' to include 'waste in the state of liquid or gas' to punish and deter the smuggling of all forms of waste into China. Second, it is expressly stated that the crime of waste smuggling can be committed by both entities (legal persons) and individuals (natural persons) to address the increasingly serious trend of corporate crimes. Third, criminal sanction is imposed based on the quantity, nature and actual or potential harm of the smuggled waste, not on the amount of evaded customs duties, as is usually applied in smuggling cases. In *Geng Yuping and Another* (2013),[55] both the person in charge and the company were prosecuted and convicted for the crime of waste smuggling.

Geng Yuping and Another (2013)

From October to December 2011, Geng Yuping, who ran Hepu Trading Co. (Hepu), had falsified customs declarations, stating that she was importing 'wastepaper Euro no. 6', for which there was no need to apply for an import permit in advance. In fact, the thirty containers she imported held more than 656 t of a variety of waste: unsorted 'wastepaper A2', which was subject to permit control, as well as second-hand clothes, waste plastics and nappies, among others, which were prohibited from being imported. Both Geng and Hepu were prosecuted for the crime of waste smuggling.

Suzhou Intermediate Court (2012) convicted both defendants of the crime of waste smuggling, the circumstances of which were especially serious, as defined by article 152(2) and (3) of the CL (2002), and articles 6 and 7 of the SPC Interpretation on Environmental Crime (2006). Hepu was fined 800,000 yuan. Geng was sentenced to six and a half years' imprisonment and fined 30,000 yuan. Geng appealed, claiming, in the hope of a more lenient sentence, that she did not know that municipal waste was mixed in with the 'wastepaper A2' , and that no environmental harm had been caused.

Jiangsu High Court (2013) dismissed Geng's appeal. It held that Geng knew that 'wastepaper A2' was subject to import restrictions and required an import permit. Hepu had no permit and Geng had falsified the declarations to evade supervision by customs. Whether Geng knew that 'wastepaper A2' was mixed with municipal waste was irrelevant, the court said. Actual environmental harm is not required if the quantity of smuggled waste reaches the prescribed range, it said. Under articles 6 and 7 of the SPC Interpretation on Environmental Crime (2006), smuggling more than 25 t of waste, the importing of which is prohibited, constitutes 'especially serious circumstances'.

[54] SPC Interpretation on the Application of Law in Smuggling Cases (II) (2006), art. 7.

[55] *Geng Yuping and Another* (2013). The judgment is available at www.pkulaw.cn.

TABLE 11.3 THE CRIME OF WASTE SMUGGLING

'serious circumstances'	'especially serious circumstances'
• Smuggling HW, the importing of which is prohibited: 1 t to 5 t; • Smuggling non-hazardous waste, the importing of which is prohibited: 5 t to 25 t; • Without permit, smuggling waste restricted by the state for use as raw material: 20 t to 100 t; • Smuggling any waste below the threshold if it is carried out: o by a criminal gang, o using special-purpose vehicles, or o causing serious pollution.	• quantity of smuggled waste exceeds quantitative range prescribed under 'serious circumstances', or • quantity reaches threshold and committed by a criminal gang, or by special vehicle or causing serious pollution incident, or • quantity does not reach threshold but a serious pollution incident is caused and consequences are especially serious.

Sources: SPC and SPP Interpretation on Smuggling (2014), art. 14.

The SPC Interpretation on Environmental Crime (2006) was repealed by the SPC and SPP Interpretation on Smuggling (2014).[56] The latter combines articles 6 and 7 of the SPC Interpretation on Environmental Crime (2006) into one article to define 'serious circumstances' and 'especially serious circumstances'.

In contrast to the prosecution and conviction of waste smuggling cases under article 339 (3), article 339 (1) and (2) are rarely used. Article 339(1) concerns on the illegal dumping, deposit or disposal of imported solid waste. The waste may have been lawfully imported for recovery or may have been smuggled into China. The party committing the crime may be the importer or smuggler or anyone who has bought the imported waste. Article 339(2) provides for the crime of illegal importing of solid waste, aiming to punish those who import solid waste of a restricted type without prior approval. However, to prosecute and convict anyone under article 339(2), there must be proof of heavy loss of public or private property or serious harm to human health. In practice, anyone who intends to import restricted solid waste without approval almost always does it by smuggling, instead of declaring it honestly to the customs authority. To prosecute or convict for the crime of waste smuggling does not require proof of actual harm and is thus always preferred by the law enforcement authorities and the courts, rendering article 339(2) useless in a practical sense.

11.4 CL AMENDMENT VIII (2011): THE CRIME OF ENVIRONMENTAL POLLUTION

Though a few high-profile cases were prosecuted and convicted under article 338 of the CL (1997),[57] the article was seldom used to impose criminal sanctions on liable parties

[56] The SPC and SPP Interpretation on Smuggling was issued by the SPC and SPP on 12 August 2014. It came into force on 10 September 2014.

[57] Examples are *Yang Junwu* (1998), *Li Jian and Others* (2005), *Chengjiang Jinye Co. and Others* (2009) and *Zijin Mining Group Ltd and Others* (2011), which are discussed in Section 11.2.1.

causing serious pollution in China in the fourteen years prior to the 2011 amendment. One of the reasons was the high threshold requirement for prosecution and conviction, i.e., proof of actual harm caused by pollution in the form of heavy loss of public or private property, or human casualties. To address the problem, article 338 was revised in 2011:

> Whoever, in violation of law, discharges, dumps or disposes of radioactive waste, waste containing pathogens of infectious disease, toxic substances or other hazardous substances and causes serious environmental pollution shall be sentenced to imprisonment of up to three years or criminal detention, and/or fined; if the consequences are especially serious, that person shall be sentenced to imprisonment of three to seven years and fined.[58]

The most significant change was the removal of the requirement of 'serious environmental pollution incidents causing heavy loss of public or private property or human casualties', which means the prosecution no longer needs to prove actual harm of 'heavy property loss' or 'human casualty'. The scope of application of article 338 was expanded to cover acts that by nature are likely to cause serious pollution and harm to both the environment and human health. In addition, 'other hazardous waste' is replaced by 'other hazardous substances' so that the subject of the discharge, dumping or disposal is not restricted to HW contained in the National Catalogue of Hazardous Waste (HW Catalogue).[59]

The SPC and SPP soon issued the Interpretation on Several Issues Concerning the Application of Law in Environmental Criminal Cases (SPC and SPP Interpretation on Environmental Crime) (2013),[60] which defines the act 'causing serious environmental pollution' by listing:[61]

(1) discharge, dumping or disposal of radioactive waste, waste containing infectious disease pathogens, or toxic substances in Grade I drinking-water-source reserves and the core area of nature reserves;
(2) illegal discharge, dumping or disposal of three tonnes or more of hazardous waste;
(3) illegal emission/discharge of pollutants containing heavy metals, persistent organic pollutants and other pollutions that seriously harm the environment and damage human health, which exceed national or local emission/discharge standards by three times;
(4) discharge, dumping or disposal of radioactive waste, waste containing infectious disease pathogens, or toxic substances by setting up hidden pipes or making use of seepage wells, seepage pits, crevices or karst caves;

[58] The CL Amendment VIII (2011) came into force on 1 May 2011.
[59] The HW Catalogue (2016) was issued by the MEP, National Development and Reform Commission (NDRC) and the Ministry of Public Security (MPS) on 14 June 2016. It came into force on 1 August 2016. It replaced the previous HW Catalogue (2008), which had repealed the HW Catalogue (1998). The Catalogue is revised and updated to accommodate the changing needs of protection of the environment and public health, and is updated as knowledge and science develop.
[60] The SPC and SPP Interpretation on Environmental Crime (2013) was issued by the SPC and SPP on 17 June 2013. It came into force on 19 June 2013 and was repealed by the SPC and SPP Interpretation on Environmental Crime (2016).
[61] SPC and SPP Interpretation (2013), art. 1.

(5) illegal discharge, dumping or disposal of radioactive waste, waste containing infectious disease pathogens or toxic substances for a third time within two years, with the previous two violations sanctioned by administrative penalty;
(6) more than 12 hours of interruption of centralized water supply from the drinking-water-source reserve at or above the township level;
(7) loss of fundamental function or permanent destruction of more than five *mu* of basic farmland, protection forestland or special-purpose forestland, or more than ten *mu* of other farmland, or more than 20 *mu* of other land;
(8) death of more than 50 m^3 of forests or other woods, or more than 2,500 saplings;
(9) loss of public or private property of more than 300,000 yuan;
(10) evacuation or relocation of more than 5,000 people;
(11) poisoning of more than 30 people;
(12) minor injury, minor disability or general dysfunction resulting from organ or tissue damage of over three persons;
(13) serious injury, moderate disability or serious dysfunction resulting from organ or tissue damage of one or more person;
(14) other circumstances that cause serious environmental pollution.

While items (6) to (13) focus on the consequences of heavy loss of public or private property and human casualties, items (1) to (5) are act-based and do not require proof of actual harm. They are the acts likely to cause pollution and harm to human health and safety.

The SPC and SPP Interpretation on Environmental Crime (2013) further defines 'especially serious consequences' as meeting one of the following criteria:[62]

(1) more than 12 hours of interruption to the centralized water supply from the drinking-water-source reserve in urban areas at or above the county level;
(2) loss of fundamental function or permanent destruction of more than 15 *mu* of basic farmland, protection forestland or special-purpose forestland, or more than 30 *mu* of other farmland, or more than 60 *mu* of other land;
(3) death of more than 150 m^3 of forests or other woods, or more than 7500 saplings;
(4) loss of public or private property of more than one million yuan;
(5) evacuation or relocation of more than 15,000 people;
(6) poisoning of more than 100 persons;
(7) minor injury, minor disability or general dysfunction resulting from organ or tissue damage of over ten persons;
(8) serious injury, moderate disability or serious dysfunction resulting from organ or tissue damage of over three persons;
(9) serious injury, moderate disability or serious dysfunction resulting from organ or tissue damage of over one person, and minor injury, minor disability or general dysfunction resulting from organ or tissue damage of over five persons;
(10) death or severe disability of one or more person;
(11) other circumstances with any especially serious consequences.

[62] SPC and SPP Interpretation (2013), art. 3.

The CL Amendment VIII (2011) and the SPC and SPP Interpretation on Environmental Crime (2013) have had a significant impact on criminal prosecutions under article 338 of the CL (2011). Prior to the SPC Interpretation on Environmental Crime (2006), fewer than ten criminal cases were concluded each year, against a backdrop of hundreds of pollution incidents reported each year from 2001 to 2006. From 2007 to 2012, approximately twenty criminal cases were concluded annually. This increased to 104 in 2013, 988 in 2014 and 1,691 in 2015.[63] The substantial increase in the number of criminal prosecutions and sanctions under article 338 is attributed to the SPC and SPP Interpretation on Environmental Crime (2013) that expressly provided for conviction based on acts, not only consequences. Article 338 has become a useful tool with which to punish and deter illegal discharge of toxic wastewater, illegal disposal of HW and illegal emission of toxic air pollutants, because prosecution and conviction are based on the nature and quantity of the waste, wastewater or air pollutants involved, the severity of the violation, the location of discharge or disposal, the means of discharge and previous convictions. In addition, measures were taken to improve transfer of cases from EPBs to PSBs so as to ensure potentially criminally liable parties are actually investigated, prosecuted and sanctioned.[64] In 2014, the number of cases transferred by EPBs to PSBs reached 2,080, twice the total number of cases transferred over the previous ten years.[65]

In *Liu Zuqing* (2016),[66] the courts in Fujian province convicted Liu for discharging wastewater containing heavy metals that seriously exceeded national standards.

Liu Zuqing (2016)

Since October 2013, Liu Zuqing had operated a factory processing shoe moulds. He had not conducted an EIA and had not installed any pollution-control facilities. The wastewater was discharged without treatment. Monitoring data showed that the concentration levels of nickel, chromium, copper and zinc were 23,199, 4.76, 35 and 25.4 times respectively of the relevant national discharge standards.

Jinjiang City Court (2016) found Liu had, in violation of law, discharged wastewater containing the heavy metals nickel, chromium, copper and zinc at levels more than three times over national discharge standards. Liu was convicted of the crime of environmental pollution. He was sentenced to imprisonment of two years and eight months and fined 50,000 yuan under article 338 of the CL

[63] Yu Haisong, *Practice and Interpretation*, at 28–9.

[64] The MEP and PBS issued the Opinion on Improving Enforcement Coordination between Environmental Protection Bureaus and Public Security Bureaus on 4 November 2013. The MPS, MEP, Ministry of Industry and Information Technology (MIIT), and the State Administration for Quality Supervision, Inspection and Quarantine (SAQSIQ) issued the Provisional Measures on the Transfer of Environmental Violation Cases for Administrative Detention by Administrative Agencies in Charge on 24 December 2014. It came into force on 1 January 2015. For more discussion on case transfer and effective enforcement, see Yuhong Zhao, 'Innovative measures'.

[65] Yu Haisong, *Practice and Interpretation*, at 28–9.

[66] SPC Eight Model Cases on Environmental Crimes (2016), case no. 1.

(2011) and under the SPC and SPP Interpretation on Environmental Crime (2013). The defendant appealed.

Quanzhou Intermediate Court (2016) dismissed the appeal and upheld the first-instance judgment which, it said, was made on clear facts, solid evidence and lawful procedure, with proper sentencing.

In *Bai Jialin and Wu Shuqin* (2016),[67] both the HW operator and generator were convicted of the crime of environmental pollution. Wu sold 50.5 t of HW to Bai Jialin, who did not have an HW operation permit.

Bai Jialin and Wu Shuqin (2016)

From October 2014 to April 2015, Bai Jialin, who did not have an HW operation permit, purchased 50.5 t of discarded barrels tainted with mineral oil, paint and organic solvent from Wu Shuqin. Bai employed workers to rinse the barrels before reselling them. The dirty water was released onto the ground and into the sewage system. According to the HW Catalogue, mineral oil was classed as HW, and discarded packaging or containers containing or tainted with HW should also be treated as HW.

Yubei District Court (2016) found that Bai, in violation of state provisions, had illegally disposed of more than 3 t of HW causing serious environmental pollution. Wu had known that Bai did not have an HW operation permit, but nonetheless provided HW to Bai for disposal, the court said, and Wu had jointly committed the crime of environmental pollution. As Wu was a first-time offender and had confessed, the court decided to convict both of the crime of environmental pollution, but with a more lenient sentence for Wu. Bai was sentenced to imprisonment of one year eight months and fined 150,000 yuan. Wu was sentenced to one year's imprisonment with a two-year suspension and was fined 80,000 yuan. Bai appealed, but subsequently applied to withdraw his appeal.

Chongqing No.1 Intermediate Court (2016) approved Bai's application to withdraw.

In *Zhejiang Huidelong Dye Chemical Co. Ltd. and Others* (2014),[68] all defendants were convicted and sanctioned under article 338 of the CL (2011) with reference to the amount of HW disposed of. There was no need to prove actual harm in the form of heavy loss of public or private property or human casualties. Under the SPC and SPP Interpretation on Environmental Crime (2013), the act of 'illegal discharge, dumping or disposal of hazardous waste of more than three tonnes' meets the threshold requirement for conviction of the crime of environmental pollution.[69]

[67] SPC Eight Model Cases on Environmental Crimes (2016), case no. 7.

[68] SPC Eight Model Cases on Environmental Crimes (2016), case no. 3.

[69] SPC and SPP Interpretation (2013), art. 1. Article 3 of the revised SPC and SPP Interpretation (2016) further provides that 'the act of illegal discharge, dumping or disposal of hazardous waste of more than 100 tonnes' meets the threshold requirement for 'especially grave circumstances' carrying the sentence of three to seven years' imprisonment.

Zhejiang Huidelong Dye Chemical Co. Ltd. and Others (2014)

Zhejiang Huidelong Dye Chemical Co. Ltd. (Huidelong) was a chemical enterprise generating toxic and hazardous wastewater. Yan Haixing was the owner of Huidelong and Pan Defeng was the general manager. From July to August 2012, Yan and Pan sent more than 5,000 t of hazardous wastewater to Tengda Dye Ltd for secret discharge through hidden pipes to the sewage system. From October 2012, Pan passed the hazardous wastewater to Ru Jianguo, who did not have an HW operation permit, for disposal at a price of 50–80 yuan/t. Yan knew of the arrangement and consented to it. Ru, assisted by others, discharged more than 18,000 t of hazardous wastewater to Hangzhou Bay, near the Shangyu Industrial Park.

Shangyu District Court (2014) found that Huidelong had collaborated with Ru and others to discharge, dump and dispose of hazardous substances, causing serious environmental pollution with especially serious consequences. They were convicted for jointly committing the crime of environmental pollution. The court considered the defendants' confessions, the fact that illegal gains had been returned and that wastewater disposal fees had subsequently been paid. Huidelong was fined 20 million yuan, while Yan was sentenced to four and a half years' imprisonment and fined 1 million yuan. Pan and Ru were each sentenced to four years' imprisonment and fined 300,000 yuan, and other individuals were also sanctioned. The defendants appealed.

Shaoxing Intermediate Court (2014) dismissed the appeal and upheld the first-instance judgment.

In *Jiantao (Hebei) Coking Co. Ltd. and Others* (2015),[70] both the company and individuals in charge and directly responsible were convicted of the crime of environmental pollution under article 338 of the CL (2011) for illegal emission of toxic air pollutants causing serious pollution.

Jiantao (Hebei) Coking Co. Ltd. and Others (2015)

In March 2014, the wastewater treatment facility at Jiantao (Hebei) Coking Co. Ltd. (Jiantao) malfunctioned and did not treat NH_3 in the wastewater produced by the plant. Instead of fixing the treatment facility, Wang Chengwu, the general manager, and Zhang Jianfu, manager of the public works division, together with others, instructed the workers to use the wastewater containing NH_3 in the coke-quenching tower, causing untreated volatile phenol to be directly emitted into the air. This resulted in serious air pollution. The volatile phenol in the water used for the coke-quenching tower is a toxic and hazardous substance and was 137 times over national standards.

Qiaodong District Court (2015) found that Jiantao had, in violation of law, emitted toxic air pollutants that seriously endangered the environment and human health. Jiantao was convicted of the crime of environmental pollution and individuals in charge and those directly responsible were also found to bear criminal liabilities. However, since Jiantao had invested substantially in an upgrade of its equipment in the aftermath, a more lenient sanction was imposed. Jiantao was fined 2.45 million yuan. Zhang was sentenced to one year's imprisonment and fined 50,000 yuan. Wang was sentenced to six months' imprisonment with a one-year suspension and was fined 20,000 yuan. Others were also sanctioned accordingly.

[70] SPC Eight Model Cases on Environmental Crimes (2016), case no. 6.

The SPC and SPP Interpretation on Environmental Crime (2013) has effectively made criminal sanction an additional tool for punishing serious environmental violations. From July 2013 to October 2016, a total of 4,636 cases of environmental crime were accepted by China's courts and 4,250 cases were concluded during the same period. Prior to 2013, the annual caseload of environmental crimes averaged twenty to thirty.[71] The substantial increase in the number of environmental criminal cases prosecuted and resulting in a conviction has revealed the new problem of inconsistency in conviction and sentencing of the crime of environmental pollution. In response, the SPC and SPP issued the SPC and SPP Interpretation on Environmental Crime (2016).[72] It addresses issues relating to the crime of environmental pollution and focuses on disposal of HW and discharge of heavy metals, crimes relating to EIA and environmental monitoring, among others. For the crime of environmental pollution, the SPC and SPP Interpretation on Environmental Crime (2016) further elaborates the definition of 'serious environmental pollution' to include: the discharge, dumping or disposal of pollutants containing lead, mercury, cadmium, chromium, arsenic, thallium or antimony at a level over three times the national or local standard; the discharge, dumping or disposal of pollutants containing nickel, copper, zinc, silver, vanadium, manganese or cobalt at a level over ten times the national or local standard; key polluting units tampering with or forging automatic monitoring data or disrupting an automatic monitoring facility, and discharging without monitoring, pollutants including chemical oxygen demand (COD), NH, sulphur dioxide (SO_2) and nitric oxide; illegally reducing the operation cost of pollution treatment facilities by more than 1 million yuan; illegal gains of more than 300,000 yuan; and serious damage to the ecological environment.[73] In the case of 'especially serious consequences', two new items are included: the illegal discharge, dumping or disposal of more than 100 t of HW; and especially serious damage to the ecological environment.[74]

11.5 KEY ISSUES OF ENVIRONMENTAL CRIMINAL LAW

This section addresses key issues of general importance to environmental criminal law, including liable parties, fault-based liability, defences, multiple parties jointly committing crimes and sanctions.

11.5.1 Liable Parties: Natural Persons and Units

The CL (1979) followed the civil law tradition of imposing criminal liability on natural persons only.[75] Criminal sanctions for serious environmental violations were imposed on individuals such as factory workers, fly-tipping truck drivers, company managers or government officers. The economic take-off and industrialization of the 1980s and 1990s

[71] Zhou Jiahai and Yu Haisong, 'Understanding and applying the judicial Interpretation on the Application of Law in Environmental Criminal Cases', *People's Adjudication (Application)*, 4 (2017), 23–9.

[72] The SPC and SPP Interpretation (2016) was issued by the SPC and SPP on 23 December 2016. It came into force on 1 January 2017 and repealed the SPC and SPP Interpretation (2013).

[73] SPC and SPP Interpretation (2016), art. 1.

[74] SPC and SPP Interpretation (2016), art. 3.

[75] Tingmei Fu, 'Legal person in China: essence and limits', *American Journal of Comparative Law*, 41 (1993), 261–97.

revealed that corporate entities were causing harm to the environment that resulted in loss of public or private property, and in human casualties, on a much larger scale and with greater severity. Criminal sanction of individuals only does not deter heavily polluting enterprises from violating the law in their pursuit of economic gain.

Significant progress was made by the CL (1997) to establish the criminal liability of units.[76] It was hoped that the prosecution of corporate offenders and the associated negative publicity would effectively deter enterprises that care about their reputation from violating the law. The CL (1997) provided that 'where a company, enterprise, institution, government body, or organization commits an act endangering society that is considered a crime committed by a unit under the law, it shall bear criminal liability'.[77] A unit liable for a criminal offence is to be fined. Any person in charge or other person directly responsible also bears relevant criminal liability.[78] Thus, where a provision specifies criminal liability of a unit, both the entity and individuals in charge or directly responsible are liable and criminal sanctions can be imposed. Under article 346, all environmental crimes contained in section 6 of chapter VI of the CL (1997) may be committed by a unit, meaning any entity including a company, enterprise, institution or organization.[79] In *Huzhou City Industrial and Medical Waste Disposal Centre and Another* (2016),[80] both the legal person and the individual in charge were convicted and sanctioned for the crime of environmental pollution. They had entrusted HW to unlicensed parties for disposal in Zhejiang province.

***Huzhou City Industrial and Medical Waste Disposal Centre and Another* (2016)**

Huzhou City Industrial and Medical Waste Disposal Centre (Huzhou Waste Disposal Centre) had an HW operation permit to collect, store and dispose of industrial and clinical waste. From 2011 to 2014, Shi Zheng, its legal representative, had both instructed and consented to its employees passing more than 5,950 t of HW it had collected to unlicensed parties, in order to benefit from their low disposal fees and increase profits. Some of the waste was randomly dumped.

Wuxing District Court (2015) found that Huzhou Waste Disposal Centre had disposed of HW in violation of law, causing serious environmental pollution. Shi was the person directly in charge and he had both instructed and consented to this illegal operation. Both the legal person and the individual in charge had committed the crime of environmental pollution with especially grave consequences. Huzhou Waste Disposal Centre was fined 400,000 yuan and illegal gains were confiscated. Shi was sentenced to imprisonment of three years and ten months and fined 150,000 yuan for the crime of environmental pollution. He was also convicted of and sanctioned for the crime of bribery. Shi appealed.

Huzhou Intermediate Court (2016) upheld the first-instance judgment with regard to the crime of environmental pollution and adjusted the sanction for the crime of bribery.

[76] CL (1997), chapter II on 'Crimes', section 4 on 'Crimes committed by a unit'. [77] CL (1997), art. 30

[78] CL (1997), art. 31.

[79] CL (1997), art. 346. It provides that 'if a unit commits the crimes stipulated under articles 338 to 345, the unit shall be fined, and any person in charge or others directly responsible shall be sanctioned in accordance with the stipulations of related articles'. The environmental crimes are: environmental pollution, waste-related crimes and crimes against natural resources.

[80] SPC Eight Model Cases on Environmental Crimes (2016), case no. 5.

At Tengger Desert, eight heavily polluting enterprises illegally discharged untreated toxic wastewater, causing serious contamination. Each of the enterprise and relevant individuals were investigated and prosecuted for criminal liability. The case of *Mingsheng Dye Chemical Co. and Another* (2015) is one of them.[81]

Mingsheng Dye Chemical Co. and Another (2015)

Mingsheng Dye Chemical Co. (Mingsheng) started operations in 2007, but had not conducted an EIA and did not have an EPB inspection approval. It discharged industrial wastewater to the Tengger Desert. Lian Xingzhong became the legal representative of Mingsheng in June 2009 and continued the practice. Mingsheng obtained a discharge permit for 2011 to 2014, which expired on 30 April 2014. However, it continued to discharge wastewater without a permit and the concentration of chemicals in the discharge far exceeded national standards. Following media exposure of the illegal operations, Mingsheng was ordered in September 2014 to shut down. The company and Lian took immediate measures to eliminate the pollution. Mingsheng paid 626,640 yuan to cover the cost of mitigating the effects of the pollution.

Zhongwei Shapotou District Court (2015) found that Mingsheng had engaged in illegal discharge and disposal of toxic substances in violation of law and had caused serious environmental pollution. Lian was the person directly in charge. Both were convicted under article 338 for the crime of environmental pollution. The court took into account the subsequent positive behaviour of the defendants, including Lian's confession and the measures Mingsheng had taken to eliminate the pollution. It fined Mingsheng 5 million yuan, while Lian was sentenced to one and a half years' imprisonment with a two-year suspension and fined 50,000 yuan.

The approach of sanctioning both the legal person and the natural persons in charge or directly responsible has been taken in many other cases, including *Zijin Mining Group Ltd and Others* (2011)[82] and *Chengjiang Jinye Co. and Others* (2009).[83] However, in the absence of express provision for corporate criminal liability, only a natural person may be criminally liable. One example of this is the crime of depositing hazardous substances under article 115 of the CL (1997).

In *Hu Wenbiao and Ding Yuesheng* (2010),[84] Biaoxin Chemical Co. was not prosecuted for its toxic wastewater discharge. Only Hu Wenbiao and Ding Yuesheng were convicted and sanctioned for the crime of depositing hazardous substances under article 115. The case has triggered intense debate among lawyers and scholars of both criminal and environmental law.

81 SPC 10 Model Criminal, Civil and Administrative Cases on Environment and Resources (2017), case no. 1.

82 SPC Four Model Cases on Environmental Crimes (2013), case no. 1. Zijin Mining Group Ltd was fined 30 million yuan and liable individuals were imprisoned and fined.

83 SPC Four Model Cases on Environmental Crimes (2013), case no. 2. Jinye Co. was fined 16 million yuan and liable individuals were imprisoned and fined.

84 SPC Four Model Cases on Environmental Crimes (2013), case no. 4.

Hu Wenbiao and Ding Yuesheng (2010)

From November 2007 to February 2009, Biaoxin Chemical Co. (Biaoxin) had discharged a large amount of toxic wastewater containing benzene and phenol into the Wuzhi River, located to the north of the plant. Hu, legal representative of Biaoxin, and Ding, head of the production division, knew that the wastewater contained the toxic substances of benzene and phenol and that the river passed multiple collection points for drinking water supply. On 20 February 2009, the drinking water supply had to be suspended for more than 66 hours, affecting more than 200,000 residents. On 21 February 2009, Hu and Ding were detained by the police for investigation. They were prosecuted on 1 July 2009 for the crime of depositing hazardous substances under article 115 of the CL (2009).

Yandu District Court (2009) found that from November 2007 to February 2009 Hu and Ding had instructed employees to discharge untreated industrial wastewater to the Wuzhi River, knowing that the wastewater was toxic and hazardous, and that the river would pass sources of drinking water supply. The total direct economic loss amounted to 5.43 million yuan. Both were convicted of the crime of depositing hazardous substances. Hu was sentenced to ten years' imprisonment and Ding to six years. Both defendants appealed.

Yancheng Intermediate Court (2010) dismissed the appeal and upheld the first-instance judgment.

In *Hu Wenbiao and Ding Yuesheng* (2010), the Jiangsu courts were keen to impose a heavier punishment proportionate to the grave consequence of environmental harm endangering public health, and to deter others from similar violations. They were of the view that the maximum penalty of seven years' imprisonment under article 338 failed to deter intentionally committed offences. The experiments of Jiangsu courts in convicting under article 115, instead of taking the conventional approach of relying on article 338, were highly controversial, and raised questions of inconsistent treatment of the same or similar environmental violations by different courts in different cities and provinces. There is also doubt as to whether article 115 can effectively deter violations. Although courts may impose heavier sanctions in the form of longer imprisonment terms or even the death penalty, corporate behaviour may not change. Article 115 does not apply to legal persons and thus the court can only punish individuals rather than imposing corporate criminal liability. Crimes contained in the article, and all other crimes against public security, carry the principle punishments [85]of criminal detention, imprisonment or the death penalty. They do not, however, impose supplementary punishment of monetary sanctions, either in the form of fines or confiscation of property.[86]

11.5.2 Fault-Based Criminal Liability

Chinese criminal law theory and legislation do not recognize strict or no-fault liability for criminal offences. *Mens rea* is required for the commission of an environmental crime.

[85] There are five principle punishments under article 33 of the CL (2009): control, criminal detention, fixed-term imprisonment, life imprisonment and the death penalty.

[86] CL (2009), art. 34. The article contains three supplementary punishments: fine, deprivation of political rights and confiscation of property.

'Where an act has caused harmful consequences, no crime is committed in the absence of an individual's intention or negligence or as a result of irresistible or unforeseeable causes.'[87] The prosecution must prove either criminal intention or negligence. 'An intentional crime is committed with clear knowledge that one's act will cause socially dangerous consequences, hoping for or being indifferent to the occurrence of such consequences.'[88] 'A negligent crime is committed where an individual should have foreseen that their act may cause socially dangerous consequences, but where they fail to do so because of carelessness or, having foreseen the consequences, readily assume they can prevent them, with the result that these consequences occur.'[89]

In the context of environmental crimes, the 'guilty mind' is not required either to have actual knowledge that pollution would cause harm or an intention to cause harm by pollution. In *Yang Junwu* (1998),[90] the court convicted Yang for the offence of causing an environmental pollution incident under article 338 because: (i) he should have known, given his experience in the paper industry, the serious consequences of discharging toxic wastewater containing volatile phenol and (ii) he intentionally discharged the wastewater to the Yellow River Water Diversion Ditch, which diverted water to the local reservoir, a source of water supply for production and consumption.

In *Yunguang Chemical and Others* (2012),[91] the court in Sichuan province held both licensed and unlicensed waste operators jointly liable for the crime of environmental pollution by illegal disposal and dumping of HW. Yunguang Chemical was a licence holder permitted to dispose of HW legally. The company, however, entrusted the waste to an unlicensed third party in order to cut costs and maximize profit. Even though it was the third party, Zhang, who dumped and disposed of the HW in a manner that caused serious environmental harm, the court held Yunguang Chemical jointly liable for the crime of environmental pollution as it was the source of the HW. The SPC and SPP Interpretation on Environmental Crime (2013) provided that 'anyone who entrusts a party, knowing that the latter has no HW operation permit or operates beyond the scope of its permit, to collect, store, utilize or dispose of HW, causing serious environmental pollution, jointly commits the crime of environmental pollution'.[92] Here, 'knowing' does not require proof of actual knowledge of a third party's lack of operation permit or of the fact that illegal dumping causes pollution. The unreasonably low fee charged by a third party for the collection of HW indicates that illegal dumping is the only viable choice. It is no secret that many enterprises, including waste generators and operators, opt for such illegal disposal by an unlicensed third party in order to cut substantially the cost of HW disposal. To punish and deter such illegal operations, the law only requires knowledge that the fee charged is substantially below HW disposal fees charged by licensed service providers.

[87] CL (1997), art. 16. [88] CL (1997), art. 14(1). [89] CL (1997), art. 15(1).
[90] *Supreme People's Court Gazette*, 2 (1999). The judgement is also available at www.pkulaw.cn.
[91] SPC Four Model Cases on Environmental Crimes (2013), case no. 3. See Chapter 7 of this book for details of the case.
[92] SPC and SPP Interpretation (2013), art. 7.

11.5.3 Defences

Typical defences to charges of environmental crimes include necessity and *force majeure*. Individuals will not be criminally liable for the damage resulting from necessary emergency measures taken to prevent existing or imminent danger to the state or public interest or to the personal rights, property rights or other rights and interests of the actor or other people.[93] The defence of necessity is limited to 'necessary' measures taken. That is, a person is liable if measures are unnecessary and cause undue harm. However, depending on the circumstances, the courts will consider reducing or not applying a punishment.[94]

The defence of *force majeure* applies where an act has objectively caused harmful consequences, but the harm was not intended, nor was it the result of negligence, but came about due to irresistible or unforeseeable causes. The act is not deemed a crime in such circumstances.[95]

11.5.4 Multiple Parties Jointly Committing Crimes

Illegal disposal of HW causing serious environmental pollution commonly involves many parties, including the waste generator and licensed and unlicensed HW operators. Due to the high cost of safe disposal of HW and the relatively small number of licensed service providers, some waste generators and permit holders are motivated by financial gain to hire unlicensed parties to dispose of their HW for a relatively small fee, resulting in waste being dumped by rivers, on farmland and on hillsides. In *Zhejiang Jinfanda Biochemical Co. and Others* (2015),[96] all relevant parties involved in the illegal disposal and dumping of HW were convicted of the crime of environmental pollution by the courts in Zhejiang province.

Zhejiang Jinfanda Biochemical Co. and Others (2015)

Zhejiang Jinfanda Biochemical Co. (Jinfanda) owned Fangbu Chemical Plant, which manufactured pesticides and generated HW. From October 2011 to May 2013, deputy general manager Du Zhongxiang had, with the general manager's agreement, entrusted more than 35,000 t of HW to several chemical companies that did not have an HW operation permit. One of those, Xinhe, agreed to collect and dispose of the waste for 80–100 yuan/t. Xinhe then paid Huang Xiaodong and Wang Fei at 50–60 yuan/t to dispose of the waste. From the beginning of 2012 until May 2013, more than 5,000 t of HW was collected and dumped in streams, on beaches and on forestland.

Longyou County Court (2015) held that Jinfanda, Xinhe, Huang, Wang and Du had jointly engaged in the illegal dumping and disposal of HW, causing serious environmental pollution. They had committed the crime of environmental pollution with especially serious consequences. The court considered the defendants' confessions and their surrender of illegal gains, and fined Jinfanda 75 million yuan and Xinhe 4 million yuan. Du was sentenced to six years' imprisonment and fined 1 million yuan. Other companies and individuals were also sanctioned. The defendants appealed.

Quzhou Intermediate Court (2015) dismissed the appeal and upheld the first-instance judgment.

[93] CL (1997), art. 21(1). [94] CL (1997), art. 21(2). [95] CL (1997), art. 16.
[96] SPC Eight Model Cases on Environmental Crimes (2016), case no. 8.

In *Tian Jianguo and Li Enguo* (2015),[97] the courts in Jiangsu province found Tian Jianguo and Li Enguo jointly liable for the crime of environmental pollution, though it was Tian who, without holding an HW operation permit, had engaged in illegal lead recovery from waste lead-acid batteries without any pollution-control measures.

Tian Jianguo and Li Enguo (2015)

Tian, who did not possess an HW operation permit, rented a lead smelting plant to recover lead from waste lead-acid batteries. He did not take any pollution-control measures. From August 2012 to October 2013, Tian processed 13,500 t of waste lead-acid batteries and caused serious pollution. Li had constructed the lead smelting plant and leased it to Tian.

Yunlong District Court (2015) found that Tian's illegal operation had generated a large amount of wastewater and air pollutants that had been discharged without treatment. The lead recovered from the operation was stockpiled on the site, causing serious pollution. Tian was convicted of the crime of environmental pollution. Li was held to have jointly committed the crime. The court considered the duration of the illegal operation, the scale of production, the extent of the pollution and the amount of discharge and emissions and classed the pollution as having especially serious consequences. Both were sentenced to four and a half years' imprisonment and fined 100,000 yuan. The defendants appealed.

Xuzhou Intermediate Court (2015) dismissed the appeal and upheld the first-instance judgment.

Li was jointly liable for providing assistance to Tian's illegal operation by constructing the lead smelting plant and leasing it to Tian.

11.5.5 Sanction: Balancing Severe Punishment with Leniency

Criminal law serves the multiple functions of punishing crime, deterring violations and reshaping human behaviour. Environmental criminal law aims to strike the right balance between severe and lenient punishment so as to effectively punish and deter serious environmental violation and change human and corporate behaviour. The SPC and SPP Interpretation on Environmental Crime (2016) combines severe punishment[98] with lenient treatment[99] to create the deterrence and incentive necessary for behavioural change.

Severe punishment is used when a crime has been committed with a high degree of malicious intention or has caused grave harm due to the location or time at which it occurred. If an offender is convicted under articles 338 or 339 of the CL in the following four circumstances, the punishment will be severe:[100]

(1) obstructing environmental supervision and inspection, or obstructing investigation of environmental emergencies;
(2) illegal discharge, dumping or disposal of radioactive waste, toxic substances, waste containing infectious disease pathogens, toxic substances or other

[97] SPC Eight Model Cases on Environmental Crimes (2016), case no. 2.
[98] SPC and SPP Interpretation (2016), art. 4. [99] SPC and SPP Interpretation (2016), art. 5.
[100] SPC and SPP Interpretation (2016), art. 4.

hazardous substances at or near densely populated areas such as hospitals, schools and residential areas;

(3) illegal discharge, dumping or disposal of radioactive waste, waste containing infectious disease pathogens, toxic substances or other hazardous substances during a period in which a heavy-pollution-weather warning has been issued, an environmental emergency has occurred, or in the period before a deadline that was given for carrying out compulsory rectification measures;

(4) illegal discharge, dumping or disposal of radioactive waste, waste containing infectious disease pathogens, toxic substances or other hazardous substances by an enterprise in possession of a HW operation permit.

Scenarios (1) and (4) focus on the attitude of the offender; they are offences committed knowingly and deliberately. Offenders under scenario (1) do not cooperate with inspection or investigation authorities and obstruct environmental enforcement, while offenders under scenario (4) have the capacity for lawful disposal of HW as permit holders, but intentionally engage in illegal disposal purely to maximize financial gains. The offences are highly reprehensible and are behaviours that are potentially more socially harmful. The scenarios under (2) and (3) focus on the potentially grave environmental harm and impact on human health caused by offences at particular locations or during particular periods.

However, if 'the circumstances are clearly minor and the harm is not substantial', the socially harmful conduct or violation will not be deemed a crime.[101] Even if an offender is prosecuted for harmful conduct or violation, criminal sanctions may not be imposed if the circumstances are not serious. Where the circumstances of a crime are minor and punishment is unnecessary, an exemption from criminal sanction may be granted. The liable party may be reprimanded, ordered to make a statement of remorse, ordered to offer an apology or pay compensation for loss, or may receive an administrative penalty.[102]

The classification of circumstances is closely linked to the degree of social harm caused by the conduct. For criminal liability to arise, the consequences or violation must reach the minimum threshold of severity. In environmental criminal law, the offender's mental state, attitude and previous violations are relevant factors, in addition to the actual or potential environmental harm. Under the SPC and SPP Interpretation on Environmental Crime (2016), where an act or consequence just reaches the threshold requirement for conviction under articles 338 and 339 of the CL, but the offender (a remorseful first-time offender) has taken timely measures to mitigate loss, eliminate pollution, make full compensation and actively restore the ecosystem, the case may be treated as one of 'minor circumstances'. The offender is exempt from criminal prosecution or criminal sanction. Where it is absolutely necessary to impose criminal sanction on the offender, punishment will be lenient.[103] The attitude of an offender is clearly of crucial importance in the prosecution, conviction and sentencing of environmental crimes. An offender who cooperates with the investigation authority by voluntarily providing details of an offence and takes immediate measures to mitigate harm and remediate damage is treated more leniently by courts. This occurred in

[101] CL (1997), art. 13. [102] CL (1997), art. 37. [103] SPC and SPP Interpretation (2016), art. 5.

Zhejiang Huidelong Dye Chemical and Others (2014),[104] *Jiantao (Hebei) Coking and Others* (2015)[105] and *Mingsheng Dye Chemical Co. and Another* (2015).[106]

The use of criminal sanction to punish serious environmental violations is part of the conventional command-and-control regulatory approach to pollution. Depending on the degree of harm, culpability and the seriousness of the circumstances, parties in violation are subject to a range of different types of administrative and criminal sanctions. Administrative penalties are provided for in environmental statutes and imposed by agencies in charge to punish less serious environmental wrongdoing that does not meet the threshold requirements of the CL. In practice, criminal sanction of environmentally damaging behaviour relies heavily on the transfer of a case by an EPB to a PSB or procuratorates.[107] Where an EPB becomes aware of a serious violation that may involve criminal liability, it is required to transfer the case to a PSB for investigation.[108] Where potential criminal liability of state personnel is involved, the EPB must transfer the case to the procuratorate for investigation.[109] Criminal law is employed to sanction polluters who deserve the stigma of a criminal conviction for seriously reprehensible acts of pollution and ecological destruction. The law not only punishes the wrongdoer and eliminates any financial gain or other benefit from the non-compliance, but also aims to change the behaviour of offenders and deter others from violating the law. Weak criminal sanctions failed to deter violations, giving rise to the increasing severity of penalties for environmental violations in China over the last four decades. An offender's state of mind matters in sentencing. Flagrant, deliberate and sustained disregard of national law and regulation deserves a heavier penalty, while a guilty plea, cooperation with enforcement authorities and abatement of harm call for more lenient treatment. While proof of actual harm is not required for all environmental crimes, both culpability and harm or risk of harm caused by pollution are key considerations in the criminal sanction of environmental violations.

[104] SPC Eight Model Cases on Environmental Crimes (2016), case no. 3. The court took into account the defendant's confession, the return of illegal gains and the payment of wastewater disposal fees as factors calling for more lenient sanctions. It fined the company 20 million yuan and penalized individuals.

[105] SPC Eight Model Cases on Environmental Crimes (2016), case no. 6. The court considered measures taken by the defendant to rectify the problem in the aftermath, including substantial investment in upgraded equipment, and fined the company 2.45 million yuan and penalized individuals.

[106] SPC 10 Model Criminal, Civil and Administrative Cases on Environment and Resources (2017), case no. 1.

[107] To ensure effective operation of the transfer system, the SEPA, MPS and SPP issued the Provisions on the Transfer of Suspected Environmental Criminal Cases by the Environmental Protection Agencies (Provisions on Environmental Case Transfer) on 17 May 2007.

[108] Provisions on Environmental Case Transfer (2007), art. 3(1).

[109] Provisions on Environmental Case Transfer (2007), art. 3(2).

12

Environmental Public Interest Litigation

Environmental public interest litigation (EPIL) aims to protect the public interest in a sound environment, rather than the private interests of individuals who suffer loss or injury caused by pollution or by agency acts or omissions. In EPIL, plaintiffs representing stakeholders in the environment sue polluters or agencies, seeking remedies including an injunction on the polluting activities, elimination of the harm, restoration and clean-up of contamination, compensation for loss of ecological function, compelling agencies to perform their statutory duties and declaring agency acts or omissions unlawful.[1] Such litigation provides remedies where private tort litigation or conventional judicial review is not applicable. It expands public participation in environmental governance and strengthens environmental law enforcement by allowing the public to play a more effective and influential role in monitoring and supervising both agencies and polluters.

Prior to the formal introduction of EPIL by national law reform, local pilot schemes were trialled under the auspices of the State Council's Decision on Implementing Scientific Development and Strengthening Environmental Protection (State Council Decision) (2005), which promotes information disclosure, public participation, development of social organizations and EPIL.[2] From 2007 until national laws began to formalize EPIL in 2012, trials took place mainly in the provinces of Guizhou, Jiangsu and Yunnan, establishing a range of rules on standing, jurisdiction and remedies. National law reform formally endorsed EPIL. The Civil Procedure Law (CPL) (2012) granted standing to authorities and relevant organizations in PIL.[3] The Environmental Protection Law (EPL) (2014) set criteria for defining a 'relevant organization' that may initiate EPIL.[4] The Joint Notice on Implementing the Environmental Civil Public Interest Litigation System (2014) was issued,[5] followed by the Interpretation on Several Issues Concerning the Application of Law in

[1] For further discussion of civil and administrative EPIL, see Wan E'Xiang, 'Establishing an environmental public interest litigation system and promoting the building of an ecological civilization', *Chinese Law and Government*, 43 (2010), 30–40; Cao Mingde and Wang Fengyuan, 'Environmental public interest litigation in China', *Asia Pacific Law Review*, 19 (2011), 217–35; Carpenter-Gold, 'Castles made of sand'; Juan Chu, 'Vindicating public environmental interest'.

[2] State Council Decision (2005), para. 27. [3] CPL (2012), art. 55. [4] EPL (2014), art. 58.

[5] The Notice on Implementing the Environmental Civil Public Interest Litigation System (2014) was issued by the SPC, the Ministry of Civil Affairs and the Ministry of Environmental Protection (MEP) on 26 December 2014.

Environmental Civil Public Interest Litigation (SPC Interpretation on Civil EPIL) (2015), which was issued by the Supreme People's Court (SPC) to guide courts of all levels in accepting and adjudicating civil EPIL.

During the development of civil EPIL, the procuratorates' function was developed to cover both civil and administrative EPIL. Soon after the EPL (2014) came into force, the National People's Congress Standing Committee (NPCSC) delegated to the Supreme People's Procuratorate (SPP) the power to launch pilot PIL schemes.[6] The two-year pilot exercise under the Reform Plan on a Pilot Project for Instituting Public Interest Litigation by Procuratorial Organs (Reform Plan on PIL Pilots) (2015)[7] and the Implementation Measures on Pilot Projects of Public Interest Litigation Initiated by People's Procuratorates (SPP Implementation Measures) (2015)[8] tested both civil and administrative PILs in designated subject areas, including environmental protection, in thirteen provinces. At the end of the two-year pilots in June 2017, the NPCSC amended both the CPL (2012) and Administrative Litigation Law (ALL) (2014) to formalize the standing of procuratorates in civil and administrative PIL in designated subject areas, including environmental protection.[9] In 2017, procuratorates acquired standing to sue in civil EPIL under the CPL (2017)[10] and administrative EPIL under the ALL (2017).[11] Then, in 2018, the SPC and SPP issued the Interpretation on Application of Law in Public Interest Litigation by Procuratorates[12] to clarify the roles of procuratorates in civil and administrative PIL and the procedural requirements for procuratorates to initiate PIL to ensure the best use of public procuratorial resources.

This chapter examines the development of EPIL in China from local pilot schemes to national law reform. Section 12.1 examines the critically important issue of standing, looking at which bodies are best suited to initiate EPIL and protect the public interest by guarding against environmental pollution and ecological destruction. Section 12.2 explores China's experiments with jurisdiction over EPIL, including the use of existing specialized maritime courts, the development of new environmental tribunals, and innovation in jurisdiction by designation, whereby a higher court designates certain lower courts to exercise jurisdiction over specific types of cases. Sections 12.3 and 12.4 investigate remedies offered by civil and administrative EPIL respectively, and their effectiveness in environmental protection. Section 12.5 discusses the role of mediation in EPIL, and procedural guarantees that protect the public interest in the outcome of judicial mediation. The chapter

[6] NPCSC, Decision on Authorizing the Supreme People's Procuratorate to Launch the Pilot Program of Initiating Public Interest Actions in Certain Areas (2015). It granted the SPP the power to launch – in thirteen provinces for two years – pilot exercises in which procuratorates initiate PIL in designated fields, including environmental protection, safeguarding of state assets, lease of state-owned land, and food and drug safety.

[7] The SPP issued the Reform Plan on PIL Pilots on 2 July 2015.

[8] The SPP issued the more detailed SPP Implementation Measures on 16 December 2015.

[9] NPCSC, Decision on Amending the Civil Procedure Law and the Administrative Litigation Law (2017). The NPCSC decision was issued on 27 June 2017. It came into force on 1 July 2017.

[10] Article 55(2) of the CPL (2017) grants standing to procuratorates in PIL in two subject areas: the protection of environment and resources and the protection of consumer rights in food and drug safety.

[11] Article 25(4) of the ALL (2017) grants standing to procuratorates in PIL in four subject areas: the protection of environment and resources, food and drug safety, the protection of state assets and transfer of state land-use rights.

[12] The SPC and SPP issued the Interpretation on Application of Law in Public Interest Litigation by Procuratorates on 1 March 2018. It came into force on 2 March 2018.

concludes with discussion of challenges that must be overcome if EPIL is to reach its full potential in China.

12.1 STANDING

Conventional rules of standing for both civil and administrative litigation in China require the plaintiff's rights and interests to have been injured or potentially to be adversely affected by the defendant's acts. New and special rules have been formulated to give a designated party the right to sue in court in order to protect the public interest in a sound and healthy environment.[13]

12.1.1 Local Pilots before the CPL (2012)

Prior to the formal endorsement of PIL by national legislation, the difficult question of standing was addressed by local rules as part of the pilot exercises. Specialized environmental tribunals have existed since 2007, with their own liberalized rules on standing allowing procuratorates, environmental protection authorities and non-governmental organizations (NGOs) to initiate civil and administrative EPIL.[14]

Environmental NGOs

Wuxi Intermediate Court and Yunnan High Court expressly allowed 'environmental organizations' to litigate as plaintiffs in EPIL,[15] offering an invaluable opportunity for green NGOs to test PIL against polluters. A small number of financially and professionally capable NGOs were actively involved in the early tests of PIL at newly established environmental tribunals in the provinces of Jiangsu, Yunnan and Guizhou. The All-China Environment Federation (ACEF) was, and still is, one of the most active players. It is a government-organized non-governmental organization (GONGO) sponsored and supervised by the Ministry of Environmental Protection (MEP, now Ministry of Ecology and Environment (MEE)) and registered with the Ministry of Civil Affairs. Its first EPIL was against Jiangsu Jiangyin Harbour Container Co. (Jiangyin Container Co.) at Wuxi Intermediate Court. The container company was a private enterprise based at Jiangyin Harbour, on the Yangtze River. It expanded its container-transport business to include loading and unloading of iron ore powder in 2003. The company exposed the iron ore powder to open air and wind and did not take any environmental protection measures. It caused serious dust and noise pollution. The dispute between residents and Jiangyin Container Co. escalated from

[13] For more on standing, see Tiantian Zhai and Yen-Chiang Chang, 'Standing of environmental public-interest litigants'; Qi Gao and Sean Whittaker, 'Standing to sue beyond individual rights: who should be eligible to bring environmental public interest litigation in China', *Transnational Environmental Law*, 8 (2019), 327–47.

[14] For further discussion of these local pilot schemes, see Bie Tao and Bie Zhi, 'Environmental public interest litigation breaking the ground', in Li Hengyuan and Chang Jiwen (eds.), *Environmental Law in China 2008* (Beijing: China Environmental Science Press, 2008), 182–8; Lin Yanmei, 'The development of environmental', 272–82; Ma Yong, 'Social organizations making an impact by promoting environmental public interest litigations' in Zeng Xiaodong and Chang Jiwen (eds.), *Environmental Law in China*, vol. A (Beijing: Law Press China, 2009), 67–73.

[15] Wuxi Intermediate People's Court approved the establishment of the environmental court in March 2008 and issued the Provisions on the Jurisdiction of the Environmental Court; Yunnan Provincial Court, Provisions on the Establishment of Environmental Courts and Environmental Adjudication (2009).

complaints beginning in 2004 to letters and petitions in 2005 and finally to violent road blockades in 2009.[16] The ACEF became aware of the dispute after one of the residents, Zhu Zhengmao, complained to the MEP hotline. The case began as a private environmental tort case and the ACEF was prepared to assist Zhu. However, the ACEF's investigation revealed that the environmental harm caused by Jiangyin Container Co. far exceeded Zhu's private claim.[17] As a result, the ACEF initiated EPIL at the newly established environmental tribunal of Wuxi Intermediate Court. The court had issued the Provisions on Jurisdiction of the Environmental Court, which stated that 'it accepts PIL initiated by procuratorates, environmental protection authorities, environmental organizations and management companies of residential premises'.[18] *Zhu Zhengmao and All-China Environment Federation* v. *Jiangsu Jiangyin Harbour Container Co.* (2009)[19] is a landmark case in EPIL.

Zhu Zhengmao and All-China Environment Federation v. *Jiangsu Jiangyin Harbour Container Co.* (2009)

Jiangsu Jiangyin Harbour Container Co. had caused severe air, water and noise pollution, adversely affecting the living environment of the general public and seriously endangering the quality of drinking water supplies of the cities of Wuxi and Jiangyin.[20] The plaintiffs sued, seeking a court order for the defendant to take measures including: (i) ceasing the infringement and eliminating harm to the affected residents; (ii) treating the wash water, which contained iron ore powder, and eliminating the danger to drinking water supplies; (iii) restoring the municipal sewage system and treating iron ore mud and (iv) paying the litigation costs, including the appraisal fee for assessing the environmental damage and the cost of remediation, and lawyers' fees.[21]

Wuxi Intermediate Court (2009) accepted the case and conducted an on-site inspection the following day. It ordered the defendant to stop the polluting operation without delay. Then, at the first court hearing, the defendant was ordered to take measures to protect the environment prior to the completion of the trial. After taking measures to control dust and clean up the sewage system, the defendant applied for court mediation. The court facilitated mediation and the parties reached agreement. The court prepared the mediation report, which stated: (i) within fifteen days of signing the mediation report, the defendant was required to carry out an environmental impact assessment

[16] Ma Yong, 'Social organizations making an impact'. Ma Yong was the head of the litigation department of the ACEF and the lead lawyer in this case. See also Qie Jianrong, 'Wuxi court accepts litigation filed by environmental organization, first NGO public interest litigation', *Legal Daily*, 9 July 2009, 6; Huang Qi, 'Public interest litigation'.

[17] Carpenter-Gold, 'Castles made of sand', at 260.

[18] Wuxi Intermediate People's Court approved the establishment of the environmental court in March 2008 and issued the Provisions on the Jurisdiction of the Environmental Court. The decision to create the environmental court was directly related to the serious contamination of Lake Tai by blue algae in the summer of 2007. It caused the water supply to the city of Wuxi to be suspended for more than a week and drew national and international attention to China's water pollution problems. The environmental court was expressly granted civil, criminal and enforcement jurisdiction to improve its efficiency and effectiveness in handling environmental cases. See Huang Qi, 'Public interest litigation'.

[19] SPC Nine Model Cases on Environment and Resources (2014), case no. 5.

[20] The storage yard was less than 50 m from residential premises. Staff rinsed iron ore powder off the site and directly into the municipal sewage system, without treating the dirty water. The drinking water for Wuxi and Jiangyin is taken from the Yangtze River, downstream of the enterprise. Qie Jianrong, 'Wuxi court', 6.

[21] Qie Jianrong, 'Wuxi court'; see also Huang Qi, '"Chinese-style dilemma" of environmental public interest litigation', *Xinmin Weekly*, 10 August 2009.

(EIA) of its iron ore powder loading and unloading operations. It was to suspend operations if it failed to obtain the EIA approval within ninety days; (ii) during the ninety-day period pending EIA approval, the defendant was to take measures to ensure that its operations did not generate dust or discharge pollutants contaminating the waters, or emit noise in excess of national maximums; (iii) the defendant was to report its performance of the tasks stipulated in the mediation report in writing to the court every thirty days from the date of signing, and was required to attach environmental monitoring reports from the local environmental protection bureau (EPB).[22]

Although the case was eventually settled by mediation, the court-prepared mediation report has the legally binding force of a judgment.[23] As China's first PIL initiated by an environmental NGO, the Jiangyin case was groundbreaking. The court affirmed the ACEF had standing due to its registration with the Ministry of Civil Affairs and its mission of environmental protection. It ordered a preliminary injunction prior to the court hearing to stop the ongoing pollution at the earliest possible date, and enforced its mediation report by requiring the defendant to submit progress reports and EPB monitoring records.

The ACEF collaborated with a local NGO, Guiyang Public Environmental Education Centre, in *All-China Environment Federation and Another* v. *Guiyang Dingba Paper Mill* (2011)[24] at Qingzhen City Court,[25] to force a paper factory to suspend operations and clean up contamination.

All-China Environment Federation and Another v. _Guiyang Dingba Paper Mill_ (2011)

Guiyang Dingba Paper Mill (Dingba) was founded in 1993 and did not have an effluent discharge permit. It kept toxic wastewater on site in two storage tanks during the day and, at night, discharged it, untreated, through karst caves to the Nanming River, causing serious water pollution. Dingba had been sanctioned by the local EPB repeatedly since 2003. However, it did not stop the illegal discharge. Two environmental NGOs, the ACEF and Guiyang Public Environmental Education Centre sued, requesting Dingba to: (i) stop its illegal discharge of wastewater; (ii) eliminate the risk of pollution and (iii) pay the litigation expenses, including testing and legal fees.

Qingzhen City Court (2011) accepted the case and, following a request by the plaintiffs, sent a team to the site to take photos and collect samples. It ordered Dingba to stop the discharge immediately. Laboratory testing of the samples confirmed that the concentration level of the ammonia nitrogen (NH) being discharged seriously exceeded the national permitted maximum, and that the water quality of the Nanming River downstream of the discharge outfall was sub-Grade V. The court found that Dingba had only obtained a permit to emit sulphur dioxide (SO_2), smoke and dust, and did not have a permit for industrial wastewater discharge or any legally constructed

22 Ma Yong, 'Social organizations making an impact', at 68.

23 CPL (2017), art. 234. A mediation report prepared by a people's court is to be enforced in the same manner as a judgment or decision of the court.

24 SPC Nine Model Cases on Environment and Resources (2014), case no. 1.

25 Qingzhen is a county-level city under the jurisdiction of Guiyang, the provincial capital of Guizhou. It established China's first specialized environmental division in 2007. See SPC, *Environment and Resources Adjudication in China* (2016), part II.

discharge outlet that was subject to monitoring. The defendant had seriously polluted the Nanming River with its secret night-time discharge of wastewater, and had endangered the public interest. The court ordered Dingba to: (i) stop discharging wastewater to the Nanming River immediately; (ii) eliminate the danger to the environment; (iii) pay 10,000 yuan in lawyers' fees and 1,500 yuan in sample-testing fees.

In addition to civil claims against polluters, the ACEF sued a local land bureau for failing to perform its statutory duties: *All-China Environment Federation* v. *Qingzhen Municipal Bureau of Land and Resources* (2009).[26] Although the litigation ended with the ACEF withdrawing its claim, it achieved its purpose of forcing the government body to perform its statutory duties.

All-China Environment Federation v. *Qingzhen Municipal Bureau of Land and Resources* (2009)

On 14 November 1994, Qingzhen Municipal Bureau of Land and Resources (Qingzhen Land Bureau) signed a contract with Li Wanxian, legal representative of the Hundred Flower Lake Cold Drink Shop, leasing to him the land-use rights for lot number four, an 800 m^2 plot near the Hundred Flower Lake, for fifty years. Li was to use the land for making cold drinks, and for offices and staff quarters. According to the lease, Li was to have constructed the premises by 15 November 1995, with a possible one-year extension depending on the circumstances. Qingzhen Land Bureau was entitled to revoke Li's lease and land-use rights and recover the land and all buildings or other fixtures on it if the construction had not been completed by the end of the extension period. More than ten years passed and the construction work was not completed, but Qingzhen Land Bureau had not repudiated the lease. The uncompleted construction was an eyesore and had adverse impact on the aesthetics of the environment, including of the Hundred Flower Lake, a scenic zone designated as such by the Guizhou provincial government. The ACEF sued Qingzhen Land Bureau for omitting to repudiate the lease and thereby placing the environment at risk, through harm to the aesthetics of the site. It sought a court order requiring the defendant to repudiate the lease and recover the plot of land and all buildings on it.

Qingzhen City Court (2009) accepted the case. Prior to the first court hearing, the defendant revoked Li's land-use rights. The ACEF applied to the court to withdraw the lawsuit, and the court approved its application.

The achievements of the ACEF in the early years of testing EPIL have instilled public confidence in EPIL, which is now viewed as a channel through which NGOs can fight pollution and protect the public interest. However, one should be cautiously optimistic, because the ACEF is government-organized and is not a grass-roots NGO. There are at most a few dozen grass-roots NGOs that are registered and have standing to sue, but most lack professional legal expertise and financial resources or are reluctant to

[26] Liu Xiaoxing, 'Administrative public interest litigation initiated by social organization concluded', *China Environment News*, 4 September 2009, 3.

fight legal battles against the government or enterprises.[27] Unregistered grass-roots NGOs and second-tier NGOs do not have the legal-person status that would allow them to initiate lawsuits in their own names.

Compared to the ACEF, grass-roots NGOs face more obstacles in bringing EPIL, including capacity, funding, accessing information and collecting evidence.[28] The first EPIL initiated by a grass-roots NGO was *Friends of Nature and Chongqing Green Volunteer League* v. *Yunnan Luliang Chemical Industry and Yunnan Luliang Peace Technology Ltd* (2020) in the aftermath of the Qujing chromium contamination.[29] Liable parties were prosecuted and convicted for the illegal dumping of 5,222 t of chromium waste in the hills near Qujing.[30] The hexavalent chromium (Cr^{6+}) spread from soil to groundwater, contaminating an underground aquifer known as 'the dragon's fountain'. The two NGOs sued at Qujing Intermediate Court on 20 September 2011, seeking compensation and clean-up.[31]

Friends of Nature and Chongqing Green Volunteer League v. *Yunnan Luliang Chemical Industry and Yunnan Luliang Peace Technology Ltd* (2020)

In September 2011, two grass-roots environmental NGOs filed a lawsuit against defendant companies in Qujing, which had dumped chromium slag in the hills near Qujing and stockpiled toxic waste at its site by the Nanpan River, contaminating the water supply and poisoning livestock. The Nanpan River is a tributary of the Pearl River, which supplies water to Guangxi, Guangdong and Hong Kong. The plaintiffs sued both defendants for the contamination, seeking remedies including: (i) cessation of pollution; (ii) clean-up of the contaminated sites; (iii) compensation for loss of eco-function of the damaged environment and (iv) payment of litigation expenses, including appraisal fees and lawyers' fees.

Qujing Intermediate Court (2020) accepted the case in October 2011 and settled the dispute by mediation in August 2020. Considering the clean-up and remediation work conducted by the two defendants from 2011 to 2019, Friends of Nature (FON) agreed to lower its claim from 10 million yuan to 3.08 million yuan. The money covers the cost of continuing remediation, monitoring and assessment. Both defendants also agreed to pay 1.32 million yuan to cover reasonable costs incurred by the two NGOs in relation to the litigation. The agreement further stipulates detailed arrangements for future remediation of the contaminated sites and the NGOs' ongoing monitoring of remediation.

27 Huang Qi, 'Public interest litigation'.

28 See Jessica Scott, 'Cleaning up the dragon's fountain: lessons from the first public interest lawsuit brought by a grassroots NGO in China', *The George Washington International Law Review*, 45 (2013), 727–62.

29 Yu Ping, 'New lessons learned from the first environmental public interest litigation', *Guangming Daily*, 10 August 2020, 2; see also 'Ten years to conclude the chromium contamination case in Qujing', 3 August 2020, www.pkulaw.cn

30 For more details of the case, see Chapter 7 of this book.

31 See Qie Jianrong, 'Revision of Environmental Protection Law stirs controversy' in Liu Jianqiang, *Chinese Research Perspectives on the Environment, Volume 3: Public Action and Government Accountability* (Leiden: Brill, 2014), 96–105; Scott, 'Cleaning up the dragon's'; Carpenter-Gold, 'Castles made of sand'; Tyler Liu, 'China's revision to the Environmental Protection Law: challenges to public interest litigation and solutions for increasing public participation and transparency', *Journal of Energy and Environmental Law*, Spring (2015), 60–70.

This was a long journey for the two NGOs. The court facilitated the mediation and, in December 2012, the two parties had reached an initial agreement, under which the defendants agreed to stop the infringement, eliminate the danger (i.e. remove the toxic waste for proper treatment and disposal, and prevent future illegal dumping) and conduct environmental remediation (i.e. clean up the contaminated site), subject to public supervision and third-party verification. However, in April 2013, the defendants refused to sign the formal mediation report that had been prepared by the court based on the December 2012 agreement. The mediation failed and the court resumed its adjudication pending an environmental appraisal report of the pollution, damage and cost of restoring the site from the plaintiffs. The plaintiffs had obtained the support of the local EPB and gained access to evidence and environmental reports, but they were unable to afford a third-party appraisal report of the damage caused by the pollution. An appraisal body quoted a fee of 7 million yuan.[32] It is common practice for Chinese courts to rely heavily on third-party appraisal reports by a qualified appraisal body, which often assess the extent and amount of environmental damage and/or the causal link between the pollution and the harm.[33] Such an appraisal report is accepted by courts as science-based and unbiased, but the prohibitively high appraisal fees often deny NGOs' access to the service.

Procuratorates

In addition to NGOs, local procuratorates also initiate EPIL to protect the environment.[34] Of the twenty-four civil EPILs filed nationwide between 2007 and 2011, procuratorates initiated and won fourteen.[35] In Guangdong province, procuratorates have, since 2008, firmly established their standing in EPIL on the basis of the EPL (1989),[36] the Organic Law of the People's Procuratorates (1986)[37] and the State Council Decision (2005). In *Haizhu District Procuratorate* v. *Chen Zhongming* (2008),[38] Guangzhou Maritime Court decided that procuratorates have standing to sue to protect the environment and natural resources where harm is caused to public or private property.

Haizhu District Procuratorate v. *Chen Zhongming* (2008)

Chen Zhongming, sole owner of XinZhongXing Laundry Factory, set up the business to process and wash jeans in September 2007 without obtaining an operation licence or a wastewater discharge

[32] Li He et al, 'Environmental public interest litigations facing various difficulties', *Science and Technology Daily*, 30 May 2013, 6.

[33] Moser and Tseming Yang, 'Environmental tort litigation', at 10899.

[34] For more on procuratorial PIL, see Jingjing Liu, 'China's procuratorate'; Yifan Shi and Benjamin van Rooij, 'Prosecutorial regulation in the global south: environmental civil litigation by prosecutors in China compared to Brazil', *Regulation & Governance*, 10 (2016), 44–57.

[35] Yang Zhaoxia, 'The role of the procuratorates', *China Environment News*, 2 July 2012, 3.

[36] Article 6 of the EPL provides that any units and individuals have a duty to protect the environment and the right to report and sue anyone who has caused pollution or environmental destruction.

[37] The Organic Law of People's Procuratorates was enacted in 1979, amended in 1983 and 1986, and substantially revised in 2018. Article 4 provides that through the exercise of procuratorial power, people's procuratorates protect the property of the state, collectives and individuals and the rights of citizens.

[38] The judgment is available at www.pkulaw.cn. The case was discussed in Li Zhiping, 'Analysis of the practice of water pollution public interest litigation: based on cases handled by the Guangzhou Maritime Court', *Vermont Journal of Environmental Law*, 13 (2012), 797–822, at 802–3.

permit. From September 2007 to May 2008, the factory discharged around 40 t of untreated industrial effluent daily. The discharge contained chemical oxygen demand (COD) at levels five times the national discharge limit, seriously contaminating the ShiLiuGang River. Haizhu District EPB hired Guangzhou Environmental Science Academy to assess the environmental damage caused to the river. The Academy assessed it at 117,289.20 yuan, which comprised direct economic losses of 109,171.20 yuan, monitoring and assessment fees of 7,806 yuan and water resources fees of 312 yuan. Instead of imposing a fine, Haizhu EPB passed the case to Haizhu District Procuratorate, who sued Chen for compensation.

Guangzhou Maritime Court (2008) accepted the case and addressed the issues of jurisdiction and standing. The court had jurisdiction as the case involved pollution of the river leading to the sea, both of which fell within its jurisdiction. On the issue of standing of Haizhu District Procuratorate, the court said that water resources belonged to the state under article 3 of the Water Law (2002), while article 73 of the General Principles of Civil Law (GPCL) provided that no organization or individual may damage state property. No unit or individual may abuse or destroy water resources owned by the state, the court said. Where harm has been caused to water resources, the state is entitled to seek compensation in court. The state's procuratorates protect state property and resources from unlawful infringement. The contaminated ShiLiuGang River in Haizhu was a state-owned water resource and therefore Haizhu procuratorate had standing to sue and claim damages on behalf of the state, the court found. Chen had violated articles 20, 21, 22 and 24 of the Water Pollution Prevention and Control Law (WPPCL) (2008) by discharging industrial effluent without a permit, without paying effluent discharge fees or installing or operating wastewater treatment facilities. The illegal discharge caused serious deterioration of the water quality of the ShiLiuGang River, the court found. It held Chen liable and ordered him to pay 117,289.20 yuan to compensate for the environmental damage and expenses incurred. The plaintiff was ordered to receive the money and hand it to the state treasury.

In this case, the court made the polluter bear the cost of environmental harm, even in the absence of loss or injury suffered by private parties. A procuratorate may sue on behalf of the state to claim damages for harm to natural resources owned by the state. Within a year, Guangzhou Maritime Court tried a second EPIL and reaffirmed procuratorate standing in *Panyu District Procuratorate* v. *Lu Pingzhang* (2009).[39]

Panyu District Procuratorate v. *Lu Pingzhang* (2009)

Lu Pingzhang, sole owner of Dongtai Tannery, registered with the industrial and commercial authority in January 2005 to process leather. On 13 July 2008, Guangzhou Environmental Inspection Division, Panyu Team received public complaints over serious water pollution at Xiadao Chong, a river. Large volumes of red effluent had been discharged from Dongtai Tannery. Further investigation found that from January to July 2008, the tannery had, on five occasions, discharged untreated wastewater directly to the municipal sewage system connected to Xiadao Chong. The

[39] The judgment is available at www.pkulaw.cn; see also 'Guangdong Panyu tannery discharges wastewater in violation of law, procuratorate becomes plaintiff', *People's Daily*, 10 August 2009.

total discharge came to 55 t. The effluent contained COD and heavy metals in excess of state limits, causing serious contamination of Xiadao Chong. Guangzhou Panyu Environmental Science Institute assessed the environmental damage and estimated the economic loss at 62,500 yuan. Panyu District Procuratorate sued Lu Pingzhang, seeking an injunction and compensation on behalf of the state.

Guangzhou Maritime Court (2009) accepted the case and addressed the issues of jurisdiction and standing. The case fell within its jurisdiction as it was an environmental dispute over pollution of water entering the sea. The water resources belonged to the state under article 3 of the Water Law (2002) and, under article 73 of the GPCL (1986), no organization or individual may damage state property. No legal or natural person may harm water resources owned by the state, the court said, adding that where water resources are damaged, the state is entitled to seek compensation in court. The procuratorates protect state property and resources from unlawful infringement, and the contaminated Xiadao Chong in Panyu district is a state-owned water resource, the court found. Consequently, Panyu District Procuratorate had standing to sue and claim damages on behalf of the state, it said. The unlawful discharge of untreated industrial effluent was caused by a worker who was in a rush to leave the office, and Dongtai Tannery had been negligent in the management and supervision of its employees, the court found. As owner of Dongtai Tannery, Lu bore the civil liability for the harm caused by the illegal discharge, it said. The court ordered Lu to stop causing water pollution immediately, including stopping the illegal discharge of industrial effluent, and pay 62,500 yuan as compensation for the environmental damage and expenses incurred to control the pollution. The procuratorate was ordered to receive the payment and pass it to the state treasury.

In both cases, Guangzhou Maritime Court confirmed the standing of local procuratorates by reference to their role as the state procuratorial organ, exercising the function of protecting state resources from damage by illegal infringement, and representing the state to sue to stop ongoing infringement and claim compensation.

In Zhejiang province, the first EPIL was filed by Pinghu City Procuratorate in 2011 against an environmental services company and four tanneries.[40]

Pinghu City Procuratorate v. *Jiaxing Lüyi Environmental Service Co. and Four Others* (2011)

Four tanneries hired Jiaxing Lüyi Environmental Service Co. (Lüyi) to dispose of more than 5,000 t of toxic chromium waste generated from the processing of leather. Lüyi did not have a hazardous waste (HW) operation permit, but nonetheless entered into contracts with four tanneries to dispose of toxic industrial waste. From September 2010, the chromium waste collected by Lüyi was dumped in a pond in a remote part of Pinghu, a county-level city. In November 2010, Pinghu EPB received complaints. The EPB inspected the site and found that the pond had been filled with toxic industrial waste, which was in fact piled 1 m high. The pond was within a Grade II Drinking-Water-Source Reserve (DWSR), was 570 m from a Grade I DWSR and 2 km away from the drinking water collection point of the water

[40] Zhou Ying, 'Zhejiang exploring environmental public interest litigation: breakthrough and impact', *China Environment News*, 19 December 2011, 3.

supply company that served Pinghu city. Pinghu EPB fined Lüyi 50,000 yuan and ordered it to clean up the contaminated site. Pinghu City Procuratorate sued Lüyi and the four tanneries, seeking payment of 541,373 yuan for the clean-up and remediation of the pond.

Pinghu City Court (2011) accepted the case and facilitated the parties to settle via mediation. Pinghu City Procuratorate claimed that the five defendants were jointly liable for the contamination of the site, for endangering the safety of drinking water and for causing serious environmental harm to the state. The four tanneries had violated the Law on the Prevention and Control of Pollution by Solid Waste (SWL) (2004) by hiring Lüyi, a company without an HW operation permit, to dispose of toxic waste. Lüyi was in serious violation of the SWL (2004) and WPPCL (2008) by engaging in HW operations without a permit and by illegally dumping toxic waste in the Grade II DWSR, thereby endangering public health and causing heavy economic losses to the state and the people of Pinghu. The parties reached a settlement agreement: Lüyi was to pay 541,373 yuan to cover the cost of clean-up, including expenses already incurred by Pinghu EPB to consult experts, remove contaminated waste and remediate the contaminated site, and future expenses incurred for post-remediation monitoring and treatment, among others. The court prepared a mediation report based on the settlement agreement.

Prior to the case of *Pinghu City Procuratorate* v. *Jiaxing Lüyi Environmental Service Co. and Four Others* (2011), procuratorates in Zhejiang province had engaged in 'supporting litigation', an important mechanism under the CPL.[41] Where a victim of a tort is unwilling or unable to sue the tortfeasor for financial or other reasons, a procuratorate may support the victim in bringing a lawsuit to seek judicial redress. The procuratorate joins the case as a party and uses its professional and financial resources to support the victim during the lawsuit. One example is the *Nanhu Cupboard Case* (2010).[42] In 2007, a cupboard factory in Nanhu district in the city of Jiaxing discharged untreated wastewater to a local river, killing fish. The factory had neither applied for a discharge permit, nor installed wastewater treatment facilities. The victims complained to Nanhu District EPB, which, in March 2008, ordered the factory to stop production, apply for a permit and install pollution-control facilities. The factory ignored the EPB's order and continued operating as usual. In December 2009, the EPB transferred the case to Nanhu District Procuratorate, which investigated and decided to support the victims in suing the factory. The case was settled before trial as the factory owner accepted the illegal nature of his operation under environmental laws and regulations. The victims were paid compensation to their satisfaction and the factory relocated.

Environmental Protection Agencies

The third category of bodies with standing to initiate EPIL under local pilot schemes are EPBs. The case of *Kunming Sannong Ltd and Another* v. *Kunming Environmental Protection Bureau* (2011)[43] is one of the very few EPIL initiated by an EPB against polluters.

[41] Article 15 of the CPL (1991) provides for supporting litigation and the article remains unchanged in the CPL amendments of 2007, 2012 and 2017. Where the civil legal rights and interests of the state, collectives or individuals have been infringed upon, any government body, social organization, enterprise or institution may support the injured unit or individual in bringing a lawsuit.

[42] Jingjing Liu, 'China's procuratorate', at 53–4.

[43] The judgment is available at www.pkulaw.cn.

***Kunming Sannong Co. Ltd. and Another* v. *Kunming Environmental Protection Bureau* (2011)**

In 2007, Yangfu Co. (Yangfu) acquired the land-use rights of 1,000 *mu* of agricultural land in Guandu district on which to establish a pig farm. In July 2008, Yangfu registered a company named Kunming Sannong Co. Ltd. (Sannong) to construct and operate the pig farm. Operations started without any inspection or approval of the wastewater treatment facilities. In November 2009, Dalong Tan, a lake and drinking water source located 1 km from the pig farm, became dark, foul-smelling and contaminated. Guandu District EPB imposed a fine of 500,000 yuan on Sannong and suspended its operations. Sannong took some temporary measures, but continued operating illegally. In early 2010, wastewater leakage from the pig farm further contaminated the groundwater. The water quality at Dalong Tan became sub-Grade V. Kunming EPB sued Sannong and Yangfu, seeking the remedies of: (i) cessation of infringement; (ii) payment of 4.17 million yuan for treatment of pollution to protect Dalong Tan; (iii) payment of 155,293 yuan for the emergency monitoring and pollution treatment appraisal fees and (iv) court acceptance fees.

Kunming Intermediate Court (2010) accepted the case and confirmed Kunming EPB had standing. As protector of the ecological and living environment of Kunming city, Kunming EPB sued polluters on behalf of the state to stop ongoing pollution and to claim compensation for environmental harm caused to society, the court said. A polluter's payment of a fine, an administrative penalty, does not exempt it from civil liabilities, it added. The court ordered Sannong and Yangfu to stop the infringement immediately, pay 4.17 million yuan for pollution treatment, and pay 132,520 yuan for assessment and appraisal. Sannong and Yangfu were also ordered to pay the court acceptance fees of 40,176.80 yuan. The two companies appealed.

Yunnan High Court (2011) dismissed the appeal and upheld the first-instance judgment.

Whether local EPBs should engage in EPIL is subject to debate. Their resources might be better used at an earlier stage on effective enforcement to ensure compliance and sanction violations, rather than on going to court to remediate the polluted environment.

12.1.2 Standing in Civil EPIL: CPL (2012), EPL (2014) and CPL (2017)

Valuable experience was gained from the local pilot PIL schemes, which led to national reform. The 2012 amendment to the CPL grants standing to government authorities and relevant organizations to protect the environment or consumers:

> Where anyone pollutes the environment, infringes upon the lawful rights and interests of a large number of consumers or otherwise damages the public interest, an authority or relevant organization as prescribed by law may sue the liable party at a people's court.[44]

It confirms the practice adopted by local pilot schemes of allowing procuratorates, local EPBs and NGOs to sue to protect the environment. The provision was, however, vague as to

[44] CPL (2012), art. 55.

the meaning and scope of 'relevant organization'.[45] The EPL (2014) clarified the issue of standing of relevant organizations in article 58, which provides that social organizations meeting certain criteria may sue any natural or legal person who pollutes the environment, damages an ecosystem and harms the public interest. The criteria are:[46]

(i) the body has registered legally with the civil administrative affairs department at or above the municipal level in cities with districts and
(ii) the body has specially engaged in environmental protection for the public good for five consecutive years or more without any record of violation of law.

Where a case is filed by an eligible social organization, courts must accept the case.[47] The EPL (2014) came into force on 1 January 2015, and reaffirmed that environmental NGOs may seek judicial redress by filing EPIL in China. However, many NGOs are excluded under article 58, because it imposes more restrictions on the standing of NGOs than the CPL (2012) did, laying down requirements on registration, years of practice, specialization and no record of violation for five consecutive years.[48] Nevertheless, the SPC has taken a more relaxed approach to the interpretation of the article 58 standing requirement through its case adjudication and judicial interpretations.

The requirement for an NGO to have been operating for five consecutive years clearly excludes many newly established NGOs from initiating EPIL. Taizhou Environment Federation, a local GONGO in Jiangsu province, was established and registered in February 2014. Had it initiated its case after 1 January 2015, when the EPL (2014) came into force, it would not have had standing to sue in the case *Taizhou Environment Federation* v. *Taixing Jinhui Chemical Co. and Five Others* (2016).[49]

Taizhou Environment Federation v. *Taixing Jinhui Chemical Co. and Five Others* (2016)

From January 2012 to February 2013, six defendants, including Taixing Jinhui Chemical Co. (Jinhui Chemical), hired third parties, none of which had an HW operation permit, to dispose of more than 25,000 t of waste acid generated in their production processes. The six defendants paid between 20 yuan/t and 100 yuan/t, much lower than reasonable toxic waste disposal fees. The waste acid was secretly and illegally discharged to major waterbodies in the cities of Taixing and Taizhou, causing severe contamination of the Rutai Canal and Gumagan River. Taizhou Environment Federation, a non-profit social organization supervised by Taizhou EPB and registered with the Taizhou Civil Affairs Bureau in February 2014, sued the six defendants. It claimed 160 million yuan to cover the cost of environmental restoration and 100,000 yuan for the assessment and appraisal fees.

Taizhou Intermediate Court (2014) accepted the case and confirmed the plaintiff's standing under article 55 of the CPL (2012). It noted that article 57(3) of the SWL (2013) prohibited anyone

[45] For more critique of the vagueness of this provision, see Tiantian Zhai and Yen-Chiang Chang, 'Standing of environmental public-interest litigants', at 375–6.
[46] EPL (2014), art. 58(1). [47] EPL (2014), art. 58(2). [48] EPL (2014), art. 58.
[49] SPC 10 Model Cases of Environmental Public Interest Litigation (2017), case no. 1; *Supreme People's Court Gazette*, 5 (2016).

from supplying or entrusting HW to parties that did not possess a permit to collect, store, utilize or dispose of such waste. Article 85 of the SWL (2013) provides that where any person has caused environmental pollution by waste, they are liable for eliminating the harm, as well as compensation and restoration, the court said. The defendants, as the generators of toxic waste, were held liable, because they entrusted the HW to unlicensed parties, thereby causing pollution. Where it is difficult to calculate the cost of restoration, an alternative formula, a 'virtual treatment cost', must be used to estimate the cost of treatment and remediation by professionals, the court said. The court held the six defendants liable to pay more than 160 million yuan in restoration fees and 100,000 yuan in assessment and appraisal fees. Jinhui Chemical and three others appealed to Jiangsu High Court, challenging: (i) the standing of Taizhou Environment Federation; (ii) causation between the disposal and the environmental harm and (iii) calculation of restoration fees.

Jiangsu High Court (2014) agreed with the first-instance court on all three issues of standing, causation and calculation of restoration fees and dismissed the appeal. In order to incentivize polluters to innovate in pollution control and treatment, the court revised the order for payment of restoration fees. It decided that liable parties could claim up to 40 per cent of the restoration fees for use at their own plants on technological improvements to treatment processes for waste acid in order to mitigate environmental risks. Jinhui Chemical petitioned to the SPC for retrial. One of the key arguments was that Taizhou Environment Federation had no standing under article 55 of the CPL (2012) or article 58 of the EPL (2014).

The SPC (2016) dismissed Jinhui Chemical's petition for retrial. On the issue of standing, it ruled that Taizhou Environment Federation was a social organization registered with Taizhou City Civil Affairs Bureau on 25 February 2014 to protect environmental public interest and to promote environmental protection in Taizhou and globally. The court noted that Taizhou Environment Federation made environmental policy recommendations, protected the environmental rights and interests of the public, and engaged in environmental public education and in policy and technology consultancy work. The court ruled that it had standing under article 55 of the CPL (2012) to file civil EPIL on 4 August 2014. The five-year practice requirement in article 58 of the EPL (2014) did not apply to this case filed in 2014 as the law was not implemented until 1 January 2015, the court found.

All three courts confirmed the standing of Taizhou Environment Federation under the CPL (2012) and emphasized that at the time the case was accepted and adjudicated, the EPL (2014) was not in force and thus did not apply.

Since the EPL (2014) has been in force, the courts have taken a liberal approach to the interpretation of article 58's five-years-of-experience rule. In *Friends of Nature and Another* v. *Xie Zhijin and Others* (2015),[50] the first EPIL case filed by an NGO under EPL (2014), standing was a disputed issue. The FON registered with Chaoyang District Civil Affairs Bureau in June 2010 and filed the case on 1 January 2015. However, the NGO had operated since 2003 under the same name, though it was previously registered with the Ministry of Civil Affairs as the Green Culture Institute of the International Academy of Chinese Culture in 1994. When interpreting article 58's rule on five years of experience,

[50] SPC 10 Model Cases on Environmental Torts (2015), case no. 1.

both Nanping Intermediate Court (the first-instance court) and Fujian High Court (second-instance) decided that the FON's experience began when it started to engage in public interest environmental protection work in the name of the FON in 2003, not in 2010 when it was registered.

The requirement of 'specially engaging in the work of environmental protection' under article 58 further restricts the number of NGOs that may initiate EPIL. In *China Biodiversity Conservation and Green Development Foundation* v. *Ningxia Ruitai Science and Technology Co. and Seven Others* (2016),[51] Zhongwei Intermediate Court and Ningxia High Court decided that the foundation[52] did not have standing, because it was not 'specially engaged in environmental protection'. The foundation first had to overcome the hurdle of standing before it could sue eight companies for their illegal discharge of untreated industrial wastewater to the Tengger Desert, which caused severe contamination.

China Biodiversity Conservation and Green Development Foundation v. *Ningxia Ruitai Science and Technology Co. and Seven Others* (2016)

China Biodiversity Conservation and Green Development Foundation (CBCGDF) sued eight companies, including Ningxia Ruitai Science and Technology Co. (Ruitai), for causing severe contamination to the Tengger Desert by discharging industrial wastewater in violation of state standards. It sought a court order requiring the defendants to: (i) stop the illegal discharge of wastewater; (ii) eliminate any risk or danger of pollution; (iii) clean up the contaminated site or set up a fund for third-party restoration; (iv) accept inspection by a court-organized joint task force that included the plaintiff and technical and legal experts, among others; (v) compensate for loss of ecological function of the contaminated desert until it was fully restored and (vi) make a public apology in the national media.

Zhongwei Intermediate Court (2015) refused to accept the case, deciding that the CBCGDF did not have standing under article 58 of the EPL (2014), which stipulated that an organization must be 'specially engaged in environmental protection'. It ruled that the CBCGDF was not eligible to initiate EPIL as there was no reference to environmental protection in its mission statement when it registered in 1997. The CBCGDF appealed.

Ningxia High Court (2015) dismissed the appeal and upheld the lower court's decision. The CBCGDF petitioned the SPC for a retrial.

The SPC (2016) decided that the CBCGDF did have standing and ordered Zhongwei Intermediate Court to accept the case. It discussed the specific criteria for determining standing in EPIL under article 58 of EPL (2014) and its own Interpretation on Several Issues Concerning the Application of Law in Environmental Civil Public Interest Litigation (SPC Interpretation on Civil EPIL) (2015). It dismissed the restrictive and narrow approach taken by the lower courts in the interpretation of article 58, and stipulated three key factors for courts to review in determining standing: (i) whether a plaintiff's mission statement and scope of business covers the protection of the environmental public interest; (ii) whether the plaintiff actually engages in the public interest work of protecting

[51] Guiding Case no. 75, promulgated by the SPC on 28 December 2016; SPC 10 Model Cases of Environmental Public Interest Litigation (2017), case no. 2.

[52] The CBCGDF was set up by a former military officer in 1985 as the China Milu Foundation and registered as an NGO in 1997 in the name of the CBCGDF. It focused on biodiversity conservation and began its legal work in 2015 when the EPL (2014) came into force.

the environment and (iii) whether the environmental interest pursued by the plaintiff in the EPIL is relevant to its mission and scope of business. The CBCGDF had presented solid evidence to prove the existence of all three elements, and therefore met the standing requirements under article 58 of EPL (2014) and the SPC Interpretation on Civil EPIL (2015), the SPC found.

Given the landmark importance of the case, it was later promulgated by the SPC as Guiding Case No. 75.[53] Although in theory there is no rule of precedent in China, guiding cases are vested with the highest possible legal authority in order to direct the adjudication work of all levels of courts in China.[54] Thus, a broad approach to the interpretation of the requirement of 'specially engaged in environmental protection for public interest' under article 58 has been firmly established and is to be followed. First, courts should not focus narrowly or mechanically on the exact wording of the mission statement or scope of business drafted at the time of establishment and registration. Even if the mission statement does not specifically include 'environmental protection for the public interest' in the environment, the plaintiff still passes the test if its scope of business involves the protection of natural or built environments that impact human survival and development. The CBCGDF's missions and activities included protecting biodiversity and promoting green development, which were to be treated as equivalent to protecting the public interest in the environment. Second, the work of protecting the public interest in the environment covers wide-ranging activities that not only include those directly improving the environment, such as planting trees, protecting endangered species, conserving energy, abating emissions and cleaning up contamination, but also includes strengthening environmental governance and capacity building, such as public education, research and training, academic exchange, legal assistance and EPIL. Since starting out in 1985, the CBCGDF had hosted symposia on environmental protection, organized ecological field trips, campaigned for environmental awareness raising and initiated EPIL. Third, the requirement for relevance between the environmental interest under litigation and the plaintiff's mission and business does not demand that the issues under litigation exactly fit into the plaintiff's mission and business. What is required is relevance between the litigated matter and the general environment or ecosystem the plaintiff was established to protect. In the CBCGDF case, the litigated issue was the severe contamination that was harming the vulnerable Tengger Desert ecosystem. This was relevant to the CBCGDF's mission and activities to protect and conserve the ecosystem in general.

The CPL (2012) was amended again in 2017 to clarify the standing of procuratorates in civil EPIL.[55] Procuratorates gained standing to initiate civil EPIL, subject to the restriction that no other eligible plaintiff has done so.[56] This was done to ensure the best use of public and procuratorial resources and allow NGOs to play a major role in civil EPIL.

[53] SPC Guiding Case No. 75, issued on 28 December 2016.
[54] SPC, Provisions on Case Guidance Work (2010).
[55] NPCSC, Decision on Amending the Civil Procedure Law and the Administrative Litigation Law (2017).
[56] CPL (2017), art. 55(2). A procuratorate may initiate PIL to protect the environment and resources or to ensure food and drug safety in the absence of another eligible body, or where no other eligible body has initiated it.

12.1.3 Standing in Administrative EPIL: Two-Year Pilots and the ALL (2017)

In China, EPIL started with a focus on civil litigation against liable parties that had polluted the environment or destroyed an ecosystem, thereby harming the public interest. However, agency omissions have aggravated environmental harm caused by pollution or eco-destruction. To better supervise agencies in performing their statutory duties and to promote effective enforcement against environmental violations, the NPCSC decided to expand the role of procuratorates in PIL, with a focus on administrative PIL. It authorized the SPP to start a two-year pilot exercise (2015–17)[57] covering thirteen provinces, autonomous regions or municipalities directly under the central government in four subject areas: (i) protection of environment and resources; (ii) protection of state assets; (iii) transfer of state-owned land-use rights and (iv) protection of food and drug safety.[58]

In 2015, the SPP issued a reform plan[59] and measures[60] to launch a two-year pilot scheme covering both civil and administrative PIL. The pilot scheme targeted civil PIL in two areas: (i) environment and resource protection and (ii) food and drug safety.[61] In the case of administrative PIL, the scheme targeted regulatory agencies in charge of three areas: (i) environment and resource protection; (ii) protection of state assets and (iii) transfer of state-owned land-use rights.[62] Thus, procuratorates were given a role to play in both civil and administrative EPIL. The SPP emphasized that the procuratorates must effectively protect the public interest by initiating civil or administrative PIL against any legal or natural person that had infringed on state interests or the public interest by pollution or resource destruction, among others.[63] In administrative PIL, cases of EPIL were to be prioritized during the two-year pilot exercise.[64]

The theoretical basis for a procuratorate's standing in PIL is its function of legal supervision.[65] Litigation is an expensive legal instrument in any society and PIL is not the only, nor the first and foremost, means used by procuratorates to supervise agencies. Litigation is not the goal, but a tool to achieve the goals of ensuring an agency performs its statutory duty lawfully and effective law enforcement. Therefore, pre-litigation procedures are prescribed to ensure the most efficient use of public and procuratorial resources. In civil PIL, a procuratorate may initiate PIL against any party harming the public interest by polluting or by infringing the interest of a large number of consumers of food and drugs, only if no other party has standing to sue or if parties with standing do not sue.[66] In administrative PIL, a procuratorate may initiate PIL against any regulatory agency for violating the law or for failing to perform its statutory duty if a citizen, legal person or any

[57] The NPCSC issued the Decision on Authorizing the Supreme People's Procuratorate to Launch the Pilot Program of Initiating Public Interest Actions in Certain Areas on 1 July 2015.

[58] The thirteen designated cities, autonomous regions and provinces were: Beijing, Inner Mongolia, Jilin, Jiangsu, Anhui, Fujian, Shandong, Hubei, Guangdong, Guizhou, Yunnan, Shaanxi and Gansu.

[59] The Reform Plan on a Pilot Project for Instituting Public Interest Litigation by Procuratorial Organs (Reform Plan on PIL Pilots) (2015) was issued by the SPP on 2 July 2015.

[60] The SPP Implementation Measures (2015) were issued by the SPP on 16 December 2015.

[61] Reform Plan on PIL Pilots (2015), part II (I); SPP Implementation Measures (2015), chapter I.

[62] Reform Plan on PIL Pilots (2015), part II (II); SPP Implementation Measures (2015), chapter II.

[63] Reform Plan on PIL Pilots (2015), part I (III). [64] Reform Plan on PIL Pilots (2015), part II (II), para. 1.

[65] The Organic Law of People's Procuratorates (1986), art. 1.

[66] Reform Plan on PIL Pilots (2015), part II (I), para. 1; SPP Implementation Measures (2015), art. 1; CPL (2017), art. 55(2).

other social organization does not or cannot sue.[67] The pre-litigation procedures for civil PIL include 'urging or supporting another relevant authority or social organization to initiate PIL',[68] and for administrative PIL include 'urging the relevant regulatory agency in violation to rectify or to perform its statutory duties by issuing procuratorial advice'.[69] In *Guizhou Liuzhi District Procuratorate* v. *Dingqi Township Government* (2016),[70] the local government was sued for using land unlawfully as a rubbish dump.

Guizhou Liuzhi District Procuratorate v. *Dingqi Township Government* (2016)

Dingqi Township Government used land at a former aeroplane manufacturing plant as a temporary site for disposing of household waste. Longtan village sent waste to the site for disposal. In November 2015, Guizhou Liuzhi District Procuratorate issued a procuratorial advice to the defendant, Dingqi Township Government, requiring it to remove the waste, restore the land within one month and stop Longtan village dumping waste there. Dingqi Township Government neither replied nor took action. The Procuratorate sued, seeking a court decision that the defendant's use of the site for waste disposal was unlawful. It also sought a court order requiring the defendant to stop Longtan village from dumping waste at the site, take remedial measures to remove the waste, and restore the site.

Qingzhen City Court (2016) found that the defendant was using the site as a temporary rubbish dump without having obtained approval from environmental and health authorities. It had taken no measures to prevent pollution from the household waste. During the trial, the defendant removed the waste from the site and told Longtan village to stop dumping there. The court held that Dingqi Township Government's decision to use the site as a rubbish dump was unlawful, ordering it to take remedial measures in accordance with expert opinions and recommendations to improve the environmental quality of the site and the affected areas surrounding it.

In *Jilin Baishan City Procuratorate* v. *Jiangyuan District Health and Family Planning Bureau and Baishan Hospital* (2016),[71] the local procuratorate filed administrative EPIL attached with civil EPIL.

Jilin Baishan City Procuratorate v. *Jiangyuan District Health and Family Planning Bureau and Baishan Hospital* (2016)

Baishan Hospital's new complex was brought into use without wastewater treatment installations. Jilin Baishan City Procuratorate found that the hospital was discharging clinical wastewater to an on-site seepage well and an off-site seepage pit, contaminating groundwater and soil. Testing showed that the discharged wastewater and the soil around the well both contained excessively high levels of pollutants, including COD. Jiangyuan District Health and Family Planning Bureau renewed the licence of Baishan Hospital following an annual inspection, despite the fact that it did

[67] Reform Plan on PIL Pilots (2015), part II (II), para. 1; SPP Implementation Measures (2015), art. 28.
[68] Reform Plan on PIL Pilots (2015), part II (I), para. 3; SPP Implementation Measures (2015), art. 13.
[69] Reform Plan on PIL Pilots (2015), part II (II), para. 3; SPP Implementation Measures (2015), art. 40.
[70] SPC 10 Model Cases of Environmental Public Interest Litigation (2017), case no. 9.
[71] SPC 10 Model Cases of Environmental Public Interest Litigation (2017), case no. 10.

not have the requisite EIA approval from the local EPB. The Procuratorate issued procuratorial advice to the Bureau, urging it to perform its statutory duty and stop the illegal discharge. The Bureau issued an order to Baishan Hospital and reported back to the Procuratorate, but the illegal discharge continued, infringing on the public interest. The Procuratorate sued both parties by initiating an administrative EPIL with a civil EPIL attached.

Baishan Intermediate Court (2016) accepted the two cases separately, conducted one single trial with the same collegiate panel, and delivered two judgments. It accepted the evidence presented by the Procuratorate and found the hospital's illegal discharge had caused contamination of groundwater and soil. It found that the Bureau had failed to perform its statutory duty in supervising the operation of the hospital. In the administrative EPIL against the Bureau, the court held that: (i) the Bureau's decision to renew the hospital's operation licence was in violation of law and (ii) the Bureau was to perform its statutory duty to supervise the hospital and ensure it improved its wastewater treatment within three months. In the civil EPIL, the court held that the hospital was to stop the illegal discharge immediately.

In this case in which one single pollution incident triggered the pursuit of different legal liabilities of different parties, the court adopted the format of administrative EPIL with a civil EPIL attached to improve efficiency and save judicial resources. That the finding of facts and acceptance of evidence was conducted by one collegiate panel avoided repeating work and wasting judicial resources.

Upon successful completion of the two-year pilot exercise in 2017, the NPCSC formally confirmed the standing of procuratorates in both civil and administrative EPIL in specified subject areas by amending the CPL (2012) and ALL (2014).[72] Procuratorates enjoy certain advantages compared to NGOs given their financial resources, professional capability and institutional status and, due to the political power relationships that exist between procuratorates, agencies and courts, are more powerful than NGOs in fighting legal battles against agencies.[73]

12.2 JURISDICTION

Chinese courts are conventionally divided into civil, criminal, administrative and enforcement divisions. Specialized environmental divisions have been set up to strengthen courts' roles in environmental protection. Prior to the systemic establishment of environmental tribunals, maritime courts in many provinces were actively involved in handling water pollution cases.

12.2.1 Maritime Courts

Maritime courts are special courts with expertise in hearing cases of maritime torts and contract disputes, and cases involving land-sourced pollution contaminating the ocean and

[72] NPCSC, Decision to Amend the Civil Procedure Law and the Administrative Litigation Law (2017).
[73] For more discussion, see Tiantian Zhai and Yen-Chiang Chang, 'Standing of environmental public-interest litigants', at 379–80.

navigable waters. They are not funded by the local governments and thus are more detached from the impact of local protectionism compared to local courts. The accumulated professional experience in resolving maritime disputes and relatively independent institutional structure put them in a suitable position to handle EPIL prior to the establishment of specialized environmental tribunals.

Guangdong province, one of China's most economically advanced and heavily industrialized regions, saw the extreme urgency of controlling pollution and protecting water resources. Consequently, the province decided that using the judicial experience and expertise of its maritime courts would be an efficient approach to handling water pollution disputes relating to the sea and waters leading to the sea.[74] Guangzhou Maritime Court took the lead by accepting the first EPIL in Guangdong province, in a case in which Haizhu District Procuratorate sued a jeans-processing laundry/factory, calling for it to stop its polluting operations and clean up the seriously contaminated river.[75] Haizhu District Procuratorate's success led to another EPIL being filed by Panyu Procuratorate.[76] In both the Haizhu (2008) and Panyu (2009) cases, Guangzhou Maritime Court established its jurisdiction over disputes caused by pollution of waters leading to the sea. However, in both cases pollution was caused by industrial operations on land. The SPC Provisions on the Scope of Cases Accepted by Maritime Courts (SPC Provisions) (2001) provides a list of cases that fall within the jurisdiction of maritime courts. These include water pollution caused by vessels, by operations at sea or within waters leading to the sea, by the building, repair or dismantling of ships, and by works or construction at a harbour.[77] The list does not expressly include water pollution caused by sources on land, such as the operation by the laundry/factory or the Panyu tannery. However, paragraph (10) of part I of the SPC Provisions (2001) covers 'any other maritime disputes', which can be interpreted broadly and therefore covered disputes such as the pollution of the ShiLiuGang River (see *Haizhu District Procuratorate* v. *Chen Zhongming* (2008)) and Xiadao Chong (see *Panyu District Procuratorate* v. *Lu Pingzhang* (2009)). In addition, Guangzhou Maritime Court finds its jurisdiction in the SPC's Several Opinions on the Development of Maritime Adjudication Work (2006), which expressly stated that 'the scope of jurisdiction of the maritime courts should be adjusted when needed and cases involving land source pollution of the sea or navigable waters leading to the sea should fall under the jurisdiction of maritime courts'.[78] Most recently, the jurisdiction of Guangzhou Maritime Court was strengthened with the implementation of the Opinion of the Guangdong High Court on Designating Certain Cases under the Jurisdiction of Guangzhou Maritime Court (for trial use), which came into force on 1 January 2012. Article 1 provides that cases involving pollution of the sea or waters leading to the sea by land-based sources fall under the jurisdiction of Guangzhou Maritime Court.[79]

[74] Wang Doudou, 'The Supreme People's Court', 5.
[75] The judgment in *Haizhu District Procuratorate* v. *Chen Zhongming* (2008) is accessible at www.pkulaw.cn. The case was further discussed in Li Zhiping, 'Analysis of the practice', at 802–3.
[76] *Panyu District People's Procuratorate* v. *Lu Pingzhang* (2009). The judgment is available at www.pkulaw.cn.
[77] SPC Provisions (2001), part I, paras. (4) and (5).
[78] SPC, Several Opinions on the Development of Maritime Adjudication Work (2006), part II, para (5).
[79] Guangdong High Court, Opinion on Designating Certain Cases under the Jurisdiction of Guangzhou Maritime Court (for trial use), art. 1(2).

12.2.2 Specialized Environmental Tribunals

The establishment of specialized environmental tribunals started under local pilot schemes. In 2007, Qingzhen Environmental Division was set up as China's first specialized environmental court. Qingzhen is a county-level city under the jurisdiction of Guiyang, the capital city of Guizhou province.[80] With the approval of Guizhou Provincial High Court, Guiyang Intermediate Court issued the Decision on Designated Jurisdictions (2007), which stipulated that all first-instance environmental cases in the city of Guiyang, including EPIL, fell under the jurisdiction of the newly established Qingzhen Environmental Court. It further stipulated that procuratorates, the management authority of two lakes and one reservoir, environmental protection authorities and forest bureaus were permitted to initiate EPIL as plaintiffs.[81] In Wuxi city in Jiangsu province, environmental divisions were set up in 2008 at both basic-level and intermediate courts to accept environmental cases filed by procuratorates, environmental protection authorities, environmental social organizations and companies managing residential premises.[82] In the city of Kunming, an environmental tribunal was set up at Kunming Intermediate Court in 2008, with jurisdiction over environmental civil, criminal, administrative and enforcement cases. Procuratorates, environmental bureaus and social organizations were permitted to initiate EPIL.[83] These were pilot schemes that trialled specialized environmental tribunals with various jurisdictions. Then, on 4 July 2014, the SPC set up the Environment and Resources Division (ERD) to hear first-instance cases within its jurisdiction and appeals from lower-level people's courts. By the end of 2018, 391 environmental courts had been established and, of those, twenty-three were located at provincial high courts.[84]

The ERD was established with civil jurisdiction over first- and second-instance civil disputes involving: (i) tort caused by air pollution, water pollution and soil contamination; (ii) mining rights; (iii) rights to develop and use natural resources, including forests, grassland, rivers, lakes, shoals and wetlands.[85] In 2016, the SPC expanded the ERD's jurisdiction to cover second-instance and review for retrial of administrative cases in which environmental agencies are defendants.[86] Since then, the ERD has had jurisdiction over both civil and administrative cases involving environment and resources. In 2017, the SPC adopted a three-in-one model at its Third Circuit Court, putting one adjudication team in charge of all civil, criminal and administrative cases involving environment and resources.[87]

80 SPC, *Environment and Resources Adjudication in China*, part II.

81 Guiyang Intermediate Court, Decision on Designated Jurisdictions (2007). The two lakes are Red Maple Lake and Hundred Flower Lake, and the reservoir is the Aha Reservoir. They provide more than 60 per cent of the water supply in Guiyang. However, as a result of industrialization, by 2007 the water quality had deteriorated to Grade V and sub-Grade V in the two lakes and Grade IV in the reservoir. The contamination threatened the safety of drinking water for more than one million people in Guiyang and thus the municipal government set up, in 2007, a special authority to manage the three waterbodies.

82 Wuxi Intermediate Court and Wuxi Procuratorate, Provisions on Handling Environmental Public Interest Litigations (for trial use) (2008).

83 Kunming Intermediate Court, Kunming Procuratorate, Kunming Municipal Public Security Bureau (PSB and Kunming Environmental Protection Bureau (EPB) issued the Decision on Establishing Environmental Protection Coordinating Mechanisms (2008).

84 SPC, *Environmental and Resources Adjudication in China 2017–18*, part III.

85 SPC, 'Fully strengthening'; see also, 'SPC establishes', *People's Court News*.

86 SPC, *Environment and Resources Adjudication in China*, part III.

87 SPC, *Environment and Resources Adjudication in China 2016–17*, part III.

The jurisdiction of the ERD was expanded again in 2018 to take in administrative cases in which agencies in charge of the eco-environment, natural resources, forestry and grassland are defendants.[88] Under the guidance of the SPC, local courts have also adopted combined jurisdictions in the form of two-in-one civil and administrative jurisdiction, three-in-one civil, administrative and criminal jurisdiction, and even three-plus-one civil, administrative and criminal, plus enforcement, jurisdiction over all environmental and resource cases.[89]

Innovation in jurisdiction that centralizes all hearings relating to environmental issues is beneficial, because it harmonizes law enforcement standards across a jurisdiction and reduces legal costs. It resolves the waste of judicial resources that occurred when one pollution case was tried separately in both a criminal division (for prosecution and sanction of an environmental crime) and a civil division (for compensation of victims or eco-remediation). In the case of *Jilin Baishan City Procuratorate* v. *Jiangyuan District Health and Family Planning Bureau and Baishan Hospital* (2016),[90] the court accepted the two cases (administrative EPIL and civil EPIL) separately, conducted one single trial using the same collegiate panel, and delivered two judgments. The trial model of administrative EPIL with an attached civil EPIL has improved efficiency and saved judicial resources. In the case of *Jinghu District Procuratorate* v. *Li and Others* (2018),[91] Jinghu District Court in Wuhu city, Anhui province tried the case as a criminal prosecution with civil EPIL attached.

Jinghu District Procuratorate v. *Li and Others* (2018)

In October 2017, Li Changhong, Huang Guanqun and Zhang Chuanjiang, none of whom possessed an HW operation permit, collected more than 2,500 t of industrial sludge from nine enterprises in Jiangsu and Zhejiang provinces for disposing of in Anhui province. They dumped the toxic sludge, which contained heavy metals, in a village by the Yangtze River, seriously contaminating the eco-environment of the river and harming surface water, soil and groundwater. An emergency response was taken, following which Jinghu District Procuratorate prosecuted Li and others (three individuals and nine companies) for the crime of environmental pollution under the CL (2011). It also initiated a civil EPIL claim, which was attached to the criminal prosecution, seeking compensation of more than 13.02 million yuan to be borne jointly by the twelve defendants. The compensation was to cover the cost of the emergency response, the remediation of the contaminated environment and appraisal fees.

Jinghu District Court (2018) found the defendants' illegal disposal of toxic sludge across the provincial boundary had caused serious contamination of the eco-environment of the Yangtze River. The court convicted the defendants of the crime of environmental pollution and sentenced them to imprisonment for terms of one and a half years to six years, and imposed fines of 10,000 yuan to 200,000 yuan. The court also held the defendants liable for the environmental harm caused by the dumping of toxic sludge, ordering them to pay 13.02 million yuan in compensation and offer a public apology via provincial media.

88 SPC, *Environment and Resources Adjudication in China 2017–18*, part III.
89 SPC, *Environment and Resources Adjudication in China*, part III.
90 SPC 10 Model Cases of Environmental Public Interest Litigation (2017), case no. 10.
91 SPP 10 Model Cases of Procuratorial Public Interest Litigation (2018), case no. 10; see also *Baoxun (Zhejiang) Ltd Co. and Others* (2018), for which the judgment is available at www.pkulaw.cn.

The establishment of specialized environmental divisions staffed with specialized judges improves the quality and efficiency of environmental adjudication, giving plaintiffs better access to judicial redress.

12.2.3 Jurisdiction by Designation

After a trial period that began in 2007 when the first environmental tribunal was established, the SPC decided to streamline the issue of jurisdiction. It expressly provided that courts of intermediate level or above at the place at which environmental pollution or eco-destruction has happened, at the place at which harm is done or where defendants have domicile have jurisdiction over first-instance civil EPIL.[92] Where necessary, an intermediate court may delegate its jurisdiction to a basic-level court, subject to prior approval of the high court.[93] Upon approval by the SPC, high courts may designate certain intermediate courts to exercise jurisdiction over first-instance civil EPIL based on the particular environmental protection needs of a province. The geographical scope of the jurisdiction of each designated intermediate court will be determined by the high court.[94] This more flexible approach of jurisdiction by designation allows a smaller number of intermediate courts to develop expertise in environmental adjudication. It also addresses the practical issues arising from the fact that the environmental caseload is lower than caseloads for other types of cases. For example, Guizhou Provincial High Court designated four intermediate courts (out of a total of nine) and five basic-level courts (out of more than eighty) to exercise jurisdiction over environment and resources cases. In 2019, the SPC approved Jiangsu High Court's request to set up a specialized environment and resources division at Nanjing Intermediate Court to exercise jurisdiction over second-instance adjudication of all environmental cases in Jiangsu province.[95] The innovation and reforms are initiated by courts in response to the challenges encountered in developing specialized environmental adjudication.

12.3 REMEDIES UNDER CIVIL EPIL

Where acts of pollution or ecological destruction harm the public interest in the environment, or threaten imminent harm to it, civil EPIL offers the remedies of injunction, removal of obstruction, elimination of danger, restoration, compensation and offer of apology.[96] The first three aim to stop ongoing infringement of public interest by pollution and prevent any risk of potential harm. Offer of apology, as a form of civil remedy, has only recently begun to be used in environmental cases. Restoration and compensation remain the major remedies in almost all civil EPILs, and these often involve technical and legal challenges in the calculation of restoration fees and loss of ecological function, the making and implementation of restoration plans, and the management and use of the money collected in damages.

[92] SPC Interpretation on Civil EPIL (2015), art. 6(1). [93] SPC Interpretation on Civil EPIL (2015), art. 6(2).
[94] SPC Interpretation on Civil EPIL (2015), art. 7.
[95] SPC, Reply to Jiangsu Provincial High Court on the Approval of Establishing a Specialized Environment and Resources Division at Nanjing Intermediate Court (2 January 2019).
[96] SPC Interpretation on Civil EPIL (2015), art. 18.

12.3.1 Injunction, Removal of Obstruction and Elimination of Danger

A court injunction to stop ongoing infringement is the most effective way of preventing further deterioration of the environment caused by pollution discharge. This is seen in the case of *Chongqing Green Volunteers Federation* v. *Hubei Huangchangping Mining Co.* (2016).[97]

Chongqing Green Volunteers Federation v. *Hubei Huangchangping Mining Co.* (2016)

Qianzhangyan Reservoir is a designated DWSR providing water to 50,000 people. The defendant's mining project, located 2.6 km from the reservoir, started operations on 10 August 2014. It discharged untreated wastewater and tailings to nearby karst caves. On 12 August 2014, villagers reported that the water in Qianzhangyan Reservoir had become abnormal and the local government activated its environmental emergency response plan. The plaintiff NGO sued, seeking a court order for the defendant to: (i) stop the infringement and prevent further pollution; (ii) carry out another EIA to assess the risks of contaminating groundwater and the reservoir (and, depending on the EIA outcome and conclusion, the local government would decide whether the defendant should relocate) and (iii) clean up the contaminated reservoir or pay 991,000 yuan.

Chongqing Wanzhou District Court (2016) found that the defendant had operated illegally and contaminated the Qianzhangyan Reservoir, threatening the supply of safe drinking water and damaging the public interest. The location of the mining project risked contaminating groundwater and no water pollution prevention and control facilities had been installed, the court found. Actual environmental damage had occurred, and there was also a risk of further pollution, it continued. The court held that: (i) the defendant was to stop the ongoing infringement immediately and conduct another EIA. It was not permitted to resume production prior to obtaining this EIA approval from the EPB and passing an inspection of the pollution-control facilities; (ii) the defendant was to prepare a remediation plan and, within 180 days, clean up the contaminated sites that held untreated wastewater and tailings. If the defendant failed to clean up the site or its remediation failed to protect the public interest in the ecological environment, it would have to pay a remediation fee of 991,000 yuan and (iii) the defendant must apologize publicly via national media. The defendant appealed.

Chongqing No.2 Intermediate Court (2016) dismissed the appeal and upheld the lower court's decision.

Courts may also issue an injunction, prior to trial, for a polluter to stop its discharge, as in the case of *All-China Environment Federation and Another* v. *Guiyang Dingba Paper Mill* (2011).[98] Upon accepting the case and at the request of the plaintiffs, Qingzhen City Court sent a team of judges to the point at which the Nanming River was being contaminated by the defendant's secret discharge. They took photos and collected samples to preserve evidence. Given the seriousness of the circumstances, the court, prior to the hearing, issued an injunction ordering Dingba to stop the discharge immediately. In its judgment, Qingzhen City Court ordered Dingba to stop the infringement and eliminate danger by suspending its discharge. Elimination of

97 SPC 10 Model Cases of Environmental Public Interest Litigation (2017), case no. 4.
98 SPC Nine Model Cases on Environment and Resources (2014), case no. 1.

danger is an order to remove a substantial threat of environmental harm. It is often ordered by a court simultaneously with an order to cease an infringement. A court's active and early intervention can contain pollution and mitigate environmental harm.

The SPC's Interpretation on Civil EPIL (2015) formalized the experiences gained in judicial practice. It provides that 'to prevent and control harm caused to the environment, the plaintiffs' request for an injunction to stop the ongoing infringement, for the removal of obstruction and elimination of danger may be supported by courts'.[99] Further, if plaintiffs have incurred costs to take reasonable measures to contain and prevent the environmental harm and subsequently request reimbursement from the defendants, the courts may support their claims and order the defendants to bear the cost.[100]

12.3.2 Restoration

Restoration, also known as remediation, refers to a clean-up of the contaminated environment, such as a river, pond or land, or remediation of the harmed eco-environment, such as by reforestation. Where restoration of the site is impossible, substitute restoration or off-site restoration may be ordered by the court. Where a plaintiff requests restoration, a court may order the defendant to restore the environment to the state and function existing prior to the pollution or ecological harm. Where full restoration is unachievable, the court may allow alternative forms of restoration.[101] A court may also decide the cost of restoration, and order liable parties to pay the restoration fees in lieu of restoration.[102] The restoration fees include expenses for making and implementing a remediation plan, and the related monitoring and supervision costs.[103]

In *Friends of Nature and Another* v. *Xie Zhijin and Others* (2015),[104] the first EPIL initiated by grass-roots NGOs under the EPL (2014), Nanping Intermediate Court offered both restoration and compensation as remedies.

Friends of Nature and Another v. *Xie Zhijin and Others* (2015)

Xie and three other defendants had, since July 2008, engaged in illegal mining without obtaining the relevant approvals, causing serious destruction of more than 28 *mu* of forestland. The defendants had been convicted of the crime of illegally occupying agricultural land in 2014, but the damaged forestland had not been attended to.[105] The revised EPL (2014), which came into force on 1 January 2015, gave standing to NGOs to seek remedies through EPIL. The FON and Fujian Green Home sued for restoration of the forestland and compensation for loss of ecological value and land function during the period from harm to recovery.

Nanping Intermediate Court (2015) accepted the case on 1 January 2015, and held trials in May, June and October. It found that the defendants' unlicensed mining had caused serious ecological

[99] SPC Interpretation on Civil EPIL (2015), art. 19(1).

[100] SPC Interpretation on Civil EPIL (2015), art. 19(2).

[101] SPC Interpretation on Civil EPIL (2015), art. 20(1).

[102] SPC Interpretation on Civil EPIL (2015), art. 20(2).

[103] SPC Interpretation on Civil EPIL (2015), art. 20(3).

[104] SPC 10 Model Cases on Environmental Torts (2015), case no. 1. The case was examined in Zander, 'How effective', at 609–14.

[105] 'Agricultural land' is defined as including forestland, among others.

damage to the trees, forestland and the forest ecosystem. It held the four defendants jointly liable for the ecological damage and allocated civil liabilities: (i) the defendants were ordered, within five months, to remove the mining sheds, equipment, rubble and mining waste from the mining site and destroyed forestland, restore 28.33 *mu* of forestland, and plant trees, and maintain and protect them for three years; (ii) in case of failure to restore the forestland and plant trees by the deadline, the defendants were to pay environmental restoration fees of 1.1 million yuan; (iii) the defendants were held liable for 1.27 million yuan in compensation for the loss of the ecological function of the forestland during the period from harm to recovery and (iv) the defendants were ordered to pay the plaintiffs 166,162 yuan to cover the appraisal fee, lawyers' fees and other reasonable litigation expenses incurred. The defendants appealed.

Fujian High Court (2015) dismissed the appeal and upheld the first-instance decision.

In addition to ordering the site to be restored to its original condition, the court also calculated the restoration fees so that it would be able to demand the money and use it to pay for third-party restoration if the defendants failed to restore by the due date. Restoration by a professional third party ensures quality remediation is conducted in a timely manner and in a way that best protects the environmental interests of the general public. It is becoming common for courts to include third-party restoration as a measure to be used if the defendant defaults, as in *All-China Environment Federation* v. *Jiangyin Liangping Pig Farm and Another* (2016).[106]

All-China Environment Federation v. *Jiangyin Liangping Pig Farm and Another* (2016)

Jiangyin Liangping Pig Farm started operations without conducting the required EIA and without inspection and approval of its pollution-control installations. Serious pollution was caused to a nearby village. The ACEF sued, seeking: a court order to stop the infringement; an apology; treatment of the animal waste to eliminate the risk of further contamination; clean-up of contaminated water and soil; and compensation for the loss of ecological function of water and soil.

Wuxi Intermediate Court (2016) accepted the case. Jiangyin Liangping Pig Farm suspended its operations and the discharge during the trial and submitted an environmental restoration plan. The court invited experts to attend the trial and examine the defendant's plan, but the experts concluded that it would not eliminate the pollution. The court then hired an appraisal body to produce a technical restoration plan and a supervision plan, and held that: (i) the defendant must clean up the contaminated soil and water in compliance with the technical restoration plan and under supervision (ii) the defendant must report to the court, within one month, on the progress of the restoration work.

[106] SPC 10 Model Cases of Environmental Public Interest Litigation (2017), case no. 5. The full text of the judgement is available: Jiangsu Provincial High Court, *Jiangsu Provincial High Court Gazette*, 6 (2017), 54–62.

The court would request a local EPB to conduct an inspection; (iii) if the defendant's restoration work failed to achieve the targets of the technical restoration plan, the court would engage a third party to conduct the restoration, for which Jiangyin Liangping Pig Farm would have to pay.

Where it is difficult to ascertain the cost of ecological restoration or where the appraisal fees are prohibitively high, the court may decide on a reasonable amount, taking into account the extent and degree of the environmental pollution and ecological destruction, the rarity of the ecosystem, the difficulty in restoring the environment, the cost of operating the pollution prevention and control equipment, and the defendants' illegal gains and fault, with reference to the opinions of EPBs and experts.[107] In *Taizhou Environment Federation* v. *Taixing Jinhui Chemical Co. and Five Others* (2016) (see Section 12.1.2), Taizhou Intermediate Court estimated the cost of restoration by reference to the virtual treatment cost calculated by professionals.[108] It ordered six defendant companies to pay 160 million yuan for having entrusted more than 25,000 t of toxic and hazardous waste acid to unlicensed parties, who secretly discharged the waste acid to the Rutai Canal and Gumagan River, causing severe toxic contamination of the water.

In addition to the use of the virtual treatment cost, the court also considers other elements including fault, illegal gains and the operation costs of pollution prevention and treatment. A defendant's fault in repeated intentional violations of law by secret discharge of untreated industrial wastewater impacts on the calculation of the restoration cost, as occurred in the case of *Xuzhou Procuratorate* v. *Xuzhou Hongshun Paper Co.* (2016).[109]

Xuzhou Procuratorate v. *Xuzhou Hongshun Paper Co.* (2016)

Routine on-site inspections of Xuzhou Hongshun Paper Co. from 2013 to 2015 found that the defendant's wastewater treatment installations were not being used and untreated industrial wastewater was being discharged by hidden pipes to the North Jiangsu Embankment River. The local EPB imposed fines of 50,000 yuan in 2014 for illegal discharge of 600 t of wastewater and 100,000 yuan in 2015 for illegal discharge of 2,000 t. Xuzhou Procuratorate sued in December 2015, seeking a court order to compel the defendant to restore the contaminated river and compensate for the loss of ecological function. It also requested that if the defendant was unable to carry out restoration, it would be required to pay a restoration fee.

Xuzhou Intermediate Court (2016) found the defendant's illegal discharge of untreated industrial wastewater contained excessive levels of COD, NH and total phosphorous. The contaminated river was connected to the Beijing–Hangzhou Grand Canal, an important source of water for irrigation, the court noted. The defendant had engaged in secret discharge through hidden pipes in order to avoid paying pollution discharge fees and save the cost of treatment, it added. On-site inspections had found secret discharge of 2,600 t of wastewater, but the secret

[107] SPC Interpretation on Civil EPIL (2015), art. 23.
[108] SPC 10 Model Cases of Environmental Public Interest Litigation (2017), case no. 1.
[109] SPC 10 Model Cases of Environmental Public Interest Litigation (2017), case no. 8.

discharging could have occurred over a longer period of time, and therefore the total discharge could have been much more, the court found. Experts estimated the virtual treatment cost of 2,600 t of wastewater at 269,100 yuan. The defendant's operations would normally generate 960 t/day of wastewater, while its discharge permit indicates a maximum 195,000 t of annual effluent discharge. Considering that the defendant had repeatedly and intentionally engaged in secret discharge in violation of the law in order to reduce treatment costs and evade agency monitoring, and that it was unable to carry out the restoration itself, the court held that Xuzhou Hongshun Paper Co. should pay 1.058 million yuan as the total sum for restoration and compensation for loss of ecological function of the contaminated river. The defendant appealed.

Jiangsu High Court (2016) dismissed the appeal and upheld the decision of the lower court.

To address the difficulties of calculating restoration fees and compensation for loss of ecological function, the court applied article 23 of the SPC Interpretation on Civil EPIL (2015), which permits courts to consider a range of key factors, including the extent and degree of contamination, the difficulty of restoration, the cost of operating pollution treatment facilities and, in particular, the defendant's unlawful gains resulting from the violation and the degree of fault. This case highlights the difficulty of putting a price on remediation and loss of ecological function, with the court not treating the restoration fee and the compensation for loss of ecological function as two separate items, but offering one lump sum of 1.058 million yuan for both.

Where on-site restoration is impossible, off-site ecological conservation may be an acceptable alternative as long as the ecological harm is more than compensated for. This can be seen in *All-China Environment Federation* v. *Wuxi Lihu Huishan Scenic Zone Management Committee* (2012).[110]

All-China Environment Federation v. *Wuxi Lihu Huishan Scenic Zone Management Committee* (2012)

From October 2009 to July 2010, Wuxi Lihu Huishan Scenic Zone Management Committee (Management Committee) constructed an eco-project in Wuxi, comprising the Wuxi Zoological and Botanical Garden and the Happy Park. However, the zoo (just one part of the Garden) and relevant roads had been built on 17,477 m^2 of forestland without prior approval. Further, the internal transport link between the Garden and the Park, and a fire safety facility occupied a further 3,677 m^2 of forestland, without prior approval. In total, the defendant had illegally occupied 21,154 m^2 of forestland, for which it paid a fine of 232,694 yuan, an administrative sanction imposed by Wuxi Binhu District Agriculture and Forestry Bureau. Also on the site, there was a 2,500 m^2 piece of land that was bare soil, a legacy of open mining in the 1980s. The ACEF sued the Management Committee, seeking the remedies of restoration of the forestland, compensation for loss of ecological function, prevention of water and soil loss by planting trees and grass on the bare soil, and better conservation of natural resources in the future.

[110] SPC Nine Model Cases on Environment and Resources (2014), case no. 8.

Wuxi Binhu District Court (2012) addressed three issues in detail and awarded remedies: (i) regarding the defendant's illegal occupation of 17,477 m^2 of forestland without approval, the court found that as the land had been used to build the Wuxi Zoological and Botanical Garden, an eco-project forming part of the city's greenery, there was no obvious environmental damage. During the trial, the defendant applied to the local agriculture and forestry bureau for approval to change the permitted use of the land and paid more than 1.14 million yuan as a forest restoration fee, which the court treated as compensation for ecological damage to the forestland; (ii) regarding the illegal occupation of the 3,677 m^2 forestland to build the link between the Garden and the Park and structures for emergency exits, the court decided that due to the important public interest involved, safety from fire, *in situ* restoration was undesirable and dismantling the completed structures would be a waste of resources. Following consultation with professionals and the public, the defendant proposed an off-site restoration plan to plant trees at a site as near to the original site as possible. The court ordered the defendant to pay a conservation fee of 794,400 yuan and complete the off-site afforestation on 4,500 m^2 of land in Yangwan, an area within the Binhu district; (iii) regarding the 2,500 m^2 of bare soil that posed a potential risk of water and soil loss, the court referred to article 120 of the Property Law (2007), which provides that 'anyone exercising land-use rights shall comply with provisions on conservation and rational exploitation and utilization of resources'. The defendant Management Committee and two of its subordinates (the management bodies of the Garden and the Park), as parties with land-use rights over the site, were ordered to take measures to provide treatment and eliminate the danger of water and soil loss. The court ordered the defendant to complete the planting of trees and grass on the 2,500 m^2 plot within six months.

While restoration is a crucial remedy to maintain the quality and function of an ecosystem, courts may take a pragmatic approach and balance different interests, especially the public interest in the protection of public safety and conservation of resources. Where *in situ* restoration is not feasible, *ex situ* conservation becomes an option, with the condition that the ecological capacity of the restored site reaches the level of the original site prior to the destruction.

12.3.3 Compensation for Loss of Ecological Function

In the case of *Friends of Nature and Another* v. *Xie Zhijin and Others* (2015)[111], in addition to restoration, Nanping Intermediate Court ordered the defendants to pay compensation for the loss of ecological values and functions of the forestland during the period from destruction to recovery.[112] Where plaintiffs claim compensation for the loss of an ecological function of a polluted environment or damaged ecosystem for the period from the time harm is done to the time restoration is completed, the courts may support the claim.[113] This remedy was offered by the court in *All-China Environment Federation* v. *Dezhou Zhenhua Co.* (2016).[114]

[111] SPC 10 Model Cases on Environmental Torts (2015), case no. 1.
[112] The appraisal report points out that one of the ecological functions of forests is to act as a carbon sink.
[113] SPC Interpretation on Civil EPIL (2015), art. 21.
[114] Guiding case no.131; SPC 10 Model Cases of Environmental Public Interest Litigation (2017), case no. 3; see also SPC 10 Model Cases on Environmental Torts (2015), case no. 2.

***All-China Environment Federation v. Dezhou Zhenhua Co.* (2016)**

Dezhou Zhenhua Co. (Zhenhua) was founded in 2000 to manufacture flat glass, glass blocks and glassware. Data from Dezhou Environmental Monitoring Centre showed its emissions of SO_2, nitrogen oxides (NOx), smoke and soot had exceeded state limits since November 2013. It had been fined by Dezhou EPB and Shandong Provincial EPB many times, but the air pollution continued. Zhenhua was located in Dezhou city, surrounded by residential premises. The company's long-term air pollution in violation of state standards had caused serious adverse impact on the residents. The ACEF sued, seeking a court order for the defendant to: (i) stop emitting air pollutants in excess of state standards; (ii) pay compensation for the harm caused by air pollution; (iii) publicly apologize in the media and (iv) pay the ACEF's expenses relating to the litigation, including the appraisal fee and the lawyers' fees.

Dezhou Intermediate Court (2016) confirmed the ACEF's standing under article 58 of the EPL (2014). The defendant suspended all production lines and decided to relocate to an industrial park away from residential premises. The court accepted the expert opinion on the harm caused to property, human health and the atmosphere by excessive emissions of SO_2, NOx, smoke and soot. It also accepted an assessment and appraisal report produced by the Environmental Planning Academy, which calculated damages based on the virtual treatment cost. The court held that the defendant must: (i) pay 21.98 million yuan as compensation for losses caused by excessive air pollution; (ii) publicly apologize via provincial media and (iii) pay an appraisal fee of 100,000 yuan.

In this case, the court focused on compensation for loss, instead of injunction, as Zhenhua had decided to relocate. The biggest challenge was the calculation of damages. The court relied heavily on expert opinion and the professional appraisal report as objective and scientific bases for the determination of damages, and estimated the air pollution treatment costs. The court accepted expert opinion that excessive emissions of particulate matters, SO_2 and NOx not only harm property and human health, but also the ecological value and function of the atmosphere. To address the challenging task of assessing pure ecological or environmental loss, the MEP has offered guidance by issuing the Recommended Methods on Appraisal and Assessment of Assess Environmental Damage (2011) and its second edition in 2014.[115]

12.3.4 Liabilities of Multiple Polluters

Environmental harm is often caused by more than one party. The rules of tort law apply in civil EPIL. Where two or more persons act jointly to infringe on another person's rights and cause that person harm, they bear joint and several liability.[116] Where multiple tortfeasors are jointly and severally liable, the injured party has the right to seek remedies against any or all of them.[117] In the context of environmental tort, where two or more polluters jointly undertake polluting activities that cause harm, they bear joint and several liability.[118] Each

[115] The Recommendation was drafted by the Chinese Academy of Environmental Planning and is not a legally binding instrument.

[116] TL (2009), art. 8. [117] TL (2009), art. 13.

[118] SPC Interpretation on Application of Laws in Adjudicating Environmental Tort Cases (2015), art. 2.

tortfeasor is potentially 100 per cent liable to the victims of pollution for all the harm caused. Among tortfeasors bearing joint and several liability, liability is apportioned by reference to each party's contribution to the harm. Where it is difficult to determine the liability of each party, each party is deemed to have equal liability.[119] If any party pays more than its share to the injured party, it is entitled to recover the cost from other joint tortfeasors.[120] In *All-China Environment Federation* v. *Tan Yaohong and Fang Yunshuang* (2015),[121] the appellate court apportioned the liability between Tan and Fang in the ratio of 80:20, and they were held jointly and severally liable to the ACEF for the cost of restoration.

All-China Environment Federation v. *Tan Yaohong and Fang Yunshuang* (2015)

Fang Yunshang had leased two fish ponds to Tan Yaohong in August 2011. In early September, Tan dumped 110 truckloads of sludge into one of the ponds. Fang, concerned by the smell, terminated the lease, spread lime over the sludge and resumed fish farming in the pond. An on-site inspection and sample testing by the local EPB found excessively high levels of heavy metals, including copper and zinc, in the pond. The ACEF sued both Tan and Fang, seeking either restoration of the fish pond to its original state prior to the sludge dumping, or the payment of environmental restoration fees of 4,092,432 yuan.

Baiyun District Court (2014) found that Tan and Fang had jointly caused heavy metal contamination of the fish pond, noting that heavy metals can enter the food chain and threaten public health. The defendants had failed to prove a lack of causation, it found. The court held Tan and Fang jointly and severally liable for the restoration of the fish pond to its original state prior to the sludge dumping. If they failed to restore the pond, the local EPB would designate a third party to carry out restoration, with the cost jointly borne by Tan and Fang, the court said. Fang appealed.

Guangzhou Intermediate Court (2015) agreed with the lower court that Tan and Fang had jointly caused heavy metal contamination and should bear joint and several liability. It was the combination of Tan's dumping of sludge and Fang's lease of the fish pond that had together caused the pollution. However, Tan had directly dumped 110 truckloads of sludge into one pond and had played a major role in causing the heavy metal contamination. Fang had provided Tan with the site and possibility, but had also later worked with the villagers' committee to stop Tan dumping more sludge. The court apportioned liability between the two defendants, finding that Tan bore 80 per cent and Fang 20 per cent. Both were required to restore the fish pond to the state it was in prior to the heavy metal contamination within six months of the effective date of the judgment. If, by the end of six months, they had failed to restore the pond to the satisfaction of the local EPB, the court would designate a qualified third party to conduct restoration at the expense of the defendants.

Tan and Fang bore joint and several liability to the ACEF to carry out restoration or pay restoration fees. If either party had paid more than his share, he would have had the right to claim reimbursement from the other party in court. As the generators of the sludge could not be traced in this case, Tan and Fang were 100 per cent liable for the harm caused.

[119] TL (2009), art. 14(1). [120] TL (2009), art. 14(2).
[121] SPC 10 Model Criminal, Civil and Administrative Cases on Environment and Resources (2017), case no. 7.

In *Changzhou Environmental Public Interest Association* v. *Chu Weiqing and Others* (2014),[122] Chu Weiqing, who directly caused land contamination, was imprisoned for four years upon conviction for the crime of environmental pollution. Holding four other defendants jointly and severally liable in civil litigation ensures timely remediation and clean-up of the contaminated site.

Changzhou Environmental Public Interest Association v. *Chu Weiqing and Others* (2014)

Chu Weiqing had engaged in illegal disposal of HW from September 2012 to December 2013, causing serious land contamination. When he was arrested in December 2013, more than 1,200 t of HW, including oil sludge and filter residue, were found on a site he had leased from BoShiEr Recycling Co. (BoShiEr). Chu had borrowed an HW operation permit from Jinke Co. (Jinke) and collected HW from Xiangyue Petroleum Products Co. (Xiangyue) and Changzhou Refinery Petrochemical Co. (Changzhou Refinery). In September 2014, Chu was prosecuted and convicted of the crime of environmental pollution, sentenced to four years' imprisonment and fined 200,000 yuan by Wujin District Court. The plaintiff sued five defendants – BoShiEr, Jinke, Xiangyue, Changzhou Refinery and Chu – as joint tortfeasors, claiming that they bore joint and several liability for damages amounting to 3,190,400 yuan. This comprised the cost of clean-up of the contaminated site (2,830,700 yuan) and the appraisal fee (359,700 yuan). BoShiEr and Jinke denied any responsibility, while Xiangyue and Changzhou Refinery each accepted their respective liability caused by their respective waste, but denied joint and several liability with Chu.

Changzhou Intermediate Court (2014) found Chu's illegal collection, storage and disposal of HW had directly caused the land contamination at and around the site leased from BoShiEr. Chu was found liable for the cost of clean-up and the appraisal fee. The other four defendants had collaborated with Chu knowing that he did not have an HW operation permit, and therefore jointly committed the tort, the court said. They were held to bear joint and several liability with Chu. BoShiEr had leased the site to Chu for disposal of HW, providing both the site and equipment for illegal storage and disposal of HW, the court noted, while Jinke had supplied a photocopy of its HW operation permit certified by its company seal. Xiangyue and Changzhou Refinery knew Chu was not licensed to handle HW, but nonetheless they hired him to dispose of their HW. They neither paid the official HW disposal fee, nor filled out the HW disposal transfer form as required by the SWL (2013). The court ordered Chu to pay 2.83 million yuan to a bank account of the plaintiff earmarked for environmental restoration, and 359,700 yuan, an appraisal fee, to Changzhou Environmental Science Co. The other four defendants were found to bear joint and several liability with Chu.

None of the parties appealed and the first-instance judgment became effective in late September 2014, when Chu was imprisoned for the crime of environmental pollution. To ensure timely clean-up of the site, the court coordinated with the procuratorate, the local EPB, the appraisal body and the four parties jointly and severally liable with Chu to formulate plans on pollution treatment and environmental remediation to be undertaken by a third party.

[122] SPC 10 Model Cases on Environmental Torts (2015), case no. 3.

12.4 REMEDIES UNDER ADMINISTRATIVE EPIL

Administrative EPIL was introduced to improve agency performance of statutory duties, ensuring they are carried out in full compliance with law, and to strengthen environmental law enforcement.[123] A procuratorate sues an agency to make it perform its statutory duty, as in *Yunyang District Procuratorate* v. *Yunyang District Forestry Bureau* (2016) in Hubei province,[124] or to make an agency rectify its unlawful act, as in *Qingliu County Procuratorate* v. *Qingliu County EPB* (2016), the events of which occurred in Fujian province.[125]

Yunyang District Procuratorate v. *Yunyang District Forestry Bureau* (2016)

In March and April 2013, Jin Xingguo, Wu Gang and Zhao Fengqiang illegally mined for stone construction materials on land designated as protected 'ecological forestland' by the state and province. They did this without the approval of the local forestry bureau and without obtaining a land-use permit. In late April and early May, Yunyang District Forestry Bureau (Yunyang Bureau) made administrative penalty decisions against Jin, Wu and Zhao, ordering them to stop their illegal acts, restore the forestland and pay fines. They paid part of the fines, but did not restore the forestland. Yunyang Bureau neither urged them to perform their duties under the administrative penalty decision, nor applied to court for the decision to be enforced. The destroyed forestland remained unrestored. In December 2015, Yunyang District Procuratorate issued a procuratorial advice to Yunyang Bureau, urging it to enforce its administrative penalty and order Jin, Wu and Zhao to restore the forestland. Yunyang Bureau neither took action to rectify nor replied in writing. In February 2016, Yunyang District Procuratorate sued, seeking a court decision that Yunyang Bureau should perform its statutory duty.

Yunyang District Court (2016) held that Yunyang Bureau had failed to follow up on its administrative penalty decision or apply to court for enforcement. It ordered Yunyang Bureau to perform its statutory duty to collect the overdue fines and penalty charges, and exercise its duty of supervision and management over the restoration of the destroyed forestland.

During the trial, Yunyang Bureau successfully urged Jin, Wu and Zhao to pay the overdue fines and the penalty charges for late payment, and to plant trees on the destroyed forestland. A court-appointed appraisal body confirmed that the species and quality of the trees planted by Jin, Wu and Zhao, as well as the planting time, density and method, met the relevant standards, but also stated that it would take a minimum of three years for the land to recover its ecological function. The Yunyang Bureau submitted to the court a draft conservation plan for the destroyed forestland, pledging to perform its duty of supervision and management over the remediation work to ensure restoration of the ecological function of the forestland.

In many cases in which an agency is sued for its unlawful omission or for failing to perform a statutory duty, it takes action during the trial to rectify. If that occurs, the plaintiff may choose to withdraw the lawsuit or may amend the claim to request a court

[123] SPC and SPP, Interpretation on Application of Law in Public Interest Litigation by People's Procuratorates (2018), art. 2.

[124] SPP 8th Batch of Guiding Cases (2016), guiding case no. 30.

[125] SPP 8th Batch of Guiding Cases (2016), guiding case no. 31.

declaration that the agency's act or omission prior to rectification was unlawful. Courts may confirm that the agency's act or omission was unlawful.[126] Instead of simply withdrawing a case, procuratorates normally choose to amend their claim and request a court decision on the legality of the agency act or omission. In *Fujian Qingliu County Procuratorate* v. *Qingliu County Environmental Protection Bureau* (2016),[127] despite Qingliu EPB's rectification during trial, the procuratorate still insisted on a court decision on the legality of the defendant EPB's handling of e-waste.

Fujian Qingliu County Procuratorate v. *Qingliu County Environmental Protection Bureau* (2016)

On 31 July 2014, Qingliu County EPB stopped Liu Wensheng's illegal operation, confiscating 28,580 kg of e-waste. The EPB first stored the e-waste at a nearby pig farm and then transferred it for storage to Dongying Company in August 2014 and Jiuli Company in May 2015. Neither company had the capacity to store HW. In July 2015, Fujian Qingliu County Procuratorate issued procuratorial advice to the EPB, urging it to treat the e-waste. The EPB replied in the same month that it would pass the e-waste to a qualified operator for safe disposal. However, in December 2015, the procuratorate found the EPB had neither disposed of the e-waste nor sanctioned Liu. It sued in December 2015, seeking a court decision that the EPB's delay in disposing of the e-waste and its failure to sanction Liu was unlawful. It also sought a court order that the EPB should perform its statutory duty.

Mingxi County Court (2016) accepted the case. During the trial, the EPB imposed an administrative penalty on Liu, ordering him to suspend operations, treat the residues left behind by the illegal burning of e-waste and pay a fine of 20,000 yuan. The EPB also passed the confiscated e-waste to a qualified third party for safe disposal. As a result, the procuratorate applied to modify its claim, seeking a court decision that Qingliu EPB's undue delay in the safe disposal of the e-waste was unlawful. The court held that the defendant had handled the situation unlawfully prior to the rectification during trial.

These administrative EPIL initiated against agencies for their failure to perform a statutory duty or for committing an unlawful act raise awareness among government bodies at higher levels, not only of specific unlawful agency acts or omissions, but of the broader picture. In the past, some agencies had believed that they had discharged their duty of enforcement by imposing administrative penalties on polluters. These cases have proved them wrong. Imposing a fine or issuing an order does not in itself count as a discharge of duty of enforcement: EPBs must also follow up. Fujian provincial government requested all EPBs within the province to strengthen and improve environmental law enforcement and rectify any unlawful acts or omissions.[128] Hubei Provincial Forestry Bureau ordered all forestry bureaus within its province to examine their own activities and rectify any unlawful acts or omissions.[129]

[126] ALL (2017), art. 74.

[127] SPP 8th Batch of Guiding Cases (2016), guiding case no. 31; SPC and SPP 10 Model Cases of Procuratorial Public Interest Litigation (2018), case no. 6.

[128] SPP 8th Batch of Guiding Cases (2016), guiding case no. 31.

[129] *Yunyang District People's Procuratorate* v. *Yunyang District Forestry Bureau* (2016), SPP 8th Batch of Guiding Cases (2016), guiding case no. 30.

Environmental agencies' statutory duty of environmental enforcement is an ongoing duty. Simply issuing an administrative order for an enterprise to suspend operations is found to be inadequate for an agency to discharge its enforcement duty. In *Guizhou Jinping County Procuratorate* v. *Jinping County Environmental Protection Bureau* (2015),[130] the court ruled that whether a local EPB has performed its statutory duty of supervision and enforcement depends on whether it has been successful in stopping the illegal operations.

Guizhou Jinping County Procuratorate v. *Jinping County Environmental Protection Bureau* (2015)

On 5 August 2014, Jinping County EPB found seven stone-processing enterprises, including Hongfa Co. and Xiongjun Co., had failed to install pollution prevention and control facilities. They discharged untreated wastewater directly to the Qingshui River, polluting it with suspended particles and oil. Jinping County EPB ordered seven enterprises to suspend their operations and rectify. The enterprises, however, continued operating and continued to discharge untreated wastewater. On 15 August 2014, on finding that the seven enterprises had not suspended operations to rectify the situation, Jinping County Procuratorate issued a procuratorial advice to Jinping EPB, urging it to follow up on the seven enterprises and impose sanctions if needed. On 16 April 2015, Jinping County Procuratorate found that Hongfa Co. and Xiongjun Co. had continued to operate and discharge without installing pollution-control facilities. It issued another procuratorial advice, urging Jinping EPB to perform its duty of supervision and enforcement to stop the violations and sanction the two enterprises. It was not until 11 November 2015 that the EPB ordered the two enterprises to suspend their operations. On 1 December 2015, the EPB imposed a fine of 10,000 yuan on both polluters. On confirming that no other citizen, legal person or social organization had sued the agency, Jinping Procuratorate initiated an administrative EPIL on 18 December 2015, seeking: (i) a court decision that the EPB's failure to perform its statutory duty of supervision and enforcement was unlawful and (ii) a court order for the EPB to perform its statutory duty.

Guizhou Fuquan City Court (2015) found that Jinping County EPB was the agency in charge of the EIA approval of the two stone-processing enterprises and was required to monitor and supervise their operation and production. It had issued an order for the enterprises to rectify, but had failed to conduct follow-up monitoring. As a result, the two enterprises continued operating in violation of law until 31 December 2015, when the county government shut down all illegal operations along the Qingshui River, including those of Hongfa Co. and Xiongjun Co. This happened during the trial and the procuratorate withdrew its second claim. The court held that Jinping EPB's failure to perform its statutory duty of environmental supervision from 5 August 2014 to 31 December 2015 was unlawful.

A court declaration that an agency act or omission is unlawful puts pressure on the agency and the individuals in charge, because it has a negative impact on performance appraisals. It is hoped that this will force agencies to try not to repeat their mistakes, but to improve their administrative performance.

[130] SPC 10 Important Administrative Cases on Environmental Protection (second batch) (2016), case no. 10. This case was issued by the SPP as guiding case no. 32 in its 8th Batch of Guiding Cases (2016).

12.5 JUDICIAL MEDIATION

Mediation is commonly practised as an effective method of dispute resolution. Courts routinely facilitate mediation between parties to civil disputes. Given that the public interest is involved, the SPC has taken extra steps to ensure that the public interest is not compromised by mediation. It stipulates that a settlement agreement between two parties must be publicized for a minimum of thirty consecutive days.[131] This requirement gives the general public and other stakeholders notice to comment on the proposed settlement agreement. Upon expiry of the public notice period, the court is required to examine the agreement to ensure that it does not harm any public interest before preparing the binding mediation report.[132] In *Friends of Nature* v. *Shandong Jinling Chemical Co.* (2016),[133] Dongying Intermediate Court in Shandong province facilitated mediation to settle the dispute in a timely manner.

Friends of Nature v. *Shandong Jinling Chemical Co.* (2016)

Between 2014 and 2015, Jinling Chemical Co. (Jinling) had been sanctioned many times by its local EPB for emitting air pollutants that violated state standards, operating without pollution-control equipment and falsifying monitoring data. It was ordered by Shandong Provincial EPB to suspend production and install desulphurization and denitrification devices. Its environmental performance was also to be directly supervised and monitored by the MEP. The FON sued, seeking a court order for the defendant to stop the excessive emissions, eliminate the danger to the atmosphere, and pay to treat the air pollution caused by its illegal emissions.

Dongying Intermediate Court (2016) accepted the case and found that, during the trial, the defendant had taken measures to ensure compliance with emission standards and had its monitoring devices inspected by Dongying EPB. The court conducted mediation and Jinling agreed to pay 3 million yuan for air pollution treatment. The court publicized the settlement agreement to the public for notice and comment. Upon expiry of the notice period, the court examined the agreement to ensure it would not harm the public interest, that the outcome would meet the aim of EPIL and that timely remedies had been offered to protect the environment. The court then prepared the mediation report, which was signed by both parties to become legally binding.

A court-prepared mediation report has the same legal force as a judgment, so the SPC requires it to record clearly the parties' claims, the basic facts of the case and the contents of the agreement.[134] Mediation is allowed for civil EPIL because it has been tested and proven to be low cost and highly efficient. It not only minimizes the risk of escalating disputes causing social unrest, but also saves judicial resources. Similarly, Pu'er Intermediate Court in Yunnan province settled a dispute by mediation in *Pu'er City Procuratorate* v. *Yunnan Jinggu Mining & Metallurgy Co.* (2017).[135]

[131] SPC Interpretation on Civil EPIL (2015), art. 25(1).
[132] SPC Interpretation on Civil EPIL (2015), art. 25(2).
[133] SPC 10 Model Cases of Environmental Public Interest Litigation (2017), case no. 6.
[134] SPC Interpretation on Civil EPIL (2015), art. 25(3).
[135] SPC and SPP 10 Model Cases of Procuratorial Public Interest Litigation (2018), case no. 9.

Pu'er City Procuratorate v. *Yunnan Jinggu Mining & Metallurgy Co.* (2017)

In March 2015, accidental fracturing of a pipe at Jinggu Mining & Metallurgy Co. (Jinggu Mining) caused the discharge of copper sulphate, which contaminated farmland and killed river fish. Jinggu County EPB ordered Jinggu Mining to suspend operations and rectify, and also imposed a fine of 160,000 yuan. Jinggu EPB paid 400,000 yuan to obtain an appraisal report from a qualified third party, which certified the environmental pollution damage to the farmland to be 528,600 yuan and the restoration cost 829,700 yuan. Jinggu Mining reached a settlement with the farmers and paid 514,928 yuan to compensate their direct economic losses. Pu'er City Procuratorate sued Jinggu Mining, seeking remedies including: (i) payment of 829,700 yuan to restore the contaminated environment and (ii) reimbursement for the 400,000 yuan appraisal fee paid by Jinggu EPB.

Pu'er Intermediate Court (2017) accepted the case and facilitated mediation. The two parties reached a settlement under which Jinggu Mining would pay both the restoration and appraisal fees, as requested by Pu'er City Procuratorate. The court publicized the civil claims and the settlement agreement on its public announcement bulletin, in the *People's Court News* and *Pu'er Daily* for thirty days. At the end of the thirty days, the court reviewed the settlement agreement to ensure its performance would not harm the public interest. It then prepared the mediation report, which was signed by both parties to become legally binding.

In this case, the court made an effort to communicate with the disputing parties to facilitate mediation and reach agreement. Effective judicial mediation improves efficiency, which is much needed both for timely environmental remediation and for the best use of judicial resources.

From local pilot exercises to national law reform, EPIL is making steady progress towards becoming an important tool with which to fight pollution and ecological destruction. Both civil and administrative EPIL supplement and fill gaps left by conventional environmental tort and administrative litigation by strengthening public supervision over polluters and administrative bodies. Courts are playing a crucial role in the legal protection of the public interest in environment and resources through institutional reform and innovation in adjudication. However, challenges remain for NGOs wishing to initiate civil EPIL. Often, NGOs lack funding and professional legal expertise. Prohibitively high litigation costs, including the court acceptance fee and the environmental damage appraisal fee effectively deter most NGOs from initiating EPIL.[136] This explains the small number of civil EPILs initiated by NGOs and the very small number of NGOs that have sued. The ACEF, FON and CBCGDF are the three main NGOs financially and professionally capable of initiating EPIL, though they also often experience difficulties in financing the high appraisal fees. In contrast, procuratorial EPIL has developed faster, as it is not constrained by a shortage of resources or personnel. Procuratorial EPIL is making an impact on agency behaviour and will continue to improve environmental law enforcement.

[136] For further discussion, see Tiantian Zhai and Yen-Chiang Chang, 'Standing of environmental public-interest litigants', at 385–6. According to a survey conducted by the ACEF and NRDC in 2013, nearly half the NGOs in China have an annual budget of less than half a million yuan. In contrast are the high litigation costs and appraisal fees. For example, in *Taizhou Environment Federation* v. *Taixing Jinhui Chemical and Five Others* (2016), the litigation costs at Taizhou Intermediate Court (the first-instance court) and Jiangsu High Court (second-instance) were 973,652 yuan and 947,298 yuan respectively. In *Friends of Nature* v. *Yunnan Luliang Chemical* (2011), the damage appraisal fee was quoted at 7 million yuan.

Bibliography

ACEF, n.d., 'All-China Environment Federation'. Online article. www.acef.com.cn/a/about/#C1

n.d., 'Environmental public interest litigation'. Online articles. www.acef.com.cn/envlaw/index.shtml.

Alford, William P. and Benjamin L. Liebman, 'Clean air, clear processes? The struggle over air pollution law in the People's Republic of China', *Hastings Law Journal*, 52:3 (2001), 703–37.

Alford, William P. and Yuanyuan Shen, 'Limits of the law in addressing China's environmental dilemma', *Stanford Environmental Law Journal*, 16 (1997), 125–48.

An Keming and Chen Yifang, 'To provide judicial guarantee for the construction of ecological civilization', *People's Court News*, 7 July 2014.

Associated Press, 'China overtakes Japan as world's second-largest economy', *The Guardian*, 16 August 2010.

Bachner, Bryan, 'Regulating pollution in the People's Republic of China: an analysis of the enforcement of environmental law', *Colorado Journal of International Environmental Law and Policy*, 7 (1996), 373.

Bao Cun-kuan et al., 'Framework and operational procedure for implementing strategic environmental assessment in China', *Environmental Impact Assessment Review*, 24 (2004), 27–46.

Barboza, David 'China passes Japan as second-largest economy', *New York Times*, 15 August 2010.

'Beijing bans fireworks within fifth ring road, good law in response to public opinion', *New Beijing News*, 2 December 2017.

Bellamy, Jeffrey M., 'Putting the boss behind bars: using criminal sanctions against executives who pollute: what China could learn from the United States', *Indiana International and Comparative Law Review*, 13 (2003), 579–604.

Beyer, Stefanie, 'Environmental law and policy in the People's Republic of China', *Chinese Journal of International Law*, 5 (2006), 185.

Bie Tao and Bie Zhi, 'Environmental public interest litigation breaking the ground', in Li Hengyuan and Chang Jiwen (eds.) *Environmental Law in China 2008* (Beijing: China Environmental Science Press, 2008), 182–8.

Bird, Thomas, 'China's bike sharing bubble has burst: drone photography captures its casualties rusting in "bicycle graveyards" ', *South China Morning Post*, 27 July 2018.

Blood, Justin, 'Energy production pollution in China: the effectiveness of two forms of Chinese governmental response to the problem', *Colorado Journal of International Environmental Law and Policy*, 19 (2008), 155.

Briggs, Adam, 'China's pollution victims: still seeking a dependable remedy', *Georgetown International Environmental Law Review*, 18 (2006), 305–33.

British Antarctic Survey, n.d., 'Ozone'. Online article. www.bas.ac.uk/about/antarctica/geography/ozone/

Brown Weiss, Edith, 'Intergenerational equity in international law', *American Society of International Law Proceedings*, 81 (1987), 126–32.

Bu Xuelin, 'Zhou Shengxian emphasizes Premier Wen Jiaobao's instruction to win environmental law enforcement victory at 2006 Environmental Protection Action Teleconference', *China Environment News*, 2 June 2006.

Cai Dingjian, 'China's major reform in criminal law', *Columbia Journal of Asian Law*, 11 (1997), 213–18.

Cai, Jane 'Restoration of palace lake hangs in balance', *South China Morning Post*, 5 April 2005, 5.

'"Cancer village" in spotlight', *China Daily*, 10 May 2004.

Cao Mingde and Wang Fengyuan, 'Environmental public interest litigation in China', *Asia Pacific Law Review*, 19 (2011), 217–35.

Carpenter-Gold, Daniel, 'Castles made of sand: public-interest litigation and China's new Environmental Protection Law', *Harvard Environmental Law Review*, 39:1 (2015), 241–74.

Carson, Rachel, *Silent Spring* (London: Hamish Hamilton, 1962).

Carter, Neil T. and Arthur P. J. Mol (eds.), *Environmental Governance in China* (London and New York: Routledge, 2007).

Center for Legal Assistance to Pollution Victims, (n.d.). Website. www.clapv.org/

Central Supervision and Inspection Office of the MEE (n.d.). Website. http://dcb.mee.gov.cn/

Chang, Qing et al., 'Ambient air pollution and daily hospital admissions for respiratory system-related diseases in a heavy polluted city in Northeast China', *Environmental Science and Pollution Research*, 27 (2020), 10055–64.

Che Xiuzhen et al., 'Strategic environmental assessment and its development in China', *Environmental Impact Assessment Review*, 22 (2002), 101–9.

Chen, Albert H. Y., *An Introduction to the Legal System of the People's Republic of China*, 4th ed. (Hong Kong: LexisNexis, 2011).

Chen Changzhi, *Report of the NPCSC Inspection Team on the Implementation of the WPPCL* (2015). www.pkulaw.cn

Chen Huamian et al., 'Heavy metal pollution in soils in China: status and countermeasures', *Royal Swedish Academy of Science*, 28 (1999), 130–4.

Chen Jining, *Report on Environmental Status and Achievement of Environmental Protection Targets* (2015).

Chen, Renjie et al., 'Association of particulate air pollution with daily mortality: the China Air Pollution and Health Effects Study', *American Journal of Epidemiology*, 175:11 (2012), 1173–81.

Chen, Stephen and Ada Lee, 'Lab tests confirm Yunnan toxic spill', *South China Morning Post*, 31 August 2011.

Chen Yu, 'Alleviating pressure on clinical waste disposal facilities', *Science and Technology Daily*, 30 April 2020, 5.

Chen Yuanyuan, 'Nine years to conclude a case: Qujing chromium case settled by mediation', *China Environment News*, 11 August 2020.

Chen, Zhu et al., 'China tackles the health effects of air pollution', *The Lancet*, 382:9909 (2013), 1959–60.

Chen, Zunxuan 'Digger' 'Tackling China's water pollution problem: a legal and institutional perspective from Taihu Lake water pollution control', *Temple Journal of Science Technology and Environmental Law*, 24 (2005), 325–50.

Cheng Xi, 'Ten thousand tonnes of cadmium tainted rice from Hunan to be on the dining tables in Guangdong', *Southern Daily*, 27 February 2013.

Cheung, Ray '"Toothless tiger" to pounce again', *South China Morning Post*, 16 March 2005, 7.

'China's economy is now the world's second largest', *BBC News*, 14 February 2011.

'China's environmental ministry acknowledges "cancer villages"', *Science*, 339:6123 (2013), 1018–19.

Choi, Christy, 'Documentary maker captures mounting waste from Chinese population boom', *South China Morning Post*, 5 December 2013.

Chu, Juan, 'Vindicating public environmental interest: defining the role of environmental public interest litigation in China', *Ecology Law Quarterly*, 45 (2018), 485–532.

Dai, Sarah, 'Winter descends on China's once-hot bike sharing market as another player goes bust', *South China Morning Post*, 27 November 2017.

Day, Kristen (ed.), *China's Environment and the Challenge of Sustainable Development* (Armonk, NY: M. E. Sharpe, 2005).

Deng Qi, 'Second round of central eco-environmental supervision and inspection starts this year', *New Beijing News*, 27 February 2019.

Deng, Yanhua and Guobin Yang, 'Pollution and protest in China: environmental mobilization in context', *The China Quarterly* 214 (2013), 321–36.

Department of Economic Construction (MOF), 23 January 2019, 'Pilot exercises on paid use and trading of pollution discharge allowances making progress'. Online article. http://jjs.mof.gov.cn/gongzuodongtai/201901/t20190118_3125090.htm

Dodwell, David, 'More than a year after China's ban on waste imports, the world is still learning to clean up after itself', *South China Morning Post*, 8 June 2019.

Dong Fanchao, 'SPP releases the procuratorial work on eco-environmental protection', *Legal Daily*, 14 February 2019.

Drenguis, Dustin D., 'Reap what you sow: soil pollution remediation reform in China', *Pacific Rim Law and Policy Journal*, 23 (2014), 171–201.

East China Inspection Bureau, MEE (n.d.). Website. https://hddc.mee.gov.cn/

Economy, Elizabeth, 'China's environmental challenge' in David B. H. Denoon (ed.), *China: Contemporary Political, Economic, and International Affairs*, (NYU Press, 2007), 204–15.

'Environmental governance: the emerging economic dimension', *Environmental Politics*, 15 (2006), 171–89.

'The great leap backward?', *Foreign Affairs*, 86 (2007), 38–59.

The River Runs Black: The Environmental Challenge to China's Future (Ithaca, NY: Cornell University Press, 2004).

Edmonds, Richard, 'The environment in the People's Republic of China 50 years on', *China Quarterly*, 159 (1999), 640–9.

Patterns of China's Lost Harmony: A Survey of the Country's Environmental Degradation and Protection (London: Routledge, 1994).

Edmonds, Richard (ed.), *Managing the Chinese Environment* (Oxford University Press, 1998).

'Enforcement cases under the new Environmental Protection Law', *China Environment News*, 3 March 2015, 3.

'Evaluation report recommends continuing with controversial lake bed lining project, but with modifications', *Xinhua General News Service*, 5 July 2005.

'Experts explore Beijing's air pollution', *China Daily*, 11 June 2012.

Fang, Kun et al., 'Protecting the public's environmental right to know: developments and challenges in China's legislative system for EEID, 2007–2015', *Journal of Environmental Law*, 29 (2017), 285–315.

Faure, Michael and Song Ying, *China and International Environmental Liability: Legal Remedies for Transboundary Pollution* (Cheltenham and Northampton, MA: Edward Elgar, 2008).

Faure, Michael G. and Liu Jing, 'Compensation for environmental damage in China: theory and practice', *Pace Environmental Law Review*, 31 (2014), 226–309.

Feng Hao and Tom Baxter, 'China's coal consumption on the rise', *China Dialogue*, 1 March 2019.

Feng, Yan et al., 'Environmental pollution liability insurance in China: compulsory or voluntary', *Journal of Cleaner Production*, 70 (2014), 211–19.

'Environmental pollution liability insurance in China: in need of strong government backing', *AMBIO: A Journal of the Human Environment*, 43:5 (2013), 1–16.

Ferris, Richard and Zhang Hongjun, 'Reaching out to the rule of law: China's continuing efforts to develop an effective environmental law regime', *William and Mary Bill of Rights Journal*, 11 (2003), 569–602.

Finder, Susan, 'Like throwing an egg against a stone? Administrative litigation in the People's Republic of China', *Journal of Chinese Law*, 3 (1989), 1–28.

'First public hearing over environment', *China Daily*, 14 April 2005.

Forti, Vanessa et al., *The Global E-waste Monitor 2020: Quantities, Flows, and the Circular Economy Potential* (Bonn, Geneva and Rotterdam: United Nations University/United Nations Institute for Training and Research, 2020). http://ewastemonitor.info/

Friends of Nature., n.d., 'Leadership'. Online article. www.fon.org.cn/index.php?option=com_k2&view=item&id=12931:leadership&Itemid=261

Friends of Nature and Yang Dongping (eds.), *Annual Report on Environment Development of China* (Beijing: Social Sciences Academic Press, 2009).
自然之友，杨东平编《中国环境发展报告》（社会科学文献出版社）

Fu, Tingmei, 'Legal person in China: essence and limits', *American Journal of Comparative Law*, 41 (1993), 261–97.

Gao, Helen, 'Chinese government admits existence of cancer villages', *Lancet Oncology*, 14 (2013), 284.

Gao, Qi and Sean Whittaker, 'Standing to sue beyond individual rights: who should be eligible to bring environmental public interest litigation in China', *Transnational Environmental Law*, 8 (2019), 327–47.

Gilbert, Natasha, 'Green protests on the rise in China', *Nature*, 488 (2012), 261–2.

Goelz, Darcey, 'China's environmental problems: is a specialized court the solution?', *Pacific Rim Law and Policy Journal*, 18 (2008), 155–87.

Golding, Wyatt F., 'Incentives for change: China's cadre system applied to water quality', *Pacific Rim Law and Policy Journal*, 20 (2011), 399–428.

Gong, Gu and Ran An, 'Progress and obstacles in environmental public-interest litigation under China's new environmental law: an analysis of cases accepted and heard in 2015', *Climate Law*, 7 (2017), 185–208.

Gong Jing, 'Toxic rice tainted by cadmium', *New Century Weekly*, 14 February 2011.

Gong Shengsheng and Zhang Tao, 'Temporal–spatial distribution changes of cancer villages in China', *China Population Resources and Environment*, 23 (2013), 156–64.

Green Earth Volunteers (n.d.). Website. http://chinagev.org/

Guan, Wei-Jie et al., 'Impact of air pollution on the burden of chronic respiratory diseases in China: time for urgent action', *The Lancet*, 388: 10054 (2016), 1939–51.

'Guangdong Panyu tannery discharges wastewater in violation of law, procuratorate becomes plaintiff', *People's Daily*, 10 August 2009.

Han, Dongmei et al., 'Deep challenges for China's war on water pollution', *Environmental Pollution*, 218 (2016), 1222–33.

Han, Zhiyong et al., 'A review of groundwater contamination near municipal solid waste landfill sites in China', *Science of the Total Environment*, 569–70 (2016), 1255–64.

Hao Xin, 'Mortality survey offers mixed message', *Science*, 321:5893 (2008), 1155.

Havis, Richard James, 'Plastic China documentary focuses on human impact of imported waste', *South China Morning Post*, 19 May 2018.

He Guangwei, 'Special report: the legacy of Hunan's polluted soils', *China Dialogue*, 7 July 2014.

He Haibo, 'The ideal and reality in the ALL Amendment', *China Law Review*, 4 (2014), 138–42. 何海波,《行政诉讼法》修改的理想与现实,《中国法律评论》2014.12 总第4期, 138–142页

'Litigations without a ruling: the predicament of administrative law in China', *Tsinghua China Law Review*, 3 (2011), 257–81.

'Hidden toxic sites', *Caijing*, 4 June 2012.

Ho, Peter, 'Sprouts of environmentalism in China?' in Christof Mauch et al., (eds.), *Shades of Green: Environmental Activism Around the Globe* (Lanham, MD: Rowman & Littlefield Publishers, 2006), 135–60.

Holdaway, Jennifer, 'Environment and health research in China: the state of the field', *The China Quarterly*, 214 (2013), 255–82.

Holder, Jane, *Environmental Assessment: The Regulation of Decision Making* (Oxford University Press, 2006).

Hong, Jinglan et al., 'Intensification of municipal solid waste disposal in China', *Renewable and Sustainable Energy Reviews*, 69 (2017), 168–76.

Hu Jintao, *Report to the 18th National Congress of the Chinese Communist Party* (2012).

Huang Jianchu et al., (eds.), *Interpreting the Solid Waste Law* (Beijing: Law Press, 2005). 黄建初等 主编《中华人民共和国固体废物污染环境防治法释义》(法律出版社)

Huang Qi, '"Chinese-style dilemma" of environmental public interest litigation', *Xinmin Weekly*, 10 August 2009.

'Public interest litigation by Chinese NGO breaking ice', *Xinmin Weekly*, 10 August 2009.

Huang, Youliang et al., 'Public acceptance of waste incineration power plants in China: comparative case studies', *Habitat International*, 47 (2015), 11–19.

Institute of Public and Environmental Affairs (n.d.). Website. www.ipe.org.cn/

International Agency for Research on Cancer (WHO), 'IARC: outdoor air pollution a leading environmental cause of cancer deaths', (press release) 17 October 2013, www.iarc.fr/wp-content/uploads/2018/07/pr221_e.pdf

IPE, (n.d.). 'Air'. wwwen.ipe.org.cn/AirMap_fxy/AirMap.html?q=1

Itakura, Takashi, 'Current issues with the regulatory framework for managing soil contamination in China', *Asia Pacific Journal of Environmental Law*, 18 (2015), 119–46.

Jahiel, Abigail, 'The contradictory impact of reform on environmental protection in China', *China Quarterly*, 149 (1997), 81–103.

'The organization of environmental protection in China', *China Quarterly*, 156 (1998), 757–87.

Jahiel, Abigail R., 'The organization of environmental protection in China' in Richard Louis Edmonds (ed.), *Managing the Chinese Environment* (Oxford and New York: Oxford University Press, 2000), 33–63.

Jeffery, Michael I. and Xiaobo Zhao, 'Developing a national contaminated land liability scheme in China: the Comprehensive Environmental Response, Compensation, and Liability Act Revisited', *Journal of Energy and Natural Resources Law*, 30 (2012), 423–65.

Jiang Bixin, 'Improvement of the administrative litigation system from a macroscopic perspective', *Frontiers of Law in China*, 9 (2014), 1–30.

'Providing judicial service and guarantee for ecological civilization in the new era', *Zi Guang Ge*, 9 (2018), 29–30.

江必新, 为新时代生态文明建设提供司法服务和保障，《紫光阁》2018年第9期29-30页。

'Reform of China's administrative adjudication', *Administrative Law Studies*, 4 (2013), 3–11.

江必新, 中国行政审判体制改革研究，《行政法学研究》2013年第4期，3–11页

Jiang Wenlai, 'The YuanMingYuan hearing is not perfect', *Green Leaf*, 4 (2005), 11.

Jin, Shuqin et al., 'Mitigating land pollution through pesticide packages: the case of a collection scheme in rural China', *Science of the Total Environment*, 622–3 (2018), 502–9.

Jin Zining, 'Environmental Impact Assessment Law in China's courts: a study of 107 judicial decisions', *Environmental Impact Assessment Review*, 55 (2015), 35–44.

Johnson, Thomas, 'The health factor in anti-waste incinerator campaigns in Beijing and Guangzhou', *The China Quarterly*, 214 (2013), 356–75.

Knup, Elizabeth, 'Environmental NGOs in China: an overview', *China Environment Series*, 1 (1997), 9–15.

LaFraniere, Sharon, 'Lead poisoning in China: the hidden scourge', *New York Times*, 15 June 2011.

Lan, Hong et al., 'Water pollution and regulatory cooperation in China', *Cornell International Law Journal*, 44 (2011), 349–83.

Landsberger, Stefan, *Beijing Garbage: A City Besieged by Waste* (Amsterdam University Press, 2019).

Larson, Christina, 'Soil pollution is a state secret in China', *Bloomberg Business Week*, 25 February 2013.

Larssen, Thorjorn et al., 'Acid rain in China', *Environmental Science and Technology*, 40:2 (2006), 418–25.

Lau, Mimi, 'How leaders and an army of staff turned Beijing's grey into APEC blue', *South China Morning Post* , 18 November 2014.

'Lead pollution: whose fault?', *CCTV*, 9 July 2011. http://news.cntv.cn/china/20110710/100502.shtml

Lee, Christine, '"Pollute first, control later" no more: combating environmental degradation in China through an approach based in public interest litigation and public participation', *Pacific Rim Law and Policy Journal*, 17 (2008), 795–823.

Levin, Dan, 'Study links polluted air in China to 1.6 million deaths a year', *New York Times*, 13 August 2015.

Li Dun, 'YuanMingYuan hearing: expose all under the sunshine', *China Newsweek*, 25 April 2005, 38–9.

(ed.), *Environmental Public Interest Litigation Observation Report for 2015* (Beijing: Law Press, 2016).

李楯主编《环境公益诉讼观察报告》(2015年卷) (法律出版社)

(ed.), *Environmental Public Interest Litigation Observation Report for 2016* (Beijing: Law Press, 2018).

李楯主编《环境公益诉讼观察报告》(2016年卷) (法律出版社)

Li Ganjie, *Report of the State Council on 2017 Environmental Status and Achievement of Environmental Targets* (2018). www.pkulaw.cn

Li He et al, 'Environmental public interest litigations facing various difficulties', *Science and Technology Daily*, 30 May 2013, 6.

Li, Heng, 'Legislation and adjudication of tort liability in environmental pollution: an empirical study based on health-related cases in China', *Hong Kong Law Journal*, 46 (2016), 961–90.

Li Jing, 'Hundreds of pupils at school near toxic site in East China fall ill, some with cancer, state TV reports', *South China Morning Post*, 17 April 2016.

'Pollution scandal brings halt to projects', *China Daily*, 2 September 2011.

'Report on mainland China's soil pollution a "state secret"', *South China Morning Post*, 26 February 2013.

'Soil pollution poisons more than farmland', *China Daily*, 10 March 2011.

Li Keqiang, *Government Work Report* (5 March 2015). www.npc.gov.cn/npc/dbdhhy/12_3/2015-03/17/content_1930436.htm

Li Shufei and Chen Tianlu, 'The senior official that blew the "environmental protection storm"', *Government and Law*, 6A (2005), 10–13.
李菽菲、陈天路, 刮起"环保风暴"的高官,《政府法制》2005.6(上)

Li, Yanwei et al., 'Government responses to environmental conflicts in urban China: the case of the Panyu waste incineration power plant in Guangzhou', *Journal of Cleaner Production*, 134 (2016), 354–61.

Li, Yedan et al., 'Understanding China's court mediation surge: insights from a local court', *Law & Social Inquiry*, 43:1 (2018), 58–81.

Li Zhanshu, NPCSC *Inspection Report on the Implementation of the Air Pollution Prevention and Control Law* (2018). www.pkulaw.cn

NPCSC Inspection Report on the Implementation of the Water Pollution Prevention and Control Law (2019). www.pkulaw.cn

Li Zhiping, 'Analysis of the practice of water pollution public interest litigation: based on cases handled by the Guangzhou Maritime Court', *Vermont Journal of Environmental Law*, 13 (2012), 797–822.

'The challenges of China's discharge permit system and effective solutions', *Temple Journal of Science, Technology & Environmental Law*, 24 (2005), 375–95.

Liebman, Benjamin, 'China's courts: restricted reform', *China Quarterly*, 191 (2008), 620–38.

'Class action litigation in China', *Harvard Law Review*, 111 (1998), 1523.

Lin Yanmei, 'The development of environmental public interest litigations from seven test cases' in Friends of Nature and Yang Dongping (eds.), *Annual Report on Environment Development of China* (Beijing: Social Sciences Academic Press (China), 2010), 272–82.

Liu Baijun, 'Trial of environmental public interest litigation on Yunnan chromium waste pollution starts soon', *Legal Net*, 23 May 2012.

Liu Hongqiao, 'The coming of cadmium epidemic', *Caixin New Century Weekly*, 3 June 2013.

'The polluted legacy of China's largest rice-growing province', *China Dialogue*, 30 May 2014.

Liu, Jingjing, 'China's procuratorate in environmental civil enforcement: practice, challenges & implications for China's environmental governance', *Vermont Journal of Environmental Law*, 13 (2011), 41–68.

Liu, Lee, 'Made in China: cancer villages', *Environment*, 52 (2010), 8–21.

Liu Qin, 'Film: how China became the world's rubbish dump', *China Dialogue*, 1 May 2014.

Liu, Tyler, 'China's revision to the Environmental Protection Law: challenges to public interest litigation and solutions for increasing public participation and transparency', *Journal of Energy and Environmental Law*, Spring (2015), 60–70.

Liu Xiang, 'Shilianghe 97 households of aquatic farming suing two polluters in Shandong for compensation' in Wang Canfa and Feng Jia (eds.), *China's Environmental Litigation* (Beijing: Chinese University of Politics and Law Press, 2015), 172–88.

Liu Xiaoxing, 'Administrative public interest litigation initiated by social organization concluded', *China Environment News*, 4 September 2009, 3.

'National soil environmental data platform launched', *China Environment News*, 27 December 2018.

Liu Yang, 'Soil at the site of Beijing Hongshi Coatings factory removed for incineration', *Beijing Daily*, 16 August 2007.

Liu Yi, 'Behind the order to suspend thirty giant projects', *People's Daily*, 27 January 2005, 16.

Liu Yuxin, 'Big developers bid for second batch of two limits housing sites', *Beijing Daily*, 12 July 2007.

Liu Wei, 'Beijing: after the subway workers fell ill', *Outlook Weekly*, 9 (2009), 49–50.

Lo, Carlos et al., 'Changes in regulatory enforcement styles among environmental enforcement officials in China', *Environment and Planning*, 41 (2009), 2706–23.

'Explaining the enforcement gap in China: local government support and internal agency obstacles as predictors of enforcement actions in Guangzhou', *Journal of Environmental Management*, 111 (2012), 227–35.

Lora-Wainwright, Anna, 'An anthropology of "cancer villages": villagers' perspectives and the politics of responsibility', *Journal of Contemporary China*, 19 (2010), 79–99.

Lora-Wainwright, Anna and Ajiang Chen, 'China's cancer villages: contested evidence and the politics of pollution' in Merrill Singer (ed.), *A Companion to the Anthropology of Environmental Health* (Chichester: Wiley Blackwell, 2016), 396–416.

Lou Jiwei, *Explanation of the Draft Bill of the Environmental Protection Tax Law*, (2016).

Lu Hao et al., (eds.), *Understanding the Law on Prevention and Control of Water Pollution* (Beijing: China Legal Publishing House, 2017).
陆浩主编《中华人民共和国水污染防治法解读》(中国法制出版社)

Lu, Hongmei and Roman Sidortsov, 'Sorting out a problem: a co-production approach to household waste management in Shanghai, China', *Waste Management*, 95 (2019), 271–7.

Lu, Yiyi, *Non-Governmental Organizations in China: The Rise of Dependent Autonomy* (London and New York: Routledge, 2009).

Lu, Yonglong et al., 'Impacts of soil and water pollution on food safety and health risks in China', *Environment International*, 77 (2015), 5–15.

Lü Zhongmei, 'Progress and dilemma of environmental public interest litigation' in Friends of Nature and Yang Dongping (eds.), *Annual Report on Environment Development of China* (Beijing: Social Sciences Academic Press, 2009), 229–37.

Lü Zhongmei (ed.), *Comments on Environmental Cases* (Beijing: Higher Education Press, 2006).
吕忠梅 主编《环境法案例辨析》（高等教育出版社）

Environmental Protection Law of the People's Republic of China (Beijing: China Planning Press, 2014).
吕忠梅主编《中华人民共和国环境保护法释义》（中国计划出版社）

Lü Zhongmei and Liu Changxing, 'Innovative development of specialization and professionalization of environmental adjudication: observation in 2017–18', *China Applied Legal Science*, 2 (2019), 1–35.

Luo Gan, *An Explanation of the State Council's Reform Proposal* (1998).

Lubman, Stanley, *China's Legal Reforms* (Oxford University Press, 1996).

Luo Aihua, 'People's will more important: Panyu residents say no to incinerator', *People's Net*, 2 November 2009.

Luo Jingyun and Zhou Hui, 'Lack of information disclosure on toxic sites, investigation of chaotic treatment sector', *21st Century Economic Report*, 29 September 2012.

Ma Jun, *China's Water Crisis* (Beijing: China Environmental Sciences Publishing House, 1999).
马军，《中国水危机》（中国环境科学出版社）

Ma, Qiusha, *Non-Governmental Organizations in Contemporary China: Paving the Way to Civil Society?* (London and New York: Routledge, 2006).

Ma, Xiaoying and Leonard Ortolano, *Environmental Regulation in China: Institutions, Enforcement, and Compliance* (Lanham, MD: Rowman & Littlefield Publishers, 2000).

Ma Yong, 'Social organizations making an impact by promoting environmental public interest litigations' in Zeng Xiaodong and Chang Jiwen (eds.), *Environmental Law in China*, vol. A (Beijing: Law Press China, 2009), 67–73.

Ma Yun, 'Dynamics in central–local division of the authority of EIA approval in China', *Journal of Environmental Law*, 31 (2019), 29–57.

Mao Yushi, Sheng Hong and Yang Fuqiang, *The True Cost of Coal* (Greenpeace, The China Sustainable Energy Programme and World Wide Fund for Nature, 2008). https://issuu.com/greenpeacechina/docs/the-true-cost-of-coal

McCurry, Justin and Julia Kollewe, 'China overtakes Japan as world's second-largest economy', *The Guardian*, 14 February 2011.

McElwee, Charles, *Environmental Law in China: Mitigating Risk and Ensuring Compliance* (Oxford University Press, 2011).

McMullin, Joseph, 'Do Chinese environmental laws work? A study of litigation as a response to the problem of fishery pollution in China', *UCLA Pacific Basin Law Journal*, 26 (2009), 142–83.

'Mediation failed in the Yunnan chromium public interest litigation due to defendants' objection', *Zhengyi Net*, 19 April 2013.

MEE, n.d., 'All-China Environment Federation'. Online article. www.mee.gov.cn/gkml/zzjg/qt/200910/t20091030_180902.htm

2017 China Ecology and Environment Gazette to *2019 China Ecology and Environment Gazette* (published in the year following the Gazette date). www.mee.gov.cn/hjzl/sthjzk/ 生态环境部，《中国生态环境状况公报》

16 November 2018, 'MEE answers reporters' questions regarding the work plan on monitoring of agriculture land by national soil environmental monitoring network'. Online article. www.mee.gov.cn/xxgk2018/xxgk/xxgk15/201811/t20181116_674167.html

7 January 2020, 'Responses to the press regarding the Catalogue (2019) and others'. Online article. www.mee.gov.cn/xxgk2018/xxgk/xxgk15/202001/t20200107_757941.html

15 May 2020, 'The Ministry of Ecology and Environment holds a regular press conference in April'. Online article. www.mee.gov.cn/xxgk2018/xxgk/xxgk15/202005/t20200515_779537.html

'Central environmental supervision and inspection follow-up visits receiving 38,000 complaints, holding 4,305 accountable', (press release) 9 July 2018. www.mee.gov.cn/gkml/sthjbgw/qt/201807/t20180709_446306.htm

'Notice on the final assessment outcome of the implementation of the Air Action Plan (2018)', (notice) 17 May 2018.

'Second batch of revisits by central eco-environmental supervision and inspection teams completed', (press release) 8 December 2018. www.mee.gov.cn/xxgk2018/xxgk/xxgk15/201812/t20181208_680881.html

Division of Law and Standards, *Handbook on the Interpretation and Application of Soil Pollution Prevention and Control Law* (Beijing: Law Press, 2018). 生态环境部法规与标准司 编写 《中华人民共和国土壤污染防治法》解读与适用手册（法律出版社）

MEE, 26 December 2018, 'National soil environmental information platform launched online'. Online article. www.mee.gov.cn/xxgk2018/xxgk/xxgk15/201812/t20181226_686129.html

Mei Hong, 'Problems of China's EIA Law and Responses', *Asia-Pacific Economic Review*, 4:July–August (2005), 93–6.

MEP, *2007 China Environment Gazette* to *2016 China Environment Gazette* (published in the year following the Gazette date). www.mee.gov.cn/hjzl/sthjzk/ 环境保护部，《中国环境状况公报》

31 May 2016, 'MEP answers reporters' questions'. Online article. www.mee.gov.cn/gkml/sthjbgw/qt/201605/t20160531_352670.htm

MEP, 'MEP signs target responsibility agreement on air pollution control with 31 provinces', (press release) 7 January 2014.

MEP and MLR, *National Soil Pollution Survey Report* , 17 April 2014. www.mee.gov.cn/gkml/sthjbgw/qt/201404/W020140417558995804588.pdf

环境保护部和国土资源部，《全国土壤污染状况调查公报》

MEP et al., *Gazette on the First National Survey of Polluting Sources* (National Bureau of Statistics, 2010).

环境保护部、国家统计局和农业部，《第一次全国污染源普查公报》

Ministry of Commerce and China Resource Recovery Association, *Report on the Development of Resource Recovery Industry in China* (Ministry of Commerce, 2019). http://ltfzs.mofcom.gov.cn/article/ztzzn/201910/20191002906058.shtml

商务部流通业发展司和中国物资再生协会，《中国再生资源回收行业发展报告》

Ministry of Ecology and Environment (n.d.). Website. www.mee.gov.cn/

Ministry of Environmental Protection (n.d.). Website. www.mep.gov.cn/zhxx/jgzn/

Ministry of Justice, 27 June 2019, 'The fourth bureau of legislation'. Online article. http://en.moj.gov.cn/2019-06/27/c_384623.htm

Minter, Adam, *Junkyard Planet: Travels in the Billion-Dollar Trash Trade* (New York: Bloomsbury Press, 2013).

Minzner, Carl, 'Riots and cover-ups: counterproductive control of local agents in China', *University of Pennsylvania Journal of International Law*, 31 (2009), 53–123.

Molina, Mario and Sherwood Rowland, 'Stratospheric sink for chlorofluoromethanes: chlorine atom-catalysed destruction of ozone', *Nature*, 249 (1974), 810–12.

Moorman, Jesse L. and Zhang Ge, 'Promoting and strengthening public participation in China's environmental impact assessment process: comparing China's EIA Law and U.S. NEPA', *Vermont Journal of Environmental Law*, 8 (2007), 281–335.

Moser, Adam and Tseming Yang, 'Environmental tort litigation in China', *Environmental Law Reporter*, 41 (2011), 10895–901.

'Most postponed projects granted go-ahead for construction', *Xinhua General News Service*, 19 February 2005.

MWR, *China Groundwater Status Monthly Report* (January 2016). www.mwr.gov.cn/sj/tjgb/dxsdtyb/201702/t20170214_860969.html

National Bureau of Statistics and SEPA/MEP/MEE, *China Statistical Yearbook on Environment* (Beijing: China Statistics Press, published annually)

国家统计局和国家环保总局/环境保护部/生态环境部，《中国环境统计年鉴》（中国统计出版社）

North China Inspection Bureau, MEE (n.d.). Website. https://hbdc.mee.gov.cn/

Northeast China Inspection Bureau, MEE (n.d.). https://dbdc.mee.gov.cn/

Northwest Inspection Bureau, MEE (n.d.). Website. https://xbdc.mee.gov.cn/

NPC, 18 April 2002, 'What is unlawful property?'. Online article. www.npc.gov.cn/npc/c2385/200204/bc7a4d5a84ec410583fd3d921f98a98e.shtml

'Nu River hydropower completes EA examination', *Wen Wei Po*, 11 January 2006.

O'Brien, Kevin J. and Lianjiang Li, 'Suing the local state: administrative litigation in rural China', *The China Journal*, 51 (2004), 75–96.

OECD, 'Council recommendation on the implementation of the polluter-pays principle', *International Legal Materials*, 14:1 (1975), 234–41.

'Recommendation on guiding principles concerning international economic aspects of environmental policies (1972)', *International Legal Materials*, 14 (1975), 236–8.

Orts, Eric, 'Environmental law with Chinese characteristics', *William & Mary Bill of Rights Journal*, 11 (2003), 545–67.

Ouyang, Yadan, 'The respiratory landscape in China: a focus on air pollution', *The Lancet Respiratory Medicine*, 5:1 (2017), 16–17.

'Over half of Chinese children suffering from lead poisoning, experts advocate legislation', *China News Net*, 31 March 2005. www.chinanews.com/news/2005/2005-03-31/26/557546.shtml

Palmer, Michael, 'Controlling the State? Mediation in administrative litigation in the People's Republic of China', *Transnational Law & Contemporary Problems,* 16 (2006), 165–87.

Pan Hongtao, 'Relocation of chemical enterprises and the building of residential housing', *China Environment News*, 25 December 2008.

Pan Yue, 'I care more about the YuanMingYuan hearing', *Legal Daily*, 24 September 2007, 1.

'Pan Yue speaks at conference on environmental culture and public participation', *Sina News*, 8 December 2003.

Patton, Dominique, 'China farm pollution worsens, despite moves to curb excessive fertilisers, pesticides', *Reuters*, 14 April 2015.

Peerenboom, Randall, 'Globalization, path dependency and the limits of law: administrative law reform and rule of law in the People's Republic of China', *Berkeley Journal of International Law*, 19 (2001), 161–264.

Pei, Minxin, 'Citizens v. mandarins: administrative litigation in China', *The China Quarterly*, 152 (1997), 832–62.

Peking University Legal Information Network (n.d.). Website. www.pkulaw.cn

Peng Xu et al, 'Haze, air pollution, and health in China', *The Lancet*, 382:9910 (2013), 2067.

Potter, Pitman (ed.), *Domestic Law Reforms in Post-Mao China* (Armonk, NY and London: M.E. Sharpe, 1994).

Qie Jianrong, 'China's first environmental information disclosure public interest litigation won by the public', *Legal Daily*, 6 April 2012.

'EIA law still young: does it need big surgery?', *Legal Daily*, 5 September 2006.

'Environmental impact report of the YuanMingYuan project approved', *Legal Daily*, 8 July 2005, 6.

'Environmental organizations sued for 10 million yuan of compensation caused by chromium waste in Qujing, Yunnan', *Legal Daily*, 20 September 2011.

'Law compliance more costly than violation: five major problems in implementing the EIA Law', *Legal Daily*, 19 September 2005.

'Let environmental protection laws be strengthened as steel', *Legal Daily*, 31 January 2005, 1.

'MEP refused disclosure on basis of state secret', *Legal Daily*, 25 February 2013.

'MEP replied to lawyer that soil pollution data will be disclosed', *Legal Daily*, 8 May 2013.

'Pan Yue: environmental authorities are ready for a lasting war [against pollution] and hope for patience and confidence from the public', *Legal Daily*, 28 February 2008, 8.

'Revision of Environmental Protection Law stirs controversy' in Liu Jianqiang, *Chinese Research Perspectives on the Environment, Volume 3: Public Action and Government Accountability* (Leiden: Brill, 2014), 96–105.

'Wuxi court accepts litigation filed by environmental organization, first NGO public interest litigation', *Legal Daily*, 9 July 2009, 6.

Qin Chuan, 'All 30 law-breaking projects building stopped', *China Daily*, 3 February 2005.

Qin Tianbao (ed.), *Research Handbook on Chinese Environmental Law* (Cheltenham: Edward Elgar, 2015).

Qiu, Xin and Honglin Li, 'China's environmental super ministry reform: background, challenges and the future', *Environmental Law Reporter,* 39 (2009), 10152–63.

Qin Xuan, 'YuanMingYuan hearing: a suddenly emerged opportunity', *China Newsweek*, 2 January 2006, 32–4.

Qu Geping, *Qu's Pursuit: China's Environmental Protection Strategy* (Beijing: China Environmental Science Press, 2010).
曲格平，《曲之求索：中国环境保护方略》（中国环境科学出版社）

'Qujing city government report on chromium waste pollution incident at press conference', *Yunnan Daily*, 5 September 2011.

Railton, W. Scott, 'The rhetoric and reality of water quality protection in China', *Pacific Rim Law and Policy Journal*, 7 (1998), 859–88.

Ramzy, Austin, 'Wang Canfa', *Time*, 17 October 2007. http://content.time.com/time/specials/2007/article/0,28804,1663317_1663320_1669921,00.html

Ross, Lester, *Environmental Policy in China* (Bloomington: Indiana University Press, 1988).

Ross, Lester and Mitchell Silk, *Environmental Law and Policy in the People's Republic of China* (London: Quorum Books, 1987).

Ryan, Erin, 'The elaborate paper tiger: environmental enforcement and the rule of law in China', *Duke Environmental Law and Policy Forum*, 24 (2013), 183–239.

Sands, Philippe et al., *Principles of International Environmental Law*, 4th ed. (Cambridge University Press, 2018).

'School campus 100 meters from the toxic site: Changzhou school chemical pollution incident', *Xinhua News*, 19 April 2016.

Scott, Jessica, 'Cleaning up the dragon's fountain: lessons from the first public interest lawsuit brought by a grassroots NGO in China', *The George Washington International Law Review*, 45 (2013), 727–62.

SEPA, *2005 China Environment Gazette* (2006) and *2006 China Environment Gazette* (2007). www.mee.gov.cn/hjzl/sthjzk/

'SEPA announcement on environmental administrative permit hearing', (SEPA announcement no. 13 of 2005) 5 April 2005.

'SEPA Deputy Head Pan Yue: hydropower construction projects must implement EIA, all thirty projects are being rectified', (press release) no. 9, 2 February 2005.

SEPA Deputy Head Pan Yue reports on the illegal construction of 30 projects and orders suspension of projects ignoring environmental impact assessment regime', (press release) no. 3, 18 January 2005.

'SEPA Deputy Head Pan Yue updates on the 30 illegal construction projects: most have suspended construction', (press release) no. 5, 24 January 2005.

'SEPA notice on environmental impact hearing of the YuanMingYuan project', (SEPA notice no. 117 of 2005), 11 April 2005.

'SEPA requests comprehensive rectification of the YuanMingYuan anti-seepage project', (press release), 7 July 2005.

SEPA/MEP/MEE, *Environmental Statistics Yearbook*. www.mee.gov.cn/hjzl/sthjzk/sthjtjnb/

SEPA and State Bureau of Statistics, 'Report on China's green GDP for 2004', *Environmental Protection*, 98 (2006), 22–9.

Shan Juan and Wang Qian, 'Exposure to smog is severe hazard', *China Daily*, 6 December 2011.

Shapiro, Judith, *China's Environmental Challenges*, 2nd ed. (Cambridge and Malden, MA: Polity Press, 2016).

Mao's War against Nature: Politics and the Environment in Revolutionary China (Cambridge University Press, 2001).

Shen Deyong (ed.), *Understanding and Applying SPC's Judicial Interpretation on Environmental Tort Liability Disputes* (Beijing: People's Court Press, 2016).
沈德咏 主编《最高人民法院环境侵权责任纠纷司法解释理解与适用》（人民法院出版社）

Shen Yueyue, *Inspection Report on the Implementation of the Environmental Protection Law* (2016). www.pkulaw.cn

Shi Jiangtao, 'Watchdog clears the way for power plant construction to restart', *South China Morning Post*, 17 February 2005, 4.

'Watchdog flexes muscles, orders work on "illegal" projects to stop', *South China Morning Post*, 19 January 2005, 6.

'Wen supports crackdown on 30 unapproved projects', *South China Morning Post*, 27 January 2005, 5.

Shi, Yifan and Benjamin van Rooij, 'Prosecutorial regulation in the global south: environmental civil litigation by prosecutors in China compared to Brazil', *Regulation & Governance*, 10 (2016), 44–57.

Sitaraman, Srini, 'Regulating the belching dragon: rule of law, politics of enforcement, and pollution prevention in post-Mao industrial China', *Colorado Journal of International Environmental Law and Policy*, 18 (2007), 267–334.

Smil, Vaclav, *The Bad Earth: Environmental Degradation in China* (London: Zed Books, 1984).

China's Environmental Crisis: An Inquiry into the Limits of National Development (Armonk, NY and London: M.E. Sharpe, 1993).

China's Past, China's Future: Energy, Food, Environment (New York: Routledge Curzon, 2004).

'Smog in Beijing US reading beyond index EPB criticized for announcement of light pollution', *Ming Pao Daily News*, 6 December 2011, A20.

'Smog spawns environmental awareness in China', *Xinhua*, 2 December 2011.

Song Jian, 'Protect environment according to law and accomplish sustainable development', *China Environment News*, 25 July 1996, 2.

Song Ying, 'International legal aspects of the Songhua River incident' in Michael Faure and Song Ying (eds.), *China and International Environmental Liability: Legal Remedies for Transboundary Pollution* (Cheltenham and Northampton, MA: Edward Elgar, 2008) 315–32.

South China Inspection Bureau, MEE (n.d.). Website. https://hndc.mee.gov.cn/

Southwest Inspection Bureau, MEE (n.d.). Website. https://xndc.mee.gov.cn/

'SPC establishes environment and resources division', *People's Court News*, 4 July 2014.

SPC, '51 cases influencing China over 65 years of SPC', *People's Court News*, 25 November 2014.

Environment and Resources Adjudication in China (2016).
最高人民法院，《中国环境资源审判》

Environment and Resources Adjudication in China 2016–2017 (Beijing: People's Court Press, 2017). www.pkulaw.cn
最高人民法院，《中国环境资源审判 (2016–2017)》

Environment and Resources Adjudication in China (2017–2018) (Beijing: People's Court Press, 2019).
最高人民法院，《中国环境资源审判 (2017–2018)》

'Fully strengthening the environment and resources adjudication work', (press release) 3 July 2014. www.pkulaw.cn

SPP, *Annual Work Report* (2014 to 2019). www.pkulaw.cn

State Council, *China's Agenda 21: White Paper on China's Population, Environment, and Development in the 21st Century* (Beijing: China Environmental Science Press, 1994).
国务院，《中国21世纪议程 – 中国21世纪人口、环境与发展白皮书》(中国环境科学出版社)

State Council, *China's Energy Policy* (2012). www.pkulaw.cn
国务院，中国的能源政策（2012）

State Council, *Environmental Protection in China* (1996). www.pkulaw.cn
国务院，中国的环境保护（1996）

State Council, *Environmental Protection in China 1996–2005* (2006). www.pkulaw.cn
国务院，中国的环境保护1996–2005（2006）

State Council, *Human Rights Development in China during Forty Years of Reform* (2018). www.pkulaw.cn

国务院，改革开放40年中国人权事业的发展进步

Stern, Rachel E., *Environmental Litigation in China: A Study in Political Ambivalence* (Cambridge University Press, 2013).

'From dispute to decision: suing polluters in China', *The China Quarterly*, 206 (2011), 294–312.

'On the frontlines: making decisions in Chinese civil environmental lawsuits', *Law & Policy*, 32 (2010), 79–103.

'The political logic of China's new environmental courts', *The China Journal*, 72 (2014), 53–74.

Sun Xiuyan, 'Pan Yue: Obstacles to the implementation of EIA of government plans come from conflict of interests', *People's Daily*, 8 November 2007, 10.

Sun Youhai (ed.), *Study on the Theory and Practice of Environmental Adjudication* (Beijing: People's Court Press, 2014).

孙佑海主编《环境司法理论与实务研究》（人民法院出版社）

Tam, Fiona, 'Yunnan plant dumped toxic dregs for two decades', *South China Morning Post*, 17 August 2011.

Tan Ee Lyn, 'China's "cancer villages" bear witness to economic boom', *Reuters*, 17 September 2009.

Tang Tao et al., 'Integrating environment into land-use planning through strategic environmental assessment in China: towards legal frameworks and operational procedures', *Environmental Impact Assessment Review*, 27 (2007), 243–65.

Tao, Tao and Kunlun Xin, 'A sustainable plan for China's drinking water', *Nature*, 511 (2014), 527–8.

Taylor, Alan, 'The bike-share oversupply in China: huge piles of abandoned and broken bicycles', *The Atlantic*, 22 March 2018.

'Ten years to conclude the chromium contamination case in Qujing', 3 August 2020, www.pkulaw.cn

'The 2006 Time 100', *Time* , 30 April 2006.

'The bad earth: the most neglected threat to public health in China is toxic soil', *The Economist*, 8 June 2017.

'The pursuit of fairness and efficiency: the YuanMingYuan environmental impact hearing in focus', *Green Leaf*, 4 (2005) 5–9.

'Toxic site clean-up at SongJiaZhuang section of subway line no. 10', *Jianghua Times*, 7 December 2009.

Tyler, Zachary, 'Transboundary water pollution in China: an analysis of the failure of the legal framework to protect downstream jurisdictions', *Columbia Journal of Asian Law*, 19 (2006), 572–613.

UN Environment Programme, (2017), *A Success in the Making*. Online report. https://unep.ch/ozone/Publications/MP_A_Success_in_the_making-E.pdf

UN Environment Programme, *Achievements in Stratospheric Ozone Protection: Progress Report 1987–2007*. Online report. https://unep.ch/ozone/Publications/MP_Achievements-E.pdf

A Review of 20 Years' Air Pollution Control in Beijing (United Nations Environment Programme, 2019).

Stockholm Convention, n.d., 'The new POPs under the Stockholm Convention'. Online article. www.pops.int/TheConvention/ThePOPs/TheNewPOPs/tabid/2511/Default.aspx

Stockholm Convention, n.d., 'What are POPs?'. Online article. www.pops.int/TheConvention/ThePOPs/tabid/673/Default.aspx

van Rooij, Benjamin, 'The authoritarian logic of regulatory pluralism: understanding China's new environmental actors', *Regulation & Governance*, 10 (2016), 3–13.

'Organization and procedure in environmental law enforcement: Sichuan in comparative perspective', *China Information*, 17 (2003), 36–64.

'The people vs. pollution: understanding citizen action against pollution in China', *The Journal of Contemporary China,* 19: 63 (2010), 55–77.

van Rooij, Benjamin and Carlos Lo, 'Fragile convergence: understanding variation in the enforcement of China's industrial pollution law', *Law & Policy,* 32 (2010), 14–37.

Vaughan, Adam, 'China burns half of coal consumption worldwide, figures show', *The Guardian,* 30 January 2013.

Wan E'Xiang, 'Establishing an environmental public interest litigation system and promoting the building of an ecological civilization', *Chinese Law and Government,* 43 (2010), 30–40.

Wang, Alex L., 'Explaining environmental information disclosure in China', *Ecology Law Quarterly,* 44 (2018), 865–923.

'The role of law in environmental protection in China: recent developments', *Vermont Journal of Environmental Law,* 8 (2007), 195–223.

'The search for sustainable legitimacy: environmental law and bureaucracy in China', *Harvard Environmental Law Review,* 37 (2013), 365–440.

'Symbolic legitimacy and Chinese environmental reform', *Environmental Law,* 48 (2018), 699–760.

Wang, Alex L. and Jie Gao, 'Environmental courts and the development of environmental public interest litigation in China', *Journal of Court Innovation,* 3 (2010), 37–50.

Wang Canfa, 'The achievement, challenges and prospects of environmental law', *Tribune of Political Science and Law,* 28:3 (2010), 106–15.

'The case of air pollution compensation caused by copper smelter in Chifeng of Inner Mongolia' in Wang Canfa and Feng Jia (eds.), *China's Environmental Litigation* (Beijing: Chinese University of Politics and Law Press, 2015), 21–39.

'Chinese environmental law enforcement: current deficiencies and suggested reforms' *Vermont Journal of Environmental Law,* 8 (2006), 159–93.

'Discussion on several issues in drafting the Chinese EIA Law', *Chinese Environment News,* 9 March 2001.

'Keynote: special functions of promoting public participation in environmental protection in aiding pollution victims', *Vermont Journal of Environmental Law,* 8 (2007), 380–92.

'Legal issues of strategic environmental assessment', *Legal Forum,* 19:3 (2004), 13–19.

'Low cost of environmental violation: causes and proposal for change', *Environmental Protection,* 9 (September 2005), 32–4.

'The rapid development of environmental protection law' in Cai Dingjian and Wang Chenguang (eds.), *China's Journey toward the Rule of Law: Legal Reform, 1978–2008* (Leiden and Boston, MA: Brill, 2010) 495–548.

'Reflections on Chinese environmental law', *Tsinghua Journal of Rule of Law,* 1 (2010), 21–32.

'Rewrite environmental legal principles to contain environmental pollution accidents', *China Law,* 3 (2010), 22–6.

Wang Canfa et al., 'Pondering over the incident of Songhua River pollution from the perspective of environmental law' in Michael Faure and Song Ying (eds.), *China and International Environmental Liability: Legal Remedies for Transboundary Pollution* (Cheltenham and Northampton, MA: Edward Elgar, 2008), 291–314.

Wang Canfa and Feng Jia (eds.), *China's Environmental Litigation* (Beijing: Chinese University of Politics and Law Press, 2015).
王灿发 主编 冯嘉 副主编《中国环境诉讼》（中国政法大学出版社）

Wang Doudou, 'The Supreme People's Court exploring public interest litigation to protect water resources', *Legal Daily,* 12 April 2010, 5.

Wang Erde, 'China's cost of pollution reached 1.5 trillion yuan in 2010', *21st Century Economic Report*, 15 January 2013.

Wang Jin, *A Comparative Study of Sino-Foreign EIA Mechanism* (Beijing: Peking University Press, 2006).
汪劲，《中外环境影响评价制度比较研究》（北京大学出版社）

Environmental Law, 4th ed. (Beijing: Peking University Press, 2018).
汪劲《环境法学》(第四版) (北京大学出版社)

Wang, Jin, 'Environmental public interest litigation: when will it flourish in China?', *Journal of Korean Law*, 7 (2007), 217–28.

Wang Jin, et al. 'Reflections from the transboundary pollution of Songhua River' in Michael Faure and Song Ying (eds.), *China and International Environmental Liability: Legal Remedies for Transboundary Pollution* (Cheltenham and Northampton, MA: Edward Elgar, 2008) 273–90.

The Principles of Chinese Environmental Law (Beijing: Peking University Press, 2000).
汪劲，《中国环境法原理》（北京大学出版社）

Wang Ming et al., *China's NGO Reform: From the Governmental Choice to Societal Choice* (Beijing: Social Science Academic Press, 2001).
王名、刘国翰、何建宇著《中国社团改革：从政府选择到社会选择》（北京: 社会科学文献出版社）

Wang Ming (ed.), *Emerging Civil Society in China, 1978–2008* (Leiden and Boston: Brill, 2008).

Wang Mingyuan, 'China's pollutant discharge permit system evolves behind its economic expansion', *Villanova Environmental Law Journal,* 19 (2008), 95–121.

Wang Mingyuan and Jin Feng, 'Some thoughts on the amendments to the Environmental Protection Law of China', *Asia Pacific Journal of Environmental Law,* 17 (2014), 191–203.

Wang Ping, 'Thirty Years of Environmental Legislation', *The People's Congress of China*, 18 (2012), 27–8.

Wang, Shanyong et al, 'Information publicity and resident's waste separation behavior: an empirical study based on the norm activation model', *Waste Management,* 87 (2019), 33–42.

Wang, Shizhou, 'Environmental crime and environmental criminal law in the People's Republic of China', *European Journal of Crime, Criminal Law and Criminal Justice,* 12 (2004), 150–65.

Wang Weimin, 'Beijing land bureau responds to query over toxic site transfer', *China Real Property News*, 20 August 2007.

Wang Xi and Lu Kun, *Environmental Law in China* (Alphen aan den Rijn, Netherlands: Wolters Kluwer, 2017).

Wang, Xixin, 'Administrative procedure reforms in China's rule of law context', *Columbia Journal of Asian Law,* 12 (1998), 251–77.

'Between dreams and the reality: making of the Administrative Procedure Act in China', *Journal of Korean Law,* 7 (2007), 157–82.

Wang, Yan et al., 'Atmospheric emissions of typical toxic heavy metals from open burning of municipal solid waste in China', *Atmospheric Environment*, 152 (2017), 6–15.

'Environmental impact assessment of projects in the People's Republic of China: new law, old problems', *Environmental Impact Assessment Review,* 23 (2003), 543–79.

Wang Yongchen, *Green Action in China* (Beijing: Foreign Languages Press, 2006).
汪永晨，《中国绿色行动》（新世界出版社）

Watts, Jonathan, 'China's "cancer villages" reveal dark side of economic boom', *The Guardian,* 7 June 2010.

'The clean-up begins on China's dirty secret: soil pollution', *The Guardian,* 12 June 2012.

WHO, n.d., 'Air pollution in China'. Online article. www.who.int/china/health-topics/air-pollution

'7 million premature deaths annually linked to air pollution', (press release) 25 March 2014. www.who.int/mediacentre/news/releases/2014/air-pollution/en/

Action Is Needed on Chemicals of Major Public Health Concern (Geneva: World Health Organisation, 2010). www.who.int/ipcs/features/10chemicals_en.pdf?ua=1.

Air Quality Guidelines for Particulate Matter, Ozone, Nitrogen Dioxide and Sulfur Dioxide: Global Update 2005: Summary of Risk Assessment (World Health Organization, 2006).

Burden of Disease from Household Air Pollution for 2012 (World Health Organization, n.d.). www.who.int/phe/health_topics/outdoorair/databases/FINAL_HAP_AAP_BoD_24March2014.pdf

Chromium in Drinking Water (Geneva: World Health Organization, 2003).

'Country profile of environmental burden of disease: China', (Geneva: World Health Organization, 2009), www.who.int/quantifying_ehimpacts/national/countryprofile/china.pdf?ua=1

Evolution of WHO Air Quality Guidelines: Past, Present and Future (Copenhagen: WHO Regional Office for Europe, 2017).

'Greater cooperation needed to win the war on pollution', (press release) 8 May 2018.

Guidelines for Drinking-Water Quality: Fourth Edition Incorporating the First Addendum (World Health Organization, 2017).

Health Risks of Heavy Metals from Long-Range Transboundary Air Pollution (Copenhagen: WHO Regional Office for Europe, 2007).

Williams, Paul N., 'Occurrence and partitioning of cadmium, arsenic and lead in mine impacted paddy rice: Hunan, China', *Environmental Science and Technology*, 43 (2009), 637–42.

Winalski, Dawn, 'Cleaner water in China? The implications of the amendments to China's Law on the Prevention and Control of Water Pollution', *Journal of Environmental Law and Litigation*, 24 (2009), 181–201.

Wong, Edward, 'Air pollution linked to 1.2 million premature deaths in China', *New York Times*, 1 April 2013.

Wong, Natalie W. M., 'Environmental protests and NIMBY activism: local politics and waste management in Beijing and Guangzhou', *China Information*, 30:2 (2016), 143–64.

Wong Young-tsu, *A Paradise Lost: The Imperial Garden Yuanming Yuan*, (Springer Singapore, 2001).

World Affairs Council of Pittsburgh, 18 April 2014, 'China's struggle to access water'. Blog. https://worldpittsburgh.wordpress.com/2014/04/18/chinas-struggle-to-access-water/

World Bank, *China: Agenda for Water Sector Strategy for North China (Summary Report)* (Washington, DC: World Bank Group, 2002).

Clear Water, Blue Skies: China's Environment in the New Century (Washington, DC: World Bank Group, 1997).

Cost of Pollution in China: Economic Estimates of Physical Damages (Washington, DC: World Bank Group, 2007).

Waste Management in China: Issues and Recommendations (Washington, DC: World Bank Group, 2005).

What a Waste: A Global Review of Solid Waste Management (Washington, DC: World Bank Group, 2012).

What a Waste 2.0: A Global Snapshot of Solid Waste Management to 2050 (Washington, DC: World Bank Group, 2018).

World Commission on Environment and Development (Brundtland Commission), *Our Common Future* (Oxford University Press, 1987).

Wright, Teresa (ed.), *Handbook of Protest and Resistance in China* (Northampton, MA: Edward Elgar, 2019).

Wu Boya, *The History of YuanMingYuan* (Beijing: *Encyclopaedia of China Publishing*, 2000). 吴伯娅，《圆明园史话》（大百科全书出版社）

Wu Changhua, 'Improving the legal and policy foundation for public access to environmental information in China', *Temple Journal of Science Technology and Environmental Law*, 24 (2005), 291–323.

Wu, Jing et al., 'Strategic environmental assessment implementation in China: five-year review and prospects', *Environmental Impact Assessment Review*, 31 (2011), 77–84.

'Study on the practice of public participation in environmental impact assessment by environmental non-governmental organizations in China', *Renewable and Sustainable Energy Reviews*, 74 (2017), 186–200.

Wu, Vivian, 'Watchdog orders halt to lake restoration', *South China Morning Post*, 1 April 2005, 8.

'Wu Xiaoqing: increased state fiscal input in energy conservation and environmental protection in 2014', *China Daily*, 8 March 2014.

Xi Jinping, *Secure a Decisive Victory in Building a Moderately Prosperous Society in All Respects and Strive for the Great Success of Socialism with Chinese Characteristics for a New Era* (2017). www.pkulaw.cn

Xi Xiaoming and Du Wanhua (eds.), *Selection of Model Environmental and Resource Cases and Comments* (Beijing: People's Court Press, 2014).
奚晓明 主编 杜万华 副主编《环境资源典型案例选编与评析》（人民法院出版社）

Xia Mingqun, 'State Environmental Protection Administration: China's sulfur dioxide emissions ranked first in the world in 2005', *Sina Finance*, 4 August 2006. http://finance.sina.com.cn/g/20060804/09052792219.shtml

Xiang Lili, 'The first environmental case: story of the Grand Canal 29 years ago', *The Beijing News*, 24 February 2008.

Xie, Jian and Fasheng Li, *Overview of the Current Situation on Brownfield Remediation and Redevelopment in China* (Washington, DC: World Bank Group, 2010).

Xie Zhenhua, *Typical Cases and Enforcement Guide of Chinese Environmental Law* (Beijing: China Environmental Science Press, 1994).
解振华《中国环境典型案例与执法提要》(中国环境科学出版社)

Xin Chunying (ed.), *Interpreting the Environmental Protection Law of the PRC* (Beijing: Law Press China, 2014).
信春鹰 主编《中华人民共和国环境保护法释义》(法律出版社)

(ed.), *Interpreting the Air Pollution Prevention and Control Law* (Beijing: Law Press, 2015).
信春鹰 主编《中华人民共和国大气污染防治法释义》(法律出版社)

Xinhua, 'Pollutants, pesticides threaten farm land', *China Daily*, 12 June 2012.

Xinhua News Agency, 'Shaanxi Fengxiang lead poisoning: 615 children confirmed blood lead levels exceed state standard', 14 August 2009. www.gov.cn/jrzg/2009-08/14/content_1391538.htm

Xu Huiying, 'Vanke won the second batch of two limits housing bids in Beijing', *First Financial Daily*, 27 July 2007.

Xu Shaoshi, *Report on Establishing the Ecological Compensation Mechanism* (2013). www.pkulaw.cn

Xu Yijie, 'Environmental protection regional cooperation in the new China: the case of Guanting Reservoir', *Contemporary China History Studies*, 22:6 (2015), 69–81.

Yan Huiqi, *Pesticide Law and Compliance Decision Making: A Case Study of Chinese Farmers* (Springer Singapore, 2017).

Yan Jie, 'Illegal dumping pollutes water', *China Daily*, 15 August 2011.

'Plant stored toxic waste, endangering residents', *China Daily*, 17 August 2018.

Yang Chunxi et al., 'China's treatment of crimes against the environment: using criminal sanctions to fight environmental degradation in the PRC', *Journal of Chinese Law*, 8 (1994), 145–84.

Yang, Fan et al, 'Adjudicating environmental tort cases in China: burden of proof, causation, and insights from 513 court decisions', *Asia Pacific Journal of Environmental Law*, 21 (2018), 171–89.

Yang, Gonghuan and Dafang Zhuang (eds.) *Atlas of the Huai River Basin Water Environment: Digestive Cancer Mortality* (Dordrecht: Springer Netherlands, 2014).

Yang, Guobin, 'Environmental NGOs and institutional dynamics in China', *The China Quarterly*, 181 (2005), 46–66.

Yang Jian, '"Cancer village" blames chrome plant', *Shanghai Daily*, 18 August 2011, A03.

'Top team in cancer scare probe', *Shanghai Daily*, 19 August 2011.

Yang Meng, 'The damaging truth about Chinese fertiliser and pesticide use', *China Dialogue*, 7 September 2012.

Yang Mingsen, *China Environment Yearbook* (Beijing: China Environment Yearbook Press, 2006) 杨明森 主编《中国环境年鉴》（中国环境年鉴社）

Yang Sujuan, 'Water pollution compensation: the Zhejiang Pinghu tadpole case' in Wang Canfa and Feng Jia (eds.), *China's Environmental Litigation* (Beijing: Chinese University of Politics and Law Press, 2015), 156–71.

Yang, Tseming and Xuehua Zhang, 'Public participation in environmental enforcement . . . with Chinese characteristics?: A comparative assessment of China's environmental complaint mechanism', *The Georgetown International Environmental Law Review*, 24 (2012), 325–66.

Yang Yan, 'Dongling smelter main cause for lead poisoning in Fengxiang', *People's Daily*, 16 August 2009, 2.

'Over one hundred children suspected of lead poisoning in Shaanxi Fengxiang', *People's Daily*, 11 August 2009, 6.

Yang Zhaoxia, 'The role of the procuratorates', *China Environment News*, 2 July 2012, 3.

Yardley, Jim, 'China announces more pollution controls', *New York Times*, 1 August 2008.

Yang Zhaofei, 'Environmental pollution liability insurance: using market instrument to address environmental management difficulties', *Green Leaf*, 10 (2010), 19–28.

Yao, Hong et al., 'Analysis of surface water pollution accidents in China: characteristics and lessons for risk management', *Environmental Management*, 57 (2016), 868–78.

Yee, Wai-Hang, Shui-Yan Tang and Carlos Wing-Hung Lo, 'Regulatory compliance when the rule of law is weak: evidence from China's environmental reform', *Journal of Public Administration Research and Theory*, 26 (2016), 95–112.

You, Mingqing, 'Changes and challenges of the 2014 revised Environmental Protection Law in the context of China's five fundamental transitions', *Hong Kong Law Journal*, 45 (2015), 621–49.

'Moratorium on EIA approvals: China's new environmental law enforcement tool', *Natural Resources Journal*, 48 (2008), 163–87.

Yu Fang et al., *Report of China's Environmental-Economic Accounting in 2007–2008* (Beijing: China Environmental Science Press, 2012).
於方 等,《中国环境经济核算研究报告2007-2008》(中国环境科学出版社)

Yu Haisong, *Practice and Interpretation of Crimes against Environment and Resources* (Beijing: Law Press, 2017).
喻海松《环境资源犯罪实务精释》(法律出版社)

Yu Ping, 'New lessons learned from the first environmental public interest litigation', *Guangming Daily*, 10 August 2020, 2.

Yu, Xia, 'Transboundary water pollution management: lessons learned from river basin management in China, Europe and the Netherlands', *Utrecht Law Review*, 7 (2011), 188–203.

Yuan Jie (ed.), *Understanding the Air Pollution Prevention and Control Law* (Beijing: China Legal Publishing House, 2015).
袁杰 主编 《中华人民共和国大气污染防治法解读》(中国法制出版社)

Zander, Sophie, 'How effective a weapon is the new EPL in China's "war against pollution"?: The past triumphs and future challenges of environmental public interest litigation', *NYU Journal of International Law and Politics,* 50 (2018), 605–36.

Zhai, Tiantian and Yen-Chiang Chang, 'Standing of environmental public-interest litigants in China: evolution, obstacles and solutions', *Journal of Environmental Law,* 30 (2018), 369–97.

Zhang, Bo et al., 'A new Environmental Protection Law, many old problems? Challenges to environmental governance in China', *Journal of Environmental Law,* 28 (2016), 325–35.

Zhang Dejiang, *Inspection Report on the Implementation of the Solid Waste Law* (2017). www pkulaw.cn

Zhang, Dongliang et al, 'Waste-to-energy in China: key challenges and opportunities', *Energies*, 8 (2015), 14182–96.

Zhang Enyin, *A Study of the History of YuanMingYuan* (Beijing: Beijing Sports College Press, 1993).
张恩荫，《圆明园变迁史探微》(北京体育学院出版社)

Zhang Hongjun and Richard Ferris, 'Shaping an environmental protection regime for the new century: environmental law and policy in the People's Republic of China', *Asia Journal of Environmental Management,* 6 (1998), 35–58.

Zhang Jingjing, 'The environmental tort case sued by 1,721 villagers of Fujian Pingnan against Rongping Chemical Company Ltd' in Wang Canfa and Feng Jia (eds.), *China's Environmental Litigation* (Beijing: Chinese University of Politics and Law Press, 2015), 68–81.

Zhang Jun, *Report on Procuratorial Public Interest Litigation* (2019). www.pkulaw.cn

Zhang Ke, 'The central environmental supervision and inspection teams: members and rules', *Environmental Education,* 194:12 (2016), 20–1.

Zhang Lujing et al., 'Powerful environmental supervision and inspection by the central authorities', *China Economic Weekly,* 43:6 November (2017), 17–29.

Zhang Qiulei, 'MEP signed agreement on air pollution prevention and control targets and responsibilities with 31 provincial-level governments', *China Environment News,* 8 January 2014, 1.

Zhang, Xuehua 'Implementation of pollution control targets in China: has a centralized enforcement approach worked?', *The China Quarterly,* 231 (2017), 749–74.

Zhang, Xuehua and Leonard Ortolano, 'Judicial review of environmental administrative decisions: has it changed the behavior of government agencies?', *The China Journal,* 64 (2010), 97–119.

'Agency empowerment through the Administrative Litigation Law: court enforcement of pollution levies in Hubei province', *The China Quarterly,* 202 (2010), 307–26.

Zhang Yanchun et al., 'Wuhan Heshan "toxic site" cleaned up at high cost', *People's Daily,* 4 January 2013, 1.

Zhang Yingying, 'The shadow over rural China', *China Dialogue,* 10 February 2011. www .chinadialogue.net/article/show/single/ch/4098-The-shadow-over-rural-China.

Zhang Yuan, 'MEP lawful in treating soil pollution data as state secret', *New Beijing News,* 9 May 2013.

Zhao, Xiaobo and Jianwei Zhang, 'Review of regulatory frameworks for contaminated land in China', *Frontiers of Law in China,* 8 (2013), 69–102.

Zhao Xin-gang et al., 'Technology, cost, a performance of waste-to-energy incineration industry in China', *Renewable and Sustainable Energy Reviews,* 55 (2016), 115–30.

Zhao Yinan, 'Court backs environmental group', *China Daily,* 20 January 2012.

Zhao Yongxin, 'A complete rectification of the YuanMingYuan anti-seepage project', *People's Daily,* 8 July 2005, 5.

'Destruction or protection? YuanMingYuan Park is laying a waterproof membrane at the bottom of the lakes', *People's Daily*, 28 March 2005, 5.

Zhao Yongxin and Liu Yi, 'Five key issues of the YuanMingYuan hearing', *People's Daily*, 14 April 2005, 5.

Zhao, Yuhong, 'Assessing the environmental impact of projects: a critique of the EIA regime in China', *Natural Resources Journal*, 49 (2009), 485–524.

'Environmental dispute resolution in China', *Journal of Environmental Law*, 16 (2004), 157–92.

'Environmental NGOs and sustainable development in China' in Robert Percival et al. (eds.), *Global Environmental Law at a Crossroads* (Cheltenham and Northampton, MA: Edward Elgar, 2014) 63–80.

'Environmental principles in China' in Ludwig Kramer and Emanuela Orlando (eds.), *Principles of Environmental Law* (Cheltenham: Edward Elgar, 2018) 424–36.

'Innovative measures to improve environmental law enforcement in China', *China–EU Law Journal*, 4 (2015), 155–72.

'Public participation in China's EIA regime: rhetoric or reality', *Journal of Environmental Law*, 22 (2010), 89–123.

Zhao Yuhong, 'Land contamination in urban China: developing a national cleanup legal regime', *Hong Kong Law Journal*, 39 (2009), 627–48.

'Mediation of environmental disputes', *Journal of Comparative Law*, 10 (2016), 237–53.

Zhao Ziyang, *Report on State Council Institutional Reform* (1982). www.pkulaw.cn

Zheng Dao, 'Rescue rice', *Caixin New Century Weekly*, 27 May 2013.

Zhong, Raymond and Carolyn Zhang, 'Food delivery apps are drowning China in plastic', *New York Times*, 28 May 2019.

Zhou Hui, 'Wuhan toxic site in city centre sold for 1.44 billion yuan', *21st Century Economic Report*, 23 December 2014.

Zhou Jiahai and Yu Haisong, 'Understanding and applying the judicial Interpretation on the Application of Law in Environmental Criminal Cases', *People's Adjudication (Application)*, 4 (2017), 23–9.
周加海和喻海松，《关于办理环境污染刑事案件适用法律若干问题的解释》的理解与适用《人民司法（应用）》 2017年第4期第23–29页。

Zhou, Kai-Yi and William R. Sheate, 'Case studies: application of SEA in provincial level expressway infrastructure network planning in China – current existing problems', *Environmental Impact Assessment Review*, 31 (2011), 521–37.

Zhou, Maigeng et al., 'Mortality, morbidity, and risk factors in China and its provinces, 1990–2017: a systematic analysis for the global burden of disease study 2017', *The Lancet*, 394:10204 (2019), 1145–58.

Zhou Qiang, *SPC's Work Report Presented to the 12th NPC at Its Third Meeting*, (2015). www.pkulaw.cn

Zhou Shengxian, *Report on Environmental Protection Work* (2011). www.pkulaw.cn

Zhou Ying, 'Zhejiang exploring environmental public interest litigation: breakthrough and impact', *China Environment News*, 19 December 2011, 3.

Zhu Rongji, *The Government Work Report* (5 March 1999). www.npc.gov.cn/npc/index.shtml and www.pkulaw.cn

Zhu Xiao, 'Formulating rules of written testimony in environmental administrative permit hearing', *Academic Journal of Zhongzhou*, 4 (2005), 75–8.

Zhu, Xiao and Kaijie Wu, 'Public participation in China's environmental lawmaking: in pursuit of better environmental democracy', *Journal of Environmental Law*, 29 (2017), 389–416.

Zhu, Xiao et al., 'Regional restrictions on environmental impact assessment approval in China: the legitimacy of environmental authoritarianism', *Journal of Cleaner Production*, 92 (2015), 100–8.

Zi Min, 'Seven penalized for the crime of environmental pollution', *China Environment News*, 22 May 2012.

Zusman, Eric, 'The river runs dry: examining water shortages in the Yellow River Basin' in *Economic, Social and Legal Issues in China's Transition to a Market Economy* (University of California, Los Angeles: Asia Institute, 2000).

Index

Introductory Note

References such as '178–79' indicate (not necessarily continuous) discussion of a topic across a range of pages. References to footnotes are in italics. Wherever possible in the case of topics with many references, these have either been divided into sub-topics or only the most significant discussions of the topic are listed. Because the entire work is about 'environmental law' and 'China', the use of these terms (and certain others which occur constantly throughout the book) as an entry point has been minimized. Information will be found under the corresponding detailed topics.

For EU product safety concerns, contact us at Calle de José Abascal, 56–1°, 28003 Madrid, Spain or eugpsr@cambridge.org.

www.ingramcontent.com/pod-product-compliance
Lightning Source LLC
LaVergne TN
LVHW081935200926
848484LV00009B/2435

* 9 7 8 1 1 0 7 0 3 9 4 4 5 *